CRIMINAL PROCEDURE HANDBOOK

CRIMINAL PROCEDURE HANDBOOK

FOURTH EDITION

by

Peet M Bekker BA LLB (Pret) LLD (Unisa)
Professor of Law, University of South Africa
Advocate of the High Court of South Africa

Tertius Geldenhuys BA (Pret) LLB LLD (Unisa)
Chief Manager Legal Assistance, National Standards and Management Services
South African Police Service
formerly Professor of Law, University of South Africa
Advocate of the High Court of South Africa

J J Joubert BA LLB (Pret) LLD (Unisa)
Professor of Law, University of South Africa
Advocate of the High Court of South Africa

J P Swanepoel BA LLB (PUCHO) LLM (Unisa)
Associate Professor of Law, University of South Africa
Advocate of the High Court of South Africa

S S Terblanche BIur (PUCHO) LLB LLD (Unisa)
Professor of Law, University of South Africa
Advocate of the High Court of South Africa

Step E van der Merwe B Iuris (UPE) LLB (Unisa) LLD (Cape Town)
Professor of Law, University of Stellenbosch
Advocate of the High Court of South Africa

Jan H van Rooyen BA LLB (Pret) MCL (Michigan)
Emeritus Professor of Law, University of South Africa
Advocate of the High Court of South Africa

EDITOR
J J Joubert

Juta & Co, Ltd
1999

First published 1994
Second Edition 1996
Third Edition 1998
Fourth Edition 1999

© Juta & Co, Ltd
PO Box 14373, Kenwyn 7790

Cover design by Joy Wrench

ISBN 0 7021 5113 0

TYPESETTING BY PETER GREEN, GREEN POINT
PRINTED AND BOUND IN THE REPUBLIC OF SOUTH AFRICA
BY CREDA COMMUNICATIONS, CAPE TOWN

Preface

Legal developments (as far as case law and statutory amendments are concerned) up to 30 June 1999 are covered in this work. Books cited repeatedly are referred to by the surname of the author(s) concerned. These are:

> E du Toit et al *Commentary on the Criminal Procedure Act* (annual revision service)
> J Dugard *South African Criminal Law and Procedure* Vol IV *Introduction to Criminal Procedure* 1977
> Gardiner and Lansdown *South African Criminal Law and Procedure* Vol I *General Principles and Procedure* 1957
> *Hiemstra: Suid-Afrikaanse Strafproses* 5 ed (1993) by J Kriegler
> J L Snyman and D W Morkel *Strafprosesreg* 2 ed 1988

Works cited only occasionally are referred to in full in the text.

Concise references to Chapter 2 (Bill of Rights) of the Constitution of the Republic of South Africa, Act 108 of 1996, have been inserted in appropriate places in the material based on the Criminal Procedure Act. Sections of the Constitution dealt with in the chapters that follow, are reproduced after the index to each chapter, with mention of the subdivision of the chapter where each section appears. Such selected sections of the Constitution are included by way of an appendix at the end of this book; also supplied is a list of the sections of the Criminal Procedure Act that are dealt with in the text, the relevant page being indicated.

Editor
Pretoria
September 1999

Contents

PREFACE   v

TABLE OF CASES   ix

**PART I   SELECTED GENERAL PRINCIPLES OF THE LAW OF
CRIMINAL PROCEDURE**

CHAPTER 1:   Basic principles, values and constitutionalism   1
CHAPTER 2:   The criminal courts of the Republic   30
CHAPTER 3:   The prosecution of crime   43
CHAPTER 4:   The right to legal assistance   73
CHAPTER 5:   The accused: his presence as a party   79

PART II   THE CRIMINAL PROCESS
PHASE ONE: PRE-TRIAL CRIMINAL PROCEDURE

CHAPTER 6:   The exercise of powers and the vindication of individual
             rights   87
CHAPTER 7:   Securing the attendance of the accused at the trial   92
CHAPTER 8:   Interrogation, interception and establishing the bodily
             features of a person   116
CHAPTER 9:   Search and seizure   123
CHAPTER 10: Bail and other forms of release   135
CHAPTER 11: Pre-trial examinations   159

PHASE TWO: THE TRIAL

CHAPTER 12: Indictments and charge sheets   169
CHAPTER 13: The court   185
CHAPTER 14: Arraignment and plea of an accused   197
CHAPTER 15: Miscellaneous matters relating to the trial   223
CHAPTER 16: Joinder and separation of trials   228
CHAPTER 17: The conduct of the trial   232
CHAPTER 18: The verdict   247

PHASE THREE: THE SENTENCE

CHAPTER 19: The sentence   255

PHASE FOUR: POST-VERDICT AND POST-SENTENCE REMEDIES

CHAPTER 20: Review   289
CHAPTER 21: Appeal   315
CHAPTER 22: Mercy, indemnity and free pardon   371

APPENDIX   375

REFERENCES TO THE CRIMINAL PROCEDURE ACT   387

SUBJECT INDEX   394

Table of cases

	Page
A 1994 (1) SACR 602 (A)	279
Abbass 1916 AD 233	174
Abdool Latieb & Co v Jones 1918 TPD 215	340
Abels 1948 (1) SA 706 (O)	333
Abraham 1964 (2) SA 336 (T)	347
Abrahams 1980 (4) SA 665 (C)	214
Abrahams 1983 (1) SA 137 (A)	346
Abrahams 1989 (2) SA 668 (E)	190, 192, 233
Abrahams 1990 (1) SACR 172 (C)	284
Abrahams 1990 (2) SACR 420 (A)	345, 369
Abrahams 1991 (1) SACR 633 (O)	305
Absalom 1989 (3) SA 154 (A)	341, 352
Acheson 1991 (2) SA 805 (Nm)	137, 138, 146
Ackerman 1973 (1) SA 765 (A)	355
Adam 1993 (1) SACR 62 (E)	214
Adam Effendi 1917 EDL 267	67
Adams 1959 (1) SA 646 (Spec Crim Ct)	174, 202
Adams 1959 (3) SA 753 (A)	329, 330, 360, 361
Adams 1986 (3) SA 733 (C)	283
Addabba; Ngeme; Van Wyk 1992 (2) SACR 325 (T)	204, 303, 305, 312
Adriantos 1965 (3) SA 436 (A)	245
Afrika 1982 (3) SA 1066 (C)	206
Afrikaner 1992 (2) SACR 408 (C)	302
Agnew 1996 (2) SACR 535 (C)	75
Ahmed 1958 (3) SA 313 (T)	27
Aimes 1998 (1) SACR 343 (C)	155
Alberts 1959 (3) SA 404 (A)	336
Alexander (1) 1965 (2) SA 796 (A)	364
Allart 1984 (2) SA 731 (T)	282
Allen v Attorney-General 1936 CPD 302	60
Alli 1958 (2) SA 50 (C)	214
Allie v De Vries NO 1982 (1) SA 774 (T)	347
Amerika 1990 (2) SACR 480 (C)	240
Anderson 1949 (4) SA 629 (C)	340
Anderson 1964 (3) SA 494 (A)	330
Anderson 1973 (2) SA 502 (O)	194
Anderson 1991 (1) SACR 525 (C)	148
Andresen v Minister of Justice 1954 (2) SA 473 (W)	131
Andrews 1948 (3) SA 577 (Spec Crim Ct)	202
Anthony 1938 TPD 602	175
AR Wholesalers 1975 (1) SA 551 (NC)	176
Aranoff 1979 (2) SA 179 (T)	208
Areff v Minister van Polisie 1977 (2) SA 900 (A)	110

Arends 1988 (4) SA 792 (E) 260
Arlow 1960 (2) SA 449 (T) 110
Assel 1984 (1) SA 402 (C) 77
Attorney-General v Magistrate, Regional Division, Natal 1967 (4) SA 680 (N) 309
Attorney-General v Van der Merwe and Bornman 1946 OPD 197 70
Attorney-General, Bophuthatswana, Ex parte 1980 (3) SA 292 (B) 314
Attorney General, Eastern Cape v Linda 1989 (2) SA 578 (E) 219
Attorney-General, Namibia, Ex parte: In re: The Constitutional Relationship between the
    Attorney-General and the Prosecutor-General 1995 (8) BCLR 1070 (NmS) 51
Attorney-General of Natal v Johnstone 1946 AD 256 314
Attorney-General, Transvaal v Botha 1993 (2) SACR 587 (A) 208, 209, 210
Attorney-General, Transvaal v Flats Milling Co (Pty) Ltd 1958 (3) SA 360 (A) 343, 352
Attorney-General, Transvaal v Kader 1991 (2) SACR 669 (A) 225
Attorney-General, Transvaal v Kader 1991 (4) SA 727 (A) 343
Attorney-General, Transvaal v Lutchman 1959 (2) SA 583 (A) 343
Attorney-General, Transvaal v Moores (SA) (Pty) Ltd 1957 (1) SA 190 (A) 362
Attorney-General, Transvaal v Nokwe 1962 (3) SA 803 (T) 343, 353
Attorney-General, Transvaal v Raphaely 1958 (1) SA 309 (A) 343
Attorney-General, Venda v Maraga 1992 (2) SACR 594 (V) 344
Attorney-General, Venda v Molepo 1992 (2) SACR 534 (V) 342
Attorney-General, Zimbabwe v Mzizi 1992 (2) SACR 582 (Z) 342
Attorney-General, Zimbabwe v Phiri 1988 (2) SA 696 (Z) 153
B 1954 (3) SA 431 (SWA) 82
B 1985 (2) SA 120 (A) 260
B 1991 (1) SACR 405 (N) 204, 207
Baba JS 376/33 (G) 37
Bagas 1952 (1) SA 437 (A) 229, 230
Bailey 1962 (4) SA 514 (E) 194, 330
Balepile 1979 (1) SA 702 (NC) 205, 207
Baloi 1949 (1) SA 523 (A) 355
Baloyi 1981 (2) SA 227 (T) 285
Bam 1972 (4) SA 41 (E) 195
Barber 1979 (4) SA 218 (D) 143
Barclays Zimbabwe Nominees (Pvt) Ltd v Black 1990 (4) SA 720 (A) 70
Barkett's Transport (Edms) Bpk 1988 (1) SA 157 (A) 177, 336
Barlow 1924 CPD 202 311
Baron 1978 (1) SA 510 (C) 205
Barnabas 1991 (1) SACR 467 (A) 264
Barnard 1986 (3) SA 1 (A) 111
Basson 1961 (3) SA 279 (T) 109, 113
Bate v Regional Magistrate, Randburg 1996 (7) BCLR 974 (W) 322
Beahan 1992 (1) SACR 307 (Z) 40
Beck 1958 (4) SA 250 (C) 334
Beckenstrater v Rottcher and Theunissen 1955 (1) SA 129 (A) 65
Beckett 1987 (4) SA 8 (C) 238
Beehari v Attorney-General, Natal 1956 (2) SA 598 (N) 143
Beer 1986 (2) SA 307 (E) 147
Bekisi 1992 (1) SACR 39 (C) 226
Bekker 1926 CPD 410 217
Belinsky 1925 AD 363 333
Benjamin 1980 (1) SA 950 (A) 181
Bennett 1976 (3) SA 652 (C) 146, 153

Bepela 1978 (2) SA 22 (B) 214
Berkowitz v Pretoria Municipality 1925 TPD 113 313
Bernardus 1965 (3) SA 287 (A) 368
Bernhardt 1967 (3) SA 174 (T) 311
Bersin 1912 CPD 969 244
Bersin 1970 (1) SA 729 (R) 276
Bester 1971 (4) SA 28 (T) 60
Bham v Lutge NO 1949 (3) SA 392 (T) 164, 244
Bhembe 1993 (1) SACR 164 (T) 275, 276
Bhulwana 1995 (12) BCLR 1579 (CC) 8
Bhulwana; Gwadiso 1995 (2) SACR 748 (CC) 8
Bidi 1969 (2) SA 55 (R) 192
Biyana 1997 (1) SACR 332 (T) 304
Bizi 1971 (1) SA 502 (RAD) 216, 218
Bkenlele 1983 (1) SA 515 (O) 227
Blaau 1973 (2) PH H(S) 116 (C) 179
Blaauw 1980 (1) SA 536 (C) 302
Black v Barclays Zimbabwe Nominees (Pvt) Ltd 1990 (1) SACR 433 (W) ... 45, 68
Blank 1995 (1) SACR 62 (A) 273
Blokland 1946 AD 940 246
Blom 1939 AD 188 .... 10, 238
Blooms 1966 (4) SA 417 (C) 74
Bokopane 1964 (1) SA 695 (O) 206, 207
Bonadei v Magistrate of Otjiwarongo 1986 (1) SA 564 (SWA) 71
Booi 1972 (4) SA 68 (NC) 246
Booysen 1988 (4) SA 801 (E) 209, 210
Bopape 1966 (1) SA 145 (C) 66
Boshoff 1981 (1) 393 SA (T) 129
Bosman 1978 (3) SA 903 (O) 220
Bosman 1988 (2) SA 485 (A) 187
Bosman, Kleinschmidt 1980 (1) SA 852 (A) 120
Botha 17 SC 297 101
Botha 1970 (4) SA 407 (T) 273
Botha 1978 (4) SA 543 (T) 301
Botha 1990 (1) SA 665 (T) 209, 210
Bothma 1957 (2) SA 100 (O) 186
Bothma 1971 (1) SA 332 (C) 192
Boya 1952 (3) SA 574 (C) 356
Brand 1975 (2) PH H138 (T) 246
Brand v Minister of Justice 1959 (4) SA 712 (A) 97
Brandt 1972 (1) PH HS17 (NC) 199
Brandt 1972 (4) SA 70 (NC) 246
Brash 1911 AD 525 342
Breakfast 1970 (2) SA 611 (E) 246
Bresler 1967 (2) SA 451 (A) 246
Breytenbach 1954 (2) SA 10 (O) 338, 339
Britz 1949 (3) SA 293 (A) 110
Britz 1963 (1) SA 394 (T) 209
Bron 1986 (4) SA 394 (C) 214
Brown 1996 (2) SACR 49 (NC) 243
Brunette 1979 (2) SA 430 (T) 303, 311
Buchanan v Voogt NO 1988 (2) SA 273 (N) 72

Budlender 1973 (1) SA 264 (C)   149
Burns 19 SC 477   219
Burns 1988 (3) SA 366 (C) 195, 305
Butcher 1986 (4) SA 1051 (O)   301
Butler 1947 (2) SA 935 (C)   309
C 1955 (1) SA 464 (T) 175, 202, 342
C 1998 (2) SACR 721 (C) 138, 158
Cairn's Executors v Gaarn 1912 AD 181   340
Calitz 1979 (2) SA 576 (SWA)   207
Callaghan v Klackers NO 1975 (2) SA 258 (E) 284, 305
Campbell 1991 (1) SACR 435 (Nm) 238, 239
Carelse 1943 CPD 242   335
Carr 1949 (2) SA 693 (A) 365, 366
Casker 1971 (4) SA 504 (N)   151
Cassidy 1978 (1) SA 687 (A)   356
Catsoulis 1974 (4) SA 371 (T)   246
Ceaser 1977 (2) SA 348 (A)   355
Cebekulu 1976 (2) PH H132 (A)   367
Cedras 1992 (2) SACR 530 (C)   305
Certification of the Constitution of the RSA 1996, In re 1996 (10) BCLR 1253 (CC)   51
Chamane 1962 (2) SA 428 (A)   228
Charlie 1976 (2) SA 596 (A)   284
Chauke 1998 (1) SACR 354 (VHC)   248
Chavulla 1999 (1) SACR 39 (C)   155
Chawe 1970 (2) SA 414 (NC)   183
Chetty 1977 (2) SA 885 (A)   113
Chetty v Cronje 1979 (1) SA 294 (O)   208
Chigwana 1976 (4) SA 26 (RA)   237
Chili 1917 TPD 61   245
Christie 1982 (1) SA 464 (A) 180, 243
Chunguete v Minister of Home Affairs 1990 (2) SA 836 (W)   143
Cine Films (Pty) Ltd v Commissioner of Police 1971 (4) SA 574 (W)   126
Citizen Newspapers (Pty) Ltd 1981 (4) SA 18 (A)   364
Clark 1931 AD 455   12
Clark, In re 1958 (3) SA 394 (A)   355
Claymore Court (Pty) Ltd v Durban City Council 1986 (4) SA 180 (N) ...   68
Cloete 1999 (2) SACR 137 (C)   154
Coales 1995 (1) SACR 33 (A)   274
Cobothi 1978 (2) SA 749 (N)   282
Coetzee 1977 (4) SA 539 (A) 333, 360
Coetzer 1976 (2) SA 769 (A) 177, 178
Cohen 1970 (2) SA 231 (N)   339
Colgate-Palmolive 1971 (2) SA 149 (T)   333
Collier 1976 (2) SA 378 (C)   336
Collier 1995 (2) SACR 648 (C)   195
Conradie 1972 (2) PH H109 (T)   345
Cooke 1959 (3) SA 449 (T)   246
Cooper 1926 AD 54   246
Cooper 1976 (2) SA 875 (T)   238
Cordozo 1975 (1) SA 635 (O)   206
Cornelissen; Cornelissen v Zeelie NO and another 1994 (2) SACR 41 (W)   225
Council of Review, South African Defence Force v Mönnig 1992 (3) SA 482 (A)   195

Crause 1959 (1) SA 272 (A) 177, 336
Cresto Machines (Edms) Bpk v Die Afdeling-Speuroffisier, Suid-Afrikaanse Polisie, Noord
    Transvaal 1972 (1) SA 376 (A) 126
Croukamp 1993 (1) SACR 439 (T) 279
D 1951 (4) SA 450 (A) 244
D 1953 (4) SA 384 (A) 345
D 1997 (2) SACR 671 (C) 76
Dabner v South African Railways and Harbours 1920 AD 583 74
Dalton 1978 (3) SA 436 (O) 301
Daly v Solicitor General 1911 EDC 399 69
Daniëls 1983 (3) SA 275 (A) 212
Daniels 1991 (2) SACR 449 (C) 204
Daniels 1997 (2) SACR 531 (C) 187
Datnis Motors (Midlands) (Pty) Ltd v Minister of Law and Order 1988 (1) SA 503 (N) 134
Dave 1954 (4) SA 736 (A) 353
David v Van Niekerk 1958 (3) SA 82 (T) 199
Davids; Dladla 1989 (4) SA 172 (N) 76
Dawid 1991 (1) SACR 375 (Nm) 195
Dayzell 1932 WLD 157 216
De Abreu 1980 (4) SA 94 (W) 143, 149
De Beer 1949 (3) SA 740 (A) 311
De Beer 1977 (2) SA 161 (O) 276
De Bruin 1987 (4) SA 933 (C) 209
De Coning 1954 (2) SA 647 (N) 175
De Freitas 1997 (1) SACR 180 (C) 66
De Jager 1965 (2) SA 612 (A) 365
De Jager v Attorney-General, Natal 1967 (4) SA 143 (D) 149
De Klerk 1992 (1) SACR 181 (W) 205
De Koker 1978 (1) SA 659 (O) 222
De Villiers 1984 (1) SA 519 (O) 210
De Vos 1970 (2) SA 590 (C) 332, 346
De Vos 1975 (1) SA 449 (O) 340
De Wet v Greeff NO 1991 (2) SACR 17 (T) 336
Deetlefs 1953 (1) SA 418 (A) 347, 364
Denysschen 1955 (2) SA 81 (O) 110
Desai 1959 (2) SA 589 (A) 175
Dhadhla 1964 (2) SA 623 (T) 366
Dhlamini 1967 (4) SA 679 (N) 284
Dhlamini 1997 (1) SACR 54 (W) 146
Dhludhla 1968 (1) SA 459 (N) 176
Dhlumayo 1948 (2) SA 677 (A) 333
Diedericks 1960 (4) SA 730 (O) 340
Diedericks 1984 (3) SA 814 (C) 181
Dimane 1987 (3) SA 146 (T) 160
Dipholo 1983 (4) SA 751 (T) 193
Disler 1933 CPD 405 304
Divisional Commissioner of SA Police, Witwatersrand Area v SA Associated Newspapers Ltd
    1966 (2) SA 503 (A) 125
Dladla 1975 (1) SA 118 (T) 27
Dladla (2) 1961 (3) SA 921 (D) 238
Dlamini; Dladla; Joubert; Schietekat 1999 (2) SACR 51 (CC) 137, 138, 144, 152, 156, 157
Dlomo 1969 (1) SA 104 (N) 304

Dockrat 1959 (3) SA 61 (D) 149
Doud 1978 (2) SA 403 (O) 205
Dozereli 1983 (3) SA 259 (C) 190, 233
Dreyer 1978 (2) SA 182 (NC) 211
Du Plessis 1957 (4) SA 463 (W) 148
Du Plessis 1969 (1) SA 72 (N) 285
Du Plessis 1978 (2) SA 496 (C) 208
Du Plessis v De Klerk 1996 (3) SA 850 (CC) 295
Du Toit 1966 (4) SA 627 (A) 347
Du Toit 1972 (1) PH H50 (E) 192
Du Toit 1979 (3) SA 846 (A) 346
Dubayi 1976 (3) SA 110 (Tk) 60
Dube 1915 AD 557 .... 193, 243
Dube 1929 AD 46 332
Duncan v Minister of Law and Order 1984 (3) SA 460 (T) 101, 105
Duncan v Minister of Law and Order 1986 (2) SA 805 (A) 99
Dyantyi 1983 (3) SA 532 (A) 150
E 1953 (3) SA 314 (A) 310
E 1979 (3) SA 973 (A) 310, 347
E 1992 (2) SACR 625 (A) 331
Ebrahim 1972 (2) SA 61 (C) 358
Ebrahim 1973 (1) SA 868 (A) 226
Ebrahim 1974 (2) SA 78 (N) 181
Ebrahim 1991 (2) SA 553 (A) 27, 40
Edward 1978 (1) SA 317 (NC) 284
Eli 1978 (1) SA 451 (E) 304
Ellis v Morgan; Ellis v Desai 1909 TS 576 299
Ellis v Visser 1954 (2) SA 431 (T) 69
Ellish v Prokureur-Generaal, WPA 1994 (2) SACR 579 (W) 156
Els v Minister of Safety and Security 1998 (2) SACR 93 (NC) ... 63
Endemann 1915 TPD 142 172
Engelbrecht 1923 CPD 586 313
Eshumael 1973 (2) PH H83 (RA) 245
Essa 1964 (2) SA 13 (N) 195
Esta 1912 TPD 7 107
Eusuf 1949 (1) SA 656 (N) 65
Evans 1981 (4) SA 52 (C) 212
Eyden 1982 (4) SA 141 (T) 200
Ex parte Chairperson of the Constitutional Assembly: In re Certification of the Constitution of
  the Republic of South Africa 1996 (4) SA 744 (CC) 4
Ex parte die Minister van Justisie: In re S v De Bruin 1972 (2) SA 623 (A) 34
Ex parte Minister of Justice: In re Duze 1945 AD 112 270
Ex parte Minister of Justice: In re R v Bolon 1941 AD 345 ... 34
Ezekiel v Kynoch NPD 13.4.1923 (cited in Gardiner and Lansdown 215) 98, 107
F 1975 (3) SA 167 (T) 177
F 1983 (1) SA 747 (O) 332, 347
F 1989 (1) SA 460 (Z) 60
Faber 1979 (1) SA 710 (NC) 205, 206
Fairfield 1920 CPD 279 36
Ferreira 1978 (4) SA 30 (T) 305
Ferreira v Levin NO 1995 (2) SA 813 (W) 297
Ferreira v Levin; Vryenhoek v Powell NO 1996 (1) SA 984 (CC) 312, 326

Fikizolo 1978 (2) SA 676 (NC) 205
Fischer 1955 (2) PH H186 (C) 332
Fisher 1973 (4) SA 121 (R) 340
Flanagan 1995 (1) SACR 13 (A) 273, 280
Foley 1926 TPD 168 365
Foley 1953 (3) SA 496 (E) 342
Ford 1974 (2) PH H39 (N) 357
Fouché 1953 (3) SA 201 (C) 305
Fourie 1947 (2) SA 574 (O) 149
Fourie 1991 (1) SACV 21 (T) 209, 210
Francis 1991 (1) SACR 198 (A) 332
Franco; Lasovsky 1974 (4) SA 496 (RA) 341
Frans 1924 TPD 419 275
Fredericks 1992 (1) SACR 561 (C) 246, 304, 336
Freedman 1921 AD 603 310
Friedman (2) 1996 (1) SACR 196 (W) 297
G 1989 (3) SA 695 (A) 330
G 1992 (1) SACR 568 (B) 237
Gaba 1981 (3) SA 745 (O) 176
Gabriel 1971 (1) SA 646 (RA) 216
Gabriel 1981 (2) SA 156 (SWA) 205
Gaika 1971 (1) SA 231 (C) 283
Gani 1957 (2) SA 212 (A) 249, 362
Gasa 1916 AD 241 342
Gasa v Regional Magistrate for the Regional Division of Natal 1979 (4) SA 729 (N) 337
Gascoyne v Paul & Hunter 1917 TPD 170 238
Gavanozis 1979 (1) SA 1020 (W) 358
Geidel v Bosman NO 1963 (4) SA 253 (T) 234
Gelderbloem 1962 (3) SA 631 (C) 184
Gerbers 1997 (2) SACR 601 (SCA) 242
Geritis 1966 (1) SA 753 (W) 226
Gibbs 1959 (2) SA 84 (C) 341
Gidi 1984 (4) SA 537 (C) 242
Gillingham v Attorney-General 1909 TS 572 60
Ginsberg v Additional Magistrate, Cape Town 1933 CPD 357 330
Giuseppe 1943 TPD 139 220
Gobozi 1975 (2) PH H99 (E) 242
Gobozi 1975 (3) SA 88 (E) 237
Goeieman 1992 (1) SACR 296 (NC) 283
Goliath 1972 (3) SA 1 (A) 360
Goncalves v Addisionele Landdros, Pretoria 1973 (4) SA 587 (T) 174, 329
Goosen 1988 (4) SA 5 (A) 229
Goras 1985 (4) SA 411 (O) 204
Gosschalk v Rossouw 1966 (2) SA 476 (C) 121
Gough 1980 (3) SA 785 (NC) 262
Gouws 1995 (1) SACR 342 (T) 273
Govazela 1987 (4) SA 297 (O) 193
Govender 1955 (2) SA 130 (N) 334
Govender v Buys 1978 (2) SA 292 (N) 205
Government of the Republic of South Africa v Basdeo 1996 (1) SA 355 (A) 109, 110, 112
Gqeba 1989 (3) SA 712 (A) 187
Gqozo 1994 (1) SACR 253 (Ck) 220

Gqulagha 1990 (1) SACR 101 (A) 192
Graham, Ex parte: In re United States of America v Graham 1987 (1) SA 368 (T) 143
Grobler 1966 (1) SA 507 (A) 179, 180
Grobler 1972 (4) SA 559 (O) 181
Groesbeek (1) 1969 (4) SA 383 (O) 230
Groesbeek (2) 1969 (4) SA 445 (O) 360
Gross 1982 (1) SA 593 (A) 331
Grotes; Jawuka 1970 (1) SA 368 (C) 193, 245
Grundlingh 1955 (2) SA 269 (A) 332, 334
Guess 1976 (1) PH H37 (C) 193
Gulyas v Minister of Law and Order 1986 (3) SA 934 (C) 100
Gumbi 1962 (1) SA 188 (D) 109, 113
Gumede 1992 (2) SACR 237 (N) 345
Gwala 1969 (2) SA 227 (N) 222
Gwebu 1988 (4) SA 155 (W) 76, 192
Gwebu, Xaba 1968 (4) SA 783 (T) 198
H 1998 (1) SACR 260 (SCA) 321, 358
H 1999 (1) SACR 72 (W) 158
Haarmeyer 1970 (4) SA 113 (O) 360
Haasbroek 1969 (1) SA 356 (O) 310
Hadebe 1998 (1) SACR 422 (SCA) 332
Hannah 1913 AD 484 182
Harbour 1988 (4) SA 921 (T) 207
Harper 1909 TS 361 231
Harricharan 1962 (3) SA 35 (N) 192
Hartkopf 1981 (1) SA 992 (T) 231
Hartzer 1933 AD 306 .... 110, 112
Hassan 1970 (1) SA 192 (C) 174
Hassen 1956 (3) SA 106 (N) 341
Hatch 1914 CPD 68 227
Hattingh 1972 (3) SA 843 (O) 209
Hattingh 1978 (2) SA 826 (A) 281
Hattingh 1992 (2) SACR 466 (N) 143
Hayman 1988 (1) SA 831 (NC) 274
Haysom v Additional Magistrate 1979 (3) SA 155 (C) 225
Hazelhurst 1984 (3) SA 897 (T) 210
Head and Fortuin v Wollaston 1926 TPD 549 195
Heita 1992 (2) SACR 285 (Nm) 194
Heller 1970 (4) SA 679 (A) 353, 373
Heller 1971 (2) SA 29 (A) 177
Hendricks 17 CTR 470 179
Hendricks 1997 (1) SACR 174 (C) 241
Hendriks 1974 (2) PH H91 (C) 192
Hendrix 1979 (3) SA 816 (D) 160, 219, 222
Hepworth 1928 AD 265 244
Herbst 1942 AD 434 362
Herbst 1980 (3) SA 1026 (E) 212, 214
Herold 1992 (2) SACR 195 (W) 283
Herschel 1920 AD 575 .... 175, 335, 336
Heskwa 1992 (2) SACR 95 (C) 301
Heugh 1998 (1) SACR 83 (ECD) 206
Heyman 1966 (4) SA 598 (A) 120, 226

Heyne (1) 1958 (1) SA 607 (W) 174
Heyns 1958 (2) SA 253 (E) 340, 343
Heyns 1976 (1) PH H48 (C) 179
Highstead Entertainment (Pty) Ltd t/a "The Club" v Minister of Law and Order 1994 (1) SA
    387 (C) 60
Hlalikaya 1997 (1) SACR 613 (SE) 75
Hlatswayo 1947 (4) SA 755 (O) 300, 309
Hlatswayo 1982 (4) SA 744 (A) 354
Hlatswayo v Attorney-General, Witwatersrand 1994 (1) SACR 232 (W) 227
Hlokulu 1988 (1) SA 174 (C) 207
Hlongwa 1979 (4) SA 112 (D) 138, 145, 146, 153
Hlongwa 1993 (2) SACR 225 (A) 334
Hlongwane 1982 (4) SA 321 (N) 193
Hlongwane 1989 (4) SA 79 (T) 143
Hlongwane 1990 (1) SACR 310 (NC) 305
Hlopane 1990 (1) SA 239 (O) 138
Hlope 1962 (2) SA 607 (T) 305, 334
Ho 1979 (3) SA 734 (W) 146, 153
Holder 1979 (2) SA 70 (A) 270
Hollenbach 1971 (4) SA 636 (NC) 77
Hoosain v Attorney-General, Cape (1) 1988 (4) SA 137 (C) 374
Hoosain v Attorney-General, Cape (2) 1988 (4) SA 142 (C) 374
Hoosen 1953 (3) SA 823 (N) 339
Horne 1971 (1) SA 630 (C) 339
Hudson 1980 (4) SA 145 (D) 145, 146, 153
Hudson 1998 (2) SACR 359 (W) 239
Hughes v Minister van Wet en Orde 1992 (1) SACR 338 (A) 112
Hugo 1976 (4) SA 536 (A) 170
Hull 1948 (4) SA 239 (C) 36
Huma 1996 (1) SA 232 (W) 122
Human 1979 (3) SA 331 (E) 346
Human 1990 (2) SACR 155 (NC) 143
I 1973 (3) SA 794 (A) 192
Imene 1979 (2) SA 710 (A) 214
Ingham 1958 (2) SA 37 (C) 182
Ingram 1995 (1) SACR 1 (A) 279
Ingram v Minister of Justice 1962 (3) SA 225 (W) 99
Isaacs 1968 (2) SA 184 (A) 337
Isaacs 1970 (4) SA 397 (NC) 310
Isaacs v Minister van Wet en Orde 1996 (1) SACR 314 (A) 106
Ismael v Durban City Council 1973 (2) SA 362 (N) 125
Jackelson 1926 TPD 685 131
Jacobs 1970 (2) PH H152 (C) 191
Jacobs 1970 (3) SA 493 (E) 77
Jacobs 1978 (1) SA 1176 (C) 204
Jacobs 1978 (3) SA 440 (E) 204
Jacobs v The Attorney-General 1918 CPD 526 340
Jada 1985 (2) SA 182 (E) 208
Jama 1998 (2) SACR 237 (N) 239
Jansen 1975 (1) SA 425 (A) 263
Jantjies 1958 (2) SA 273 (A) 354, 355
Jantjies 1982 (4) SA 790 (C) 183

January; Prokureur-Generaal, Natal v Khumalo 1994 (2) SACR 801 (A)   338
Jasat 1997 (1) SACR 489 (SCA)   248
Jatham 1968 (3) SA 311 (N)   367
Jhazbai 1931 AD 480   177
Jija 1991 (2) SA 52 (E) 67, 236
Joale 1998 (1) SACR 293 (O)   303
Johannesburg Consolidated Investment Company v Johannesburg Town Council 1903 TS 111   293, 294
Jonas 1998 (2) SACR 677 (SECLD)   158
Jones 1952 (1) SA 327 (E)   103
Joone 1973 (1) SA 841 (C)   139
Jooste NO v Minister of Police 1975 (1) SA 349 (E)   109
Joseph 1967 (2) SA 539 (N)   334
JT Publishing (Pty) Ltd v Minister of Safety and Security 1996 (12) BCLR 1599 (CC)   314
Julies 1996 (7) BCLR 899 (CC)   8
Julius 1983 (2) SA 442 (C)   61
K 1956 (3) SA 353 (A) 193, 243
K 1974 (3) SA 857 (C)   245
K 1982 (4) SA 422 (B)   213
K 1997 (1) SACR 106 (C)   188
Kabele 1974 (3) SA 223 (NC)   231
Kabinet van die Tussentydse Regering van Suidwes-Afrika v Katofa 1987 (1) SA 695 (A) . . .   107
Kahita 1983 (4) SA 618 (C)   200
Kalase JS 315/17 (C)   99
Kalogoropoulos 1993 (1) SACR 12 (A)   333
Kamffer 1965 (3) SA 96 (T)   246
Kamte 1992 (1) SACR 677 (A)   67
Kannigan 1975 (4) SA 639 (N)   209
Kantor 1964 (3) SA 377 (W)   153
Kashire 1978 (4) SA 166 (SWA)   356
Keller and Parker 1914 CPD 791   236
Kellerman 1997 (1) SACR 1 (A) 344, 346
Kelly 1993 2 SACR 492 (A)   269
Kennedy 1967 (1) SA 297 (C)   337
Kerr (1907) 21 EDC 324   217
Keulder 1994 (1) SACR 91 (A)   274
Key v Attorney-General, Cape Provincial Division 1996 (4) SA 187 (CC); 1996 (6) BCLR 788
  (CC) 241, 312
Kgatlane 1978 (2) SA 10 (T)   219
Kgogong 1980 (3) SA 600 (A)   60
Kgolane 1959 (4) SA 483 (A) 356, 366
Kgoloko 1991 (2) SACR 203 (A)   171
Khaile 1975 (3) SA 97 (O)   333
Khalpy 1958 (1) SA 291 (C)   337
Khambule 1991 (2) SACR 277 (W) 193, 236, 262
Khan 1961 (1) SA 282 (N)   337
Khan v Koch NO 1970 (2) SA 403 (R)   195
Khanyile 1988 (3) SA 795 (N) 76, 78
Khiba 1978 (2) SA 540 (O)   205
Khoali 1990 (1) SACR 276 (O)   76
Khoele 1984 (2) SA 480 (O)   61
Khomo 1975 (1) SA 344 (D)   193
Khoza 1989 (3) SA 60 (T) 64, 217

Khumalo 1978 (4) SA 516 (N) 207
Khumalo 1979 (3) SA 708 (T) 210
Khomunala 1998 (1) SACR 362 (VHC) 243
Khuzwayo 1981 (1) SA 481 (N) 38
Kibido 1988 (1) SA 802 (C) 214
Kirsten 1988 (1) SA 415 (A) 335
Kistesamy 1947 (4) SA 788 (N) 114
Klaasen 1978 (1) SA 355 (C) 212
Klein 1995 (3) SA 848 (W) 241
Klein v Attorney-General and Another (1995)2 SACR 210 (W) 368
Kleyn 1937 CPD 288 .... 97, 103
Klink v Regional Magistrate NO [1996] 1 All SA 191 (SECL) 224
Kloppers 1986 (3) SA 478 (T) 301
Klumalo 1972 (4) SA 500 (O) 245
Kock 1988 (1) SA 37 (A) 330
Koekemoer 1973 (1) PH H20 (N) 181
Komani 1974 (2) PH H85 (C) 245
Komo 1947 (2) SA 508 (N) 207
Kondile 1974 (3) SA 774 (Tk) 237
Kotze 1994 (2) SACR 214 (O) 279
Kramer 1983 (2) PH H120 (A) 138
Kristusamy 1945 AD 549 332
Kritzinger 1952 (2) SA 401 (W) 238
Kritzinger 1952 (4) SA 651 (W) 230
Kroon 1997 (1) SACR 525 (SCA) 188, 359
Kroukamp 1927 TPD 412 175
Kruger 1954 (3) SA 816 (C) 326
Kruger 1970 (2) SA 233 (N) 339
Kruger 1989 (1) SA 785 (A) 39
Kruger v Minister of Correctional Services 1995 (1) SACR 375 (T) 372
Kumalo 1991 (2) SACR 694 (W) 245
Kungeka 1954 (4) SA 76 (E) 342
Kuse 1990 (1) SACR 191 (E) 176, 192
Kuzwayo 1949 (3) SA 761 (A) 355
Kuzwayo 1960 (1) SA 340 (A) 180
Kwinika 1989 (1) SA 896 (W) 245
L 1960 (3) SA 503 (A) 355
L 1988 (4) SA 757 (C) 77
Labuschagne 1960 (1) SA 632 (A) 112
Laher, Ex parte: In re Laher 1960 (2) SA 32 (W) 360
Lakier 1934 TPD 250 108
Lalsing 1990 (1) SACR 443 (N) 277
Langa 1963 (4) SA 941 (N) 236
Langa 1981 (3) SA 186 (A) 340
Larsen 1994 (2) SACR 149 (A) 279
Lawrence 1991 (2) SACR 57 (A) 201
Lawrence 1997 (4) SA 1176 (CC) 358
Lawrence v ARM Johannesburg 1908 TS 525 220
Lebokeng 1978 (2) SA 674 (O) 204
Leeb 1993 (1) SACR 315 (T) 279
Leepile (5) 1986 (4) SA 187 (W) 224
Leeuwner 1972 (1) PH H51 (E) 193

Lehnberg 1976 (1) SA 214 (C) 365
Lekaoto 1978 (4) SA 684 (A) 189
Lekgoale 1983 (2) SA 175 (B) 276
Lemmert 1969 (2) PH H210 (NC) 231
Leopeng v Meyer NO 1993 (1) SACR 292 (T) 162
Leseana 1993 (2) SACR 264 (T) 193
Lesias 1974 (1) SA 135 (SWA) 236
Letaoana 1997 (11) BCLR 1581 (W) 145
Lethopa 1994 (1) SACR 553 (O) 160, 219
Letuli 1953 (4) SA 241 (T) 367
Letweli 1982 (2) SA 666 (NC) 334
Levin v Whitelaw 1928 TPD 357 227
Levy v Benatar 1987 (4) SA 693 (Z) 70
Li Kui Yu v Superintendent of Labourers 1906 TS 181 75
Libaya 1965 (4) SA 249 (O) 229
Lipschitz 1921 AD 282 243
Liscoxo 1974 (2) SA 356 (O) 231
Loate 1983 (3) SA 400 (T) 331
Loggerenberg 1984 (4) SA 41 (E) 209
Lombard 1951 (3) SA 842 (E) 338
Lombard 1994 (3) SA 776 (T) 74
Londi 1985 (2) SA 248 (E) 204
Long 1958 (1) SA 115 (A) 216
Long 1988 (1) SA 216 (NC) 213
Lotzoff 1937 AD 196 174
Loubscher 1979 (3) SA 47 (A) 357
Loubser 1977 (4) SA 546 (T) 100
Louw 1981 (4) SA 939 (E) 313
Louw 1990 (3) SA 116 (A) 346, 367
LSD Ltd v Vachell 1918 WLD 127 .... 90, 131
Lubbe 1925 TPD 219 183
Lubbe 1989 (3) SA 245 (T) 160, 219
Lubisi 1980 (1) SA 187 (T) 221, 308
Lukas 1923 CPD 508 244
Lukas 1991 (2) SACR 429 (E) 148, 153
Lukele 1978 (4) SA 450 (T) 208, 263
Lulane 1976 (2) SA 204 (N) 145, 153
Lusu 1953 (2) SA 484 (A) 343
M 1970 (3) SA 20 (RA) 237
M 1976 (3) SA 644 (A) 331
M 1976 (4) SA 8 (T) 237
M 1979 (2) SA 167 (T) 248
M 1979 (4) SA 1044 (B) 213
M 1982 (1) SA 240 (N) 204
M 1989 (3) SA 887 (W) 200
M 1989 (4) SA 517 (B) 269
M 1990 (2) SACR 131 (B) 242
M 1990 (2) SACR 217 (T) 301
M 1993 (1) SACR 126 (A) 270
M 1998 (1) SACR 384 (C) 281
M, S 1979 (2) SA 959 (T) 150
M, S 1980 (4) SA 404 (O) 160, 161

Mabaso 1980 (2) SA 20 (N) 205
Mabaso 1980 (2) SA 790 (O) 250
Mabaso 1990 (3) SA 185 (A) 75, 76
Mabona 1973 (2) SA 614 (A) 234
Mabona v Minister of Law and Order 1988 (2) SA 654 (SE) 101
Mabote 1983 (1) SA 745 (O) 246
Mabuza 1991 (1) SACR 636 (O) 191, 233, 313
Mabuza 1996 (2) SACR 239 (T) 152
Macaba 1939 AD 66 332
MacDonald 1978 (4) SA 200 (T) 301
MacDonald v Kumalo 1927 EDL 293 140
Mache 1980 (3) SA 224 (T) 272
Mackenzie, In re 1933 AD 367 35
Mackeson 1939 PH L21 (C) 338
Macu v Du Toit 1982 (1) SA 272 (C) 98
Macu v Du Toit 1983 (4) SA 629 (A) 107, 113
Madizela 1992 (1) SACR 125 (N) 275
Madlelana 1936 EDL 140 304
Maelane 1978 (3) SA 528 (T) 284
Maepa 1974 (1) SA 659 (A) 364
Mafungo 1969 (2) SA 667 (G) 175
Magadhla 1947 (3) SA 585 (N) 175
Magano v District Magistrate, Johannesburg (1) 1994 (2) SACR 307 (W) 156, 295, 298
Magidson 1984 (3) SA 825 (T) 281
Magistrate, Regional Division 1972 (3) SA 377 (N) 61
Magmoed v Janse Van Rensburg 1990 (2) SACR 476 (C) 361
Magmoed v Janse Van Rensburg 1993 (1) SACR 67 (A) 333
Magoda 1984 (4) SA 462 (C) 64, 237
Magongo 1987 (3) SA 519 (A) 200
Magqabi v Mafundityala 1979 (4) SA 106 (E) 223
Magubane v Van der Merwe NO 1969 (2) SA 417 (N) 196, 221
Magxwalisa 1984 (2) SA 314 (N) 188, 240
Mahabeer 1980 (4) SA 491 (N) 82
Maharaj 1958 (4) SA 246 (A) 365, 373
Maharaj 1960 (4) SA 256 (N) 192
Maharaj 1976 (3) SA 205 (D) 153
Mahlangu 1997 (1) SACR 338 (T) 177, 311
Mahlatse 1949 (4) SA 455 (O) 103
Mahlongwana v Kwatinidubu Town Council 1991 (1) SACR 669 (E) 105
Mahobe 1898 NLR 56 63
Mahomed 1994 (2) SACR 171 (N) 216
Majola 1971 (3) SA 804 (N) 183
Majola 1982 (1) SA 125 (A) 242, 330
Makabane 1981 (3) SA 1028 (O) 201
Makaula 1993 (1) SACR 57 (Tk) 148
Makebe 1967 (1) SA 464 (N) 304
Makgetle 1980 (4) SA 256 (B) 222
Makhae 1974 (1) SA 578 (O) 284
Makhali v Minister of Justice 1957 (4) SA 322 (T) 354
Makhanya v Bailey NO 1980 (4) SA 713 (T) 69
Makhele 1981 (4) SA 956 (NC) 82
Makhubele 1987 (2) SA 541 (T) 305

Makhutla 1968 (2) SA 768 (O) 39
Makhutla 1969 (2) SA 490 (O) 218
Makofane 1998 (1) SACR 603 (T) 239
Makoni 1976 (1) SA 169 (R) 222
Makoula 1978 (4) SA 763 (SWA) 272
Makwanyane 1995 (6) BCLR 665 (CC); 1995 (2) SACR 1 (CC) 1995 (3) SA 391 (CC) 4, 22, 23,
                                                                         113, 264, 296
Makwasie 1970 (2) SA 128 (T) 65
Malakwana 1975 (3) SA 94 (O) 308
Malatji 1998 (2) SACR 622 (W) 240
Malcolm 1999 (1) SACR 49 (SEC) 143
Malesa 1990 (1) SACR 260 (T) 250, 251
Malgas 1996 (1) SACR 73 (NC) 189
Malikhethla 1978 (3) SA 11 (O) 205
Malili 1988 (4) SA 620 (T) 208
Malinde 1990 (1) SA 57 (A) 329
Malindi 1990 (1) SA 962 (A) 187, 188, 195
Malindisa 1961 (3) SA 377 (T) 111
Mall 1953 (1) SA 118 (SWA) 340
Mall 1960 (2) SA 340 (N) 238, 239
Malope 1991 (1) SACR 458 (B) 246
Mamba 1957 (2) SA 420 (A) 353
Mamkeli 1992 (2) SACR 5 (A) 356, 359, 369, 373
Mampa 1985 (4) SA 633 (C) 180
Mampie 1980 (3) SA 777 (NC) 195
Manaka 1978 (1) SA 287 (T) 241
Manasewitz 1933 AD 165, 1934 AD 95 .... 215, 217
Manekwane 1996 (2) SACR 264 (EC) 240
Mangqu 1977 (4) SA 84 (E) 172
Mankaji 1974 (4) SA 113 (T) 246
Mannheim 1943 TPD 169 174
Manupo 1991 (2) SACR 447 (C) 201, 226
Maqungu v Assistant Magistrate, Whittlesea 1977 (2) SA 359 (E) 153
Marais 1959 (1) SA 98 (T) 330
Marais 1966 (2) SA 514 (T) 336
Marimo, Ndhlovu 1973 (2) SA 442 (R) 198
Marion 1981 (1) SA 1216 (T) 82
Maritz 1996 (1) SACR 405 (A) 280
Martins 1986 (4) SA 934 (T) 204
Martinus 1990 (2) SACR 568 (A) 104, 109
Marwane 1981 (3) SA 588 (B) 320
Marx 1989 (1) SA 222 (A) 190, 233, 260, 309, 331
Marx 1996 (2) SACR 140 (W) 75
Maseki 1981 (4) SA 374 (T) 38, 39
Maseko 1990 (1) SACR 107 (A) 195
Maseko 1993 (2) SACR 579 (A) 237
Maseti 1992 (2) SACR 459 (C) 344
Mashele 1990 (1) SACR 678 (T) 240
Masike 1996 (2) SACR 245 (T) 210
Masilela 1990 (2) SACR 116 (T) 198
Masina 1990 (4) SA 709 (A) 265
Masinda 1981 (3) SA 1157 (A) 358

Mataboge 1991 (1) SACR 539 (B) 146
Mathabula 1969 (3) SA 265 (N) 39
Mathe 1981 (3) SA 644 (NC) 208
Mathebula 1978 (2) SA 607 (A) 183
Mathebula 1997 (1) SACR 10 (W) 75, 239
Mathogo 1978 (1) SA 425 (O) 206, 211, 214
Mathope 1982 (3) SA 33 (B) 213
Matisonn 1981 (3) SA 302 (A) 120
Matlou v Makhubedu 1978 (1) SA 946 (A) 113
Matonsi 1958 (2) SA 450 (A) 242
Matsane 1978 (3) SA 821 (T) 305
Matsatebe 1949 (2) SA 105 (O) 356
Matsego 1956 (3) SA 411 (A) 188, 359
Matshoba 1977 (2) SA 671 (A) 345
Matthys 1999 (1) SACR 117 (C) 242
Mavhungu 1981 (1) SA 56 (A) 353, 355
Maweke 1971 (2) SA 327 (A) 243
Maxekwa 1978 (1) SA 419 (O) 205
Mayedwa 1978 (1) SA 509 (E) 211
Mayekiso 1988 (4) SA 738 (W) 202
Mayekiso 1996 (1) SACR 510 (C) 189
Mayekiso 1996 (2) SACR 298 (C) 129, 133
Mayisa 1983 (4) SA 242 (T) 221
Mayongo 1968 (1) SA 443 (E) 176
Mazeka v Minister of Justice 1956 (1) SA 312 (A) 110, 112
Mazibuko 1978 (4) SA 563 (A) 355
Mazwi 1982 (2) SA 344 (T) 208, 210
Mbaka 1964 (2) SA 280 (E) 186
Mbata 1956 (4) SA 735 (N) 244
Mbatha 1982 (2) SA 145 (N) 248
Mbatha 1996 (3) BCLR 293 (CC) 8
Mbatha; Prinsloo 1996 (2) SA 464 (CC) 296
Mbelu 1974 (1) PH H38 (N) 231
Mbombo 1984 (1) SA 390 (D) 283
Mbothoma 1978 (2) SA 530 (O) 205
Mboyany 1978 (2) SA 927 (T) 302
Mbulawa, Tandawupi 1969 (1) SA 532 (E) 180, 181
Mchunu 1974 (1) SA 708 (N) 262
McInnes 1946 WLD 386 151
McKenna 1998 (1) SACR 106 (C) 76
Mcwera 1960 (1) PH H43 (N) 176
Mdau 1991 (1) SA 169 (A) 271
Mdlalose 1972 (1) PH H10 (A) 365
Mdodana 1978 (4) SA 46 (E) 240
Mdunge v Minister of Police 1988 (2) SA 809 (N) 134
Mei 1982 (1) SA 299 (O) 248
Melani 1991 (2) SACR 611 (NC) 302
Melani 1996 (1) SACR 335 (E) 75
Mene 1978 (1) SA 832 (A) 360, 361
Metelerkamp 1959 (4) SA 102 (E) 110, 111
Meyer 1948 (3) SA 144 (T) 184
Meyer 1950 (1) PH H88 (O) 338

Meyers 1946 AD 57   220
Meyers 1988 (3) SA 917 (O)   160
Mfazi 1978 (4) SA 28 (T)   201
Mgcina v Regional Magistrate, Lenasia 1997 (2) SACR 711 (T)   74
Mgilane 1974 (4) SA 303 (Tk)   219
Mgotywa 1958 (1) SA 99 (E)   244
Mgwenya 1925 TPD 288   108
Mhalati 1976 (2) SA 426 (Tk)   241
Mhlanga 1959 (2) SA 220 (T)   222
Mhlongo 1935 AD 133   366
Mhlongo 1970 (2) SA 235 (N)   339
Mhlongo 1991 (2) SACR 207 (A)   187
Mhlungu 1995 (2) SACR 277 (CC)   328
Milne and Erleigh (3) 1950 (4) SA 599 (A)   355
Milne and Erleigh (6) 1951 (1) SA 1 (A)   373
Minister of Justice v Desai NO 1948 (3) SA 395 (A)   126
Minister of Justice v Ntuli 1997 (2) SACR 19 (CC) 307, 319, 341
Minister of Justice v Ntuli 1997 (3) SA 772 (CC)   319
Minister of Justice, Ex parte: In re Duze 1945 AD 102   283
Minister of Justice, Ex parte: In re R v Bolon 1941 AD 345   34
Minister of Justice, Ex parte: In re R v Demingo 1951 (1) SA 36 (A)   229
Minister of Justice, Ex parte: In re R v Moseme 1936 AD 52   178
Minister of Law and Order v Kader 1991 (1) SA 41 (A) 97, 105
Minister of Law and Order v Parker 1989 (2) SA 633 (A) 97, 98
Minister van Justisie, Ex parte: In re S v De Bruin 1972 (2) SA 623 (A) 35, 337
Minister van Justisie, Ex parte: In re S v Suid-Afrikaanse Uitsaaikorporasie 1992 (2) SACR
    618 (A)   363
Minister van Polisie v Chetty 1977 (2) SA 885 (A)   109
Minister van Polisie v Goldschagg 1981 (1) SA 37 (A)   94
Minister van die SA Polisie v Kraatz 1973 (3) SA 490 (A) 97, 99, 100
Minister van Veiligheid en Sekuriteit v Rautenbach 1996 (1) SACR 720 (A)   99
Minister van Wet en Orde v Van der Heever 1982 (4) SA 16 (C)   99
Mitchell v Attorney-General, Natal 1992 (2) SACR 68 (N)   61
Mitondo 1939 EDL 110   251
Mjoli 1981 (3) SA 1233 (A)   212
Mjoli, In re 1994 (1) SACR 336 (T)   302
Mjware 1990 (1) SACR 388 (N)   283
Mkenkana 1972 (2) SA 200 (E)   170
Mkhafu 1978 (1) SA 665 (O)   205
Mkhise 1988 (2) SA 868 (A) 204, 368
Mkhize 1978 (1) SA 264 (N)   205
Mkhize 1978 (3) SA 1065 (T) 199, 210
Mkhize 1981 (3) SA 585 (N) 205, 206
Mkhuzangewe 1987 (3) SA 248 (O)   218
Mkize 1960 (1) SA 276 (N) 231, 239, 240
Mkize 1978 (2) SA 249 (N)   211
Mkohle 1990 (1) SACR 95 (A)   332
Mlakaza 1996 (2) SACR 187 (C)   75
Mlangeni 1976 (1) SA 528 (T)   207
Mlilo 1985 (1) SA 74 (T)   181
Mlooi 1925 AD 131   249
Mlumbi 1991 (1) SACR 235 (A)   332

Mmatli 1988 (2) SA 533 (T) 205
Mnanzana 1966 (3) SA 38 (T) 91, 112
Mngadi 1973 (4) SA 540 (N) 245
Mngadi 1991 (1) SACR 313 (T) 274, 277
Mngomezulu 1983 (1) SA 1152 (N) 237
Mnyamana 1990 (1) SACR 137 (A) 220
Mnyanda 1976 (2) SA 751 (A) 201
Moabi 1979 (3) SA 648 (B) 251
Moekazi v Additional Magistrate, Welkom 1990 (2) SACR 212 (O) 153
Moeti 1991 (1) SACR 462 (B) 138
Mofokeng 1962 (2) SA 385 (A) 364
Mofokeng 1962 (3) SA 551 (A) 364, 373
Mofokeng 1992 (2) SACR 261 (O) 66
Mofokeng v Prokureur-Generaal, OVS 1958 (4) SA 519 (O) 356
Mogatsi 1970 (1) PH H74 (B) 216
Mogora 1990 (2) SACR 9 (T) 284
Mogoregi 1978 (3) SA 13 (O) 211, 212
Mohamed 1977 (2) SA 531 (A) 143, 148
Mohapi 1990 (1) SACR 573 (O) 334
Mohase 1998 (1) SACR 185 (O) 245
Mohlabane 1969 (2) PH H137 (O) 193
Moilwa 19797 (1) SACR 188 (NC) 241
Mokgeledi 1968 (4) SA 335 (A) 345
Mokgoetsi 1943 AD 622 174
Mokgoje 1999 (1) SACR 233 (NC) 158
Mokie 1992 (1) SACR 14 (T) 226
Mokoa 1985 (1) SA 350 (O) 81, 200
Mokoena 1981 (1) SA 148 (O) 207
Mokoena 1983 (2) SA 312 SA 312 (O) 294
Mokoena 1984 (1) SA 267 (O) 310
Mokoena v Commissioner of Prisons 1985 (1) SA 368 (W) 75
Mokoena v Minister of Justice 1968 (4) SA 708 (A) 373
Mokubung; Lesibo 1983 (2) SA 710 (O) 301
Mokwaka 1969 (2) SA 484 (O) 285
Molala 1988 (2) SA 97 (T) 277
Molauzi 1984 (4) SA 738 (T) 205
Molele 1978 (2) SA 668 (O) 211
Molelekeng 1992 (1) SACR 604 (T) 211
Molobi 1976 (2) SA 301 (W) 225
Moloinyane 1965 (2) SA 109 (O) 176
Molorane 1954 (2) PH H150 (O) 332
Moloto 1980 (3) SA 1081 (B) 181
Moloto 1982 (1) SA 844 (A) 181
Moloto 1991 (1) SACR 617 (T) 225
Molotsi 1976 (2) SA 404 (O) 337, 338
Moloyi 1978 (1) SA 516 (O) 211
Monchanyana 1968 (1) SA 56 (O) 309
Mondlane 1987 (4) SA 70 (T) 239
Monnanyane 1977 (3) SA 976 (O) 199
Montsoa 1952 (3) SA 511 (T) 250
Moodie 1961 (4) SA 752 (A) 346, 354, 355, 360, 367
Moodie 1962 (1) SA 587 (A) 217, 218

Moos 1998 (1) SACR 401 (W) 76
Morapedi v Springs Municipality 1946 TPD 105 104
Morgan 1993 (2) SACR 134 (A) 310, 347
Morris 1992 (1) SACR 537 (A) 204, 205
Morris 1992 (2) SACR 365 (C) 310
Morten 1991 (1) SACR 483 (A) 182
Mosala 1968 (3) SA 523 (T) 367
Moseli (1) 1969 (1) SA 646 (O) 77
Mosia 1971 (2) PH H135 (A) 355
Mosia 1988 (2) SA 730 (T) 277
Mosterd 1991 (2) SACR 636 (T) 362
Motaung 1980 (4) SA 131 (T) 240
Motha 1987 (1) SA 374 (T) 347
Mothlaping 1988 (3) SA 757 (NC) 211, 212
Mothopeng 1965 (4) SA 484 (T) 199
Mothopeng 1979 (4) SA 367 (T) 224
Motlatla 1975 (1) SA 814 (T) 80
Motloutsi 1996 (1) SA 584 (C) 133
Motsepa 1982 (1) SA 304 (O) 216, 221
Moyage 1958 (3) SA 400 (A) 277
Mpanza 1974 (2) SA 298 (N) 114
Mpeta 1912 AD 568 333
Mpetha (1) 1981 (3) SA 803 (C) 171, 174
Mpetha (1) 1983 (1) SA 492 (C) 64
Mphala 1998 (1) SACR 388 (W) 75
Mphela 1994 (1) SACR 488 (A) 226
Mpika JS 253/41 (E) 38
Mpofu 1970 (2) SA 162 (RA) 81, 193, 199, 241
Mpompotshe 1958 (4) SA 471 (A) 354
Mpongoshe 1980 (4) SA 593 (A) 199
Mpopo 1978 (2) SA 424 (A) 336
Msibi 1992 (2) SACR 441 (W) 211
Msimango 1972 (3) SA 145 (N) 270
Msiza 1979 (4) SA 473 (T) 285
Mthenjane 1979 (2) SA 105 (A) 225
Mthetwa 1970 (2) SA 310 (N) 218, 219
Mthetwa 1978 (2) SA 773 (N) 204
Mthwana 1989 (4) SA 368 (N) 76
Mtombeni 1946 TPD 401 305
Mtungwa 1931 TPD 466 106
Mtungwa 1990 (2) SACR 1 (A) 330
Mtyuda 1995 (5) BCLR 646 (E) 292
Mugwedi 1988 (2) SA 814 (V) 208
Mukama 1934 TPD 134 195
Mulayo 1962 (2) SA 522 (A) 360
Muller 1957 (4) SA 642 (A) 355
Mullins and Meyer v Pearlman 1917 TPD 639 .... 69, 70
Muniohambo 1983 (4) SA 791 (SWA) 306, 341
Murbane 1992 (1) SACR 298 (NC) 180
Muruven 1953 (2) SA 779 (N) 77
Mushimba 1977 (2) SA 829 (A) 190, 233
Mutambanengwe 1976 (2) SA 434 (RA) 246

Mutawarira 1973 (3) SA 901 (R) 182
Muzikayifani 1979 (3) SA 661 (D) 212
Mvelase 1996 (8) BCLR 1055 (N) 369
Mwambazi 1991 (2) SACR 149 (Nm) 293
Mweuhanga v Cabinet of the Interim Government of SWA 1989 (1) SA 976 (SWA) 70
Myburgh 1922 AD 249 335
Myende 1985 (1) SA 805 (A) 357
Mzo 1980 (1) SA 538 (C) 192
N 1979 (3) SA 308 (A) 181
N 1988 (3) SA 450 (A) 357, 367
N 1991 (2) SACR 10 (A) 352, 356
N 1992 (1) SACR 67 (Ck) 205
Nabote 1978 (1) SA 648 (O) 282
Nagel 1998 (1) SACR 218 (O) 204
Naidoo 1962 (2) SA 625 (A) 234
Naidoo 1962 (4) SA 348 (A) 217, 218, 360, 368, 370
Naidoo 1974 (3) SA 706 (A) 77
Naidoo 1985 (2) SA 32 (N) 204
Naidoo 1987 (3) SA 834 (N) 346
Nambela 1996 (1) SACR 356 (E) 180
Namib Wood Industries (Pty) Ltd v Mutiltha 1992 (1) SACR 381 (Nm) 236
Nangutuuala 1973 (4) SA 640 (SWA) 174
Nathaniel 1987 (2) SA 225 (SWA) 202
Nathanson 1959 (1) SA 258 (N) 210
National Coalition for Gay & Lesbian Equality v Minister of Justice 1998 (2) SACR 5556
    (CC) 329
National High Command 1964 (1) SA 1 (T) 174, 175
National Union of South African Students v Divisional Commissioner, South African Police,
    Cape Western Division 1971 (2) SA 553 (C) 126
Ncaphayi 1990 (1) SACR 472 (A) 359, 360
Ncobo 1988 (3) SA 954 (N) 275, 276
Ncube 1981 (3) SA 511 (T) 208
Ncukutwana v Acting Additional Magistrate, Lady Frere 1968 (1) SA 140 (E) 330
Ndaba 1993 (1) SACR 637 (A) 280
Ndara 1955 (4) SA 182 (A) 104
Ndhlovu 1991 (2) SACR 322 (W) 336
Ndiwe 1988 (3) SA 972 (NC) 208
Ndlovu 1987 (3) SA 827 (N) 210
Ndlovu 1998 (1) SACR 599 (W) 303
Ndou 1971 (1) SA 668 (A) 163, 217
Ndwandwe 1970 (4) SA 502 (N) 229, 231
Ndwandwe 1976 (1) SA 323 (N) 248
Ndzeku 1996 (1) SACR 301 (A) 36
Nel 1960 (4) SA 228 (O) 341
Nel 1974 (2) SA 445 (NC) 77
Nel 1987 (4) SA 276 (O) 325, 326
Nel v Le Roux 1996 (3) SA 562 (CC) 121
Nell 1967 (4) SA 489 (SWA) 91, 109, 111, 112
Nell 1969 (1) SA 143 (A) 226
Nene (1) 1979 (2) SA 520 (D) 241
Neumann 1949 (3) SA 1238 (Spec Crim Ct) 172
Ngcobo 1966 (1) SA 444 (N) 94

Ngcobo 1985 (2) SA 319 (W) 188
Ngcube 1976 (1) SA 341 (N) 240
Ngema; Cele 1960 (1) SA 137 (A) 373
Ngidi 1972 (1) SA 733 (N) 97, 114
NGJ Trading Stores (Pty) Ltd v Guerreiro 1974 (1) SA 51 (O) 65
NGJ Trading Stores (Pty) Ltd v Guerreiro 1974 (4) SA 738 (A) 65, 82
Ngobe 1978 (1) SA 309 (NC) 206
Ngobeni 1981 (1) SA 506 (B) 213, 231
Ngutshane 1952 (4) SA 608 (N) 235
Ngwatya 1949 (1) SA 556 (E) 231
Ngwenya 1991 (2) SACR 520 (T) 139, 152
Ngwenya 1998 (2) SACR 503 (W) 75
Ngxitho 1979 (1) SA 1037 (O) 336
Nhantsi 1994 (1) SACR 26 (Tk) 192
Nhlabathli v Adjunk Prokureur-Generaal, Transvaal 1978 (3) SA 620 (W) 107
Nichas 1977 (1) SA 257 (C) 145, 146, 153
Niesewand (1) 1973 (3) SA 581 (RA) 224
Nigrini 1948 (4) SA 995 (C) 62
Njaba 1966 (3) SA 140 (A) 364, 366
Njadayi 1994 (5) BCLR 90 (E) 156
Nkala 1964 (1) SA 493 (A) 366
Nkambule 1993 (1) SACR 136 (A) 260
Nkete, Ex parte 1937 EDL 231 146
Nkibane 1989 (2) SA 421 (NC) 242
Nkiwani 1970 (2) SA 165 (R) 175
Nkombani 1963 (4) SA 877 (A) 245
Nkosi 1963 (4) SA 87 (T) 337
Nkosi 1978 (1) SA 548 (T) 211
Nkosi 1984 (3) SA 345 (A) 213
Nkosi 1987 (1) SA 581 (T) 150
Noah 1959 (3) SA 530 (E) 339
Nocuse 1995 (1) SACR 510 (Tk) 324
Noemdoe 1993 (1) SACR 264 (C) 311
Nomakhalala 1990 (1) SACR 300 (A) 193
Nomzaza 1996 (2) SACR 14 (A) 155
Nongila 1970 (3) SA 97 (E) 76
Nqula 1974 (1) SA 801 (E) 77
Nqumba v State President 1987 (1) SA 456 (E) 97
Nqunelo 1948 (4) SA 428 (O) 186, 220
Ntakatsane 1990 (2) SACR 382 (NC) 276
Ntjoro 1959 (4) SA 447 (T) 177, 178
Ntomane 1978 (3) SA 596 (T) 205
Ntshingila 1980 (3) SA 883 (N) 304
Ntswakele 1982 (1) SA 325 (T) 182
Ntswayi 1991 (2) SACR 397 (C) 292
Ntuli 1975 (1) SA 429 (A) 361
Ntuli 1978 (2) SA 69 (A) 231
Ntuli 1996 (1) BCLR 141 (CC) 292
Ntuli 1996 (1) SACR 94 (CC) 306, 319, 341
Nxane 1975 (4) SA 433 (O) 301
Nxumalo 1992 (2) SACR 268 (O) 276
Nyambe 1978 (1) SA 311 (NC) 206

Nyati 1972 (4) SA 11 (T) 217
Nzama 1997 (1) SACR 542 (D) 224
Nzuza 1952 (4) SA 376 (A) 230
Nzuza 1963 (3) SA 631 (A) 209, 235
O'Brien 1970 (3) SA 405 (C) 367
O'Carroll 17 ECD 79 220
October 1991 (1) SACR 455 (C) 211
Offerman 1976 (2) PH H215 (E) 237
Olckers 1978 (4) SA 169 (SWA) 208
Omar 1935 AD 230 244
Omar 1982 (2) SA 357 (N) 191
Omar 1993 (2) SACR 5 (C) 278, 280
Onward 1972 (1) PH H68 (R) 210
Oosthuizen 1961 (1) SA 604 (T) 109, 112
Osborne 1978 (3) SA 173 (C) 208
P 1972 (2) SA 513 (NC) 338
Papenfus 1978 (4) SA 32 (T) 207
Park-Ross v Director: Office for Serious Economic Offences 1995 (2) SA 148 (C) 125
Parmanand 1954 (3) SA 833 (A) 246
Parry 1924 AD 401 249
Pastoors 1986 (4) SA 222 (W) 224
Patel 1970 (3) SA 565 (W) 145, 153
Pauline 1928 TPD 643 81
Peerkhan and Lalloo 1906 TS 798 249
Pennington 1997 (4) SA 1076 (CC) 320, 325
Penrose 1966 (1) SA 5 (N) 220
Persotam 1934 TPD 253 194
Peta 1982 (4) SA 863 (E) 240
Peter 1989 (3) SA 649 (CkA) 346
Peterson 1992 (2) SACR 52 (C) 145
Petro Louise Enterprises 1978 (1) SA 271 (T) 342
Phakati 1978 (4) SA 477 (T) 207
Pheka 1975 (4) SA 230 (NC) 176
Phewa 1962 (3) SA 370 (N) 347
Phikwa 1978 (1) SA 397 (E) 204
Philips v Botha 1999 (1) SACR 1 (SCA) 69, 70
Phillips 1949 (2) SA 671 (O) 338
Phillips 1984 (4) SA 536 (C) 181
Phiri 1958 (3) SA 161 (A) 242
Phundula 1978 (4) SA 855 (T) 206
Phuravhatha 1992 (2) SACR 544 (V) 239
Pienaar 1992 (1) SACR 178 (W) 153
Pieters 1987 (3) SA 717 (A) 259, 331
Pieterse 1982 (3) SA 678 (A) 201
Pietersen 1947 (1) SA 56 (W) 230
Piliso 1991 (2) SACR 354 (Tk) 40
Pillay 1958 (4) SA 27 (N) 341
Pillay 1975 (1) SA 919 (N) 170, 177
Pillay 1977 (4) SA 531 (A) 330
Pineiro 1992 (1) SACR 287 (Nm) 360
Pineiro (1) 1992 (1) SACR 577 (Nm) 144, 149
Pitso v Additional Magistrate, Krugersdorp 1976 (4) SA 553 (T) 209, 312

Pogrund 1974 (1) SA 244 (T) 120
Pokela 1968 (4) SA 702 (E) 218
Polelo 1981 (2) SA 271 (NC) 182
Ponyana 1981 (1) SA 139 (Tk) 368
Potgieter 1994 (1) SACR 61 (A) 279
Pratt 1960 (4) SA 743 (T) 201
Preller 1952 (4) SA 452 (A) 335
President of the RSA v Hugo 1997 (1) SACR 567 (CC) 371, 372
Pretoria Timbers Co (Pty) Ltd 1950 (3) SA 163 (A) 367
Pretorius 1991 (2) SACR 601 (A) 363
Prinsloo 1970 (3) SA 550 (O) 348
Prinsloo v Newman 1975 (1) SA 481 (A) 125
Prokureur-Generaal, Noord-Kaap v Hart 1990 (1) SA 49 (A) 346
Prokureur-Generaal, Transvaal, Ex parte 1978 (4) SA 15 (T) 314
Prokureur-Generaal, Transvaal, Ex parte 1980 (3) SA 516 (T) 105
Prokureur Generaal, Venda v Magistraat Streekafdeling 1982 (2) SA 659 (V) 207, 222
Prokureur-Generaal, Vrystaat v Ramokhosi 1997 (1) SACR 127 (O) 143, 152
Punshon v Wise NO 1948 (1) SA 81 (N) 221
Purcell-Gilpin 1971 (3) SA 548 (RA) 111
Quinta 1979 (2) SA 326 (O) 207
Qozeleni v Minister of Law and Order 1994 (2) SACR 340 (E); 1994 (3) SA 625 (E) 296, 322
R 1993 (1) SACR 209 (A) 278, 279, 280
Rabie 1975 (4) SA 855 (A) 260
Radebe 1954 (3) SA 785 (O) 175
Radebe 1968 (4) SA 410 (A) 27
Radebe 1973 (1) SA 796 (A) 196
Radebe 1973 (4) SA 244 (O) 80
Radebe 1988 (1) SA 191 (T) 76, 193
Raftopulos 1952 (4) SA 85 (T) 337
Rakanang 1978 (1) SA 591 (NC) 206, 211
Rall 1982 (1) SA 828 (A) 191, 368
Raloso v Wilson 1998 (2) SACR 298 (NC) 113
Ramakulukusha v Commander, Venda National Force 1989 (2) SA 813 (V) ... 97
Ramgobin 1985 (4) SA 130 (N) 61, 139, 149
Randell 1995 (1) SACR 404 (O) 273
Raphatle 1995 (2) SACR 452 (T) 303, 313
Rapholo v State President 1993 (1) SACR 421 (T) 372
Rautenbach 1991 (2) SACR 700 (T) 172
Rens 1996 (1) SACR 105 (CC) 324
Rheeders v Jacobsz 1942 AD 395 340
Riet 1970 (1) PH H94 (NC) 231
Robinson 1968 (1) SA 666 (A) 332
Roopsingh 1956 (4) SA 509 (A) 245
Rosenthal 1927 TPD 470 108
Rossouw 1971 (3) SA 222 (T) 240
Rost 1980 (2) SA 528 (SWA) 334
Rothman 1990 (1) SACR 170 (O) 303
Rousseau 1979 (3) SA 895 (T) 80
Rousseau v Boshoff 1945 CPD 135 109
Roux 1974 (2) SA 452 (N) 345
Rudman 1992 (1) SA 343 (A) 199, 292
Rudman 1992 (1) SACR 70 (A) 217, 218

Rudman; Mthwana 1992 (1) SACR 70 (A) 78
Rudolf 1950 (2) SA 522 (C) 131
Runds 1978 (4) SA 304 (A) 330
Russell 1978 (1) SA 223 (C) 149
S 1978 (4) SA 374 (T) 161
S 1981 (3) SA 377 (A) 180
S 1987 (2) SA 307 (A) 270
S 1988 (1) SA 120 (A) 331
S 1991 (2) SA 93 (A) 182
S 1995 (2) SACR 421 (T) 336
SA Motor Acceptance Corporation v Oberholzer 1974 (4) SA 808 (T) 195
Sadeke 1964 (2) SA 674 (T) 174
Saib 1975 (3) SA 994 (N) 342
Salie 1986 (2) SA 295 (C) 199, 213
Sallem 1987 (4) SA 772 (A) 190, 193, 233
Salusbury 1934 (1) PH H83 (T) 67
Sambo v Milns 1973 (4) SA 312 (T) 109, 112
Sanderson v Attorney-General, Eastern Cape 1998 (1) SACR 227 (CC); 1998 (2) SA 38 (CC) ... 227
Sangster 1991 (1) SA 240 (O) 301
Sarjoo 1978 (4) SA 520 (N) 176
Sas 1918 CPD 346 228
SASOL III (Edms) Bpk v Minister van Wet en Orde 1991 (3) SA 766 (T) 125
Scagell v Attorney-General of the Western Cape 1996 (11) BCLR 1446 (CC) .. 8
Schawol 1956 (1) SA 310 (T) 353
Schoba 1985 (3) SA 881 (A) 187
Scholtz 1974 (1) SA 120 (W) 110
Scholtz 1996 (2) SACR 40 (NC) 243
Scholtz 1996 (2) SACR 623 (C) 322
Schutte 1926 TPD 172 311
Seals 1990 (1) SACR 38 (C) 225
Sebatana 1983 (1) SA 809 (O) 193, 237
Sebe v Magistrate, Zwelitsha 1984 (3) SA 885 (Ck) 150
Sebiya 1994 (1) SACR 129 (O) 281
Second 1970 (1) PH H5 (RA) 76
Seedat 1971 (1) SA 789 (N) 80, 192
Seekoei 1982 (3) SA 97 (A) 343, 361
Sefatsa v Attorney-General, Transvaal 1988 (4) SA 297 (T) 374
Sefatsa v Attorney-General, Transvaal 1989 (1) SA 821 (A) .. 319, 369, 373, 374
Segal 1949 (3) SA 67 (C) 195
Seheri 1964 (1) SA 29 (A) 76, 227
Sejake 1981 (1) SA 1215 (O) 206
Sekete 1980 (1) SA 171 (N) 224
Selane 1979 (1) SA 318 (T) 212
Selebogo 1984 (2) SA 486 (NC) 214
Seleke 1978 (1) SA 993 (T) 246
Seleke 1980 (3) SA 745 (A) 211, 215
Selemana 1975 (4) SA 908 (T) 193, 242
Sellars 1991 (1) SACR 491 (N) 207
Semenya 1978 (2) SA 110 (T) 211
Sepiri 1979 (2) SA 1168 (NC) 211, 216
September 1959 (4) SA 256 (C) 114
Serumala 1978 (4) SA 811 (NC) 205

Serumula 1962 (3) SA 962 (A) 359
Sesetse 1981 (3) SA 353 (A) 212
Sethoga 1990 (1) SA 270 (A) 207, 214
Sethole 1984 (3) SA 620 (O) 234
Sethuntsa 1982 (3) SA 256 (O) 214
Shabalala 1982 (2) SA 123 (T) 208
Shabalala 1984 (2) SA 234 (N) 272
Shabalala 1995 (2) SACR 761 (CC) 156
Shabalala v Attorney-General 1995 (12) BCLR 1593 (CC) 170
Shaban 1965 (4) SA 646 (W) 140
Shabangu 1976 (3) SA 555 (A) 76
Shaffee 1952 (2) SA 484 (A) 355
Shange 1983 (4) SA 46 (N) 82
Shaw v Collins (1883) 2 SC 389 140
Shein 1925 AD 6 238
Shelembe 1955 (4) SA 410 (N) 181
Shezi 1984 (2) SA 577 (N) 308
Shirindi 1974 (1) SA 481 (T) 263
Shivute 1991 (1) SACR 656 (Nm) 212
Shuma 1994 (4) SA 583 (ECD) 230, 231
Shuping 1983 (2) SA 119 (B) 239
Sias v Minister of Law and Order 1991 (1) SACR 420 (E) 106
Sibande 1958 (3) SA 1 (A) 365, 373
Sibeko 1990 (1) SACR 206 (T) 139, 194
Sibia 1947 (2) SA 50 (A) 240
Sibisi 1972 (2) SA 446 (N) 193
Sibiya 1957 (1) SA 247 (T) 339
Sibiya 1980 (2) SA 457 (N) 205
Sibuya 1979 (3) SA 193 (T) 150
Sibuyi 1993 (1) SACR 235 (A) 279
Sigwahla 1967 (4) SA 566 (A) 245
Sikeliwe 1962 (1) SA 408 (E) 251
Sikhindi 1978 (1) SA 1072 (N) 206
Sikosana 1980 (4) SA 559 (A) 355
Sikumba 1955 (3) SA 125 (E) 238
Silber 1952 (2) SA 475 (A) 194
Simango 1979 (3) SA 189 (T) 105
Simbi 1975 (4) SA 700 (RA) 210
Simelane 1958 (2) SA 302 (N) 306
Simxadi 1997 (1) SACR 169 (C) 241
Sinama 1998 (1) SACR 255 (SCA) 349
Singh 1986 (4) SA 263 (C) 160, 219, 222
Singh 1990 (1) SA 123 (A) 160, 216, 219
Singh v Blomerus NO 1952 (4) SA 63 (N) 171
Sinkankanka 1963 (2) SA 531 (A) 243
Sisulu 1963 (2) SA 596 (W) 347
Sita v Olivier 1967 (2) SA 442 (A) 314
Sitebe 1934 AD 56 277
Sithole 1966 (2) SA 335 (N) 231
Sithole 1974 (2) SA 572 (N) 245
Sithole 1979 (2) SA 67 (A) 276
Sithole 1988 (4) SA 177 (T) 309

Sithole 1991 (4) SA 94 (W) 225
Sitlu 1971 (2) SA 238 (N) 246
Sittig 1929 TPD 669 365
Siwela 1981 (2) SA 56 (T) 294
Skeyi 1981 (4) SA 191 (E) 200
Skwati 1942 TPD 115 114
Slabbert 1958 (1) SA 275 (O) 336
Slabbert 1968 (3) SA 318 (O) 177
Slabbert 1985 (4) SA 248 (C) 184
Smile 1998 (1) SACR 688 (SCA) 369
Smit v Van Niekerk NO 1976 (4) SA 293 (A) 121
Smit v Van Niekerk NO 1976 (4) SA 304 (E) 120, 226
Smith 1971 (4) SA 419 (T) 263
Smith 1985 (2) SA 152 (T) 82
Smith (2) 1987 (4) SA 768 (A) 331
Smith 1996 (1) SACR 250 (E) 270, 271
Smith, Tabata & Van Heerden v Minister of Law and Order 1989 (3) SA 627 (E) 126
Snyman 1999 (8) BCLR 931 (C) 154
Solani 1987 (4) SA 203 (NC) 263
Solo 1995 (1) SACR 490 (E) 369
Solomon 1934 CPD 94 230
Solomon 1966 (3) SA 145 (A) 334
Solomon v Magistrate, Pretoria 1950 (3) SA 603 (T) 70, 71
Solomons 1959 (2) SA 352 (A) 189, 361
Somciza 1990 (1) SA 361 (A) 230
Somyali 1979 (2) SA 274 (E) 205
Sonday 1994 (2) SACR 810 (C) 332
Sonday 1995 (1) SA 497 (C) 234, 241
Soni 1973 (1) PH HS20 (N) 245
Sotiralis 1950 (4) SA 481 (T) 103
Sparks 1972 (3) SA 396 (A) 189
Stanfield 1997 (1) SACR 221 (C) 138, 148
Steenkamp 1960 (3) SA 680 (N) 109
Steenkamp 1973 (2) SA 221 (NC) 65
Stevens 1981 (1) SA 864 (C) 246
Stevens 1983 (3) SA 649 (A) 367
Steyn 1981 (4) SA 385 (C) 366
Stone 1976 (2) SA 279 (A) 189
Strowitzki 1995 (1) SASCR 414 (NmH) 324
Strowitski 1995 (2) SA 525 (NmHC) 241
Strydom 1994 (2) SACR 456 (W) 280
Suid-Afrikaanse Uitsaaikorporasie 1991 (2) SA 698 (W) 343
Suliman 1969 (2) SA 385 (A) 192, 196, 221
Summers 1956 (2) SA 786 (A) 352
Swanepoel 1945 AD 444 346
Swanepoel 1979 (1) SA 478 (A) 163, 359
Swanepoel 1980 (2) SA 81 (NC) 64
Swanepoel 1985 (1) SA 576 (A) 110
Swarts 1983 (3) SA 261 (C) 208
Swartz 1991 (2) SACR 502 (NC) 250
Sweigers 1969 (1) PH H110 (A) 328
T 1940 CPD 14 180

T 1990 (1) SACR 57 (T) 236
T 1997 (1) SACR 496 (SCA) 271
Taitz 1970 (3) SA 342 (N) 177
Talie 1979 (2) SA 1003 (C) 212
Taljaard, Ex parte 1942 OPD 66 146
Tampart 1990 (1) SACR 282 (SWA) 194
Tembani 1970 (4) SA 395 (E) 242
Thane 1925 TPD 850 171
Theunissen 1952 (1) SA 201 (A) 364
Thielke 1918 AD 373 342
Thipe 1988 (3) SA 346 (T) 183
Thobakgale 1998 (1) SACR 703 (W) 321
Thomas 1978 (2) SA 408 (B) 211
Thompson 1911 EDL 98 313
Thornhill (2) 1998 (1) SACR 177 (C) 143
Thos 1976 (2) SA 408 (O) 341
Tieties 1990 (2) SA 461 (A) 164, 216
Tito 1984 (4) SA 363 (Ck) 204
Tladi 1978 (2) SA 476 (O) 205
Tladi 1989 (3) SA 444 (B) 347
Tlailane 1982 (4) SA 107 (T) 222
Tola 1974 (1) SA 115 (W) 111
Tom 1991 (2) SACR 249 (B) 201
Toms; Bruce 1990 (2) SA 802 (A) 260
Tranter v Attorney-General and the First Criminal Magistrate of Johannesburg 1907 TS 415   63
Tremearne 1917 NPD 117 338
Trope v Attorney-General 1925 TPD 175 143
Tsane 1978 (4) SA 161 (O) 241
Tsankobeb 1981 (4) SA 614 (A) 162
Tsatsinyana 1986 (2) SA 504 (T) 277
Tsawane 1989 (1) SA 268 (A) 358
Tsedi 1984 (1) SA 565 (A) 352, 356
Tshabalala 1998 (2) SACR 259 (C) 147, 156
Tshaki 1985 (3) SA 373 (O) 283
Tshapo 1967 (3) SA 100 (N) 334
Tshivhule 1985 (4) SA 48 (V) 176
Tshoko 1988 (1) SA 139 (A) 330
Tshuke 1965 (1) SA 582 (C) 180
Tshumi 1978 (1) SA 128 (N) 204
Tsose v Minister of Justice 1951 (3) SA 10 (A) 100, 101
Tucker 1953 (3) SA 150 (A) 175, 335, 360
Tuge 1966 (4) SA 565 (A) 368
Turner 1976 (1) PH H107 (A) 366
Tyebela 1989 (2) SA 22 (A) 199
Union Government v Bolstridge 1929 AD 240 101
V 1953 (3) SA 314 (A) 347
Van Deventer 1978 (3) SA 97 (T) 204
Van Deventer v Reichenberg 1996 (1) SACR 119 (C)   70
Van H 1959 (3) SA 648 (T) 354
Van Heerden 1949 (4) SA 949 (N) 342
Van Heerden 1956 (1) SA 366 (A) 365
Van Heerden 1958 (3) SA 150 (T) 91, 109

Van Heerden 1972 (2) PH H74 (E) 330
Van Heerden v De Kock 1979 (3) SA 315 (E) 209
Van Niekerk 1924 TPD 486 171
Van Niekerk 1967 (4) SA 269 (SWA) 340
Van Niekerk 1981 (3) SA 787 (T) 242
Van Niekerk v Van Rensburg 1976 (2) SA 471 (T) 305
Van Rensburg 1963 (2) SA 343 (N) 66, 236
Van Rensburg 1969 (1) SA 215 (G) 176
Van Rensburg 1978 (4) SA 481 (T) 270, 282
Van Rooyen 1994 (2) SACR 823 (A) 275
Van Schoor 1995 (2) SACR 515 (E) 324
Van Sitters 1962 (4) SA 296 (C) 304
Van Staden 1975 (2) PH H103 (T) 302
Van Vuuren 1992 (1) SACR 127 (A) 284
Van Wyk 1960 (2) SA 106 (C) 343
Van Wyk 1972 (1) SA 787 (A) 76
Van Wyk 1981 (3) SA 228 (C) 66
Van Zyl 1949 (2) SA 948 (C) 178
Vanmali 1975 (1) SA 17 (N) 284
Vaz 1975 (1) SA 52 (T) 338
Veenendal v Minister of Justice 1993 (1) SACR 154 (T) 143, 148
Velela 1979 (4) SA 581 (C) 248
Venter 1990 (2) SACR 291 (NC) 357, 367
Verity-Amm 1934 TPD 416 175
Vermaas 1997 (2) SACR 454 (T) 246
Vermaas; Du Plessis 1995 (3) SA 293 (CC); 1995 (2) SACR (CC) 74, 328
Verster 1952 (2) SA 231 (A) 309, 311
Vezi 1963 (1) SA 9 (N) 240
Victor 1970 (1) SA 427 (A) 269
Viljoen 1923 AD 90 248
Viljoen 1989 (3) SA 965 (T) 310
Visser 1975 (2) SA 342 (C) 138, 139, 148
Visser; Nkwandla 1990 (1) SACR 183 (E) 273
Vlok 1931 CPD 181 180
Von Molendorff 1987 (1) SA 135 (T) 338
Vorster 1961 (4) SA 863 (O) 217
Vorster 1976 (2) PH H202 (A) 182
Vorster, In re 1997 (1) SACR 269 (EC) 226
Vos 1914 CPD 139 338
Vries 1996 (2) SACR 628 (Nm) 261
Wahlhaus v Additional Magistrate, Johannesburg 1959 (3) SA 113 (A) . . . 329
Waite 1978 (3) SA 896 (O) 220
Waites 1991 (2) SACR 388 (NC) 180
Watson 1970 (1) SA 320 (R) 217
Webb 1956 (2) SA 208 (A) 353
Weber v Regional Magistrate, Windhoek 1969 (4) SA 394 (SWA) 174
Wegener 1938 EDL 3 179
Wehr 1998 (1) SACR 99 (C) 181
Wells 1990 (1) SA 816 (A) 251
Wessels 1996 (3) SA 737 (C) 225
Wessels 1966 (4) SA 89 (C) 74, 226
Weyer 1958 (3) SA 467 (G) 121

White 1952 (2) SA 538 (A) 355
Whitehead 1970 (4) SA 424 (A) 330
Whitney 1975 (3) SA 453 (N) 246
Wild v Hoffert 1998 (2) SACR 1 (CC) 227
Wilken 1971 (3) SA 488 (A) 334
Willemse 1988 (3) SA 836 (A) 269
Williams 1963 (1) SA 761 (T) 334
Williams [1977] 1 WLR 400 (CA) 199
Williams 1995 (7) BCLR 861 (CC); 1995 (2) SACR 251 (CC) 20, 268
Williams v Janse van Rensburg (1) 1989 (4) SA 485 (C) 71
Williams v Janse van Rensburg (2) 1989 (4) SA 680 (C) 70
Wise 1975 (1) SA 597 (RA) 236
Witbooi 1978 (3) SA 590 (T) 206
Witbooi 1980 (2) SA 911 (NC) 183
Witbooi 1994 (1) SACR 44 (Ck) 230
Wolman v Springs Town Council 1941 TPD 104 66
Wolpe v Officer Commanding South African Police, Johannesburg 1955 (2) SA 87 (W) 127
Wood v Ondangwa Tribal Authority 1975 (2) SA 294 (A) 107
Wronsky v Prokureur-Generaal 1971 (3) SA 292 (SWA) 60
X, Ex parte 1938 AD 244 335
Xaba 1978 (1) SA 646 (O) 197
Xaba 1983 (3) SA 717 (A) 236, 359, 360
Xhaba 1971 (1) SA 232 (T) 283
Xolo v Attorney-General of the Transvaal 1952 (3) SA 764 (W) 231
Xungu 1978 (1) SA 663 (O) 211
Young 1977 (1) SA 602 (A) 274
Yuill v Yuill [1945] 1 All ER 183 215
Yusuf 1968 (2) SA 59 (A) 357, 368
Zackey 1945 AD 505 .... 227, 311
Zantsi v The Council of State 1995 (4) SA 615 (CC) 328
Zenzile 1975 (1) SA 210 (E) 181
Zimba 1975 (2) PH H122 (N) 227
Zimmerie 1989 (3) SA 484 (C) 240
Zive 1960 (3) SA 24 (T) 339
Zoko 1983 (1) SA 871 (N) 342, 343
Zondi 1974 (3) SA 391 (N) 284
Zondi 1995 (1) SACR 18 (A) 262
Zonele 1959 (3) SA 319 (A) 230, 262
Zulu 1967 (4) SA 499 (T) 309, 310
Zulu 1990 (1) SA 655 (T) 240
Zuma 1995 (1) SACR 568 (CC) 8, 76
Zuma 1995 (4) BCLR 401 (CC); 1995 (2) SACR 152 (CC); 1995 (2) SA 652 (CC) 9, 10, 19, 24, 293, 296, 320, 326, 369
Zuma [1996] 3 All SA 334 (N) 192
Zungu 1984 (1) SA 376 (N) 191, 294
Zuny 1919 TPD JS 345 181
Zwane (1) 1987 (4) SA 369 (W) 182
Zwane v Magistrate, Maphumulo 1980 (3) SA 976 (N) 300
Zwayi 1997 (2) SACR 772 (Ck) 75
Zwela 1981 (1) SA 335 (O) 209

PART I

SELECTED GENERAL PRINCIPLES OF THE LAW OF CRIMINAL PROCEDURE

CHAPTER 1

Basic principles, values and constitutionalism

		Page
1	INTRODUCTION	4
2	LAW; THE LAW OF CRIMINAL PROCEDURE	5
3	PRESUMPTION OF INNOCENCE; LEGAL GUILT	6
4	PRIVILEGE AGAINST SELF-INCRIMINATION/RIGHT TO SILENCE	8
5	RIGHTS AND POWERS; DELIMITATION	10
6	DOUBLE-FUNCTIONAL NATURE OF SOME RULES	13
7	CRIMINAL PROCEDURE AS A SYSTEM	14
8	THE HISTORY OF SOUTH AFRICAN CRIMINAL PROCEDURE; VARIOUS MODELS OF CRIMINAL PROCEDURE	15
9	A BILL OF RIGHTS: CONSTITUTIONAL CRIMINAL PROCEDURE	18
	9.1 General	18
	9.2 Section 9: Equality	21
	9.3 Section 10: Human dignity	21
	9.4 Section 11: Life	22
	9.5 Section 12: Freedom and security of the person	23
	9.6 Section 13: Slavery, servitude and forced labour	23
	9.7 Section 14: Privacy	23
	9.8 Section 32: Access to information	23
	9.9 Section 34: Access to courts	24
	9.10 Section 35: Arrested, detained and accused persons	24
	9.11 Section 28: Children	24
	9.12 Section 37: States of emergency	24
10	REMEDIES	25
11	CONCLUSION	29

1

The Constitution and this chapter:

Section 1—Republic of South Africa

The Republic of South Africa is one, sovereign, democratic state founded on the following values:

. . .

(c) Supremacy of the constitution and the rule of law.

See 1 and 9.1, below.

Section 2—Supremacy of Constitution

This Constitution is the supreme law of the Republic; law or conduct inconsistent with it is invalid, and the obligations imposed by it must be fulfilled.

See 9.1, below.

Section 8—Application of Bill of Rights

8(2) A provision of the Bill of Rights binds a natural or a juristic person if, and to the extent that, it is applicable, taking into account the nature of the right and the nature of any duty imposed by the right.

See 9.1, below.

Section 9—Equality

9(1) Everyone is equal before the law and has the right to equal protection and benefit of the law.

See 9.2, below.

Section 10—Human dignity

Everyone has inherent dignity and the right to have their dignity respected and protected.

See 9.3, below.

Section 11—Life

Everyone has the right to life.

See 9.4, below.

Section 12—Freedom and security of the person

12(1) Everyone has the right to freedom and security of the person, which includes the right—

　　(a) not to be deprived of freedom arbitrarily or without just cause;

　　(b) not to be detained without trial;

　　(c) to be free from all forms of violence from either public or private sources;

　　(d) not to be tortured in any way; and

　　(e) not to be treated or punished in a cruel, inhuman or degrading way.

See 9.5, below.

Section 13—Slavery, servitude and forced labour

No one may be subjected to slavery, servitude or forced labour.

See 9.6, below.

Section 14—Privacy

Everyone has the right to privacy, which includes the right not to have—

(a) their person or home searched;

(b) their property searched;

(c) their possessions seized; or

(d) the privacy of their communications infringed.

See 9.7, below.

Section 28—Children

28(1) Every child has the right—

. . .

(g) not to be detained except as a measure of last resort, in which case, in addition to the rights a child enjoys under sections 12 and 35, the child may be detained only for the shortest appropriate period of time, and has the right to be—

(i) kept separately from detained persons over the age of 18 years; and

(ii) treated in a manner, and kept in conditions, that take account of the child's age.

See 9.11, below.

Section 32—Access to information

32(1) Everyone has the right of access to—

(a) any information held by the state; and

(b) any information that is held by another person and that is required for the exercise or protection of any rights.

See 9.8, below.

Section 34—Access to courts

Everyone has the right to have any dispute that can be resolved by the application of law decided in a fair public hearing before a court or, where appropriate, another independent and impartial tribunal or forum.

See 9.9, below.

Section 35—Arrested, detained and accused persons

see the Appendix "Selected sections, Constitution . . ."

See 4, 9.1, 9.10 and 10 below—and *passim* in this book

Section 36—Limitation of rights

see the Appendix "Selected sections, Constitution . . ."

See 9.1, below.

Section 37—States of emergency

see the Appendix "Selected sections, Constitution . . ."

See 9.1 and 9.12, below.

Section 38—Enforcement of rights

see the Appendix "Selected sections, Constitution . . ."

See 9.1, below.

Section 39—Interpretation of Bill of Rights

see the Appendix "Selected sections, Constitution . . ."

See 9.1, below.

Section 165—Judicial authority

165(2) The courts are independent and subject only to the Constitution and the law, which they must apply impartially and without fear, favour or prejudice.

See 10, below.

> '(Penal law) is the law on which men place their ultimate reliance
> for protection against all the deepest injuries that human
> conduct can inflict on individuals and institutions. By the same
> token, penal law governs the strongest force that we permit official
> agencies to bring to bear on individuals. Its promise as an
> instrument of safety is matched only by its power to destroy.
> If penal law is weak or ineffective, basic human interests are in
> jeopardy. If it is harsh or arbitrary in its impact, it works a gross
> injustice on those caught within its toils. The law that carries
> such responsibilities should surely be as rational and just as law
> can be. Nowhere in the entire legal field is more at stake for the
> community or for the individual.'
> —Wechsler 'The Challenge of a Model Penal Code'
> 1952 Harvard Law Review 1097, 1098.

1 INTRODUCTION

In this chapter we deal with a number of preliminary topics, viewpoints and approaches as a backdrop to the main body of the book; the chapter in a sense can provide a set of spectacles (or plural, sets of spectacles) through which to view the rest of the book, ie ways of thinking about aspects of criminal procedure. We want to move away from a totally positivistic study of legal procedural rules; on the other hand, we do not want to propose a total paradigmatic scheme or philosophy (such as could be provided, for instance, by the Critical or Neo-Marxist approaches in criminology or penology). The chapter is not intended to be a complete prolegomenon to the study of criminal procedure. It is an 'introduction'.

No modern South African book on criminal procedure can ignore the existence or provisions of the Constitution of the Republic of South Africa, Act 108 of 1996. This constitution (and its predecessor, the 'Interim Constitution' Act 200 of 1993) created a new legal order in South Africa, fundamentally restructuring the legal system from one in which Parliament reigned supreme to one in which the supremacy of the *Constitution* and the rule of law are founding values (see section 1(c) of the Constitution). State power is limited, being subordinate to the Constitution as interpreted by the Constitutional Court. The state has, so to speak, been brought under the discipline of the 'rule of law'. Section 2 of the Constitution reads: 'This Constitution is the supreme law of the Republic; law or conduct inconsistent with it is invalid, and the obligations imposed by it must be fulfilled.' As will be seen, this has profound implications for criminal procedure.

The first judgment relating to the 1996 Constitution is *Ex parte Chairperson of the Constitutional Assembly: In re Certification of the Constitution of the Republic of South Africa* 1996 (4) SA 744 (CC), which contains important principles and clarifications regarding the present Constitution. In this chapter, we shall use the case in which the death sentence was abolished, *Makwanyane* 1995 (3) SA 391 (CC); 1995 (2) SACR 1 (CC), as our main illustration of constitutional criminal procedural litigation and the impact of the Constitution on the law of criminal procedure. Although this case deals with the interpretation of the Interim Constitution, the principles contained therein would be applicable *mutatis mutandis* under the present Constitution.

Since we aim in this chapter to further perspective, we do not often cite authority for our views. Sometimes there will be no authority for our views, precisely because they are views or perspectives and not statements of law. Where statements of law are made (eg on *onus* and *quantum* of proof, below), they tend to be trite; authority may be found in later chapters of this book or in the standard books on the law of criminal procedure and evidence.

We regrettably can also not indulge much in empirical criminal justice, although we are acutely aware that a realistic picture of what actually happens in real life practice is not only different from the impressions that a mere study of the rules will create, but is also important. The importance of (empirical) realism as opposed to idealistic or ideological dreaming in criminal justice has been well illustrated in *Makwanyane* (above) as well as in the fate of the so-called 'drastic process' (see below). The scope of this work, however, must be limited.

2 LAW; THE LAW OF CRIMINAL PROCEDURE

Human beings generally live in a community, in society. Various social mechanisms exist to help them live together in an acceptably orderly fashion, such as rules of etiquette, custom, morality, ethics and religion. Law is a highly formalised set of rules which also help to regulate and enforce human conduct, backed by state power and enforced through a variety of institutions such as the police, the courts and correctional services. (Human conduct includes the conduct of humans-in-association, eg legal persons such as companies, and the state.)

Law can be classified in various categories for analytical and study purposes; there is nothing absolute or eternal in these classifications—they are but human constructs and they can differ from person to person. Two of the categories into which we classify law are substantive (material) law and adjectival (formal) law. Substantive law comprises all the norms which define rights and duties; in criminal law, for instance, substantive law defines exactly what theft means. Substantive law by itself would not be of much use; if a country had the most excellent Criminal Law Code, it would still need a mechanism to apply that code, ie to put it into action. Substantive criminal law is static. The mere threat of criminal sanctions would not have a strong general deterrent effect on the population as a whole. Accordingly, adjectival law is needed to make the substantive criminal law dynamic, ie to make it work. The two branches of adjectival law which correspond closely with substantive criminal law are the Law of Criminal Procedure and the Law of Evidence. Criminal procedure regulates, *inter alia*, the workings of the entire prosecutorial machinery—the courts' structure, the structure of prosecution, the position of suspects or accused persons, police powers, pre-trial procedure, detention, bail, charge sheets/indictments, pleading, the trial, verdict, sentencing, post-trial remedies (such as appeal and review), and executive action (eg mercy, indemnification and free pardon).

The law of evidence is very closely connected with criminal procedure; it regulates the manner in which relevant issues may be proved in court. Rules of evidence may have a definitive effect on criminal procedure and vice versa. For instance, non-compliance in the pre-trial (investigative) phase by the police of evidential rules or guidelines (such as the Judges' Rules regarding interrogation or guidelines regarding the proper holding of an identification parade) may lead to the exclusion/ inadmissibility of the evidence which they obtained as a result of their improper procedure. Evidential exclusion thus becomes a sanction against wrongful or improper police conduct; it also (and, perhaps, more importantly) vindicates the principle of legality or the Rule of Law, viz the principle that the conduct of the processes of criminal justice should always conform to the requirements of the law and that the courts will enforce this; and finally it ensures integrity in criminal justice: the courts will not dirty their hands by becoming party to the illegal conduct of other functionaries of the criminal justice system.

The interrelationship between the law of criminal procedure and the law of evidence is clear, although for analytical, teaching and study purposes they are often separated.

Overarching all areas of law is the Constitution. The present handbook deals first and foremost with criminal procedure as such, but has to pay attention to the constitutional context and the relevant provisions of the Constitution, as well as to aspects of the law of evidence, albeit in a limited way.

3 PRESUMPTION OF INNOCENCE; LEGAL GUILT

It is important to note that criminal procedure does not deal with the detection, investigation and prosecution of *criminals*, but of *suspects and accused persons*. ('Suspect' generally refers to a person who has not yet been charged, eg an arrested person who is being taken to the police station; 'accused' refers to a person who has been charged. The terms are not mutually exclusive, nor is the term 'suspect' a legally defined one. In this handbook, we shall use 'accused' in wide terms to include suspects as well as charged persons, or in narrow terms to include only the latter; the meaning should be clear from the context.)

Due to the presumption of innocence, every person is regarded as innocent until properly convicted by a court of law. The adverb 'properly' involves, *inter alia*, compliance with the rules of evidence and criminal procedure. A conviction is an objective and impartial official pronouncement that a person has been proved legally guilty by the State (prosecution) in a properly conducted trial, in accordance with the principle of legality, ie in a trial where the State obeyed the rules of criminal law, criminal procedure, evidence, and the Constitution. A person may in the public's subjective view be factually or morally guilty of a crime, but that does not say that he will or can be proved to be legally guilty. In a state under the rule of law (*Rechtsstaat*), only legal guilt counts; to 'convict' a person in any other way may amount to vigilantism, mob trials and even anarchy. If an accused is convicted by a trial court, but is acquitted on appeal because the higher court finds that a rule of evidence required some evidence, which is crucial to the State's case, to have been excluded at the trial (eg evidence improperly obtained after the accused was tortured by the police), it would be wrong to say that the rule of evidence has caused a criminal to go free; it has simply caused a person who had been presumed to be innocent from the outset to continue to be presumed (labelled) innocent because the State could not prove his guilt with due regard to the requirements of the principle of legality—the *status quo ante* remains.

Accordingly, in criminal procedure, although the purpose of a criminal investigation, court trial and post-trial procedures is to find the truth in order to convict the guilty and acquit the innocent, truth as such is not an absolute and not even the highest value. Sometimes truth will be excluded in pursuit of higher values. This can be illustrated by referring to the concept of privilege in the law of evidence; certain evidence must be excluded because it is privileged, even though it is highly relevant and reliable, eg certain communications between legal representative and client. The reason is that there are values or interests at stake that are higher than truth; in this case the fostering of free and open communication between attorneys and their clients without fear of its being revealed and used in court. The exclusion of improperly or illegally obtained admissions/confessions and other illegally obtained evidence is likewise based on the notion of legality; the court is unwilling to become part of illegal state action against its citizens and therefore excludes the illegally obtained evidence (even though the evidence may be highly relevant and reliable) in the interests of the Rule of Law or legality. (Although this type of exclusionary rule is embedded in the Constitution—see section 35(5)—it should be kept in mind that it has not yet, at the time of writing, been the subject of litigation before and interpretation by the Constitutional Court. See further below.)

In order to obtain a conviction, the prosecution must prove the accused's guilt beyond a reasonable doubt. The onus or burden of proof rests on the prosecution because of the above-mentioned presumption of innocence regarding the accused. This means that an accused person does not have to prove that he is innocent. The prosecution must cover adequately every substantive element of the crime as defined in criminal law and which the accused is alleged in the charge sheet/indictment to have perpetrated, by presenting concrete and admissible evidence in order to prove *prima facie* that the accused is guilty. As has been mentioned, the elements which make up each offence are defined in substantive criminal law. If but a single element is not proved by the prosecution beyond a reasonable doubt, the accused can in no way be convicted and may in fact be discharged at the end of the state's case, without even being required to proceed with the defence case, as will be seen below. If the State does succeed in proving a *prima facie* case and the accused does nothing to disturb that case, the *prima facie* proof may 'harden' into proof beyond reasonable doubt and the accused may be convicted—simply because there is nothing which reasonably (ie not in a far-fetched or purely speculative way) produces a doubt in the court's mind about the guilt of the accused on each and every element of the alleged crime. If, on the other hand, the accused can make the court doubt reasonably that one (or more) of the required elements has been proved, he must be acquitted. The accused can raise a reasonable doubt through cross-examining a State witness, objecting to the admissibility of certain evidence, producing his own witness(es), or testifying himself. Whereas the quantum of proof in a criminal case is 'beyond reasonable doubt', in civil matters it is 'on a balance or preponderance of probabilities', which is a much smaller quantum of proof. The smaller quantum in a civil case means that if the court is in doubt at the end of, say, a suit for damages, it will assess the probabilities; if the plaintiff's version seems more likely or probable than that of the defendant, in the light of human experience and other factors, the plaintiff will win. Not so in a criminal case: even if the State's version is more likely or probable than the defendant's, he will be acquitted if there is a reasonable possibility that his version may be true; this 'possibility' need not be a probability. If there is a reasonable doubt that every single element of the offence has been proved, the defendant gets the benefit of it. *In dubio pro reo.*

Although we do not propose to deal with ethics as such in this book, it may be mentioned here that it should by now be clear that there are no ethical problems involved per se in 'defending the guilty'. The accused is by law presumed innocent; the label of legal guilt can be affixed to him only by a court after a proper process has been completed in accordance with the requirements of the principle of legality; the onus of proof rests on the prosecution; the quantum is big. The function of the defence lawyer is, *inter alia*, to check and challenge the prosecution's performance. If the latter fails, the accused remains legally innocent. Moral and/or factual guilt (how determined?), are irrelevant to the earthly criminal justice process.

The fundamental right to be presumed innocent until found guilty in a manner as stated above, is guaranteed in section 35(3)*(h)* of the Constitution: 'Every accused person has a right to a fair trial, which includes the right . . . to be presumed innocent, to remain silent, and not to testify during the proceedings'.

The presumption of innocence has a profound impact on the validity of presumptions in the law of evidence (which, of course, is closely related to the law of criminal procedure) which purport to shift the burden of proof (onus) to the accused. For instance, in *Zuma* 1995 (1) SACR 568 (CC), *Bhulwana* 1995 (12) BCLR 1579 (CC), *Mbatha* 1996 (3) BCLR 293 (CC), *Julies* 1996 (7) BCLR 899 (CC) and *Scagell v Attorney-General of the Western Cape* 1996 (11) BCLR 1446 (CC) statutory presumptions which shift the onus from the state to the accused were struck down by the Constitutional Court since they infringed the right to be presumed innocent until the state proves guilt above reasonable doubt.

4 PRIVILEGE AGAINST SELF-INCRIMINATION/RIGHT TO SILENCE

Not unrelated to the presumption of innocence is the rule that an accused can never be forced to testify; he has a right to silence, which is also called his privilege against self-incrimination or his right to a passive defence. This applies not only to the trial phase but also to the pre-trial stage (ie the investigative or police phase, as well as the pleading phase). Accordingly, the Constitution guarantees the right of every *arrestee* to remain silent (s 35(1)*(a)*) and not to be compelled to make a confession or admission which could be used in evidence against him or her (s 35(1)*(c)*), as well as the right of every *accused* to remain silent and not to testify during the proceedings (s 35(3)*(h)* and *(j)*). At the root of this is the fact that the suspect/accused is in our law a full legal subject and not merely an object of enquiry. The interrelatedness of the presumption of innocence and the right to silence is apparent in section 35(3)*(h)* and was explored in *Zuma* 1995 (4) BCLR 401 (SA), which declared unconstitutional the reverse onus in the then section 217(1)*(b)*(ii) of the Criminal Procedure Act which required an accused to prove that a confession was not freely and voluntarily made. The presumption of innocence is the basis for the rule that the onus in criminal cases should always rest on the State. Section 21(1)*(a)*(i) of the Drugs and Drug Trafficking Act 140 of 1992, which places the burden of proof on the accused under certain circumstances, is therefore an unconstitutional infringement of the right entrenched in s 35(1)*(a)* — *Bhulwana; Gwadiso* 1995 (2) SACR 748 (CC).

In medieval criminal procedure, objects were tried — black cats, cocks that crowed at the wrong times, roof tiles that fell on people's heads, etc. The accused (often suspected witches) were likewise regarded as objects without any rights or dignity. The confession was regarded as the queen of evidence; different degrees of torture were permitted by law in order to coerce accused persons to confess (hence the term 'third degree'—see below). An accused could, for instance, be pressed under layer upon layer of slabstone in order to make him or her speak, until he literally cracked (hence the present idiomatic or figurative expressions 'he was hard pressed for an answer' and 'he cracked under questioning'). Not so any more: as has been stated, the accused is now a full legal subject. As such he is entitled to participate in his trial according to his own autonomous decisions and to be assisted, if he so wishes, by a legal representative. (When we mention an accused's right to counsel, we refer in general to his right to be legally represented by an attorney or advocate or any other permissible legal adviser or practitioner. See the Constitution s 35(2)*(b)* and *(c)* and s 35(3)*(f)* and *(g)*.) Since an accused is now viewed as a legal subject, he must be able to participate meaningfully (ie with understanding), as he wishes, in the criminal process. His counsel will assist him in this. If he is unrepresented, he should at all crucial decision-making or option-choosing stages in the process be informed of his rights and options, as well as their implications—eg his right to counsel, right to silence, right to call witnesses, right to cross-examine and so forth; otherwise his status as legal subject is empty and useless. His position as full legal subject in the modern criminal process also implies that he cannot be tried if he is mentally unable to understand enough to participate meaningfully and communicate with his lawyer (see s 77 of the Criminal Procedure Act). In medieval times insane persons were tried in the same way as other 'objects', tortured and, if convicted, punished (often by being burned at the stake on the ground that they were 'demon-possessed').

Many of the rights of accused persons can be traced to the above two fundamental points of departure—viz the presumption of innocence (including the privilege against self-incrimination) and the status of the accused as legal subject—coupled with the notion of legality (ie that the state is not absolute, but is limited or ruled by law)—for example the right to be informed of his rights and about the reasons for restrictions of his rights (eg the reasons for arrest, or the contents of a search warrant); the right to pre-trial release (bail, etc); the right to contact family, friends and counsel upon arrest; the right to a specified place of detention (lest he be made to disappear; he must be locatable in order that he may effectively exercise his other rights); the right not to be coerced into talking; the right to an interpreter; the right to obtain a copy of a search or arrest warrant; the right to be brought speedily before a judicial officer (ie the right to judicial supervision and control); the right to be fully informed of the charges against him; the right to have pre-trial action against him or against his possessions based upon principles of reasonableness—to mention but a few (see the Constitution s 35 and cf further below).

If a person has certain rights, obviously he should not be penalised for exercising those rights, otherwise the rights in reality amount to nothing at best and to liabilities or traps at the worst. A person who exercises his right to silence at his trial should accordingly not be penalised for the exercise of the right as such; no adverse inference should be drawn against his decision not to testify, for two reasons: first, no such inference *could* be drawn, for there may be a multitude of reasons why he does not wish to testify (he may think the State case is so weak that it does not merit an answer; he may not trust the court or legal system, or be afraid or ignorant as to strategy; or he may simply want to exercise the right to silence about which he has been informed); secondly, no such inference could *logically* be drawn to fill gaps in the State case: if an element of a crime (eg identity in the case of robbery) has not been covered by prima facie proof, the nothingness of the accused's silence cannot logically fill that gap in the State's case. (Regarding the very important cardinal rules of logic, see *Blom* 1939 AD 188.)

The foregoing, however, does not mean that an accused's defence cannot be severely or fatally damaged by his silence. It can happen like this: If the State has proved a *prima facie* case against the accused, ie it has covered each and every element of the crime (as defined by substantive criminal law) by evidence (whether verbal or documentary, lay or expert, direct or circumstantial) and the accused has not raised a reasonable doubt on any of these elements (for example by shaking a state witness in cross-examination), and he then does not testify (ie he does not put another version before the court), the court as a matter of fact only has the uncontroverted State evidence to go on; the *prima facie* proof hardens into sufficient evidence for a conviction. But note that this happens simply because the defence did not 'disturb' the State's case; the silence of the defence did not add anything positively to the State's case. The inference is not really an inference in the strict sense of the word, but simply an observation or conclusion that the accused could not or would not disturb the State's *prima facie* case, with the result that the latter stands uncontroverted and becomes proof beyond a reasonable doubt.

As will be discussed in more detail below, criminal procedure must be viewed as a *system*. This means, *inter alia*, that what happens in the earlier stages of the system is relevant in the later stages; it gets passed on. The pre-trial (investigatory or police) phase can be seen as the gatehouse to the mansion of the trial. It would be ludicrous to recognise, respect and protect the rights of the accused at the mansion but deny those same rights at the gatehouse. The right to silence or privilege against self-incrimination must accordingly also be protected in the pre-trial stage, for instance, during police interrogation. This is accomplished by, *inter alia*, the rules regarding the admissibility of admissions and confessions, supplemented by the Judges' Rules which inform a suspect of his rights, including his right to silence (with emphasis on non-coercion, voluntariness and informed waiver of rights).

The right to silence or privilege against self-incrimination must furthermore be protected at the pleading stage. If an accused pleads guilty, he is abdicating virtually all his rights, including the presumption of innocence. Questioning him in terms of s 112 of the Criminal Procedure Act can accordingly only help him, for instance if he was unaware that he may have a valid defence of, say, self-defence to a charge of assault or culpable homicide. If an accused, on the other hand, pleads not guilty, he is opting to retain all his rights and to put the prosecution to prove his guilt on its own, without his help. Questioning him in terms of s 115 can sometimes damage him, since it may lead to his making admissions and even formal admissions, incriminating himself and absolving the State from the obligation to prove all its allegations. He should, accordingly, be properly instructed as to his rights and cautioned before he is so questioned. (Sections 112 and 115 are fully discussed later in the book.)

On the presumption of innocence and the right to silence in general, see *Zuma* 1995 (4) BCLR 401 (SA).

5 RIGHTS AND POWERS; DELIMITATION

An accused person of course does not only have rights; he also has duties, for example the duty to submit to lawful arrest. The content of a right of an accused is in inverse proportion to a power of the state; the greater or stronger the state power (eg the power to search), the smaller or weaker the accused's property rights or right to privacy. If the state were to have absolute powers, it would probably be able to curb criminality to a very large extent, but we would be living under a tyranny and we would have no rights; we would be objects, not legal subjects. If the individual's rights, on the other hand, were absolute, the state would be powerless and unable to cope with crime or operate a criminal justice system. One of the tasks of the law of criminal procedure is to devise a balance between powers and rights which makes life bearable and acceptable to citizens and which nevertheless can control crime at a tolerable level. (Crime can, of course, never be eradicated; there are no 'solutions' to the crime problem—there are only better or worse ways of managing it, *inter alia* through the criminal justice system, but mainly through long-term socio-economic and political management. The key word is management.)

Considerations such as legitimacy, time in history and culture, perceived crime problems, emphasis on human rights, war, and states of emergency will play a role in determining the relationship between right and powers in a particular country at a particular time. The pendulum always swings; it is never stagnant. In South Africa's not too distant past the emphasis was on powers; right now, under the new constitution with its emphasis on human rights, it may well be swinging somewhat towards more rights, with concomitant limitations on powers.

The dilemma of the law of criminal procedure—in its constitutional context—in finding the correct, or rather, acceptable balance between rights and powers, is sometimes erroneously perceived to be a conflict between the community's interests (to fight crime, etc versus the individual's interest.) Thus it is sometimes said that the individual's interest in privacy and property rights should give way before the community's interest in crime control through search and seizure, and that mass searches (eg sweeping whole neighbourhoods at night without warrants) should accordingly be justified. Those who defend the individual's rights are then often described as bleeding heart liberals. In our view, this is a wrong analysis. What is at stake here is not the community versus the individual, but two competing community interests, viz the community's interest in crime control and the community's interest in fair treatment of its members; we are interested in less crime AND we are interested in the protection of human rights. Both interests are community interests; absolute statism, despotism, totalitarianism or any form of dictatorship have never been in the interests of the community at large. It should be borne in mind that freedom is indivisible; one cannot make strict rules of criminal procedure and think that they will be applied only to 'criminals'. Especially in the case of pre-trial (investigative) criminal procedure, the peace officers (the police) operate on tentative and often untested grounds, which in turn means that many innocent people will be drawn into their power and brought under their control. The more power, the fewer rights—and that may well include the reader of this, his/her beloved ones, children and friends. Once again: the rights of the suspect/accused do not amount to the mollycoddling of criminals at all; rules of criminal procedure are for everybody, not just for 'criminals'—therefore those rules must be so just and fair and tolerable that we all can live with and under them. Freedom is indivisible. In the eyes of the law everybody, not just some, are regarded as legally not guilty before a final judgment is given by a court of law—and happily so, for we are all potential suspects or accused persons and not one of us would like to be regarded and treated as guilty before we have been tried and found guilty by a court after a fair process.

At the same time, however, the rules of criminal procedure and the relevant constitutional provisions must give enough powers to the police so that they can operate with an acceptable measure of efficiency. (Crime prevention depends more on effective policing than on severe punishment.) This dilemma of constitutional law and the law of criminal procedure accordingly requires compromises:

'It is to the public good that the police should be strong and effective in preserving law and order and preventing crime; but it is equally to the public good that police power should be controlled and confined so as not to interfere arbitrarily with personal freedom' (our emphasis)— *Royal Commission on the Police Report* (Cmnd 1728 1962) 9.

In *Clark* 1931 AD 455 458 it is emphasised that procedural guarantees 'are not primarily for the benefit of the accused, but in the interests of the public—to prevent the police from disturbing the privacy of people' (our emphasis).

We shall give an illustration of how a balance is struck. First, it should be realised that the converse of a police power is a duty on the part of the citizen to submit; the exercise of the power diminishes or shrinks the citizen's rights, albeit often only temporarily. If a peace officer has reasonable grounds for searching a suspect and the latter's premises, finds the relevant objects and seizes them (and all the other legal requirements for a lawful search and seizure are complied with), the suspect will not be able to sue the officer or the state if it later turns out that the seized objects were innocent and that the suspect, too, is innocent. Since the exercise of police powers was in the circumstances lawful, the innocent citizen's property rights and right to privacy shrunk in inverse proportion to the police powers and the citizen simply had to submit to, or tolerate, the state action. Thus it is possible for an innocent person to be arrested, searched, fingerprinted and lined-up for an identification parade quite lawfully; if the criminal procedural requirements have been met, he has a duty to submit. If, on the other hand, the police acted unlawfully by going beyond the provisions of law or by not complying therewith, the suspect has a whole variety of remedies, such as resistance, suing for damages, obtaining an interdict, instituting the *rei vindicatio* to get his property back, laying criminal charges against the police, as well as other possibilities.

In the above illustration, the key to the lawful exercise of police powers and the duty of the citizen to submit lies in the concept 'reasonable grounds'. The law of criminal procedure has used this concept to determine where the balance between rights and powers lies in a number of instances; many references to the concept can be found in the pre-trial provisions of criminal procedure—sometimes as 'reasonably', 'on reasonable suspicion' and various other formulations. (See e g sections 19–21, 23, 40, 42, 43 and 49 of the Criminal Procedure Act.) These phrases all have the same meaning; they set up a reasonableness standard for the dividing line between (suspects') rights and (police) powers in various circumstances. This standard requires some elucidation.

The term 'reasonable grounds' (for suspicion, arrest, search, seizure or whatever action) as such is clearly a misnomer. Grounds are facts; they simply exist and cannot be categorised as reasonable or otherwise. Accordingly the term must be analysed and construed. It should be noted that it consists of two components:

(1) *Grounds*. These are facts which can be ascertained or perceived by the five senses of seeing, hearing, feeling, smelling and tasting. The facts are objective in the

sense that they exist in the outside world of reality whether a human being is aware of them or not. Ms Traffic Officer, for example, sees a car driving very slowly at night. It stops at a red light; when the light turns green, the car remains stationary. Upon investigation, she finds the driver slumped over the steering wheel. She knocks on the window but gets no response. When she opens the door, he falls out, but scrambles to his feet. He is unsteady, has slurred speech and bloodshot eyes, and reeks of liquor. The grounds or facts which she perceived by seeing, hearing and smelling are quite clear. (There must always be concrete grounds, not mere hunches, suspicions or vibes.)

(2) *Reasonableness*. This refers to the quality, not of the grounds, but of the inference which is drawn from the grounds (facts) that have been ascertained. The inference is subjective in the sense that it is a conclusion which is drawn in Ms Traffic Officer's head; the quality of reasonableness, on the other hand, is based on an objective test. An inference will be unreasonable if it is far-fetched, ie not in accordance with normal human experience. This means that the standard for evaluating the reasonableness of the inference is an objective community standard, the standard of average persons in the community, the notional reasonable person test. Since reasonable people would also have concluded from Ms Traffic Officer's grounds that the driver was intoxicated, her (subjective) inference, drawn from the objective facts, gets labelled reasonable.

However, the story continues: When she arrested him and took him first to a police station and then to a district surgeon, it transpired that he was a teetotaller; at an office party he was mocked and had brandy poured over him; he left in a huff and suffered a stroke in the car, which accounts for all the symptoms. This outcome will not transform Ms Traffic Officer's lawful action into unlawful arrest. When she acted, the criminal procedural basis for her action existed. Accordingly, she is fully protected; the driver, although innocent, had a duty to submit. By positioning the dividing line between rights and powers where it did by means of the reasonable grounds formula, the law of arrest does not require an arrestor to be correct, only to be reasonable; the subject's rights shrink accordingly.

Just as it is possible for an innocent citizen to be arrested (or subjected to other forms of force) lawfully, it is possible for 'guilty' persons to be arrested unlawfully, since the criteria must be applied at the time of the action and cannot be retroactively be made unlawful or lawful by what transpires later. If an arrest was unlawful (in that, for example, there were no reasonable grounds for suspicion), the fact that the accused is later convicted of the relevant crime will not make the arrest lawful in retrospect.

Suspicion on reasonable grounds that someone has committed an offence must exist before arrest; it is insufficient if there is only a (vague) suspicion that a crime might possibly have been committed which the arrestor wants to investigate after arrest—such an arrest would be unlawful.

The limitation of fundamental rights, as regulated by the Constitution, is discussed further in 9, below.

6 DOUBLE-FUNCTIONAL NATURE OF SOME RULES

From the foregoing it will be noted that many rules of criminal procedure are double-functional in the sense that apart from regulating procedure, they also operate as grounds of justification in substantive law, ie substantive criminal as well as civil law. Thus, if a peace officer infringes a suspect's interests in privacy by searching him in terms of the provisions of criminal procedure, the act of searching is both a regular procedural action and a lawful limitation of the suspect's right to privacy; in terms of substantive law the suspect can neither successfully charge the peace officer with an offence nor sue him in a delictual matter. If, on the other hand, the search was illegal (for example, in that it was not permitted by the law of criminal procedure), then, in terms of criminal procedure and the consequences of procedural actions, and if an exclusionary rule is introduced in our law, the procedural/ evidential consequences of the action will be that the evidence thus obtained will not be admissible; the substantive consequences may be a criminal charge against the officer as well as an action for damages.

Conversely, grounds of justification in substantive law may also be double-functional and may be used to great effect in criminal procedure. For instance, if a peace officer may lawfully arrest a suspect and the latter attacks the officer, the officer may rely on the law of self-defence and defend himself. While self-defence as such is primarily a ground of justification in substantive criminal and civil law (meaning that action which would otherwise be unlawful is rendered lawful in the circumstances), it here also empowers the officer to act in a criminal procedural sense. (The office may, of course, also rely on relevant provisions in the law of criminal procedure, viz the rules relating to overcoming resistance in arrest.) In a similar way, functionaries in criminal procedure may where appropriate rely on any of the recognised grounds of justification. (See in general handbooks on substantive criminal law and the law of delict. Many reported cases on, eg unlawful arrest and/or excessive use of force, actually appear in the law reports as civil cases for damages or other relief, eg interdict.)

7 CRIMINAL PROCEDURE AS A SYSTEM

In addition to other possible models (see below), criminal procedure should also be viewed as a system, namely a step-by-step process which moves along according to set legal rules. The various stages in the process have their own characteristics. Later stages are also to a large extent dependent upon earlier stages. If, for instance, poor quality work done by the police in the investigatory phase (eg a coerced confession) is fed into the trial phase by the prosecution, it may contaminate the trial and even, if it is not excluded at the trial, have repercussions at the appeal or review stage, leading to the eventual acquittal of the accused. Pre-trial criminal procedure is accordingly just as important as trial procedure.

Criminal procedure as a system can also be viewed as a system of case decay or attrition; if a picture is used to illustrate this, it would look like a funnel with many holes in its sides, apart from the proper spout. Many complaints are fed into the system funnel; it leaks a great deal; sometimes no more than a drop emerges at the spout end. For example, if there are 25 000 murder dockets opened by the police per year (ie there are 25 000 murder 'complaints'), there would typically be about 3 000 murder convictions and 100 death sentences (or 100 sentences of life imprisonment if there exists no death sentence). Many factors contribute to this phenomenon, which is called case decay or attrition—such as poor investigative work in the pre-trial phase. However, some legitimate sifting also takes place; many of the 25 000 will, for instance, have been found guilty of lesser offences (eg culpable homicide or assault, due to plea bargaining or other reasons), some will have left the system for the mental health system (see ss 77–79 of the Criminal Procedure Act), some will have been acquitted, and so on.

Standards of proof differ in the various stages of the criminal procedure system. In the pre-trial phase, the general criterion for interfering with individual liberties is that of reasonable grounds (see above). At the bail phase, considerations such as danger of flight, danger of tampering with witnesses or evidence, or danger of repetition of serious criminality may play a role. At the end of the State case, the question is whether the prosecution has presented enough evidence upon which the accused could be convicted (ie whether each and every element of the substantive crime has been covered by *prima facie* evidence)—if not, the accused may be discharged without having to answer the State. At the end of the trial, the full burden of proving legal guilt beyond a reasonable doubt, rests upon the State (see above). Thus, the more tentative State action is (for instance, early in the system), the lighter the burden it must prove before it can interfere with individual rights; the more final it becomes (for example, at the end of the trial), the tougher it gets. Among other things, this helps to prevent people from having the label of legal guilt, with all its implications, wrongly attached to them.

The realisation that criminal procedure is a dynamic *system*, in the sense outlined above, has profound implications for rational criminal justice policy planning. For instance, if policy-makers are concerned about an unacceptably high crime rate, then increased state intervention at the *earlier* phases of the system rather than at the *end* of the system would have a superior *deterrent* (ie crime-preventing) effect; for instance, tactics early in the system, such as police roadblocks, searches, and confiscation of illegal firearms, would have a greater effect in reducing the incidence of car hijacking than merely severely punishing some convicted hijackers at the far end of the system. While an increase by the legislature of the quantum of punishment may seem to the public to be 'real action' against crime (and, for that reason, be a favourite expedient of politicians seeking popular approval), it usually is, by itself, a cheap and hollow 'solution' having less to do with the concerns of criminal justice and crime prevention than with politics. Crime prevention and deterrence should focus primarily on the earlier phases of the criminal justice system. (This does not, of course, imply that punishment should not *also* be adequate and credible—and, of course, in line with the Constitution.)

8 THE HISTORY OF SOUTH AFRICAN CRIMINAL PROCEDURE; VARIOUS MODELS OF CRIMINAL PROCEDURE

Regarding the history and antecedents of South African criminal procedure, see in general *Dugard South African Criminal Law and Procedure* vol 4: *Introduction to Criminal Procedure* (Cape Town, Juta, 1977) 1–56.

The roots of South African criminal procedure may be found in the Roman, Roman-Dutch and English law. Before expounding on aspects of this, some distinctions between various models of criminal procedure must first be pointed out, namely accusatorial and inquisitorial systems, and due process and crime control systems. The word model implies that we are here discussing ideal, conceptual or intellectual structures, not necessarily systems that exist in real life exactly as we describe them; most real-life systems show features of more than one model and they also change and fluctuate over periods of time. A model is accordingly simply an analytical tool.

The essential difference between the accusatorial and inquisitorial models of criminal procedure lies in the functions of the parties, ie the judicial officer, the prosecution and the defence. In an inquisitorial system (as a modern example of which we may cite France) the judge is the master of the proceedings (*dominus litis*) in the sense that he himself actively conducts and even controls the search for the truth (see above and below) by dominating the questioning of witnesses and the accused. (We use the term judge generically here, to include any judicial officer: judges, magistrates, etc.) After arrest, the accused is questioned primarily by the investigating judge, not by the police. In the trial, the presiding judge primarily does the questioning, not the counsel for the prosecution or the defence. Conversely, in accusatorial systems (the modern examples of which are the Anglo-American systems), the judge is in the role of detached umpire, who should not enter the arena of the fight between the prosecution and the defence for fear of his becoming partial or losing perspective as a result of all the dust caused by the fray. The police are the primary investigative force; they pass the collected evidence on to the prosecution in dossier (file) format, who then becomes *dominus litis*; the prosecution decides on the appropriate charges, the appropriate court, etc. In court, the trial takes the form of a contest between two theoretically equal parties (the prosecution and the defence) who do the questioning, in turn leading their own witnesses and cross-examining the opposition's witnesses.

As has been pointed out, no real-life system conforms exactly to a model. South African criminal procedure, as will be seen in later chapters of this book, has basically been accusatorial. But in certain circumstances a judge may, and sometimes even must, call witnesses of his own. The procedure of questioning that may take place under s 115 (plea of not guilty), contains inquisitorial elements, as does part of s 112 (questioning pursuant to a plea of guilty); on the other hand, the fact that an accused can be found guilty solely on his plea of guilty without the judge doing any questioning to investigate the 'truth', is a strong accusatorial element (even though it can happen only in the case of relatively minor offences).

A due process model presupposes that a suspect or an accused is a full legal subject with rights (such as privacy, dignity, integrity of person and property) and powers (such as to obtain a lawyer and to make decisions) and that state power is circumscribed and limited by law. Of paramount importance is the presumption of innocence. A crime control model is exactly the opposite. The suspect or accused is a mere object of enquiry with no rights; the state is all-powerful. In extreme models, there is a presumption of guilt; the accused may be tortured in order to extract a confession of that guilt and he may be expected to prove his innocence in extraordinary ways, for example by floating when thrown into a river with weights attached to his legs.

Historically, the European inquisitorial systems of criminal procedure were all based on the crime control model. It need not, of course, be so. Modern Western European systems, for instance, are due process inquisitorial systems. In Germany, an accused has all the rights that an accused has under Anglo-American systems, if not more: the presumption of innocence is fully operative—if the court has reasonable doubt that any element of an offence has been adequately proved by the prosecution, the accused will be acquitted; the accused has the right to silence and no adverse inferences may be drawn from the exercise of that right; evidence wrongfully obtained, eg through trick or torture, is inadmissible.

Not all accusatorial systems are necessarily also due process systems. In the not-too-distant past it was possible under South African criminal procedure for a person to be detained indefinitely *incommunicado*, without access to a lawyer or to the courts; illegally obtained evidence was fully admissible; in terrorism cases the accused had, under certain circumstances, to prove his innocence beyond reasonable doubt.

Modern South African criminal procedure will shift increasingly towards the due process model as a consequence of the new constitutional order. This will be interesting to watch.

Western European inquisitorial criminal procedure had a forerunner in the decree of Pope Innocentius III in 1198 of which the cornerstones were, *inter alia*, the compulsory interrogation of the accused, the abolition of the right to silence or the privilege against self-incrimination, and the legitimisation and institutionalisation of torture. This canonical or clerical procedure in due course had its impact on secular criminal procedure, influencing, for instance, the very important *Constitutio Criminalis Carolina*, a code of criminal procedure instituted by Charles V in 1532, also called the *Peinliche Gerichtsordnung*, the CCC or simply the *Carolina*. Commentators such as Carpzovius, Bartoldus, Baldus, Clarus, Wielant and Damhouder helped to spread the crime control inquisitorial process with its institutionalised torture all over Europe, including the Netherlands.

In the Netherlands of the seventeenth and eighteenth centuries, criminal procedure was based on an Ordinance which Philip II of Spain issued in 1570. Torture was regulated in detail; Huber writes (quoted by Dugard at 8): 'The method of torture consists among us of three kinds of degrees: first, the application of thumb-screws; second, of the boot; and third, the racking of the limbs.' The term 'third degree' has become part of the English language, referring to (illegal) torture during interrogation (especially by the police).

Some Roman-Dutch writers of the eighteenth century, eg Van der Linden, deplored the harshness of the system. Legalised torture was eventually abolished in Holland in 1798, due, inter alia, to the pervasive influence of the Italian Cesare de Beccaria (1738–94), who was himself a product of the Enlightenment and who wrote a brilliant little booklet on crime and punishment, *Dei delitti e delle pene* (1764), in which he attacked, *inter alia*, torture and the death sentence. This booklet eventually changed the face of criminal justice in all of Western Europe.

With the Dutch occupation of the Cape in 1652, the system of criminal procedure based on the Philip II Ordinance of 1570 was introduced. Torture was widely practised. Punishments were equally severe and included hanging, strangling, breaking on the wheel, burning, drowning, whipping, branding, keelhauling, dismemberment and the pillory.

The first British occupation (1795–1803) saw the abolition of legalised torture in 1796—two years before it was abolished in the Netherlands. After the second British occupation (1806), the Roman-Dutch law of criminal procedure nevertheless remained in force in the Cape. The structure of the courts was, however, subject to several amendments, which resulted in uncertainty as to which procedure the newer courts should follow. This led to the Chief Justice and the members of

the Court of Justice issuing a code of criminal procedure in 1819, which document—
introducing elements of English criminal procedure—became known as *Crown Trial*. Eventually all prosecutions in the Cape fell under the authority of an official called the fiscal. In 1827, a commission of enquiry recommended that the system of criminal procedure in the Cape should approximate even more closely that of England. The recommendations were largely accepted, resulting in the *First Charter of Justice* in 1827, which was replaced by a very similar *Second Charter of Justice* in 1832. The *First Charter of Justice* was followed by Ordinances 40 (1828) (on criminal procedure) and 72 (1830) (on evidence), which virtually completed the anglicisation of the law of criminal procedure and evidence and which form the foundation of our modern law, putting an end to the inquisitorial system and replacing it with the accusatorial English procedure; the trial 'now took the form of an open confrontation between prosecutor and accused with the court acting as arbiter'—Dugard at 26. Theoretically, however, the Roman-Dutch law of criminal procedure still remains the South African law of criminal procedure.

After the establishment of the Union of South Africa in 1910, the Criminal Procedure and Evidence Act 31 of 1917 was enacted, which was a comprehensive code of criminal procedure, popularly also called 'The Code'. Many amendments followed, the one of 1935 being the most important. The Judges' Rules were formulated by a conference of judges in 1931 as guidelines intended to protect the accused's privilege against self-incrimination during police interrogation. A consolidating Criminal Procedure Act (Act 56 of 1955) replaced the 1917 Act. Trial by jury, already exceptional in practice, was abolished de jure by the Abolition of Juries Act 34 of 1969. The present Criminal Procedure Act 51 of 1977 came into force on 22 July 1977. The Constitution, Act 108 of 1996, also contains important provisions affecting criminal procedure.

Various important commissions of enquiry dealing with criminal justice matters have brought out reports through the years, eg the Lansdown Commission (Report UG 47 of 1947), the Rumpff Commission (RP 69 of 1967), the Botha Commission (RP 78 of 1971), the Viljoen Commission (RP 78 of 1976)—to mention but a few.

The sources of present-day South African Criminal Procedure are statutory as well as common law. Apart from the Criminal Procedure Act 51 of 1977, various other statutes have been of importance in that they also made provisions for aspects of criminal procedure, for example legislation relating to the courts, the police, correctional services, extradition, dangerous weapons, drugs, mail interception and telephone tapping, entrapment, and, more recently, of course the Constitution. In this handbook we attempt to paint a picture of the general criminal procedure of South Africa. There are numerous special provisions which fall outside the scope of this book; in practice it should always be investigated whether some legislation contains provisions regarding or affecting criminal procedure.

9 A BILL OF RIGHTS: CONSTITUTIONAL CRIMINAL PROCEDURE

9.1 General

For criminal procedure, the most fundamental structural change that has been brought about by the new legal order under the Constitution (Act 108 of 1996), is that the Constitution and the Bill of Rights (contained in chapter 2 of the Constitution) create a Higher Law—a law above the law, so to speak. Parliament no longer has the sovereignty to do as it pleases. Its laws are subject to scrutiny and challenge in court in terms of the Constitution and the Bill of Rights, and ultimately constitutional matters are decided upon by the Constitutional Court, which is the highest court dealing with the Constitution and Bill of Rights. See the Constitution sections 1, 2 and 7.

It is now possible to have legislation which conflicts with the Constitution and Bill of Rights set aside—declared null and void for unconstitutionality. The Bill of Rights operates like a protective umbrella over all areas of law and state action. Section 2 of the Constitution explicitly states that the Constitution is the supreme law of the Republic; law or conduct inconsistent with it is invalid, and the obligations imposed by it must be fulfilled. The Bill of Rights applies to all law, and binds the legislature, the executive, the judiciary and all organs of state— section 8(1). (See also chapter 8 of the Constitution which further regulates the declaration of a law as unconstitutional and which regulates the powers of the courts in constitutional matters.)

Constitutions or Bills of Rights are not self-executing or self-explanatory; they have to be interpreted authoritatively—this is called the principle of justiciability. Reported judgments relating to "constitutional criminal procedure" accordingly have to be studied well. *Zuma* 1995 (4) BCLR 401 (SA) emphasises that the Constitution is to be interpreted so as to give clear expression to the values it seeks to nurture. Constitutional interpretation involves interpretation of a written document. Due regard must be paid to the express language which is used, since a less rigorous approach entails the danger that the Constitution may be taken to mean whatever one wishes it to mean.

A few preliminary points are important: *First*, in a Bill of Rights, the criminal procedural provisions usually have 'vertical' operation; they do not regulate relationships between equal persons, but between the state-as-power-wielder and the subject, or rather, between the community's interest in state power and the community's interest in individual rights and liberties—ie between the two competing sets of community interests already discussed. However, the present Constitution in section 8(2) also provides for 'horizontal' operation of the Bill of Rights: 'A provision of the Bill of Rights binds a natural or a juristic person if, and to the extent that, it is applicable, taking into account the nature of the right and the nature of any duty imposed by the right.' (See also s 8(3) in this regard.) *Secondly*, constitutional criminal procedural provisions usually are stated negatively, ie they are limitations on state powers, prohibiting the state from infringing certain fundamental rights. (Only occasionally may they be mandatory provisions, for instance, requiring that free counsel be provided to indigent accused persons by the state.) In this way they may also be limitations on *democracy*; if, for instance, the Bill of Rights forbids torture, then torture will remain illegal even if a sounding majority of the people want it legitimised and even if Parliament purports to legitimise it. South Africa does not have an unlimited democracy, but one limited *inter alia* by the Bill of Rights. *Thirdly*, the Bill of Rights recognises that most rights are not absolute and may under certain circumstances be curtailed or limited, as we shall indicate below. *Lastly*, without the principle of justiciability (see above), a Bill of Rights would be useless; this principle requires a strong and independent Bench. Sometimes the judges will have to go against popular sentiments in interpreting the Bill of Rights. For a discussion on the nature of the South African democracy created by the constitution, see Van Rooyen 'Discoursing about legality, democracy and the death sentence in South Africa' in Joubert (ed) *Essays in honour of SA Strauss* 312 (1995).

Chapter 2 of the Constitution of the Republic of South Africa Act 108 of 1996 (which is called the 'Bill of Rights'), consisting of sections 7 to 39, is organised as follows:

- *Section 8* regulates the application of the chapter, ie its vertical and horizontal operation (see above).

- *Sections 9–35* state the fundamental rights, ranging from the right to equality to the rights of arrested, detained and accused persons.

- *Section 36* is the so-called limitation clause; it regulates the scope of the rights and how they may be limited (eg how the right to privacy may be limited so as to allow search as seizure in the course of criminal procedure). The section *inter alia* provides that entrenched rights may be limited by law only to the extent that such limitation is reasonable and justifiable in an open and democratic society based on human dignity, equality and freedom, taking into account all relevant factors, including—
  - the nature of the right;
  - the importance of the purpose of the limitation;
  - the nature and extent of the limitation;
  - the relation between the limitation and its purpose; and
  - less restricted means to achieve the purpose.

It should be noted that the listing of certain rights in the Bill of Rights does not mean that other rights (eg accorded by common law) are negated— section 39(3).

Early rulings of the Constitutional Court (in terms of the limitation clause and the Bill of Rights of the 'interim' Constitution, Act 200 of 1993) include *Williams* 1995 (7) BCLR 861 (CC), in which corporal punishment was held to violate the right to human dignity and the protection against cruel, inhuman or degrading punishment, and could not be saved by the limitation clause; and *Zuma* 1995 (4) BCLR 401 (SA), which held that it is not permissible that constitutional rights which have been conferred without express limitation be cut down by reading implicit restrictions into them so as to bring them into line with the common law. Fundamental rights provisions should be interpreted generously.

- *Section 37* provides for derogation from the Bill of Rights following the declaration of a state of emergency—only to the extent that the derogation is strictly required by the state of emergency; that the legislation is consistent with the Republic's obligations under international law applicable to states of emergency (s 37(4); and that the derogation does not affect the rights listed and qualified in the Table of Non-Derogable Rights following section 37(5). It is important to note that any competent court may enquire into the validity of a declaration of a state of emergency as well as any action taken under such declaration (section 37(3)). The 'absolute' rights in the Table of Non-Derogable Rights which may *never* be limited or abolished at all, are the rights to human dignity and life.

- *Section 38* lists those who have *locus standi* in constitutional litigation where fundamental rights have allegedly been violated or threatened: anyone acting in their own interest; anyone acting on behalf of another person who cannot act in their own name; anyone acting as a member of, or in the interest of, a group or class of persons; anyone acting in the public interest; and an association acting in the interest of its members.

- *Section 39* contains certain important provisions relating to the interpretation of the Bill of Rights, *inter alia* requiring that courts must, in interpreting this chapter, 'promote the values which underlie an open and democratic society based on human dignity, quality and freedom' and must consider international law. In addition, courts *may* have consider foreign law. Courts must promote the spirit, purport and objects of the Bill of Rights. (It is accordingly not enough that students and practitioners of criminal procedure be experts in criminal procedure itself—they must also at least be conversant with constitutional law, criminal law, law of evidence, law of interpretation, international law, comparative law, and jurisprudence/legal philosophy.)

In what follows, some of the specific rights contained in the chapter on fundamental rights will be discussed or mentioned briefly. As we stated above, we shall mainly use *Makwanyane* as illustration.

9.2 Section 9: Equality

Section 9 of the Constitution provides that every person is equal before the law and has the right to equal protection and benefit of the law. This is sometimes called the 'equal justice' provision. Section 9(3) *inter alia* specifies that the state may not unfairly discriminate directly or indirectly against anyone on the ground of race (etc). Section 9(5) states that discrimination on one or more of the grounds listed in subsection (3) is unfair unless it is established that the discrimination is fair. Unequal justice was one of the grounds upon which the death sentence was declared unconstitutional—see *Makwanyane* 1995 (6) BCLR 665 (CC). There existed concrete evidence of various unacceptable degrees of discrimination or unequal justice in the history of the administration of the death sentence, eg on the basis of race, or depending on who the judge is. See eg Zimring, Van Vuren and Van Rooyen 'Selectivity and racial bias in a mandatory death sentence dispensation: a South African case study' 1995 *CILSA* 107 and Van Rooyen 'Toward a new SA without the death sentence—struggles, strategies, and hopes' 1993 *Florida State University Law Review* 737 (referring to the 'Curlewis revelations'). If, in a future constitutional amendment, it is purported to reintroduce the death sentence, it would accordingly not be sufficient to 'write in' the death sentence as an exception to the right to life, as some are currently proposing; an exception to the equal justice clause would also have to be created, otherwise the new death sentence dispensation might once again be declared unconstitutional on *this* ground (ie denial of equal justice).

9.3 Section 10: Human dignity

Section 10 provides that everyone has inherent dignity and also the right to have their dignity respected and protected. This provision *inter alia* will have consequences as far as the treatment of suspects, accused persons, complainants, witnesses, convicted persons (etc) are concerned, for instance in arrest and detention, interrogation, identification parades, search and seizure, and punishment. From *Makwanyane* 1995 (6) BCLR 665 (CC) it appears that this section may serve as yet another ground for invalidating the death sentence.

9.4 Section 11: Life

The Constitution (in section 11) states the most fundamental right, the right to life, very simply, as follows: 'Everyone has the right to life'. The question arises whether this right can be 'limited' or whether it is an absolute right. At first glance, it seems as if it must be a relative right, ie a limitable one; one may, for instance, under certain circumstances kill an attacker in self-defence. However, one can argue that in such a case it is not a *limitation* as such of the attacker's life that is construed, but a *choice between the maintenance of two competing rights to life*, viz a choice between the protection of either the right to life of the defender or the right to life of the attacker. When faced with such a choice in a situation of immediacy where there are no other options available, the right to life of the attacker must give way—hence killing that person could be permissible.

The same situational conflict which exists in the foregoing self-defence scenario does, however, not arise in the case of the death sentence. The death sentence accordingly is unconstitutional in terms of the right to life, too (in addition to the other grounds for unconstitutionality mentioned above)—see *Makwanyane* 1995 (6) BCLR 665 (CC); the death sentence is not saved by the limitation clause (s 36).

It accordingly seems evident that the right to life cannot be limited; life either exists or it does not.

Someone may ask, 'Yes, but what about the right to life of the victim of murder?' The sad answer is that that life has been irretrievably lost; the victim's right to life has been destroyed—which is why the perpetrator must be punished in terms of the criminal law. However, the *form* of punishment chosen must be legal in terms of the Constitution. Since the literal application of the idea of 'an eye for an eye and a tooth for a tooth' (rape for rape, etc!) is not permissible in terms of the Constitution (*inter alia* because of the prohibition of cruel and inhuman punishment), surrogate punishments must be implemented, eg imprisonment.

Note once again, that even if a constitutional amendment were to create an exception to the right to life, thereby permitting the reintroduction of some death sentence dispensation, legislation passed in the wake of such a constitutional amendment would still be justiciable for possible unconstitutionality on other grounds, for instance that on the basis of statistics there is a risk of unacceptable discriminatory practices; or that the legislation allows unacceptable disparities (ie unequal justice) in that it does not give adequate guidelines for regulating judicial discretion, with the result that the same set of facts might result in a death sentence before some judges but not before a number of others; or that the preceding procedures and/or the method of execution amounts to cruel and unusual punishment; or that the quality of defence services (eg *pro deo* counsel, interpreters, access to medico-psychiatric and social science experts) is so low as to amount to a denial of fair trial standards—which standards might be set higher by the Constitutioonal Court for an absolute sentence (death) than for relative sentences (such as fines or imprisonment). In sum, if in terms of an amended constitution, Parliament were to purport to construct a new death sentence dispensation (viz through amending the Criminal Procedure Act), such legislation would certainly again be subject to challenge by way of constitutional litigation. The purportedly resuscitated death sentence may again fail to pass constitutional muster.

9.5 Section 12: Freedom and security of the person

Section 12(1) provides that everyone has the right to freedom and security of the person, which includes the right—

- not to be deprived of freedom arbitrarily or without just cause;
- not to be detained without trial;
- to be free from all forms of violence from either public or private sources;
- not to be tortured in any way; and
- not to be treated or punished in a cruel, inhuman or degrading way.

The latter prohibition reminds one of the American Bill of Rights's prohibition of 'cruel and unusual' punishment, and was used by the South African Constitutional Court as a fourth—indeed, main—ground for declaring the death sentence unconstitutional—*Makwanyane* 1995 (6) BCLR 665 (CC).

Retentionists of the death sentence would accordingly have to cater through constitutional amendment for exceptions to at least *all four* of the relevant constitutional rights—equality; dignity; freedom from cruel, inhumane or degrading treatment and punishment; and life—if they want to be successful in reinstating the death sentence. But even then there may be other constitutional grounds for invalidating the death penalty.

9.6 Section 13: Slavery, servitude and forced labour

Section 13 provides that no one may be subjected to slavery, servitude or forced labour. This *inter alia* may have implications for prison labour. One should here, as in the case of *all* the rights, keep in mind the existence of the limitation clause (section 36) as well as section 39.

9.7 Section 14: Privacy

Section 14 provides that everyone has the right to privacy, which includes the right not to have their person or home searched; their property searched; their possessions seized; or the privacy of their communications infringed. As far as criminal procedure is concerned, this section *inter alia* has implications for the rules relating to search and seizure, and interception of communications. The provisions of section 14 are not absolute—they may be limited in accordance with sections 36 and 39 of the Constitution. The validity of existing criminal procedural provisions will accordingly have to be tested against these sections.

9.8 Section 32: Access to information

This section provides that everyone has the right of access to any information held by the state and any information that is held by another person and that is required for the exercise or protection of any rights. The matter is to be regulated further by statute. This provision has implications *inter alia* for access to the basis for search warrants, the contents of police dockets (containing for instance witness statements), particulars relating to charge sheets and so forth—which we shall discuss later in this book.

9.9 Section 34: Access to courts

Section 34 provides that everyone has the right to have any dispute that can be resolved by the application of law decided in a fair hearing before a court or, where appropriate, another independent and impartial tribunal or forum.

9.10 Section 35: Arrested, detained and accused persons

This section contains provisions of great importance for criminal procedure, relating to some of the basic principles that have been discussed earlier in this chapter (eg presumption of innocence, right to silence) as well as other procedural rights. *The section is reproduced in the appendix to this book.* The various subsections will be discussed in the course of the rest of the book. *Zuma* 1995 (4) BCLR 401 (SA) confirmed that the right to a fair trial embraces *more* than what is contained in the list of specific rights enumerated in section 35(3)*(a)–(o)* of the Constitution. The right to a fair trial requires that criminal trials be conducted in accordance with notions of basic fairness and justice, and it is the duty of criminal courts to give contents to these notions.

9.11 Section 28: Children

Section 28(1)*(g)* stipulates that every child (ie person under the age of 18 years— s 28(3)) has the right not to be detained except as a measure of the last resort, in which case, in addition to the rights a child enjoys in terms of section 12 and 35, the child may be detained only for the shortest appropriate period of time, and has the right to be kept separately from detained persons over the age of 18 years and treated in a manner, and kept in conditions, that take account of the child's age. In all matters concerning a child, his or her 'best interests' are of paramount importance— section 28(2).

9.12 Section 37: States of emergency

All modern constitutional states recognise that in exceptional cases of emergency it may become necessary temporarily to amend the existing rules of criminal procedure in the interest of the safety of the state, so that the rights of individuals may be greatly restricted and the powers of the police considerably extended, but they all also state limits and make provision for controls, especially judicial control.

In the past, a state of emergency in South Africa could even exclude judicial supervision over state action, to create a situation—

> 'where order is well maintained, but where the policy and practice of legality is not evident. Such a situation is probably best illustrated by martial rule, where military authority may claim and exercise the power of detention without warrant. If, in addition, the writ of habeas corpus, the right to inquire into these acts, is suspended, as it typically is under martial rule, the executive can exercise arbitrary powers. Such a system of social control is efficient, but does not conform to generally held notions about the "rule of law"'— Skolnick *Justice without Trial* (John Wiley & Sons 1967) 95.

Starting in the 1960's the South African legislature created, on a permanent basis, a 'drastic procedure' which infringed most of the principles discussed in this chapter;

for instance it introduced detention without trial, abolition of judicial review of executive action, curtailment of the right to counsel, reversal of the onus in criminal cases—thus opening the doors for torture, murder, wrongful convictions and executions, and more abuse (some of which have in the meantime become public through the work of the Truth and Reconciliation Commission). Some lawyers had warned against this; others, however, had supported the trend. Justification for supporting the government was sought *inter alia* in a perceived threat to national security which stemmed from external as well as internal opposition to government policies. Because of the transition to a new constitutional order and a Bill of Rights dispensation which culminated in the present Constitution, we do not propose to discuss the old drastic process here. Suffice it to mention that, since criminal procedure must be viewed as a *system*, it should never be forgotten that pre-trial procedure influences the trial itself. The existence of the drastic process had a markedly adverse effect upon our accusatorial trial procedure:

> 'This system (ie the accusatorial system) assumes that both sides in any legal dispute will have the fullest opportunity to present their case in its strongest form before an impartial arbiter. When one party is confined in an isolation cell, interrogated without legal restraint and deprived during this detention of legal assistance, his ability to present a forceful case is greatly diminished. If, in addition, the witnesses for the other side have been detained and subjected to similar treatment, the whole balance upon which the validity of the system depends is destroyed. This is so even if the subsequent court proceedings are conducted with immaculate regard for standard procedures'—Mathews *Law, Order and Liberty in South Africa* (Juta, 1971) 162–3.

The drastic process had the potential for undermining our entire system of criminal justice. The present approach of change and the safeguards contained in section 37 of the Constitution ('States of emergency') must accordingly be welcomed. The section is reproduced in the appendix and should be read. Note especially the Table of Non-Derogable Rights. This table provides *inter alia* that even in a state of emergency the rights to human dignity (s 10) and life (s 11) are absolute; they are *always* non-derogable.

10   REMEDIES

We have discussed the proposition that suspects and accused persons are accorded certain rights and that the powers of the authorities are subjected to limitations in the criminal procedure; particular attention has been given to criminal procedure prior to trial. It has become evident that it is in society's interest that the police should act lawfully and that meaningful control should be exercised over the actions of the executive (including law enforcement officials) in the criminal process. We have called this part of the principle of legality in pre-trial criminal procedure: the conduct and actions of executive officers in the criminal process ought to conform to the general requirements of the law, whether written or unwritten.

Apart from any new protective measures that may be developed under the Bill of Rights, the rights of the suspect are maintained and protected, and lawful conduct by state officials is encouraged, by a continuum of sanctions ranging from informal social sanctions to formal legal sanctions. The following are more or less familiar: civil action for damages, for example, on the ground of wrongful arrest, wrongful detention, physical injury, etc; criminal sanctions, eg on the ground of assault; the interdict; the writ of *habeas corpus*, or rather, its local Roman-Dutch equivalent, the interdictum *de libero homine exhibendo*; rules of evidence (for example, regarding the admissibility of admissions and confessions, privilege, and exclusionary rules); judicial criticism of police action; newspaper reporting and editorial comment; internal disciplinary measures by the police; even public protest, to mention but a few.

It is clear that judicial supervision and control are of the utmost importance for the maintenance of the principle of legality in the modern state under the Rule of Law (the *Rechtsstaat*). In the liberal-democratic Rule of Law state there is a

'general assumption that a degree of scrutiny and control must be exercised with respect to the activities of law enforcement officers, that the security and privacy of the individual may not be invaded at will. It is impossible to imagine a society in which even lip service is not paid to this assumption. Nazi Germany approached but never quite reached this position. But no one in our society would maintain that any individual may be taken into custody at any time and held without any limitation of time during the process of investigating his possible commission of crimes, or would argue that there should be no form of redress for violation of at least some standards for official investigative conduct'—Packer *The Limits of the Criminal Sanction* (Stanford University Press, 1968) 156.

The importance of the courts for the maintenance of legality can be expressed as follows:

'In the countries to which the term police state is applied opprobriously, police power is controlled by the government; but they are so called not because the police are nationally organized, but because . . . the citizen cannot rely on the courts to protect him. Thus in such countries the foundations upon which liberty rests do not exist'—*Royal Commission on the Police Report* 45.

The judiciary is indeed the ultimate guardian of the principle of legality, and access to an independent and strong bench is the highest guarantee of respect for and maintenance of the rights of the individual. As has been pointed out, the Constitution and its Bill of Rights acknowledge this; section 165(2) states that the courts are independent and subject only to the Constitution and the law. Section 167 states *inter alia* that the Constitutional Court has the final say on all matters relating to the Constitution (see section 167(3)).

We now wish to draw attention briefly to some remedies for infractions or threatened infractions of fundamental rights.

(1) *The writ of* habeas corpus (or rather the *interdictum de libero homine exhibendo*)

This is an important remedy which may be resorted to in the course of the criminal process to obtain judicial review of police action and thus to protect the subject against unlawful deprivation of his liberty. The court is asked for an order that the respondent (who may be the Minister, the commanding officer, the chief warder, etc) produce the body of X (the detainee) before the court at a certain date and time. This order is coupled with a rule *nisi* that the respondent must show reason why X should not be released. *Prima facie* reasons for believing that the detention is wrongful must be adduced. The application is usually heard by a single judge in a civil court where it enjoys preference on the roll. The application may be made *ex parte*. The return date is as early as possible and the case may be dealt with summarily, on the strength of oral evidence. It is quite possible, for example, that by special arrangement the application is made at 7 am; that the return date is set for 10 am the same day; and that, after argument, the detainee obtains his release at 1 pm (see Kentridge

'Habeas Corpus Procedure in South Africa' 1962 *SALJ* 283). It is immediately apparent how important inter alia the following rights are for the successful implementation of this remedy: specified place of detention; information as to reasons of arrest; and access to friends, counsel etc.

(2) *A civil action for damages*

An action for damages, eg on the ground of wrongful arrest, is an example of delictual liability which may arise in the course of the criminal process and which may be used by suspects to compensate them for any abuse which they suffered. See textbooks on the law of delict for a fuller discussion.

(3) *The interdict*

This is an order of court whereby a person is prohibited from acting in a certain way. Since its purpose is to limit or prevent harm or damage, it may even be obtained where harm has not yet occurred but is threatening. This legal remedy can be fruitfully employed during criminal proceedings to obtain relief, for example for detainees.

(4) *Mandamus*

This is the reverse of an interdict; it is a positive order that a functionary perform his or her duty (eg furnish an accused with proper particulars relating to the charges), whereas an interdict is an negative order that a person refrain from doing something.

(5) *The exclusionary rule*

This evidential 'remedy' is recognised in section 35(5) of the Constitution: 'Evidence obtained in a manner that violates any right in the Bill of Rights must be excluded if the admission of that evidence would render the trial unfair or otherwise be detrimental to the administration of justice.' Note that exclusion is not automatic but is contingent on a finding that admission would be unfair or detrimental to the administration of justice. We thus have a guided discretion to exclude or to admit.

The exclusionary rule, in any of its forms, is a remedy that properly belongs to the sphere of the law of evidence. It was developed in the USA and aims, inter alia, to deter unlawful police conduct in the pre-trial criminal procedure by rendering inadmissible in a court any evidence which was obtained by state officials by unlawful means—eg during illegal detention, or as a result of an unlawful search, or as a result of overbearing questioning (infringement of the right to silence) or torture (third-degree methods), or through denial of the right to (pre-trial) counsel. In our view it is more satisfactory to view this remedy as a means of maintaining and vindicating the principle of legality than just as a police deterrent—see above. Traditionally the rule had no place in our law; all relevant evidence was admissible. However, the courts began to hint that they, in their discretion, may well exclude evidence that was grossly illegally obtained—cf *Dladla* 1975 (1) SA 118 (T); *Radebe* 1968 (4) SA 410 (A) at 418–19; *Ahmed* 1958 (3) SA 313 (T); *Ebrahim* 1991 (2) SA 553 (A).

The exclusionary rule must be understood in the light of the concept of legal guilt (see above):

'A person is not to be held guilty of crime merely on a showing that in all probability, based upon reliable evidence, he did factually what he is said to have done. Instead, he is to be held guilty if and only if these factual determinations are made in a procedurally regular fashion and by authorities acting within competencies duly allocated to them'—Packer *The Limits of the Criminal Sanction* (1968) 166.

A further theoretical basis for the exclusionary rule may be found in the idea of 'privilege' which is well known in the law of evidence: because of respect for a higher value, relevant evidence is excluded (eg state privilege, marital communications, the legal professional privilege). In the instance of the exclusionary rule, one can argue along similar lines: in the interest of legality an accused is privileged from being convicted on illegally obtained evidence—such evidence should accordingly be excluded; the higher value in question is legality, ie that the authorities should not be law-breakers themselves.

The exclusion of confessions/admissions made under duress (eg while being tortured) was traditionally not viewed as a case where the exclusionary rule as such is applied; the ratio for exclusion was rather the fact that such coerced evidence is inherently unreliable, and unreliable evidence should not be admitted (this is called the 'Wigmore rule'). When the exclusionary rule is applied, however, exclusion takes place on other grounds; the question of whether the evidence to be excluded is reliable or not is irrelevant, as we have pointed out above—the rationale for exclusion is akin to privilege. Highly reliable evidence may be excluded.

The argument sometimes raised against the exclusionary rule, viz that it lets criminals go free, is without substance for two reasons. First, it shows no understanding of the concept 'legal guilt' (see above); secondly, it loses sight of the fact that if the police had acted lawfully, the 'criminal' would in any case have gone free, as the following illustration will show: In terms of s 22*(b)* of the Criminal Procedure Act (search without a warrant) a policeman who has a mere suspicion (vibes!) that the delay in obtaining a warrant would defeat the purposes of the search, may not search without a warrant: a belief on reasonable grounds is required. Therefore the law-abiding policeman who knows that, objectively speaking, he has no reasonable grounds to rely on, will restrain himself even if he has a strong subjective notion, sixth sense or suspicion as a basis for action. He will first obtain a warrant. In the meantime, the culprit disappears with all the evidence. This possible result is a calculated risk that we must run if we value our personal liberty and human rights so highly that we are not prepared to deliver ourselves to the mere suspicions of peace officers. The exclusionary rule *ex post facto* compels the same result: '[I]f the criminal goes free in order to serve a larger and more important end, then social justice is done, even if individual justice is not'—Goldstein 'The State and the Accused: Balance of Advantage in Criminal Procedure' 1960 *Yale Law Journal* 1149.

(6) *Informal remedies*
An informal way of obtaining relief is to resist unlawful arrest or to escape from unlawful custody. In practice this resort may, of course, be risky.

(7) *Constitutional mechanisms*
Various mechanisms for the promotion of the maintenance of human rights and legality as against overbearing state action are contained in the Constitution. Section 38, for instance, lists those who may approach a competent court to allege that a right in the Bill of Rights has been infringed or threatened (see above).

Further 'state institutions supporting constitutional democracy' are listed in chapter 9 of the Constitution, including the office of Public Protector, and the Human Rights Commission. Of great importance are also many private (ie non-governmental) organisations which offer help to citizens.

11 CONCLUSION

This chapter has been an introduction only. It does not treat constitutional principles exhaustively. Yet it provides a framework against which the ensuing chapters must be read and/or studied. It will be noted that at the outset of each chapter there will be an indication of the constitutional principles involved in that chapter. Selected sections from the Constitution are reprinted in an appendix.

The criminal courts of the Republic

		Page
1	INTRODUCTION	31
2	THE CONSTITUTIONAL COURT	31
3	SUPERIOR COURTS	32
	3.1 The Supreme Court of Appeal	32
	3.2 The High Court	32
	3.2.1 Provincial divisions of the High Court	32
	3.2.2 Local divisions of the High Court	32
	3.2.3 High Courts of erstwhile independent states	33
	3.3 Special superior courts	33
4	LOWER COURTS	33
	4.1 Magistrates' courts and regional courts	33
5	JURISDICTION OF CRIMINAL COURTS	34
	5.1 Appellate jurisdiction	34
	5.1.1 The Supreme Court of Appeal	34
	5.1.2 Provincial divisions of the High Court	35
	5.1.3 Local divisions of the High Court	35
	5.2 Jurisdiction in respect of offences	35
	5.2.1 The Supreme Court of Appeal	35
	5.2.2 Provincial and local divisions of the High Court	35
	5.2.3 Special superior court	35
	5.2.4 District court	35
	5.2.5 Regional court	35
	5.3 Jurisdiction in respect of offences committed on South African territory	35
	5.3.1 The Supreme Court of Appeal	35
	5.3.2 Provincial divisions of the High Court	35
	5.3.3 Local divisions of the High Court	36

    5.3.4 Regional courts and district courts 36

           5.3.4.1 Summary trials 37

           5.3.4.2 Preparatory examinations 39

  5.4 Jurisdiction in respect of offences committed outside South Africa . 39

  5.5 Jurisdiction with regard to sentencing 41

    5.5.1 General 41

    5.5.2 The High Court and special superior courts 41

    5.5.3 Regional courts 41

    5.5.4 District courts 42

  5.6 Jurisdiction to pronounce upon the validity of statutory provisions 42

The Constitution and this chapter:

Section 165—Judicial authority

(1) The judicial authority of the Republic is vested in the courts.

(2) The courts are independent and subject only to the Constitution and the law, which they must apply impartially and without fear, favour or prejudice.

See 1, below.

---

1 INTRODUCTION

The judicial authority of the Republic is vested in the courts (s 165(1) of the Constitution of the Republic of South Africa Act 108 of 1996). The courts are independent and subject only to the Constitution and the law, which they must apply impartially and without fear, favour or prejudice (s 165(2) of the Constitution). Of importance, for present purposes, are the Constitutional Court and the criminal courts. The latter can be divided into superior and lower courts.

2 THE CONSTITUTIONAL COURT

The Constitutional Court (with its seat in Johannesburg) consists of a president, deputy president and nine other judges (s 167(1) of the Constitution). A matter before the Constitutional Court must be heard by at least eight judges—s 167(2). This court is the highest court in all constitutional matters. It may decide only constitutional matters (and issues connected with decisions on constitutional matters) and makes the final decision whether a matter is a constitutional matter or whether an issue is connected with a decision on a constitutional matter— s 167(3). (A constitutional matter includes any issue involving the interpretation, protection or enforcement of the Constitution—s 167(7).) In terms of s 167(4) only the Constitutional Court may decide on—

- disputes between organs of state in the national or provincial sphere concerning the constitutional status, powers or functions of any of those organs of state;
- the constitutionality of any parliamentary or provincial Bill;

- the constitutionality of any amendment to the Constitution; or
- the question as to whether Parliament or the President has failed to fulfil a constitutional obligation.

The Constitutional Court makes the final decision whether an Act of Parliament, a provincial Act or the conduct of the President is constitutional. It must confirm any order of invalidity made by the Supreme Court of Appeal, a High Court or a court of similar status, before that order has any force—s 167(5).

Access to the Constitutional Court is regulated by the Constitution and is further dealt with in chapter 20 (1.2.4) and chapter 21 (also 1.2.4), below.

3 SUPERIOR COURTS

In terms of s 1 of the Criminal Procedure Act 51 of 1977, 'superior court' means a provincial or local division of the High Court. It accordingly does not include the Supreme Court of Appeal. The Constitution, moreover and as far as superior courts are concerned, in s 166 distinguishes between the Constitutional Court, the Supreme Court of Appeal and High Courts. The last mentioned courts include include any high court of appeal that may be established by and Act of Parliament to hear appeals from High Courts. Apart from the High Court, provision is also made for the institution of a 'special superior court'. The term 'special superior court' refers to a court instituted in terms of s 148, Act 51 of 1977.

3.1 The Supreme Court of Appeal

The Supreme Court of Appeal (with its seat in Bloemfontein—s 4(1), Supreme Court Act 59 of 1959) may decide appeals in any matter. It is the highest court of appeal except in constitutional matters (in which respect the Constitutional Court is the highest court). Initially it was possible to appeal from the Appellate Division (as the Supreme Court of Appeal was known until 1996) to the British Privy Council, but from 1950 this was no longer possible. In terms of s 21(1) of the Supreme Court Act a quorum of the Supreme Court of Appeal ordinarily consists of five judges for all criminal matters. In practice, three judges of appeal usually hear a criminal appeal.

3.2 The High Court

The High Court of South Africa consists of six provincial divisions, three local divisions (s 2 of the Supreme Court Act) as well as the High Courts of Bophuthatswana, Ciskei, Transkei and Venda. Local circuit divisions may also be instituted in all the provinces—s 7, Act 59 of 1959.

3.2.1 *Provincial divisions of the High Court*

The High Court consists of six provincial divisions. They are the following, with their respective seats in parentheses: Cape of Good Hope (Cape Town), Eastern Cape (Grahamstown), Northern Cape (Kimberley), Natal (Pietermaritzburg), Orange Free State (Bloemfontein), and Transvaal (Pretoria).

3.2.2 *Local divisions of the High Court*

In some areas local divisions were instituted in addition to the provincial divisions for the sake of convenience. The local divisions thus instituted are as follows:

(1) the Witwatersrand Local Division (sitting at Johannesburg);

(2) the Durban and Coast Local Division (sitting at Durban); and

(3) the South Eastern Cape Local Division (sitting at Port Elizabeth).

3.2.3 *High Courts of erstwhile independent states*

The courts of erstwhile independent states within the Republic of South Africa— currently known as the Bophuthatswana High Court, Ciskei High Court, Transkei High Court and Venda High Court—have their seats at Mmabatho, Bisho, Umtata and Thohoyandou, respectively.

3.3 Special superior courts

Where a director of public prosecutions decides to arraign an accused before a superior court upon a charge which relates to the security of the state or to the maintenance of public order, and the Minister is of the opinion that the interests of justice or public order will be better served if the accused is tried by a superior court which is specially constituted for the trial, the President may, in terms of s 148 of Act 51 of 1977, constitute a special superior court to conduct the trial. Such a court consists of three judges from any provincial division and the decision or finding of the majority of the members of the court shall be the decision or finding of the court. The court may sit at any place within the area of jurisdiction of the provincial division in respect of which the director of public prosecutions has been appointed. Such a court has jurisdiction to try the charge referred to above and may sentence the accused to any punishment which may by law be imposed in respect thereof. The procedure at a trial before a special superior court is exactly the same as that in a criminal trial before a division of the High Court. An appeal against the judgment of a special criminal court is determined by the same rules regulating appeals from judgments of provincial or local divisions of the High Court.

4 LOWER COURTS

4.1 Magistrates' courts and regional courts

In terms of s 1 of the Criminal Procedure Act 'lower court' means any court established under the provisions of the Magistrates' Courts Act 32 of 1944. The courts so established are the magistrates' courts with ordinary jurisdiction and the regional courts—s 2 of the Magistrates' Court Act. In s 2(1)*(j)* of the Magistrates' Courts Act provision is also made for the institution of periodical courts.

The magistrate's court is instituted for a district (we shall, for the sake of brevity, refer to it as the *district court*), and a court for a regional division (to which we shall refer simply as the *regional court*) was instituted in terms of s 2 of the Magistrates' Court Act.

Periodical courts are magistrates' courts which sit at regular intervals at places other than the seats of fixed permanent district courts. Periodical courts perform the same function in large and sparsely populated areas as circuit courts in the case of the High Court. The jurisdiction of a periodical court is exactly the same as that of a district court, except that there are certain limitations as regards its territorial jurisdiction. However, no person shall, without his consent, be liable to appear as an accused before any periodical court unless he resides nearer to the place where the periodical court is held than to the seat of the magistracy of the district—s 91(1)*(b)* of the Magistrates' Court Act.

5   JURISDICTION OF CRIMINAL COURTS

With regard to the jurisdiction of the criminal courts of the Republic, the following may be distinguished: appeal jurisdiction; jurisdiction in respect of offences, territory, punishment and the validity of the provisions of any Act.

5.1   Appellate jurisdiction

5.1.1   *The Supreme Court of Appeal*

The Supreme Court of Appeal the authority by law to hear an appeal against any judgment of a high court and to decide on such appeal—s 21, Act 59 of 1959 and s 315, Act 51 of 1977. This means that the Supreme Court of Appeal has jurisdiction to hear and determine an appeal from any decision of a high court (ie a provincial or local division)—s 21(1A) of Act 59 of 1959. Persons who have been found guilty by a superior court may not automatically appeal to the Supreme Court of Appeal. The general principle is that leave has first to be sought from the High Court before an appeal can be made to the Supreme Court of Appeal.

In addition to the jurisdiction just discussed, the Supreme Court of Appeal also has certain powers in terms of s 333, Act 51 of 1977. This section lays down that whenever the Minister of Justice has any doubt as to the correctness of any decision given by any high court in any criminal case on a question of law, or whenever a decision in any criminal case on a question of law is given by any division of the High Court which is in conflict with a decision in any criminal case on a question of law given by any other division of the High Court, he may submit that decision or, as the case may be, such conflicting decisions to the Supreme Court of Appeal and cause the matter to be argued before it, in order that it may determine the said question for the future guidance of all courts (except, as far as constitutional matters are concerned, the Constitutional Court). A previous judgment of another court is not reversed or amended in any way by such a decision of the Supreme Court of Appeal, although the Executive, as distinct from the Judiciary, may be prepared in special cases to show clemency to a convicted person when, in the light of such a decision, it appears that his conviction was not a justifiable one.

An example of the application of this section is seen in *Ex parte Minister of Justice: In re R v Bolon* 1941 AD 345. In this case the Minister referred to the Supreme Court of Appeal (known at that time as the Appellate Division) the question of what degree of proof was required from an accused when a statute stated that the onus of proof was on the accused. The Supreme Court of Appeal held that such an onus was the same as that in a civil trial; the accused had to discharge the onus on a balance of probabilities (not beyond reasonable doubt). The Minister has repeatedly made use of s 333 to obtain a final verdict from the Supreme Court of Appeal on conflicting decisions of Provincial and Local Divisions. Another example in this connection is *Ex parte die Minister van Justisie: In re S v De Bruin* 1972 (2) SA 623 (A).

5.1.2 *Provincial divisions of the High Court*

The provincial divisions have appeal and review jurisdiction in respect of criminal proceedings emanating from lower courts. Furthermore the provincial divisions, when sitting as a 'full court' (ie, two or three judges), have appellate jurisdiction to hear an appeal in a criminal case decided by a single judge if the questions of law and of fact and other considerations involved in the appeal are of such a nature that the appeal does not require the attention of the Supreme Court of Appeal. (The appellate and reviewing jurisdiction of the provincial divisions will be discussed in Chapters 20 and 21.)

5.1.3 *Local divisions of the High Court*

The Witwatersrand Local Division has exactly the same appellate jurisdiction as a provincial division. All other local divisions have no appellate jurisdiction.

5.2 Jurisdiction in respect of offences

5.2.1 *The Supreme Court of Appeal*

The Supreme Court of Appeal may act as a court of appeal only, except in cases of contempt in *facie curiae*, where the court has an inherent power summarily to impose a sentence—see *Snyman & Morkel* 37; *In re Mackenzie* 1933 AD 367.

5.2.2 *Provincial and local divisions of the High Court*

Provincial and local divisions have original jurisdiction in respect of all offences.

5.2.3 *Special superior court*

A special superior court has jurisdiction only in respect of the offence for which it was instituted.

5.2.4 *District court*

A district court has jurisdiction to try all crimes except treason, murder and rape. In terms of the Internal Security Act 74 of 1982, a district court may even try the serious offences of terrorism, subversion and sabotage.

5.2.5 *Regional court*

A regional court may try all crimes except treason—see s 89, Act 32 of 1944. A regional court may thus try murder and rape.

5.3 Jurisdiction in respect of offences committed on South African territory

5.3.1 *The Supreme Court of Appeal*

The Supreme Court of Appeal has jurisdiction to hear an appeal against any judgment of a high court in South Africa and to decide on such appeal—s 21, Act 59 of 1959 and s 315, Act 51 of 1977.

5.3.2 *Provincial divisions of the High Court*

The provincial divisions have original jurisdiction in respect of all offences committed within their respective areas as defined in the Supreme Court Act 59 of

1959. The Cape of Good Hope Provincial Division does not have concurrent jurisdiction in the areas of the Eastern and Northern Cape Divisions.

The rule that provincial divisions exercise jurisdiction in respect of offences committed within their respective areas has been extended in the following respects:

(1) In *Hull* 1948 (4) SA 239 (C), it was held that a division of the High Court has jurisdiction to put into effect a suspended sentence imposed by another division or magistrate's court.

(2) The legislature sometimes enacts that in respect of specific offences, such offence shall for the purposes of jurisdiction be deemed to have been committed in any place where the accused happens to be. An example is found in s 4 of the Civil Aviation Act 10 of 1972.

(3) In *Fairfield* 1920 CPD 279, it was held that if an Act creates an offence and confers jurisdiction merely on a lower court in respect of such offence, the jurisdiction of a high court is not ousted in respect of the offence (unless, of course, there is an express provision in the Act to this effect).

(4) Section 111 of the Criminal Procedure Act empowers the Minister of Justice to order a trial in a court within the area of a director of public prosecutions although the offence was committed within the area of another director. All that is required is that the Minister must deem such removal in the interests of the administration of justice. The direction of the Minister is final and not subject to appeal to any court. This section is clearly applicable to lower as well as to high courts. See *Ndzeku* 1996 (1) SACR 301 (A). According to section 22(3) of Act 32 of 1998, furthermore, where the national director of public prosecutions or deputy director of public prosecutions authorised thereto in writing by the national director deems it in the interest of the administration of justice that an offence committed as a whole or partially within the area of jurisdiction of one director be investigated and tried within the area of jurisdiction of another director, he or she may, subject to the provisions of section 111 of the Criminal Procedure Act, in writing direct that the investigation and criminal proceedings in respect of such offence be conducted and commenced within the area of jurisdiction of such other director.

5.3.3 *Local divisions of the High Court*

The area of jurisdiction of each of the local divisions includes a number of magisterial districts—ss 2 and 6 and the First Schedule to Act 59 of 1959. In the areas of jurisdiction of local divisions, the provincial divisions have concurrent jurisdiction. The result is that a prosecution for an offence committed in an area falling under the jurisdiction of a local division, may be instituted in either the provincial division or in that local division.

The Judge-President of a provincial division may, by way of notices published in the *Government Gazette*, divide the area of jurisdiction of that provincial division into circuit districts. Circuit courts (also known as circuit local divisions) must sit at least twice yearly—s 7 of Act 59 of 1959.

5.3.4 *Regional courts and district courts*

Here we must distinguish between a summary trial and a preparatory examination. In a summary trial the accused is charged in the magistrate's court and this court itself decides whether he is guilty or not guilty. In the case of a preparatory examination, there is a hearing in which the accused is not tried; the magistrate does not judge whether he is guilty or not guilty, but only hears the evidence which is then sent to the director of public prosecutions who will decide whether to institute a prosecution or not, and in which court.

5.3.4.1 Summary trials

Section 90 of the Magistrates' Court Act lays down that a district court and a regional court have jurisdiction to hear trials of persons who are charged with an offence committed within the district or within the regional division (consisting of a number of districts) respectively. This principle has been extended by the further provisions of s 90 as follows:

(1) When any person is charged with any offence—

　(a) committed within the distance of four kilometres (formerly two miles) beyond the boundary of the district, or of the regional division; or

　(b) committed in or upon any vessel or vehicle on a voyage or journey, any part whereof was performed within a distance of four kilometres from the boundary of the district or the regional division;

　(c) committed on board any vessel on a journey upon any river within the Republic (or forming the boundary of any part thereof) and such journey or part thereof was performed in the district or regional division or within four kilometres of it;

　(d) committed on board any vessel on a voyage within the territorial waters of the Republic, and the said territorial waters adjoin the district or regional division; or

　(e) begun or completed within the district or within the regional division, such person may be tried by the court of the district or of the regional division as the case may be, as if he had been charged with an offence committed within the district or within the regional division respectively.

With regard to the four kilometres rule, a person may be tried in a particular area for an offence committed in another province but within four kilometres beyond the boundary of the particular area if it is an offence under the common law (implicit in the decision in *Baba* JS 376/33 (G)) and probably also if it is an offence in terms of statutory law operative in both provinces concerned. The court cannot, however, by virtue of this rule, apply statutory law operative in its own area if the act or omission concerned took place in another province where the particular statutory provision is not applicable, even, it would appear, if there is a similar statutory provision applicable in that other province. In *Baba* (above) the court decided that a person could not be tried in Kimberley, in the Cape Province, for the offence of resisting the police contrary to the provisions of a Cape Act where the person's act took place in the district of Boshof, in the Free State, within two miles beyond the boundary of the district of Kimberley; the fact that there was a similar Act operative in the Free State did not affect the issue.

　The question whether the court could apply statutory law operative in the province where the act or omission took place, but not operative in its own province (eg, in the case of *Baba* (above) whether Baba could have been tried in Kimberley for a transgression of the Free State Act committed in the district of Boshof) has correctly been decided in the negative in *Mpika* JS 253/41 (E). The position is similar if the two offences are the same but in the one area a mandatory minimum sentence should be imposed after conviction while this is not the case in the other area—*Khuzwayo* 1981 (1) SA 481 (N).

Subject to the remarks on extra-territorial jurisdiction below, a South African court does not have jurisdiction to adjudicate upon an offence committed in a foreign state and the four kilometres rule is thus not applicable—*Maseki* 1981 (4) SA 374 (T).

(2) Where it is uncertain in which of several jurisdictions an offence has been committed, it may be tried in any of such jurisdictions.

(3) A person charged with an offence may be tried by the court of any district or any regional division, as the case may be, wherein any act, omission or event which is an element of the offence took place.

(4) A person charged with theft of property or of obtaining property by an offence, or of an offence which involves the receiving of any property by him, may also be tried by the court of any district or regional division, as the case may be, wherein he has or had part of the property in his possession.

(5) A person charged with kidnapping, child-stealing or abduction may also be tried by the court of any district or of any regional division as the case may be, through or in which he conveyed or concealed or detained the person kidnapped, stolen or abducted.

(6) Where by any special statutory provision a magistrate's court has jurisdiction in respect of an offence committed beyond the local limits of the district (or of the regional division, as the case may be) such court is not deprived of such jurisdiction by any of the provisions of s 90 of the Magistrates' Courts Act.

(7) Where an accused is alleged to have committed various offences within different districts within the area of jurisdiction of any attorney-general, the latter may in writing direct that criminal proceedings be commenced in a magistrate's court within his area of jurisdiction as if such offence has been committed within the area of jurisdiction of such court. A regional court within whose area of jurisdiction such magistrate's court is situated, shall likewise have jurisdiction in respect of such offence if the offence may be tried by a regional court—s 90(8), Act 32 of 1944.

(8) In one instance the accused may even, upon a written order of the director of public prosecutions, be charged in the court of any district or regional division of the province or area for which that director holds office. This may happen when the director of public prosecutions deems it expedient owing to the number of accused involved in any criminal proceedings or with a view to avoiding excessive inconvenience or the disturbance of the public order—s 90(9), Act 32 of 1944.

(9) In terms of the provisions of s 110(1) of the Criminal Procedure Act, if a person is, as far as territorial jurisdiction is concerned, wrongly charged before a particular court, and fails to object timeously, such court will thereby acquire jurisdiction to try him.

(10) There are specific statutory provisions in terms of which a magistrate's court may exercise jurisdiction. Thus s 18 of the Aviation Act 74 of 1962 provides that in respect of any offence under that Act and in respect of any offence committed on a South African aircraft, the offence is deemed for the purpose of criminal jurisdiction to have been committed in any place where the accused happens to be. The Internal Security Act contains a similar provision—see s 68, Act 74 of 1982, and cf s 4 of the Civil Aviation Offences Act 10 of 1972.

(11) Lastly, s 111 of the Criminal Procedure Act 51 of 19 confers upon the Minister of Justice an unlimited discretion to order a trial to take place in the area of another director of public prosecutions. Note the extension in s 22(3) of Act 32 of 1998 — item (4) in 5.3.2, above.

5.3.4.2 Preparatory examinations

Section 125 regulates the jurisdiction of magistrates' courts. A preparatory examination is conducted in a magistrate's court within whose area of jurisdiction the offence has allegedly been committed. The director of public prosecutions may, however, if it appears to him expedient on account of the number of accused involved or in order to avoid excessive inconvenience or a possible disturbance of the public order, direct that the preparatory examination be held in another court within the area of his jurisdiction.

5.4 Jurisdiction in respect of offences committed outside South Africa

The general principle is that the courts of the Republic will exercise jurisdiction with regard to offences committed on South African territory only—cf *Makhutla* 1968 (2) SA 768 (O); *Mathabula* 1969 (3) SA 265 (N); and *Maseki* 1981 (4) SA 374 (T). However, there are a number of exceptions. The exceptions apply with regard to the following offences:

(1) High treason. By its very nature high treason is an offence which is frequently committed on foreign territory, eg where a South African citizen in wartime happens to be resident in an enemy country and joins the enemy army.

(2) A South African court will have jurisdiction to hear a charge of theft (which is a continuing offence) committed in a foreign state—not because it is regarded as theft in the foreign country, but because an accused is regarded to continue to appropriate the stolen object with the necessary intention in South Africa— *Kruger* 1989 (1) SA 785 (A).

(3) Offences committed on ships. Here one has to distinguish between offences committed on South African ships on the open sea or on other ships by South African citizens (by virtue of the Merchant Shipping Act 57 of 1951), on the one hand, and offences committed within the territorial waters of the Republic and piracy, on the other. As Hiemstra (277) quite correctly points out, the territorial waters of a state must by virtue of international law be considered as part of that state, so that legislation in this regard is unnecessary. (Section 90(2) of Act 32 of 1944 now regulates the jurisdiction of magistrates' courts regarding offences committed within adjacent territorial waters. See 4.3.4.1 above.)

(4) Offences committed on aircraft. One has to distinguish between offences committed on South African aircraft, wherever they might be in the world,

either in the air or on land (see s 18 of the Aviation Act 74 of 1962 and Hiemstra 277–8) and certain offences (generally related to hijacking) committed outside the Republic on board aircraft other than South African. In respect of the latter category it is required that

(a) such aircraft lands in the Republic with the offender still on board; or

(b) that the principal place of business or permanent residence of the lessee of such aircraft is in the Republic; or

(c) that the offender be present in the Republic—s 3(2) of the Civil Aviation Offences Act 10 of 1972.

(5) Offences committed on territory which is subsequently annexed by the Republic—Hiemstra 280.

(6) Offences committed on South African aircraft, wherever they might be, and whether in the air or on land—s 18 of the Aviation Act 74 of 1962 and Hiemstra 277–8.

(7) Offences committed by South African citizens in Antarctica are justiciable in South Africa. For the purposes of the administration of justice, Antarctica is deemed to be situated within the magisterial district of Cape Town—s 2 of the South African Citizens in Antarctica Act 55 of 1962.

(8) Offences deemed to be committed where the accused happens to be. Examples are: first, the Internal Security Act 74 of 1982, which makes punishable specified acts committed outside the Republic by residents or ex-residents of the Republic, eg to undergo training which could be of use in overthrowing or endangering the state authority in the Republic. Section 68 of that Act provides that any offence under the Act is deemed to have been committed at the place where the accused happens to be. The last-mentioned provision enables the High Court to exercise jurisdiction over an accused arrested in the Republic. By way of a second example, an offence committed in contravention of s 2 of the Simulated Armaments Transactions Prohibition Act 2 of 1976, is deemed to have been committed in any place in the Republic where the accused may find himself—s 3 of the Act. (Section 2 *inter alia* prohibits a person who poses as the state or one of its organs, from acquiring weapons, information or concessions with regard to the acquisition of weapons.) However, an accused's mere presence does not always settle the matter: when an accused is illegally abducted from a foreign State by agents of the South African authorities and subsequently handed over to the South African police, the court before which such abducted person is arraigned has no jurisdiction to try such person— *Ebrahim* 1991 (2) SA 553 (A); *Piliso* 1991 (2) SACR 354 (Tk) and *Beahan* 1992 (1) SACR 307 (ZS).

(9) Embassies have traditionally been regarded as part of the territory of the state represented, but this notion has fallen into disrepute over the years on account of malpractices (eg harbouring of criminals). The Vienna Convention of 1961 provides for diplomatic immunity from criminal jurisdiction in countries where diplomatic agents represent their own states. Diplomats of course remain subject to the jurisdiction of their home states—s 31(4) of the said Convention reads as follows:

The immunity of a diplomatic agent from the jurisdiction of the receiving state does not exempt him from the jurisdiction of the sending state.

Generally speaking, it would appear (although the practice may vary in different countries) as if domicile is accepted as the decisive test and that diplomats are regarded as remaining domiciled on the territory of the sending state.

5.5 Jurisdiction with regard to sentencing

5.5.1 *General*

The fact that the various courts mentioned below have the jurisdiction to impose any of the respective sentences as indicated below, does not mean that they may do so whenever they feel like it. The Criminal Procedure Act lays down specific rules with regard to the offences for which, the persons upon whom and the circumstances in which some of these sentences may or may not be imposed. Apart from that, several Acts of Parliament, ordinances and regulations contain provisions prescribing theminimum or maximum sentences that may be imposed for certain offences. In addition thereto, a whole body of case law have been built up over the years in which guidelines have been laid down concerning the way in which a court should exercise its discretion in sentencing an accused. The rules and guidelines with regard to the exercise by the court of its sentencing discretion, will be discussed in more detail in chapter 19.

5.5.2 *The High Court and special superior courts*

The Supreme Court of Appeal will only impose a sentence as court of first instance where it convicts a person of contempt *in facie curiae*. In such a case the court will be able to impose any sentence that may by law be imposed for that offence.

If the Supreme Court of Appeal, a provincial division or the Witwatersrand Local Division, after having heard an appeal in a criminal case, decides to change the conviction of the appellant to a conviction of another offence or to confirm a conviction but to impose a different sentence from the one originally imposed by the court of first instance, the jurisdiction of the court is limited to impose a sentence that may by law have been imposed by the court of first instance.

The Supreme Court of Appeal, provincial and local divisions, as well as special superior courts, may impose the following sentences:

(1) imprisonment, including imprisonment for life;

(2) periodical imprisonment;

(3) declaration as an habitual criminal;

(4) committal to a treatment centre;

(5) a fine;

(6) correctional supervision; and

(7) imprisonment from which the person may be placed under correctional supervision—s 276 of the Criminal Procedure Act.

5.5.3 *Regional courts*

A regional court may impose the following sentences and no other:

(1) imprisonment not exceeding a period of fifteen years;

(2) periodical imprisonment;

(3) declaration as an habitual criminal;

(4) committal to a treatment centre;

(5) a fine not exceeding the amount determined by the Minister from time to time by notice in the *Cazette*; (The amount determined with effect from 28 September 1998 is R300 000.)

(6) correctional supervision; and

(7) imprisonment from which the person may be placed under correctional supervision—s 276 of the Criminal Procedure Act.

5.5.4 *District courts*

A district court may impose the following sentences and no other:

(1) imprisonment not exceeding a period of three years; (If an Act has conferred an increased jurisdiction upon the magistrates' courts, these courts may impose such sentence notwithstanding the fact that such punishment exceeds the jurisdiction of the magistrates' courts.)

(2) periodical imprisonment;

(3) committal to a treatment centre;

(4) a fine not exceeding the amount determined by the Minister from time to time by notice in the *Gazette*; (The amount determined with effect from 28 September 1998 is R60 000.)

(5) correctional supervision; and

(6) imprisonment from which the person may be placed under correctional supervision—s 276 of the Criminal Procedure Act.

5.6 Jurisdiction to pronounce upon the validity of statutory provisions

Section 110 of the Magistrates' Courts Act provides that no magistrate's court shall be competent to pronounce upon the validity of a provincial ordinance or of a statutory proclamation issued by the President and every such court shall assume that every such ordinance or proclamation is valid. However, every such court shall be competent to pronounce upon the validity of any statutory regulation, order or by-law.

Where an accused pleads not guilty in a lower court and his defence is based on the alleged invalidity of a provincial ordinance or a proclamation issued by the President, the accused must be committed for summary trial before a superior court having jurisdiction—s 117.

CHAPTER 3

The prosecution of crime

		Page
1	INTRODUCTION	45
2	PUBLIC AND PRIVATE PROSECUTIONS	46
3	CRIMINAL PROSECUTIONS AND CIVIL ACTIONS	46
4	PUBLIC PROSECUTIONS	47
	4.1 Constitutional provisions and the National Prosecuting Authority Act 32 of 1998	47
	4.2 Structure and composition of the single national prosecuting authority	49
	4.2.1 Investigating directorates and appointment of investigating directors	50
	4.2.2 Appointment of special directors	50
	4.3 The power to institute and conduct criminal proceedings (s 20(1) of Act 32 of 1998)	50
	4.4 The authority and hierarchy of power to institute criminal proceedings	51
	4.5 The national director of public prosecutions (NDPP) and deputy national directors of public prosecutions (DNDPPs)	51
	4.5.1 Appointment	51
	4.5.2 Qualifications for appointment as NDPP or DNDPP	52
	4.5.3 Term of office of the NDPP and a DNDPP	52
	4.5.4 The NDPP and a DNDPP: suspension and removal from office	52
	4.5.5 Powers, functions and duties of the NDPP and a DNDPP	53
	4.5.6 Prosecution policy and issuing of policy directives	55
	4.5.7 Accountability to Parliament	56
	4.5.8 Ministerial responsibility over the prosecuting authority	56
	4.6 The directors of public prosecutions (DPPs)	57
	4.6.1 Appointment, qualifications, term of and removal from office and accountability	57
	4.6.2 Powers, duties and functions of a DPP and a DDPP	57

4.7   Prosecutors   59
        4.7.1   Appointment   59
        4.7.2   Powers, duties and functions of prosecutors   59
4.8   The prosecuting authority and the judiciary   60
4.9   Extraordinary powers of a DPP   61
4.10   Control over local prosecutors   61
4.11   The prosecution and the police   62
4.12   The prosecution, the police, the public and the reporting of crime   63
4.13   The prosecution as *dominus litis*   64
4.14   The discretion to prosecute   64
        4.14.1 The exercise of a discretion   64
        4.14.2 The distinction between withdrawal of a charge and
                stopping of the prosecution   66
4.15   Prescription of the right to prosecute   66
4.16   The prosecution and legal ethics   66
4.17   The prosecution and the assistance of a private legal practitioner .   67
4.18   Diversion of the criminal trial   67

5   PRIVATE PROSECUTIONS   67
    5.1   Introduction   67
    5.2   Private prosecution under statutory right   67
    5.3   Private prosecution by an individual on a certificate *nolle prosequi*   68
          5.3.1   Introduction   68
          5.3.2   Locus standi of a private prosecutor   69
          5.3.3   The certificate nolle prosequi   70
          5.3.4   Security by private prosecutor   71
          5.3.5   Failure of private prosecutor to appear   71
          5.3.6   Costs of successful private prosecution   72
          5.3.7   Costs of accused in an unsuccessful private prosecution . .   72
          5.3.8   Intervention by the state in a private prosecution   72

The Constitution and this chapter:

Section 9 — Equality

9(1) Everyone is equal before the law and has the right to equal protection and
benefit of the law.

See 4.14.1, below.

Section 179 — Prosecuting authority

See the full text of s 179 as cited in 4.1 below

1 INTRODUCTION

In primitive societies all wrongs were private wrongs, and private vengeance could lawfully be taken by the wronged against the wrongdoer — *Black v Barclays Zimbabwe Nominees (Pvt) Ltd* 1990 (1) SACR 433 (W) 434E. This right to exact private vengeance — which had often escalated into blood-feuds between clans or tribes — was gradually displaced by the idea that there had to be some form of officially enforced system of criminal justice in terms of which the guilt of an alleged perpetrator could be established, and in terms of which punishment could be meted out without the direct involvement of the individual victim concerned. There was a need for what we would today call 'legality' or 'due process of law'. Several factors contributed to this development.

First, societies became progressively more civilised. They began to view private vengeance (personal retaliation, self-help) as a disruptive method of exacting retribution and as a most ineffective means of seeking to restore harmony between wrongdoer and victim, and between wrongdoer and society.

Secondly, the formation of organised forms of government and the development of political units known as states, made it possible to transfer 'private vengeance' to a faceless entity which had the necessary resources, and which could create the appropriate structures, publicly to enforce justice on behalf of society, thereby indirectly accommodating or satisfying in a non-personal manner man's primitive but perhaps natural urge to seek retribution. This progress was accelerated when it became clear that there had to be a distinction between a private wrong and a public wrong, the latter being a wrong of such a nature that it required the state to intervene in the public interest. These 'public wrongs' were identified as crimes, and also contributed to the distinction between private and public law.

Thirdly, as soon as the state became responsible for the enforcement of criminal law, it was no longer possible to tolerate self-help. In fact, it then became unlawful to exact private vengeance.

Fourthly, the due and proper administration of criminal justice requires that the state should in principle shoulder the prosecutorial task. There can be no fair and equal administration of the criminal justice system if prosecutions for crime are entirely left to the whim, initiatives or resources of individual victims concerned. This is one of the reasons why in our local criminal justice system it is possible for the prosecuting officials, in the exercise of their discretion to prosecute, to decide to proceed with the institution of a prosecution despite the victim's or complainant's wish to have the case withdrawn. Wider public interests are at stake. On the same basis the prosecuting officials may refuse to institute a prosecution against the wishes of the victim. However, to avoid private vengeance, the victim may then in certain circumstances institute a private prosecution (see paragraphs 2 and 5 below).

Fifthly, in most legal systems there are also so-called victimless crimes. In other words, certain human activities have been criminalised on the basis that they are harmful to a larger public interest even though there usually is no readily identifiable victim or complainant. It falls upon the state and its officials to prosecute these crimes where necessary.

Section 179(2) of the Constitution determines that the prosecuting authority has the power to institute criminal proceedings on behalf of the state, and to carry out any necessary functions incidental to instituting criminal proceedings. Section 20 of the National Prosecuting Authority Act 32 of 1998 gives more detailed effect to this constitutional provision. See paragraph 4.3 below. For all practical purposes, it is the state which — through its appointed officials — prosecutes those who transgress the rules of substantive criminal law.

Charge sheets accordingly read 'The State *versus* Jones'. And indictments in the High Court mention that the director of public prosecutions is prosecuting on behalf of the state. When South Africa was still a Union, we followed the fiction which had originated in England, namely that the formal head of state (the King or the Queen as the case might have been) was injured by every crime. Public prosecutions were therefore instituted in the name of the King (*Rex*) or the Queen (*Regina*), depending on who reigned at the relevant time. The usual abbreviation used in the law reports up to 31 May 1961, was *R v Jones*. And up to this date the prosecuting authority was commonly known as 'the Crown'. After 31 May 1961 criminal cases have been reported as *State versus Jones*, or as *S v Jones* in abbreviated form. The prosecuting authority is now commonly referred to as 'the state'. In this work we use the terms 'state', 'prosecution', 'prosecutor' and 'public prosecutor' interchangeably; and for the sake of brevity, we simply use *Jones* to denote *R v Jones* or *S v Jones*, as the case may be.

2   PUBLIC AND PRIVATE PROSECUTIONS

When individuals relinquished to the state their right to private vengeance, they did so on the tacit understanding that the state would dutifully prosecute crime. However, most states do not adhere to the principle of compulsory prosecution. Prosecuting officials are vested with a discretion whether to prosecute or not. There are good reasons why prosecuting authorities should have a discretion (see par 4.14.1 below). However, an official refusal to prosecute might occasionally aggrieve an individual who happens to be the victim of a crime (and who, of course, has now been deprived of his ancient right to self-help). In order to avoid a deadlock of this nature and in an attempt to suppress or accommodate man's primitive urge to resort to self-help, some states have in addition to their system of public prosecution also created a system of private prosecution. This is a system in terms of which the aggrieved individual may in certain circumstances in his personal capacity proceed against the perpetrator in an attempt to prove the latter's guilt beyond reasonable doubt in a court of law and have him punished within the ambit of legitimate procedures which were created by the state and which were also available to the state had it not declined to prosecute. The South African Criminal Procedure Act makes provision for private prosecutions in certain instances. Private prosecutions are dealt with in paragraph 5 below. Public prosecutions, however, represent the vast majority of prosecutions.

3   CRIMINAL PROSECUTIONS AND CIVIL ACTIONS

Having regard to the evolution from private vengeance to public prosecution, most modern states perceive the commission of a crime as a violation of the public interest. Punishment is in principle sought on behalf of society, and only in an incidental way in respect of an individual who has suffered some personal harm or damages in consequence of a crime. It is therefore considered proper that the state should in principle perform the necessary prosecutorial functions even in those circumstances where an identifiable victim clearly suffered some personal harm to his legitimate interests, for example, the patrimonial (economic) loss suffered by the victim of a theft. But this does not mean that a prosecution — whether public or private — deprives the injured party of any civil remedies he might have. In our example the victim of the theft might still seek to recover his losses in a civil court. This is a private law matter, and does not involve punishment through the application of procedural and substantive criminal law rules. The civil action is a matter between two individuals: the victim as plaintiff and the alleged thief as defendant. The civil action is in principle possible irrespective of the outcome of the criminal case. Section 342 provides that a conviction or an acquittal in respect of any offence shall not bar a civil action for damages at the instance of any person who has suffered damages in consequence of the commission of that offence. The exception to this rule is where the criminal court has ordered a convicted accused to pay compensation to the complainant or to return stolen property. See ss 300 and 301, discussed in greater detail in Chapter 19. The victim (plaintiff) cannot be compensated twice in respect of one and the same loss.

Section 342 also determines that an *acquittal* of an accused shall not bar a civil action. This is not a peculiar provision. It must be understood in the light of the differences between civil and criminal cases. In a criminal court the prosecution must prove its case *beyond reasonable doubt*. The prosecution will be unsuccessful if it fails to meet this standard of proof. But in a civil case the plaintiff will achieve success if the lesser standard of proof *upon a balance of probabilities* is met. To revert to our hypothetical theft case: In the absence of proof beyond reasonable doubt, the alleged thief must be acquitted. But the victim of the theft can in his capacity as plaintiff in a civil action instituted by him, possibly still achieve success because he need only prove his case on a balance of probabilities (the lesser standard).

The institution of a civil action based on certain facts against a specific person, does not preclude the institution of a public (or private) prosecution against the same person, arising out of the same facts. Once again, to return to our theft case: The fact that the victim has instituted a civil action to recover his losses cannot prevent the criminal justice system from taking its course and proceeding with a charge of theft. However, if the victim has (in his capacity as plaintiff in the civil action) successfully recovered his losses, the criminal court can in the event of a conviction not make any compensatory order. It should merely impose some form of punishment and not order compensation or return of property as envisaged by ss 300 and 301.

4 PUBLIC PROSECUTIONS

4.1 Constitutional provisions and the National Prosecuting Authority Act 32 of 1998

Section 179 of the Constitution (which should be read with schedule 6 item 18(1) of the Constitution and s 108 of the interim Constitution) provides as follows:

(1) There is a single national prosecuting authority in the Republic, structured in terms of an Act of Parliament, and consisting of —

　　(a) a national director of public prosecutions, who is the head of the prosecuting authority, and is appointed by the President, as head of the national executive; and

(b) directors of public prosecutions and prosecutors as determined by an Act of Parliament.

(2) The prosecuting authority has the power to institute criminal proceedings on behalf of the state, and to carry out any necessary functions incidental to instituting criminal proceedings.

(3) National legislation must ensure that the directors of public prosecutions —

(a) are appropriately qualified; and

(b) are responsible for prosecutions in specific jurisdictions, subject to subsection (5).

(4) National legislation must ensure that the prosecuting authority exercises its functions without fear, favour or prejudice.

(5) The national director of public prosecutions —

(a) must determine, with the concurrence of the Cabinet members responsible for the administration of justice, and after consulting the directors of public prosecutions, prosecution policy, which must be observed in the prosecution process;

(b) must issue policy directives which must be observed in the prosecution process;

(c) may intervene in the prosecution process when policy directives are not complied with; and

(d) may review a decision to prosecute or not to prosecute, after consulting the relevant director of public prosecutions and after taking representations within a period specified by the national director of public prosecutions, from the following:

(i) The accused person.

(ii) The complainant.

(iii) Any other person or party whom the national director considers to be relevant.

(6) The Cabinet member responsible for the administration of justice must exercise final responsibility over the prosecuting authority.

(7) All other matters concerning the prosecuting authority must be determined by national legislation.

Section 179 provides the constitutional framework which must govern public prosecutions: Legislative or common law provisions which conflict with this framework, are unconstitutional.

Parliament has passed the National Prosecuting Authority Act 32 of 1998 (hereafter referred to as 'Act 32 of 1998'). Act 32 of 1998 seeks to give effect to the provisions of s 179 of the Constitution — and it also regulates further matters governing the prosecution of crime at the instance of the state. The whole of the Attorney-General Act 92 of 1992 — which previously governed the appointment and essential powers of officials responsible for public prosecutions — has been repealed by s 44 of Act 32 of 1998.

An important transitional provision is contained in s 45 of Act 32 of 1998: Any reference in any law to an attorney-general or deputy attorney-general, shall be construed as a reference to a director of public prosecutions or deputy director of public prosecutions. This means, for example, that a reference to an attorney-general in the Criminal Procedure Act, must be read as a reference to a director of public prosecutions appointed in terms of Act 32 of 1998.

Section 8 of Act 32 of 1998 provides that the need for the prosecuting authority to reflect broadly the racial and gender composition of South Africa must be considered when members of the prosecuting authority are appointed.

All members of the prosecuting authority must take an oath or make an affirmation to the effect that they will 'uphold and protect the Constitution and the fundamental rights entrenched therein' — s 32(2) of 32 of 1998.

Section 32(1) provides as follows:

(a) A member of the *prosecuting authority* shall serve impartially and exercise, carry out or perform his or her powers, duties and functions in good faith and without fear, favour or prejudice and subject only to the *Constitution* and the law.

(b) Subject to the *Constitution* and Act 32 of 1998, no organ of state and no member or employee of an organ of state nor any other person shall improperly interfere with, hinder or obstruct the *prosecuting authority* or any member thereof in the exercise, carrying out or performance of its, his or her powers, duties and functions.

4.2 Structure and composition of the single national prosecuting authority

In the past South Africa had attorneys-general (head of prosecutions) at various divisions of the High Court. These attorneys-general acted independently of each other. There was no single national prosecuting authority.

Section 2 of Act 32 of 1998 — as read with s 179 of the Constitution — establishes a single national prosecuting authority.

The structure of the single prosecuting authority consists of the office of the national director of public prosecutions (see s 3*(a)* of Act 32 of 1998) and the various offices of the prosecuting authority at the High Courts and established in terms of s 6(1) of Act 32 of 1998 (see s 3*(b)* of Act 32 of 1998).

In terms of s 4 of Act 32 of 1998, the prosecuting authority comprises the following: *(a)* the national director of public prosecutions (hereafter referred to as the 'NDPP'); *(b)* the deputy national directors of public prosecutions (hereafter the 'DNDPPs'); *(c)* the directors of public prosecutions (the former attorneys-general and hereafter the 'DPPs'); *(d)* the deputy directors of public prosecutions (the former deputy attorneys-general and hereafter the 'DDPPs') and *(e)* prosecutors.

The office of the NDPP (as established in terms of s 5(1)) shall (in terms of s 5(2)) consist of the following: *(a)* the NDPP who is the head of and controls the office; *(b)* DNDPPs (who may not be more than three — s 11(1)); *(c)* investigating directors (see paragraph 4.2.1 below) and special directors (see paragraph 4.2.2 below) and *(d)* other members of the prosecuting authority appointed or assigned to the office of the NDPP.

Section 6(1) establishes offices of the national single prosecuting authority at seats of the High Court. In terms of s 6(2) each of these offices consists of a DPP (or DDPP) who is head of and controls the office concerned; DDPPs; prosecutors and persons contemplated in s 38(1), ie, persons appointed on an *ad hoc* basis on account of their qualifications and experience to perform services in *specific* cases. If a DDPP is appointed as head of one of these offices, he shall exercise his functions subject to the control and directions of a DPP appointed in writing by the NDPP — s 6(3).

4.2.1 *Investigating directorates and appointment of investigating directors*

The President may, by proclamation in the *Gazette* and with the concurrence of the Minister of Justice and the NDPP, establish not more than three investigating directorates in the office of the NDPP, specifying the categories of offences for which such a directorate has been established — s 7(1), (2) and (3) of Act 32 of 1998. The person in control of such a directorate is known as an investigating director and performs the functions, power and duties of the directorate subject to the control of the NDPP — s 7(3).

The President — after consultation with the Minister of Justice and the NDPP — must, in respect of each investigating directorate, appoint a DPP as the head of such a directorate — s 13(1)*(b)*. When it comes to the decision to prosecute, an investigating director acts only after consultation with the DPP who has jurisdiction, ie, after having heard the views of the relevant DPP — s 24(2)*(b)*. However, the ultimate decision rests with the NDPP — s 22(2)*(c)*. See further paragraph 4.5.5 below.

The power, duties and functions relating to investigating directorates are also governed by the provisions of Chapter 5 of Act 32 of 1998. These special provisions are not discussed in this work, except to point out that investigating directors have special powers to hold formal enquiries (s 28) and enter premises (s 29). It should also be noted that the whole of the Investigation of Serious Economic Offences Act 117 of 1991 — which created the office for serious economic offences — has been repealed by s 44 of Act 32 of 1998. However, an investigating directorate for serious economic offences has been established as a transitional arrangement in terms of s 43(7) and operates in accordance with the provisions of Chapter 5.

An investigating directorate in respect of organized crime has been established in terms of s 7.

4.2.2 *Appointment of special directors*

The President — after consultation with the Minister of Justice and the NDPP — may appoint special directors of public prosecutions to exercise certain powers, carry out certain duties and perform certain functions conferred or imposed on or assigned to these persons by the President by proclamation in the *Gazette* — s 13(1)*(c)*. A special director remains subject to the directions of the NDPP — s 24(3). When it comes to the decisions to prosecute, a special director must act in consultation with the DPP who has jurisdiction, ie, with the concurrence of the DPP concerned — s 24(3). But the ultimate decision still rests with the NDPP who may in accordance with s 22(2)*(c)* review the decision. See further paragraph 4.5.5 below.

4.3 The power to institute and conduct criminal proceedings (s 20(1) of Act 32 of 1998)

The above section provides that the power as contemplated in s 179(2) and all other relevant sections of the *Constitution*, to *(a)* institute and conduct criminal proceedings on behalf of the State: *(b)* carry out any necessary functions incidental to instituting and conducting such criminal proceedings; and *(c)* discontinue criminal proceedings, vests in the *prosecuting authority* and shall, for all purposes, be exercised on behalf of the *Republic*.

4.4 The authority and hierarchy of power to institute criminal proceedings

The hierarchy of power — within the single national prosecuting authority — is governed by s 20(2) to s 20(6)*(c)* of Act 32 of 1998.

Any DNDPP shall exercise the powers referred to in s 20(1) subject to the control and directions of the NDPP — s 20(2) of Act 32 of 1998.

Subject to the provisions of the *Constitution* and Act 32 of 1998, any DPP shall, subject to the control and directions of the NDPP, exercise the powers referred to in s 20(1) in respect of *(a)* the area of jurisdiction for which he or she has been appointed; and *(b)* any offences which have not been expressly excluded from his or her jurisdiction, either generally or in a specific case, by the NDPP — s 20(3) of Act 32 of 1998.

Subject to the provisions of Act 32 of 1998, any DDPP shall, subject to the control and directions of the DPP concerned, exercise the powers referred to in s 20(1) in respect of *(a)* the area of jurisdiction for which he or she has been appointed; and *(b)* such offences in such courts, as he or she has been authorised in writing by the NDPP or a person designated by the NDPP — s 20(4) of Act 32 of 1998.

Any *prosecutor* shall be competent to exercise any of the powers referred to in s 20(1) to the extent that he or she has been authorised thereto in writing by the NDPP, or by a person designated by the NDPP — s 20(5) of Act 32 of 1998. A written authorisation referred to in s 20(5) shall set out *(a)* the area of jurisdiction; *(b)* the offences; and *(c)* the court or courts, in respect of which such powers may be exercised — s 20(6) of Act 32 of 1998.

4.5 The national director of public prosecutions (NDPP) and the deputy national directors of public prosecutions (DNDPPs)

4.5.1 *Appointment*

The President as head of the national executive appoints the NDPP — s 10 of Act 32 of 1998 as read with s 79(1)*(a)* of the Constitution. In *Ex parte Attorney-General, Namibia: In re: The Constitutional Relationship between the Attorney-General and the Prosecutor-General* 1995 (8) BCLR 1070 (NmS) the Namibian Supreme Court warned against the danger of political appointees having control over prosecutorial matters. At 1088F it was said that such interference 'is not the product of a rechsstaat and is not compatible with the Grundnorm relating to the separation of powers. It paves the way for executive domination and State despotism. It represents a denial of the cardinal values of the Constitution.'

In *In re: Certification of the Constitution of the RSA 1996* 1996 (10) BCLR 1253 (CC) the Constitutional Court was satisfied that appointment of the NDPP by the President did not compromise the independence of the prosecuting authority and did not violate the separation of powers. In paragraph [141] of the judgment it was noted that the prosecuting authority is not part of the judiciary. In paragraph [146] it was pointed out that in terms of s 179(4) of the Constitution national legislation must ensure that the prosecuting authority exercises its function without fear, favour or prejudice: Section 179(4) provides a constitutional guarantee of independence, and any legislation or executive action inconsistent therewith would be subject to constitutional control by the courts. See further paragraphs 4.5.4, 4.5.7 and 4.5.8 below. It is submitted that Act 32 of 1998 is consistent with s 79 of the Constitution. The President may, after consultation with the Minister of Justice and the NDPP, appoint no more than three persons, as DNDPPs — s 11(1).

4.5.2   *The qualifications for appointment as NDPP or DNDPP*

The power of the President to appoint the NDPP and a DNDPP is qualified by s 9 of Act 32 of 1998. This section provides that any person to be appointed as NDPP or DNDPP must possess qualifications that would entitle him or her to practise in all courts in the Republic and, furthermore, must be a fit and proper person, with due regard to his or her experience, conscientiousness and integrity, to be entrusted with the responsibilities of the office concerned — s 9(1)*(a)* and *(b)*. A NDPP must also be a South African citizen — s 9(2).

4.5.3   *Term of office of the NDPP and a DNDPP*

The NDPP shall hold office for a non-renewable term of 10 years, but must vacate office on attaining the age of 65 — s 12(1). A DNDPP must also vacate his or her office on attaining the age of 65 but is not subject to the 10 year period which applies in respect of the NDPP — s 12(2) as read with 12(1). In certain circumstances the President may direct that the NDPP or a DNDPP who has attained the age of 65, be retained. Such retention, however, may not exceed a period of two years or periods which in the aggregate exceed two years — and the rule that the term of office of the NDPP may not exceed 10 years, remains applicable (s 12(4)).

4.5.4   *The NDPP and a DNDPP: suspension and removal from office*

The independence of the prosecuting authority — as alluded to in paragraph 4.5.1 above — is enhanced by strict rules governing suspension and removal. In order to minimize and prevent possible executive interference in prosecutorial matters, the NDPP and a DNDPP must enjoy strong security of tenure. The same applies to a DPP (see paragraph 4.6.1 below). In terms of s 12(5) of Act 32 of 1998 the NDPP and a DNDPP shall not be suspended or removed from office except in accordance with the provisions of s 12(6), 12(7) and 12(8). The latter section deals with removal from office at the request of NDPP or a DNDPP. Sections 12(6) and 12(7) deals with executive action and provide as follows:

(6)   *(a)*   The President may provisionally suspend the NDPP or a DNDPP from his or her office, pending such enquiry into his or her fitness to hold such office as the President deems fit and, subject to the provisions of this subsection, may thereupon remove him or her from office —

   (i)   for misconduct;

   (ii)   on account of continued ill-health;

   (iii)   on account of incapacity to carry out his or her duties of office efficiently; or

   (iv)   on account thereof that he or she is no longer a fit and proper person to hold the office concerned.

(b) The removal of the NDPP or a DNDPP, the reason therefor and the representations of the NDPP or DNDPP (if any) shall be communicated by message to Parliament within 14 days after such removal if Parliament is then in session or, if Parliament is not then in session, within 14 days after the commencement of its next ensuing session.

(c) Parliament shall, within 30 days after the message referred to in paragraph *(b)* has been tabled in Parliament, or as soon thereafter as is reasonably possible, pass a resolution as to whether or not the restoration to his or her office of the NDPP or DNDPP so removed, is recommended.

(d) The President shall restore the NDPP or DNDPP to his or her office if Parliament so resolves.

(e) The NDPP or a DNDPP provisionally suspended from office shall receive, for the duration of such suspension, no salary or such salary as may be determined by the President.

(7) The President shall also remove the NDPP or a DNDPP from office if an address from each of the respective Houses of Parliament in the same session praying for such removal on any of the grounds referred to in s 12(6)*(a)*, is presented to the President.

Certain provisions relating to the salaries of the NDPP, DNDPPs and DPPs also enhance the independence of the prosecuting authority in that the salaries of the afore-mentioned officials are linked to and form percentages of the remuneration that judges receive — s 17. Practically speaking, it means that their income may only be reduced by an Act of Parliament. See also s 18(6) as regards the salaries of DDPPs and prosecutors.

4.5.5 *Powers, functions and duties of the NDPP and a DNDPP*

Any DNDPP may exercise or perform any of the functions, powers or duties of the NDPP which he or she has been authorised by the NDPP to exercise or perform — s 23.

The powers, duties and functions of the NDPP are set out in s 22. This section provides as follows:

(1) The NDPP, as the head of the *prosecuting authority*, shall have authority over the exercising of all the powers, and the performance of all the duties and functions conferred or imposed on or assigned to any member of the *prosecuting authority* by the *Constitution*, Act 32 of 1998 or any other law.

(2) In accordance with s 179 of the *Constitution*, the NDPP —

(a) must determine prosecution policy and issue policy directives as contemplated in s 21 (see further paragraph 4.5.6 below);

(b) may intervene in any prosecution process when policy directives are not complied with; and

(c) may review a decision to prosecute or not to prosecute, after consulting the relevant DPP and after taking representations, within the period specified by the NDPP, of the accused person, the complainant and any other person or party whom the NDPP considers to be relevant (see also s 179(5)*(d)* of the Constitution).

(3) Where the NDPP or a DNDPP authorised thereto in writing by the NDPP deems it in the interest of the administration of justice that an offence committed as a whole or partially within the area of jurisdiction of one DPP be investigated and tried within the area of jurisdiction of another DPP, he or she may, subject to the provisions of s 111 of the Criminal Procedure Act 51 of 1977, in writing direct that the investigation and criminal proceedings in respect of such offence be conducted and commenced within the area of jurisdiction of such other DPP.

(4) In addition to any other powers, duties and functions conferred or imposed on or assigned to the NDPP by s 179 or any other provision of the *Constitution*, Act 32 of 1998 or any other law, the NDPP, as the head of the *prosecuting authority* —

(a) with a view to exercising his or her powers in terms of s 22(2), may —

(i) conduct any investigation he or she may deem necessary in respect of a prosecution or a prosecution process, or directives, directions or guidelines given or issued by a DPP in terms of Act 32 of 1998, or a case or matter relating to such a prosecution or a prosecution process, or directives, directions or guidelines;

(ii) direct the submission of and receive reports or interim reports from a DPP in respect of a case, a matter, a prosecution or a prosecution process or directions or guidelines given or issued by a *director* in terms of Act 32 of 1998; and

(iii) advise the Minister of Justice on all matters relating to the administration of criminal justice;

(b) shall maintain close liaison with the DNDPPs, the DPPs, the *prosecutors*, the legal professions and legal institutions in order to foster common policies and practices and to promote co-operation in relation to the handling of complaints in respect of the *prosecuting authority*;

(c) may consider such recommendations, suggestions and requests concerning the *prosecuting authority* as he or she may receive from any source;

(d) shall assist the DPPs and *prosecutors* in achieving the effective and fair administration of criminal justice;

(e) shall assist the DNDPPs, DPPs and *prosecutors* in representing their professional interests;

(f) shall bring the United Nations Guidelines on the Role of Prosecutors to the attention of the DPPs and *prosecutors* and promote their respect for and compliance with the above-mentioned principles within the framework of national legislation;

(g) shall prepare a comprehensive report in respect of the operations of the *prosecuting authority*, which shall include reporting on —

(i) the activities of the NDPP, DNDPPs, DPPs and the prosecuting authority as a whole;

(ii) the personnel position of the *prosecuting authority*;

(iii) the financial implications in respect of the administration and operation of the *prosecuting authority*;

    (iv) any recommendations or suggestions in respect of the *prosecuting authority*;

    (v) information relating to training programmes for *prosecutors*; and

    (vi) any other information which the NDPP deems necessary;

(h) may have the administrative work connected with the exercise of his or her powers, the performance of his or her functions or the carrying out of his or her duties, carried out by administrative staff referred to in s 37 of Act 32 of 1998; and

(i) may make recommendations to the Minister of Justice with regard to the *prosecuting authority* or the administration of justice as a whole.

(5) The NDPP shall, after consultation with the DNDPPs and the DPPs, advise the Minister of Justice on creating a structure, by regulation, in terms of which any person may report to such structure any complaint or any alleged improper conduct or any conduct which has resulted in any impropriety or prejudice on the part of a member of the *prosecuting authority*, and determining the powers and functions of such structure.

(6) *(a)* The NDPP shall, in consultation with the Minister of Justice and after consultation with the DNDPPs and the DPPs, frame a code of conduct which shall be complied with by members of the *prosecuting authority*.

(b) The code of conduct may from time to time be amended, and must be published in the *Gazette* for general information.

(7) The NDPP shall develop, in consultation with the Minister of Justice or a person authorised thereto by the *Minister*, and the DPPs, training programmes for *prosecutors*.

(8) The NDPP or a person designated by him or her in writing may —

(a) if no other member of the *prosecuting authority* is available, authorise in writing any suitable person to act as a prosecutor for the purpose of postponing any criminal case or cases;

(b) authorise any competent person in the employ of the public service or any local authority to conduct prosecutions, subject to the control and directions of the NDPP or a person designated by him or her, in respect of such statutory offences, including municipal laws, as the NDPP, in consultation with the Minister of Justice, may determine.

(9) The NDPP or any DNDPP designated by the NDPP shall have the power to institute and conduct a prosecution in any court in the *Republic* in person.

4.5.6 *Prosecution policy and issuing of policy directives*

In accordance with ss 179(5)*(a)* and 179(5)*(b)* of the Constitution, the NDPP must — with the concurrence of the Minister of Justice and after consulting the DPP — determine prosecution policy — s 21(1)*(a)*. The NDPP must also issue policy directives — s 21(1)*(b)*. The prosecution policy and directives must be observed in the prosecution process — s 21. The NDPP may intervene where these are not observed — s 22(2)*(b)*. See further paragraph 4.14.2 below.

4.5.7 *Accountability to Parliament*

The prosecuting authority is accountable to Parliament — s 35(1).

A refined prosecutorial system would seek to ensure that there are checks and balances, and that someone who holds such immense prosecutorial powers as the NDPP should be accountable. Section 35(2) of Act 32 of 1998 accordingly provides as follows:

(a) The NDPP must submit annually, not later than the first day of June, to the Minister of Justice a report referred to in s 22(4)*(g)*, which report must be tabled in Parliament by the *Minister* within 14 days, if Parliament is then in session, or if Parliament is not then in session, within 14 days after the commencement of its next ensuing session.

(b) The NDPP may, at any time, submit a report to the *Minister* or Parliament with regard to any matter relating to the *prosecuting authority*, if he or she deems it necessary.

4.5.8 *Ministerial responsibility over the prosecuting authority*

Closely linked to the prosecuting authority's accountability to Parliament (as set out in paragraph 4.5.7 above), is the provision that the Minister of Justice has the final responsibility over the prosecuting authority — s 33(1). Section 33(2) of Act 32 of 1998 provides as follows:

To enable the *Minister* to exercise his or her final responsibility over the *prosecuting authority*, as contemplated in s 179 of the *Constitution*, the NDPP shall, at the request of the *Minister* —

(a) furnish the *Minister* with information or a report with regard to any case, matter or subject dealt with by the NDPP or a DPP in the exercise of their powers, the carrying out of their duties and the performance of their functions;

(b) provide the *Minister* with reasons for any decision taken by a DPP in the exercise of his or her powers, the carrying out of his or her duties or the performance of his or her functions;

(c) furnish the *Minister* with information with regard to the prosecution policy referred to in s 21(1)*(a)*;

(d) furnish the *Minister* with information with regard to the policy directives referred to in s 21(1)*(b)*;

(e) submit the reports contemplated in s 34 to the *Minister*; and

(f) arrange meetings between the *Minister* and members of the prosecuting authority.

It should be noted that neither s 33 nor any other section in Act 32 of 1998, provides for ministerial control of or intervention in the decisions of the NDPP or a DPP. There is a difference between ministerial *responsibility* and ministerial control and intervention. The problem, however, is that the present absence of ministerial control and intervention stems from Act 32 of 1998 and not necessarily from the provisions of the Constitution. See the critical analysis by D'Oliviera 'The Prosecuting Authority: Seeking a Bridle for the Unicorn' in Carpenter (ed) *Suprema Lex* (1998) 71. At 86 the author points out that there is no indication in our Constitution of the relationship between the responsible Minister and the NDPP.

But it is to be hoped that legislative blurring of the distinction between ministerial responsibility over the prosecuting authority and the prosecutorial functions of the NDPP, can be prevented on the basis of the decision of the Constitutional Court in *In re: Certification of the Constitution of the RSA 1996* as cited and discussed in paragraph 4.5 above.

The procedure created by s 33 cuts both ways: It also gives a NDPP an opportunity to explain a particular decision which might on the face of it, and to someone not familiar with all the facts of the case, have seemed a peculiar decision.

Various prosecutorial models and the extent to which the official who is at the head of prosecutions can be controlled by ministerial interference, are referred to in *Ex parte Attorney-General, Namibia: In re: The Constitutional Relationship between the Attorney-General and the Prosecutor-General* (cited in paragraph 4.5.1 above).

4.6 The directors of public prosecutions (DPPs)

4.6.1 *Appointment, qualifications, term of and removal from office and accountability*

The President, after consultation with the Minister of Justice and the NDPP, may appoint a DPP at the seat of each High Court of the Republic — s 13(1)*(a)*.

Qualifications for appointment as a DPP are the same as those for appointment of a NDPP — s 9(1). See further paragraph 4.5.2 above. But a DPP, like a DNDPP, need not be a South African citizen.

A DPP must vacate office at the age of 65 — s 14(1). A DPP may, like a DNDPP, be re-appointed for a period which does not exceed (or periods which in the aggregate do not exceed) two years — s 14(2) as read with s 12(4). See also paragraph 4.5.3 above.

Suspension and removal of a DPP must be dealt with as if he or she were the NDPP or a DNDPP — s 14(3) as read with s 12(3), (4), (6), (7), (8) and (9). The suspension and removal of the NDPP and a DNDPP are discussed in paragraph 4.5.4 above.

A DPP must and may report to the NDPP. Section 34 provides:

(1) A DPP must annually, not later than the first day of March, submit to the NDPP a report on all his or her activities during the previous year.

(2) The NDPP may at any time request a DPP to submit a report with regard to a specific activity relating to his or her powers, duties or functions.

(3) A DPP may, at any time, submit a report to the NDPP with regard to any matter relating to the *prosecuting authority*, if he or she deems it necessary.

4.6.2 *Powers, duties and functions of a DPP and a DDPP*

Section 24 provides as follows:

(1) Subject to the provisions of s 179 and any other relevant section of the *Constitution*, Act 32 of 1998 or any other law, a DPP referred to in s 13(1)*(a)* has, in respect of the area for which he or she has been appointed, the power to —

    (a) institute and conduct criminal proceedings and to carry out functions incidental thereto as contemplated in s 20(3);

    (b) supervise, direct and co-ordinate the work and activities of all DDPPs and *prosecutors* in the Office of which he or she is the head;

(c) supervise, direct and co-ordinate specific investigations; and

(d) carry out all duties and perform all functions, and exercise all powers conferred or imposed on or assigned to him or her under any law which is in accordance with the provisions of Act 32 of 1998.

(2) In addition to the powers, duties and functions conferred or imposed on or assigned to an *investigating director*, such an *investigating director* or any person authorized thereto by him or her in writing may, for the purposes of criminal prosecution —

(a) institute an action in any court in the *Republic*; and

(b) prosecute an appeal in any court in the *Republic* emanating from criminal proceedings instituted by the *investigating director* or the person authorised thereto by him or her:

Provided that an *investigating director* or the person authorized thereto to him or her shall exercise the powers referred to in this subsection only after consultation with the DPP of the area of jurisdiction concerned. See also paragraph 4.2.1 above.

(3) A *special director* shall exercise the powers, carry out the duties and perform the functions conferred or imposed on or assigned to him or her by the President, subject to the directions of the NDPP: Provided that if such powers, duties and functions include any of the powers, duties and functions referred to in s 20(1), they shall be exercised, carried out and performed in consultation with the DPP of the area of jurisdiction concerned. See also paragraph 4.2.1 above.

(4) In addition to any other powers, duties and functions conferred or imposed on or assigned to him or her by s 179 of the Constitution, Act 32 of 1998 or any other law, a DPP referred to in s 13(1) —

(a) shall, at the request of the NDPP, submit reports to the NDPP or assist the NDPP in connection with a matter referred to in s 22(4)*(a)*(ii);

(b) shall submit annual reports to the NDPP pertaining to matters referred to in s 22(4)*(g)*;

(c) may, in the case of a DPP referred to in s 13(1)*(a)*, give written directions or furnish guidelines to —

    (i) the Provincial Commissioner of the police service referred to in s 207(3) of the *Constitution* within his or her area of jurisdiction; or

    (ii) any other person who within his or her area of jurisdiction —

        (åa) conducts investigations in relation to offences; or

        (ab) other than a private prosecutor, institutes or carries on prosecutions for offences; and

(d) shall, subject to the directions of the NDPP, be responsible for the day to day management of the DDPP and *prosecutors* under his or her control.

(5) Without limiting the generality of s 24(4)*(c)* and subject to the directions of the NDPP, directions or guidelines under that subsection may be given or furnished in relation to particular cases and may determine that certain offences or classes of offences must be referred to the DPP concerned for decisions on the

institution or conducting of prosecutions in respect of such offences or classes of offences.

(6) The *director* shall give to the NDPP a copy of each direction given or guideline furnished under s 24(4)*(c)*.

(7) Where a DDP

    (a) is considering the institution or conducting of a prosecution for an offence; and

    (b) is of the opinion that a matter connected with or arising out of the offence requires further investigation,

the DPP may request the provincial commissioner of the police service referred to in s 24(4)*(c)*(i) for assistance in the investigation of that matter and where the DPP so requests, the provincial commissioner concerned shall, so far as practicable, comply with the request.

(8) The powers conferred upon a DPP under s 20(1) shall include the authority to prosecute in any court any appeal arising from any criminal proceedings.

(9) *(a)* Subject to s 20(4) and the control and directions of a DPP, a DDPP at the Office of a DPP referred to in s 13(1), has all the powers, duties and functions of a DPP.

    (b) A power, duty or function which is exercised, carried out or performed by a DDPP is construed, for the purposes of Act 32 of 1998, to have been exercised, carried out or performed by the DPP concerned.

The appointment of a DDPP is governed by s 15 of Act 32 of 1998.

4.7 Prosecutors

4.7.1 *Appointment*

The appointment of prosecutors is governed by s 16 which provides as follows:

(1) *Prosecutors* shall be appointed on the recommendation of the NDPP or a member of the *prosecuting authority* designated for that purpose by the NDPP, and subject to the laws governing the public service.

(2) *Prosecutors* may be appointed to —

    (a) the *office of the NDPP*;

    (b) offices established by s 6(1);

    (c) *investigating directorates*; and

    (d) lower courts in the *Republic*.

(3) The Minister of Justice may from time to time, in consultation with the NDPP and after consultation with the DPPs, prescribe the appropriate legal qualifications for the appointment of a person as *prosecutor* in a lower court.

4.7.2 *Powers, duties and functions of prosecutors*

Section 25 of Act 32 of 1998 determines the powers, duties and functions of prosecutor. This section provides as follows:

(1) A *prosecutor* shall exercise the powers, carry out the duties and perform the functions conferred or imposed on or assigned to him or her —

(a) under Act 32 of 1998 and any other law of the *Republic*; and .

(b) by the head of the office or *investigating directorate* where he or she is employed or a person designated by such head; or

(c) if he or she is employed as a *prosecutor* in a lower court, by the DPP in whose area of jurisdiction such court is situated or a person designated by such DPP.

(2) Notwithstanding the provisions of the Right of Appearance in Courts Act 62 of 1995, or any other law, any *prosecutor* who —

(a) has obtained such legal qualifications as the *Minister* after consultation with the NDPP may prescribe; and

(b) has at least three years' experience as a *prosecutor* of a magistrates' court of a regional division,

shall, subject to s 20(6), have the right to appear in any court in the *Republic*.

4.8   The prosecuting authority and the judiciary

Courts have on rare occasions expressed their disapproval of the fact that a prosecution was instituted — *F* 1989 (1) SA 460 (ZH); *Bester* 1971 (4) SA 28 (T).

However, courts can in principle not interfere with a *bona fide* decision of the prosecuting authority. It is irregular to do so — *Dubayi* 1976 (3) SA 110 (Tk). Courts can at most, in the event of a conviction, impose a lenient sentence reflecting their opinion that the prosecution was unwarranted. If convinced of the triviality of the case, the court may acquit the accused — *Kgogong* 1980 (3) SA 600 (A). However, such an acquittal is based on the substantive criminal law principle *de minimis non curat lex* (the law is not concerned with trivialities). And the acquittal should therefore not be seen as interference with the prosecution. But it is, of course, a clear indication that there should never have been a prosecution in the first place — Snyman 1980 *SACC* 313 at 314.

On the whole, courts are reluctant to comment on the discretion exercised by the prosecuting authority — Richings 1977 *SACC* 143 144. Courts do not interfere with the prosecuting authority's *bona fide* exercise of its discretion because the prosecuting authority has the power to decide and, once an accused is on trial, the accused will have the fullest opportunity to put his defence to the court, to cross-examine prosecution witnesses and to rely on his right not to be convicted unless the prosecution can prove his guilt beyond reasonable doubt based on admissible evidence and presented in terms of a regular procedure. Accordingly, a court will not interdict the prosecuting authority from prosecuting where it has decided to do so — *Allen v Attorney-General* 1936 CPD 302. Nor will it issue a *mandamus* (court order to act) to compel the prosecuting authority to prosecute — *Gillingham v Attorney-General* 1909 TS 572. And it has been held that a court cannot compel the prosecuting authority to decide within a specified period whether it intended prosecuting certain accused — *Wronsky v Prokureur-Generaal* 1971 (3) SA 292 (SWA). The prosecuting authority's discretion to prosecute, however, does not fall beyond the jurisdiction of a court of law and the latter can intervene where such discretion is *improperly* exercised — *Highstead Entertainment (Pty) Ltd t/a 'The Club' v Minister of Law and Order* 1994 (1) SA 387 (C).

The prosecuting authority's discretion can, of course, be reviewed by the courts on the basis of ordinary administrative law grounds of review, for example, where *mala fides* can be proved, or where it can be proved that the prosecuting authority never applied its mind to the matter or acted from an ulterior motive — see generally *Mitchell v Attorney-General, Natal* 1992 (2) SACR 68 (N). Likewise, the courts will on the basis of administrative law principles be able to interfere where the prosecuting authority exceeds its powers. Control by the courts is also justified on administrative law grounds where a DPP delegates a function which he himself should have performed — *Julius* 1983 (2) SA 442 (C); *Khoele* 1984 (2) SA 480 (O).

4.9 Extraordinary powers of a DPP

The function of a DPP is of course prosecutorial and not judicial — *Ramgobin* 1985 (4) SA 130 (N) at 130J–131D. Anything that concerns the liberty of a person is in principle something to be determined by the court.

A DPP has in certain limited circumstances the power to detain a prospective State witness for a period of up to seventy-two hours without a judge having so ordered — s 185(1)*(b)*, Act 51 of 1977. A State witness can be detained for a longer period on the basis of an order given by a judge in chambers in consequence of a DPP's application — s 185(2), (3), (4).

4.10 Control over local prosecutors

Local public prosecutors are as a rule permitted to exercise their own discretion in deciding whether to prosecute. It is impossible for a DPP (let alone a NDPP) to have full knowledge of each and every criminal matter in his or her jurisdiction. However, there are at least the following formal and informal ways in which a DPP can direct and control the decisions of public prosecutors in his or her jurisdiction:

(1) In practice DPPs issue internal circulars to their prosecutors, providing guidelines to the latter in the exercise of their discretion with regard to certain cases or certain types of crimes. See also s 24(5) of Act 38 of 1998 (as referred to in paragraph 4.6.2 above).

(2) A DPP may also, in an internal circular, direct his prosecutors not to prosecute in respect of certain offences without his prior approval. It has been suggested that a prosecution instituted contrary to such an instruction would be null and void. There is some authority to the contrary — *Magistrate, Regional Division* 1972 (3) SA 377 (N). At any rate, all prosecutions must comply with the prosecution policy and policy directives of the NDPP — s 21(1) of Act 32 of 1998. See paragraph 4.5.6 above. In terms of s 22(2)*(b)* the NDPP may intervene in any prosecution where policy directives have not been complied with. It would seem that in such an instance the NDPP may even stop the prosecution. See paragraph 4.14.2 below.

(3) There are a few statutes which require that in respect of certain offences no prosecution may be instituted without the written authority of the DPP who has jurisdiction. Prosecutions instituted without such authority are null and void.

(4) Complaints made to a DPP by members of the public and which relate to some decision taken by a local public prosecutor may also draw the attention of the DPP to a specific case. The DPP may then call for the police docket and require

the local prosecutor to advance reasons for the decision taken by him. The DPP may then consider the matter afresh and exercise his own discretion. He may confirm the prosecutor's decision. Or he may overrule the local prosecutor's withdrawal of the charge, and direct that a prosecution be instituted. He may even stop a prosecution which has already begun but which has not as yet resulted in a conviction — s 6*(b)* of Act 51 of 1977. See also the discussion in paragraph 4.14.2 below.

(5) Prosecutors should (and they often do) refer difficult, sensitive or borderline cases to the DPP concerned, setting out their viewpoints on the particular cases and requesting the DPP concerned to take the final decision.

4.11   The prosecution and the police

The Republic of South Africa has a national police force which is an independent government department and which is under the ultimate control of the relevant member of the cabinet. The structure and functions of the department are governed by statute. The main statutory functions of the police are to preserve internal security, to maintain law and order, to investigate any crime or alleged crime and to prevent crime. As far as prosecutions are concerned, the police do in practice exercise a discretion of their own and often refrain from bringing trivial matters and allegations, which are not adequately supported by evidence, to the attention of the public prosecutor. All investigations completed by the police for purposes of a prosecution must be submitted to the prosecuting authorities as the police do not have the final say on whether a prosecution should be instituted. The final decision rests with the DPP concerned or his local public prosecutors, as the case may be. Obviously, the NDPP may also intervene. This separation between officials who investigate crime and those who decide to prosecute and actually do prosecute crime is an important one. It promotes objectivity and provides the criminal justice system with a process in terms of which the results of a police investigation can (to some extent) be evaluated independently before the grave step of instituting a prosecution is taken. Courts have disapproved of the combination in one person of investigator and prosecutor — *Nigrini* 1948 (4) SA 995 (C).

There is, in practice, some loose but very essential form of co-operation between the police and prosecutors in the investigation of a case and its preparation for trial. The initial investigation is conducted by the police. They do so upon their own initiative or as a result of a complaint received from the public. Or they may do so in consequence of instructions received from the prosecuting authorities. See s 24(4)*(c)*(i) of Act 32 of 1998. The police prepare a docket (file, dossier) for submission to the public prosecutor who takes the decision whether to prosecute or not. The prosecutor, in the exercise of his discretion to prosecute, examines the witnesses' statements and documentary evidence contained in the docket, together with such real evidence as might be available, for example, weapons, fingerprints and clothing. At this stage the prosecutor may also direct and control the investigation by giving specific instructions to the investigating officer, that is, the police official charged with the investigation of the crime. The prosecutor may, for example, call for further statements from potential State witnesses, or he may direct that certain scientific analyses be done. But he himself does not, in principle, actively participate in any investigative work. The prosecutor should avoid a situation where he becomes a potential State witness, as it is most undesirable that a prosecutor in a case should also testify on behalf of the State in the same case — see generally *Mahobe* 1898 NLR 56.

If finally satisfied on all the available evidence that there is a *prima facie* case and if satisfied that there is no other compelling reason not to prosecute, the prosecutor has a duty to institute a criminal action and take such further steps as might be legally required (such as having the necessary summons issued — s 54) and legally permitted (such as having a pre-trial interview with a prospective State witness). The prosecutor determines the charges and is, in this respect, *dominus litis* — a concept which is explained in paragraph 4.13 below.

4.12 The prosecution, the police, the public and the reporting of crime

Obviously, any criminal justice system which employs a system of public prosecutions must to a large extent depend for its effectiveness on the willingness of members of the public to report crime to the authorities. And yet there is *no* general legal duty (as opposed to a possible moral duty) on members of the public to report crime. A legal duty (that is, where non-reporting is punishable) exists only in certain exceptional instances. The only common-law example is that a legal duty rests upon all who owe allegiance to the state to provide information on acts of high treason. There are scattered statutory provisions which also impose a duty to report in certain cases. One such example is that any person who has reason to suspect that another person has died of an unnatural cause must report this to a policeman as soon as possible, unless he has reason to believe that such a report was made or will be made by someone else — s 2, Inquests Act 58 of 1959.

Members of the public might at times, for fear of reprisals, be most reluctant to report the activities of criminals. However, the criminal justice system makes use of a so-called 'informer's privilege' to meet this situation. This privilege is dealt with in greater detail in the course on the law of evidence. For present purposes, it is sufficient to note that the identity of a private individual who has secretly given information to the police concerning the commission of a crime may as a rule not be disclosed in a court of law — see further Schmidt *Bewysreg* 3 ed (1989) 546; Hoffmann & Zeffertt *The South African Law of Evidence* 4 ed (1988) 274–7. And the contents of the individual's communication enjoy a similar protection — Van Niekerk, Van der Merwe & Van Wyk *Privilegies in die Bewysreg* (1984) 260. The purpose of the privilege is 'to encourage information as to the commission of crime by placing the informer in a condition of security' — *Tranter v Attorney-General and the First Criminal Magistrate of Johannesburg* 1907 TS 415 425; see also Schwikkard, Skeen & Van der Merwe *Principles of Evidence* (1997) 134–7. The informer's privilege was held constitutional in *Els v Minister of Safety and Security* 1998 2 SACR 93 (NC).

A further method aimed at encouraging a member of the public to come forward and report crime and ultimately to testify if necessary, is the witness protection system as created by s 185A.

The mere fact that an individual is under no general duty to report crime does not mean that he may in all instances lawfully refuse to co-operate once it is likely that he could be a potential State witness. As noted earlier, the law generally tolerates the inaction of the individual in reporting crime. But no criminal justice system can operate effectively in the absence of coercive measures in securing statements from potential State witnesses once a crime has been reported. An example of a measure of this nature can be found in s 205 of the Criminal Procedure Act as discussed in Chapter 8 of this work.

4.13 The prosecution as *dominus litis*

The prosecution can be described as *dominus litis* ('master of the case'). However, no exaggerated importance should be given to this concept. It merely means that the prosecution can do what is legally permissible to set criminal proceedings in motion, such as determining the charges and the date and venue of the trial. A measure of residual control by the courts over decisions taken by the prosecution as *dominus litis*, remains essential. Fairness to the accused is an important guideline in exercising this control. The following examples illustrate this point:

(1) In *Khoza* 1989 (3) SA 60 (T) it was held that the prosecution, precisely because it is *dominus litis*, should formulate and consolidate all its charges, in relation to a particular set of facts, to be tried in a single case. It may therefore not proceed in a piecemeal fashion by bringing successive prosecutions on different charges in relation to one broad incident. The case was struck off the roll (that is, the four accused concerned were not acquitted but the court declined to proceed with the case). The procedure adopted by the prosecution was considered unfair.

(2) Similarly, although the prosecution can as *dominus litis* determine the numerical order in which several accused are named in the charge or indictment, the court may, in the interests of justice, right and fairness, order that the sequence in which the accused present their evidence be varied — *Swanepoel* 1980 (2) SA 81 (NC) at 84D. The defence has no right to determine the sequence of State witnesses and the prosecution should therefore not have a final right to determine the sequence of accused who wish to testify as defence witnesses. After all, the adversarial (accusatorial) nature of the criminal trial demands that parties should as far as possible be given equal opportunities in the presentation of their cases — *Mpetha (1)* 1983 (1) SA 492 (C) at 494A–C.

(3) A presiding judicial officer in a criminal case does not have the authority to close the State's case if the prosecutor is unwilling to do so. But if the prosecutor, after an application by him for the postponement of the trial has rightfully been rejected by the court, refuses to adduce evidence or to close the State's case, the judicial officer will continue with the proceedings as if the prosecutor had indeed closed the State's case — *Magoda* 1984 (4) SA 462 (C). This case illustrates, once again, that decisions taken by the prosecution as *dominus litis*, may be overruled by the court in the interests of fairness to the accused. In this instance the accused's right to a reasonably speedy completion of the trial against him formed the basis upon which the court interfered with the prosecution's right to decide when to close its case.

4.14 The discretion to prosecute

4.14.1 *The exercise of a discretion*

South Africa does not, in principle, follow a system of compulsory prosecution.

A prosecutor has a duty to prosecute if there is a *prima facie* case and if there is no compelling reason for a refusal to prosecute. In this context '*prima facie* case' would mean the following: The allegations, as supported by statements and real and documentary evidence available to the prosecution, are of such a nature that if proved in a court of law by the prosecution on the basis of admissible evidence, the court should convict. Sometimes it is asked: Are there reasonable prospects of success? The prosecution, it has been held, does not have to ascertain whether there is a defence, but whether there is a reasonable and probable cause for prosecution — see generally *Beckenstrater v Rottcher and Theunissen* 1955 (1) SA 129 (A) at 137. The prosecution must at the trial be able to furnish proof beyond a reasonable doubt.

In exercising his discretion, the prosecutor must respect the individual's right not to be harassed by a prosecution which has no reasonable prospects of success. The fact that the prosecutor doubts the strength of the State case is no good ground for fixing an admission of guilt fine in a summons in the hope that the accused might pay the admission of guilt fine and thereby relieve the State of the burden of proving its case — *Eusuf* 1949 (1) SA 656 (N) at 656–7. This is an important point because, as was pointed out in *NGJ Trading Stores (Pty) Ltd v Guerreiro* 1974 (1) SA 51 (O) at 53H–54A, many accused persons pay an admission of guilt fine in order to be rid of the worry, inconvenience and expense of fighting a petty criminal charge and not because they are in fact guilty. It is improper for the prosecution to secure a 'successful prosecution' in this manner because the payment of an admission of guilt fine does for criminal record purposes amount to a previous conviction — see generally *NGJ Trading Stores (Pty) Ltd v Guerreiro* 1974 (4) SA 738 (A) at 746A.

On rare occasions there might be good grounds for refusing to prosecute despite the fact that a *prima facie* case exists. Such grounds may be the triviality of the offence — see generally Snyman 1980 *SACC* 313 at 314; the advanced age or very young age of an accused — Stoker & Van der Merwe 1981 *SACC* 73; the antiquated nature of the offence — see generally *Steenkamp* 1973 (2) SA 221 (NC); or the tragic personal circumstances of an accused, for example, a father who has through his negligent driving caused the death of his young children — see generally Richings 1977 *SACC* 143. A former DPP has described the discretion to prosecute as

'a very valuable safeguard, because one has to take into account . . . what the consequences to [an accused] may be, apart from any penalty which a court of law might inflict. If, in our view, the consequences are out of all proportions to the gravity of the offence committed, we are permitted to exercise our discretion and decline to prosecute' — Yutar 1977 *SACC* 135 at 136.

Two fundamental principles of criminal justice govern the exercise of the discretion to prosecute. First, the police and prosecuting authorities should not knowingly allow a pattern of contravention of a certain statute to develop and then, most unexpectedly, arrest and prosecute. This is what happened in *Makwasie* 1970 (2) SA 128 (T) where the conviction was unfortunately confirmed on appeal. Such an approach does not promote legal certainty, offends the principle of legality, is unfair to citizens and undermines the deterrent function of the criminal law — Van Rooyen 1975 *Acta Juridica* 70 83. Secondly, discretionary prosecution is no licence for discriminatory prosecution. This means that in the exercise of the discretion to prosecute there must be no selective enforcement or non-enforcement of the criminal law, amounting to unjustifiable distinctions between persons in similar circumstances. Discriminatory prosecution not only conflicts with the equal protection and due process principles or ideals of the criminal justice system, but also with s 9(1) of the Constitution:

'Every person is equal before the law and has the right to equal protection and benefit of the law.'

There is a rule of practice in terms of which an accused, or his legal representative acting upon his instructions, may make written representations to a DPP or the local public prosecutor to decline to prosecute.

4.14.2   *The distinction between withdrawal of a charge and stopping of the prosecution*

The prosecuting authority may withdraw a charge before the accused has pleaded to such a charge — s 6*(a)* of Act 51 of 1977. However, the accused is in these circumstances not entitled to a verdict of acquittal. He may be prosecuted again on the same or related charges, for example, where new evidence is discovered. A prosecutor may withdraw a charge without the consent of his DPP. The reason for this is that a DPP, if dissatisfied with the prosecutor's withdrawal of the charge, may charge the accused afresh.

Before an accused pleads, the prosecution can also withdraw a summons and issue another — *Wolman v Springs Town Council* 1941 TPD 104.

A DPP may at any time *after an accused has pleaded, but before conviction*, stop the prosecution in respect of that charge. If this is done, the accused is entitled to an acquittal — s 6*(b)* of Act 51 of 1977. This means that in any subsequent prosecution in respect of the same facts, the accused can successfully rely on a plea of previous acquittal (*autrefois acquit*). This plea is dealt with in greater detail in Chapter 14.

However, a public prosecutor may not stop a prosecution without the consent of the DPP or any person authorised thereto by such a DPP — s 6*(b)*; *Van Wyk* 1981 (3) SA 228 (C). The mere fact that a prosecutor indicates to the court that on the evidence as presented in court he is unable to support a conviction, does not amount to a stopping of the prosecution — *Bopape* 1966 (1) SA 145 (C). The prosecutor's acceptance of an accused's plea is discussed in Chapter 14.

4.15   Prescription of the right to prosecute

The right to institute a prosecution for any offence shall, unless some other period is expressly provided by law, lapse after the expiration of a period of twenty years from the time when the offence was committed — s 18 of Act 51 of 1997. However, in terms of the same section the following crimes have no prescription period: murder; treason committed when the Republic is in a state of war; robbery, if aggravating circumstances were present; kidnapping; child-stealing and rape. The date of commencement of s 18 is 27 April 1994 — s 27 of Act 105 of 1997. Prior to this date, the right to prosecute could not have lapsed in respect of capital crimes. With the abolition of the death penalty, it became necessary to amend s 18. See generally *De Freitas* 1997 (1) SACR 180 (C).

4.16   The prosecution and legal ethics

A public prosecutor must display the highest degree of fairness to an accused. This duty is for obvious reasons more pronounced in respect of the unrepresented accused — *Mofokeng* 1992 (2) SACR 261 (O) at 264C.

Information favourable to the defence must be disclosed — *Van Rensburg* 1963 (2) SA 343 (N). If there is a serious discrepancy between a State witness's oral testimony in court and his earlier written statement made during the investigation of the case, the prosecutor must draw attention to this fact and make the written statement of the witness available to the defence for purposes of cross-examination — *Kamte* 1992 (1) SACR 677 (A). The court must also have access to such a statement.

It is not the task of the prosecutor to seek to secure a conviction at all costs. In *Jija* 1991 (2) SA 52 (E) at 68A it was said that a prosecutor 'stands in a special relation to the Court. His paramount duty is not to procure a conviction but to assist the Court in ascertaining the truth . . .'.

4.17 The prosecution and the assistance of a private legal practitioner

A private practitioner who has no authority to prosecute, may not assist the state prosecutor by cross-examining defence witnesses on behalf of the prosecution or by addressing the court on behalf of the prosecution — *Adam Effendi* 1917 EDL 267.

Nevertheless, it would seem as if no irregularity is committed where a private practitioner who was given a watching brief by an interested party, renders some other assistance on an *informal* basis to the prosecution, such as suggesting to the prosecutor that certain questions should be put — *Salusbury* 1934 (1) PH H83 (T). But in the final analysis the prosecution must be in full control of the presentation of the case for the State.

4.18 Diversion of the criminal trial

There are certain procedures or methods in terms of which a criminal trial can be avoided — whether partially or as a whole, temporarily or permanently. This can be called diversion of the criminal process. One encounters several such diversions in the law of criminal procedure. Examples are the conversion of a trial to children's court procedure — s 254; conversion of a trial into an enquiry with a view to committing an accused to a rehabilitation centre — s 255; and an enquiry into mental illness — ss 77, 78 and 79.

5 PRIVATE PROSECUTIONS

5.1 Introduction

The South African Criminal Procedure Act refers to two forms of private prosecution, namely a private prosecution by an individual on the basis of a certificate *nolle prosequi* (s 7) and a private prosecution under statutory right (s 8). However, in the present chapter it will be shown that the latter is not a true 'private prosecution' even though it is identified as a 'private prosecution' in the Criminal Procedure Act. Unlike a private prosecution in terms of s 7, it does not involve an individual who is aggrieved by the fact that the prosecuting officials have declined to prosecute. See also paragraphs 1 and 2 above and cf paragraphs 5.2 and 5.3 below.

5.2 Private prosecution under statutory right

Any body upon which or person upon whom the right to prosecute in respect of any offence is expressly conferred by law may institute and conduct a prosecution in respect of such offence in any court competent to try that offence — s 8(1) of Act 51 of 1977. Some municipalities prosecute in terms of this section. However, a body which or a person who intends exercising a right of prosecution under s 8(1) shall exercise such right only, first, after consultation with the DPP concerned and, secondly, after the DPP has withdrawn his right of prosecution in respect of any specified offence or any specified class or category of offences with reference to which such body or person may by law exercise such right of prosecution — s 8(2).

A DPP may, under s 8(2), withdraw his right of prosecution on such conditions as he may deem fit, including a condition that the appointment by such body or person of a prosecutor to conduct the prosecution in question shall be subject to the approval of the DPP, and that the DPP may at any time exercise with reference to any such prosecution any power which he might have exercised if he had not withdrawn his right of prosecution — s 8(3). It is clear, therefore, that private prosecutions under statutory right remain under the control of the DPP and NDPP. Large municipalities often have the necessary expertise to conduct prosecutions for contraventions of municipal regulations. In practice it is therefore convenient for a DPP to allow these municipalities to prosecute their regulatory offences in terms of s 8, providing him and his public prosecutors more time to concentrate on crimes of a more serious nature. A s 8 prosecution is reported in the name of the parties, as in *Claymore Court (Pty) Ltd v Durban City Council* 1986 (4) SA 180 (N). In this case it was also held that a prosecution in terms of s 8 must be instituted and conducted, and all process in connection therewith issued, in the name of the prosecutor. This is peremptory in terms of s 10. The NDPP may also in writing authorise any local authority to conduct certain prosecutions. See s 22(8)*(b)* of Act 32 of 1998 as cited in paragraph 4.5.5 above.

5.3   Private prosecution by an individual on a certificate *nolle prosequi*

5.3.1   *Introduction*

The origin and rationale of having a system in terms of which an aggrieved individual may in certain circumstances institute a private prosecution (that is, proceed in lieu of the state), were discussed in paragraph 2 above. The historical background is dealt with in more detail by Smit J in *Black v Barclays Zimbabwe Nominees (Pvt) Ltd* 1990 (1) SACR 433 (W). By way of summary, it may be said that an individual's statutory power to institute a private prosecution is a 'safety valve', so to speak, in the machinery of the law. It is also to some extent an indirect method of controlling corruption or incompetence in the state's prosecutorial services. It has furthermore been said that a

'system of private prosecution can be justified in terms of both society's interest in increased law enforcement and the individual's interest in vindication of personal grievances. Full participation by the citizen as a private prosecutor is needed to cope with the serious threat to society posed by [the prosecuting authority's] improper action and inaction' — Comment (1955) 65 *Yale Law Journal* 209 at 227.

It has also been argued that a system of private prosecutions demonstrates 'the value of citizen/victim participation in the criminal justice system and serves to reinforce . . . the integrity of basic democratic values' — *Private Prosecutions: Working Paper 52 of the Law Reform Commission of Canada* (1986) 4. Private prosecutions are rare but essential.

A system of private prosecution is not an isolated instance of citizen participation in the criminal justice system. Private persons — even though totally disinterested in a matter — must in certain circumstances assist in an arrest when called upon to do so by a police official — s 47. And private persons not personally involved in a case, may be called upon and agree to sit as assessors in criminal trials — see, for example, s 93*ter* of the Magistrates' Courts Act 32 of 1944 as discussed in Chapter 13.

A private prosecution must be instituted and conducted in the name of the private prosecutor — s 10(1) of Act 51 of 1977. All process must also be issued in the name of and at the expense of the private prosecutor — s 10(1) and 14. The indictment or summons, as the case may be, must describe the private prosecutor with certainty and precision and must be signed by such prosecutor or his legal representative — s 10(2). A private prosecution is reported in the names of the parties, for example, *Smith v Jones*.

A private prosecution shall — except as otherwise stated in the present chapter — be proceeded with in the same manner as if it were a prosecution at the instance of the state — s 12(1). This means that an accused enjoys all those procedural rights which would have been available to him had he been prosecuted at the instance of the state. He enjoys the additional privilege that he may be brought before the court only by way of summons in the case of a lower court or an indictment in the case of the supreme court — see the proviso in s 12(1).

5.3.2 Locus standi *of a private prosecutor*

In any case in which a DPP has declined to prosecute for an alleged offence, the following persons may, subject to certain other procedural requirements, either in person or through a legal representative institute and conduct a prosecution in respect of such offence in any court competent to try that offence:

(1) any private person who proves some substantial and peculiar interest in the issue of the trial arising out of some injury which he individually suffered in consequence of the commission of the said offence — s 7(1)*(a)*; or

(2) a husband, if the said offence was committed in respect of his wife — s 7(1)*(b)*; or

(3) the wife or child or, if there is no wife or child, any of the next of kin of any deceased person, if the death of such person is alleged to have been caused by the said offence — s 7(1)*(c)*; or

(4) the legal guardian or curator of a minor or lunatic, if the said offence was committed against his ward — s 7(1)*(d)*.

In the absence of an injury cognisable under s 7(1), there is no room on the part of a private prosecutor for any interest (substantial and peculiar or otherwise) in the issue of the trial — *Phillips v Botha* 1999 (1) SACR 1 (SCA).

The question whether a private person has in terms of s 7(1)*(a)* 'some substantial and peculiar interest in the issue of the trial arising out of some injury which he individually suffered in consequence of the commission of the . . . offence', is a question of law as well as fact. An obvious example is the victim of an alleged theft — *Daly v Solicitor General* 1911 EDC 399. In *Mullins and Meyer v Pearlman* 1917 TPD 639 at 643 and *Ellis v Visser* 1954 (2) SA 431 (T) at 438 it was held that the right to institute a private prosecution does not exist where there is no right of civil redress. However, in *Makhanya v Bailey NO* 1980 (4) SA 713 (T) at 717C it was correctly held that where it is clear that a legal right of a person has been infringed by an offence, then the question of a civil remedy arising from it is no longer a relevant consideration and the provisions of s 7(1)(a) would then be satisfied. It is submitted that s 7(1)(a) should in principle not be interpreted restrictively. After all, the purpose of a private prosecution is to reduce 'the temptation to an aggrieved person to take the law into his own hands' — *Solomon v Magistrate, Pretoria* 1950 (3) SA 603 (T) at 609H. The state should not have a monopoly of the right to prosecute — Van Zyl Smit 1981 *SACC* 78 at 79. At the same time, however, it is clear that s 7 does place important restrictions on the right to institute a private prosecution. It follows that not every case in which a DPP declines to prosecute, will necessarily give rise to a private prosecution — see also generally Morkel and Labuschagne 1980 *SACC* 160 at 168. In *Attorney-General v Van der Merwe and Bornman* 1946 OPD 197 at 201 it was said that restrictions are necessary

> 'to prevent private persons from arrogating to themselves the function of a public prosecutor and prosecuting in respect of offences which do not affect them in any different degree than any other member of the public; to curb, in other words, the activities of those who would otherwise constitute themselves public busybodies'.

In *Solomon v Magistrate, Pretoria* (above) the court held that it was competent to entertain and grant an application for an order restraining the magistrate and the private prosecutor from continuing with an unfounded prosecution. The onus of proving that the prosecution is unfounded rests on the applicant. *Van Deventer v Reichenberg & another* 1996 (1) SACR 119 (C) is an example of a case where the high court interdicted the respondent from instituting an unfounded prosecution.

The Supreme Court of Appeal has held that the High Court's inherent power to prevent abuse of its process by frivolous or vexatious proceedings — and which is usually asserted in civil proceedings — also applies where the process abused is that provided for in the conduct of private prosecutions — *Phillips v Botha* 1999 (1) SACR 1 (SCA). However, in this case it was held that there was no abuse of process. Even though the court was satisfied that the private prosecutor had played a protracted game of cat-and-mouse with the accused, it was also found that the dominant motive of the private prosecutor was to have justice done to a wrongdoer.

A private prosecutor has the burden of proving his *locus standi* if it is disputed — see generally *Levy v Benatar* 1987 (4) SA 693 (Z). A widow has the necessary peculiar interest — *Mweuhanga v Cabinet of the Interim Government of SWA* 1989 (1) SA 976 (SWA) at 982. Companies and other legal persons do not fall within the ambit of s 7(1)(a) — *Barclays Zimbabwe Nominees (Pvt) Ltd v Black* 1990 (4) SA 720 (A).

In *Mullins and Meyer v Pearlman* 1917 TPD 639 a full bench held that only persons who can prove that they have suffered actual damage as a result of the commission of the alleged offence are entitled to institute a private prosecution. The mere apprehension of injury or of an invasion of rights which may possibly cause damage in the future, is insufficient.

Two or more persons may not prosecute in the same charge, except where two or more persons have been injured by the same offence — s 10(3); *Williams v Janse van Rensburg* (2) 1989 (4) SA 680 (C).

5.3.3   *The certificate* nolle prosequi

No private prosecutor wishing to proceed in terms of s 7 can obtain the process of any court for summoning any person to answer any charge unless such private prosecutor produces a so-called 'certificate *nolle prosequi*' to the officer authorised by law to issue such process. A certificate *nolle prosequi* is a certificate signed by a DPP and in which he confirms, first, that he has examined the statements or affidavits on which the charge is based and, secondly, that he declines to prosecute at the instance of the state — s 7(2)*(a)*.

A DPP must, at the request of the person intending to prosecute, grant the certificate *nolle prosequi* in every case in which he has declined to prosecute. It would seem as if the DPP is not entitled to investigate whether the person requesting the certificate has the necessary locus standi as envisaged in s 7(1)*(a)* to 7(1)*(d)*. At the trial the accused can raise lack of locus standi of the private prosecutor.

In *Solomon v Magistrate, Pretoria* (above) it was held that a DPP cannot be required to particularise or identify the charges on which he declines to prosecute. If the accused can show at the trial that the certificate *nolle prosequi* does not relate to the charges preferred against him by the private prosecutor, he is entitled to a discharge.

In terms of s 7(2)*(c)* a certificate *nolle prosequi* shall lapse unless proceedings in respect of the offence in question are instituted by the issue of the required process within three months of the date of the certificate.

5.3.4 Security by private prosecutor

No private prosecutor may take out or issue any process commencing the private prosecution unless he deposits the sum of one thousand rand with the magistrate's court in whose area of jurisdiction the offence was committed — s 9(1). This amount serves as security that the private prosecutor will prosecute the charge to a conclusion without undue delay — s 9(1)*(a)*. The amount is forfeited to the state in the event of such a delay — s 9(3). Forfeiture to the state also takes place where the charge against the accused is dismissed because of the private prosecutor's failure to appear — s 9(3) as read with s 11.

The magistrate's court in whose area of jurisdiction the offence was committed may determine a further amount to be deposited as security for the costs which the accused may incur in respect of his defence to the charge — s 9(1)*(b)*. The accused may, when he is called upon to plead to the charge, apply to the trial court to review the amount which was determined in terms of s 9(1)*(b)* — *Bonadei v Magistrate of Otjiwarongo* 1986 (1) SA 564 (SWA); s 9(2). The trial court must then, before the accused pleads, reassess the amount and may require the private prosecutor to deposit any additional amount, as determined by the court, with the magistrate's court where the initial s 9(1)*(b)* deposit was made — s 9(2)*(a)*. The court may, as an alternative to a further deposit, direct that the private prosecutor enter into a recognisance, with or without sureties, in such additional amount as the court may determine — s 9(2)*(b)*.

The reference to costs in s 9 is concerned only with the actual costs which an accused will probably incur personally in conducting his defence — *Williams v Janse van Rensburg (1)* 1989 (4) SA 485 (C).

5.3.5 Failure of private prosecutor to appear

If the private prosecutor does not appear on the day set down for the appearance of the accused in the magistrate's court or for the trial of the accused, the charge against the accused shall be dismissed unless the court has reason to believe that the private prosecutor was prevented from being present by circumstances beyond his control, in which event the court may adjourn the case to a later date — s 11(1). Where the charge is so dismissed, the accused shall forthwith be discharged. He may not in respect of that charge be prosecuted privately again. But the DPP or a public prosecutor with the consent of the DPP may at the instance of the state prosecute the accused in respect of that charge — s 11(2).

5.3.6 *Costs of a successful private prosecution*

The general rule is that the costs and expenses of a private prosecution must be paid by the prosecutor — s 15(1). But the court may, having regard to all the circumstances of the case, order a person convicted upon a private prosecution to pay the costs and expenses of the prosecution, including the costs of any appeal against such conviction or any sentence — s 15(2). It is also possible for the court to order that the costs and expenses of the successful private prosecution, including the costs of an appeal arising from such prosecution, must be paid by the state — s 15(2). An order of this nature should be made where the court is convinced that the DPP should not have declined to prosecute at the instance of the state. The taxation of costs is regulated by s 17.

5.3.7 *Costs of accused in an unsuccessful private prosecution*

Where the charge against the accused is dismissed or the accused is acquitted or a decision in favour of the accused is given on appeal, the court dismissing the charge or acquitting the accused or deciding in favour of the accused on appeal, may order the private prosecutor to pay to such accused the whole or any part of the costs and expenses incurred by him in connection with the prosecution or the appeal, as the case may be — s 16(1). Where the court is of the opinion that a private prosecution was unfounded and vexatious, it shall award to the accused at his request such costs and expenses incurred by him as it may deem fit — s 16(2). A court should be slow in coming to a decision mulcting in costs under s 16(2) if a prosecutor *bona fide* has sought justice in a private prosecution — *Buchanan v Voogt NO* 1988 (2) SA 273 (N). Taxation of costs is also governed by s 17.

5.3.8 *Intervention by the state in a private prosecution*

A DPP (or a local public prosecutor acting on the instructions of the DPP) may in respect of any private prosecution apply by motion to the court before which the private prosecution is pending to stop all further proceedings in the case in order that a prosecution for the offence in question may be instituted or continued at the instance of the state, as the case may be — s 13. The court must make such an order — s 13. Intervention in terms of s 13 is in the discretion of the DPP. However, where an accused in a private prosecution pleads guilty to the charge, the prosecution must be continued at the instance of the state — s 12(2).

CHAPTER 4

The right to legal assistance

		Page
1	INTRODUCTION AND HISTORICAL BACKGROUND	74
2	THE RIGHT TO ASSISTANCE IN THE PRE-TRIAL STAGE OF THE CRIMINAL PROCEDURE	75
3	THE RIGHT TO ASSISTANCE DURING THE TRIAL	76
	3.1 General	76
	3.2 The duty to inform the accused of the right to legal representation	76
	3.3 The duty to afford the accused an opportunity to obtain legal representation	76
	3.4 The role of the legal representative and others in providing the accused with assistance	77
4	THE ACCESSIBILITY OF LEGAL REPRESENTATION	77

The Constitution and this chapter:

Section 35—Arrested, detained and accused persons

(2) Everyone who is detained, including any sentenced prisoner, has the right—

. . .

(b) to choose, and to consult with, a legal practitioner, and to be informed of this right promptly;

(c) to have a legal practitioner assigned to the detained person by the state and at state expense, if substantial injustice would otherwise result, and to be informed of this right promptly; . . .

. . .

See 2, below.

(3) Every accused person has a right to a fair trial, which includes the right—

. . .

(f) to choose, and be represented by, a legal practitioner, and to be informed of this right promptly;

(g) to have a legal practitioner assigned to the accused person by the state and at state expense, if substantial injustice would otherwise result, and to be informed of this right promptly; . . .

See 1 and 3.1, below.

---

1 INTRODUCTION AND HISTORICAL BACKGROUND

One of the most important rights of a person suspected of the commission of an offence, whether he has been formally charged with the offence or not, is to be assisted by counsel (attorney or advocate) and friends. This right, of common-law origin, is of exceptional importance since the effective exercise of other rights and the employment of various remedies such as the interdict, *habeas corpus*, civil action for damages, and bail may depend on it. This right may quite correctly be termed 'an accused's most pervasive right'.

Vroman *Tractaat de Foro Competenti* (1721) 2.4.3 contends that the right to counsel originates in the law of nature and God. It may not be denied anyone, says Vroman—not even irrational animals! He continues: 'Yes, not even (may it be denied) the devil, if he were to appear before the judgment throne' (our translation)—cf *Wessels* 1966 (4) SA 89 (C); *Blooms* 1966 (4) SA 417 (C).

In South Africa an accused could not always as of right demand that he be defended by an attorney or advocate: it was only in 1819 that a proclamation was issued providing that a person accused of a serious offence has the right, if he so wishes, to employ a legal practitioner to defend him (cf *Wessels* (above) at 91G–H).

In 1920 a general right to counsel was accepted, without reference to any authority, by the Supreme Court of Appeal in *Dabner v SA Railways and Harbours* 1920 AD 583. The court stated:

> 'That a person who is charged with an offence before any court in judicial proceedings in this country is entitled to appear by a legal adviser is a proposition which no one will dispute.'

Today this right is entrenched in s 35(2) and (3) of the Constitution as set out above. Furthermore, ss 73(1) and (2) of the Criminal Procedure Act confirm this fundamental procedural right to legal representation, whereas s 73(3) provides for some qualified form of assistance that may be rendered by third parties other than legal qualified counsel. Section 74 provides for the presence of a parent or guardian at the trial of an accused who is under eighteen years of age.

The right to legal representation is not confined to the accused but is extended to witnesses in appropriate cases.

The effect of s 35(2)*(c)* and (3)*(g)* of the Constitution is that an arrested person as well as an accused, must be provided with legal representation at the expense of the state if substantial injustice would otherwise result. 'Substantial injustice' is not defined, but in *Lombard* 1994 (3) SA 776 (T) the court stated that, at the least, it means that an accused who is charged with an offence in respect of which he may be sentenced to imprisonment if convicted and who cannot afford legal representation, should be entitled to legal representation at state expense. Also compare *Mgcina v Regional Magistrate, Lenasia and Another* 1997 (2) SACR 711. An accused must, however, accept the legal representative appointed by the state and has no choice as to the latter's identity—*Vermaas; Du Plessis* 1995 (3) SA 293 (CC).

On legal representation generally, see 1965–1966 *Acta Juridica* 53; 'Fokus' 1989 *SACJ* 47–77; Steytler *The Undefended Accused*.

2 THE RIGHT TO ASSISTANCE IN THE PRE-TRIAL STAGE OF THE CRIMINAL PROCESS

A powerful statement of the importance that outsiders should have access to persons who are held in custody is contained in *Li Kui Yu v Superintendent of Labourers* 1906 TS 181 at 188:

> 'I think it is quite clear that the only way of preventing a person being illegally done away with and illegally treated is to uphold to the fullest extent the right of every person to have any of his friends come and see him who choose to do so. I am not now dealing with solicitors, I am thinking of the ordinary question of friends; I think to prevent the access of friends to any person is a most serious infringement of the liberty of any subject.'

The court continued by stating that it is even more serious to withhold access to an attorney. (See also Wides 'An Arrested Person's Right of Access to His Lawyer—A Necessary Restatement of the Law' 1964 *SALJ* 513.)

In *Mabaso* 1990 (3) SA 185 (A) it was already suggested that the legislature should provide for legislation in terms of which an arrested person should be informed of his right to legal representation upon arrest.

The right of a detained person to choose and consult with a legal practitioner and to be *promptly* informed of this right, is now entrenched in s 35(2)*(b)* of the Constitution. A person who has been arrested is in detention from the moment of his or her arrest and therefore immediately qualifies for this right. Furthermore, the accused may exercise this right at any stage during his or her detention, whether before, during or after the trial—cf *Melani* 1996 (1) SACR 335 (E).

The arrested person must be informed of this right in a manner that it can reasonably be supposed that he understood the right and the importance thereof—*Melani* 1996 (1) SACR 335 (E).

The right of a detained person to be informed of this right not only requires the state to inform him or her *at the time of his or her arrest* of this right, but also at every further stage of the investigation into the alleged offence where his or her co-operation is sought, such as when he or she is being questioned, a statement is taken from him or her; he or she makes a confession or is required to take part in an identification parade—*Marx* 1996 (2) SACR 140 (W); *Mlakaza* 1996 (2) SACR 187 (C); *Mathebula* 1997 (1) SACR 10 (W); and *Agnew* 1996 (2) SACR 535 (C). However, see *Ngwenya and Others* 1998 (2) SACR 503 (W) where the opposite was held. See also *Hlalikaya* 1997 (1) SACR 613 (SE) and *Zwayi* 1997 (2) SASV 772 (Ck) where it was held that when an identification parade by means of photographs is held in the absence of the legal practitioner of the suspect, evidence concerning the identification parade will still be admissible. In *Mphala and Another* 1998 (1) SACR 388 (W) the accused were not informed, before making confessions, that an attorney who had been appointed for them had requested that they should not make statements before consulting with him. The waiver by the accused of their right to legal representation was accordingly held to have been uninformed and therefore invalid.

The right to legal representation includes the right to confidentiality during consultation with the legal practitioner. A detainee therefore has the right to consult with his legal adviser without the conversation being overheard—*Mokoena v Commissioner of Prisons* 1985 (1) SA 368 (W).

3   THE RIGHT TO ASSISTANCE DURING THE TRIAL

3.1   General

The right to legal representation in criminal trials is now universally recognised in most civilised societies. This fundamental right of an accused is inherent in the principle that an accused must have a fair trial—*Davids; Dladla* 1989 (4) SA 172 (N); *Khanyile* 1988 (3) SA 795 (N); *Zuma* 1995 (2) SA 642 (CC).

3.2   The duty to inform the accused of the right to legal representation

A right is of no use to a person if he is not aware of it. The Constitution accordingly provides in section 35(3)*(b)* that the accused person must be *promptly* informed of the right to choose and be represented by a legal practitioner of his or her choice. A judicial officer therefore has a duty to inform an unrepresented accused that he has a right to be legally represented.

A failure on the part of a judicial officer to inform an unrepresented accused of his legal rights, including the right to legal representation, can lead to a complete failure of justice—*Radebe* 1988 (1) SA 191 (T); *Mabaso* 1990 (3) SA 185 (A) at 204 (cf in particular the minority judgment of Milne JA: the failure to inform the accused about his right to legal representation automatically invalidates the criminal proceedings); *D en Andere* 1997 (2) SACR 671 (C); *Moos* 1998 (1) SACR 401 (W).

It has long been realised that only to inform the accused about his right to legal representation would be worthless if he is in any event too poor to afford it. It was therefore decided by some courts that the accused should furthermore be informed of his right to legal aid—see the majority decision in *Davids* (above) and cf also *Mthwana* 1989 (4) SA 368 (N). The Constitution now requires that an accused must be informed *promptly* that he or she has a right to have a legal representative assigned to him or her at state expense if substantial injustice would otherwise result—s 35(3)*(g)*.

3.3   The duty to afford the accused an opportunity to obtain legal representation

If the right to legal representation is to have any meaning, it must include the right to be afforded a reasonable opportunity of securing it—*McKenna* 1998 (1) SACR 106 (C).

The court must always carefully consider an application by an accused for a postponement in order to enable him or her to obtain legal representation. A refusal to grant such a postponement may in certain circumstances amount to an irregularity—*Seheri* 1964 (1) SA 29 (A); *Van Wyk* 1972 (1) SA 787 (A).

Where an accused's legal representative withdraws from the case, the court should ask the accused whether he wishes to have the opportunity to instruct another legal representative and/or whether he is ready to undertake his own defence—failure to do so is irregular and invalidates the proceedings—*Khoali* 1990 (1) SACR 276 (O). The absence of duly instructed counsel may well be due to the indifference of the latter and refusal to grant a postponement will prejudice the accused—*Shabangu* 1976 (3) SA 555 (A); *Gwebu* 1988 (4) SA 155 (W). Where, however, an accused has ample opportunity to obtain legal representation and fails to arrange this, he cannot subsequently attack the proceedings unless he can furnish an acceptable explanation for his failure—*Second* 1970 (1) PH H5 (RA) and cf *Nongila* 1970 (3) SA 97 (E).

If at higher instance a refusal to grant a postponement for the purpose of enabling the accused to obtain counsel is held to have been irregular, the irregularity is of the kind that *per se* must have prejudiced the accused and, accordingly, the conviction will be set aside by the court of higher instance without further ado (cf *Nqula* 1974 (1) SA 801 (E). Cf also *Nel* 1974 (2) SA 445 (NC)).

3.4 The role of the legal representative and others in providing the accused with assistance

Apart from assistance by a trained *legal* representative, an accused under the age of 18 years may be assisted by his parent or guardian, in terms of the Criminal Procedure Act. Such assistance is not synonymous with legal representation and the parent or guardian has no greater right than a legal representative to decide how a case should be conducted—*Assel* 1984 (1) SA 402 (C). Cf *L* 1988 (4) SA 757 (C) 760 with regard to the nature of assistance by a guardian.

The Criminal Procedure Act further provides that 'any accused person who in the opinion of the court requires the assistance of another person may, with the permission of the court, be so assisted'—s 73. (It has happened that a magistrate authorised an articled clerk (candidate attorney) to assist an accused in terms of this section.) Assistance in terms of s 73 cannot be foisted on an accused either by a court's order that he has to be represented, or by appointment of a representative for such a purpose if he does not seek it—*L* (above).

A court will not allow the same advocate to defend two accused with interests which conflict in material respects—*Moseli* (1) 1969 (1) SA 646 (O); *Jacobs* 1970 (3) SA 493 (E); *Hollenbach* 1971 (4) SA 636 (NC).

There may be circumstances in which it may even be proper for the representative of the State to direct the attention of his opponent or of the presiding official to the question whether counsel for the defence should not retire from the case because of the conflict of interest between his clients—*Naidoo* 1974 (3) SA 706 (A).

As a general rule an accused is bound by what is done by his legal representative in the execution of his mandate during the course of the trial—*Muruven* 1953 (2) SA 779 (N).

The effect of the entrenchment of the right to legal representation in the Bill of Rights may, as has happened in the United States, possibly be that a detained or accused person now has the right to *effective* or *competent* legal representation (see e g *McMann v Richardson* 397 US 759 (1970); *Cuyler v Sullivan* 446 US 335 (1980); and *Strickland v Washington* 466 US 668 (1984)). Whether this right wil be interpreted in a similar way in South Africa, is debatable.

4 THE ACCESSIBILITY OF LEGAL REPRESENTATION

The right to counsel is part of a broader requirement of procedural equality of all citizens, rich and poor. The rich have always enjoyed their right to purchase their own defence services and have always enjoyed effective remedies. The plight of the indigent accused who is too poor to afford legal services has been recognised in the practice of appointing *pro Deo* counsel for accused in certain serious cases: a step forward in making legal services accessible to the poor.

If the charge against an accused who cannot afford legal representation is not of such a serious nature that a *pro Deo* counsel would be appointed automatically, the court has a duty in certain cases (depending on the facts) to determine before the commencement of the trial whether the absence of legal representation would prejudice the accused to such an extent that continuation of the trial without legal representation would clearly result in an unfair trial. If the court comes to the conclusion that the accused should be assisted by a legal representative, it should refer the matter to a legal aid scheme or an association of lawyers willing to offer assistance *pro bono*. (Legal *aid*—as distinguished from legal *assistance*—denotes the provision of the means to acquire legal representation.) The court should decline to continue with the trial until such time as legal representation is procured—cf *Khanyile* 1988 (3) SA 795 (N).

The Legal Aid Act 22 of 1969 introduced a Legal Aid Board which has as its aims the granting or making available of legal aid to needy persons. The Board has the capacity, inter alia, to procure the services of legal practitioners and to stipulate the conditions under which legal aid is to be given. In Johannesburg there are also public defenders who defend needy accused free of charge in certain cases.

In *Rudman; Mthwana* 1992 (1) SACR 70 (A) it was stated that a worthy ideal to be pursued in any criminal justice system is the principle that each person who is accused of a serious crime and is not able to afford legal representation should be provided with legal representation at the expense of the state in order to avoid an unfair trial. Although the present circumstances in South Africa are such that this cannot be attained, it does not detract from the fact that the ideal should be pursued vigorously.

CHAPTER 5

The accused: his presence as a party

		Page
1	THE GENERAL RULE	79
2	EXCEPTIONS TO THE RULE	80
	2.1 Trial in absence of accused on account of his misbehaviour	80
	2.2 Absence of accused where there is more than one accused	81
	2.3 Payment of fine without appearance in court (admission of guilt)— s 57	81
3	COMPOUNDING OF MINOR OFFENCES—s 341	82

The Constitution and this chapter:

Section 34—Access to courts

Everyone has the right to have any dispute that can be resolved by the application of law decided in a fair public hearing by a court or, where appropriate, another independent and impartial tribunal or forum.

See 1, below.

Section 35—Arrested, detained and accused persons

(3) Every accused person has a right to a fair trial, which includes the right—

. . .

(c) to a public trial before an ordinary court;

. . .

(e) to be present when being tried;

. . .

(i) to adduce and challenge evidence

. . .

See 1, below.

---

1 THE GENERAL RULE

It is a basic principle of the law of criminal procedure in every civilised community that the trial of an accused must take place in his presence and that the verdict of the court and the sentence that it imposes, must be announced in his presence. This general rule was written into ss 34 and 35(3)*(c)* and *(e)* of the Constitution, safeguarding access to court and including (as part of the right to a fair trial) the right to a public *trial* before an ordinary court of law. The principle is also contained in s 158 of the Criminal Procedure Act and is scrupulously upheld by the superior courts. The following are examples of the application of this principle:

- In *Seedat* 1971 (1) SA 789 (N) the accused was convicted of an offence in terms of the Insolvency Act. Prior to sentencing the accused, the magistrate called a certain C as an expert witness in regard to certain bookkeeping matters. This step the magistrate took as a result of a discussion which he had with the prosecutor in the absence of the accused and his legal representative. This procedure, it was held upon appeal, amounted to a serious irregularity offending against the aforementioned basic principle. The court of appeal disregarded C's evidence altogether for purposes of imposing a proper sentence.

- In *Radebe* 1973 (4) SA 244 (O) the magistrate altered the suspension order on the accused's driver's licence in his absence. On review it was held that the magistrate acted irregularly.

- In *Rousseau* 1979 (3) SA 895 (T) a medical practitioner testified in court. The magistrate thereafter consulted another medical practitioner and obtained an opinion from him concerning the testimony of the medical practitioner. Neither the accused nor his legal representative was present during this consultation. This procedure, it was held, amounted to a serious irregularity and the accused's conviction and sentence were set aside.

Note that the above basic principle means more than that an accused must merely *know* what the state witnesses have said; it requires that there should be a *confrontation*: he must see them as they testify against him so that he can observe their demeanour, and they must give their evidence in the face of a present accused. The denial of this fundamental right of an accused in itself amounts to a failure of justice that will lead to the setting aside of the accused's conviction on appeal or review—s 35(3)*(i)* of the Constitution and *Motlatla* 1975 (1) SA 814 (T).

There are, however, a number of exceptions to this rule. First, in the case of certain trivial offences, a so-called admission of guilt fine can be paid which will result in the accused being convicted in his absence. Secondly, the accused can by his behaviour during the trial make it impossible for the court to carry on with the trial in his presence. Thirdly, circumstances may make it necessary for a trial, in which there are more than one accused, to continue in the absence of one or more co-accused. These cases will now be dealt with.

2   EXCEPTIONS TO THE RULE

2.1   Trial in absence of accused on account of his misbehaviour

If the accused conducts himself in such a manner as to render the continuance of the proceedings in his presence impracticable, the court may order him to be removed and may direct that the trial proceed in his absence—s 159(1) of the Criminal Procedure Act. The court will, however, make use of its powers under this section only as a last resort and only if it cannot avoid doing so. The court would prefer to postpone the matter or grant a temporary adjournment and then continue with the case at a later stage in the presence of the accused. If the court does make use of its powers in terms of s 159(1), it ought first to warn the accused and to note its warning. Even after the accused has been removed, it is advisable to give him a further opportunity and have him brought before the court after the leading of evidence has been completed and to ask him whether he wishes to give any evidence—cf *Mpofu* 1970 (2) SA 162 (R); *Pauline* 1928 TPD 643; *Mokoa* 1985 (1) SA 350 (O) and Hiemstra 410.

2.2 Absence of accused where there is more than one accused

If two or more accused appear jointly at criminal proceedings, the court may, at any time after the commencement of the proceedings, upon application by the accused or his legal representative, authorise the absence of an accused on the following grounds:

(a) that the physical condition of the accused is such that he is unable to attend or that it is undesirable that he should attend the trial; or

(b) that circumstances in connection with the illness or death of a member of the accused's family have arisen which make his absence from the proceedings necessary—s 159(2)*(a)*.

Furthermore, if any of the accused is absent from the proceedings, whether as a result of his removal in terms of s 159(1) or with or without leave of the court, the court may direct that the proceedings be proceeded with in the absence of the accused concerned. The court will make such an order only if in its opinion the trial cannot be postponed without undue prejudice, embarrassment or inconvenience to the prosecution or any co-accused or any witness—s 159(2).

The court may also, in lieu of directing that the proceedings be proceeded with in the absence of the accused, upon the application of the prosecution direct that the proceedings in respect of the absent accused be separated from the proceedings in respect of the accused who are present. When such accused is again in attendance, the proceedings against him shall continue from the stage at which he became absent and the court shall not be required to be differently constituted—s 159(3).

If the proceedings continue in the absence of the accused he may, if he later again attends the proceedings and has not been legally represented during his absence, examine a witness who testified during his absence and inspect the record of the proceedings. (Cf also the provisions of s 160(2) and (3).) It is clear that the proceedings in respect of the absent accused may be concluded only after his reappearance and after he has been given the opportunity of leading evidence and closing his case.

2.3 Payment of fine without appearance in court (admission of guilt)—s 57

A public prosecutor or the clerk of the court who issues a summons in terms of s 54 to an accused person to appear in court, may, if he believes on reasonable grounds that a magistrate's court, on convicting the accused of the offence in question, will not impose a fine exceeding the amount determined by the Minister by notice in the *Government Gazette* (at present R1 500), endorse the summons to the effect that the accused may admit his guilt in respect of the offence and that he may pay a fine stipulated on the summons in respect of such offence without appearing in court— s 57(1).

After an accused has appeared in court but before he has pleaded, a public prosecutor may, if he believes on reasonable grounds that a magistrate's court (on convicting the accused of the offence he is alleged to have committed) will not impose a fine exceeding the amount determined by the Minister by notice in the *Government Gazette* (at present R1 500), hand to the accused a written notice, or cause such notice to be delivered to the accused by a peace officer, containing an endorsement in terms of section 57 that the accused may admit his guilt in respect of such offence and pay a stipulated fine in respect thereof without appearing in court again—s 57A(1).

A peace officer may, in terms of s 56(1), hand a written notice to an accused person to appear in court. This notice may contain a similar endorsement, provided the peace officer holds a similar belief based on reasonable grounds—s 56(1)*(c)*.

An accused who receives a summons or written notice as aforesaid, may, without appearing in court, admit his guilt in respect of the offence in question by paying the admission of guilt fine either to the clerk of the magistrate's court which has jurisdiction or at any police station within the area of jurisdiction of that court. The summons or written notice may stipulate that the admission of guilt fine must be paid before a date specified—s 57(1).

After the clerk of the court concerned has received such a document, he enters it in the criminal record book of the court and the accused is then deemed to have been convicted and sentenced by the court of the offence concerned. Such an admission of guilt amounts to a previous conviction for the purposes of all offences—*NGJ Trading Stores (Pty) Ltd v Guerreiro* 1974 (4) SA 738 (A).

The judicial officer may in certain instances set aside the conviction and sentence and direct that the accused be prosecuted in the ordinary course—s 57(7). After the judicial officer has found the documents in order, he is *functus officio* and he may not consider representations by the accused—*Marion* 1981 (1) SA 1216 (T); *Makhele* 1981 (4) SA 956 (NC); contra *Mahabeer* 1980 (4) SA 491 (N); *Shange* 1983 (4) SA 46 (N).

A public prosecutor may also reduce an admission of guilt fine on good cause shown—s 57(4). Where a prosecutor withdrew a charge after the accused had already paid an admission of guilt fine which was confirmed by the magistrate, the conviction and sentence were set aside on review because of considerations of justice and equity—*Smith* 1985 (2) SA 152 (T).

Although s 57 does not stipulate the kind of offences in respect of which an admission of guilt fine may be set, it has been held that this procedure should be limited to statutory offences and should not be used for offences under common law—*B* 1954 (3) SA 431 (SWA). This procedure is very often (as is generally known to motorists!) used for traffic offences. For the consequences of an accused's failure to appear in court in accordance with a summons in respect of which he could have paid an admission of guilt fine (which he did not pay)—see chapter 5 (5.3).

Some Acts prohibit the acceptance of admission of guilt fines with regard to certain offences.

3 COMPOUNDING OF MINOR OFFENCES—s 341

A distinction must be drawn between admission of guilt and compounding of offences. In the case of an admission of guilt, the accused is summoned or a written notice is handed to the accused. The prosecution is therefore actually initiated. By signing an admission of guilt, an accused is deemed to have been convicted and sentenced. Compounding of an offence, on the other hand, means that the offender pays a certain amount to some or other body (for example a municipality) in order not to be prosecuted for some minor offence which he has committed. This procedure is generally used with traffic offences.

Compounding is regulated by s 341 of the Criminal Procedure Act which limits this procedure to certain minor traffic offences and contraventions of the rules and regulations of local authorities.

PART II

THE CRIMINAL PROCESS

PHASE ONE:
PRE-TRIAL CRIMINAL PROCEDURE

CHAPTER 6

The exercise of powers and the vindication of individual rights

		Page
1	INTRODUCTION	88
2	THE REQUIREMENT OF REASONABLENESS IN THE EXERCISE OF POWERS	90

The Constitution and this chapter:

Section 10—Human dignity

Everyone has inherent dignity and the right to have their dignity respected and protected.

See 1, below.

Section 12—Freedom and security of the person

(1) Every person shall have the right to freedom and security of the person, which includes the right—

    (a) not to be deprived of freedom arbitrarily or without just cause;

    (b) not to be detained without trial;

    (c) to be free from all forms of violence from either public or private sources;

    (d) not to be tortured in any way; and

    (e) not to be treated or punished in a cruel, inhumane or degrading way.

See 1, below.

Section 14—Privacy

Everyone has the right to privacy, which includes the right not to have—

(a) their person or home searched;

(b) their property searched;

(c) their possessions seized; or

(d) the privacy of their communications infringed.

See 1, below.

Section 25—Property

(1) No one may be deprived of property except in terms of a law of general application, and no law may permit arbitrary deprivation of property.

See 1, below.

Section 35—Arrested, detained and accused persons

(3) Every accused person has a right to a fair rial, which includes the right—

. . .

(h) to be presumed innocent

. . .

(5) Evidence obtained in a manner that violates any right in the Bill of Rights must be excluded if the admission of that evidence would render the trial unfair or otherwise be detrimental to the administration of justice.

See 1, below.

Section 36—Limitation of rights

(1) The rights in the Bill of Rights may be limited only in terms of law of general application to the extent that the limitation is reasonable and justifiable in an open and democratic society based on human dignity, equality and freedom, taking into account all relevant factors, including—

(a) the nature of the right;

(b) the importance of the purpose of the limitation;

(c) the nature and extent of the limitation;

(d) the relation between the limitation and its purpose; and

(e) less restrictive means to achieve the purpose.

(2) Except as provided in subsection (1) or in any other provision of the Constitution, no law may limit any right entrenched in the Constitution.

See 1, below.

1 INTRODUCTION

The law jealously protects the personality and property rights of individuals. These rights include every person's right to his body, freedom, honour, dignity and privacy, as well as his rights with regard to property. Accordingly, these interests are fully protected by the Constitution (see ss 10, 12, 14 and 25 quoted immediately above).

Sometimes, however, society's wider interest in the combating of crime necessitates the limitation of these rights. It may, for instance, be necessary to arrest persons and thereby encroach upon their freedom of movement or to seize property. Despite this, the law constantly strives towards achieving a balance between society's demands, on the one hand, to bring offenders to justice, and, on the other hand, to uphold the personality and property rights of the individual. (The latter, after all, until found guilty in a court of law, is presumed innocent—see s 35(3)*(h)* of the Constitution, quoted above.) To achieve this, the law (and in particular the law of criminal procedure) lays down strict rules with regard to the circumstances in which a limitation of these rights will be permissible to investigate crime or to bring offenders to justice. The constitutionality of these limitations can only be determined by measuring them against the limitation clause in section 36 of the Constitution (quoted above).

Section 36 lays down certain requirements with which such limitations must comply before they could be regarded as constitutional. According to these requirements the limitation—

(a) must be contained in a law of general application; and

(b) must be *reasonable* and *justifiable* in an open and democratic society based on human dignity, equality and freedom.

In considering whether a particular limitation complies with these requirements, a court has to take into account all relevant factors, including—

(a) the nature of the right;

(b) the importance of the purpose of the limitation;

(c) the nature and extent of the limitation;

(d) the relation between the limitation and its purpose; and

(e) less restrictive means to achieve the purpose.

These factors will indicate whether the limitation could be considered as being *proportional* to the purpose of the limitation. Simply stated, it means that a court will have to determine what purpose the limitation sets out to achieve, whether this purpose is sufficiently important to justify a limitation of the right, whether the limitation will be effective to achieve the purpose and, finally, whether the purpose could be achieved in another, less restrictive, manner. (Cf the Canadian case of *Oakes* [[1986] 26 DLR (4th) 201].)

The rules of criminal procedure aim to protect the safety and security of all members of society by enabling the effective investigation of offences to identify the offenders and to bring them to justice.

The rules of criminal procedure are very strict in order to prevent arbitrary action by the police or private persons. Persons who act outside the limits laid down by these rules, act unlawfully, whether they do so to investigate crime or to bring offenders to justice or not. Accordingly, in our law it can, as a general rule, be assumed that the search of persons or premises, the seizure of objects and the arrest of persons will invariably be unlawful, unless such action complies with the aforementioned rules or is justified by some ground of justification (such as consent to the search). The consequences of such unlawful conduct are threefold:

(a) Firstly, a person unlawfully arrested or whose property was unlawfully searched or seized, may institute a civil claim against the person effecting the arrest, search or seizure and, in some instances even against his or her employer (eg the state, if the person who acted unlawfully was a state official, such as a police official).

(b) Secondly, in appropriate circumstances an unlawful search, seizure or arrest may even constitute an offence.

(c) Finally, section 35(5) of the Constitution provides that evidence obtained in a manner that violates any right in the Bill of Rights, must be excluded if the admission of that evidence would render the trial unfair or otherwise be detrimental to the administration of justice. This means that if evidence is obtained during an unlawful search or by unlawfully arresting a person, such evidence will be excluded and may not be taken into account by the court during the trial, if its admission would have one of the aforementioned effects. This may result in the acquittal of the accused.

2 THE REQUIREMENT OF REASONABLENESS IN THE EXERCISE OF POWERS

In Chapter 1 mention was made of the policy considerations relating to the requirement of reasonableness of government action that can be gleaned from the judgments
of our courts. The application of these principles in practice in the exercise of powers
during the pre-trial phase of the criminal process now calls for some explanation.

The various statutory provisions providing for the power to conduct searches, to
seize articles and to arrest persons, repeatedly refers to 'reasonableness' in their
description of the circumstances in which these powers may be exercised. Section 20
provides that certain articles may be seized if they are 'on reasonable grounds
believed to be' articles of a certain nature. Section 21(1)(a) authorises the issuing of
search warrants where it appears from information on oath that there are
'reasonable grounds for believing' that certain articles will be found at a certain
place. Section 22(1)(b) authorises a police official to conduct a search if he 'on
reasonable grounds believes' that certain circumstances exist. In terms of s 24 a
person in charge of or occupying premises may conduct a search and seize articles
provided he 'reasonably suspects' certain circumstances to exist. Sections 26 and 48
authorise the entry of premises where the person 'reasonably suspects' that a certain
state of affairs exists. Sections 41 to 43 empowers certain persons to arrest persons
'reasonably suspected' of having committed certain offences. Section 41 authorises
peace officers to require that certain persons provide certain information if they are
'reasonably suspected' of having committed offences.

Apart from the above, certain statutory provisions also empower certain persons
to use such force as may be 'reasonably necessary' to gain entry to premises (see s 27
which authorises the use of such force that may be 'reasonably necessary' to gain
entry to premises and s 49 in terms of which such force as may be 'reasonably
necessary' may be used to overcome resistance against an arrest or to prevent the
arrested person from fleeing).

The question is often posed how one is supposed to determine exactly when a
suspicion may be said to be a 'reasonable suspicion', or when one could be said to
have 'reasonable grounds' to believe, or what force would be 'reasonably necessary'
to achieve a certain objective. Although it would be impossible to lay down any hard
and fast rules in this regard, the following guidelines may be followed:

(1) In each of the aforementioned instances the requirement of reasonableness may
     be described as a requirement that there be 'reasonable grounds' from which a
     certain inference can be drawn. It can for instance only be said that force is
     'reasonably necessary' to achieve a certain goal, if there are 'reasonable
     grounds' to believe that such force is actually necessary to achieve the goal. A
     person can furthermore only be said to have a 'reasonable suspicion' that a
     certain state of affairs exists if he has 'reasonable grounds' to believe that that
     state of affairs exists. (Cf in general in this regard *LSD v Vachell* 1918 WLD 127
     at 134.)

(2) A person will only be said to have 'reasonable grounds' to believe or suspect
     something or that certain action is necessary if:

     (a) he really 'believes' or 'suspects' it;

     (b) his belief or suspicion is based on certain 'grounds'; and *(c)* in the circumstances and in view of the existence of those 'grounds', any reasonable person would have held the same belief or suspicion.

(3) The word 'grounds' as it is used here, refers to 'facts'. This means that there will only be 'grounds' for a certain suspicion or belief if the suspicion or belief is reconcilable with the available facts. The existence or otherwise of a 'fact' is objectively determined—cf *Van Heerden* 1958 (3) SA 150 (T) at 152 and *Nell* 1967 (4) SA 489 (SWA) at 494–6). This means that one will have to look at the facts as they really are and not as someone may 'think' they are. To determine what the facts really are, a person will make use of his five senses. This means that the person will determine the true facts by looking, hearing, smelling, touching and tasting.

(4) Once a person has established what the facts really are, he will evaluate them and make an inference from those facts with regard to the existence or otherwise of other facts, which he is at the time, for whatever reason, unable to establish. This means that he will consider the true facts and will then decide whether the true facts are in his view sufficient to warrant a belief that the other facts also exist—cf *Mnanzana* 1966 (3) SA 38 (T) at 43.

(5) Once he has made the inference that the other facts exist, it can be said that the person himself 'believes' or 'suspects' that such facts exist.

(6) However, the mere fact that a certain person believes or suspects that certain facts exist is not sufficient to regard his belief as one based on 'reasonable grounds' as required by the law. This will only be the case if it can be said that any reasonable person would have held the same belief or suspicion in the circumstances—cf *Van Heerden* (above). The words 'any reasonable person', as they are used in this regard, refer to any other person who has more or less the same background knowledge (such as training and experience) as the person who actually entertains the belief or suspicion.

(7) A person can therefore be said to have 'reasonable grounds' to believe or suspect something if he actually believes or suspects it, his belief or suspicion is based on facts from which he has drawn an inference, and if any reasonable person would, in view of those facts, also have drawn the same inference. This is a factual question that will have to be answered with reference to the factual circumstances that are present in each case.

In the discussion of the various provisions of the Criminal Procedure Act which provides for powers to search, seize or arrest, it will be pointed out how these guidelines are applied.

CHAPTER 7

Securing the attendance of the accused at the trial

		Page
1	INTRODUCTION	93
2	SUMMONS	94
3	WRITTEN NOTICE TO APPEAR	95
4	INDICTMENT	96
5	ARREST	96
	5.1 General	96
	5.2 The requirements for a lawful arrest	97
	5.3 Arrest with a warrant	98
	5.3.1 General	98
	5.3.2 The issue of a warrant of arrest	98
	5.3.3 The execution of a warrant of arrest	99
	5.4 Arrest without a warrant	99
	5.4.1 General	99
	5.4.2 The power to arrest without a warrant	100
	5.4.2.1 Powers of peace officers	100
	5.4.2.2 Powers of private persons	104
	5.4.2.3 Special statutory powers of certain officials	104
	5.5 Procedure after arrest	105
	5.6 The effect of an arrest	107
	5.7 The duty to arrest	108
	5.8 Resisting arrest and attempts to flee	108
	5.8.1 Use of force in effecting an arrest to overcome resistance	108
	5.8.2 Justifiable homicide	109
	5.9 Escape from lawful custody	113
	5.10 Arrest and detention for interrogation	114
6	OTHER METHODS	114
7	EXTRADITION	114

The Constitution and this chapter:

Section 12—Freedom and security of the person

(1) Everyone has the right to freedom and security of the person, which includes the right—

   (a) not to be deprived of freedom arbitrarily or without just cause;

   ...

See 5.1, below.

Section 21—Freedom of movement

(1) Everyone has the right to freedom of movement.

See 5.1, below.

Section 35

(1) Everyone who is arrested for allegedly committing an offence has the right—

   ...

   (b) to be informed promptly—

     (i) of the right to remain silent; and

     (ii) of the consequences of not remaining silent;

   ...

   (d) to be brought before a court as soon as reasonably possible, but not later than—

     (i) 48 hours after the arrest; or,

     (ii) the end of the first court day after the expiry of the 48 hours, if the 48 hours expire outside ordinary court hours or on a day which is not a court day;

   (e) at the first court appearance after being arrested, to be charged or to be informed of the reason for the detention to continue, or to be released;

   ...

See 5.5, below.

(2) Everyone who is detained, . . . , has the right—

   (a) to be informed of the reason for being detained;

   ...

   (d) to challenge the lawfulness of the detention in person before a court and, if the detention is unlawful, to be released;

   ...

See 5.2, below.

---

1 INTRODUCTION

There are various means by which an accused's attendance at the trial may be secured. The most important are a summons, a written notice to appear, an indictment, or the arrest of the accused—s 38 of the Criminal Procedure Act. The rules relating to each of these will now be discussed, whereafter brief reference will be made to the warning of the accused to appear and extradition as a means of ensuring that an accused appears in court in another country.

2 SUMMONS

This is used for a summary trial in a lower court where the accused is not in custody or about to be arrested. In cases where there is no reason to suppose that such an accused will abscond, attempt to hamper the police investigation, or attempt to influence State witnesses, it is preferable to secure his attendance by means of a summons and not to subject him to the indignity of an arrest. An accused may, of course, be arrested even after a summons to appear on a certain date has been served on him. This step may have to be taken when it becomes clear that he will attempt to defeat the ends of justice.

To secure the attendance of an accused at a summary trial in a lower court by means of a summons, the following procedure is followed:

(1) The prosecutor draws up the charge and hands it, together with information relating to the name, address and occupation or status of the accused, to the clerk of the court—s 54(1).

(2) The clerk of the court issues a document (known as a 'summons') containing the charge and the information handed to him by the prosecutor, and specifying the place, date and time for the appearance of the accused in court—s 54(1).

(3) The clerk of the court hands the summons (together with so many copies thereof as there are accused) to a person empowered to serve a summons—s 54(1). (Persons empowered to serve a summons include police officials—s 329.)

(4) The summons is served by delivering it to the person named therein or, if he cannot be found, by delivering it at his residence or place of employment or business to a person apparently over the age of sixteen years and apparently residing or employed there—s 54(2)(a). A summons is in force throughout the Republic and may be served anywhere in the Republic—s 328. It may be transmitted by telegraph and service of a telegraphic copy has the same effect as that of the original—s 330. Service must take place at least fourteen days (Sundays and public holidays excluded) before the date fixed for the trial—s 54(3).

A return by the person who served the summons that the service has been effected in terms of s 54(2)(a) may, upon the failure of the person concerned to attend the proceedings, be handed in at the trial as prima facie proof of service—s 54(2)(b).

If the person summoned fails to appear at the place on the date and at the time specified or fails to remain in attendance, he is guilty of an offence and liable to punishment of a fine or imprisonment for a period not exceeding three months—s 55(1). The court may, if satisfied from the return of service that the summons was duly served (cf *Ngcobo* 1966 (1) SA 444 (N) and *Minister van Polisie v Goldschagg* 1981 (1) SA 37 (A)) and that the accused has failed to appear or to remain in attendance, issue a warrant for his arrest. In terms of s 55(2A), the court must endorse the warrant of arrest to the effect that the accused may admit his guilt in respect of the offence in question and may pay the fine stipulated in the summons without appearing in court. The court may make a further endorsement on the warrant of arrest to the effect that the accused may, upon arrest, admit his guilt in respect of the failure to appear in answer to the summons and pay the amount stipulated on the warrant. The amount so stipulated shall not exceed the amount of the admission of guilt fine that could have been imposed for such an offence.

If an accused fails to pay the admission of guilt as stipulated on the warrant and appears in court on the due date, the court may summarily enquire into his failure to appear. It may then convict him of the abovementioned offence—unless the accused satisfies the court that his failure was not due to any fault on his part—s 55(2). The proviso to this section, however, provides for the following two instances where the accused need not be arrested in terms of the warrant, viz:

(1) Where it appears to the person executing the warrant that the accused received the summons and that he will appear in court in accordance with a warning under s 72 (see below), he may release the accused on such warning. In this respect the official thus has a discretion.

(2) Where it appears to the person executing the warrant that the accused did not receive the summons or that the accused has paid an admission of guilt fine in terms of s 57 or that there are other grounds on which it appears that the failure of the accused to appear on the summons was not due to any fault on the part of the accused (for which purpose he may require the accused to furnish an affidavit or affirmation), he must release the accused on warning under s 72. In this instance the official has no discretion.

If an accused failed to appear on a summons and it was permissible for him in terms of s 57 to admit his guilt in respect of that summons and to pay a fine without appearing in court, s 55(3) provides that, where a warrant of arrest was issued and the accused was arrested in the area of jurisdiction of a magistrate's court other than the district in which the warrant of arrest was issued, such other magistrate's court— if satisfied that the accused has, since the date on which he failed to appear on the summons, admitted his guilt and has paid a fine in respect thereof without appearing in court—may summarily enquire into his failure to appear. Unless the accused satisfies the court that his failure was not due to any fault on his part, s 55(1) (see above) takes effect. (In proceedings in the magistrate's court of the district where he was arrested, it is presumed, upon production of the warrant of arrest, that the accused failed to appear on the summons, unless the contrary is proved— s 55(3)*(b)*.) The effect of this section may be illustrated by the following example:

> A person (X) commits a minor traffic offence in Town A. Town A is one thousand kilometres away from his home town (Town B). X receives a summons to appear in the magistrate's court in Town A. The summons makes provision for the accused to pay an admission of guilt fine at the magistrate's court or police station in Town A. X forgets about the summons and fails either to pay the admission of guilt fine or to appear in court on the specified date. A warrant for his arrest is issued. X is arrested in Town B. In terms of this provision X may now pay the admission of guilt fine in Town B and may be tried in the magistrate's court of Town B for his failure to appear in court. It is therefore not necessary to take him to Town A and have his case heard in the court there.

3 WRITTEN NOTICE TO APPEAR

If a peace officer on reasonable grounds believes that a magistrate's court, on convicting an accused of an offence, whether the accused is in custody or not, will not impose a fine exceeding the amount determined by the Minister from time to time by notice in the *Government Gazette* (at present this amount is R1 500), he may hand to the accused a written notice

(1) specifying the name, residential address and occupation or status of the accused;

(2) calling upon the accused to appear at a place and on a date and at a time specified in the written notice to answer a charge of having committed the offence in question;

(3) containing an endorsement in terms of s 57 that the accused may admit his guilt in respect of the offence and that he may pay a stipulated fine without appearing in court; and

(4) containing a certificate signed by the peace officer that he has handed the original notice to the accused and explained the import thereof to him—s 56(1). (See also subsections (2), (3) and (4) of this section as well as s 57A(4) in respect of the written notice referred to in that section.)

If an accused fails to respond to the written notice in question, the provisions of s 55—with regard to a summons (see above) apply *mutatis mutandis*—s 56(5).

A written notice to appear differs from a summons as follows:

First, a written notice to appear is prepared, issued and handed directly to the accused by a peace officer, whereas a summons is prepared by the prosecutor, issued by the clerk of the court and served on the accused by a messenger of the court or a police official (see s 329).

Secondly, whereas a written notice to appear always offers the accused the option of paying a set admission of guilt fine in order to avoid a court appearance, a summons need not provide this option. The purpose of this procedure is clearly to expedite the course of justice in the case of minor offences.

4 INDICTMENT

At a trial in a superior court the charge is contained in a document known as an indictment, which is drawn up in the name of the director of public prosecutions. The indictment contains the charge against the accused, his name, address, sex, nationality and age. It may be accompanied by a summary of the substantial facts of the case and a list of the names and addresses of state witnesses—s 144(1), (2) and (3).

The indictment, together with a notice of trial, must be served on the accused at least ten days (Sundays and public holidays excluded) before the date of the trial, unless the accused agrees to a shorter period. It is served by handing it to the accused in substantially the same manner as a summons (discussed above)—see s 144(4)*(a)*—or is handed to the accused by the magistrate or regional magistrate who commits him to the superior court for trial. A return of service is prima facie proof of the service—s 144(4)*(b)*.

Failure to appear is *mutatis mutandis* governed by s 55(1) and (2).

5 ARREST

5.1 General

Arrest constitutes one of the most drastic infringements of the rights of an individual (eg his right not to be deprived of his freedom arbitrarily or without just cause or his right to freedom of movement (ss 12(1)*(a)* and 21(1) respectively of the Constitution). It is therefore not surprising that the Criminal Procedure Act lays down strict rules concerning when a person may be arrested.

In terms of the Criminal Procedure Act an arrest should preferably be effected only after a warrant for the arrest has been obtained. It is only in exceptional circumstances that private individuals, or even the police, are authorised to arrest anyone without the authority of a warrant. Any arrest without a warrant which is not specifically authorised by law, will be unlawful. Even a police official who executes a warrant for the arrest of a person must exercise proper care in doing so. If he negligently arrests the wrong person, he may, in an action for wrongful arrest, be compelled to pay such person a large amount in damages. Apart from that, should an arrestee challenge the validity of his arrest and detention, the onus to prove the lawfulness thereof is on the arrestor or the person who ordered the arrest—*Minister of Law and Order v Parker* 1989 (2) SA 633 (A) and *Ramakulukusha v Commander, Venda National Force* 1989 (2) SA 813 (V).

However, if a person is authorised to arrest another, a bad motive for the arrest will not make an otherwise lawful arrest unlawful—*Minister van die SA Polisie v Kraatz* 1973 (3) SA 490 (A).

5.2 The requirements for a lawful arrest

Lawful arrest and lawful continued detention after arrest are based upon four 'pillars':

(1) The first pillar is that the arrest (with or without a warrant) must have been properly authorised, ie there must be a statutory provision authorising the arrest. We shall discuss this requirement in detail under paragraphs 5.3 and 5.4 below.

(2) The second pillar is that the arrestor must exercise physical control over the arrestee. He must therefore limit the latter's freedom of movement. Unless the arrestee submits to custody, an arrest is effected by actually touching his person or, if the circumstances so require, by forcibly confining his person—s 39(1). The amount of force—both lethal and non-lethal—that may be used legally will be discussed below.

(3) The third pillar is the informing of the arrestee of the reason for his arrest: s 39(2) requires that an arrestor must, at the time of effecting the arrest or immediately thereafter, inform the arrestee of the reason for his arrest or, if the arrest took place by virtue of a warrant, hand the arrestee a copy of the warrant upon demand. This requirement is also entrenched in the Constitution (s 35(2)*(a)*, quoted above).

An arrestee's custody will be unlawful if this requirement is not complied with—see *Kleyn* 1937 CPD 288 and *Ngidi* 1972 (1) SA 733 (N).

The question whether the arrestee was given an adequate reason for his arrest depends on the circumstances of each case, particularly the arrested person's knowledge concerning the reason for his arrest. The exact wording of the charge which will later be brought against the arrestee need not be conveyed at the time of the arrest—*Minister of Law and Order v Kader* 1991 (1) SA 41 (A) and cf *Brand v Minister of Justice* 1959 (4) SA 712 (A).

Although the arrestee's detention will be unlawful if he was not informed of the reason for his arrest at the time of his arrest, his detention will become lawful if he is later informed of the reason—*Nqumba v State President* 1987 (1) SA 456 (E). Detailed information relating to something that the arrestee ought

to know, need not be given, especially when the arrestee is caught in the act—
Macu v Du Toit 1982 (1) SA 272 (C) and *Minister of Law and Order v Parker*
1989 (2) SA 633 (A).

(4)   The final pillar is the requirement that the arrestee be taken to the appropriate
authorities as soon as possible. Section 50(1)*(a)* provides that an arrestee must
as soon as possible be brought to a police station or, if the arrest was made in
terms of a warrant, to the place stipulated in the warrant. In *Ezekiel v Kynoch*
NPD 13.4.1923 (cited in Gardiner & Lansdown 215) a person was detained for
20 hours pending investigation of a theft at a place five kilometres from the
police station; this was held to be unlawful, and he was awarded damages.
Section 50 will be discussed in detail below.

5.3   Arrest with a warrant

5.3.1   *General*

A warrant for the arrest of a person is a written order directing that the person
described in the warrant be arrested by a peace officer in respect of the offence set
out in the warrant and that he be brought before a lower court in terms of s 50
(which governs the procedure after arrest)—s 43(2).

Unless it is imprudent or inconvenient in the circumstances to obtain a warrant or
the summary arrest of the offender is necessary or advisable in the circumstances, it
is desirable that a warrant should be obtained before the liberty of a person is
infringed.

5.3.2   *The issue of a warrant of arrest*

A magistrate or justice of the peace may issue a warrant for the arrest of a person
upon the written application of a director of public prosecutions, a public prosecutor
or police officer. Such application must

(1)   set out the offence alleged to have been committed;

(2)   allege that such offence was committed within the area of jurisdiction of such
magistrate, or in the case of a justice of the peace, within the area of jurisdiction
of the magistrate within whose district or area application is made to the justice
for such warrant, or where the offence was not committed within his area of
jurisdiction, that the person in respect of whom the application is made, is
known or is on reasonable grounds suspected to be within such area of
jurisdiction;

(3)   state that from information taken upon oath there is a reasonable suspicion that
the person in respect of whom the warrant is sought has committed the alleged
offence.

A warrant may be issued on any day and remains in force until it is cancelled by the
person who issued it or until it is executed—s 43(3).

A warrant issued in one district is valid in all other districts throughout the
Republic without any further formalities having to be complied with—s 328. In
terms of s 45, a telegraphic or similar written or printed communication from any
magistrate, justice of the peace or peace officer stating that a warrant has been issued
for the arrest of a person shall be sufficient authority to any peace officer to arrest
and detain the said person.

If an application is made for a warrant but it is intended to execute such warrant only under certain circumstances, the warrant is not void by virtue of this fact only: the official to whom it is issued is not totally deprived of his discretionary powers— *Minister van die SA Polisie v Kraatz* 1973 (3) SA 490 (A) at 509–10; *Duncan v Minister of Law and Order* 1986 (2) SA 805 (A) at 819.

5.3.3 *The execution of a warrant of arrest*

A warrant of arrest is executed by a peace officer—s 44.

In terms of s 1 (which contains the definitions), 'peace officer' includes a magistrate, justice of the peace, police official, member of correctional services and certain persons declared by the Minister of Justice to be peace officers for specified purposes—cf s 334. 'Police official' means a member of the SA Police Service as defined in s 1 of the South African Police Service Act 68 of 1995.

Sections 46 and 331 make provision for the exemption from liability of a person who is authorised to execute or assist in the execution of a warrant of arrest and who, in the reasonable belief that he is arresting the person mentioned in the warrant, arrests another or who acts under a warrant which is invalid due to a defect in the substance or form thereof, provided that he has no knowledge of such defect. The arrestor is placed in the position he would have been in had the warrant been valid. In the case of the arrest of the wrong person, without the arrestor having been negligent, the arresting person is placed in the same position he would have been in had he arrested the correct person. The test is whether a person of ordinary intelligence, who takes reasonable care, would have believed that the arrestee was the person named in the warrant—*Ingram v Minister of Justice* 1962 (3) SA 225 (W) and *Minister van Wet en Orde v Van der Heever* 1982 (4) SA 16 (C).

The Criminal Procedure Act, therefore, does not deprive a person who has been maliciously and wrongfully arrested of his civil remedy of a claim for damages.

A charge of resisting an arrest made in terms of a warrant will not fail merely because the police officials were not in uniform, provided it appears that the warrant was shown and explained to the arrestee and that he knew or was informed that it was being executed by the police—*Kalase* JS 315/17 (C).

In terms of s 39 the person arrested, hand him a copy of the warrant. In *Minister van Veiligheid en Sekuriteit v Rautenbach* 1996 (1) SACR 720 (AD), it was held that if the person effecting the arrest is not in possession of the warrant of arrest and realises that he will not be able to comply with a demand made in terms of s 39(2), the arrest will be unlawful. In this case the policeman intended to take the arrested person to the police station and hand him the copy of the warrant at the police station. According to the court, this would have taken too long and would not have complied with the requirements of s 39(2).

5.4 Arrest without a warrant

5.4.1 *General*

Although it is preferable that an arrest be effected only by virtue of a warrant, circumstances may arise where the delay caused by obtaining a warrant will enable the suspect to escape. It is therefore imperative that provision be made for the arrest of suspects without a warrant in certain circumstances.

The protection of the liberties of the individual stretches so far that a public-spirited person who conceives it to be his duty to arrest another person, without first having studied the Criminal Procedure Act, may seem to be embarking on a perilous undertaking. However, the provisions of the Criminal Procedure Act are based on sound common sense and, on the whole, empower persons to arrest in circumstances in which any right-thinking citizen would normally feel morally obliged to intervene on the side of law and order, so that a citizen would be reasonably safe in obeying his instincts in deciding whether or not he should effect an arrest. As was already stated, private individuals and even the police may without a warrant arrest persons believed to have committed an offence, only if there are special circumstances justifying this form of arrest.

A study of the rules relating to arrest will show that the powers to arrest of peace officers are wider than those of private individuals, and that wider powers are conferred in respect of the arrest of persons who are caught *in flagrante delicto* (ie caught in the act), than in respect of persons merely *suspected* of the commission of an offence. It will also be noticed that not any suspicion is sufficient to justify an arrest. It must be a *reasonable* suspicion and the crimes in respect of which arrest upon suspicion is possible are generally of a more serious nature. The question what is meant by the term 'reasonable suspicion', has already been discussed in Chapter 6.

Before setting out in detail the circumstances in which a person may be arrested without a warrant, a very important general principle on the exercise of the power to arrest, which was laid down by the Supreme Court of Appeal, must be mentioned. In the case of *Tsose v Minister of Justice* 1951 (3) SA 10 (A) it was held that 'If the object of an arrest, though professedly to bring an arrested person before the court, is really not such, but is to frighten or harass and so induce him to act in a way desired by the arrestor, without his appearing in court, the arrest is unlawful. But if the object of the arrestor is to bring the arrested person before court in order that he may be prosecuted to conviction and so may be led to cease to contravene the law, the arrest is not rendered illegal because the arrestor's motive is to frighten and harass the arrested person into desisting from his illegal conduct.' 'Punitive arrest' (ie arrest to punish the offender) is therefore illegal. In Tsose's case the police repeatedly arrested an unlawful squatter on a farm, allegedly with a view to compelling him to leave—cf also *Minister van die SA Polisie v Kraatz* 1973 (3) SA 490 (A) at 507–8.

The statutory provisions prescribing the circumstances in which an arrest without a warrant may be effected will now be discussed.

5.4.2 *The power to arrest without a warrant*

5.4.2.1 Powers of peace officers

In terms of s 40 every peace officer may, without a warrant, arrest

(1) Any person who commits or attempts to commit any offence in his presence cf *Loubser* 1977 (4) SA 546 (T) and *Gulyas v Minister of Law and Order* 1986 (3) SA 934 (C).

(2) Any person whom he reasonably suspects of having committed an offence referred to in the First Schedule, other than the offence of escaping from lawful custody.

Comment

(a) The First Schedule includes the serious offences and will be discussed in greater detail below. A list of offences committed in terms of Schedule I is set out as an annexure at the end of the book.

(b) With regard to the provision that a peace officer may arrest someone whom he reasonably suspects of having committed an offence mentioned in the First Schedule of the Act, the peace officer must be certain that the suspected act does in fact constitute a crime—*Union Government v Bolstridge* 1929 AD 240.

(c) The words 'reasonably suspects' do not imply that there must be a *prima facie* case against the suspect. The section requires only a reasonable suspicion and not a certainty. The suspicion must, however, have a factual basis. The reasonable man would therefore analyse and assess the quality of the information at his disposal critically and he would not accept it lightly or without checking it where it can be checked—*Mabona v Minister of Law and Order* 1988 (2) SA 654 (SE).

(d) The peace officer, when effecting the arrest, need not necessarily have the intention of bringing the arrested person to court to be prosecuted. A reasonable suspicion, coupled with the intention to make further inquiries before deciding whether the case merits prosecution, will suffice. A further investigation is especially necessary in a case where information is obtained from an informer (whose evidence must be regarded with caution)—*Mabona v Minister of Law and Order* (above). The possibility of an arrested person being released before his appearance in court is not anomalous: it arises from the difference between the test laid down for a lawful arrest without a warrant and the practical requirement of a *prima facie* case for a prosecution—*Duncan v Minister of Law and Order* 1984 (3) SA 460 (T).

(e) Telegraphic information from the police that a warrant has been issued somewhere else is sufficient ground for arrest in terms of this paragraph—*Botha* 17 SC 297.

(f) As was held in *Tsose's* case (above), the motive of deterring the offender is not in itself sufficient to make the arrest lawful.

(3) Any person who has escaped or who attempts to escape from lawful custody. A 'reasonable suspicion' that a person has escaped is not sufficient for an arrest in terms of this provision. A person who effects an arrest in terms of this provision must *know* that the person he arrests has escaped from lawful custody.

(4) Any person who has in his possession any housebreaking implement or carbreaking implement, as referred to in the Third General Law Amendment Act of 1993, and who is unable to account for such possession to the satisfaction of the peace officer. The possession of housebreaking or carbreaking implements in suspicious circumstances constitutes an offence in terms of the said Act.

(5) Any person who is found in possession of anything which the peace officer reasonably suspects to be stolen property or property dishonestly obtained, and whom the peace officer reasonably suspects of having committed an offence with respect to such thing.

(6)   Any person who is found at any place at night in circumstances which afford reasonable grounds for believing that such person has committed or is about to commit an offence. The purpose of the arrest provided for in this provision is to enable the peace officer to conduct an investigation to find out whether the person has committed an offence or not. If it appears that no offence has been committed, the person will have to be released.

(7)   Any person who is reasonably suspected of being or having been in unlawful possession of stock or produce as defined in any law relating to the theft of stock or produce.

(8)   Any person who is reasonably suspected of committing or of having committed an offence under any law governing the making, supply, possession or conveyance of intoxicating liquor or of dependence-producing drugs or the possession or disposal of arms or ammunition.

(9)   Any person found in a gambling house or at a gambling table in contravention of any law relating to the prevention or suppression of gambling or games of chance.

(10) Any person who obstructs him in the execution of his duty.

(11) Any person who has been concerned in or against whom a reasonable complaint has been made or credible information has been received or a reasonable suspicion exists that he has been concerned in any act committed outside the Republic which, if committed in the Republic, would have been punishable as an offence, and for which he is, under any law relating to extradition of fugitive offenders, liable to be arrested or detained in custody in the Republic. Extradition will be discussed below.

(12) Any person who is reasonably suspected of being a prohibited immigrant in the Republic in contravention of any law regulating entry into or residence in the Republic.

(13) Any person who is reasonably suspected of being a deserter from the South African Defence Force.

(14) Any person who is reasonably suspected of having failed to observe any condition imposed in postponing the passing of sentence or in suspending the operation of any sentence under this Act. The purpose with the arrest in this instance is to bring the person before the court to enable the court to determine whether the sentence should be imposed or be put into operation.

(15) Any person who is reasonably suspected of having failed to pay any fine or part thereof on the date fixed by order of court under this Act.

(16) Any person who fails to surrender himself in order that he may undergo periodic imprisonment when and where he is required to do so under an order of court or any law relating to prisons.

A peace officer is given the further power to call upon any person

   (a) whom he has power to arrest;

   (b) whom he reasonably suspects of having committed any offence or of having attempted to commit any offence (ie not only offences listed in the First Schedule to the Act); or

  (c) who may, in his opinion, be able to give evidence in regard to the commission or suspected commission of any offence,

to furnish his full name and address—s 41(1).

If such person fails to furnish his full name and address, the peace officer may forthwith arrest him. If the peace officer reasonably suspects that a false name or address has been given to him, he may arrest such person and detain him for a period not exceeding twelve hours until the name and address so furnished have been verified—s 41(1).

The failure by a person to furnish his name and address in the abovementioned circumstances and the furnishing of an incorrect or false name and address, constitute offences and are punishable by a fine or imprisonment without the option of a fine for a period of three months—s 41(2).

In the case of *Kleyn* 1937 CPD 288 the accused were charged with (1) using obscene, abusive and threatening language in a public street, and (2) resisting arrest. The State case was stopped by the magistrate in view of the strong evidence in support of the accused's denial and he acquitted them on these charges. The State, however, proceeded with a third charge of assault. The third charge was based on the following facts: The constable who had attempted to arrest the accused on the first charge went to the police station and returned with a sergeant to look for the accused, who were found in a private house. After having spoken to them, the sergeant demanded their names and addresses. They made no reply. The constable then identified the accused to the sergeant as the persons who had been swearing in the public street and placed his hand on their shoulders and told them he was arresting them for that offence. They refused to accompany the sergeant quietly and he thereupon ordered the constable to handcuff them and remove them. They resisted and, although handcuffed, assaulted the constable. The magistrate convicted and sentenced them on this charge. On appeal it was held that the crime of swearing in the public street had not been committed in the presence of the sergeant who had ordered the arrest or in the presence of the constable and, as no warrant for the arrest was obtained, the arrest was unlawful and the accused were entitled to resist arrest. The magistrate convicted them on the ground that the arrest was justified since the predecessor to s 41(1) provided that a peace officer may forthwith arrest a person who is reasonably suspected of having committed an offence and who fails to furnish his full name and address to him on demand. The court rejected the decision of the magistrate since the sergeant who had ordered the arrest *did not purport to act under this section* but had indicated to the accused through the constable that they were being arrested for swearing in a public street and since s 41(1) requires that the arrestee be informed that he is being arrested for failing to furnish his name and address, that section accordingly did not apply. The court pointed out that every man has the right to offer reasonable resistance to unlawful aggression upon his person and, if unlawfully arrested, is entitled to do anything reasonable to free himself. The court accordingly held that the assault was justified and set aside the conviction.

This case demonstrates the importance attached by the High Court to the personal liberty of the individual. As is clear from this case, a court will only allow a person to be deprived of his personal liberty in those circumstances expressly provided for by the law.

The case of *Kleyn* has been followed in numerous other cases such as *Mahlatse* 1949 (4) SA 455 (O), *Jones* 1952 (1) SA 327 (E) and *Sotiralis* 1950 (4) SA 481 (T).

In the latter case it was held that it is no defence, when a person fails to give his name and address on demand, to prove that he had been advised by his legal representative to say nothing—cf *Ndara* 1955 (4) SA 182 (A). The legislature has shown the same concern for the personal liberty of an individual as are not entitled to detain a person for more than 12 hours in order to verify a name and address furnished in terms of s 41(1).

5.4.2.2 Powers of private persons

In terms of s 42 a private person may, without a warrant, arrest the following persons:

(1) Any person who commits or attempts to commit in his presence or whom he reasonably suspects of having committed a First Schedule offence; (the private person may pursue that person and any other private person to whom the purpose of the pursuit has been made known, may join and assist therein— s 42(2));

(2) Any person whom he reasonably believes to have committed any offence and to be escaping from and to be hotly pursued by a person whom such private person reasonably believes to have authority to arrest that person for the offence;

(3) Any person whom he is by any law authorised to arrest without warrant in respect of any offence specified in that law. In terms of s 9(1) of the Stock Theft Act 57 of 1959 a private person may, for instance, arrest another without a warrant where there is a reasonable suspicion that the latter has committed any one of certain offences created by the Act;

(4) Any person whom he sees engaged in an affray;
     (The aforementioned grounds of arrest are authorised by s 42(1).)

(5) The owner, lawful occupier or person in charge of property on or in respect of which any person is found committing any offence, and any person authorised thereto by such owner, etc may without a warrant arrest the person so found— s 42(3).

The power conferred upon a private citizen to arrest without a warrant should be exercised sparingly and with great circumspection—cf *Martinus* 1990 (2) SACR 568 (A). The tendency of the courts to protect the liberty of the individual is demonstrated in the case of *Morapedi v Springs Municipality* 1946 TPD 105. Here a municipal constable, on finding the appellants unlawfully in the possession of liquor, endeavoured to effect an arrest but was forcibly resisted. The appellants were charged with and convicted of obstructing the constable in the execution of his duty. The court held that the constable was not a peace officer. Moreover the constable did not have the power to arrest without a warrant as a private person, as this right extended only to offences involving the *supply* of liquor and *not* to *mere possession*.

5.4.2.3 Special statutory powers of certain officials

Section 52 specifically provides that nothing contained in the Act in regard to arrest shall be construed as taking away or diminishing any authority specially conferred by any other law to arrest, detain or place any restraint on any person.

It is impossible to refer to all statutory provisions conferring special powers of arrest on private persons or officials. The following are, however, a few instances:

(1) An officer appointed by the Board of Trustees of National Parks has powers of arrest similar to those of peace officers in terms of the Criminal Procedure Act—s 27(1) of the National Parks Act 57 of 1976.

(2) An officer of a society for the prevention of cruelty to animals may arrest without a warrant any person reasonably suspected of having contravened a provision of the Animal Protection Act 71 of 1962, if there is reason to believe that the ends of justice will be defeated by the delay in obtaining a warrant— s 8(1)*(b)* of Act 71 of 1962.

(3) If the commander of an aircraft in flight has reasonable grounds to believe that a person on board the aircraft has done or is about to do any act which jeopardises the safety of the aircraft or persons on board the aircraft or which in the opinion of the commander is a serious offence under the law in force in the country in which the aircraft is registered, the person may be detained for disembarkation or delivery to a police or immigration officer—s 6 of the Civil Aviation Offences Act 10 of 1972.

5.5 Procedure after arrest

An arrested person has to be brought to a police station as soon as possible after his arrest. The purpose of bringing an arrestee to a police station is to ensure that he is in the custody of the South African Police 'as soon as possible' and that he be detained by the police for a period not exceeding 48 hours. There is no purpose in bringing an arrested person to a police station unless his further detention is entrusted to the police. The custody envisaged by s 50 consists of two periods: the first is that period following the arrest but before the arrival at the police station and the second is that period after he has been brought to the police station. It is the first period which is governed by the words 'as soon as possible'.

Law enforcement officers other than police officials who have the power to arrest in terms of s 40 have no powers of detention in terms of s 50 other than during the first period, that is until the arrested person is brought to a police station. They cannot assume the power of detention (ie the second period) merely because the South African Police cannot or will not exercise its powers of detention— *Mahlongwana v Kwatinidubu Town Council* 1991 (1) SACR 669 (E) (in casu the arrested person was unlawfully detained overnight in the back of a municipal police van because the police cells at the police station were full).

If an arrestee is not released because no charges are to be brought against him (eg where the police discover that he is indeed innocent), he may not be detained for longer than 48 hours unless he is brought before a lower court. This is called the 'first appearance'. The 'first appearance' in terms of s 50(1) normally does not signify the beginning of the arrested person's trial (see Chapter 14 and cf *Minister of Law and Order v Kader* 1991 (1) SA 41 (A)). At this first appearance he may be remanded in custody pending further investigation or for his trial, or be released on bail or on warning.n an alleged offence—eg for not having paid a fine—the court may, at this first appearance, adjudicate upon the cause of the arrest—see *Simango* 1979 (3) SA 189 (T) and *Duncan v Minister of Law and Order* 1984 (3) SA 460 (T). Although a charge need not be put to an accused at his first appearance and he need not plead, it is important that he should know, at least in general terms, why he is being detained—*Ex parte Prokureur-generaal, Transvaal* 1980 (3) SA 516 (T).

If a person is unlawfully arrested, his detention after the arrest will also be unlawful. However, once such person has, in accordance with the provisions of s 50(1), been brought before a court and his further detention has been ordered, the further detention, after the hearing, will be lawful detention, although the suspect will retain his right to institute an action for damages as a result of the unlawful arrest and initial detention—see *Isaacs v Minister van Wet en Orde* 1996 (1) SACR 314 (AD).

The 48-hour period is considerably extended by s 50(1)*(d)*(i)–(iii):

If the 48-hour period expires

(a) on a day which is not a court day, or on any court day after 4 pm (16h00), then the said period is deemed to expire at 4 pm (16h00) on the next court day (this means that if a person is arrested on a Wednesday evening, the 48-hour period is *deemed* to expire the next Monday at 4 pm (16h00));

(b) on any court day before 4 pm (16h00), *then* the said period is deemed to expire at 4 pm (16h00) on such court day;

(c) at a time when the arrestee is outside the area of jurisdiction of the court and he is at such time of expiry *in transit* from the place of detention to the court, then the said period is deemed to expire at 4 pm (16h00) on the next court day after the day on which the arrestee was brought into the court's area of jurisdiction;

(d) or is deemed to expire at a time when the arrestee cannot, because of his *physical illness or other physical condition*, be brought before a court, *then* that court may upon application by the prosecutor order that the arrestee be detained at a place specified by the court (eg a hospital) for such period as the court may deem necessary so that he may recuperate (release on bail or warning, etc may, of course, also be considered—see below) in order to prevent abuse; the application by the prosecutor must set out the circumstances relating to the illness or other condition and must be supported by a certificate from a medical practitioner.

For the purposes of s 50, a 'court day' means a day on which the court in question normally sits as a court—s 50(2).

The court of a district within which the area of a periodical court is situated retains concurrent jurisdiction with the periodical court over such area. If the 48-hour period expires on a day on which the periodical court is not in session, an arrested person ought to be brought before a district court having jurisdiction over the area of the periodical court—*Sias v Minister of Law and Order* 1991 (1) SACR 420 (E); cf s 26 of the Magistrates' Courts Act.

Section 50(3) specifically provides that, subject to subsections (6) and (7), nothing in the section shall be construed as modifying any provisions whereby a person may be released on bail or on a written notice to appear. The police may release certain arrestees even before the 48-hour period lapses—see Chapter 10.

The time limit of 48 hours detention must be strictly observed and any further detention is unlawful. This was held in *Mtungwa* 1931 TPD 466, where an accused escaped from custody after having been arrested without a warrant and after he had been detained for more than 48 hours. The court held that the accused could not be convicted of the crime of escaping from custody.

The 48 hour-rule features prominently in the list of the rights of an arrestee, as guaranteed by the Constitution—see s 35(1)*(d)*, quoted at the beginning of this chapter. The entrenchment of this right in the Constitution emphasises the fact that an arrested person must be brought before a court *as soon as reasonably possible.* Despite the fact that s 50 of the Criminal Procedure Act seems to allow the detention of an arrested person for 48 hours, the Constitution requires that he either be released or be brought before a court as soon as is reasonably possible to do so. This can be explained by means of the following example:

> If X is arrested at 21:00 on a Wednesday evening and the police make such progress with their investigation that, by 24:00 that same evening, they are satisfied that X is innocent and that no charge will be brought against him, X must immediately be released. If the police continue to detain X until the next Monday and release him just before 16:00 on that Monday (when the 48 hours expire), his further detention after 24:00 on that Wednesday evening will be unlawful. Similarly, if the police make such progress with their investigation that, by 24:00 that same Wednesday evening, they are satisfied that they have sufficient evidence to bring a charge against X, X must be taken to court on Thursday. To continue to detain X until the Monday before he is taken to court will mean that his detention after Thursday will be unlawful.

5.5.1 *Detention of unconvicted young persons*

Legislation is presently under consideration which will lay down specific rules with regard to the detention of children, Note that a 'child' is a person below the age of 18 years.

5.6 The effect of an arrest

The effect of a lawful arrest is that the arrestee will be in lawful custody (unless that custody subsequently becomes unlawful, e g as in *Ezekiel's* case (above)) and may be detained until he is lawfully discharged or released—s 39(3). See also *Nhlabathli v Adjunk Prokureur-Generaal, Transvaal* 1978 (3) SA 620 (W).

The fact that an arrest or detention is unlawful will obviously not affect the liability of an accused in so far as the offence is concerned in connection with which he is detained (or has been arrested illegally)—*Esta* 1912 TPD 7. In the case of unlawful detention the detainee may apply to the court for an order for his release. A detainee will obviously be unable to bring such an application himself. Such an application may accordingly be brought on his behalf by an interested person, such as a family member, friend, partner, co-member of a society, church or political party—cf *Wood v Ondangwa Tribal Authority* 1975 (2) SA 294 (A). In such an application the question is whether the person concerned is unlawfully being deprived of his liberty.

In dealing with such an application, uncertainty prevailed whether to apply the principles of the *habeas corpus* remedy of English law or the Roman-Dutch *interdictum de libero homine exhibendo*, especially since in terms of the habeas corpus procedure, the rule existed until recently in English law that a person or interested person against whom an order had been made, could not appeal against such an order. In *Kabinet van die Tussentydse Regering van Suidwes-Afrika v Katofa* 1987 (1) SA 695 (A) at 722E the court held that the principles of *habeas corpus* are not part of South African law, that the principles of the *interdictum de libero homine exhibendo* must apply and that parties against whom such orders have been made, may appeal against them.

The powers and duties of persons authorised by a warrant to arrest another are co-extensive with such powers and duties of a person arresting another without a warrant in the following respects:

(a) the placing of objects found on the arrested person in safe custody;

(b) the general powers necessary for the purposes of effecting an arrest; and

(c) the right to require third persons to assist in the arrest.

5.7 The duty to arrest

As a general rule there is no obligation on a private individual to arrest someone. The exception to this rule is that every male inhabitant of the Republic between the ages of 16 and 60 is, when called upon by a police official to do so, *required* to assist such police official in arresting and detaining a person—s 47(1). Failure to render assistance is an offence punishable by a fine or imprisonment for a period not exceeding three months—s 47(2).

In *Mgwenya* 1925 TPD 288, it was held that lameness may exempt the accused from criminal liability. *Mens rea* has been held to be an element of the crime of contravening this section. In *Lakier* 1934 TPD 250, a detective endeavouring to retain custody of an arrested person requested the accused, L, to assist. L had been called to the scene on information that two white men were fighting. The detective was in plain clothes, but informed L that he was a detective. L refused to assist since he believed that he was being bluffed. The person arrested then said he was willing to accompany the detective and L then realised his mistake and did thereafter render assistance. The court held on appeal that, assuming that there was a presumption of mens rea when L first refused assistance, that presumption was refuted by his explanation and subsequent conduct. L was therefore acquitted.

In order to secure a conviction under s 47, the State must discharge the onus of proving that the police official had authority to effect the arrest—*Rosenthal* 1927 TPD 470.

5.8 Resisting arrest and attempts to flee

5.8.1 *Use of force in effecting an arrest to overcome resistance*

Section 49(1) of the Criminal Procedure Act reads as follows:

'If any person authorised under this Act to arrest or to assist in arresting another, attempts to arrest such person and such person

(a) resists the attempt and cannot be arrested without the use of force; or

(b) flees when it is clear that an attempt to arrest him is being made, or resists such attempt and flees,

the person so authorised may in order to effect the arrest, use such force as may in the circumstances be reasonably necessary to overcome the resistance or to prevent the person concerned from fleeing.'

The onus rests on the arrestor (the person making the arrest) to prove the following:

(1) that he was lawfully entitled to arrest the suspect;

(2) that he attempted to arrest him;

(3) that the suspect attempted to escape by fleeing or offering resistance;

(4) that a degree of force was reasonably necessary to effect the arrest.

(Cf *Van Heerden* 1958 (3) SA 150 (T); *Steenkamp* 1960 (3) SA 680 (N); *Gumbi* 1962 (1) SA 188 (D); *Sambo v Milns* 1973 (4) SA 312 (T).)

'Reasonably' (cf *Van Heerden* (above); *Nell* 1967 (4) SA 489 (SWA) and *Rousseau v Boshoff* 1945 CPD 135) requires an objective approach.

The courts have stressed that an arrestor should not indiscriminately have recourse to force. In *Basson* 1961 (3) SA 279 (T), B, a constable, fired at night at a motor car he had signalled to stop, and wounded one of the passengers. It appeared that the police had been informed of two armed convicts who were fleeing in a stolen Chevrolet motor car. A Ford came past at high speed, and did not react to B and other police officials' signs to stop. B then fired. According to the finding of the court, B did not have reasonable grounds to think that the convicts could be in the Ford. In terms of a Transvaal Ordinance, it was an offence for the driver of a motor vehicle to refuse or fail to stop if instructed to do so by a police officer. The driver of the Ford therefore committed an offence in B's presence. The court held that under certain circumstances it would be lawful to shoot at a motor car in order to arrest persons in that motor car, where the driver had refused or failed to stop. According to the court, however, there is no general power to shoot. The court approved the view that to seriously assault the offender for this type of offence, before he had been informed of the intention to arrest him, and without his having offered resistance or attempted to escape, could not be justified. B was therefore found guilty of assault with intent to commit grievous bodily harm—cf too *Oosthuizen* 1961 (1) SA 604 (T) and *Government of the Republic of South Africa v Basdeo* 1996 (1) SA 355 (A).

In *Martinus* 1990 (2) SACR 568 (A) the Supreme Court of Appeal warns the private citizen to exercise the powers conferred upon him in terms of ss 42 and 49 sparingly and with extreme circumspection. The use of a firearm as a method of exercising force to affect an arrest should be resorted to with great caution. A private citizen contemplating the use of force in terms of s 49(1) should bear in mind that his actions will be judged according to the objective standard of the reasonable man and not according to his own *bona fide* subjective evaluation of the situation.

Regarding police dogs, there are no special statutory provisions regulating their use by the police; accordingly, the general principles set out in this chapter apply *mutatis mutandis*. Where a suspect was bitten by a police dog in the course of being arrested, in circumstances which did not justify the use of such force, damages was awarded—*Jooste NO v Minister of Police* 1975 (1) SA 349 (E). Cf also *Minister van Polisie v Chetty* 1977 (2) SA 885 (A).

Section 49(1) has been substituted by section 7 of the Judicial Matters Second Amendment Act 122 of 1998. Section 7 will be put into operation by proclamation.

5.8.2 *Justifiable homicide*

Section 49(2) of the Criminal Procedure Act provides as follows:

> 'Where a person is to be arrested for an offence referred to in Schedule 1 or is to be arrested on the ground that he is reasonably suspected of having committed such an offence, and the person authorised under this Act to arrest or to assist in arresting him cannot arrest him or prevent him from fleeing by other means than by killing him, the killing shall be deemed to be justifiable homicide.'

By virtue of this section the killing of a person who committed a crime or who is suspected of having committed a crime, is justified. It is a serious matter to kill a person in these circumstances because he may be absolutely innocent. The Criminal Procedure Act accordingly lays down very strict requirements which must be complied with—*Mazeka v Minister of Justice* 1956 (1) SA 312 (A). Where an accused has killed another and claims the protection afforded by s 49(2) the onus is upon him to show on a preponderance of probabilities that the requirements of this section were complied with—*Britz* 1949 (3) SA 293 (A); *Swanepoel* 1985 (1) SA 576 (A). Compare *Arlow* 1960 (2) SA 449 (T). In *Scholtz* 1974 (1) SA 120 (W) at 124 it was pointed out that it is an important aspect of life in a state under the rule of law that the police do not exceed the limits of their powers in terms of s 49(2). (Cf also *Government of the Republic of South Africa v Basdeo* 1996 (1) SA 355 (A).) Accordingly, every facet of police action under s 49(2) must be carefully analysed and measured against the requirements of this section. These requirements are:

(1) The power to kill exists only in respect of specified serious offences, namely those which are mentioned in the First Schedule of the Act.

The First Schedule contains the more serious offences—as well as conspiracy, incitement or attempt to commit these offences—such as treason, sedition, murder, culpable homicide, rape, robbery, arson, fraud, offences—except the offence of escaping from lawful custody in circumstances other than the circumstances referred to below—the punishment for which may be a period of imprisonment exceeding six months without the option of a fine (the Supreme Court of Appeal in *Areff v Minister van Polisie* 1977 (2) SA 900 (A) held that the last-mentioned item does not include common-law crimes) and escaping from lawful custody, where the person concerned is in such custody in respect of any offence referred to in that Schedule or in respect of the offence of escaping from lawful custody.

The protection afforded by s 49(2) relates to serious crimes. It was not the intention of the legislature to allow persons to kill with impunity offenders who flee after the commission of a trivial offence. An interesting situation arose in *Denysschen* 1955 (2) SA 81 (O). The deceased trespassed on the accused's land to hunt hares. The accused had the deceased arrested by an employee of his. The deceased ran away and the accused shot and killed him. Although trespassing on the accused's land was a trivial offence, the accused as owner of the land had the power in terms of the predecessor to s 42(3) to arrest the deceased. However, because it was not a 'First Schedule offence' he could not claim to justify the killing on the ground of that offence. Counsel for the accused argued, however, that escape from arrest is an independent offence in terms of the predecessor to s 51(1) which falls under the First Schedule and which gave the accused the power to re-arrest the deceased. The court upheld this argument and the accused was acquitted.

In *Metelerkamp* 1959 (4) SA 102 (E) the correctness of the decision in *Denysschen's* case was doubted in an *obiter dictum* by De Villiers JP, who expressed the opinion that the legislature could never have intended that if a police official or a private person arrests a person for a trivial offence and such person then runs away, that such police official or private person would then have the power to shoot him. To justify extreme action the original arrest must be an arrest for an offence falling under the First Schedule—cf also *Hartzer* 1933 AD 306 at 309 (also *obiter*). A situation of this nature will, of course, nowadays be dealt with in accordance with the wording of the First Schedule with regard to escaping from lawful custody.

This Schedule lists the following as a First Schedule offence: 'Escaping from lawful custody, where the person concerned is in such custody in respect of any offence referred to in this Schedule or is in such custody in respect of the offence of escaping from lawful custody.' This implies that if a person arrested for a petty offence escapes, he may not be killed. If, however, he is re-arrested and escapes again, he may be killed in terms of s 49(2)—provided, of course, that all the other requirements of that section are met.

(2) Where the person effecting the arrest is doing so on a suspicion, the fugitive must reasonably be suspected of having committed a First Schedule offence. In deciding this, the test is objective, ie the circumstances should be such that a reasonable person would have come to the same conclusion—*Nell* 1967 (4) SA 489 (SWA), Hiemstra 104–5; *Purcell-Gilpin* 1971 (3) SA 548 (RA).

(3) The person who arrests or attempts to arrest—with or without a warrant— must have the power to arrest the offender or to assist in his arrest for such 'First Schedule offence'.

(4) A person who claims protection under s 49(2) must have attempted to arrest the offender—cf *Metelerkamp*. He cannot merely kill without any attempt on his part to arrest the offender. The popular belief that the owner of a house may shoot an offender who has trespassed on his premises and then runs away, after having warned him three times to stop, is erroneous. Such action clearly does not in all circumstances amount to an attempt to arrest.

(5) The person who wishes to avail himself of the protection afforded by the section, must have had the intention to arrest the offender. This means that he must have had the intention of bringing the offender to justice—see *Malindisa* 1961 (3) SA 377 (T). Malindisa had shot and killed a person whom he suspected of having stolen his dagga. He did not have the intention of bringing the accused to justice. He just wanted to get hold of him and deal with him in his own manner. The court held that Malindisa could not rely upon the protection of this section.

(6) The offender must have fled or resisted arrest.

(7) The offender must be aware of the arrestor's intention to arrest him (and be informed thereof) and then flee. The arrestor, therefore, may not take it for granted that the arrestee knows that somebody is attempting to arrest him. In *Barnard* 1986 (3) SA 1 (A) the deceased discovered that he could cause his pickup van to make exploding noises by switching the vehicle's engine on and off whilst driving. One night he tore through the streets of Pietermaritzburg where, shortly before, there had been a terrorist attack on the court building. B, a police official, heard the bangs made by the deceased's vehicle in the vicinity of the court building and hurried over. He was under the impression that terrorists were making their escape in the 'bakkie', gave chase in the police vehicle and fired when the persons in the 'bakkie' failed to react to his signals to stop. The deceased was killed, unaware to the end that he had been pursued. The court held that it must be clear to the person about to be arrested that the arrestor is attempting to arrest him, otherwise it would lead to the untenable result that lesser requirements would be laid down for justifiable homicide than, for

example, a slight wounding within the framework of s 49(1)—cf *Hughes v Minister van Wet en Orde* 1992 (1) SACR 338 (A).

(8) There must be no other means to effect the arrest of the offender. Whether this requirement has been complied with, depends of course upon the facts of each individual case. In *Mazeka's* case Van den Heever JA made this statement:

> 'Where a fit young man of 24 intends to arrest a person much more than ten years his senior, who has only a few yards start and is admittedly not running very fast, where such a young man promptly avails himself of the *ultima ratio legis* without essaying any other means of effecting an arrest—especially where he has information which points to the likelihood of the arrestee being identified, located and arrested—I do not think it is enough for him to say that he thought there were no other means of preventing the escape.'

In *Metelerkamp* De Villiers JP stated that 'as in the case of self-defence, we as the judges of fact, must get out of the armchairs on the Bench and place ourselves in the position of the accused at the time when the conduct complained of took place'. 'Escaping', according to the judge, 'does not mean escaping or getting away for one yard or two yards or just out of a man's clutches. You must bear in mind and consider what the prospects are of the fugitive escaping from justice or of being brought to justice.' Therefore, reasonable action may be taken: '(R)eason is (not) to be disregarded in deciding whether it was possible to arrest the deceased and prevent him from escaping without killing him. What could have been done means what could in reason have been done, having regard to the facts which the killer knew or ought to have known'—*Labuschagne* 1960 (1) SA 632 (A) at 635G and cf *Sambo v Milns* 1973 (4) SA 312 (T) at 317–18.

(9) The force used must of course be directed against the suspected offender. Where A on reasonable grounds suspects B of having committed a 'First Schedule' offence and B is one of the occupants of a vehicle, among whom there may also be innocent persons, A may not shoot indiscriminately at the occupants— *Government of the Republic of South Africa v Basdeo* 1996 (1) SA 355 (A).

Before the enactment of s 49 (as a whole) in its present form, the question, whether the predecessor to s 49(2) applied to a case where only wounding or injury and not death had resulted, arose on more than one occasion. This question was answered in the affirmative in *Hartzer* 1933 AD 306, *Britz* 1949 (3) SA 293 (A), *Oosthuizen* 1961 (1) SA 604 (T), *Mazeka v Minister of Justice* 1956 (1) SA 312 (A), *Nell* 1967 (4) SA 489 (SWA), *Mnanzana* 1966 (3) SA 38 (T), *Tola* 1974 (1) SA 115 (W), and *Sambo v Milns* 1973 (4) SA 312 (T). This question arose because there was no provision similar to the existing s 49(1) which empowered persons to use force which only results in the injury or wounding of a fugitive. The courts accordingly argued that the predecessors to s 49(2) should be interpreted to apply in those instances as well. This view was based on the consideration that the legislature could not have intended that a person who kills a fugitive must be in a more favourable position than one who injures a fugitive; the greater includes the lesser. Contrariwise, the opinion was expressed that one should keep to the wording of the Act ('killing' and 'homicide') and that the predecessor to s 49(2) should not be applied in cases of wounding or injury. Such cases were dealt with in terms of the predecessors to the existing s 39 by arguing that that section, by implication, authorised force (ie wounding or injury) with less strict requirements than in the case of killing. This approach was accepted by implication in *Basson* 1961 (3) SA 279 (T) and was expressly accepted in *V Gumbi* 1962 (1) SA 188 (N)—cf further De Wet in 1966 *THRHR* 351. Since the promulgation of the Criminal Procedure Act, ss 49(1) and 39(1) (above), expressly provide for the use of force in effecting an arrest (although without explicitly referring to wounding or injury) and one may perhaps assume that, in future, our courts will restrict the application of s 49(2) to cases of killing. However, see also *Matlou v Makhubedu* 1978 (1) SA 946 (A).

When police action is not related to arrest in a criminal procedural sense, the police may not rely on s 49. However, the general common-law defences of necessity and self-defence, still remain at their disposal—see textbooks on criminal law and delict, and cf *Chetty* 1977 (2) SA 885 (A) in connection with the use of dogs to control mobs.

For a detailed discussion of the use of force in the course of an arrest by a private person (with reference to ss 39, 42 and 49) see *Macu v Du Toit* 1983 (4) SA 629 (A).

The Constitutional Court has not yet had the opportunity of expressing itself on the constitutionality of the provisions of s 49(2). In *Makwanyane & Another* 1995 (3) SA 391 (CC), the Constitutional Court made an *obiter* remark that the effect of declaring the death penalty unconstitutional, as was done in that case, may necessitate a re-look at s 49(2). The court, however, refrained from expressing itself on the constitutionality of the provision since the question was not before it. Cf also *Raloso v Wilson and Others* 1998 (2) SACR 298 (NC).

Section 49(2) places a severe limitation on several rights protected in the Bill of Rights. These include the right to equality (s 9); the right to life (s 11); the right to freedom and security of the person (s 12); the right of access to the court (s 34); and the right to a fair trial (s 35(3)). Whether s 49(2) in its present form will withstand an attack on its constitutionality, remains to be seen. In order to be held constitutional, it will have to be found to be a limitation permitted in terms of s 36 of the Constitution. It is interesting to note, however, that the South African Police Service has issued instructions to its members in terms of which its members may no longer discharge their firearms at a suspect in order to effect the arrest of the suspect, unless the suspect is suspected of having committed an offence which appears on a list of offences included in the instructions. The list of offences include only the most serious offences and is far more limited than the First Schedule to the Criminal Procedure Act. Offences such as theft (except in certain limited circumstances), fraud, forgery, uttering and malicious injury to property, which are included in the First Schedule, do not figure in the list.

Section 49(2) has been substituted by section 7 of the Judicial Matters Second Amendment Act 122 of 1998. Section 7 will be put into operation by proclamation.

5.9 Escape from lawful custody

The effect of an arrest is that the arrestee is in lawful custody and detained until he is lawfully discharged or released from custody—s 39(3).

Escaping from lawful custody or an attempt thereto is a serious offence. Section 51 of the Criminal Procedure Act provides that any person who, having been arrested and being in lawful custody but not having yet been lodged in any prison, police-cell or lock-up, escapes or attempts to escape from such custody shall be guilty of an offence. Any person who rescues or attempts to rescue from lawful custody any other person who has been arrested, but is not yet lodged in any prison or similar place, or who aids such person to escape, or who harbours or conceals or assists in harbouring or concealing him, is likewise guilty of an offence—cf *Mpanza* 1974 (2) SA 298 (N).

Before an accused may be convicted it is incumbent upon the State to prove that the person who was assisted by the accused to escape, was in lawful custody— *Skwati* 1942 TPD 115; *Kistesamy* 1947 (4) SA 788 (N) and *Ngidi* 1972 (1) SA 733 (N). We have seen that a private person who arrests another must forthwith inform the latter of the reason for the arrest. What is the position now of a person who wants to effect an arrest, touches the body of another and the latter frees himself and runs away before the person arresting him has reasonably had the chance to inform him of the charge? It was held in *September* 1959 (4) SA 256 (C) that in this case too the offender is guilty of escape from lawful custody. The informing of the accused of the reason for the arrest is not part of the arrest itself, according to Bloch J, but something which must be done as soon as is reasonably possible after the arrest has been effected.

5.10   Arrest and detention for interrogation

Section 185 of the Criminal Procedure Act contains important provisions relating to the arrest and detention of certain persons. This form of arrest is not directly intended to bring a suspected offender before a court, and does not strictly fall under the type of arrest which forms the subject of this chapter. But because the section regulates, *inter alia*, arrest without a warrant, it may properly be mentioned here.

6   OTHER METHODS

Apart from the above four methods for securing the attendance of the accused at the trial (specifically mentioned by the Criminal Procedure Act in this regard), there is also the possibility of release on warning in terms of s 72. If an accused is in custody in respect of an offence and a police official or a court may release him on bail under ss 59 or 60, the police official or court may in lieu of bail and with regard to certain offences (cf s 72(1)) release the accused from custody and warn him to appear before a specified court at a specified time on a specified date. If the accused is under the age of eighteen years, he is placed in the care of the person in whose custody he is, and such person is warned to bring the accused to a specified court on a fixed date. A police official who releases an accused in terms of this section must, at the time of the release of the accused, hand to him a written notice on which must be entered the offence, the court before which and the time and date on which the accused must appear. Strictly speaking, therefore, we only deal with an oral warning in cases where the court releases an accused on warning. Section 72 spells out the consequences of an accused's failure to appear, or the failure of the person in whose custody the accused is, to bring him to court.

7   EXTRADITION

Although extradition is, strictly speaking, not a way of securing the attendance of an accused at his trial, it is discussed here since it is a way of ensuring that the accused is handed over to the authorities of another state in order to allow them to take the accused to the court of that state.

This topic will be discussed only in its broadest outline, avoiding detail and technical information.

In terms of international law principles, the government of every sovereign state has exclusive authority over everything happening within the borders of that state. Consequently every state has the right to try crimes committed within its area of jurisdiction. Generally speaking, it has no power to punish persons who have committed crimes in the area of jurisdiction of another (foreign) state.

Therefore, where a person commits a crime in one state and flees to another state and then fails to return of his own accord in an attempt to escape the consequences of his act, the state where the crime was committed is powerless to act. *Extradition* makes provision for such a person to be extradited to the state in whose area of jurisdiction the crime was committed. In this manner criminals are prevented from escaping liability.

States are not obliged to extradite criminals. An obligation to extradite can only come into being in terms of an agreement. A state may, however, if it deems it proper because of mutual ties of friendship, for example, extradite a criminal to a foreign state on that state's request. Nevertheless a state will not easily extradite its own citizens, except in terms of an agreement to do so.

Extradition agreements or treaties usually have certain corresponding principles:

(1) Extradition is granted only in respect of serious crimes or according to the principles of double criminality, in terms of which extradition is granted only in respect of crimes which are punishable in terms of the law of both states.

(2) A person is not extradited to a foreign state if he is charged with a crime of a political nature.

(3) According to the principle of speciality a person is tried in the state to which he is extradited only for the crime in respect of which he has been extradited except if the extraditing state consents to a further new charge.

(4) Extradition is refused if the crime for which extradition is sought, is punishable by the death sentence in terms of the law of the state requesting extradition and if the law of the state to which the request is made, does not make provision for the death sentence for such a crime.

(5) An extradition agreement usually contains a *ne bis in idem* rule which corresponds with pleas of autrefois acquit and autrefois convict.

In South Africa extradition is regulated by the Extradition Act 67 of 1962 which makes provision for the entering into of extradition agreements with foreign states.

The procedure to be followed for the extradition of a person or persons in the Republic is set out in ss 4 to 21 of the Act.

A person whose extradition is requested has to be brought before a magistrate who then conducts an enquiry with a view to the possible extradition of such a person to the state concerned.

In the case of an application by an 'associated state' (ie an African state with which South Africa has an extradition treaty), the magistrate may make an extradition order directly (provided, of course, that all the requirements are present). In the case of a 'foreign' state, the magistrate refers his finding to the Minister of Justice for the latter's decision.

CHAPTER 8

Interrogation, interception and establishing the bodily features of a person.

		Page
1	INTERROGATION	117
1.1	General powers with regard to interrogation	118
1.1.1	Entry to premises to interrogate persons—ss 26–7	118
1.1.2	Obtaining the name and address of a person—s 41	119
1.1.3	Detention for the purposes of interrogation	119
1.2	Powers relating to possible witnesses	120
1.3	Powers relating to suspects and accused	121
2	INTERCEPTION AND MONITORING	121
3	ASCERTAINMENT OF BODILY FEATURES OF ACCUSED	121

The Constitution and this chapter:

Section 10—Human dignity

Everyone has inherent dignity and the right to have their dignity respected and protected.

See 3, below.

Section 12—Freedom and security of the person

(1) Everyone has the right to freedom and security of the person, which includes the right—

    (a) not to be deprived of freedom arbitrarily or without just cause;

    (b) not to be detained without trial;

    . . .

    (e) not to be treated . . . in a cruel, inhuman or degrading way.

(2) Everyone has the right to bodily and psychological integrity, which includes the right—

    . . .

    (b) to security in and control over their body;

    . . .

See 1 and 3, below.

Section 13—Privacy

Everyone has the right to privacy, which includes the right not to have—

. . .

(d) the privacy of their communications infringed

See 2, below.

Section 35—Arrested, detained and accused persons

(1) Everyone who is arrested for allegedly committing an offence has the right—

(a) to remain silent;

. . .

(c) not to be compelled to make any confession or admission that could be used in evidence against that person;

(3) Every accused person has a right to a fair trial, . . .

See 1, below.

1   INTERROGATION

In terms of s 205 of the Constitution, one of the objects of the South African Police Service is to investigate crime.

It sometimes happens that a crime is committed in the presence of the police or that the police arrive at the scene of a crime after the crime has been committed but before it is reported to the police. Normally, however, the police will become aware that a crime has been committed only once the victim or another member of the public reports it to them.

Once the police become aware that a crime has been committed, an important part of their investigation will consist in asking persons questions in order to obtain information relating to the commission or alleged commission of the offence.

If the police become aware of the commission of an offence when someone reports it to them, they will rely on that person to furnish them with information concerning exactly what happened during the alleged commission of the offence. The police will accordingly also ask such person questions and, in the light of his answers, decide how to proceed with the investigation. A person who reports a crime to the police normally does so voluntarily and will, therefore, in most cases be prepared to co-operate with the police and to answer their questions fully.

If the police become aware of the alleged commission of the offence in some other way, they will also interrogate any person that may possibly have information relating to the commission of the offence.

The police do not need any special power to interrogate. Nothing prohibits the police or anyone else from interrogating another person. There is no need, therefore, for any provision providing the police with special powers of interrogation.

The need for special powers arises only when a person refuses to grant the police access to someone they wish to interrogate, refuses to respond to police questioning or answers the questions but refuses to furnish them with his name and address in order to be subpoenaed to testify in court.

Before the powers conferred on the police in this respect are discussed, it is necessary to point out that there is no general legal duty on persons to furnish information that they may have concerning the commission of an offence to the police. It is only in exceptional circumstances that a person will be under such a legal duty. The only common-law offence in respect of which such a legal duty exists is high treason. A person who is aware that someone has committed high treason or plans to do so and who fails to furnish this information to the authorities, will himself be guilty of high treason. In so far as statutory offences are concerned, there are several statutory provisions that require persons who have information relating to specified statutory offences at their disposal, to provide this information to the police. Examples of such provisions are s 10 of the Drugs and Drug Trafficking Act 140 of 1992 and s 7 of the Protection of Information Act 84 of 1982. If a person has information relating to the offences mentioned in these provisions and which he fails to convey to the authorities (even without the police requesting him to do so), such a person will be guilty of an offence. Other statutory provisions provide that a person who, upon the request of the authorities, fails to furnish them with any information that may be at his disposal relating to certain offences, will be guilty of an offence. Examples of such provisions are s 157 of the Liquor Act 27 of 1989 and s 119 of the Road Traffic Act 129 of 1989.

In discussing the special powers of the police with regard to the interrogation of persons, it is necessary to distinguish between those powers of the police to interrogate any person (irrespective of whether such person is a potential witness or the person suspected of having committed the offence), and those powers that may be exercised only with regard to possible witnesses or only with regard to persons suspected of having committed offences.

1.1 General powers with regard to interrogation

1.1.1 *Entry to premises to interrogate persons—ss 26 and 27*

Although the police may question any person regarding an offence that they are investigating, it occasionally happens that the person whom they wish to question is on private premises and the person in charge of the premises refuses to allow the police to enter the premises in order to question him. This may effectively prevent the police from asking the person any questions and thus from obtaining from him any information that he may have. In order to solve this problem, s 26 of the Criminal Procedure Act 51 of 1977 was enacted.

In terms of s 26 a police official may, in the investigation of an offence or alleged offence where he reasonably suspects that a person who may furnish information with regard to any such offence is on any premises, enter such premises without a warrant for the purpose of interrogating such person and obtaining a statement from him. There is, however, the proviso that a police official may not enter any private dwelling without the consent of the occupier thereof.

The reason for the proviso is to prevent a police official from entering a private dwelling without having requested permission to do so. Such conduct may amount to a serious infringement of the privacy of the residents inside such dwelling (see s 14 of the Constitution, quoted above). However, this once again leaves open the possibility that the occupier of the dwelling may refuse the police entry to the premises which may also hamper the police investigation.

In terms of s 27(1), a police official who may lawfully enter any premises under s 26 may use such force as may be reasonably necessary to overcome any resistance against such entry, including the breaking of any door or window of such premises. In terms of a proviso to the subsection, such a police official shall first audibly demand admission to the premises and notify the purpose for which he seeks to enter such premises.

In considering the powers provided for in s 27, it is necessary to draw the attention to s 1 which contains a definition of the word 'premises'. In terms of this definition 'premises' refers not only to land or buildings but also to vehicles, ships and aircraft.

1.1.2 *Obtaining the name and address of a person—s 41*

As will appear from the discussion below, provision has been made to oblige persons who, despite a request to this effect, refuse to furnish the police with information relating to an offence or alleged offence, or to provide the court with this information. Apart from this, provision has also been made for persons who are suspected of having committed certain minor offences, in certain circumstances not to be arrested, but to be brought before the court by means of a summons. However, each of these provisions requires that at least the name and address of the person concerned be known. If a person to whom the aforementioned provisions are applicable, refuses to give his name and address to the police upon their request, he will make it impossible to apply the said provisions to him. To prevent this from taking place, s 41 confers certain powers on peace officers. (All police officials are regarded as peace officers—s 1.)

In terms of s 41(1) a peace officer is given the power to call upon

(a) any person whom he has power to arrest;

(b) any person reasonably suspected of having committed any offence or of having attempted to commit any offence (ie not only offences enumerated in the first schedule of the code); and

(c) any person who may, in his opinion, be able to give evidence in regard to the commission or suspected commission of any offence, to furnish his full name and address.

Furthermore, if such person refuses to furnish his full name and address, the peace officer may forthwith arrest him. If the peace officer reasonably suspects that a false name or address has been given to him, he may arrest such person and detain him for a period not exceeding *twelve hours until the name and address so furnished have been verified.*

The refusal by a person to furnish his or her name and address in the above-mentioned circumstances and the furnishing of an incorrect or false address, constitute offences and are punishable by a fine or imprisonment without the option of a fine for a period of three months—s 41(2).

1.1.3 *Detention for the purposes of interrogation*

In the case of certain serious offences, the legislature has empowered the police to arrest persons and to detain them for the purposes of interrogation. The following is an example of such a provision.

Section 12 of the Drugs and Drug Trafficking Act 140 of 1992 contains drastic powers for the detention of persons for interrogation under warrant issued by a magistrate. These powers exist with regard to persons suspected of having committed drug offences or of having information relating thereto. Such persons may be detained indefinitely, subject to being brought before a magistrate within 48 hours after arrest and thereafter not less than once every 10 days. Where such a detainee appears before a magistrate in terms of s 12(4)*(a)*, he is entitled to legal representation—s 12(4)*(c)* and 12(6)*(a)*(ii).

Section 12 of the Drugs and Drug Trafficking Act 140 of 1992 and all similar provisions constitute limitations on the right not to be detained without trial, which is included in s 12 of the Constitution (quoted above). Furthermore, they constitute a limitation on the right to a fair trial set out in s 35(3) of the Constitution (quoted above). The Constitutional Court has not yet had the opportunity of expressing itself on the constitutionality of any of these provisions. However, it is doubtful whether they will withstand constitutional scrutiny.

1.2 Powers relating to possible witnesses

A judge of the High Court, a regional court magistrate or a magistrate may, upon the request of a director of public prosecutions or public prosecutor, authorised thereto in writing by the director, require the attendance before him or any other judge, regional court magistrate or magistrate, for examination by the director of public prosecutions or the public prosecutor, authorised thereto in writing by the director, of any person who is likely to give material or relevant information as to any alleged offence, whether or not it is known by whom the offence was committed. Provided such person furnishes that information to the satisfaction of the director of public prosecutions or public prosecutor concerned prior to the date on which he is required to appear before the judicial official mentioned, he shall be under no further obligation to appear before such judicial official—s 205(1). Such examination can be conducted privately at any place designated by the judicial official (s 205(3)) and need not be held in court. If such a person should, however, refuse or fail to give the information, he or she shall not be sentenced to imprisonment as contemplated in s 189, unless the judicial official concerned is also of the opinion that the furnishing of such information is necessary for the administration of justice or the maintenance of law and order—s 205(4).

It is not necessary to summon a person to appear; he may be informally requested to appear on a date specified. The advantages of a summons to appear (subpoena) are self-evident—*Matisonn* 1981 (3) SA 302 (A).

Section 205 is specially designed to compel a person to reveal his knowledge of an alleged crime, which knowledge he has refused to disclose to the police.

If such a witness refuses to give the necessary information or refuses to answer the questions, the court may, in a summary manner, enquire into such refusal or failure—s 189. The witness is not obliged to answer self-incriminating questions, except where he has been warned in terms of s 204—Hiemstra 440; *Bosman, Kleinschmidt* 1980 (1) SA 852 (A). Section 205 provides for an examination and does not grant the prosecutor the right to cross-examine the witness. The witness is entitled to legal representation—*Smit v Van Niekerk* 1976 (4) SA 304 (E); *Heyman* 1966 (4) SA 598 (A); Hiemstra 439.

The questioning may take place in private. The following sections with regard to witnesses apply *mutatis mutandis* (cf chapter 15): 162 to 165, 179 to 181, 187 to 189, 191 and 204.

In *Smit v Van Niekerk NO* 1976 (4) SA 293 (A) at 304 it was held that if a witness should refuse to answer a question and thus be required in terms of s 189 to show a 'just excuse' for his refusal, he is entitled to the assistance of a legal adviser. In this case it was held that a clergyman does not have a right to silence. Cf also *Nel v Le Roux* 1996 (3) SA 562 (CC).

No witness however, is obliged to answer self-incriminating questions—s 203.

In terms of s 185, the director of public prosecutions may, in certain specified instances, issue a warrant for the arrest and detention of a potential state witness—see chapter 15.

In *Nel v Le Roux* 1996 (3) SA 562 (CC) the Constitutional Court held that, in principle, s 205 is not inconsistent with the Constitution, although the application thereof in a particular case, may be inconsistent with the Constitution. According to the court, every case will have to be considered on its own merits.

1.3 Powers relating to suspects and accused

In pre-trial criminal procedure, the right to remain silent (set out in s 35(1)*(a)* of the Constitution, quoted above), must be distinguished from the right not to be questioned. Suspects and accused persons have the former right but not the latter. It was held in *Gosschalk v Rossouw* 1966 (2) SA 476 (C) at 490–3 that once the police have lawfully obtained access to a suspect (eg by virtue of lawful arrest or his permission) they may question him within reasonable limits. He is not, however, obliged to answer these questions—*Gosschalk v Rossouw* (above) at 491H and *Weyer* 1958 (3) SA 467 (G) at 470–2. No adverse inference may be drawn from his silence.

2   INTERCEPTION AND MONITORING

The interception of post and private conversations between persons constitute serious infringements of the privacy of individuals. Strict measures were accordingly laid down to maintain the confidentiality of the post and private conversations, and these are reflected in s 14 of the Constitution, in terms of which every person has the right not to be subject to the violation of private communications.

Since the aforementioned measures to protect the confidentiality of communications sent by the post, by telegram or telephone, may hamper the investigation of crime, express provision was made for certain exceptions. These exceptions provide that postal articles which may further the commission of an offence, may afford evidence of the commission of an offence or may prevent the detection thereof, may be detained and, in certain circumstances, be handed over to a public prosecutor—s 118 of the Post Office Act 44 of 1958. Furthermore, provision was made that a judge may issue a mandate to a police official to intercept, examine, listen to and record certain postal articles, telegraphic or telephonic communications, provided the judge is of the opinion that the interception is necessary to investigate a 'serious offence' which cannot be investigated in any other manner—ss 3(1) and 4 of the Prohibition on Interception and Monitoring Act 127 of 1992. The term 'serious offence' is defined in s 1 of the said Act.

3   ASCERTAINMENT OF BODILY FEATURES OF ACCUSED

Section 37 of the Criminal Procedure Act regulates the obtaining of data through the following means: finger-, palm- and foot-printing; conducting identity parades;

ascertaining of bodily features; taking of blood samples and taking of photographs.

In *Huma* 1996 (1) SA 232 (W) the court held that the taking of fingerprints does not violate the accused's right to remain silent or his right to have his dignity being respected and protected.

Note that only suspects or accused persons or convicted persons may be finger-, palm- or foot-printed. Only medical or nursing staff may take blood samples.

In terms of common-law principles, samples of handwriting may also be taken; likewise, a person may be subjected to a 'voice identification parade'. The administering of so-called 'truth serum', however, is impermissible. The courts have laid down extensive guidelines for the conduct of identity parades—cf in general in this regard Hiemstra on s 37. (The evidentiary aspects relating to the matters discussed here are dealt with in textbooks on the law of evidence.)

Finally, s 37 provides for the destruction of data if a person is acquitted or criminal proceedings are not continued.

Section 27 should be approached in view of ss 10 and 12(1) and (2) of the Constitution. Section 10 recognises the right to respect for and protection of the dignity of the individual. Section 12(1) protects the freedom and security of the person and proscribes *degrading treatment* of the individual. Section 12(2) protects the right to security in and control over one's body.

CHAPTER 9

Search and seizure

		Page
1	INTRODUCTION	124
2	ARTICLES THAT ARE SUSCEPTIBLE TO SEIZURE	124
3	SEARCH IN TERMS OF A SEARCH WARRANT	125
	3.1 General rule	125
	3.2 The discretion of a judicial officer to issue a warrant	125
	3.3 General search warrants	126
	3.4 Warrants to maintain internal security and law and order	127
	3.4.1 Background	127
	3.4.2 Warrant in terms of s 25	127
	3.5 General information requirements with regard to warrants	128
4	SEARCH WITHOUT A WARRANT	128
	4.1 Introduction	128
	4.2 Powers of the police	129
	4.2.1 Consent to search and/or to seize	129
	4.2.2 Searches and seizures where a delay would defeat the object thereof	129
	4.2.3 Searches and seizures for the purposes of border control	129
	4.2.4 Search and seizure in a cordoned off area	129
	4.2.5 Search and seizure at a roadblock or checkpoint	130
	4.3 Powers of the occupiers of premises	130
	4.4 Search for the purpose of effecting an arrest	130
	4.5 Review of the actions of the person conducting the search	131
5	SEARCH OF AN ARRESTED PERSON	131
6	THE USE OF FORCE IN ORDER TO CONDUCT A SEARCH	131
7	GENERAL REQUIREMENT OF PROPRIETY WITH REGARD TO SEARCHING	132
8	UNLAWFUL SEARCH	132
	8.1 Formal-law consequences of unlawful action by the authorities	132
	8.2 Substantive-law consequences of unlawful action by the authorities	133
9	DISPOSAL AND FORFEITURE OF SEIZED ARTICLES	133

omit {

The Constitution and this chapter:

Section 12—Freedom and security of the person

(1) Everyone has the right to freedom and security of the person, which includes the right—

. . .

(e) not to be treated . . ., in a cruel, inhuman or degrading way.

(2) Everyone has the right to bodily and psychological integrity, which includes the right—

. . .

(b) to security in and control over their body; . . .

See 1, below.

Section 14—Privacy

Everyone has the right to privacy, which includes the right not to have—

(a) their person or home searched;

(b) their property searched;

(c) their possessions seized; . . .

See 1, below.

Section 35(5)—Exclusionary rule

(5) Evidence obtained in a manner that violates any right in the Bill of Rights must be excluded if the admission of that evidence would render the trial unfair or otherwise be detrimental to the administration of justice.

See 1, below.

1 INTRODUCTION

At the first glance the searching of persons and premises, seizure and related matters seem to go against the spirit and content of ss 12 and 14 of the Constitution, quoted immediately above. However, in terms of s 36 of the Constitution, these rights may be limited by reasonable and justifiable limitations imposed by law of general application. (Section 36 is included in the appendices at the end of this book.) Search, seizure, etc are regulated by chapter 2 (s 19 *et seq*) of the Criminal Procedure Act 51 of 1977.

The Criminal Procedure Act embodies the general provisions with regard to searching; specific provisions are contained in many other Acts. It is impossible to refer to all these Acts. Section 19 of the Criminal Procedure Act states explicitly that chapter 2 of the Act shall not derogate from any power conferred by any other Act to enter any premises or to search any person, container or premises or to seize any matter, to declare any matter forfeited or to dispose of any matter.

2 ARTICLES THAT ARE SUSCEPTIBLE TO SEIZURE

The Criminal Procedure Act confers powers to search only where the object of the search is to find a certain person or to seize an article which falls into one of three classes of articles, including documents, which may be seized by the state in terms of the provisions of the Criminal Procedure Act. These are:

(1) articles which are concerned in or are on reasonable grounds believed to be concerned in the commission or suspected commission of an offence, whether within the Republic or elsewhere;

(2) articles which may afford evidence of the commission or suspected commission of an offence, whether within the Republic or elsewhere; or

(3) articles which are intended to be used or are on reasonable grounds believed to be intended to be used in the commission of an offence—s 20.

Under normal circumstances an article or document falling into one of the abovementioned categories may be seized by the state. The only exceptions relate to documents which are privileged and in respect of which the holder of the privilege has not yet relinquished his privilege. An example of this would be where the document consists of a communication between an attorney and his client. Such a document is subject to legal professional privilege and may not be handed in to the court without the consent of the client. If the state had the power to seize such a document the whole object of the privilege would be defeated. In *Prinsloo v Newman* 1975 (1) SA 481 (A) at 493F–G and *SASOL III (Edms) Bpk v Minister van Wet en Orde* 1991 (3) SA 766 (T) it was accordingly held that such a document may not be seized.

3 SEARCH IN TERMS OF A SEARCH WARRANT

3.1 General rule

Searches and seizures should, whenever possible, be conducted only in terms of a search warrant, issued by a judicial officer such as a magistrate or judge—cf the wording of s 21(1). This will ensure that an independent judicial officer stands between the citizen and the law enforcement official (police official)—*Park-Ross v Director: Office for Serious Economic Offences* 1995 (2) SA 148 (C) (at 172). For this reason the provisions that provide for the issue of search warrants require that the judicial officer must himself decide whether or not there are 'reasonable grounds' for the search.

3.2 The discretion of a judicial officer to issue a warrant

In deciding whether there are reasonable grounds for the search, the judicial officer exercises a discretion similar to the discretions he exercises in granting bail, remanding a case or sentencing an accused, etc. This discretion must be exercised in a judicial manner. This simply means that he must exercise the discretion in a reasonable and regular manner, in accordance with the law and while taking all relevant facts into account—*Ismael v Durban City Council* 1973 (2) SA 362 (N). Before issuing a search warrant he must therefore decide whether the article that will be searched for is one which may be seized in terms of s 20 and whether it appears from the affidavit that there are reasonable grounds to believe that the article is present at a particular place. As far as the concept 'reasonable grounds' is concerned, see the discussion of the requirement of reasonability in Chapter 6.

Government action is required to be objectively and demonstrably reasonable. This laudable principle was unfortunately undermined by the decision in *Divisional Commissioner of SA Police, Witwatersrand Area v SA Associated Newspapers* 1966

(2) SA 503 (A), where it was held that the merits of the decision by a justice of the peace, that there are objective grounds upon which a warrant may be issued, may not be contested in court (contrary to where a search without a warrant is conducted by the police). The decision to issue a search warrant may, in terms of this decision, be set aside only on administrative grounds (such as male fides on the part of the judicial officer) and not on the merits. This decision was quoted with approval in *Cresto Machines v Die Afdeling-Speuroffisier SA Polisie, Noord-Transvaal* 1972 (1) SA 376 (A) 396; cf further *Cine Films (Pty) Ltd v Commissioner of Police* 1971 (4) SA 574 (W) 581.

3.3 General search warrants

The procedure with regard to search warrants is governed by s 21. Subsection (1) provides that, subject to ss 22, 24 and 25 (see below), an article referred to in s 20 shall be seized only by virtue of a search warrant issued

(1) by a magistrate or justice of the peace, if it appears to such magistrate or justice from information on oath that there are reasonable grounds for believing that any such article is in the possession or under the control of any person or upon or at any premises within his area of jurisdiction; or

(2) by a judge or judicial officer presiding at criminal proceedings, if it appears to such judge or judicial officer that any such article in the possession or under the control of any person or upon or at any premises is required in evidence at such proceedings.

Section 21(2) stipulates that a warrant must direct a police official to seize the article in question and must to that end authorise such police official to search any person identified in the warrant, or to enter and search any premises identified in the warrant and to search any person found on or at such premises.

It is an important principle of the law of criminal procedure that a warrant should be strictly interpreted to protect the individual against excessive interference by the state—*National Union of South African Students v Divisional Commissioner South African Police* 1971 (2) SA 553 (C) and *Pogrund* 1974 (1) SA 244 (T).

Even though s 21 does not require that the suspected offence be set out in the warrant, it is desirable to do so in order to facilitate the interpretation of the warrant—cf *Cine Films v Commissioner of Police* (above).

The warrant must clearly define the purpose of the search and the articles that must be seized. A court will find that the judicial officer did not apply his mind properly to the question whether there had been sufficient reason to interfere with the liberty of the individual, if the search warrant only specifies the articles that were supposed to be seized, in broad and general terms—*Smith, Tabata & Van Heerden v Minister of Law and Order* 1989 (3) SA 627 (E). The defect is not cured by an instruction that such a police official must search for documents which 'may' afford evidence of the commission of the crime—cf *Minister of Justice v Desai* 1948 (3) SA 395 (A).

The powers conferred by s 21 constitute grave infringements on the privacy of the individual. To limit this infringement, s 21(3)*(a)* provides that a search warrant must be executed (ie acted upon) by day, unless the judicial officer who issues it, gives written authorisation for it to be executed by night.

A warrant may be issued and be executed on a Sunday, as on any other day, and remains in force until it is executed or is cancelled by the person who issued it or, if such person is not available, by a person with like authority—s 21(3)*(b)*.

3.4 Warrants to maintain internal security and law and order

3.4.1 *Background*

In *Wolpe v Officer Commanding South African Police, Johannesburg* 1955 (2) SA 87 (W) members of the police entered a hall in which a conference was being held by the 'South African Congress of Democrats' in co-operation with other organisations. The chairman requested the police to leave the meeting and explained that it was a private meeting. The police refused to do so. Members of the Congress of Democrats thereupon brought an urgent application to the court for an interdict prohibiting the police from attending the meeting. They argued that the police do not have greater powers than any other individual, except in so far as they are vested with wider powers by statute. The application was refused. Rumpff J held that the basic duties of the police are not confined to those mentioned in statutes. The basic duties of the police flow from the nature of the police as a civil force in the state. According to him it was not the intention of the legislature by s 7 of the (previous) Police Act to revoke the basic duties of the police and to supplant them with statutory duties. The judge dealt fully with the duties of the police and came to the conclusion that if there were a suspicion that as a result of the holding of a meeting, a disturbance of public order would occur on the same day, the police are entitled to attend the meeting in order to prevent a disturbance of order, even though the meeting was private. If the police had reasonable grounds for suspecting that seditious speeches would be made at such meeting, and that their presence would prevent them from being made, it would be a reasonable exercise of their duty for the police to attend the meeting, notwithstanding the fact that there would be no immediate disturbance of the peace. According to Rumpff J the liberty of the individual must in such circumstances give way to the interests of the state. He suggested, however, that the legislature should define the duties and powers of the police in connection with the combating of what the state from time to time considered to be dangerous.

This eventually led to the inclusion of s 25 in the Criminal Procedure Act.

3.4.2 *Warrant in terms of s 25*

Section 25(1) stipulates that if it appears to a magistrate or justice from information on oath that there are reasonable grounds for believing

(a) that the internal security of the Republic or the maintenance of law and order is likely to be endangered by or in consequence of any meeting which is being held or is to be held in or upon any premises within his area of jurisdiction; or

(b) that an offence has been or is being or is likely to be committed or that preparations or arrangements for the commission of any offence are being or are likely to be made in or upon any premises within his area of jurisdiction he may issue a warrant authorising a police official to enter the premises in question at any reasonable time for the purpose

  (i) of carrying out such investigations and of taking such steps as such police official may consider necessary for the preservation of the internal security of the Republic or for the maintenance of law and order or for the prevention of any offence;

(ii) of searching the premises or any person in or upon the premises for any article referred to in s 20 and which such police official on reasonable grounds suspects to be in or upon or at the premises or in the possession or under the control of such person; and

(iii) of seizing any such article.

A warrant under subsect (1) may be issued on any day and shall remain in force until it is executed or is cancelled by the person who issued it or, if such person is not available, by a person with like authority—subsec (2).

A warrant issued in terms of s 25(1) confers wide powers on the police. The fact that a police official who acts in terms thereof may take any steps that he 'consider[s] necessary' for the preservation of the internal security of the Republic or for the maintenance of law and order or for the prevention of any offence, means that the police official's discretion in this respect will have to be considered *subjectively*. The question will therefore not be whether the steps he took were *really* necessary, but whether he subjectively thought that he had reason to believe that they were necessary.

3.5 General information requirements with regard to warrants

When law enforcement officials act in terms of a warrant, it is desirable that the subject involved has access to the document which infringes upon his private rights. The effective execution of legal remedies, eg an interdict, or even the institution of the *rei vindicatio* is, to a large extent, dependent thereon. Section 21(4) therefore stipulates that a police official who executes a warrant in terms of ss 21 or 25 must, once the warrant has been executed and upon the request of any person whose rights are affected by the search or seizure of an object in terms of the warrant, provide such a person with *a copy of the warrant*. We are of the opinion that two objections may be raised against this subsection which is laudable in other respects. In the first place a copy of the warrant should, whenever possible (ie if the subject is present at the time of the execution of the warrant), be provided *before* the search and/or seizure. Secondly, the delivery of a copy of the warrant should not be dependent on the *request* of the subject. Many subjects, through lack of knowledge of the law, will not make such a request and thus act to their potential detriment.

4 SEARCH WITHOUT A WARRANT

4.1 Introduction

Although it is preferable, as mentioned above, that searches should only be conducted on the authority of a search warrant issued by a judicial officer, it is quite conceivable that circumstances may arise where the delay in obtaining such warrant would defeat the object of the search. It is therefore necessary that provision be made for the power to conduct a search without a warrant.

While search warrants empower only police officials to conduct searches and to seize objects, both private persons and police officials are empowered to conduct searches or to seize objects without a warrant.

4.2 Powers of the police

4.2.1 *Consent to search and/or to seize*

In terms of s 22*(a)* a police official may search any person, container or premises for the purpose of seizing any article referred to in s 20, if the person concerned *consents* to the search for and the seizure of the article in question, or if the person who may consent to the search of the container or premises *consents* to such search and the seizure of the article in question.

4.2.2 *Searches and seizures where a delay would defeat the object thereof*

In terms of s 22*(a)* a police official may search any person, container or premises for the purpose of seizing any article referred to in s 20, if the police official believes, on reasonable grounds,

(1) that a search warrant will be issued to him under s 21(1)*(a)* if he applies for such warrant; and

(2) that the delay in obtaining such warrant would defeat the object of the search.

The belief of the police official must be objectively justified on the facts— *Mayekiso en Andere* 1996 (2) SACR 298 (C).

Section 25(3) allows a police official to act without a warrant if he believes, on reasonable grounds,

(1) that a warrant will be issued to him under s 25(1)*(a)* or *(b)* if he applies for such warrant; and

(2) that the delay in obtaining such warrant would defeat the object thereof.

A police official's powers in terms of s 25(3) are the same as the powers he would have had by virtue of a warrant (cf (i) to (iii) above and *Boshoff* 1981 (1) SA 393 (T).)

Certain objections to s 25 are discussed in chapter 1.

4.2.3 *Searches and seizures for the purposes of border control*

Section 13(6) of the South African Police Service Act 68 of 1995, empowers a police official to, for the purposes of border control or to control the import or export of any goods, without a warrant search any person, premises, other place, vehicle, vessel, ship, aircraft or any receptacle of whatever nature, at any place in the Republic within ten kilometres or any reasonable distance from any border between the Republic and any foreign state, or from any airport or at any place in the territorial waters of the Republic or inside the Republic within ten kilometres from such territorial waters and seize anything found upon such person or upon or at or in such premises, other place, vehicle, vessel, ship, aircraft or receptacle which may lawfully be seized.

4.2.4 *Search and seizure in a cordoned off area*

The National or a Provincial Commissioner of the South African Police Service may, in terms of s 13(7) of the South African Police Service Act 68 of 1995, where it is reasonable in the circumstances in order to restore public order or to ensure the safety of the public in a particular area, authorise that the particular area or any part thereof be cordoned off. This is done by issuing a written authorisation which must also set out the purpose of the cordoning off. Any member of the Service may, in order to achieve the purpose set out in the authorisation, without a warrant, search any person, premises, vehicle or any receptacle or object of whatever nature in that area and seize any article referred to in s 20 of the Criminal Procedure Act found by him or her upon such person or in that area: Provided that a member executing a search in terms of s 13(7), must, upon demand of any person whose rights are or have been affected by the search or seizure, exhibit to him or her a copy of the written authorization by such commissioner.

4.2.5 *Search and seizure at a roadblock or checkpoint*

The National or a Provincial Commissioner of the South African Police Service may, in terms of s 13(8) of the South African Police Service Act 68 of 1995, where it is reasonable in the circumstances in order to exercise a power or perform a function of the Service, in writing authorise a member under his or her command, to set up a roadblock or roadblocks on any public road in a particular area or to set up a checkpoint or checkpoints at any public place in a particular area. Any member of the Service may, without a warrant, search any vehicle and any person in or on such vehicle at such a roadblock or checkpoint and seize any article referred to in s 20 of the Criminal Procedure Act found by him or her upon such person or in or on such vehicle. A member executing a search in terms of s 13(8), must, upon demand of any person whose rights are or have been affected by the search or seizure, exhibit to him or her a copy of the written authorization by such commissioner.

Section 13(8)*(d)* authorises any member of the Service to set up a roadblock on a public road without a written authorisation in certain specified circumstances where the delay in obtaining a written authorisation will defeat the object with the setting up of the roadblock.

4.3 Powers of the occupiers of premises

In terms of s 24 of the Criminal Procedure Act any person who is lawfully in charge or occupation of any premises and who reasonably suspects that

(1) stolen stock or produce, as defined in any law relating to the theft of stock or produce, is on or in the premises concerned, or that

(2) any article has been placed thereon or therein or is in the custody or possession of any person upon or in such premises in contravention of any law relating to

  (a) intoxicating liquor,

  (b) dependence-producing drugs,

  (c) arms and ammunition, or

  (d) explosives,

may at any time, if a police official is not readily available, enter such premises for the purpose of searching such premises and any person thereon or therein, and if any such stock, produce or article is found, he shall take possession thereof and forthwith deliver it to a police official.

4.4 Search for the purpose of effecting an arrest

In the event of a search of premises in order to find and arrest a suspect, exactly the same powers are conferred on police officials and private persons.

In terms of s 48, a peace officer or private person who is authorised by law to arrest another in respect of any offence and who knows or reasonably suspects such other person to be on any premises, may, if he first audibly demands entry into such premises and states the purpose for which he seeks entry and fails to gain entry, break open and enter and search such premises for the purpose of effecting the arrest.

A number of court decisions on the forerunner of s 48 still apply to s 48. These include the following: In *Jackelson* 1926 TPD 685 it was held that persons who had ejected a police official who had entered premises without first demanding and being refused admission, could not be convicted of obstructing such police official in the execution of his duty. In *Rudolf* 1950 (2) SA 522 (C) a police official had seen a man drinking wine in a public place and wished to arrest him. The man ran into a house pursued by the constable and was arrested at the foot of the stairs. The two accused attempted to rescue the wine-drinker from the custody of the police official. It was contended, *inter alia*, that the wine-drinker had not been in 'lawful custody' because the police official had made an unlawful entry when he entered the premises without first demanding admission in terms of the predecessor to the present s 48. The court held, however, that the constable had been justified, in the circumstances of the case, in entering the house to arrest the wine-drinker and consequently the arrest was a lawful one. The court distinguished *Jackelson* mainly on the ground that the accused in *Jackelson* had ejected the constable before he had effected an arrest, while in *Rudolf* the arrest had been effected when the accused attempted to rescue the wine-drinker—cf also *Andresen v Minister of Justice* 1954 (2) SA 473 (W).

4.5 Review of the actions of the person conducting the search

In cases where action is taken *without* a warrant, the actions of the person conducting the search may be reviewed by a court of law on the merits—cf eg *LSD Ltd v Vachell* 1918 WLD 127.

5 SEARCH OF AN ARRESTED PERSON

This matter is governed by s 23. That section provides that on the arrest of any person, the person making the arrest may, provided that he is a peace officer, search the person arrested and seize any article referred to in s 20 which is in the possession or under the control of the arrested person.

If the person making the arrest is not a peace officer he has no power to search the arrested person. He does, however, have the power to seize an article referred to in s 20 which is in the possession or under the control of the arrested person. Such a private person must forthwith hand the seized article to a police official. (This also applies to a peace officer who is not a police official.)

On the arrest of any person, the person effecting the arrest may place in safe custody any object found on the arrested person and which may be used to cause bodily harm to himself or others—s 23(2).

6 THE USE OF FORCE IN ORDER TO CONDUCT A SEARCH

The use of force is regulated by s 27 as far as this chapter is concerned.

In terms of s 27(1), a police official who may lawfully search any person or any premises may use such force as may be reasonably necessary to overcome any resistance against such search or against entry of the premises, including the breaking of any door or window of such premises.

In terms of a proviso to this subsection, such a police official shall first audibly demand admission to the premises and state the purpose for which he seeks to enter such premises. This proviso does not apply where the police official concerned is, on reasonable grounds, of the opinion that any article which is the subject of the search may be destroyed or disposed of if the proviso is first complied with—s 27(2). The latter is known as the 'no-knock clause' and is particularly helpful to the police where the search will be for small objects which may easily be swallowed or flushed down a toilet.

7   GENERAL REQUIREMENT OF PROPRIETY WITH REGARD TO SEARCHING

Section 29 stipulates that a search of any person or premises shall be conducted with strict regard to decency and order, and a woman shall be searched by a woman only, and if no female police official is available, the search shall be made by any woman designated for the purpose by a police official.

In order to comply with the requirement of propriety in terms of s 29, it can certainly be assumed, in terms of the general principles of the interpretation of statutes, that a male person should be searched by a male only. We suggest that any divergence from these provisions would be unlawful and that 'consent' by the person being searched to this divergence would be invalid as it would be *contra bonos mores*.

8   UNLAWFUL SEARCH

The provisions of the law of criminal procedure which regulate searching are 'double-functional': from a substantive law viewpoint they constitute grounds of justification, while in formal law they regulate the procedural steps whereby an eventual legal decision may validly be reached. In the latter case the principle of legality (cf chapter 1) and the concept 'legal guilt' are of paramount importance in that, unless a 'factually guilty' person can be brought to justice within the bounds of the provisions of the law of criminal procedure (ie in strict compliance with the prescribed rules and limitations), he must, according to law, go free—(see Chapter 1).

The question now arises as to what the effect is of unlawful action by the authorities with regard to these pre-trial procedural rules. As these provisions are double-functional, it is necessary to differentiate between the substantive and formal law consequences:

8.1   Formal-law consequences of unlawful action by the authorities

In terms of s 35(5) of the Constitution, evidence obtained in a manner that violates any right in the Bill of Rights must be excluded if the admission of that evidence would render the trial unfair or otherwise be detrimental to the administration of justice.

This so-called 'exclusionary rule' gives a clear signal to all state officials that it is futile to gather evidence in an unlawful manner, since evidence so obtained will not be taken into account by the court in reaching a verdict. (Cf *Motloutsi* 1996 (1) SA 584 (C) and *Mayekiso en Andere* 1996 (2) SACR 298 (C).)

The exclusionary rule is discussed in more detail in handbooks dealing with the law of evidence and was briefly dealt with in Chapter 1.

8.2 Substantive-law consequences of unlawful action by the authorities

This aspect is governed partly by s 28. In terms of subsec (1) a police official commits an offence and is liable on conviction to a fine or to imprisonment for a period not exceeding six months:

(1) when he acts contrary to the authority of a search warrant issued under s 21 or a warrant issued under s 25(1); or

(2) when he, without being authorised thereto,

  (a) searches any person or container or premises or seizes or detains any article; or

  (b) performs any act contemplated in s 25(1).

Subsection (2) stipulates that where any person falsely gives information on oath for the purposes of ss 21(1) or 25(1) and a warrant is issued and executed on such information, and such person is in consequence of such false information convicted of perjury, the court convicting such person may, upon the application of any person who has suffered any damage in consequence of the unlawful entry, search or seizure, or upon the application of the prosecutor acting on the instructions of such a person, award compensation in respect of such damage, whereupon the provisions of s 300 shall mutatis mutandis apply with reference to such award. (Section 300 is fully dealt with in Chapter 19.)

Even a *police official* who is held criminally liable in terms of s 28(1) is also subject to such an order for compensation.

9 DISPOSAL AND FORFEITURE OF SEIZED ARTICLES

Sections 30 to 36 of the Criminal Procedure Act provide in detail for the disposal and forfeiture of seized articles.

A police official who seizes any article referred to in s 20 or to whom any such article is delivered in accordance with the provisions of the Criminal Procedure Act, has various powers relating to the disposal thereof. Normally such an article will be kept in police custody and, if required for criminal proceedings, will be handed to the clerk of the magistrate's court or registrar of the High Court for safe custody.

At the conclusion of the criminal proceedings the presiding judicial officer must make an appropriate order in respect of the disposal of the article (cf s 34(1))—eg that it should be returned to the person entitled thereto, or that it be forfeited to the state.

If no criminal proceedings are instituted in connection with a seized article, or if it appears that such an article is not required for purposes of evidence or for purposes of an order of court, the article shall be returned to the person from whom it was seized (if he may lawfully possess it) or, if he may not lawfully possess it, it shall be returned to the person who may lawfully possess it—s 31(1)*(a)*. If no person may lawfully possess the article or if the police do not know of any person who may lawfully possess it, the article is forfeited to the state—s 31(1)(b). A person who may lawfully possess the article, must be notified that he may take possession of the article and if he fails to take delivery thereof within thirty days, it shall be forfeited to the state—s 31(2).

If the owner of a stolen object which has been seized fails to lay claim to it after he has been informed of its recovery, he has to be considered to have abandoned his rights of ownership. The object is therefore no longer regarded as stolen property and may then be restored to the person from whom it was forfeited, if he bought it from another. The former person is then considered as 'the person who may lawfully possess it'—*Mdunge v Minister of Police* 1988 (2) SA 809 (N); *Datnis Motors (Midlands) (Pty) Ltd v Minister of Law and Order* 1988 (1) SA 503 (N).

After the conviction of an accused, the court has, in terms of s 35(1) and in certain circumstances, the power to forfeit to the state certain objects which were used in the commission of the particular crime. Section 36 deals with the circumstances under which, and the manner in which articles may be delivered to the police of another country.

There are also various other laws which make provision for the forfeiture of articles, eg the Liquor Act 27 of 1989; the Drugs and Drug Trafficking Act 120 of 1992.

Restitution should be distinguished from forfeiture. Restitution is dealt with in Chapter 19.

CHAPTER 10

Bail and other forms of release

		Page
1	INTRODUCTION	137
	1.1 The effect of bail	137
	1.2 The constitutional right to bail and the need for and nature of bail as a method of securing liberty pending the outcome of a trial	137
	1.3 Bail and some fundamental principles of criminal justice	138
2	BAIL GRANTED BY POLICE BEFORE FIRST COURT APPEARANCE OF ACCUSED	139
	2.1 Introduction	139
	2.2 Procedure concerning police bail	139
	2.3 Police bail: the limitations	140
	2.4 The discretion	140
3	BAIL GRANTED BY PROSECUTION	140
4	BAIL APPLICATIONS IN COURT	141
	4.1 General provisions	141
	4.2 The provisions of s 50(6)	141
	4.3 Appeal by accused to High Court against a lower court's decision concerning bail	142
	4.4 Appeal by director of public prosecutions against decision of court to release accused on bail	143
	4.5 The High Court: power to regulate bail matters where statutes are silent	143
5	THE RISKS AND FACTORS WHICH MUST BE CONSIDERED IN DETERMINING A BAIL APPLICATION	144
	5.1 The potential risks	144
	5.2 When is the refusal of bail in the interests of justice?	144
	5.2.1 The ground in s 60(4)*(a)*: factors which the court may consider (s 60(5))	144
	5.2.2 The ground in s 60(4)*(b)*: factors which the court may consider (s 60(6))	145
	5.2.3 The ground in s 60(4)*(c)*: factors which the court may consider (s 60(7))	146

5.2.4   The ground in s 60(4)*(d)*: factors which the court may
        consider (s 60(8))   146

5.2.5   The ground in s 60(4)*(e)*: factors which the court may
        consider (s 60(8A))   147

5.2.6   The interests of justice and the personal freedom of and
        possible prejudice to an accused (s 60(9))   147

5.2.7   Additional factors to be considered in a bail application
        pending an appeal against conviction or sentence   147

5.2.8   The amount of bail   148

5.2.9   Some irrelevant factors   148

6   BAIL CONDITIONS   148

7   PAYMENT OF BAIL MONEY   149

8   CANCELLATION OF BAIL AND FORFEITURE OF BAIL
     MONEY   150

8.1   Failure to observe conditions of bail   150

8.2   Failure to appear: procedure and consequences   150

8.3   Cancellation of bail where accused about to abscond   151

8.4   Cancellation of bail at request of accused   151

8.5   Forfeiture and remission   151

8.6   Criminal liability on the ground of failure to appear or to comply
      with a condition of bail   152

9   PROCEDURAL AND EVIDENTIARY RULES RELATING TO
     BAIL APPLICATIONS   152

9.1   The pro-active (inquisitorial) role of the court   152

9.2   Application of a free system of evidence   153

9.3   Proof of previous convictions   153

9.4   The subsequent trial and the admissibility of the record of bail
      proceedings   154

9.5   The relationship between s 60(11B)*(c)* and s 235   155

9.6   Access to information held by the prosecution   155

9.7   The burden and standard of proof in bail applications   156

9.8   The provisions of s 60(11)*(a)* and s 60(11)*(b)*   156

9.9   The meaning of 'exceptional circumstances' as used in s 60(11)*(a)*   157

10   RELEASE OTHER THAN ON BAIL   158

10.1 Release of juvenile accused   158

10.2 Release on warning   158

The Constitution and this chapter:

Section 35(1)*(f)*

(This section is quoted in full in 1.2 below.)

1 INTRODUCTION

1.1 The effect of bail

When bail is granted, an accused who is in custody shall be released from custody upon payment of, or the furnishing of a guarantee to pay the sum of money determined for his bail—s 58. He must then appear at the place and on the date and at the time appointed for his trial, or to which the proceedings relating to the offence in respect of which the accused is released on bail are adjourned—s 58. His release shall, unless sooner terminated under certain circumstances, endure until a verdict is given by a court in respect of the charge to which the offence in question relates, or, where sentence is not imposed forthwith after conviction and the court in question extends bail, until sentence is imposed—s 58. However, s 58 contains a proviso to the effect that where a court convicts an accused of an offence contemplated in Schedule 5 or 6, the court shall—in considering the question whether the accused's bail should be extended pending imposition of sentence—apply the provisions of s 60(11)(a) or s 60(11)(b), as the case may be, and the court shall take into account (a) the fact that the accused has been convicted of an offence referred to in Schedule 5 or 6, and (b) the likely sentence which the court might impose. Schedules 5 and 6 are cited in the appendix to this work; and the provisions of s 60(11)(a) and s 60(11)(b) are discussed in paras 9.7, 9.8 and 9.9 below.

An accused's failure to appear in court or to comply with any of the other conditions of his bail, may ultimately result in cancellation of bail, forfeiture of bail money to the state and the re-arrest of the accused. Failure to appear in court or to comply with a specific condition of bail, is also a criminal offence punishable by a fine or imprisonment not exceeding one year—s 67A. See further para 8.6 below.

1.2 The constitutional right to bail and the need for and nature of bail as a method of securing liberty pending the outcome of a trial

The need for a 'mechanism' such as bail must be understood in the light of the following:

(1) Everyone who is arrested for allegedly committing an offence has the right to be released from detention if the interests of justice permit, subject to reasonable conditions—s 35(1)(f) of the Constitution. In the Constitutional Court case *S v Dlamini; S v Dladla & others; S v Joubert; S v Schietekat* 1999 (2) SACR 51 (CC)—and hereafter cited as '*Dlamini etc*'—the following observation was made in para [6] of the judgment:

> '[Section] 35(1)(f) postulates a judicial evaluation of different factors that make up the criterion of interests of justice, and . . . the basic objective traditionally ascribed to the institution of bail, namely to maximise personal liberty, fits snugly into the normative system of the Bill of Rights.'

(2) An accused is, in the absence of a conviction by a court of law, also constitutionally presumed to be innocent. See s 35(3)(h) of the Constitution. There is an obvious area of tension between this presumption and deprivation of liberty pending the verdict of a court of law. Bail is a method of securing a compromise. In *Acheson* 1991 (2) SA 805 (Nm) at 822A–B Mahomed J said:

> 'An accused cannot be kept in detention pending his trial as a form of anticipatory punishment. The presumption of the law is that he is innocent until his guilt has been established in Court. The Court will therefore ordinarily grant bail to an accused person unless this is likely to prejudice the ends of justice.'

(3) It has been said that the purpose of bail is to strike a balance between the
interests of society (the accused should stand his trial and there should be no
interference with the administration of justice) and the liberty of an accused
(who, pending the outcome of his trial, is presumed to be innocent)—Du Toit
et al 9–1. See also *S v C* 1998 (2) SACR 721 (C) where Conradie J also referred
to the relevance of s 12(1)*(a)* of the Constitution which provides:

> 'Everyone has the right to freedom and security of the person, which includes the right
> . . . not to be deprived of freedom arbitrarily or without just cause. . . .'

(4) The legislature has determined that the refusal to grant bail shall be in the
interests of justice where one or more of the grounds referred to in s 60(4)*(a)* to
s 60(4)*(e)* are established—see the discussion of s 60(4) in para 5.2 below.

(5) The whole issue turns on what is in the best interests of justice. Obviously, it is
not in the best interests of justice to grant bail to an accused who will not stand
his trial or who might otherwise abuse his liberty pending verdict, for example,
by intimidating State witnesses. However, it must be appreciated that it is also
not in the best interests of justice to refuse bail to an accused who will stand his
trial and who will not otherwise interfere with the administration of justice. See
C above. In (1967) 27 *Maryland Law Review* 154 at 166 some of the
disadvantages of being deprived of liberty pending the outcome of a trial, were
put as follows:

> 'The . . . accused who . . . is presumed to be innocent, is subject to the punitive aspect
> of detention. The effect of remaining incarcerated will probably result in the loss of his
> job, of his respect in the community . . . even if [later] acquitted. In addition, the
> [accused's] defense [sic] is put to a serious handicap. He will not be free to help locate
> important witnesses. He will not have the opportunity to frequently contact his
> attorney. And if detention had resulted in the loss of the [accused's] job, he may not be
> able to even retain an attorney. The [accused] who is denied the right to bail will feel
> that effect at the most important level of criminal procedure—at the trial level. . . .'

In para [101.15] in *Dlamini etc* as referred to in para 1.2(1) above, the
Constitutional Court said:

> 'Bail serves not only the liberty interest of the accused, but the public interest by
> reducing the high number of awaiting-trial prisoners clogging our already over-
> crowded correctional system, and by reducing the number of families deprived of a
> breadwinner.'

1.3 Bail and some fundamental principles of criminal justice

Bail is non-penal in character—*Acheson* 1991 (2) SA 805 (Nm). See also generally
S v Stanfield 1997 (1) SACR 221 (C) 233*g–i* and *C* 1998 (2) SACR 721 (C). Neither
the amount determined for bail nor the refusal of bail may therefore be influenced by
punitive notions, for example, to punish the alleged offender or to deter other
possible offenders—*Visser* 1975 (2) SA 342 (C). In terms of s 60(5)*(f)* the court
may, however, consider the prevalence of a particular type of offence.

It is undesirable that an accused person should be deprived of pre-trial liberty if
the sentence likely to be imposed will be in the form of a fine or one other than
imprisonment—*Moeti* 1991 (1) SACR 462 (B) at 463H.

Each case must be considered on its merits. The prosecutor must make an
independent assessment of the case and ought not blindly to follow the police's
recommendation that bail should be refused—*Hlopane* 1990 (1) SA 239 (O) at 242.

The court, too, should not act as a mere 'rubber stamp' in confirming the viewpoint of the police and prosecution—*Visser* 1975 (2) SA 342 (C).

Release on bail is not a substitute for an accused's right to be brought to trial within a reasonable period—Du Toit *et al* 9–3.

The issue concerning release on or refusal of bail, should not be used as an inducement to obtain a statement from an accused—*Joone* 1973 (1) SA 841 (C) at 846H.

A court must inform an unrepresented accused of his right to apply for bail, as well as the nature of the procedure to be followed—*Ngwenya* 1991 (2) SACR 520 (T); Steytler 1982 *SACC* 3–17. See also s 60(1)*(c)*.

In *Sibeko* 1990 (1) SACR 206 (T) a magistrate who had earlier recorded an out-of-court confession of an accused, also presided at the bail application of the accused. Kriegler J held that this had constituted a gross irregularity nullifying the proceedings. A bail application is—like a trial—also governed by principles regulating the recusal of a presiding officer. Recusal is dealt with in Chapter 13.

2 BAIL GRANTED BY POLICE BEFORE FIRST COURT APPEARANCE OF AN ACCUSED

2.1 Introduction

The question whether bail should be refused or granted is essentially a judicial one, that is, one that must in principle be determined by a court of law—*Ramgobin* 1985 (4) SA 130 (N). However, bail may in certain limited circumstances be granted by the police—s 59. This kind of bail is in practice (and hereinafter) referred to as 'police bail'. Its purpose is not to oust a judicial decision but to ensure that pre-trial release on bail can in respect of relatively trivial offences be secured as soon as possible—that is, even before the first appearance in a lower court. At any rate, if police bail cannot be granted in terms of s 59 or if it can be granted but is refused, an accused has every right to apply to a lower court for bail even before his first compulsory appearance as required in terms of s 50—see para 3(2) below and the discussion of s 50 in Chapter 7. Bail granted by the prosecution pending an accused's first appearance in court, is also possible. See further the discussion of s 59A in para 3 below.

2.2 Procedure concerning police bail

An accused who is in custody in respect of any offence, other than an offence referred to in Part II or Part III of Schedule 2, may be released on bail in respect of such offence by any police official of or above the rank of non-commissioned officer, if the accused deposits at the police station the sum of money determined by such police official—s 59(1)*(a)*. Schedule 2 is cited in the appendix to this work. The police official who has the power to determine police bail is, however, statutorily required to consult with the police official charged with the investigation, ie, the so-called 'investigating officer'—s 59*(a)*. The police official concerned must, at the time of releasing the accused on bail, complete and hand to the accused a recognizance on which a receipt shall be given for the sum of money deposited as bail and on which the offence in respect of which the bail is granted and the place, date and time of the trial of the accused are entered—s 59(1)*(b)*. The police official must forthwith forward a duplicate original of such recognizance to the clerk of the court which has jurisdiction—s 59(1)*(c)*.

The police must grant an accused a reasonable opportunity to communicate with his legal representative, family or friends in order to obtain the amount fixed as police bail.

2.3 Police bail: the limitations

Only cash payments can be received in payment of police bail. Sureties cannot be accepted.

Release on police bail can only take place before an accused's first appearance in a lower court—s 59(1)*(a)*. This limitation is essential in order to ensure that courts remain in direct and exclusive control over release on bail once the case is on the roll.

Discretionary special conditions (these are conditions other than the essential bail conditions concerning appearance in court on a specific time and date and at a specific venue) as provided for in s 62, cannot be added by the police when releasing an accused on police bail—see Van der Berg *Bail—A Practitioner's Guide* (1986) 29. However, a court of law may upon a prosecutor's application add special conditions to police bail—s 59(2) as read with s 62 which is discussed in para 5 below. In other respects, police bail shall, if it is in force at the time of the first appearance of the accused in a lower court, remain in force after such appearance in the same manner as bail granted by a court—s 59(2).

Police bail is not possible in respect of offences referred to in Part II or Part III of Schedule 2 of Act 51 of 1977. Parts II and III include virtually all serious common-law crimes, for example, treason, sedition, murder, rape, arson, kidnapping, robbery, theft, fraud, and assault (when a dangerous wound has been inflicted). Part II also refers to certain serious statutory offences, for example, drug offences and offences relating to coinage. Contraventions of ss 1 and 1A of the Intimidation Act 72 of 1982 are referred to in Part III. See further Parts II and III of Schedule 2 (as cited in the appendix to this work) for the remainder of crimes in respect of which police bail is not possible.

2.4 The discretion

It has been held that, since in principle a theoretically innocent person should not be deprived of his liberty, an application for police bail should—like an ordinary bail application—neither be frustrated by an excessive amount nor be refused in the absence of substantial cause for such refusal—*MacDonald v Kumalo* 1927 EDL 293. It has been suggested that an action for damages will lie should police bail be refused on malicious grounds, or where the properly authorised official had simply refused to exercise his discretion—*Shaw v Collins* (1883) 2 SC 389.

3 BAIL GRANTED BY PROSECUTION

A director of public prosecutions (hereafter 'DPP'), or a prosecutor authorised thereto in writing by the DPP concerned, may, in respect of the offences referred to in Schedule 7 (see appendix to this work) and in consultation with the police investigating officer, authorise the release of an accused on bail—s 59A(1). This kind of bail is hereafter referred to as 'prosecutorial bail'. Section 59A(3) provides that the effect of prosecutorial bail is that the person who is in custody shall be released from custody

'(a) upon payment of, or the furnishing of a guarantee to pay, the sum of money determined for his or her bail at his or her place of detention contemplated in section 50(1)(a);

(b) subject to reasonable conditions imposed by the attorney-general or prosecutor concerned; or

(c) the payment of such sum of money or the furnishing of such guarantee to pay and the imposition of such conditions.'

For purposes of exercising the functions as contemplated in s 59A(1) and 59A(3), a DPP may—after consultation with the minister of justice—issue directives. An accused who is released on prosecutorial bail, must appear on the first court day at the court and at the time determined by the prosecution; and the release of the accused shall endure until he appears before the court on the first day—s 59A(4). Prosecutorial bail proceedings must be recorded in full, including the conditions imposed—s 59A(6) as read with s 64. In terms of s 59A(7) prosecutorial bail shall be regarded as bail granted by a court in terms of s 60. See para 4 below. However, it must be pointed out that prosecutorial bail only lasts until the accused's appearance on the first court day. At this first court appearance judicial intervention or approval is required. Section 59A(5) provides that at the first appearance in court of a person released on prosecutorial bail, the court

'(a) may extend the bail on the same conditions or amend such conditions or add further conditions as contemplated in section 62; or

(b) shall, if the court does not deem it appropriate to exercise the powers contemplated in paragraph (a), consider the bail application and, in considering such application, the court has the jurisdiction relating to the powers, functions and duties in respect of bail proceedings in terms of section 60.'

4 BAIL APPLICATIONS IN COURT

4.1 General provisions

An accused who is in custody in respect of an offence shall, subject to the provisions of s 50(6), be entitled to be released on bail at any stage preceding his conviction in respect of such offence, unless the court finds that it is in the interests of justice that he be detained in custody—s 60(1)(a). If a court refers an accused to another court for trial or sentencing, the court referring the accused retains jurisdiction relating to the powers, functions and duties in respect of bail until the accused appears in such other court for the first time.

4.2 The provisions of s 50(6)

The procedure which follows an arrest was discussed in para 5.5 of Chapter 7 above. This procedure is governed by s 50. However, certain important provisions which relate to bail, are contained in s 50(6).

An accused is at his first appearance in court entitled to apply for release on bail—s 50(6)(i)(bb). He is not entitled to bring a bail application outside ordinary court hours—s 50(6)(b).

The bail application of a person charged with a Schedule 6 offence must be considered by a regional court—s 50(6)(c). However, in terms of a proviso in s 50(6)(c) a DPP or prosecutor authorised thereto by the DPP may—where a regional court is, due to exceptional circumstances, not available—direct that the accused's bail application be heard by any other available lower court within the area of jurisdiction of such regional court.

Any lower court before which a person is brought in terms of s 50(6), may—in terms of s 50(6)(d)—postpone any bail proceedings or bail application to any date or court, for a period not exceeding seven days at a time, on the terms which the court may deem proper and which are not inconsistent with any provision of the Act, if

'(i) the court is of the opinion that it has insufficient information or evidence at its disposal to reach a decision on the bail application;

(ii) the prosecutor informs the court that the matter has been or is going to be referred to an attorney-general for the issuing of a written confirmation referred to in section 60(11A);

(iii) the prosecutor inform the court that the person is going to be charged with an offence referred to in Schedule 6 and that the bail application is to be heard by a regional court;

(iv) it appears to the court that it is necessary to provide the State with a reasonable opportunity to—

(aa) procure material evidence that may be lost if bail is granted; or

(bb) perform the functions referred to in section 37; or

(v) it appears to the court that it is necessary in the interests of justice to do so.'

4.3 Appeal by accused to High Court against a lower court's decision concerning bail

An accused who considers himself aggrieved by the refusal of a lower court to admit him to bail or by the imposition by such court of a condition of bail, including a condition relating to the amount of bail money and including an amendment or supplementation of a condition of bail, may appeal against such refusal or the imposition of such condition to the High Court having jurisdiction or to any judge of that court if the court is not then sitting—s 65(1)(a). The appeal may be heard by a single judge—s 65(1)(b). A local division of the High Court shall have jurisdiction to hear an appeal in terms of s 65(1)(a) if the area of jurisdiction of the lower court in question or any part thereof falls within the area of jurisdiction of such local division—s 65(1)(c).

The accused must serve a copy of the notice of appeal on the director of public prosecutions and on the magistrate or the regional magistrate, as the case may be. The notice of appeal must set out the specific grounds upon which the appeal is lodged—Ho 1979 (3) SA 734 (W) at 738B–C. The magistrate or regional magistrate concerned must forthwith furnish the reasons for his decision to the court or judge, as the case may be—s 65(3).

An appeal shall not lie in respect of new facts which arise or are discovered after the decision against which the appeal is brought, unless such new facts are first placed before the magistrate or regional magistrate against whose decision the appeal is brought and such magistrate or regional magistrate gives a decision against the accused on such new facts—s 65(2).

The court or judge hearing the appeal shall not set aside the decision against which the appeal is brought unless such court or judge is satisfied that the decision was wrong, in which event the court or judge shall give the decision which in its or his opinion the lower court should have given—s 65(4); *Barber* 1979 (4) SA 218 (D); *De Abreu* 1980 (4) SA 94 (W) at 96H-97A.

A further appeal against an order of the high court sustaining a magistrate's refusal of bail, is possible—see generally *Mohamed* 1977 (2) SA 531 (A). But this may be done only with leave of the high court concerned and, if such leave is refused, with the leave of the Supreme Court of Appeal.

Bail appeals are prima facie urgent (*Prokureur-Generaal, Vrystaat v Ramokhosi* 1997 (1) SACR 127 (O)).

4.4   Appeal by director of public prosecutions against decision of court to release accused on bail

A DPP may appeal to the High Court against the decision of a lower court to release an accused on bail or against the imposition of a condition of bail—s 65A(1)*(a)*. A DPP may also appeal to the Supreme Court of Appeal against the decision of a superior court to release an accused on bail—s 65A(2)*(a)*. In both instances the court hearing the appeal may order that the state should pay the accused concerned the whole or any part of the costs which the accused may have incurred in opposing the appeal. In the event of a successful appeal against release on bail, the court which heard the appeal shall issue a warrant for the arrest of the accused—s 65A(3).

4.5   The High Court: power to regulate bail matters where statutes are silent

In *Hattingh* 1992 (2) SACR 466 (N) it was held that a High Court has no statutory power to grant bail to an accused who has been refused leave to appeal to the Supreme Court of Appeal and who wishes to petition the Chief Justice for leave to appeal to the Supreme Court of Appeal. However, it was concluded that a High Court has the power to grant bail as an incident of its common-law power to control its own decisions—see also *Human* 1990 (2) SACR 155 (NC). See also generally, *S v Malcolm* 1999 (1) SACR 49 (SEC). In *Veenendal v Minister of Justice* 1993 (1) SACR 154 (T) at 158I–J reference was made to the 'inherent jurisdiction' of the High Court to grant bail in the absence of statutory provisions authorising such a course. In this case it was accordingly held that a High Court has inherent jurisdiction to grant bail to a person committed by a magistrate to prison in terms of s 10(1) of Act 67 of 1962. See also generally *Thornhill (2)* 1998 (1) SACR 177 (C) 180*e–g* where Ngcobo J stated (at 180*j*–181*a*) that s 35(1)*(f)* of the Constitution 'reaffirms the common-law inherent jurisdiction of the High Court to grant bail'.

It is clear, however, that after the refusal of an appeal by the Supreme Court of Appeal, no court has any statutory or common-law power to release a sentenced prisoner on bail—*Chunguete v Minister of Home Affairs* 1990 (2) SA 836 (W); *Hlongwane* 1989 (4) SA 79 (T) and cf generally *Beehari v Attorney-General, Natal* 1956 (2) SA 598 (N).

No court has the power to order that a person who anticipates arrest should be released on bail if arrested—*Trope v Attorney-General* 1925 TPD 175.

A lower court's power concerning bail is entirely regulated by statute—*Ex parte Graham: In re United States of America v Graham* 1987 (1) SA 368 (T).

5 THE RISKS AND FACTORS WHICH MUST BE CONSIDERED IN DETERMINING A BAIL APPLICATION

5.1 The potential risks

In *Pineiro (1)* 1992 (1) SACR 577 (Nm) at 580B–D Frank J cited the following passage in Du Toit *et al* 9–8B:

'In the exercise of its discretion to grant or refuse bail, the court does in principle address only one all-embracing issue: Will the interests of justice be prejudiced if the accused is granted bail? And in this context it must be borne in mind that if an accused is refused bail in circumstances where he will stand his trial, the interests of justice are also prejudiced. Four subsidiary questions arise. If released on bail, will the accused stand his trial? Will he interfere with State witnesses or the police investigation? Will he commit further crimes? Will his release be prejudicial to the maintenance of law and order and the security of the state? At the same time the court should determine whether any objection to release on bail cannot suitably be met by appropriate conditions pertaining to release on bail. . . .'

5.2 When is the refusal of bail in the interests of justice?

Section 60(4) provides that the refusal to grant bail and the detention of an accused in custody shall be in the interests of justice where one or more of the following grounds are established: *(a)* Where there is the likelihood that the accused, if he or she were released on bail, will endanger the safety of the public or any particular person will commit a Schedule 1 offence; or *(b)* where there is the likelihood that the accused, if he or she were released on bail, will attempt to evade his or her trial; or *(c)* where there is the likelihood that the accused, if he or she were released on bail, will attempt to influence or intimidate witnesses or to conceal or destroy evidence; or *(d)* where there is the likelihood that the accused, if he or she were released on bail, will undermine or jeopardise the objectives or the proper functioning of the criminal justice system, including the bail system; or *(e)* where in exceptional circumstances there is the likelihood that the release of the accused will disturb the public order or undermine the public peace or security.

The grounds in ss 60(4)*(a)* to 60(4)*(e)*—as referred to above—must be evaluated in conjunction with the various guidelines (factors, considerations) which the legislator has identified in ss 60(5) to 60(9) and which are set out in paragraphs 5.2.1 to 5.2.5 below. In *Dlamini etc* (see para 1.2(1) above) the Constitutional Court had the opportunity to consider the constitutional validity of ss 60(4) to 60(9). These sections were held constitutional, and in para [43] of *Dlamini etc* it was said:

'Such guidelines are no interference by the Legislature in the exercise of the judiciary's adjudicative function; they are a proper exercise by the Legislature of its functions, including the power and responsibility to afford the judiciary guidance where it regards it as necessary. What is more, it is not only a proper exercise of legislative power, but a very welcome one. Here, in conveniently tabulated form, the CPA now first provides (in s 60(4)*(a)* to *(e)*) a check-list of the main criteria to be considered against the grant of bail and then proceeds (in ss (5) to (8A)) to itemise considerations that may go to make up those criteria. Then, in ss (9) it provides a list of personal criteria pointing towards the grant of bail.'

On the meaning of 'interest of justice' as used in s 60(4) and other related sections, see *Dlamini etc*.

5.2.1   *The ground in s 60(4)*(a): *factors which the court may consider (s 60(5))*

In considering whether the ground in s 60(4)*(a)*—as cited in paragraph 5.2 above— has been established, the court may in terms of s 60(5) take the following factors into account where applicable, namely, the degree of violence towards others implicit in the charge against the accused—s 60(5)*(a)*; any threat of violence which the accused may have made to any person—s 60(5)*(b)*; any resentment the accused is alleged to harbour against any person—s 60(5)*(c)*; any disposition to violence on the part of the accused, as is evident from his or her past conduct—s 60(5)*(d)*; any disposition of the accused to commit offences referred to in Schedule 1, as is evident from his or her past conduct—s 60(5)*(e)*; the prevalence of a particular type of offence—s 60(5)*(f)*; any evidence that the accused previously committed an offence referred to in Schedule 1 while released on bail—s 60(5)*(g)*; or any other factor which in the opinion of the court should be taken into account—s 60(5)*(h)*.

Bail can properly be refused if the court is satisfied that an accused has a propensity to commit the crime with which he is charged and that he might continue to perpetrate such crimes if released on bail—*Patel* 1970 (3) SA 565 (W). This approach must be understood in the light of what was said by Cooper J in *Peterson* 1992 (2) SACR 52 (C) at 55E–F, namely, that the purpose of granting bail to an accused is to minimize interference in his lawful activities and, accordingly, if there is a risk of a repetition of the same criminal conduct if the accused were released on bail, the 'interests of society outweigh the rights of the lawless individual'.

5.2.2   *The ground in s 60(4)*(b)*: factors which the court may consider (s 60(6))*

In *S v Letaoana* 1997 (11) BCLR 1581 (W) it was confirmed that s 60(4)*(b)* should be read with s 60(6).

A further ground that the court must consider, is the likelihood of the accused attempting to evade his trial if released on bail—see s 60(4)*(b)* as cited in para 5.2 above. In considering this ground the court may, where applicable, take into account the following factors: the emotional, family, community or occupational ties of the accused to the place at which he or she is to be tried—s 60(6)*(a)*; the assets held by the accused and where such assets are situated—s 60(6)*(b)*; the means, and travel documents held by the accused, which may enable him or her to leave the country—s 60(6)*(c)*; the extent, if any, to which the accused can afford to forfeit the amount of bail which may be set—s 60(6)*(d)*; the question whether the extradition of the accused could readily be effected should he or she flee across the borders of the Republic in an attempt to evade his or her trial—s 60(6)*(e)*; the nature and the gravity of the charge on which the accused is to be tried—s 60(6)*(f)*; the strength of the case against the accused and the incentive that he or she may in consequence have to attempt to evade his or her trial—s 60(6)*(g)*; the nature and gravity of the punishment which is likely to be imposed should the accused be convicted of the charges against him or her—s 60(6)*(h)*; the binding effect and enforceability of bail conditions which may be imposed and the ease with which such conditions could be breached—s 60(6)*(i)*; or any other factor which in the opinion of the court should be taken into account—s 60(6)*(j)*.

It has repeatedly been held that in assessing the risk of flight, courts may properly take into account not only the strength of the case for the prosecution and the probability of a conviction (*Lulane* 1976 (2) SA 204 (N) at 213C–F) but also the seriousness of the offence charged and the concomitant likelihood of a severe sentence—*Nichas* 1977 (1) SA 257 (C) at 263. The obvious reason for this approach is that 'the expectation of a substantial sentence of imprisonment would undoubtedly provide an incentive to the appellant to abscond'—*Hudson* 1980 (4) SA 145 (D) at

146H. The risk of absconding increases where a severe sentence has in fact been imposed and a bail application is lodged pending an appeal—*Ho* 1979 (3) SA 734 (W) at 740B.

The risk that an accused may take flight should also be weighed in the light of factors such as the mobility of an accused and his access to overseas travel (*Nichas* (above)); the fact that an accused is a foreign national (*Hudson* (above)); the absence of border formalities at certain international borders (*Mataboge* 1991 (1) SACR 539 (B)) and the depth of emotional, occupational, financial and family roots that the accused has within the country where he is to stand trial—*Acheson* 1991 (2) SA 805 (Nm) at 822.

5.2.3 *The ground in s 60(4)(c): factors which the court may consider (s 60(7))*

The likelihood that an accused, if released on bail, will attempt to influence or intimidate witnesses or conceal or destroy evidence, is a ground for refusing bail— s 60(4)*(c)* as referred to in para 5.2 above. In terms of s 60(7) the court may, in considering whether this ground has been established, take into account the following factors where applicable: *(a)* the fact that the accused is familiar with the identity of witnesses and with the evidence which they may bring against him or her; *(b)* whether the witnesses have already made statements and agreed to testify; *(c)* whether the investigation against the accused has already been completed (see *S v Dhlamini* 1997 (1) SACR 54 (W)); *(d)* the relationship of the accused with the various witnesses and the extent to which they could be influenced or intimidated; *(e)* how effective and enforceable bail conditions prohibiting communication between the accused and witnesses are likely to be; *(f)* whether the accused has access to evidentiary material which is to be presented at his or her trial; *(g)* the ease with which evidentiary material could be concealed or destroyed; or *(h)* any other factor which in the opinion of the court should be taken into account.

In *Hlongwa* 1979 (4) SA 112 (D) it was held that bail for an accused can be refused 'if, on all the evidence, there is a reasonable possibility that he would tamper with one or more State witnesses if he were released'. In assessing this risk, the court may take into account the relationship between the accused and prosecution witnesses (*Ex parte Taljaard* 1942 OPD 66), whether or not the accused is aware of the identity of State witnesses or the nature of their statements (*Acheson* (above) at 822), whether or not any bail condition preventing communication between State witnesses and an accused can effectively be policed (*Acheson* (above) at 822), whether or not State witnesses have been threatened by the accused (*Ex parte Nkete* 1937 EDL 231) and, further, the nature of the accused's criminal record, 'particularly if it includes a conviction for defeating or obstructing the ends of justice by tampering with a State witness'—*Hlongwa* (above) at 113H.

In *Bennett* 1976 (3) SA 652 (C) Vos J formulated the following test for purposes of determining the presence or absence of a reasonable possibility of future interference (at 655G–H, emphasis in the original):

> '[A]s [the] applicant has thus far not interfered with the investigation, the proper approach should be that, unless the state can say that there is a real risk that he *will*, not merely *may*, interfere, there does not appear . . . to be a reasonable possibility of such interference.'

5.2.4 *The ground in s 60(4)(d): factors which the court may consider (s 60(8))*

Refusal of bail shall be in the interests of justice if it is established that there is a likelihood that the accused, if released on bail, will undermine or jeopardise the objectives or proper functioning of the criminal justice system, including the bail system—s 60(4)*(d)*. Section 60(8) provides that when considering whether the ground in subsection (4)*(d)* has been established, the court may, where applicable, take into account the following factors, namely *(a)* the fact that the accused, knowing it to be false, supplied false information at the time of his or her arrest or during the bail proceedings (see also s 60(11B); *(b)* whether the accused is in custody on another charge or whether the accused is on parole; *(c)* any previous failure on the part of the accused to comply with bail conditions or any indication that he or she will not comply with any bail conditions; or *(d)* any other factor which in the opinion of the court should be taken into account.

5.2.5 *The ground in s 60(4)*(e): *factors which the court may consider (s 60(8A))*

Section 60(8A) provides that a court—when considering the provisions in s 60(4)*(e)*—may, where applicable, take into account the following factors: *(a)* whether the nature of the offence or the circumstances under which the offence was committed is likely to induce a sense of shock or outrage in the community where the offence was committed; *(b)* whether the shock or outrage of the community might lead to public disorder if the accused is released; *(c)* whether the safety of the accused might be jeopardized by his or her release; *(d)* whether the sense of peace and security among members of the public will be undermined or jeopardized by the release of the accused; *(e)* whether the release of the accused will undermine or jeopardize the public confidence in the criminal justice system; or *(f)* any other factor which in the opinion of the court should be taken into account.

5.2.6 *The interests of justice and the personal freedom of and possible prejudice to an accused (s 60(9))*

Section 60(9) determines that the court must weigh the interests of justice against the right of an accused to his personal freedom and in particular the prejudice such an accused will suffer if bail is refused. In doing so, the court is also in terms of s 60(9) required to take the following factors into account: *(a)* the period for which the accused has already been in custody since his or her arrest; *(b)* the probable period of detention until the disposal or conclusion of the trial if the accused is not released on bail; *(c)* the reason for any delay in the disposal or conclusion of the trial and any fault on the part of the accused with regard to such delay; *(d)* any financial loss which the accused may suffer owing to his or her detention; *(e)* any impediment to the preparation of the accused's defence or any delay in obtaining legal representation which may be brought about by the detention of the accused; *(f)* the state of health of the accused; or *(g)* any other factor which in the opinion of the court should be taken into account.

If the prosecution has failed to show a likelihood of one or more of the grounds contemplated in s 60(4)*(a)* of s 60(4)*(e)*, the provisions of s 60(9) will rarely be of assistance to the prosecution because the latter section mentions factors favouring the accused—*Tshabalala* 1998 (2) SACR 259 (C).

5.2.7 *Additional factors to be considered in a bail application pending an appeal against conviction or sentence*

In an application for bail pending appeal against conviction or sentence, the absence of reasonable prospects of success on appeal may justify refusal of bail—*Beer* 1986

(2) SA 307 (SE). It has been suggested, however, that where there is no risk of an accused absconding and the appeal is against sentence only, the test should merely be whether 'the appeal against sentence is reasonably arguable and not manifestly doomed to failure'—*Anderson* 1991 (1) SACR 525 (C) 527E. There is merit in this suggested lesser test where sentence is concerned, as success on appeal can be a hollow victory if the accused has started serving a prison sentence which is eventually reduced or wholly suspended on appeal. In *Makaula* 1993 (1) SACR 57 (Tk) it was held that an application for bail pending an appeal against sentence should generally be granted where the accused has been sentenced to less than one year's imprisonment.

5.2.8   *The amount of bail*

An excessive sum which practically speaking amounts to a refusal of bail, should not be fixed—*Shaban* 1965 (4) SA 646 (W). The guideline is to fix bail at an amount that can not only be paid but will make it more advantageous to the accused to stand his trial rather than flee and forfeit his money—*Du Plessis* 1957 (4) SA 463 (W). Accordingly, there must be a careful investigation of the means and resources of the accused, especially in the absence of legal representation—*Mohamed* 1977 (2) SA 531 (A). Individualisation is important—*Visser* 1975 (2) SA 342 (C). The court is entitled to fix a high amount of bail where the accused is clearly a man of vast financial resources (*S v Stanfield* 1997 (1) SACR 221 (C) 234F).

5.2.9   *Some irrelevant factors*

In deciding a bail application, a court should ignore an accused's threat to continue his hunger strike if bail is refused—*Veenendal v Minister of Justice* 1993 (1) SACR 154 (T). The fact that an accused may receive indemnity from prosecution on the basis of an agreement between the government and political bodies, is also irrelevant in determining bail—*Lukas* 1991 (2) SACR 429 (E).

6   BAIL CONDITIONS

The court may make the release of an accused on bail subject to conditions which in the court's opinion, are in the interests of justice—s 60(12). These conditions may be referred to as discretionary special conditions.

The distinction between discretionary special conditions of bail (as provided for in terms of s 62) and the essential conditions of bail (as determined by s 58) was noted in para 2(3) (above). The court must establish whether any possible objection to release on bail can suitably be met by setting one or more special conditions which can, in conjunction with the essential conditions, govern an accused's release on bail. In terms of s 62 any court before which a charge is pending in respect of which bail has been granted, may at any stage, whether the bail was granted by that court or any other court, on application by the prosecutor, add any further condition of bail (1) with regard to the reporting in person by the accused at any specified time and place to any specified person or authority; (2) with regard to any place to which the accused is forbidden to go; (3) with regard to the prohibition of or control over communication by the accused with witnesses for the prosecution; (4) with regard to the place at which any document may be served on him under the Act; (5) which, in the opinion of the court, will ensure that the proper administration of justice is not placed in jeopardy by the release of the accused.

Practical examples of such discretionary special bail conditions are that the accused must report to a specified police station once or twice a day, or that he must hand his passport over to the police, or that he may not leave a specified magisterial district without informing the police official charged with the investigation of the case. Good examples of such conditions can be found in *Ramgobin* 1985 (4) SA 130 (N) 132, *De Abreu* 1980 (4) SA 94 (W) at 101 and *Pineiro* (1) 1992 (1) SACR 577 (Nm) at 581.

In terms of s 62(*f*) a court may also add a condition that the accused be placed under the supervision of a probation officer or a correctional official.

Bail conditions added in terms of s 62 must be practically feasible (*Fourie* 1947 (2) SA 574 (O) at 577) and should be neither vague nor ambiguous (*Budlender* 1973 (1) SA 264 (C) at 271A) nor ultra vires (*Russell* 1978 (1) SA 223 (C) at 226E). Such conditions may also not be *contra bonos mores*. A bail condition prohibiting a husband from communicating with his wife who happens to be the complainant, is not contra bonos mores—*De Jager v Attorney-General, Natal* 1967 (4) SA 143 (D).

In the ordinary course of events a condition which prohibits communication with a state witness should be taken to include a potential State witness—*Dockrat* 1959 (3) SA 61 (D) at 62.

Any court before which a charge is pending in respect of which bail has been granted may, upon the application of the prosecutor or the accused, increase or reduce the amount of bail determined under ss 55, 59 and 60 or amend or supplement any conditions imposed under s 60 or s 62, whether imposed by that court or any other court. Where the application is made by the prosecutor and the accused is not present when the application is made the court may issue a warrant for the arrest of the accused and, when the accused is present in court, determine the application—s 63(1).

7 PAYMENT OF BAIL MONEY

A prerequisite for release on bail granted by a court, is that the accused must deposit the sum of money as determined by the court. The deposit must be made with the clerk of the magistrate's court concerned or with the registrar of the superior court concerned, as the case may be, or with a member of the correctional services at the prison where the accused is in custody, or with any police official at the place where the accused is in custody—s 60(13)(*a*). In terms of s 60(13)(*b*) the court may order an accused to furnish a guarantee, with or without sureties, that he will upon breach of the relevant bail pay and forfeit to the state the sum of money as determined or as increased or reduced under s 63(1).

A third person may pay bail money for the benefit of the accused—s 69(1). However, no person shall be allowed to deposit for the benefit of an accused any bail money if the official concerned has reason to believe that such person, at any time before or after depositing such bail money, has been indemnified or will be indemnified by any person in any manner against loss of such bail money or that he has received or will receive any financial benefit in connection with the deposit of such bail money—s 69(3).

Bail money, whether deposited by an accused or any other person for the benefit of the accused must, notwithstanding that such bail money or any part thereof may have been ceded to any person, be refunded only to the accused or the depositor, as the case may be—s 69(2).

A legal representative should in principle not pay bail money for the benefit of his client. It is generally considered unethical. Lewis *Legal Ethics* (1982) 202 claims that the following rule of the Natal Law Society reflects the general position of attorneys in South Africa:

'Although it is permissible for an attorney in exceptional circumstances to stand security for bail or to advance bail for an accused person he should not make a practice of doing so.'

Paragraph 3.5.1 of the *Uniform Rules of Professional Ethics of the General Council of the Bar* determines that counsel should not become personally associated with his client's interests and should, therefore, for example, not pay bail for his client.

8 CANCELLATION OF BAIL AND FORFEITURE OF BAIL MONEY

8.1 Failure to observe conditions of bail

If the prosecutor applies to lead evidence to prove that the accused has failed to comply with a condition of bail, the court before which the charge is pending must, if the accused is present and denies that he failed to comply with the condition or that his failure to comply was due to fault on his part, proceed to hear such evidence as the prosecutor and the accused may place before it—s 66(1). If the accused is not present when the prosecutor applies to the court, the court may issue a warrant for his arrest in order to hear evidence in his presence—s 66(2). The court may, if it finds that the failure by the accused was due to fault on his part, cancel the bail and declare the bail money forfeited to the state—s 66(3). No appeal lies against an order for the cancellation of bail—*Sebe v Magistrate, Zwelitsha* 1984 (3) SA 885 (Ck).

8.2 Failure to appear: procedure and consequences

If an accused who is released on bail fails (1) to appear at the place and on the date and at the time appointed for his trial or to which the proceedings were adjourned, or (2) to remain in attendance, the court must cancel the bail provisionally, declare the bail money provisionally forfeited to the state and issue a warrant for the arrest of the accused—s 67(1). If the accused does not appear within fourteen days of the issue of the warrant for his arrest (or within such extended period as the court may on good cause determine) or if the accused does appear but fails to satisfy the court that his failure to appear or to remain in attendance was not due to fault on his part, the provisional cancellation of the bail and provisional forfeiture of the bail money become final. However, if the accused satisfies the court that his failure was not due to fault on his part, the provisional cancellation and forfeiture lapse—s 67(2); *Sibuya* 1979 (3) SA 193 (T); *Dyantyi* 1983 (3) SA 532 (A). A withdrawal of bail and forfeiture of bail money in terms of s 67 do not preclude a new application for bail in terms of s 60. The fact that the bail was withdrawn will, however, be a relevant fact which may be taken into account in the consideration of the new application for bail—*Nkosi* 1987 (1) SA 581 (T).

8.3 Cancellation of bail where accused about to abscond

Any court before which a charge is pending in respect of which the accused has been released on bail may, upon information on oath that the accused is about to evade justice or is about to abscond in order to evade justice, or that the accused interferes or threatens or attempts to interfere with witnesses, or that the accused defeats the ends of justice or that he or she poses a threat to the safety of the public or a particular person, or that it is in the public interest to do so, issue a warrant for the arrest of the accused and make such order as it may seem proper, including an order that the bail be cancelled and that the accused be committed to prison until the conclusion of the relevant criminal proceedings—s 68(1)*(a)* to s 68(1)*(d)*. In terms of s 68(1)*(e)* to s 68(1)*(g)* a similar procedure may be followed where the accused has not disclosed or has not correctly disclosed all his or her previous convictions in the bail proceedings or where his or her true list of previous convictions has come to light after his or her release on bail; or where further evidence has since become available or factors have arisen, including the fact that the accused has furnished false information in the bail proceedings, which might have affected the decision to grant bail; or it is in the interests of justice to do so.

Such a warrant may also be issued by any magistrate upon the application of a peace officer, where it is not practicable to approach the relevant court. See s 68(2). The committal to prison in this instance remains in force until the conclusion of the trial unless the court before which proceedings are pending reinstates the bail at an earlier stage—s 68(2). The decision of a magistrate under s 68 is subject to appeal—*McInnes* 1946 WLD 386; *Casker* 1971 (4) SA 504 (N).

8.4 Cancellation of bail at request of accused

Any court before which a charge is pending in respect of which the accused has been released on bail may, upon application by the accused, cancel the bail and refund the bail money if the accused is in custody on any other charge or is serving a sentence—s 68A.

8.5 Forfeiture and remission

Forfeiture has the same effect as a civil judgment upon the accused and can be executed in the ordinary way. It should be noted, however, that such forfeiture is not always ordered, for example when such an order would subject the sureties to undeserved or undue hardship.

Apart from the court concerned, the minister of justice or any officer acting under his authority may remit the whole or any part of bail money—s 70.

Although it is within the power of the prosecutor (with the permission of the attorney-general) to abandon prosecution at any stage, it is contrary to the purpose for which bail can be granted for the prosecutor, in any but trivial cases, to abandon the prosecution owing to the non-appearance of an accused. Even if a substantial sum may thus accrue to the state, a warrant for the arrest of the accused may still be issued and executed. The prosecution can then be proceeded with, while the question of forfeiture is left for the decision of the court in the proper exercise of its discretion.

8.6 Criminal liability on the ground of failure to appear or to comply with a condition of bail

Any person who has been released on bail and who fails without good cause to appear on the date and at the place determined for his appearance, or to remain in attendance until the proceedings in which he must appear have been disposed of, or who fails without good cause to comply with a condition of bail imposed by the court in terms of section 60 or 62, including an amendment or supplementation thereof in terms of section 63, shall be guilty of an offence and shall on conviction be liable to a fine or to imprisonment not exceeding one year—s 67A. For purposes of s 67A a charge sheet must be drawn up and a proper trial held (*S v Mabuza* 1996 (2) SACR 239 (T)).

9 PROCEDURAL AND EVIDENTIARY RULES RELATING TO BAIL APPLICATIONS

9.1 The pro-active (inquisitorial) role of the court

A court hearing a bail application should not act as a 'passive umpire'. See para [10] of the Constitutional Court decision in *Dlamini etc* (as cited in para 1.2(1) above).

If the question of the possible release of an accused on bail is not raised by the accused or the prosecutor, the court should mero motu ascertain from the accused whether he wishes bail to be considered by the court—s 60(1)*(c)*. See also generally *Ngwenya* 1991 (2) SACR 520 (T).

Apart from postponing bail proceedings as provided for in s 50(6) and explained in para 4.2 above, the court may—in respect of matters which are not in dispute between the accused and the prosecution—acquire in an informal manner the information that is needed for its decision or order regarding bail—s 60(2)*(a)* and s 60(2)*(b)*. If matters are in dispute, the court may require the prosecutor or the accused, as the case may be, to adduce evidence—s 60(2)*(c)*. The court, it seems, therefore has the power to decide who should lead evidence first.

Where the prosecutor does not oppose bail in respect of matters referred to in s 60(11)*(a)* and s 60(11)*(b)*, the court must require of the prosecutor to place on record the reasons for not opposing the bail application—s 60(2)*(d)*. This is another inquisitorial feature of bail proceedings. The provisions of s 60(11) are discussed in paras 9.8 and 9.9 below.

In bail proceedings the court should not play a passive role in the presentation of evidence. This much is clear from s 60(3) which provides that if the court is of the opinion that it does not have reliable or sufficient information or evidence at its disposal or that it lacks certain important information to reach a decision on the bail application, the presiding officer shall order that such information or evidence be placed before the court—s 60(3). The traditional adversarial right of the parties to be selective in their presentation of facts in support of their respective cases, has been curtailed by s 60(3). A further active role is given to the court by s 60(10). This section provides that the court '. . . has the duty . . . to weigh up the personal interests of the accused against the interests of justice . . .' despite the fact that the prosecution does not oppose the granting of bail. See further *Prokureur-Generaal, Vrystaat v Ramokhozi* 1997 (1) SACR 127 (O).

9.2 Application of a free system of evidence

The strict rules of evidence are relaxed for purposes of a bail application. Hearsay may be received more readily than at a trial—*Maharaj* 1976 (3) SA 205 (D). However, a careful assessment of such evidence is necessary. In *Maqungu v Assistant Magistrate, Whittlesea* 1977 (2) SA 359 (E) the court refused to rely on a young constable's evidence that he had received information that the accused were planning to flee. The source of the constable's information was an informer whom he had lawfully declined to identify in terms of the informer's privilege as explained in para 4.6 in Chapter 3. There are obvious risks in relying upon hearsay of this nature.

Ex parte statements (oral statements made by the defence and prosecution from the bar) may be received as 'it is desirable that . . . [bail] . . . applications should be dealt with expeditiously—to prepare affidavits or find witnesses may cause delay . . . [and] . . . [t]he absence of legal representation may also tip the balance in favour of informality'—*Nichas* 1977 (1) SA 257 (C) at 261A–B. However, this easy-going procedure has disadvantages: Very little of substance is on record in the event of an appeal and ex parte statements also carry less weight than oral evidence. Oral evidence on oath is preferable (*Nichas* (above) at 262F–G) because the witness concerned can then be cross-examined. This advantage, inherent in oral evidence, does not mean that a court may disallow affidavits—*Pienaar* 1992 (1) SACR 178 (W). In *Moekazi v Additional Magistrate, Welkom* 1990 (2) SACR 212 (O) it was held that bail applications can be brought on affidavits and that the State—should it wish to oppose the application—can file answering affidavits and adduce oral evidence. The probative value of affidavits is less than oral evidence, even though affidavits do carry more weight than a statement from the bar—*Pienaar* (above) at 180H–I.

The court may, depending upon the circumstance of the case, rely on the opinion of the investigating police official, for example, the latter's opinion that the accused will interfere with State witnesses—*Hlongwa* 1979 (4) SA 112 (D). In *Lukas* 1991 (2) SACR 429 (E) at 437B–C it was, however, warned that a

> 'court should . . . be astute not to simply accept the ipse dixit of the investigating officer or other policeman who testify on behalf of the state and should consider the possibility that such witnesses may have an improper motive in opposing bail'.

The personal opinion of a director of public prosecutions (as opposed to that of any of his prosecutors) is a relevant consideration because of a DPP's experience and the responsibilities of his office—*Kantor* 1964 (3) SA 377 (W). None the less, his opinion cannot be substituted for the court's discretion—*Bennett* 1976 (3) SA 652 (C) at 654H–655A. A DPP's opinion, moreover, becomes irrelevant once the court is in as good a position as the DPP concerned to assess the likelihood or otherwise of an accused absconding—*Lulane* 1976 (2) SA 204 (N) at 211F–G.

Due consideration should be given to an accused's testimony that he has no intention of absconding—*Hudson* 1980 (4) SA 145 (D) at 148E. Still, great reliance cannot be placed on an accused's mere *ipse dixit* to the effect that he will not abscond, since an accused who has such an intention is hardly likely to admit it—*Hudson* (supra) at 148E–F.

9.3 Proof of previous convictions

Previous convictions may be proved by the state in the course of a bail application—*Patel* 1970 (3) SA 565 (W) at 566B–C; *Ho* 1979 (3) SA 734 (W); *Attorney-General, Zimbabwe v Phiri* 1988 (2) SA 696 (ZHC); *Mdleleni* 1992 SACJ 197.

The accused or his legal adviser is also compelled to inform the court whether the accused has previously been convicted of an offence—s 60(11B)*(a)*(i). Any charges pending against the accused must also be disclosed by him or his legal representative and there is also a duty to inform the court whether the accused has been released on bail pending those charges—s 60(11B)*(a)*(ii). Where the legal representative submits the required information, whether in writing or orally, the accused shall be required by the court to declare whether he confirms such information or not—s 60(11B)*(b)*. An accused who wilfully fails or refuses to comply with the provisions of s 60(11B)*(a)* commits an offence and is liable on conviction to a fine or to imprisonment for a period not exceeding two years—s 60(11B)*(d)*(i). The same applies to an accused who wilfully furnishes false information—s 60(11B)*(d)*(ii). It is submitted that the offences referred to in s 60(11B)*(d)* may not be tried summarily.

The fact that an accused is on parole or knowingly supplied false information at the bail proceedings, may be taken into account in determining the issue of release on bail—s 60(5)*(b)* and s 60(5)*(c)* as read with s 60(4)*(a)*. See also para 5.2.1. above.

9.4   The subsequent trial and the admissibility of the record of the bail proceedings

The record of the bail proceedings—excluding the information relating to previous convictions, pending charges and release on bail in respect of pending charges—forms part of the record of the trial of the accused following upon such bail proceedings—s 60(11B)*(c)* as read with s 60(11B)*(a)*. This means that the trial court shall as a rule have access to all the evidence led at the bail application. However, s 60(11B)*(c)* contains a proviso to the effect that if the accused elects to testify during the bail proceedings the court must inform him that anything he says, may be used against him at his subsequent trial and such evidence becomes admissible in any subsequent proceedings. The result is that before s 60(11B)*(c)* can be invoked to prove the oral testimony given by an accused in the course of his bail application, it must be clear that the accused was properly informed at the bail application of his constitutional right to silence and privilege against self-incrimination—*Cloete* 1999 (2) SACR 137 (C). The proviso protects the constitutional right to a fair trial—*Snyman* 1999 (8) BCLR 931 (C).

The Constitutional Court has held that s 60(11B)*(c)* is not unconstitutional—*Dlamini etc* as referred to in para 1.2(1) above. In para [99] of this case it was said:

'Provided trial courts remain alert to their duty to exclude evidence that would impair the fairness of the proceedings before them, there can be no risk that evidence unfairly elicited at bail hearings could be used to undermine accused persons' rights to be tried fairly. It follows that there is no inevitable conflict between s 60(11B)*(c)* of the CPA and any provision of the Constitution. Subsection (11B)*(c)* must, of course, be used subject to the accused's right to a fair trial and the corresponding obligation on the judicial officer presiding at the trial to exclude evidence, the admission of which would render the trial unfair. But it is not only trial courts that are under a statutory and constitutional duty to ensure that fairness prevails in judicial proceedings. The command that the presiding judicial officer ensure that justice is done applies with equal force to a bail hearing. There the presiding officer is duty bound to ensure that an accused who elects to testify, does so knowing and understanding that any evidence he or she gives may be admissible at trial.'

In para [101] the Constitutional Court made it clear that even though s 60(11B)*(c)* is constitutional, the record of bail proceedings 'is neither automatically excluded from nor included in the evidentiary material at trial. Whether or not it is to be excluded is governed by the principles of a fair trial.' It is submitted that this approach leaves ample room for the trial court to exclude or ignore evidence (contained in the record of bail proceedings) which—in terms of the normal rules of evidence—should be excluded, such as hearsay, character and opinion evidence. The trial court is concerned with guilt or innocence. The bail proceedings concern the issue of liberty pending the outcome of the trial. Evidence received in terms of the free system of evidence which applies in bail proceedings (see para 9.2 above) and which becomes part of the trial record on account of the provisions of s 60(11B)*(c)*, would be ignored by the trial court if the admission of such evidence would be in conflict with the ordinary rules of evidence which govern criminal trials. Ultimately, the right to a fair trial must remain intact.

In *Aimes* 1998 (1) SACR 343 (C)—which was decided before s 60(11B)*(c)* came into operation—Desai J held that the admission of accused number one's bail evidence which had been obtained in breach of his right to be advised to remain silent, would violate his right to a fair trial. But it was also clear that, in the circumstances of the case, the exclusion of accused number one's bail evidence would have infringed accused numbers two's right to adduce evidence, which in turn would have violated the latter's right to a fair trial. Desai J then ruled that accused number one's bail evidence could be used by accused number two for purposes of cross-examining accused number one or any other purpose, provided that accused number one's bail evidence could not be used to prove the truth of its contents against number one. It was held that it was unnecessary to decide whether the issue had to be dealt with in terms of the interim Constitution or the provisions of s 35(5) of the Constitution, as the result would have been the same.

9.5 The relationship between s 60(11B)*(c)* and s 235

Bail proceedings may also be proved by relying on s 235. But here, too, inadmissible evidence contained in the bail record should be excluded—*Nomzaza* 1996 92) SACR 14 (A); *Chavulla* 1999 (1) SACR 39 (C).

It would seem as if s 60(11B)*(c)*—which seeks to ensure that a bail record should in principle automatically be part of the trial record—was specifically designed to ensure that oral evidence given by a bail applicant should not at his subsequent trial be received in breach of his right to silence and privilege against self-incrimination. A bail applicant's affidavit (as opposed to his oral evidence—see para 9.2 above) is not specifically covered by legislation. It is submitted, however, that a trial court should ignore a self-incriminating affidavit handed in by an accused at bail proceedings, unless the trial court is satisfied that the accused at the time when he made and handed in his affidavit, did voluntarily, knowingly and intelligently waive his relevant constitutional rights. It is submitted that this approach is necessary to ensure a fair trial.

9.6 Access to information held by the prosecution

Section 60(14) provides as follows:

'Notwithstanding anything to the contrary contained in any law, no accused shall, for the purpose of bail proceedings, have access to any information, record or document relating to the offence in question, which is contained in, or forms part of, a police docket, including any information, record or document which is held by any police official charged with the investigation in question, unless the prosecutor otherwise directs: Provided that this subsection shall not be construed as denying an accused access to any information, record or document to which he or she may be entitled for purposes of his or her trial.'

This section was held constitutional by the Constitutional Court in *Dlamini etc* as referred to in para 1.2(1) above. In para [82] it was pointed that *Shabalala* 1995 (2) SACR 761 (CC) is no authority for the proposition that bail applicants, or their legal representatives, are entitled to access to the police docket. *Shabalala* was concerned with access for purposes of the *trial* and the fairness of the *trial*.

9.7 The burden and standard of proof in bail applications

The standard of proof required from an accused where he bears the burden of proof as provided for in ss 60(11)*(a)* and 60(11)*(b)*, is the civil standard, namely proof on a balance of probability. Both these sections are dealt with more fully in para 9.8 below.

In all cases falling outside the ambit of ss 60(11)(a) *and 60(11)*(b), the burden of proof is on the prosecution and the standard of proof is on a balance of probability. See further *S v Tshabalala* 1998 (2) SACR 259 (C). Proof beyond a reasonable doubt is not necessary because guilt or innocence in respect of the charge is not the issue. Section 25(2)*(d)* of the interim Constitution provided that every person arrested for the alleged commission of an offence shall, in addition to the rights which he has as a detained person, have the right 'to be released with or without bail, unless the interests of justice require otherwise.' This former constitutional provision—which is echoed by s 60(1)*(a)* of the Act—placed the burden of proof on the state. See generally *Njadayi* 1994 (5) BCLR 90 (E) at 96C–D and *Magano v District Magistrate, Johannesburg* (1) 1994 (2) SACR 304 (W) and compare *Ellish v Prokureur-generaal, WPA* 1994 (2) SACR 579 (W). It is submitted that s 35(1)*(f)* of the new Constitution has not altered the position. See also *Tshabalala* above.

9.8 The provisions of s 60(11)*(a)* and s 60(11)*(b)*

Section 60(11) provides as follows:

'Notwithstanding any provision of this Act, where an accused is charged with an offence referred to—

(a) in Schedule 6, the court shall order that the accused be detained in custody until he or she is dealt with in accordance with the law, unless the accused, having been given a reasonable opportunity to do so, adduces evidence which satisfies the court that exceptional circumstances exist which in the interests of justice permit his or her release;

(b) in Schedule 5, but not in Schedule 6, the court shall order that the accused be detained in custody until he or she is dealt with in accordance with the law, unless the accused, having been given a reasonable opportunity to do so, adduces evidence which satisfies the court that the interests of justice permit his or her release.'

Section 60(11)*(a)* is constitutional even though it places a formal onus (burden of proof) on the accused to adduce evidence which satisfies the court that exceptional circumstances (see para 9.9 below) exist which in the interest of justice permit release—*Dlamini etc* as referred to in para 1.2(1) above. In para [77] of this case, the Constitutional Court also held that the requirement 'exceptional circumstances' limits the right in s 35(1)*(f)* of the Constitution, but that it is a constitutionally permissible limitation in terms of the limitation provisions contained in s 36 of the Constitution.

In *Dlamini etc* the Constitutional Court was not required to determine the constitutionality of s 60(11)(b). However, the remarks made by the court in para [65] of its judgment, are instructive and emphasise the differences between s 60(11)(a) and s 60(11)(b). In para [65] it was said that the latter section

'stipulates that an accused must satisfy a magistrate that the "interests of justice" permit his or her release. It clearly places an *onus* upon the accused to adduce evidence. However, apart from that, the exercise to determine whether bail should be granted is no different to that provided for in ss 60(4)–(9) or required by s 35(1)(f). It is clear that an accused on a Sch 5 offence will be granted bail if he or she can show, merely, that the interests of justice permit such grant. The additional requirement of 'exceptional circumstances' imposed by s 60(11)(a) is absent. A bail application under s 60(11)(a) is more gravely invasive of the accused person's liberty right than that under s 60(11)(b). To the extent, therefore, that the test for bail established by s 60(11)(a) is more rigorous than that contemplated by s 35(1)(f) of the Constitution, it limits the constitutional right.

In paras [80] and [84] the Constitutional Court referred to the importance of the words 'having been given a reasonable opportunity to do so' as used in s 60(11)(a) and s 60(11)(b). These words imply that a court may—despite the provisions of s 60(14) as cited in para 9.5 above—order that certain information be released to the accused in order to assist him in trying to meet the requirements of s 60(11).

Section 60(11) must be read with s 60(11A). The latter section facilitates proof of the so-called 'jurisdictional fact', ie, the fact that is necessary to bring a bail applicant within the ambit of s 60(11). Section 60(11A) provides as follows:

'(a) If the director of public prosecutions intends charging any person with an offence referred to in Schedule 5 or 6 the director of public prosecutions may, irrespective of what charge is noted on the charge sheet, at any time before such person pleads to the charge, issue a written confirmation to the effect that he or she intends to charge the accused with an offence referred to in Schedule 5 or 6.

(b) The written confirmation shall be handed in at the court in question by the prosecutor as soon as possible after the issuing thereof and forms part of the record of that court.

(c) Whenever the question arises in a bail application or during bail proceedings whether any person is charged or is to be charged with an offence referred to in Schedule 5 or 6, a written confirmation issued by a director of public prosecutions under paragraph (a) shall, upon its mere production at such application or proceedings, be *prima facie* proof of the charge to be brought against that person.'

9.9 The meaning of 'exceptional circumstances' as used in s 60(11)(a)

In para [76] of its judgment in *Dlamini etc*, the Constitutional Court observed as follows:

'In requiring that the circumstances proved to be exceptional, the subsection does not say they must be circumstances above and beyond, and generally different from those enumerated. Under the subsection, for instance, an accused charged with a Sch 6 offence could establish the requirement by proving that there are exceptional circumstances relating to his or her emotional condition that render it in the interests of justice that release on bail be ordered notwithstanding the gravity of the case. Other examples are readily to hand in the small body of case law that has already been established in the short period since the 1997 amendment came into operation on 1 August 1998. Thus an otherwise dependable man charged with consensual sexual intercourse with a 15-year-old girl, and who has a minor previous conviction dating back many years, would technically fall within the ambit of ss (11)(a). Yet a prudent judicial officer could find those circumstances sufficiently exceptional to warrant bail provided there were no other factors adverse to the grant.'

In *Jonas* 1998 (2) SACR 677 (SECLD) the court gave the following examples of what would constitute 'exceptional circumstances' for purposes of s 60(11)*(a)*: a bail applicant's terminal illness, urgent medical operation or cast-iron alibi. In this case it was held that 'exceptional circumstances' are present where an accused has adduced acceptable evidence that the prosecution's case against him is non-existent or subject to serious doubt. It should be noted that in this case the prosecution had led no evidence to contradict the accused's testimony.

In *C* 1998 (2) SACR 721 (C) Conradie J took the view that in interpreting the words 'exceptional circumstances', a court should bear in mind that it could not have been the intention of the legislator that an alleged offender must be kept in custody when he has established conclusively that he will attend his trial, will not interfere with the administration of justice and will commit no further wrong-doing (ie, the usual circumstances that arise for consideration in a bail application): To require more of a bail applicant, would mean that the procedure becomes punitive—and this cannot be reconciled with constitutional provisions and the fact that bail is non-penal in character as explained in para 1.3 above. Compare generally *H* 1999 (1) SACR 72 (W) and *Mokgoje* 1999 (1) SACR 233 (NC). In the latter case it was held that the following facts do *not* constitute 'exceptional circumstances' for purposes of s 60(11)*(a)*: (i) postponement of trial for five months; (ii) prior release on bail of co-accused before s 60(11)*(a)* came into operation; (iii) value of stolen goods appearing far less than value initially alleged by the prosecution; and (iv) the fact that the bail applicant's business was suffering because of his detention.

10 RELEASE OTHER THAN ON BAIL

10.1 Release of juvenile accused

If an accused under the age of eighteen years is in custody in respect of any offence, and a police official or a court may in respect of such offence release the accused on bail under ss 59 or 60, as the case may be, such police official or court may, instead of releasing the accused on bail or detaining him in custody, place the accused in a place of safety as defined in s 1 of the Child Care Act 74 of 1983, or place him under the supervision of a probation officer or a correctional official, pending his appearance or further appearance before a court in respect of the offence in question or until he is otherwise dealt with in accordance with law—s 71.

10.2 Release on warning

Release on warning is provided for in terms of s 72 which was also referred to in Chapter 7. The gist of s 72 is that an accused may be released by the court or a police official and warned to appear before a specified court at a specified time and date. The accused's release does not depend on the deposit of money or certain conditions. This procedure is followed with lesser offences where there is no reason to expect that the accused will abscond or try to evade justice. Section 72A makes provision for the cancellation of release on warning. The grounds for cancellation are similar to those which apply in respect of cancellation of bail. See s 72A as read with s 68.

CHAPTER 11

Pre-trial examinations

		Page
1	INTRODUCTION	159
2	PLEA IN MAGISTRATE'S COURT ON A CHARGE JUSTICIABLE IN THE REGIONAL COURT	160
3	PLEA IN MAGISTRATE'S COURT ON A CHARGE JUSTICIABLE IN THE HIGH COURT	160
4	PREPARATORY EXAMINATIONS	162
4.1	What is a preparatory examination?	162
4.2	When a preparatory examination is held	163
4.3	Powers of the director of public prosecutions after conclusion of the preparatory examination	165

1 INTRODUCTION

Once the investigation into an offence has been completed and steps have been taken to ensure the presence of the accused at the trial, the charges against the accused will be formulated and the trial will normally commence.

If the decision has been taken to charge the accused in the regional court or to indict him before the High Court, certain procedures be followed before the trial actually starts. These are that the accused be brought before a magistrate's court and be required to plead to the charges or that a preparatory examination be held.

In order to draw a clear distinction between a summary trial and a pre-trial examination, the former will be discussed briefly in view of the fact that it is repeatedly referred to further on in this chapter.

A trial is referred to as a summary trial when it was not preceded by a preparatory examination. The director of public prosecutions or any person authorised thereto by him, eg the public prosecutor, may designate any court which has jurisdiction, as the forum for a summary trial — s 75(1)(c) of the Criminal Procedure Act 51 of 1977. This may or may not be the same court in which the accused has appeared for the first time. In deciding where to hold the summary trial, no court is consulted. Once the court has been designated, the accused will be brought before that court and the trial will commence.

When the accused is in custody he must first be brought before a lower court even though that court may have no jurisdiction to try him. When this occurs, s 75(1)(b) read with s 75(2) applies. At the prosecutor's request the accused is then referred for a summary trial to a court with jurisdiction. That court may be a regional court or a superior court.

Section 75 is subject to ss 119, 122A and 123, which in effect means that, before the summary trial commences in a superior court, the director of public prosecutions may either order that a preparatory examination be held or that the accused be required to plead in a magisttrate's court to the charge against him, although that court does not have jurisdiction to try the offence or to impose what the director of public prosecutions considers to be an appropriate punishment — s 119. Similarly, before the start of the summary trial in the regional court, the prosecutor may require the accused to plead to a charge before a magistrate's court although that court does not have jurisdiction to try the offence or does not have jurisdiction to impose the punishment which, in the opinion of the prosecutor, would be the appropriate punishment to impose upon the accused — s 122A.

2 PLEA IN MAGISTRATE'S COURT ON A CHARGE JUSTICIABLE IN THE REGIONAL COURT

When an accused appears in a magistrate's court and the alleged offence may be tried by a regional court but not by a magistrate's court, or the prosecutor informs the court that he is of the opinion that the offence is of such a nature or magnitude that it merits punishment in excess of the jurisdiction of the magistrate's court but not of the jurisdiction of the regional court, the prosecutor may put the relevant charge and any other charge to the accused, who shall be required by the magistrate to plead to it — s 122A.

If the accused pleads not guilty, the magistrate may question him in terms of s 115 and thereafter commit him for a summary trial to the regional court concerned — s 122D. On a plea of guilty the accused is questioned in terms of s 112 and the magistrate, if he is satisfied that the accused is guilty, refers the accused for sentence to the regional court — s 122C(1). If he is not satisfied that the accused is guilty, he will enter a plea of not guilty and submit the accused for a summary trial to the regional court — s 122C(2) and cf *M; S* 1980 (4) SA 404 (O); *Dimane* 1987 (3) SA 146 (T). See also *Meyers* 1988 (3) SA 917 (O).

The pleas, recorded in terms of s 122A, differ from the pleas of 'guilty' or 'not guilty' in terms of s 106 (in that the accused is not entitled to demand that he be convicted or acquitted), and the first-mentioned plea proceedings cannot be regarded as the commencement of or part of the subsequent trial. It follows, therefore, that a plea of *autrefois acquit/convict* cannot be sustained. The accused must accordingly be asked to plead afresh at the subsequent trial, irrespective of what he has pleaded in the magistrate's court — *Lubbe* 1989 (3) SA 245 (T); *Singh* 1990 (1) SA 123 (A); cf *Hendrix* 1979 (3) SA 816 (D); *Singh* 1986 (4) 263 (C).

Where a charge that was temporarily withdrawn after the accused hd to plead again in the district court on the same charge, but must be summarily referred to the correct court for trial in terms of s 75. If the accused were to be asked to plead in the district court again, it would constitute an irregularity — *Lethopa* 1994 (1) SACR 553 (O).

3 PLEA IN MAGISTRATE'S COURT ON A CHARGE JUSTICIABLE IN THE HIGH COURT

This procedure is sometimes referred to as the 'ingekorte voorlopige ondersoek' (curtailed preparatory examination). It is sometimes also called a 'mini-preparatory examination'.

The purpose of this procedure is to ease the workload of the High Court and of the director of public prosecutions. It is a sifting process whereby a preparatory examination or a superior court trial may be eliminated in certain cases where, on account of the possible co-operation of the accused at an early stage, the charge proves to be of a less serious nature than was initially thought.

When an accused appears in a magistrate's court and the alleged offence may be tried by a superior court only, or is of such a serious nature and magnitude that it merits punishment in excess of the jurisdiction of a magistrate's court, the prosecutor may, on the instructions of the director of public prosecutions, put the charge to the accused in the magistrate's court — cf *S* 1978 (4) SA 374 (T). The magistrate does not determine the charge upon which the accused must stand trial. The proceedings only serve as an aid to the director of public prosecutions in determining the charge and, in terms of the provisions of s 122(1), decisions regarding the prosecution rests with him — *M; S* 1979 (2) SA 959 (T). The magistrate directs the accused to plead to the charge — s 119. (The proceedings commence by lodging the charge-sheet with the clerk of the court — s 120 read with s 76(2) and (3).)

Where an accused pleads guilty, the magistrate questions him in order to ascertain whether he admits the allegations in the charge — s 121(1) read with s 112(1)*(b)*. If the magistrate is satisfied that the accused admits the allegations, he stops the proceedings pending the decision of the director of public prosecutions. The director may decide to arraign the accused for sentence before the superior court or any other court having jurisdiction — including the court in which the proceedings were stopped — s 121(2)*(a)* and (3). (If the magistrate is not satisfied that the accused admits the allegations in the charge-sheet, he must, in terms of s 121(2)*(b)*, record in what respect he is not so satisfied, enter a plea of not guilty and deal with the matter in terms of s 122(1), below.) The magistrate must advise the accused of the decision of the director of public prosecutions. If the decision is that the accused be arraigned for sentence —

(1) in the magistrate's court concerned, the court must dispose of the case and the proceedings continue as though no interruption occurred;

(2) in a regional or superior court, the magistrate must adjourn the case for sentence by such court — s 121(4). This court may convict the accused on his plea of guilty of the offence concerned and impose any competent sentence — s 121(5). Nothing prevents the prosecutor or accused from presenting evidence on any aspect of the charge, or the court from questioning the accused for the purposes of determining an appropriate sentence — s 121(7). If the accused satisfies the court that the plea of guilty or an admission was incorrectly recorded, however, or if the court is not satisfied that the accused is guilty or has no valid defence to the charge, it records a plea of not guilty and proceeds with the trial as if it is a summary trial in that court. An admission by the accused, the recording of which took place with the agreement of the accused, stands as proof of the fact thus admitted — s 121(6).

Where an accused pleads not guilty, s 122(1) provides that the court must act in terms of s 115: the magistrate asks the accused whether he wishes to make a statement indicating the basis of his defence. Where the accused does not make a statement, or does so and it is not clear from the statement to what extent he denies or admits the allegations, the court may question him in order to establish which allegations in the charge the accused disputes. The court may in its discretion put any question to the accused in order to clarify any of the above-mentioned aspects and must enquire from the accused whether an allegation which is not placed in issue by the plea of not guilty, may be recorded as an admission. When s 115 has been complied with, the magistrate must stop the proceedings and adjourn the case pending the decision of the director of public prosecutions. The latter may —

(1) arraign the accused on any charge at a summary trial before a superior court or any other court having jurisdiction (including the magistrate's court in which the proceedings were adjourned); or

(2) institute a preparatory examination against the accused.

The director of public prosecutions advises the magistrate's court concerned of his decision and the court notifies the accused accordingly.

If the decision is that the accused be arraigned in the magistrate's court in which the proceedings were adjourned, the court must proceed from the stage at which adjournment took place as if no interruption occurred. If the accused is arraigned on a charge different from the charge to which he has pleaded, he must plead to that charge. (The court must then deal with the matter in accordance with s 115 if the plea is one of not guilty, or in terms of s 112 in the case of a plea of guilty — cf in this regard the chapter on arraignment and plea.)

If the director of public prosecution's decision is that the accused be arraigned in a regional court or a superior court, the magistrate must, after having notified the accused of the decision, commit the accused for a summary trial before such court — s 122(3).

Although the Criminal Procedure Act does not provide for transmission of the record of the proceedings to the director of public prosecutions (express provision is made in the case of preparatory examinations — s 137), one may assume that this will actually happen in practice; there is indeed no other way for a director of public prosecutions to reach the decision which is mentioned several times in ss 121 and 122. (With regard to the evidentiary value of the record of the respective proceedings, cf ss 121(5)*(aA)* and 122(4) as well as *Tsankobeb* 1981 (4) SA 614 (A).)

The pleas recorded in terms of s 119 differ from the pleas of 'guilty' or 'not guilty' in terms of s 106, and the first-mentioned plea proceedings cannot be regarded as the commencement of or part of the subsequent trial — as is the case with the pleas recorded in terms of s 122A, above. A plea of *autrefois acquit/convict* can, once more, not be sustained and the accused must be asked to plead afresh at the subsequent trial.

A request for further particulars in relation to a charge such as murder may be enforced before the accused is required to plead in terms of s 119. Section 87 is also applicable to proceedings in terms of s 119 — *Leopeng v Meyer NO* 1993 (1) SACR 292 (T).

4 PREPARATORY EXAMINATIONS

Chapter 20 of the Act (ss 123–143) is applicable to preparatory examinations.

4.1 What is a preparatory examination?

In terms of s 1 a preparatory examination is a criminal proceeding. A preparatory examination is not a trial because the final decision in the proceedings rests with the director of public prosecutions and not with the court. It is an examination which is held before a magistrate to determine whether the evidence presented before him justifies a trial before a superior court or any other court which has jurisdiction. The accused is not on trial. He is not requested to plead at the commencement of the proceedings, as at a trial, but only at the conclusion, after all the evidence to the charge or charges has been led — s 130. The magistrate (or regional magistrate) asks the accused to plead to the charge(s) — s 131. The magistrate (or regional magistrate) does not make a finding of guilty or not guilty. If a trial is instituted after a preparatory examination, it is a separate proceeding because the criminal proceeding (preparatory examination) is terminated when the accused is committed for trial — *Swanepoel* 1979 (1) SA 478 (A).

A preparatory examination is inherently irreconcilable with the s 119 or s 122A procedure, as discussed in para 2 and 3 above, because the purpose of the latter is to arraign an accused as soon as possible without the accused knowing on what evidence the State's case is founded. The purpose of the preparatory examination, on the other hand, is to enable the director of public prosecutions to determine whether the prosecution has a case and whether it is a case which should be prosecuted in a superior court or another court.

If the director of public prosecutions decides on the evidence presented, to prosecute the accused in a particular court, the accused is then *tried* by that court. It is at the director of public prosecutions' discretion to arraign the accused for sentence where he has pleaded guilty, or for trial, if the accused has pleaded not guilty in any court other than the superior court.

If the magistrate discharges the accused at the conclusion of the examination, this does not have the effect of an acquittal. If however, the accused is informed by the magistrate that the director of public prosections has decided not to prosecute him, he may, if charged with the same crime again, plead that he has previously been acquitted (*autrefois acquit*) — s 142. This creates the impression that he has been acquitted during a trial, but is only a statutory extension of the application of the rules relating to *autrefois acquit* — cf also *Ndou* 1971 (1) SA 668 (A) and Chapter 14 below).

4.2 When a preparatory examination is held

Before the coming into operation of s 152*bis* of Act 37 of 1963, a preparatory examination had to precede every superior court trial. Under s 152*bis* the director of public prosecutions was given the discretion to decide whether a summary trial should be held without a preceding preparatory examination, only if he was of the opinion that there was any danger of interference with or intimidation of witnesses or if he deemed it in the interest of the safety of the state or in the public interest. The opinion was held at that time that a preparatory examination afforded an accused an unfair advantage in that he was able to hear all the State's evidence without having to testify himself or to call witnesses or to cross-examine them and that it was time-consuming an opinion which still finds support today. See *Commission of Inquiry into the Structure and Functioning of the Courts* (Hoexter Commission), Fifth and Final Report, Part III 199.

Section 123 regulates the present position. It lays down that if an director of public prosecutions is of the opinion that it is necessary for the more effective administration of justice, he may decide to order the holding of a preparatory examination before the accused is tried in a superior or other court with jurisdiction. He may take this decision at the following stages:

(1) following s 119 procedure in which the accused has pleaded guilty, if the director of public prosecutions is in doubt regarding the accused's guilt or if he feels that the facts do not fully appear from the record — ss 121(3)*(c)* and 123*(a)*;

(2) following s 119 procedure in which the accused has pleaded not guilty — ss 122(2)(ii) and 123*(a)*; or

(3) at any stage before conviction during the course of a trial in the magistrate's court or regional court — s 123*(b)*. In such a case the trial will be converted into a preparatory examination. (In *Tieties* 1990 (2) SA 461 (A) the Supreme Court of Appeal held that, notwithstanding the wording of s 123*(b)*, it was the intention of the Legislature to provide for a conversion of a trial into a preparatory examination only before conviction and that any other interpretation would be a departure from existing principles of law. Should an accused person's trial be converted into a preparatory examination in terms of s 123*(b)* after conviction, the accused will be entitled to plead *autrefois convict* if he is required to plead on the same charges at a trial subsequent to the preparatory examination.)

The decision to institute a preparatory examination is at the director of public prosecutions' exclusive discretion and neither the magistrate nor the accused can interfere with it. The director of public prosecutions will institute a preparatory examination if he is of the opinion —

(1) that the crime is too serious to be tried by a lower court, in which case he may, in terms of s 139, refer the case to the High Court on an even more serious charge; or

(2) that there is a fatal deficiency in the State's case after the closure of the State's case at the end of the trial and that it might be remedied by converting the trial into a preparatory examination — cf *Bham v Lutge NO* 1949 (3) SA 392 (T).

The record of the proceedings held in any of the instances referred to in (1), (2) and (3) above, and which have been adjourned awaiting the director of public prosecutions' decision, forms part of the preparatory examination which is subsequently held — s 124*(a)*. The examination proceeds on the charge to which the accused has pleaded. However, evidence may be led which relates to further crimes allegedly committed by the accused, other than the charge to which he has pleaded — s 124*(b)*.

The accused pleads to the charge(s) after all the evidence for the State has been led. He may object to the charge in terms of s 85 or plead mental illness in terms of ss 77, 130 and 131. Where a summary trial has been converted into a preparatory examination the evidence already led has the same legal force and effect as if it had been led at the preparatory examination. A witness who has already testified may be recalled by the court. New witnesses may be called to testify to the charge(s) to which the accused has pleaded in the summary trial, and also to allegations of further crimes committed by the accused — ss 127 and 128.

4.3 Powers of the director of public prosecutions after conclusion of the preparatory examination

In terms of s 139 the director of public prosecutions may, after considering the record of a preparatory examination transmitted to him under s 137, arraign the accused for sentence, arraign him for trial, or decline to prosecute. The director of public prosecutions must advise the court in which the examination was held of his decision.

(1) Where an accused is arraigned for *sentence*, the magistrate or regional magistrate of the court in which the preparatory examination was held must advise the accused of the decision of the director of public prosecutions and, if the decision is that the accused be arraigned —

   (a) in the court concerned, dispose of the case on the charge on which the accused is arraigned, or

   (b) in another court, adjourn the case for sentence by such other court. The latter court may — with certain provisos — convict the accused on his plea of guilty — cf s 140.

(2) Where the accused is arraigned for *trial*, he is advised by the court of the director of public prosecutions' decision (as in the preceding paragraph) and if he is to be arraigned in some other court, he is committed for trial by such other court. The case is dealt with in all respects as a summary trial. See s 141 for further details.

(3) Where the director of public prosecutions *declines* to prosecute an accused, he advises the magistrate of the district in which the preparatory examination was held of his decision and the magistrate must forthwith have the accused released from custody, or if he is not in custody, advise him in writing of the director of public prosecutions' decision. No criminal proceedings may again be instituted against the accused in respect of the charge in question — s 142. The director of public prosecutions' decision to decline to prosecute should for all practical purposes be equated to an acquittal on the merits by a court of law, ie the accused will at a 're-trial' in respect of the same subject-matter be able to rely on the plea of *autrefois acquit* — Du Toit *et al* 20–8.

PHASE TWO: THE TRIAL

CHAPTER 12

Indictments and charge sheets

		Page
1	LODGEMENT AND SERVICE OF INDICTMENTS AND CHARGE SHEETS	170
	1.1 Introduction	170
	1.2 In superior courts	171
	1.3 In the lower courts	171
2	FORM AND SUBSTANCE OF CHARGES AND INDICTMENTS	171
	2.1 Terminology	171
	2.2 Necessary averments in the charge sheet	172
	2.3 Negativing exceptions, exemptions, provisos, excuses or qualifications	173
	2.4 Inclusion of unnecessary averments	173
	2.5 The obligation to provide particulars	174
3	DEFECT IN INDICTMENT OR CHARGE CURED BY EVIDENCE	175
4	CORRECTION OF ERRORS IN CHARGE	176
5	THE SPLITTING OF CHARGES OR DUPLICATION OF CONVICTIONS	178
	5.1 A single act constitutes more than one statutory offence, or statutory and common-law offences	179
	5.2 A single act constitutes more than one offence at common law	179
	5.3 More than one act of the same nature or of more or less the same nature is committed practically simultaneously, constituting more than one offence (whether a statutory or common-law offence)	180
	5.4 Conduct of the perpetrator is spread over a long period of time and amounts to a continuous repetition of the same offence	181
6	JOINDER OF OFFENCES	183
7	THE JOINDER OF SEVERAL ACCUSED	183

The Constitution and this chapter:

Section 32 — Access to information

(1) Everyone has the right of access to —

(a) any information held by the state; and

(b) any information that is held by another person and that is required for the exercise of protection of any rights.

See 1.1, below.

Section 35 — Arrested, detained and accused persons

(3) Every accused person has a right to a fair trial, which includes the right —

. . .

(a) to be informed of the charge with sufficient detail to answer it; . . .

See 1.1, below.

---

1 LODGEMENT AND SERVICE OF INDICTMENTS AND CHARGE SHEETS

1.1 Introduction

Everyone has the right of access to any information held by the state and any information that is held by another person and that is required for the exercise of protection of any rights — s 32 of the Constitution. This principle applies to various facets of the criminal process:

- an accused is, in principle and for example, entitled to have access to documents in the police file (which will form the basis of the case for the prosecution) — see *Shabalala v Attorney-General* 1995 (12) BCLR 1593 (CC);

- more specifically (as far as the present chapter is concerned), an accused has the right (included in his right to a fair trial) to be informed of the charge with sufficient detail to answer it — s 35(3)*(a)* of the Constitution.

In order to avoid uncertainty concerning the facts which must be proved, our law stipulates strict requirements which have to be satisfied when an indictment or charge is drawn up. (The term 'indictment' is used in connection with prosecutions in a superior court, while 'charge' refers to a prosecution in a lower court.) These documents, in which it is alleged that the accused is guilty of a specific crime or crimes, furnish specific information, as it is essential that the accused should know exactly what the charge against him is — *Hugo* 1976 (4) SA 536 (A). The legislature, nevertheless, has endeavoured to avoid criminal trials being rendered abortive merely because of insignificant mistakes made by the persons who draw up indictments and charge sheets. In the past the requirements for indictments were so strict that the slightest technical error often vitiated proceedings. Our legislature, therefore, has enacted provisions through the years in order to bring about a less formalistic practice. However, this does not mean that an indictment or charge sheet may be slovenly drawn — *Mkenkana* 1972 (2) SA 200 (E): the golden rule remains that an indictment or charge sheet should inform the accused in clear and unmistakable language of the charge he has to meet — *Pillay* 1975 (1) SA 919 (N) and cases cited there.

1.2 In superior courts

Having decided to indict an accused, the director of public prosecutions must lodge an indictment with the registrar of the High Court. This is a document presented in the name of the director of public prosecutions whereby he informs the court that the accused is guilty of the crime therein alleged. The document further sets out the date and place at which the crime was allegedly committed, together with certain personal particulars of the accused — s 144(1), (2). Where no preparatory examination has been held, the indictment must be accompanied by a summary of the salient facts of the case, in order to inform the accused of the allegations against him, provided that this will not be prejudicial to the administration of justice or the security of the state. The purpose of the summary of substantial facts is to fill out the rather terse picture almost inevitably presented by the indictment — *Mpetha* (1) 1981 (3) SA 803 (C). The State is not bound by the summary, however, and cannot be precluded from leading evidence which contradicts it — *Kgoloko* 1991 (2) SACR 203 (A). A list of the names and addresses of persons the director of public prosecutions intends calling must also be supplied, although this may be withheld if the director of public prosecutions is of the opinion that the witnesses may be tampered with or intimidated — s 144(3).

The indictment must then be served on the accused in accordance with the rules of court. Service of the indictment, together with a notice of trial, must take place at least ten days before the date appointed for the trial, unless the accused agrees to a shorter period. Service is effected either in terms of the rules of court, or by the magistrate handing the documents to the accused when committing him to the superior court — s 144(4).

1.3 In the lower courts

Unless an accused has been summoned to appear in court the proceedings at a summary trial in a lower court are commenced by lodging a charge sheet with the clerk of the court — s 76(1). Unlike an indictment, this is not served on the accused, but is presented in court. The accused may examine this at any stage of the relevant criminal proceedings — s 80. The accused in such a case is brought to court, as we have seen, on written notice, by summons, or under arrest.

Where an accused is brought to court on written notice or under arrest, he may be required to appear upon very short notice, but where a summons is served upon an accused this must take place at least 14 days (Sundays and holidays excluded) before the day of trial — s 54(3). If the accused or his adviser finds that this period leaves the accused insufficient time within which to prepare his defence he may apply for, and the court will in appropriate cases grant, a postponement for that purpose — *Thane* 1925 TPD 850 and *Van Niekerk* 1924 TPD 486. In *Singh v Blomerus NO* 1952 (4) SA 63 (N) it was held that short service to which no objection had been made at the trial could not be relied on before the appeal court.

2 FORM AND SUBSTANCE OF CHARGES AND INDICTMENTS

2.1 Terminology

Because the requirements as to the form and substance of indictments and charge sheets are the same, the shorter term 'indictment' (or simply 'charge') will, for the sake of convenience, be used from now on.

2.2 Necessary averments in the charge sheet

Charge sheets should be kept as simple as possible. It should be intelligible and a case that can be paraphrased in simple terms must not be made intricate — *Rautenbach* 1991 (2) SACR 700 (T).

Section 84(1) sets out the requirements with which a charge sheet should comply. In short, this section provides that the relevant offence should be set forth in the charge sheet in such a manner that the accused is sufficiently informed of the nature of the charge brought against him. Briefly, it can be said that all the elements of the offence should be mentioned in the charge sheet, or to put it differently, that the charge sheet should disclose an offence. Section 84(1) specifically requires that sufficient particulars as to the time and place at which the offence is alleged to have been committed, the person (if any) against whom and the property (if any) in respect of which the offence is alleged to have been committed, should be furnished in the charge sheet.

Compliance with the foregoing requirements of a charge sheet can be practically demonstrated by referring to a typical charge of murder. (In the High Court a charge sheet is referred to as an indictment.) Such a charge normally reads as follows:

> That the accused is guilty of the crime of murder in that on or about 1 August 1999 and at or near Sunnyside in the district of Pretoria, the accused did intentionally and unlawfully kill John Smith, an adult male.

Particulars furnished, are:

(1) the name of the offence for which the accused is indicted (murder);

(2) all the elements of the crime murder (intention, unlawfulness, killing of another human being);

(3) the time, and place where the offence was allegedly committed; and

(4) the person against whom the offence was allegedly committed.

In this case the accused is charged with a common-law offence. In such an instance the offence must be described in clear legal terms, and if legal appellation for the offence exists, it must be set forth by such appellation, or otherwise it should be strictly and accurately described — *Endemann* 1915 TPD 142 and *Neumann* 1949 (3) SA 1238 (Spec Crim Ct). In s 84(3) it is specifically provided that the description of a statutory offence will be sufficient if the words of the enactment, or similar words, are used. Those who draft indictments should not slavishly follow the wording of a statute, but should confine the charge to that which is relevant — *Mangqu* 1977 (4) SA 84 (E).

With regard to averments as to the time at which the offence is alleged to have been committed, s 92(1)*(c)* provides that if time is not of the essence of the offence, an indictment is not necessarily deficient as a result of failure to state the time at which the offence was committed. If the time of the offence is indeed mentioned, but it is proved that the act or offence was committed on any other day or time not more than three months before or after the day or period alleged, such proof will be taken to support such allegation as to the time of the offence, provided that time is not of the essence of the offence — s 92(2).

If the accused raises an *alibi* as a defence (in other words, that at the time of the commission of the alleged crime he was elsewhere) and the court considers that the accused might be prejudiced in making such defence if proof were to be admitted that the act or offence had been committed on some day or time other than the day or time stated in the indictment, then the court must reject such proof (even though the time proposed to be proved is within the aforesaid three-month period). The accused will then be in the same position as if he had not pleaded.

The place where the crime was committed may also be of the essence of an offence. For example, some offences can be committed only in a public place, eg negligent driving of a motor vehicle (which offence can take place only on a public road). In such a case a charge is defective if it does not allege that the offence was committed in such a place.

In the above example of an indictment of murder, you will notice that it is specifically mentioned that the accused acted intentionally. Where it is an essential feature of an offence that it be committed in circumstances showing a particular mental attitude (*animus*) of the offender — for example, that it was done intentionally (as in the case of murder), knowingly, maliciously or negligently — such mental attitude should be averred, otherwise the charge does not disclose an offence.

2.3 Negativing exceptions, exemptions, provisos, excuses or qualifications

Sometimes statutory provisions contain exceptions or provisos in terms whereof certain persons are exempted from the operation of a statutory provision. In terms of s 90 it is not necessary for the state to specify or negative such exceptions, etc in the charge. If the prosecutor (unnecessarily) does this, it need not be proved by the prosecution. It is for the accused to prove that he is protected by such an exception, exemption, etc.

A distinction should be drawn between a necessary averment concerning the offence, and an exception. In this regard the golden rule is that incriminating factors must be proved by the prosecution and exculpatory factors by the accused. While incriminating facts *must* be mentioned in the charge, exculpatory facts need not be mentioned.

The application of this rule can be explained as follows: If the accused is charged with the offence of driving a motor vehicle without a licence, the fact that the accused did not possess a licence is a substantial element of the relevant offence. Driving a vehicle as such is not an offence, but driving it *without a licence* is. The averment that the accused was not in possession of a licence is, in other words, incriminatory and must be included in the charge. However, if a person is charged with the unlawful possession of prohibited dependence-producing medicine, (eg dagga), the prosecution need not allege that the accused was not authorised in terms of the Drugs and Drug Trafficking Act 140 of 1992 to be in possession of such medicine. If the accused should allege that he was indeed authorised to be in possession of such medicine, this fact constitutes an *exculpatory factor* which must be raised by the accused and it need not be included in the charge.

2.4 Inclusion of unnecessary averments

When, during a trial, it appears that any words or particulars in an indictment or charge are superfluous, an amendment may be made if it does not prejudice the accused — s 86(1). If such amendment is not made, the validity of the proceedings will not be affected, unless the amendment has been refused by the court. Such surplusage, if it does not embarrass the accused in his defence, will as a general rule be disregarded; for example a charge which needlessly and inaccurately specified an exception was upheld in *Mannheim* 1943 TPD 169. Inaccurate averments in a charge may seriously prejudice the State's case — *Hassan* 1970 (1) SA 192 (C).

2.5 The obligation to provide particulars

If the accused feels that the particulars in the indictment are too scanty to inform him properly of the charge against him, he or his legal representative may request particulars or further particulars from the prosecutor — s 87. Even if a charge complies with the requirement set out in the preceding paragraphs of this chapter, the court is still competent to grant an order for further particulars which may be required by the accused to enable him to prepare his defence — *Mokgoetsi* 1943 AD 622 at 627. The court may (either before or at the trial but before evidence has been led) in its discretion direct particulars to be delivered to the accused. Where the accused genuinely requires particulars of the substantive allegation against him in order to ascertain the true nature of the case he has to meet, the court will order the prosecution to furnish such particulars unless this is shown to be impracticable — *Abbass* 1916 AD 233. The prosecutor must deliver the particulars free of charge. In determining whether a particular is required or not and whether a defect in an indictment is material to the substantial justice of the case or not, the court may refer to the preparatory examination or summary of substantial facts in terms of s 144(3)*(a)*.

In *Weber v Regional Magistrate Windhoek* 1969 (4) SA 394 (SWA), the South West Africa Division granted a mandamus directing that the magistrate order the prosecutor to deliver to the applicants further particulars regarding the charges against them. The High Court will intervene in unconcluded proceedings in magistrates' courts only if it is necessary to prevent a grave injustice. In this case the High Court rejected the proposition that postponements and recalling of witnesses could serve as a substitute for the right of an accused to be sufficiently informed of the charges before he pleads and before he presents his defence — *Nangutuuala* 1973 (4) SA 640 (SWA). Generally speaking, the courts are very reluctant to issue a *mandamus* directing the furnishing of further particulars — *Goncalves v Addisionele Landdros, Pretoria* 1973 (4) SA 587 (T).

If a charge sufficiently discloses an offence, but is lacking in adequate narration of particulars, the accused is deemed to have waived his right to apply for particulars and cannot set up such defect on appeal if he has failed to apply for such particulars at the trial — *Lotzoff* 1937 AD 196.

In a summary trial the accused is not entitled to be supplied with the evidence which the state proposes to lead, eg statements of witnesses, documents, etc — *National High Command* 1964 (1) SA 1 (T) (the so-called 'Rivonia trial') and *Heyne* (1) 1958 (1) SA 607 (W) at 609.

The function of particulars is to define the issues and not to enlarge them. The prosecutor must give particulars with regard to the evidence which is to be led. He is not entitled to set out an endless series of alternatives — *Sadeke* 1964 (2) SA 674 (T) and *Mpetha* (1) 1981 (3) SA 803 (C). In *Adams* 1959 (1) SA 646 (Spec Crim Ct) it was held that where further particulars are applied for the State may not merely refer to the record of the preparatory examination if such record is voluminous. Nor may the

State reply to a request for particulars by stating simply that the particulars sought 'are matters peculiarly within the knowledge of the accused'. Such reply may lead to the indictment being quashed — *National High Command* 1964 (1) SA 1 (T). Where there is more than one count, the particulars applicable to each count must be set out — *Nkiwani* 1970 (2) SA 165 (R).

Where particulars are given, the State must prove the charge as particularised (*Anthony* 1938 TPD 602) and where a conviction is based on evidence not covered by the particulars supplied, the conviction may be set aside on review — *Kroukamp* 1927 TPD 412. In a charge of negligent driving of a motor vehicle, for instance, the general allegation is made that the accused drove the car in a negligent manner. The accused requests the prosecutor to furnish particulars with regard to the manner in which it is alleged he drove negligently. The prosecutor, in response to this request, informs the defence that the accused was negligent 'in that he failed to keep a proper look-out'. If it appears in the course of the trial that the accused actually did keep a proper look-out, but that he failed to apply his brakes, he cannot be convicted (in the absence of an amendment of the charge) — cf *Kroukamp* (above) and *Mafungo* 1969 (2) SA 667 (G).

If the trial court has refused an application for particulars and it appears on appeal that the accused has been prejudiced by such refusal and that it cannot be said that no failure of justice has resulted, the court will set aside the accused's conviction — *Verity-Amm* 1934 TPD 416; *De Coning* 1954 (2) SA 647 (N) and *C* 1955 (1) SA 464 (T).

3 DEFECT IN INDICTMENT OR CHARGE CURED BY EVIDENCE

When discussing the requirements with which indictments must comply, we have more than once referred to s 88 of the Criminal Procedure Act, which was enacted in 1959. This section has very far-reaching effects. Before 1959 the courts consistently required indictments to disclose an offence, ie that they disclose facts which, if proved, would render the accused guilty of an offence. See, eg, *Desai* 1959 (2) SA 589 (A). Where a material element of the crime in question was omitted (for example where the prosecutor failed to allege that the offence was committed in a public place, or that the offence was committed with a particular *animus*) the accused could not be found guilty, even though the evidence at the trial proved the element omitted in the charge. This was also the case where the accused had pleaded guilty. If the accused was convicted in such a case he could be sure that the conviction would be quashed on appeal. The leading case in this connection is Herschel 1920 AD 575. Cf Tucker 1953 (3) SA 150 (A); *Magadhla* 1947 (3) SA 585 (N); *Radebe* 1954 (3) SA 785 (O). The court had the power, of course, to amend the indictment, but up to 1959 our courts held the view that an indictment could not be amended unless it disclosed an offence.

To put an end to prosecutions being rendered abortive because of such 'technical' errors made by persons drawing up charges, the legislature then introduced s 179*bis* (now s 88) into the Criminal Procedure Act by s 15 of Act 16 of 1959. This section provides:

> 'Where a charge is defective for the want of an averment which is an essential ingredient of the relevant offence, the defect shall, unless brought to the notice of the court before judgment, be cured by evidence at the trial proving the matter which should have been averred.'

This means that the accused can now be found guilty even though the indictment does not disclose an offence, as long as the evidence proves the offence. This arrangement greatly alleviates the burden of prosecutors. It is open to criticism, however. The charge may be so defective that the accused is not properly informed of the charge brought against him and that he is consequently prejudiced in his defence; but in such a case, of course, he may always object to it (see below) or ask for particulars.

The following comments concerning this section are noteworthy:

(1) The language of the section indicates that, at the very least, the offence with which the accused is charged should be named in the indictment — *Mcwera* 1960 (1) PH H43 (N). The words 'the offence', which are used repeatedly, should undoubtedly be construed as meaning the offence with which the accused is charged and of which he is convicted. If the prosecutor wants to charge the accused with theft, he should, it is submitted, at the very least use the word 'theft' in the indictment. Where a statutory offence is alleged, the number of the section should at least be described accurately if the prosecutor wants to rely on s 88. There must, in other words, be indicated in the charge some recognisable offence, although no offence is, technically speaking, disclosed — *Dhludhla* 1968 (1) SA 459 (N); see also *Mayongo* 1968 (1) SA 443 (E). Therefore, where two offences are contained in a section and the accused is charged with only one of them (no reference being made in the charge sheet to the other offence), s 88 cannot be invoked to convict the accused of such other offence — *Moloinyane* 1965 (2) SA 109 (O); *Van Rensburg* 1969 (1) SA 215 (G).

(2) Even though an accused may now be convicted upon an indictment which does not disclose an offence, the prosecutor should exercise caution by framing the indictment in such terms that it does disclose an offence. If he fails to do so the accused can before pleading raise an exception against the charge.

(3) If the accused before judgment brings the want of averment to the notice of the court and the court then refuses to order the charge to be amended, the rule in *Herschel's* case still applies, ie the accused may rely upon the defect on appeal, if he has been convicted by the trial court — *Gaba* 1981 (3) SA 745 (O).

(4) A defect can be cured only by evidence proper, not, for example, by the invocation of statutory provisions and presumptions — *AR Wholesalers* 1975 (1) SA 551 (NC) (this case contains a thorough exposition regarding s 88); *Pheka* 1975 (4) SA 230 (NC). The replies of an accused (who has pleaded guilty) to questioning in terms of s 112(1)*(b)* may, for the purposes of s 88, be treated as 'evidence' capable of curing a defect in the charge — *Tshivhule* 1985 (4) SA 48 (V).

(5) Section 88 does not authorise replacement of one offence by another offence proved by evidence — *Sarjoo* 1978 (4) SA 520 (N). (Substitution of 'jersey' for 'meat' in a theft charge, would amount to substitution of a charge — *Kuse* 1990 (1) SACR 191 (E)).

4 CORRECTION OF ERRORS IN CHARGE

Section 86(1) makes provision for the amendment of an indictment in the following three situations:

(1) where it is defective for want of an essential averment;

(2) where there is a variance between the averment in the charge and the evidence offered in proof of such averment; or

(3) where words have been omitted, or unnecessarily inserted, or any other error is made.

Before 1959 it was generally assumed, on the strength of an *obiter dictum* of the Supreme Court of Appeal in *Jhazbai* 1931 AD 480, that a charge could be amended only where it disclosed an offence. If it did not disclose an offence, it was considered fatally defective. In 1959, however, the Supreme Court of Appeal in *Crause* 1959 (1) SA 272 (A) held that this was incorrect and that the trial court could correct the indictment even though it did not disclose an offence. This decision was confirmed by an express provision to this effect in s 16, Act 16 of 1959, which amended s 180(1) of the 1955 Code — *Ntjoro* 1959 (4) SA 447 (T). The present s 86(1) contains a similar stipulation.

The following points regarding the amendment of a charge are to be noted:

(1) In terms of s 86(1) the court may order an amendment only if it considers that the making of the amendment will not prejudice the accused in his defence — *Taitz* 1970 (3) SA 342 (N). In a summary trial of great complexity which involves a number of counts, a court will be very loath, at a late stage of the proceedings, to sanction any radical departure from the indictment for fear of prejudicing the accused — *Heller* 1971 (2) SA 29 (A) at 53C–D. There will not be prejudice if there is but a slight variance or where it is clear that the *defence would have remained exactly the same* had the State originally presented the charge in the amended form. Where application to amend a charge is made on appeal, the court must be satisfied that the defence would have remained the same if the charge had originally contained the necessary particulars. On appeal the court would accede to an application for an amendment of a charge only if it were satisfied that there was no reasonable doubt that the appellant would not be prejudiced — *F* 1975 (3) SA 167 (T) at 170. Thus the question of prejudice depends upon an examination of the facts and circumstances in each particular case — *Pillay* 1975 (1) SA 919 (N) and *Coetzer* 1976 (2) SA 769 (A).

(2) Section 86 makes provision for amendment of the charge — not for replacement thereof by an altogether new charge — *Barkett's Transport (Edms) Bpk* 1988 (1) SA 157 (A). The approach to adopt is to establish whether the proposed amendment differs to such an extent from the original charge that it is in essence another charge. If the proposed amended charge does not correspond at all to the original charge, then one can talk of a substitution and not of an amendment. If only the citation of a charge has to be amended (eg replacing a charge of bribery — which has been repealed and substituted by a statutory offence — with a statutory provision under the Corruption Act 94 of 1992) and the essential of the charge will be essentially the same, the defence will not be affected thereby — *Mahlangu* 1997 (1) SACR 338 (T). Should a new charge be framed in the course of a trial, the possibility of prejudice to the accused is strong; the accused comes to court prepared to meet a particular charge, and will now be faced with a different issue — *Slabbert* 1968 (3) SA 318 (O).

(3) Section 86(4), however, provides that the fact that a charge has not been amended as provided in this section shall not, unless the court has refused to

allow the amendment, affect the validity of the proceedings thereunder. This subsection may be misleading. According to our courts it must be interpreted in such a way that if an amendment would have been in order by virtue of subsection (1), ie *if it would not have prejudiced the accused in his defence*, the failure to effect the amendment will not invalidate the proceedings, except where the court refused to allow the amendment — *Coetzer* 1976 (2) SA 769 (A) at 772. The peremptory words in s 88 now state expressly that the omission of an essential element is automatically cured by evidence. The need for amendment has thus fallen away altogether in such a case (see *Ntjoro* (above)), so that subsec (4) and the question of prejudice are irrelevant, except where the want of an essential averment was brought to the notice of the court. If this has occurred, the 'automatic cure' of s 88 does not become operative and the charge will have to be amended. The interpretation referred to in the italicised words above is still in force as regards the insertion of superfluous words and any discrepancy between the averment in the charge and the evidence adduced.

5 THE SPLITTING OF CHARGES OR DUPLICATION OF CONVICTIONS

It happens frequently that *one and the same* act of a person constitutes more than one offence. If a man, for instance, assaults a female idiot below the age of 16 years and has forcible intercourse with her, his conduct may constitute any of the following offences: common assault; assault with intent to rape; rape; connection with a girl below the age of 16 years in contravention of s 14, Act 23 of 1957. General considerations of fairness militate against the perpetrator being charged with *and* convicted of all these offences.

The further possibility exists that a person commits more than one offence, (i) by conduct which is spread over a period, for instance a person who for a year continuously pretends to be a medical doctor and treats patients; (ii) through the same series of actions, for instance a man who attacks a woman, rapes her and then runs away with her handbag, thereby committing within a brief period of time assault, assault with intent to commit rape, rape, robbery and theft. May the perpetrator be charged with all these offences?

Subject to the qualification that the accused *should not be convicted* of all these offences, the answer to the question above is in the affirmative. Section 83 provides that if by reason of any uncertainty as to the facts which can be proved, or for any other reason it is doubtful which of several offences is constituted by the facts which can be proved, the accused may be charged with *having committed all or any of those offences* and any number of such charges may be tried at once, or the accused may be charged in the alternative with having committed any number of those offences.

The courts developed a rule against the so-called splitting (or duplication) of charges. (For a historical review, see Hiemstra 199.) In *Ex parte Minister of Justice: In re R v Moseme* 1936 AD 52 at 60 it was questioned whether this provision does not draw a veil over the whole series of decisions dealing with splitting of charges and whether the prosecution's rights regarding the splitting of charges were not enlarged. The Supreme Court of Appeal did not decide this point, however. In *Van Zyl* 1949 (2) SA 948 (C) it was held that in view of the provisions of s 83 the old tests are now applicable only to convictions and not charges. Gardiner and Lansdown accordingly state (at 298):

'It is the duplication of convictions to which attention must be directed: save where there can be no reasonable doubt as to the offence to be charged, the duplication of charges, but not of convictions, is permitted by the section.'

The leading case on 'splitting of charges' is *Grobler* 1966 (1) SA 507 (A). In this decision the origin and application of the rule is extensively traced and the opinion is expressed that s 83 deals with the procedure which may be adopted in the formulation of charges and not with the statutory and common-law principles regarding conviction and punishment. The rule against the splitting of charges was in fact always directed at the duplication of *convictions* and designed to apply in the field of punishment. The effect of the section is only that when there is uncertainty about the facts which can be proved, or where it is doubtful for any other reason, including legal uncertainty, which of several offences is constituted by the facts which can be proved, the State may formulate as many charges as the available facts justify, and no exception can be taken against the charge sheet if the accused is charged with more than one offence in respect of one punishable fact. If, however, it appears at the end of the trial that according to the proven facts, two charges comprise one and the same punishable fact, the court will convict the accused on one charge only — cf *Heyns* 1976 (1) PH H48 (C).

The rule against the duplication of convictions is to be approached on the basis of the following possibilities:

5.1   A single act constitutes more than one statutory offence, or statutory and common law offences

Section 336 provides that where an act (or omission) constitutes an offence under two or more statutory provisions or is an offence against a statutory provision and the common law, the perpetrator may be prosecuted and punished under either the statutory provision or the common law. The perpetrator may not, however, be held liable to more than one punishment for the act or omission constituting the offence. Illustrations of the application of this principle are:

(1) Where a man is charged with incest on the ground of connection with his daughter (who is under the age of 16) as well as with connection with a girl (the same daughter) who is under the age of 16 arising out of the same act of carnal intercourse, this will amount to undue splitting).

(2) There is undue splitting of charges if the accused is charged (in actual fact convicted) in respect of the same act with assault and with committing the statutory offence of pointing a firearm — *Wegener* 1938 EDL 3 and cf *Blaau* 1973 (2) PH H(S)116 (C).

Section 336 deals only with cases where there was a single act (or omission) and where at least one of the offences is a statutory offence.

Our courts, however, apply the same principle in the following situations.

5.2   A single act constitutes more than one offence at common law

Illustrations:

(1) Where the accused was found stripping lead from a roof intending to steal it, his conviction on a charge of malicious injury to property was held incompetent, since, in respect of the same act, he had been convicted of theft — *Hendricks* 17 CTR 470.

(2) Where the accused was charged with both rape and incest, arising from the same act of intercourse, he was convicted of only one of these offences — *T* 1940 CPD 14.

(3) Where two persons are killed in the same road accident, it is improper to convict the accused on two counts of culpable homicide. A single charge should make reference to both the deceased — *Mampa* 1985 (4) SA 633 (C).

5.3 More than one act of the same nature or of more or less the same nature is committed practically simultaneously, constituting more than one offence (whether a statutory or common-law offence)

The test applied by our courts in this type of case is: Were the acts done with a single intent and were they part of one continuous transaction *or* does the evidence required to prove the one charge necessarily involve proof of the other? See Hiemstra 220. The tests are in the alternative: they need not both be answered in the affirmative. If the answer to one of the questions is in the affirmative, it is said to be an improper splitting.

These tests are rather arbitrary and it is hardly surprising to find many conflicting decisions. The tests are, in any event, only guiding principles and not conclusive. In every case the ultimate rule is that the court must judge whether, according to the difference in nature and degree of the facts, one or more offences have been proved — *Grobler* 1966 (1) SA 507 (A), 511G–512H — a case where a conviction of both murder and robbery was upheld. In *Kuzwayo* 1960 (1) SA 340 (A) it was pointed out that there are borderline cases which may not be covered precisely by the tests and in such cases the decision of the issue will depend on the judicial officer's common sense and sense of fair play. Cf also *Mbulawa, Tandawupi* 1969 (1) SA 532 (E); *Christie* 1982 (1) SA 464 (A) and *Nambela* 1996 (1) SACR 356 (E).

If the totality of the accused's criminal conduct can be accommodated in one single charge, the accused may not be convicted of multiple charges. For example: if an accused, in the act of committing rape, tears the victim's jacket, he may not be convicted of rape and malicious injury to property. But should the accused after the completion of the rape take the victim's purse which has dropped from her jacket, the accused commits the further act of theft. Where the nature of the separate acts that have been committed, and the intent with which each act has been committed, differ to such an extent that it is impossible to accommodate all the acts within one offence only, conviction on multiple charges would not constitute an improper duplication of convictions — *Waites* 1991 (2) SACR 388 (NC). See also *Murbane* 1992 (1) SACR 298 (NC).

Further illustrations for the application of these principles:

(1) If a man breaks into a house with intent to steal and thereupon commits theft from the house, he should be charged only with housebreaking with intent to steal and theft — *s* 1981 (3) SA 377 (A) at 380H. However, when a burglar breaks into different premises under one roof — various flats in one block, for example — this will amount to different offences — *Tshuke* 1965 (1) SA 582 (C).

(2) If an assault is committed pursuant to, and in the course of, an attempt to escape, the accused should be convicted one of these offences only — *Vlok* 1931 CPD 181.

(3) If an act of rape is accompanied by robbery of the victim, the accused may be convicted of both these crimes — *N* 1979 (3) SA 308 (A).

(4) If a person breaks into premises with intent to commit an offence, and *thereafter* 'breaks out' again (eg by breaking a door) in order to escape, he may be convicted of both housebreaking with intent to commit a crime and malicious injury to property — *Shelembe* 1955 (4) SA 410 (N).

(5) Where an accused drives under the influence of intoxicating liquor, and through his negligent driving causes the death of other persons, he may be convicted of both culpable homicide and driving under the influence of intoxicating liquor — *Grobler* 1972 (4) SA 559 (O) and *Koekemoer* 1973 (1) PH H20 (N). Simultaneous convictions of driving under the influence of liquor and negligent driving, may be appropriate where on the proven facts both forms of culpable conduct can be distinguished — *Mlilo* 1985 (1) SA 74 (T). If, however, evidence relating to the negligent driving is used as probative material to prove that the driver's judgment and skill were affected by the consumption of liquor, then the accused can only be convicted of driving under the influence of liquor. Common sense and considerations of reasonableness, dictated the finding that otherwise an unwarranted duplication of convictions would occur — *Wehr* 1998 (1) SACR 99 (C).

(6) Where an accused is caught selling dagga, he may be convicted only of selling and not also of possession of the rest of the (unsold) dagga — *Ebrahim* 1974 (2) SA 78 (N). The courts are not unanimous as to whether dealing in or possession of dagga and mandrax at the same time constitutes one or two offences — *Diedericks* 1984 (3) SA 814 (C) and *Phillips* 1984 (4) SA 536 (C).

(7) Where there is no evidence that an accused armed himself with the intention to commit an eventual assault, he may be convicted of both the unlawful possession of a dangerous weapon (in terms of s 2(1) of Act 71 of 1968) and assault — *Zenzile* 1975 (1) SA 210 (E) and *Mbulawa* 1969 (1) SA 532 (E).

(8) In cases where an act of assault does indeed constitute an element of attempted murder, a conviction of attempted murder and robbery will result in an accused being convicted twice of the same act of assault if the same complainant in both offences was shot with a firearm and robbed — *Benjamin* 1980 (1) SA 950 (A). Cf however, *Moloto* 1980 (3) SA 1081 (BH). If, however, it was proved beyond reasonable doubt that the accused also had the intention to kill and not merely to use force, the court is entitled to find him guilty of the two separate offences — *Moloto* 1982 (1) SA 844 (A).

5.4 Conduct of the perpetrator is spread over a long period of time and amounts to a continuous repetition of the same offence

As to whether such conduct should form the subject of one conviction only, the decisions of our courts are conflicting.

Illustrations:

(1) A separation into two counts of keeping an eating-house in a disorderly way on four consecutive days amounts to an unlawful splitting — *Zuny* 1919 JS §345.

(2)   Once the fact had been established that a person was wrongfully practising as a medical practitioner, each act of treating a patient, separate in respect of time and place, was regarded as a separate contravention — *Hannah* 1913 AD 484.

(3)   Where an accused had made an arrangement with S, an officer of the public service, that he would pay S a certain amount in respect of each motor vehicle ordered by the Administration from the accused, it was held that every subsequent individual transaction could properly form the subject of a separate charge of bribery — *Ingham* 1958 (2) SA 37 (C) and cf *Vorster* 1976 (2) PH H202 (A).

(4)   Where failing to report the presence of terrorists in the neighbourhood over a period of time was separated into several offences, it was held that splitting of charges had taken place — *Mutawarira* 1973 (3) SA 901 (R).

(5)   Where an accused has stolen goods from two complainants living in the same room he can only be convicted on one charge of theft — *Polelo* 1981 (2) SA 271 (NC) and *Ntswakele* 1982 (1) SA 325 (T).

(6)   The state is entitled to rely on a course of conduct on the part of the accused in order to charge the accused on the ground of a series of acts done in pursuance of one criminal design as a single crime. The various alleged acts are not mentioned as separate charges in the charge sheet, but by means of particulars in respect of a single charge, e g one charge of treason or sedition, based on a series of acts — *Zwane* (1) 1987 (4) SA 369 (W).

Prejudice to the accused, if he is convicted on more than one charge arising from one and the same punishable fact contrary to the above-mentioned rule, could result in one or both of the following ways: first, the combined punishment imposed by a magistrate in respect of the various charges could exceed that which it would have been competent for him to impose if the accused were to have been found guilty of one charge only (the magistrate's jurisdiction in respect of maximum punishment relates to every single charge separately) and, secondly. the number of convictions could affect the accused adversely on a subsequent conviction, considering the effect of previous convictions regarding permissible punishment — see Chapter 19. Further to the above: in sentencing, courts are also enjoined to guard against the duplication of punishment which could result where two convictions arise out of the same incident (e g rape/robbery and murder, where the victim is killed in the act of being raped/robbed). Although many of the facts relevant to one conviction may also be relevant to the other, taking the same facts into account in sentencing an accused for each of the two different offences could result in such a duplication of punishment — *Morten* 1991 (1) SACR 483 (A) and s 1991 (2) SA 93 (A).

Should the prosecutor in the same indictment bring a whole series of charges against the accused, for example incest, rape and connection with a female below the age of 16 years, all arising out of the same act of intercourse, the accused may not, as a rule, object to the indictment, but may object to conviction of more than one of the offences.

If an accused had been convicted (or acquitted) of offence X and the prosecutor thereafter charges him with offence Y, which, if it had been brought against him when he was charged with X, would have amounted to a splitting of charges (as we understand this expression now), the accused may raise the plea of *autrefois convict* or *acquit* (as the case may be). To give an example: A is charged with rape of a 15-year-old girl. He is found not guilty. He cannot subsequently be charged with unlawful connection with a girl below the age of 16 years. Should he be charged thus, he can plead *autrefois acquit*. (*Autrefois convict* and *autrefois acquit* will be dealt with below.)

6 JOINDER OF OFFENCES

In practice the prosecutor usually charges the accused with the most serious crime as main charge, and the lesser offences as alternative charges.

Apart from undue splitting, which we have just discussed, any number of offences may be charged against the same accused in one indictment — s 81(1). It must, however, take place at any time before any evidence has been led in respect of any particular charge. If this provision is not complied with, the proceedings are void, not merely voidable — *Thipe* 1988 (3) SA 346 (T). The court may, however, direct that the charges thus joined be tried separately, if in its opinion this will be in the interests of justice — s 81(2). It is desirable that where the state has knowledge of a number of charges against a person, it should endeavour as far as is reasonably possible to bring such charges before the court in one indictment so that they are tried together — *Lubbe* 1925 TPD 219 and *Jantjies* 1982 (4) SA 790 (C). But the trial of separate charges may not take place separately on the basis of 'trials within the main trial' — *Majola* 1971 (3) SA 804 (N).

Up to 1963 a charge of murder could not be joined in the same indictment with any other charge, but this limitation has now been removed — see, for example, *Mathebula* 1978 (2) SA 607 (A).

No additional charges can be joined after questioning of the accused in terms of s 112(1)*(b)* (*see the discussion of the plea of guilty* below) has commenced — *Witbooi* 1980 (2) SA 911 (NC).

7 THE JOINDER OF SEVERAL ACCUSED

Section 155 provides that any number of participants in the *same offence* may be tried together, as well as any number of accessories after the fact to an offence, or both participants and accessories in respect of the same offence. The section further provides that a receiver of property obtained by means of an offence shall be deemed to be a participant in the offence in question. The first part of this section requires that the co-accused took part in the same offence. Where, on a charge of having been found in the possession of meat reasonably suspected to have been stolen and not being able to give a satisfactory account of such possession, it appeared that separate meat was involved, it constituted a misjoinder to charge the two accused jointly — *Chawe* 1970 (2) SA 414 (NC).

Section 156 provides that whenever it is alleged in a charge that two or more persons have committed separate offences at the same place and time, or at about the same time, and the prosecutor informs the court that any evidence which is in his opinion admissible at the trial of one of those persons is in his opinion also admissible at the trial of the other person or persons, such persons may be tried jointly for those offences on that charge. Thus persons who through participation in the same transaction, commit different offences may be jointly charged and tried, for example, where a man procures and furnishes premises in which women carry on prostitution, on the proceeds whereof he lives, he and they may be charged and tried together: he with living on the proceeds of prostitution, and they with carrying on the practice. Prior to the enactment of s 156 it was held that where a passenger was killed as a result of a collision between two motor cars, there were two separate offences and that joinder of the two drivers was irregular — *Meyer* 1948 (3) SA 144 (T). But s 156 leaves little doubt that such joinder would no longer be irregular. In *Gelderbloem* 1962 (3) SA 631 (C), however, it was held that where two persons were charged with having pointed a firearm at the complainant each person's conduct constituted a separate transaction and that joinder was irregular. It is submitted that this decision is correct. Although separate offences were committed at the same time and place, evidence that X had pointed a gun would not be admissible in a charge that Y had pointed a gun, or vice versa. But it must be noted that the section makes proper joinder dependent upon the *opinion* of the public prosecutor as to admissibility. It is submitted that a court should satisfy itself that the prosecutor's opinion is *bona fide* and based on a reasonable interpretation of the rules of evidence.

Two or more persons alleged to have committed offences of sabotage at the same time and place, or at the same place and approximately the same time, may be charged jointly with such offences — s 67*(a)*, Act 74 of 1982. The intention of the legislature was obviously to make provision for the joinder of several accused persons who are charged with *different acts* of sabotage.

The provisions of the Criminal Procedure Act and Act 74 of 1982 regarding joinder are not peremptory. The prosecutor need not, therefore, join the said persons. The provisions are merely permissive. Furthermore, there is no provision for the addition of further accused *during* the trial; such a procedure would, in respect of that accused, offend against s 158 (principle of confrontation; trial in presence of accused — see Chapter 5).

The replies to the questioning of an accused in terms of s 112(1)*(b)* are not 'evidence' in terms of s 157(1), and further accused can therefore be joined after an accused has been questioned in terms of s 112(1)*(b)* — *Slabbert* 1985 (4) SA 248 (C).

In terms of s 332(5) directors of a company may be charged jointly with the company. The subsection also makes provision for separate trials.

The right of persons who are jointly charged to apply for separate trials will be discussed later.

CHAPTER 13

The court

		Page
1	VENUE OF THE COURT	186
2	CONSTITUTION OF THE COURT . . . . , ...	186
	2.1 Lower courts	186
	2.2 Superior courts	187
	2.3 Rights and duties of assessors	188
	2.4 Trial by jury	189
3	IMPARTIALITY AND FAIRNESS	190
	3.1 General	190
	3.1.1 Introduction	190
	3.1.2 Impartiality and courtesy	191
	3.1.3 *Audi alteram partem*	192
	3.1.4 Decisions solely upon evidence; the oath	192
	3.2 Fairness to the accused	192
	3.3 Recusal	194
	3.3.1 General	194
	3.3.2 Application for recusal of judicial officer	194

Omit 2.4

The Constitution and this chapter:

Section 9 — Equality

(1) Every one is equal before the law and has the right to equal protection and benefit of the law.

See 3.1.2, below.

Section 34 — Access to courts

Every one has the right to have any dispute that can be resolved by the application of law decided in a fair public hearing before a court or, where appropriate, another independent and impartial tribunal or forum.

See 3.1.2 and 3.3.1, below.

Section 35 — Arrested, detained and accused persons

(3) Every accused person has a right to a fair trial, which includes the right —
. . .

(*h*) to be presumed innocent, to remain silent, and not to testify during the proceedings;

(*i*) to adduce and challenge evidence; . . .

See 3.1.3 and 3.2, below.

---

1 VENUE OF THE COURT

For superior courts the venue of the court is fixed at the permanent seat of the provincial and local divisions or is specified in the proclamation constituting circuit courts. Lower courts must sit at the places assigned by the President in terms of s 2 of the Magistrates' Court Act 32 of 1944. Certain exceptions are allowed with juvenile accused and with patients in leper asylums, etc, where the venue of the court may be changed respectively to a room other than the regular courtroom or to the asylum.

If the accused is brought before a court which lacks jurisdiction to try him, he may object to the jurisdiction of that court. However, if he fails to object and the trial, having run its normal course, ends in a conviction, the fact that the venue was wrong will not avail the accused on appeal — see s 110, Act 51 of 1977, which applies to both superior and lower courts; and see *Nqunelo* 1948 (4) SA 428 (O).

Section 149 makes provision for the removal of a criminal case from one *superior court* to another on application of the prosecution or of the accused. The effect of such removal may be to confer jurisdiction upon a court which would not normally have been competent to try the accused.

Such an application for removal will not be granted unless the applicant can show that the change of venue would be in the interests of justice, for example where it may reasonably be feared that the evidence may be lost or tampered with if the trial has to stand over for months until the next session of the circuit court. In *Bothma* 1957 (2) SA 100 (O), it was held that the mere saving of time would not be considered a valid ground for removal. It should be noted that s 149 applies only to superior courts.

A court can order the removal of a trial to another venue in order to protect witnesses whose lives are threatened — see *Mbaka* 1964 (2) SA 280 (E), where the court made its order by virtue of s 169.

According to section 22(3) of Act 32 of 1998 where the national director or a deputy director authorised thereto in writing by the national director deems it in the interest of the administration of justice that an offence committed as a whole or partially within the area of jurisdiction of one director be investigated and tried within the area of jurisdiction of another director, he or she may, subject to the provisions of section 111 of the Criminal Procedure Act, in writing direct that the investigation and criminal proceedings in respect of such offence be conducted and commenced within the area of jurisdiction of such other director.

2 CONSTITUTION OF THE COURT

2.1 Lower courts

These courts are presided over by magistrates. In a district or regional court trial the magistrate may, if he deems it expedient for the administration of justice, in the case of any application for bail or proceedings concerning the imposition of a sentence upon a convicted person, summon one or two assessors to assist him or her at the proceedings. At the trial of an accused in respect of murder, rape, robbery or rape (in both instances where bodily harm has been inflicted on the victim) and indecent assault, the judicial officer must summon two assessors to assist him or her. In considering whether summoning assessors would be expedient for the administration of justice, the judicial officer shall take into account factors like the cultural, social and educational background of the accused, the nature and seriousness of the offence, the interests which the community may have in the adjudication of the matter concerned, etc. The assessors commence with their functions after the plea has been recorded. With regard to matters of fact the decision of the court is that of the majority thereof. Matters of law (and deciding whether a matter for decision is a matter of law) are decided by the judicial officer — s 93*ter* Act 32 of 1944.

2.2 Superior courts

Criminal cases in superior courts are tried either by a judge sitting alone, or by a judge and one or two assessors. The presiding judge generally has a discretion whether or not to sit with assessors. (The advantages which the assistance of assessors may render a judge at a trial should, however, not be underestimated — *Mhlongo* 1991 (2) SACR 207 (A).)

In practice, the trial judge is obliged to rely, to a certain extent, on the recommendation of the director of public prosecutions or a member of his staff (counsel for the State). In the final analysis, it is the trial judge who has to come to a conclusion in this matter, and the opinion of the director of public prosecutions is but one factor to be taken into account for this purpose, along with other information (eg the summary of salient facts accompanying the indictment — see Chapter 12) — *Schoba* 1985 (3) SA 881 (A). In *Bosman* 1988 (2) SA 485 (A), after counsel for the State had given certain information to the trial judge, the latter decided that it was unlikely that the death sentence would be imposed, and decided not to appoint assessors. The trial, however, took an unforeseen turn when the appellant adopted a different defence to that which the state had expected. The court found that there were no extenuating circumstances and imposed the death penalty. The Supreme Court of Appeal found that in the circumstances no irregularity had been committed.

An assessor is a person who, in the opinion of the presiding judge, has experience in the administration of justice or skill in any matter which may be considered at the trial — s 145(1)*(b)*. Usually the judge procures the services of advocates for this purpose, but occasionally magistrates (especially retired magistrates), attorneys and professors of law serve in this capacity. In cases in which expert evidence on a particular topic is expected to be led, the judge may sit with an assessor who is professionally qualified in the field in question (eg in medicine, engineering, accountancy, etc). Section 147(1)*(a)* provides that if an assessor dies or, in the opinion of the presiding judge, becomes unable to act as assessor at any time during a trial, the presiding judge may direct that the trial proceed before the remaining member or members of the court, or that the trial begin *de novo*. In terms of s 147(1), the words *unable to act* embrace not only physical disabilities but also mental disabilities. An assessor who is subjected to serious and continued emotional stress during a trial in which he is sitting as an assessor may, because of such stress, become *unable to act* as an assessor. Pressing commitments elsewhere cannot constitute an inability to act as an assessor within the meaning of the word — *Gqeba* 1989 (3) SA 712 (A).The Court has no power to dispense with his/her presence and proceed without him/her; not even with the consent of the accused — *Daniels* 1997 (2) SACR 531 (C). The inability to act in the context of s 147(1) is not applicable to a situation where an assessor is legally incompetent to continue to act in a case because of some act or occurrence which warranted the assessor's recusal — *Malindi* 1990 (1) SA

962 (A). If the mental capability and/or competency of the assessor to fulfil his duties are in issue, the matter has to be decided on the common law basis of the duty of a judicial officer to recuse himself. However, the test of reasonable perception or suspicion of the parties as to impartiality is not applicable. The assessor's competence or lack thereof can be established objectively — *Kroon* 1997 (1) SACR 525 (SCA).

Where a judge, acting in terms of s 147(1), finds an assessor has become unable to act as such, it is incumbent upon him to hear the parties on the question of how the proceedings will be conducted further (ie with one assessor or *de novo*). In general, the parties are entitled to be heard before the judge comes to the decision that an assessor has become unable to act — *Malindi* (above); *K* 1997 (1) SACR 106 (C).

2.3 Rights and duties of assessors

Before the trial commences, the assessors must take an oath that they will give a true verdict, according to the evidence upon the issues to be tried. As soon as this oath has been administered by the judge, the assessors are members of the court, with the following provisos:

(1) Subject to para (2) and (3) below and s 217(3)*(b)*, the decision or finding of the majority of the members of the court upon any question of fact or upon the question referred to in para (2), shall be the decision or finding of the court, except when the presiding judge sits with only one assessor, in which case the decision or finding of the judge shall, in the case of a difference of opinion, be the decision or finding of the court;

(2) If the presiding judge is of the opinion that it would be in the interests of the administration of justice that the assessor(s) assisting him do not take part in any decision upon the question whether evidence of any confession or other statement made by an accused is admissible as evidence against him, the judge alone shall decide upon such question, and he may for this purpose sit alone. It is clear that the judge may now, in his discretion, together with the assessors determine the admissibility of a confession or other statement made by the accused — s 145(4)*(a)* and *(b)*; *Ngcobo* 1985 (2) SA 319 (W);

(3) The presiding judge alone shall decide upon any other question of law or upon any question whether any matter constitutes a question of law or a question of fact, and he may for this purpose sit alone — s 145(4). An application at the close of the State's case for the accused's discharge in terms of s 174 is one of law, and the decision is that of the judge alone — *Magxwalisa* 1984 (2) SA 314 (N);

(4) A judge presiding at a criminal trial in a superior court shall give the reasons for his decision where he decides any question of law or whether any matter constitutes a question of law or a question of fact. The judge shall also give the reasons for the decision or finding of the court upon any question of fact or the question referred to in par (2) above, whether he sits with or without assessors. Where the judge sits with assessors and there is a difference of opinion upon any question of fact or upon the question referred to in para (2), he shall give the reasons for the minority decision — s 146.

As soon as an assessor receives information detrimental to the accused which has not been proved in evidence, he must retire from the case — *Matsego* 1956 (3) SA

411 (A). In *Solomons* 1959 (2) SA 352 (A) the irregularity in the case was that the assessors had gained information that the accused had at an earlier stage of that same evening been involved in knife-assaults. This information did not form part of the evidence at the trial. An assessor must show absolute impartiality: his or her expressing an opinion about a particular witness before the accused has been called to state his defense, will be grossly irregular — *Mayekiso* 1996 (1) SACR 510 (C). Cf also *Stone* 1976 (2) SA 279 (A).

The function of assessors is limited to the hearing of the trial, and since the trial is the determination of the matters put in issue and ends with the verdict, the assessors have no part with the judge in the assessment or the imposition of the sentence; although, according to Hiemstra 361, it is not irregular for the judge to seek the advice of his assessors in the matter of sentence. In practice this is frequently done — cf *Sparks* 1972 (3) SA 396 (A) and *Lekaoto* 1978 (4) SA 684 (A); *Malgas* 1996 (1) SACR 73 (NC).

Cf in general Richings 1976 *Criminal Law Review* 107–16; Dugard 1 (2) *Crime, Correction & Punishment* 55–9 (Nov 1972); Bekker 'Assessore in Suid-Afrikaanse strafsake' *Huldigingsbundel vir WA Joubert* (1988) 32–49; Watney 1992 *THRHR* 465.

2.4 Trial by jury

The jury system in South Africa meant that all criminal trials in the superior court, (except those in the former Natal Native High Court and special courts) took place before a judge and nine jury members. Only white males could become members of a jury. In 1931 provision was made for juries consisting of women only when it was requested by a female accused or an accused under the age of eighteen years. Initially the decision of jury members had to be unanimous. Later a majority of seven votes out of nine was required.

The jury system was introduced in South Africa in 1827 via Britain but was eventually abolished by the Abolition of Juries Act 34 of 1969.

By 'jury' is meant a panel of laymen who act in criminal cases as the sole judges of the *facts*. Judgment on legal questions and the eventual imposition of sentences are matters for the judge alone. A jury may give judgment of 'guilty' or 'not guilty', or a special judgment on the facts. The accused or the prosecutor may object to the members of the jury as a group or as individuals.

The jury system exists in several countries, *inter alia* Canada, England, Australia, New Zealand and the USA. In England and the USA the system is regarded as the cornerstone of an impartial and acceptable system of justice, because the cold logic of criminal law is tempered by the logic of a group of independent and theoretically impartial ordinary citizens of the country who come from all strata of society.

The main objection to the jury system is that it is a cumbersome and inefficient system and that judicial decisions should be left in the hands of specialists, ie trained judges. Where the jury system was introduced in Continental legal systems, it was generally abandoned for a system of trials by a bench consisting of trained judges and lay assessors who decide jointly on the questions of guilt, innocence and sentence, eg France, Belgium, Germany, Italy and Spain.

Owing to the complex composition of South African society, the jury system in South Africa changed from a trial with jury members to a trial where the accused could demand to be tried without jury members. In such a case the judge could obtain two assessors to sit with him in an advisory capacity on the facts. At a later stage it became compulsory by statute to have two assessors in trials where the charge was treason, sedition, murder or rape or where the Minister of Justice had ordered a trial without a jury. After 1959 the compulsory taking of assessors was abolished and it was left to the discretion of the judge. In 1954 the jury system suffered a serious setback when the onus of requesting a trial by jury was placed on the accused. Magistrates were obliged, when committing an accused for trial after a preparatory examination, to inform him of his right to demand a trial by jury — a right which was exercised less and less frequently until it was realised that the system had become unsuitable for South Africa and it was abolished in 1969.

The jury system did not pass unnoticed but strongly influenced especially our law of evidence with its complicated rules. Its demise does not seem to be entirely irreversible: the reintroduction of the system in South Africa's future legal dispensation is the subject of speculation from time to time.

On the jury system in general see: W R Cornish *The Jury* (1968); Kalven & Zeisel *The American Jury* (1966); S A Strauss 1960 *Acta Juridica* 164 and S A Strauss 1973 *West Australian Law Journal* 133; E Kahn 1992 *BML* 135, 163 and 201 as well as 1992 (109) SALJ 307; J P J Coetzer 1992 *Consultus* 124.

3 IMPARTIALITY AND FAIRNESS

3.1 General

3.1.1 *Introduction*

The Criminal Procedure Act lays down certain rules of procedure which should be observed, but the trial is otherwise subject to the management of the judicial officer presiding over it. All orders given in the judicial discretion of the presiding judge or other judicial officer for the proper conduct of the trial must be obeyed by the parties, the court staff and the public, who are all, in the event of wilful disobedience, liable to be committed or fined summarily for contempt of court.

A famous formulation regarding the course of a criminal trial is that of Lord Hewart in *Sussex Justices* (1924) 1 KB 256 at 259:

> '. . . [I]t is not merely of some importance, but of fundamental importance, that justice should both be done and be manifestly seen to be done . . . The rule is that nothing is to be done which creates even a suspicion that there has been an improper interference with the course of justice.'

This eloquent passage has been repeated frequently, sometimes in a modified form by our courts — cf *Sallem* 1987 (4) SA 772 (A) and *Marx* 1989 (1) SA 222 (A) at 225. One facet of the maxim that justice must be seen to be done is the requirement that witnesses and accused persons must be treated courteously by the court, the defence and the prosecution — cf *Abrahams* 1989 (2) SA 668 (E).

The concept of 'justice' in its procedural sense is closely related to the idea of legality (see Chapter 1); it is not a concept which presupposes that the accused is not guilty, but rather one which refers to a quality of the proceedings — cf *Mushimba* 1977 (2) SA 829 (A) at 844. It is clearly illustrated in *Dozereli* 1983 (3) SA 259 (C), where an accused was asked, contrary to s 197, why he had been in prison before (this section prohibits information regarding previous convictions, with certain exceptions, in the trial stages prior to sentencing). The reviewing court stated that this is not excusable, even though the magistrate affirmed that he had not based the conviction on this information; it also does not matter whether the accused is really guilty or not. The only question is whether the basic right of the accused to a fair trial has been affected by the irregularity to such a degree that it cannot in principle be said that justice was done. (In casu the reviewing court set the conviction aside.) Apart from what is stated in the following paragraph the standards which a judicial officer should maintain in the questioning of witnesses and the accused have been summarised in *Mabuza* 1991 (1) SACR 636 (O) as follows:

(1) The court should not conduct its questioning in such a manner that its impartiality can be questioned or doubted.

(2) The court should not take part in the case to such an extent that its vision is clouded by the 'dust of the arena' and is then unable to adjudicate properly on the issues.

(3) The court should not intimidate or upset a witness or the accused so that his answers are weakened or his credibility shaken.

(4) The court should control the trial in such a way that its impartiality, its open-mindedness, its fairness and reasonableness are manifest to all who have an interest in the trial, in particular the accused.

A judicial officer can only properly fulfil his demanding and socially important duties if he guards against his own actions, is attentive to his own weaknesses (such as impatience), personal opinions and whims, and continually restrains them.

3.1.2 *Impartiality and courtesy*

The presiding judge or magistrate must endeavour to be absolutely fair to both the prosecution and the defence. The individual has the right to equality before the law and to equal protection of the law (s 8 of the Constitution) and to have justiciable disputes settled by a court of law or, where appropriate, *another* independent and impartial forum — s 22 of the Constitution. (Every criminal court, therefore, is presupposed to be impartial.)

In *Jacobs* 1970 (2) PH H152 (C) two witnesses who had initially stated that they did not know the accused, having been threatened by the magistrate with a whipping in the cells unless they told the truth, then identified the accused. On the review it was held that the procedure adopted constituted such a serious irregularity that a failure of justice *per se* had resulted. Setting aside the conviction and sentence the judge said:

> 'I think that it is hardly necessary for me to say that what happened in this case constituted a very gross irregularity. While it is true that it is the function of a criminal court to determine the guilt or innocence of the accused, *it performs this function in accordance with certain accepted norms of procedure. These involve, inter alia, the concepts of fairness to the accused, courtesy to witnesses and an adherence to certain civilized standards of behaviour.* It has never been recognized in the courts of this country that, because guilty persons should be punished, any procedure, however unfair or unseemly, may be employed if it helps to establish the guilt of the accused' (at 291, our emphasis).

In *Rall* 1982 (1) SA 828 (A) the Supreme Court of Appeal stated some of the limitations within which judicial questioning of witnesses should be confined. Cf also *Omar* 1982 (2) SA 357 (N) regarding unfair cross-examination of an accused and *Zungu* 1984 (1) SA 376 (N) regarding doubts as to a presiding judicial officer's impartiality as a result of circumstances arising after the conclusion of a trial and before its reopening. Witnesses and accused persons should not be addressed by means of the impersonal terms 'witness' and 'accused', but should be addressed by surname, eg 'Mr Gwebu' — *Gwebu* 1988 (4) SA 155 (W); *Abrahams* 1989 (2) SA 668 (E); *Gqulagha* 1990 (1) SACR 101 (A); *T* 1990 (1) SACR 57 (T). It is also disrespectful, if not degrading, to address an adult as a juvenile (*in casu* by addressing him by his first name) — *Kuse* 1990 (1) SACR 191 (E).

3.1.3 *Audi alteram partem*

No ruling of any importance, either on the merits or on procedural points, should be made without giving both parties the opportunity of expressing their views — *Suliman* 1969 (2) SA 385 (A). The principle of *audi alteram partem* should always be observed — *Bidi* 1969 (2) SA 55 (R); *Zuma* [1996] 3 All SA 334 (N). Indeed, in terms of s 25(3)*(d)* of the Constitution every accused has the right to adduce and challenge evidence.

3.1.4 *Decisions solely upon evidence; the oath*

Judicial officers must base their decisions solely upon evidence heard in open court in the presence of the accused. A judicial officer should have no communication whatever with either party in a case before him except in the presence of the other, and no communication with any witness except in the presence of both parties — *Maharaj* 1960 (4) SA 256 (N); *Harricharan* 1962 (3) SA 35 (N); *Seedat* 1971 (1) SA 789 (N). Nor may a judicial officer take notice of documentary information (eg contained in the police docket) which had not been tendered as evidence — *Du Toit* 1972 (1) PH H50 (E).

Evidence must be given upon oath or upon a solemn affirmation in lieu of an oath or upon a serious admonition to speak the truth — ss 162–4. In *I* 1973 (3) SA 794 (A) the complainant was a 5-year-old girl who did not know the difference between the truth and untruth. Her evidence was inaudible except to her mother who repeated it to the court. The mother was unsworn. On appeal the conviction was set aside on account of such irregularity.

It is the duty of the court to be impartial; the presiding judicial officer or, in the case of a superior court, the presiding judge or the registrar of the court shall administer the oath in respect of witnesses — s 162(1). The prosecutor may not do so — *Bothma* 1971 (1) SA 332 (C); cf s 112 of the Magistrates' Courts Act. An interpreter, in the presence of the judge or magistrate, may naturally also be used — s 165.

Witnesses must be allowed to give evidence in their own words in their own way and at their own tempo. Only in that way can the truth be ascertained, and this is usually all the more so when the court is dealing with those who are less knowledgeable and sophisticated — *Hendriks* 1974 (2) PH H91 (C).

3.2 Fairness to the accused

Where the accused is undefended the court should ensure that the accused is aware of his rights at all times and that he is given every opportunity of conducting his defence adequately; cf *Nhantsi* 1994 (1) SACR 26 (Tk). These rights have to be explained to the accused by the presiding judicial official (not, for instance, by the interpreter) — *Mzo* 1980 (1) SA 538 (C). Likewise, his duties, such as the duty to discharge a particular onus in certain cases, should be carefully explained to him — *Sibisi* 1972 (2) SA 446 (N). In certain circumstances such an explanation should be given even before pleading — *Guess* 1976 (1) PH H37 (C).

The accused's rights include the right to cross-examine (*Sebatana* 1983 (1) SA 809 (O); *Dipholo* 1983 (4) SA 751 (T)) this includes also the right to give evidence and cross-examine in the language of his choice irrespective of his apparent race — *Leseana* 1993 (2) SACR 264 (T); the putting of his defence to State witnesses during cross-examination (*Govazela* 1987 (4) SA 297 (O)); to call witnesses (*Selemana* 1975 (4) SA 908 (T)); *Hlongwane* 1982 (4) SA 321 (N)); to produce relevant documents, facts and figures, to record the evidence if he so wishes (*Mohlabane* 1969 (2) PH H137 (O)); to testify and to present argument to the court and to make representations regarding sentence (cf *Sibisi*, above). At the close of the State's case he must be fully informed of his legal rights — *Radebe* 1988 (1) SA 191 (T).

The presiding officer should be patient with the accused and be courteous at all times — *Mpofu* 1970 (2) SA 162 (R). If the accused is unduly hampered by the court in his cross-examination of State witnesses, it may result in his conviction being set aside upon review or appeal — *Leeuwner* 1972 (1) PH H51 (E). In T 1990 (1) SACR 57 (T) the conviction was set aside owing to the magistrate's obstruction of the cross-examination of an undefended accused. In *Sallem* 1987 (4) SA 772 (A) a conviction was set aside where the magistrate had not controlled his impatience and had thereby committed a series of irregularities and misdirections. A conviction will also be set aside if an unrepresented accused is prejudiced by a failure of the judicial officer to inform him of his legal rights — *Radebe* 1988 (1) SA 191 (T); *Khambule* 1991 (2) SACR 277 (W).

It is a general principle of our law, stemming from its accusatorial character, that the court is not entitled to question the accused on the merits of the case unless he *suo motu* testifies under oath. This principle must be respected in the course of the trial — *Grotes*; *Jawuka* 1970 (1) SA 368 (C). The accused, therefore, may 'defend' himself by keeping silent. This is his procedural right. However, while an accused is not compelled to speak, in certain circumstances his silence may damage his case: it is a factor which may be taken into account in assessing the weight of the evidence in its totality. But where the State's case depends, for example, upon the drawing of inferences from circumstantial evidence, the accused's silence may well be explained as resulting from his confidence that the evidence adduced by the State does not establish guilt and does not require to be answered. Cf *Khomo* 1975 (1) SA 344 (D), and the textbooks on the law of evidence. See also *K* 1956 (3) SA 353 (A) at 358, and *Dube* 1915 AD 557; *Nomakhalala* 1990 (1) SACR 300 (A).

The accused's 'right to silence' (or more correctly, the 'right not be questioned') has been qualified only by s 115 relating to the 'plea explanation' procedure — see chapter 14 below. Such questioning by the presiding officer, however, may take place *only* on arraignment and not during the course of the trial. After an accused has been convicted, the court is entitled to know, and it is the duty of the prosecution to inform it, of the previous convictions of the accused, in order to assist it in assessing the proper punishment to impose on the accused. However, during the trial all knowledge of previous convictions of the accused should be withheld from the court, since such knowledge may influence the court to the prejudice of the accused — see s 211. The prosecution is entitled only in exceptional circumstances to prove such previous convictions before verdict, such as where the accused has attacked the character of a State witness or has given evidence of his own good character — s 197. It may be pointed out in passing that it will in practice not always be possible to keep from a judge the fact that an accused has a previous criminal record. If, for instance, an accused is indicted in the High Court for a petty offence, it should be evident to anyone with any knowledge of procedure that the accused's record of previous convictions must be considerable to have justified his trial in the High Court and not in the magistrate's court.

The accused will, however, not be entitled to complain of such inferential knowledge, whereas, if such information is improperly disclosed to the court, the conviction will generally be set aside even though the magistrate might state that he had not been influenced by the information (*Persotam* 1934 TPD 253), *unless* the court of appeal is, in the circumstances of the particular case, satisfied that no failure of justice has resulted from such disclosure — s 322. Of course, if during the trial, the fact of the accused's previous convictions is revealed by the defence, such knowledge will, as a rule, not invalidate the conviction of the accused.

3.3 Recusal

3.3.1 *General*

It is a clear rule of our law that no person who has an interest in or harbours any prejudice in respect of the matter to be tried should adjudicate on such matter. (See the remarks on impartiality in 3.1.2, above.)

Since the Criminal Procedure Act does not contain any provisions on the subject of recusal, the common-law rules must be applied in applications for the recusal of judges, magistrates, or, it is suggested, assessors.

3.3.2 *Application for recusal of judicial officer*

Such application should, if possible, be made at the commencement of the trial in order to obviate unnecessary complications, such as a discontinuation of a partly heard trial and the necessity of starting it *de novo*. If unavoidable, such an application may be made in the course of the trial — *Silber* 1952 (2) SA 475 (A). Such application must, however, be made in respectful and courteous terms and must not be wilfully insulting as the application in the case of *Silber* was held to be.

As a general rule, any magistrate or judge who is aware that he has any feeling of partiality, enmity or any motive which might actuate him or be commonly supposed to actuate him in deciding a matter, would of his own motion recuse himself and cause a substitute to try the matter. Where, for instance, a magistrate has in a previous capacity as a public prosecutor been concerned with the merits of a case, he should recuse himself, for, as it has been put, justice must not only in fact be done but must also appear to be done. Cf *Bailey* 1962 (4) SA 514 (E); *Anderson* 1973 (2) SA 502 (O); *Tampart* 1990 (1) SACR 282 (SWA); *Heita* 1992 (2) SACR 285 (Nm). Similarly it is grossly irregular for a presiding officer to hear an application for bail when he has previously taken down a confession from the same accused. The presiding officer should be an impartial, open-minded and uninformed adjudicator in the sense that he takes cognisance of only those facts about the case which are proven in court in the usual way — *Sibeko* 1990 (1) SACR 206 (T). The principle involved in an application for recusal is that no reasonable man should, by reason of the situation or action of a judicial officer, have grounds for suspecting that justice will not be administered in an impartial and unbiased manner — *Herbst* 1980 (3) SA 1026 (E). The fact that in reality the judicial officer was impartial or is likely to be impartial is not the test. It is the reasonable perception of the parties as to his impartiality that is important — *Malindi* 1990(1) SA 962 (A) 969G–I; *Council of Review, South African Defence Force v Mönnig* 1992 (3) SA 482 (A). The criterion for recusal is an objective one, ie whether the presiding officer's conduct leaves a right-thinking observer or litigant the impression that the accused did not receive a fair trial — *Maseko* 1990 (1) SACR 107 (A).

A relationship with one or other of the parties to a case also affords grounds for recusal, by reason of the not unnatural bias which may reasonably *be supposed* to result — *Head and Fortuin v Wollaston* 1926 TPD 549. Cf *Bam* 1972 (4) SA 41 (E). Irregularity in the questioning of a witness by the trial court does not mean that the presiding officer is necessarily biased — *Dawid* 1991 (1) SACR 375 (Nm). The mere fact that the judge and the accused belong to different race groups will obviously not amount to a ground for recusal — *Collier* 1995 (2) SACR 648 (C).

In *Segal* 1949 (3) SA 67 (C), it was held that it is undesirable for a magistrate who has conducted an inquest to preside at the trial arising from such inquest, unless there is no other judicial officer available.

When two judicial officers are attached to the same bench as colleagues, irrespective of order of rank, and one of them is a litigant or an accused, then there is a reasonable ground for the other to be recused from trying the action — *SA Motor Acceptance Corporation v Oberholzer* 1974 (4) SA 808 (T).

The interest on which an application for recusal is based should not, however, be so trifling or the association so remote that it would be unreasonable to suppose that it could have any effect upon the mind of the judge or magistrate concerned.

It has been held, for instance, that a magistrate is not disqualified because previously in his judicial capacity he dealt with a similar charge against the accused, although it may be better, on the whole, especially where a strong view has been expressed, that another magistrate should try the case — *Mukama* 1934 TPD 134. His mere knowledge of facts involved in the trial will not necessarily disqualify the presiding officer from hearing the case, where he brings it to the notice of the parties, and where there is no issue between him and the accused about the correctness of that knowledge — *Essa* 1964 (2) SA 13 (N). The fact that a judge has knowledge of facts obtained in civil proceedings in which the accused was concerned does not disqualify him from presiding at the subsequent criminal trial — *Mampie* 1980 (3) SA 777 (NC). Nor does knowledge of an accused's previous convictions *ipso facto* disqualify a judicial officer from trying a case — *Khan v Koch NO* 1970 (2) SA 403 (R). It is, however, preferable to incline towards granting an application for recusal in cases of uncertainty. If it could not be said that an accused could not harbour a reasonable fear that the court would reject his evidence because of a finding on his credibility in another trial, it would be preferable for the judicial officer to recuse himself — *Dawid* 1991 (1) SACR 375 (Nm).

Should a judicial officer refuse to recuse himself in a case where he should properly have done so, his refusal would create a good ground for review of the case. The case will, however, only be submitted for review after conviction, because the court will interfere with unterminated proceedings only in rare instances — *Burns* 1988 (3) SA 366 (C).

Threatening a judicial officer will not materially affect his impartiality, and his refusal to recuse himself is not irregular — *Radebe* 1973 (1) SA 796 (A).

Where a judge recuses himself *mero motu* and the accused is then charged before and convicted by another judge, such recusal will not readily be construed as a failure of justice as regards the accused — *Suliman* 1969 (2) SA 385 (A). But a judicial officer should not recuse himself unless he has asked the defence to make its submissions — *Suliman* (above).

Note that a judicial officer who recuses himself becomes *functus officio*. The whole trial becomes void and an accused may accordingly not claim that he be either acquitted or found guilty, in terms of s 106(4). A new trial may thus be instituted — *Magubane v Van der Merwe NO* 1969 (2) SA 417 (N).

CHAPTER 14

Arraignment and plea of an accused

		Page
1	ARRAIGNMENT	198
2	WHEN PLEA BY ACCUSED MAY BE DISPENSED WITH	199
2.1	Refusal to plead	199
2.2	Ambiguity in plea	200
2.3	Obstructive and rowdy behaviour	200
2.4	Mentally abnormal accused	200
2.5	Objections to the charge	201
3	PLEAS WHICH MAY BE RAISED BY ACCUSED	202
3.1	Pleas mentioned in the Act	202
3.2	Guilty	203
3.2.1	General	203
3.2.1.1	Questioning by the presiding official	204
3.2.1.2	Accused's version	205
3.2.1.3	The prosecutor's role	206
3.2.2	Statement by accused instead of questioning	207
3.2.3	Evidence or questioning with regard to sentence	207
3.2.4	Correction of plea of guilty	207
3.2.5	Committal for sentence by regional court	208
3.2.6	Amendment of plea from 'guilty' to 'not guilty'	209
3.3	Not guilty	210
3.3.1	Explanation of plea	210
3.3.2	Admissions made in the course of explanation of plea	211
3.3.3	Accused's participation	212
3.3.4	Committal to regional court	213
3.3.5	Amendment of plea of not guilty	214
3.3.6	procedure in essence	214
3.4	Prior conviction or acquittal	215
3.4.1	Basic principle	215
3.4.2	*Autrefois convict*	215

        3.4.3 *Autrefois acquit*   216
        3.4.4 Section 106 and the pleas *autrefois acquit/convict*   219
    3.5 Pardon by the President   219
    3.6 Plea to the jurisdiction of the court   219
    3.7 Discharge from prosecution   220
    3.8 Lack of authority of the prosecutor   220
    3.9 *Lis pendens*   221
    3.10 Pleas in the case of criminal defamation   221
    3.11 Plea as to an order of court on an unreasonable delay in a trial . .   221
4 AFTER PLEADING, ACCUSED ENTITLED TO VERDICT   221

The Constitution and this chapter:

Section 35 — Arrested, detained and accused persons

(3) Every accused person has a right to a fair trial, which includes the right —

   . . .

   (m) not to be tried for any offence in respect of an act or omission for which
   that person has previously been either acquitted or convicted; . . .

See 3.4, below.

Section 84 — Powers and functions of President: reprieve

(1) The President has the powers entrusted by the Constitution and legislation,
including those necessary to perform the functions of Head of State and head
of the national executive.

(2) The President is responsible for —

   . . .

   (j) pardoning or reprieving offenders and remitting any fines, penalties or
   forfeitures; . . .

See 3.5, below.

---

1 ARRAIGNMENT

This term is not defined in the Act. It is defined by Gardiner & Lansdown (at 350) as:

'The calling upon the accused to appear, the informing him of the crime charged against
him, the demanding of him whether he be guilty or not guilty, and the entering of his
plea . . . His plea having been entered he is said to stand arraigned.'

Where a number of accused are charged with the same offence on separate
charges, each individual charge must be read out to each of the accused. The
presiding officer should ensure that each accused should know exactly what he is
required to plead to — *Gwebu, Xaba* 1968 (4) SA 783 (T).

A conviction will be set aside if an accused is arraigned on a serious charge at such
short notice that he could not have been afforded sufficient time to prepare his
defence or to seek legal representation — *Masilela* 1990 (2) SACR 116 (T).

The holding of a 'mass trial' of a number of accused at one and the same time on
charges which are in no way related to each other, is highly irregular — *Marimo,
Ndhlovu* 1973 (2) SA 442 (R).

Nothing in the Act prescribes the place where the accused should stand. As a matter of practice he stands in the dock, but the court has a discretion to allow him to stand at another suitable place — *Mpofu* 1970 (2) SA 162 (R). An accused should be addressed courteously and not as 'Accused' — *Tyebela* 1989 (2) SA 22 (A). The basic concept of our legal system is that an accused must be fairly tried. That presupposes that the trial be conducted in accordance with the rules and principles of the law of criminal procedure. A trial should not be tainted by an irregularity or illegality, that is a departure from the formalities, rules and principles of procedure according to which our law requires a criminal trial to be initiated or conducted — *Rudman* 1992 (1) SA 343 (A).

The general principle of our criminal procedure is that the accused must be informed of the charge in open court and required to plead instantly thereto — s 105. Formal objections to the indictment or charge must be taken before the accused has pleaded, not afterwards (s 85). If he has already pleaded an objection cannot be raised and the trial must proceed. The defect, if any, can, however, be rectified during the trial in terms of s 86. If not, the point can still be raised at the end of the trial as a reason for acquittal — *David v Van Niekerk* 1958 (3) SA 82 (T). When an accused is requested to plead he can do so himself or his legal representative can plead on his behalf provided he is duly instructed and not prohibited by law from appearing — *Mpongoshe* 1980 (4) SA 593 (A).

When the legal adviser replies in writing or orally to any question by the court in terms of s 115(3) (see the discussion of the plea of not guilty) the accused must also confirm this but the court may not require of the accused to answer the questions personally — *Salie* 1986 (2) SA 295 (C). An accused's plea must be recorded, otherwise a conviction cannot stand — *Brandt* 1972 (1) PH HS17 (NC); *contra Williams* 1977 [1] WLR 400 (CA) where the English Court of Appeal held that where an accused intended to plead not guilty, but by an oversight had not been asked to plead, the defective arraignment had not invalidated the ensuing trial.

2 WHEN PLEA BY ACCUSED MAY BE DISPENSED WITH

2.1 Refusal to plead

The court shall enter a plea of not guilty if the accused will not plead or answer directly to the charge — *Monnanyane* 1977 (3) SA 976 (O). Such a plea entered by the court has the same effect as if the accused had actually pleaded (s 109). In *Mothopeng* 1965 (4) SA 484 (T) the opinion is expressed that the provisions of s 109 should not be invoked where an accused *bona fide* refuses to plead. Where the case was formally postponed to a certain date, but thereafter brought on before such date, and the accused, on being required to plead, refused to do so because he would thereby have been prejudiced in his right to request further particulars or to object to the charge sheet, the correct procedure would have been not to enter a plea of not guilty, but to let the matter stand down until the date to which it had originally been postponed.

To insist that an accused should plead after he has informed the court that he wishes to consult a legal representative, constitutes a gross departure from the established rules of procedure, and is in conflict with the fundamental right of an accused to have legal assistance — *Mkhize* 1978 (3) SA 1065 (T).

2.2 Ambiguity in plea

If, upon being required to plead, the accused does not do so directly, but makes a statement in which he admits certain facts, or pleads guilty adding reservations and refutations (eg guilty, but he attacked me first) the court should enter a plea of not guilty and then question the accused in terms of s 115 to ascertain what facts he is prepared to admit.

2.3 Obstructive and rowdy behaviour

If the accused's refusal to plead is accompanied by such improper behaviour that it obstructs the conduct of the proceedings of the court, the court may order him to be removed and may direct the trial to proceed in his absence — s 159(1). This power must be exercised with circumspection. A warning to the effect that if he should disrupt the proceedings, it would be competent for the judicial officer to complete the trial in his absence must, if possible, be given to the accused as it might influence him to change his attitude and state his case — *Mokoa* 1985 (1) SA 350 (O).

2.4 Mentally abnormal accused

If, when the accused is called upon to plead to a charge, it appears to be uncertain for any reason whether he is capable of understanding the proceedings at the trial, so as to be able to make a proper defence, an enquiry into his mental state should be made in accordance with the procedure laid down in ss 77 and 79. In terms of these sections, the investigation is made by the medical superintendent of a psychiatric hospital designated by the court, or by a psychiatrist appointed by him, at request of the court. Where, however, in any particular case the court so directs, the enquiry must be made by three persons: the medical superintendent (or his designate), a psychiatrist appointed by the court (who is not in the full-time service of the state) and a psychiatrist appointed by the accused, if he so wishes (cf *Magongo* 1987 (3) SA 519 (A)). For the purposes of this enquiry the accused may be committed to a psychiatric hospital for periods not exceeding thirty days at a time. When the period of committal is extended for the first time, such extension may be granted in the absence of the accused unless the accused or his legal representative requests otherwise — s 79(2)*(b)*. (Cf Chapter 5.) The report of the enquiry must include a diagnosis of the mental condition of the accused and a finding as to whether the accused is capable of understanding the proceedings so as to make a proper defence.

If the finding in the report is unanimous and is not disputed by either the prosecutor or the accused the court may determine the matter without hearing further evidence, but if the finding is not unanimous, or is disputed by the prosecutor or the accused the court must determine the matter after hearing evidence. (In either case the accused must, however, be present in court — *Eyden* 1982 (4) SA 141 (T); *Kahita* 1983 (4) SA 618 (C).) If the court finds that the accused is capable of understanding the proceedings, the proceedings continue in the ordinary way, but if the court finds that he is not so capable, it must direct that the accused be detained in a psychiatric hospital or prison pending the signification of the decision of a judge in chambers — *Skeyi* 1981 (4) SA 191 (E). Note that the mandatory provisions of ss 77(6)*(a)* and 78(6)*(b)* do not prohibit the attorney-general from stopping the proceedings against the accused in terms of s 6*(b)*. This procedure could be followed if the accused were a juvenile, or in case of a minor offence — *M* 1989 (3) SA 887 (W).

An accused is permitted to appeal against a finding that he was capable of understanding the proceedings if he is subsequently convicted, or against a finding that he is incapable provided that he did not himself allege this at the trial. Note that where an accused is declared incapable of understanding the proceedings he may later, on becoming so capable be indicted and tried for the offence in question.

The court ought to tend in the direction of an enquiry in terms of the Act if there is any measure of reasonable doubt concerning the mental state of the accused, and especially in a case where the accused is unrepresented — *Manupo* 1991 (2) SACR 447 (C).

An example of an instance where the accused was found to be incapable of understanding the proceedings by reason of mental illness is the case of *Pratt* 1960 (4) SA 743 (T), who was indicted for the attempted assassination of the then Prime Minister, Dr Verwoerd. A similar finding was made in the case of *Tsafendas* who assassinated Dr Verwoerd in 1966 (the case is not reported, but a full, translated version of the judgment is printed in G C Steyl *Regters aan die Woord* (1971) (7).

The so-called psychopath is generally capable of standing trial as well as being criminally liable (he does not fall under the provisions of ss 77 to 79) — *Mnyanda* 1976 (2) SA 751 (A); *Pieterse* 1982 (3) SA 678 (A); *Lawrence* 1991 (2) SACR 57 (A); see 1976 *CILSA* 1–56.

If it appears reasonably possible that an accused might not fully understand the nature of the proceedings and also might possibly not have been criminally responsible at the time when he committed the offence or, at least, that his moral blameworthiness might have been considerably reduced, having regard to his mental state at the time of the commission of the offence, the court is obliged by s 78(2) of the Act to direct that an enquiry into the mental condition of the accused be undertaken — *Tom* 1991 (2) SACR 249 (B).

If a court finds that the accused committed the act in question but, by reason of mental illness or mental defect (as the case may be), he was not criminally responsible, the court must find the accused not guilty and direct that he be detained pending the signification of the decision of a judge in chambers. Cf further *Mfazi* 1978 (4) SA 28 (T); *Makabane* 1981 (3) SA 1028 (O). If the court so finds after conviction but before sentence, it must set aside the conviction, find the accused not guilty and direct that the accused be detained pending the signification of the decision of a judge in chambers — s 78(6) and s 77(6)*(b)*. (The said sections allow the presiding officer to set the proceedings aside without the intervention of a court of review.) These provisions are peremptory and the court *must* declare the accused a State Patient.

2.5 Objections to the charge

Before the introduction of the Criminal Procedure Act, 1977, objections to a charge or indictment went under varying appellations, depending upon the defect or omission complained of. Thus, in the case of a formal defect (eg the accused incorrectly named) one *objected* to the charge. Where the charge disclosed no offence, one *excepted* to it. Where the charge was lacking in particularity so as to prejudice or embarrass the accused in his defence, he had to bring a *motion to quash* it. This antiquated terminology has now been abolished, and the term 'objection' now embraces all these instances.

Section 85(1) provides:

'An accused may, before pleading . . . object to the charge on the ground —

(a) that the charge does not comply with the provisions of this Act relating to the essentials of a charge;

(b) that the charge does not set out an essential element of the relevant offence;

(c) that the charge does not disclose an offence;

(d) that the charge does not contain sufficient particulars of any matter alleged in the charge . . .; or

(e) that the accused is not correctly named or described in the charge.'

Reasonable notice must, however, be given to the prosecution that the accused intends raising an objection. If the court upholds the objection it may order the prosecution to amend the charge or to deliver particulars to the accused. Where the prosecution fails to comply with such an order, the court may quash the charge — s 85(2); *Nathaniel* 1987 (2) SA 225 (SWA). As a matter of procedure an objection in terms of s 85 should properly have been raised before the accused pleaded to the charge. However, there is nothing which precludes an accused from raising such a point of law at the close of the case for the prosecution. Cf *Mayekiso* 1988 (4) SA 738 (W).

An example of a case where the court quashed an indictment is *Andrews* 1948 (3) SA 577 (Spec Crim Ct). The accused had been charged with sedition. In reply to a request for further particulars as to 'the acts by which it was alleged that the various accused took part in the seditious acts alleged', the director of public prosecutions had referred the accused to the preparatory examination record. Before pleading, all the accused objected to the indictment.

The court held that as the indictment was embarrassing to all the accused, the court was bound either to quash the indictment or to order it to be amended in the manner applied for by the Crown. Accordingly, the court held that as the amendment would cause prejudice to the accused the indictment should be quashed and leave granted to the Crown to frame an indictment afresh. See also *C* 1955 (1) SA 464 (T).

In the great treason trial before a special court in Pretoria during the fifties in which a large number of accused were charged, the defence objected to the indictment on the ground that the accused persons would be prejudiced by its lack of particularity. Upon the facts the court quashed one of the charges, but refused at that stage to quash the remaining charges, provided that the Crown delivered further particulars — *Adams* 1959 (1) SA 646 (Spec Crim Ct).

Section 88 (discussed above) does not affect the accused's right to object to an indictment.

3 PLEAS WHICH MAY BE RAISED BY ACCUSED

3.1 Pleas mentioned in the Act

Section 106 provides that the accused may plead:

(1) that he is guilty of the offence charged or of any offence of which he may be convicted on the charge;

(2) that he is not guilty;

(3) that he has already been convicted of the offence with which he is charged (*autrefois convict*);

(4) that he has already been acquitted of the offence with which he is charged (*autrefois acquit*);

(5) that he has received a free pardon from the President for the offence charged;

(6) that the court has no jurisdiction to try the offence; or

(7) that he has been discharged from prosecution in terms of s 204 after giving satisfactory evidence for the State;

(8) that the prosecutor has no title to prosecute; or

(9) that the prosecution may not be resumed or instituted owing to an order by a court under s 342A(3)*(c)*.

The section further provides that two or more pleas may be pleaded together, except that the plea of guilty cannot be pleaded with any other plea to the same charge.

Truth and public benefit: In terms of s 107 the accused may plead this where the charge is one of criminal defamation. This defence must be specially pleaded and may be pleaded with any other plea except the plea of guilty. It is noteworthy that the Act does not make provision for the plea that the defamatory words were excused as fair comment or that they were privileged or spoken in jest.

Lis pendens (that the issue before the court is the subject of adjudication before another court): This is not specially provided for in the Act and the admissibility of such a plea will be discussed below.

3.2 Guilty

3.2.1 *General*

Generally speaking, where an accused pleads guilty at his trial there is no issue between him and the State and he may be convicted and sentenced, there and then, on his plea.

Before the coming into operation of the Criminal Procedure Act of 1977, an accused who pleaded guilty before a superior court to any offence, other than murder, could be convicted without any evidence being led. As the judge generally had the preparatory examination record before him, he would be familiar with the circumstances of the case and be in a position to pass sentence. A lower court, on the other hand, having no preparatory examination record, could generally only convict an accused who pleaded guilty where there was proof (in the form of evidence) that the offence had been committed — though it was not necessary to show that it was the accused who had committed it. (This latter provision was commonly known as the 'evidence *aliunde*' rule.)

The above procedures were replaced in 1977 by s 112, which abolishes the distinction between proceedings before superior and lower courts, as well as the *aliunde* rule.

Section 112(1) lays down two different procedures where an accused at a summary trial in any court pleads guilty to the offence charged, or to an offence of which he may be convicted on the charge, and the prosecutor accepts such plea: one for serious offences and one for less serious offences.

If the presiding official is of the opinion that the offence does not merit the death sentence, imprisonment or any other form of detention without the option of a fine, whipping or a fine exceeding the amount determined by the Minister from time to time by notice in the *Gazette* (from 1 May 1992 the amount so determined is R1 500), he *may* convict the accused on his plea of guilty only and impose a sentence other than those mentioned above — s 112(1)*(a)*. Section 112(1)*(a)* must be used sparingly and only where it is certain that no injustice will result from its application. It is still intended for minor matters, as its predecessor always was — *Addabba* 1992 (2) SACR 325 (T).

If the presiding official is of the opinion that the offence does merit one of the above-mentioned sentences, or if he is requested thereto by the prosecutor, he *must* question the accused with reference to the alleged facts of the case in order to ascertain whether he admits the allegations in the charge to which he has pleaded guilty. If satisfied that the accused is guilty of the offence to which he has pleaded guilty, he may convict and sentence him — s 112(1)*(b))*.

Section 112(2) not only requires a series of admissions but also the facts upon which those admissions are based — *B* 1991 (1) SACR 405 (N). From this factual basis the court must be satisfied as to the guilt of the accused. It is, therefore, on a charge of reckless driving not enough to admit that you drove recklessly. It is necessary to admit facts from which the court can draw the conclusion that the accused did in fact drive recklessly — *Morris* 1992 (1) SACR 537 (A). An accused may also admit an element of an offence of which he bears no personal knowledge, eg a certificate indicating the alcohol level in his blood — *Martins* 1986 (4) SA 934 (T); *Goras* 1985 (4) SA 411 (O).

Where only s 112(1)*(a)* proceedings take place, the court may not sentence an accused to imprisonment (even if it is totally suspended) without the option of a fine — *Daniels* 1991 (2) SACR 449 (C).

Note the following aspects with regard to s 112(1):

3.2.1.1 Questioning by the presiding official

An uneducated and unrepresented accused may plead guilty to an offence, meaning no more than that he performed the act (eg stabbing) alleged in the charge sheet. With the provision in the 1977 Code for questioning an accused who pleads guilty, the danger of a wrong conviction has been considerably diminished.

This procedure should be applied with caution — *Van Deventer* 1978 (3) SA 97 (T); *Phikwa* 1978 (1) SA 397 (E). The magistrate's questions must be directed at satisfying himself that an accused fully understands all the elements of the charge when pleading guilty and that his answers reveal that he has in fact committed the actual offence to which he has pleaded guilty — *Tshumi* 1978 (1) SA 128 (N); *Jacobs* 1978 (3) SA 440 (E); *Lebokeng* 1978 (2) SA 674 (O); *Mthetwa* 1978 (2) SA 773 (N); *Jacobs* 1978 (1) SA 1176 (C); *Tito* 1984 (4) SA 363 (Ck); *Naidoo* 1985 (2) SA 32 (N); *Londi* 1985 (2) SA 248 (E). This is especially the case when an accused is illiterate and unsophisticated and has no legal assistance, and even more so when he is a young child with a limited grasp of the proceedings — *M* 1982 (1) SA 240 (N). The primary purpose of this questioning is to protect an accused against the consequences of an incorrect plea of guilty. It is not correct to rely on inferences in order to determine the guilt of the accused. The accused's answers cannot be used as 'evidence' to draw unfavourable inferences which establish the required conviction that he/she is guilty — *Nagel* 1998 (1) SACR 218 (O). The provisions of s 112(1)*(b)* are intended to eliminate the need to present evidence (and thereby unnecessary costs). The intention is certainly not to make a trial a mere formality when an accused pleads guilty. The presiding judicial officer must still — particularly in cases where heavy sentences are possible — ensure that sufficient information is placed before him to enable him to impose sentence properly — *Serumala* 1978 (4) SA 811 (NC).

Where possible, questions from the bench should be as few as possible, and preferably only those necessary *(a)* to elucidate what the accused has volunteered, *(b)* to canvass any allegations in the charge not mentioned by the accused, and, of course, *(c)* to confine the accused to the relevant detail. Leading questions should, as far as possible, be avoided. It is totally inadequate for the court simply to ask the accused whether he admits, one by one, each of the allegations in the charge — *Mkhize v The State* 1981 (3) SA 585 (N). It must be clear that the accused understands the nature of the offence, its elements and the nature and effect of the admissions he has made. In questioning the accused no purpose is served by putting legal conclusions to him. Facts must be established which can form the basis for legal conclusions — *N* 1992 (1) SACR 67 (Ck); *De Klerk* 1992 (1) SACR 181 (W); *Morris* 1992 (1) SACR 537 (A).

Section 112 applies not only where a plea of guilty is tendered before the commencement of a trial but also when an accused changes his plea to one of guilty during the course of the trial.

Questioning in terms of s 112(1)*(b)* is peremptory and can also operate in favour of the accused. Failure to comply with the requirements of this section will result in the conviction and sentence being set aside (*Fikizolo* 1978 (2) SA 676 (NC); *Molauzi* 1984 (4) SA 738 (T)) or that the case be remitted under s 312(1) in order to comply with the provisions of s 112 — *Govender v Buys* 1978 (2) SA 292 (N); *Malikhethla* 1978 (3) SA 11 (O); *Gabriel* 1981 (2) SA 156 (SWA); *Mmatli* 1988 (2) SA 533 (T). (Admissions made at the first trial may be used as part of the evidential material at the *de novo* trial — *Mbothoma* 1978 (2) SA 530 (O).)

If, in the course of questioning of the accused, it appears that he is not guilty of the offence charged but that he admits his guilt to a lesser offence, the court should record a plea of not guilty in terms of s 113 — if the plea of guilty on the lesser charge is not accepted by the State. (*Tladi* 1978 (2) SA 476 (O) at 480B–C. Cf also *Mabaso* 1980 (2) SA 20 (N); *Sibiya* 1980 (2) SA 457 (N)) and see below.

The use of a roneoed form for the questioning of an accused in terms of s 112(1)*(b)* is highly undesirable — *Ntomane* 1978 (3) SA 596 (T). See also *Baron* 1978 (2) 510 (C).

Co-accused should be questioned separately — *Faber* 1979 (1) SA 710 (NC). The questions to answers must be fully recorded — *Maxekwa* 1978 (1) SA 419 (O); *Khiba* 1978 (2) SA 540 (O).

3.2.1.2 Accused's version

An accused should be encouraged to tell his version. The court's function is not to evaluate the answers as if it were weighing evidence or to judge their truthfulness or plausibility. It is simply to interpret them to see whether they substantiate the plea. The test, in short, is what the accused has said, not what the court thinks of it — *Mkhize* 1978 (1) SA 264 (N). See also *Mkhafu* 1978 (1) SA 665 (O); *Doud* 1978 (2) SA 403 (O); *Somyali* 1979 (2) SA 274 (E).

If the accused's version does not accord with that of the State, a plea of not guilty must be entered (see s 113 below), except where the dispute does not concern the crux or substance of the offence, and affects sentence only — *Balepile* (above).

Cf also 1978 *SACC* 71; 1979 *De Iure* 175. The judicial officer must determine whether the accused admits the allegations in the charge concerning the time and place of the offence, incorporated in the charge in terms of s 84(1), even if such allegations are not elements of the offence charged. Section 113 should be applied where such allegations are not admitted — *Heugh* 1998 (1) SACR 83 (ECD).

As in the case of s 115 (see below; note in particular *Mathogo* 1978 (1) SA 425 (O)), the court should also, in a s 112 procedure, explain to an undefended accused that exculpatory statements, made in consequence of the court's s 112 questioning, do not constitute evidence for the defence; the latter can be given in the usual way only after the State's case — cf *Afrika* 1982 (3) SA 1066 (C).

3.2.1.3   The prosecutor's role

The prosecutor should give the court a brief summary of what the State's case is. If the summary reveals the offence charged, the magistrate is obliged to question the accused. Without such summary, the court has no idea of the seriousness of the offence, on which to assess an appropriate sentence. The fact that such a summary as well as the contents thereof have been furnished must be noted on the record because it is part of the proceedings in court — *Sejake* 1981 (1) SA 1215 (O). And, if the accused disputes the details of the State's case, the prosecutor will have to tender evidence to prove them — *Ngobe* 1978 (1) SA 309 (NC); *Rakanang* 1978 (1) SA 591 (NC); *Sikhindi* 1978 (1) SA 1072 (N). See also *Witbooi* 1978 (3) SA 590 (T); *Faber* 1979 (1) SA 710 (NC). In *Mkhize v The State* 1981 (3) SA 585 (N) it was stated that in nearly all cases it would be far better for the court to hear what the accused has to say with reference to the charge *before* inviting the prosecutor to outline the case.

The acceptance of a plea of guilty by the prosecutor is of importance only where the accused pleads guilty, not to the offence with which he is charged, but to an offence of which he can be convicted on the charge, and the prosecutor does not wish to proceed with the offence charged. If, however, the prosecutor wishes to proceed with the offence charged, and therefore does not accept the plea, the presiding judicial officer must note a plea of not guilty and act in terms of s 115 — *Phundula* 1978 (4) SA 855 (T). The punctuation marks in s 112(1) make it clear that the prosecutor's acceptance of a plea at the time of pleading is necessary only where an accused pleads guilty, not to the offence charged, but to a lesser offence of which he can, on the charge, be convicted. Thus, when an accused pleads guilty to the offence charged, acceptance of the plea by the prosecutor is unnecessary — *Nyambe* 1978 (1) SA 311 (NC).

It may happen that on arraignment, an accused tenders a plea of guilty to a lesser offence which is a competent verdict (see below) on the main charge (eg a plea of guilty to common assault where the charge is assault with intent to do grievous bodily harm). Here, the prosecutor may accept the plea of guilty without the leave of the court — *Cordozo* 1975 (1) SA 635 (O). The position is the same where the accused pleads guilty to an alternative count — *Bokopane* 1964 (1) SA 695 (O). The acceptance of a plea of not guilty to a serious charge, (eg murder) and the acceptance of a plea of guilty to a less serious charge (eg culpable homicide) is neither a withdrawal of the main charge in terms of s 6(a) nor a stopping of the prosecution in terms of s 6(b). It is rather a *sui generis* act performed by the prosecutor which limits the extent of the *lis* between State and accused, in accordance with the accused's plea. The accused can thus only be convicted of the less serious offence.

(See *Hlokulu* 1988 (1) SA 174 (C).) Once the trial is in progress, however, the situation is different. The leave of the court is then necessary if the prosecutor wishes to accept a subsequent plea of guilty to a lesser or an alternative offence. The prosecutor cannot compel the court to convict in such a case — *Komo* 1947 (2) SA 508 (N); *Mlangeni* 1976 (1) SA 528 (T). *Contra Bokopane* (above). See, in general, Hiemstra 303–4); *Papenfus* 1978 (4) SA 32 (T); *Mokoena* 1981 (1) SA 148 (O); *Prokureur Generaal, Venda v Magistraat Streekafdeling* 1982 (2) SA 659 (V); *Sethoga* 1990 (1) SA 270 (A).

3.2.2 *Statement by accused instead of questioning*

The court may, in lieu of the questioning under s 112(1)*(b)*, convict the accused and sentence him (in terms of this subsection) on the strength of a written statement by the accused (handed in to court by the accused or his legal adviser) in which he sets out the facts which he admits and on which he has pleaded guilty. The court must be satisfied that the accused is guilty of the offence to which he has pleaded guilty, and may put any question to the accused in order to clarify any matter raised in the statement — s 112(2). A written statement which is simply a regurgitation of what appears in the charge sheet, is not sufficient. The statement must set out not only a series of admissions but also the facts upon which those admissions are based — *B* 1991 (1) SACR 405 (N).

A statement of the accused made verbally by his legal representative is not a statement as intended by s 112(2) — *Calitz* 1979 (2) SA 576 (SWA). Section 112(2) does not stipulate who should draft the written statement. A statement prepared by the prosecutor and signed by the accused theoretically complies with the requirements of s 112(2), but due to the inherent danger of abuse, strict safeguards are required when resorting to this procedure — *Sellars* 1991 (1) SACR 491 (N).

3.2.3 *Evidence or questioning with regard to sentence*

For the purposes of an appropriate sentence, the prosecutor may present evidence on any aspect of the charge, and the court may hear evidence (including evidence or a statement by or on behalf of the accused) or question the accused on any aspect of the case — s 112(3). This subsection relates only to evidence. The court is not entitled to have regard to evidence given in terms of s 112(3) in considering whether or not the accused is guilty *Khumalo* 1978 (4) SA 516 (N); *Balepile* 1979 (1) SA 703 (NC); *Quinta* 1979 (2) SA 326 (O); *Phakati* 1978 (4) SA 477 (T). Where a magistrate has convicted an accused in terms of s 112, another magistrate may in the absence of the aforementioned, sentence the accused at a later stage — s 275. Cf also *Harbour* 1988 (4) SA 921 (T).

3.2.4 *Correction of plea of guilty*

If the court at any stage of the proceedings under s 112 and before sentence is passed is in doubt whether the accused is (1) in law guilty of the offence to which he has pleaded guilty, or is satisfied that (2) the accused does not admit an allegation in the charge, or (3) the accused has incorrectly admitted any such allegation or (4) the accused has a valid defence to the charge, or, (5) the court is of the opinion for any other reason that the accused's plea of guilty should not stand, the court *shall* record a plea of not guilty and require the prosecutor to proceed with the prosecution —

s 113. The conviction aparently lapses automatically — *Osborne* 1978 (3) SA 173 (C). See also *Du Plessis* 1978 (2) SA 496 (C); *Olckers* 1978 (4) SA 169 (SWA); *Lukele* 1978 (4) SA 450 (T); *Chetty v Cronje* 1979 (1) SA 294 (O); *Aranoff* 1979 (2) SA 179 (T); *Mazwi* 1982 (2) SA 344 (T); *Jada* 1985 (2) SA 182 (E). Admissions already made stand as proof of the relevant facts. Where such admissions embrace all the facts the State must prove in order to establish the offence and the guilt of the accused in respect thereof, the accused can be convicted — *Ncube* 1981 (3) SA 511 (T). The court must weigh the accused's admissions and his failure to testify in order to decide whether all the elements of the offence have been proved — *Mathe* 1981 (3) SA 644 (NC). A prosecutor may not substantially contradict the version of an accused who has pleaded guilty, unless a plea of not guilty is noted — *Swarts* 1983 (3) SA 261 (C). Note that *doubt* and not a *probability* is sufficient to compel the court to record a plea of not guilty and that the provisions of s 113 are mandatory. On the other hand, the phrase 'is satisfied' in s 113(1) postulates no other test than that the court must be in *reasonable doubt* whether the accused admits an allegation in the charge, or has correctly admitted such allegation, or is reasonably left in doubt whether the accused has a valid defence to the charge — *Attorney-General, Transvaal v Botha* 1993 (2) SACR 587 (A). The question whether the accused's non-admission of an allegation in the charge sheet is false or not, is not relevant at this stage of the proceedings — *Malili* 1988 (4) SA 620 (T).

Allegations, other than allegations incorrectly admitted by the accused, admitted by the accused up to the stage at which the court records a plea of not guilty, stand as proof in any court of such allegation — s 113(1).

Where an accused has pleaded guilty to the charge but a plea of not guilty has been entered, the trial could be resumed before another magistrate in terms of s 118 — *Ndiwe* 1988 (3) SA 972 (NC).

The following may serve as an example of the implementation of s 113: on a charge of being found in possession of property suspected of being stolen, and failing to afford a reasonable explanation of his possession, the feelings of the finder are an element of the case for the State. He should, therefore, give evidence, and a conviction in terms of s 112 without evidence and only on a plea of guilty is not possible. The court should record a plea of not guilty in terms of s 113 in order to hear at least the evidence of the finder — *Shabalala* 1982 (2) SA 123 (T). The correction of a plea of not guilty must be effected on the front page of the charge sheet. In order to give a true reflection of what transpired, the plea must be noted as follows: 'Guilty (changed to "not guilty" in terms of s 113)' — *Mugwedi* 1988 (2) SA 814 (V). If the court records a plea of not guilty before any evidence has been led the prosecution shall proceed on the original charge laid against the accused, unless the prosecutor explicitly indicates otherwise — s 113(2).

3.2.5 *Committal for sentence by regional court*

If a magistrate's court, after conviction following on a plea of guilty but before sentence, is of the opinion (1) that the offence is of such a nature or magnitude that it merits punishment in excess of the jurisdiction of a magistrate's court, or (2) that the previous convictions of the accused are such that the offence merits punishment in excess of the jurisdiction of a magistrate's court, or (3) that the accused is a dangerous criminal (as referred to in s 286A(1)), the court shall stop the proceedings and commit the accused for sentence by a regional court having jurisdiction —

s 114(1). The accused is then sentenced by the regional court. If the regional court is satisfied, however, that the plea of guilty by the accused was incorrectly recorded or is not satisfied that the accused is guilty of the offence or he has no valid defence to the charge, the court shall enter a plea of not guilty and proceed with the trial as a summary trial — s 114(3)*(b)*.

The record of the proceedings in the magistrate's court is, upon proof thereof in the regional court, received by the latter court, and forms part of the record of that court — s 114(2). Cf *Loggerenberg* 1984 (4) SA 41 (E).

Note that there is no provision for committing an accused to the High Court for sentence. This is because it is highly unlikely that the accused in such a case would be arraigned before a district magistrate's court in the first place. In the past it was the practice, where an accused pleaded guilty to murder, for the court to enter a plea of not guilty — *Nzuza* 1963 (3) SA 631 (A). (This practice originated in England, where conviction on a charge of murder resulted in a mandatory death sentence.)

3.2.6 *Amendment of plea from 'guilty' to 'not guilty'*

The accused may, with the leave of the court, withdraw his plea of guilty. At common law, this will be allowed only if he can give a reasonable explanation why he pleaded guilty and now wishes to change his plea. A reasonable explanation could be, for example, that the plea was induced by fear, fraud, duress, misunderstanding or mistake. (Cf *Britz* 1963 (1) SA 394 (T).)

An application by an accused who had no legal representation when he pleaded but is represented when his trial starts, to alter his plea from guilty to not guilty, should not succeed where there is no indication that the accused did not understand the charge and where the trial court offers the accused an opportunity to give an explanation by way of evidence which the accused, without any reason for his refusal, declines to use *Hattingh* 1972 (3) SA 843 (O). An application to change a plea of guilty to one of not guilty may be brought after conviction but before sentence. In such a case there is an onus on the accused to show on a balance of probabilities that the plea was not voluntarily made — *De Bruin* 1987 (4) SA 933 (C). See also *Booysen* 1988 (4) SA 801 (E) at 804. A contrary decision was given in the full court judgment in *Botha* 1990 (1) SA 665 (T) where it was held that at common law, an application for amendment of a plea of guilty, brought before sentencing, does not shift the onus to the accused. The explanation of the accused must be reasonable and more persuasive if the application to amend the guilty plea is brought at a late stage in the proceedings. The decision in *Botha* was confirmed on appeal — *Attorney-General, Transvaal v Botha* 1993 (2) SACR 587 (A). Cf also *Fourie* 1991 (1) SACR 21 (T). The court is not *functus officio* until the sentence has been imposed — *Van Heerden v De Kock* 1979 (3) SA 315 (E).

Even when an explanation as to why the accused pleaded guilty is somewhat improbable, the court should not refuse an amendment to the plea unless it is satisfied not only that the explanation is improbable but that it is beyond reasonable doubt false. If there is any reasonable possibility of his explanation being true then he should be allowed to withdraw his plea of guilty — *Kannigan* 1975 (4) SA 639 (N); *Pitso v Additional Magistrate, Krugersdorp* 1976 (4) SA 553 (T); *Zwela* 1981 (1) SA 335 (O).

Where the application for amendment of plea from guilty to not guilty rests upon two bases, namely coercion on the one hand and actual innocence on the other, the merits of the matter in relation to the guilt or innocence of the accused must also be taken into account. The trial court will at least have to decide whether there is a reasonable possibility that the accused is innocent and that the application is *bona fide*. It is permissible to have regard to the accused's statements during explanation of plea in terms of s 112(1)*(b)* — *De Villiers* 1984 (1) SA 519 (O).

Only in the most exceptional circumstances will such a change of plea from guilty to not guilty be allowed after verdict. Cf *Onward* 1972 (1) PH H68 (R). Where, however, the accused pleads guilty to certain charges in order to obtain advantages with regard to the other charges, the court may refuse to allow him subsequently to change his plea — *Nathanson* 1959 (1) SA 258 (N). Cf in general *Simbi* 1975 (4) SA 700 (RA); *Booysen* 1988 (4) SA 801 (E) at 804C.

In *Mazwi* 1982 (2) SA 344 (T) the view taken was that the test to be applied in deciding whether to grant an application to withdraw a plea of guilty is that set out in s 113 (see above), and that there is no room for a common-law withdrawal of a plea of guilty. In *Hazelhurst* 1984 (3) SA 897 (T), however, it was held that s 113 is applicable only in proceedings in terms of s 112 (ie in the course of questioning the accused to determine whether he admits the allegations in the charge to which he pleaded guilty) and the magistrate, without an application on the part of the accused, must change the plea to one of not guilty if certain facts emerge from the questioning. Section 113 does not supersede or exclude common law — *Attorney-General, Transvaal v Botha* 1993 (2) SACR 587 (A). Where a matter arises for which s 113 does not make provision, the common-law position, (see above) still applies. The accused is then only required to offer a reasonable explanation for having initially pleaded guilty. The court should reject the explanation only if it is convinced beyond reasonable doubt that it is false — *Botha* 1990 (1) SA 665 (T). There is no onus on the accused — *Fourie* 1991 (1) SACR 21 (T).

3.3 Not guilty

3.3.1 *Explanation of plea*

Where an accused at a summary trial pleads not guilty, the presiding official may ask him whether he wishes to make a statement indicating the basis of his defence — s 115(1). Where the accused does not make a statement, as he is entitled to — *Mkhize* 1978 (3) SA 1065 (T), (see also *Khumalo* 1979 (3) SA 708 (T)), or does so and it is not clear from the statement to what extent he denies or admits the issues raised by the plea, the court *may* question the accused in order to establish which allegations in the charge are in dispute — s 115(2)*(a)*. This discretion is to be exercised judicially — *Herbst* 1980 (3) SA 1026 (E); *Masike* 1996 (2) SACR 245 (T).

The court must inform the accused that he is not obliged to answer any questions. Failure to do this constitutes an irregularity, the effect of which would depend upon the circumstances. The nature of the information thus given by the court to the accused must appear clearly from the record. The state is entitled to rectify the record by leading the evidence of the magistrate and interpreter in order to show that the accused's statement and admissions are admissible — *Ndlovu* 1987 (3) SA 827 (N).

The court may, in its discretion, put any question to the accused in order to clarify any matter with regard to the statement made to indicate the basis of his defence, or his replies to questions put to him in order to establish which allegations in the charge are in dispute — s 115(2)*(b)*. The questioning by the court should not go beyond the matters in issue in the case and should be limited to those issues in respect of which the accused's statement is unclear and require clarification. To go beyond that only creates material for possible later cross-examination, and to do that is not permissible — *Msibi* 1992 (2) SACR 441 (W). The conviction and sentence will be set aside where the questioning by the court bordered on cross-examination, seriously prejudiced the accused and would not be categorised as questions in clarification of the plea — *Molelekeng* 1992 (1) SACR 604 (T).

It is not required of an accused that his statement intended to indicate the basis of his defence be made under oath — *Xaba* 1978 (1) SA 646 (O).

It is important that presiding officers bring home to accused, especially where they are unrepresented, that the statement in clarification of the plea is still not evidence under oath, but only directed at preventing unnecessary evidence being led by the State — *Mothlaping* 1988 (3) SA 757 (NC). The explanation of plea is, therefore, not evidential material upon which a conviction can be based — *October* 1991 (1) SACR 455 (C). The manner in which the accused ought to lay his account of events before the court, if he wants to do so, is by way of giving evidence after the State's case has been closed — *Mathogo* (above). See also *Dreyer* 1978 (2) SA 182 (NC); *Mkize* 1978 (2) SA 249 (N); *Thomas* 1978 (2) SA 408 (B); *Mogoregi* 1978 (3) SA 13 (O); *Moloyi* 1978 (1) SA 516 (O); *Nkosi* 1978 (1) SA 548 (T); *Molele* 1978 (2) SA 668 (O).

The procedure prescribed in s 115 must be completed after plea and before the commencement of the State's case. The magistrate should record *verbatim* the questions put by him to the accused and the accused's reply to each question. Meticulous care in recording both such questions and answers will leave no doubt as to what facts have been formally admitted by the accused and what facts still remain to be proved by the leading of evidence — *Mayedwa* 1978 (1) SA 509 (E). See also *Xungu* 1978 (1) SA 663 (O); *Semenya* 1978 (2) SA 110 (T) at 113; *Rakanang* 1978 (1) SA 591 (NC); *Sepiri* 1979 (2) SA 1168 (NC).

See *Mothlaping* 1988 (3) SA 757 (NC) for the court's findings on the evidential value of an explanation of plea.

3.3.2 *Admissions made in the course of explanation of plea*

The court must enquire from the accused whether an allegation which is not placed in issue by the plea of not guilty may be recorded as an admission and, if the accused consents, such admission is duly recorded — s 115(2)*(b)*. The accused can reduce the total number of facts which are put in issue by a plea of not guilty and which have to be proved by the State, by admitting facts which will then no longer be in issue. If he consents thereto, that admission will be recorded and deemed to be an admission in terms of s 220. Such an admission is sufficient proof of the relevant facts and absolves the State of the burden of proving these facts. Sufficient proof is naturally not conclusive proof, and can later be rebutted by the accused, e g on the grounds of duress or mistake or by other legally acceptable facts — *Seleke* 1980 (3) SA 745 (A). An accused is not obliged to consent to his admission being recorded. Where he does not consent, the onus remains on the State to prove by admissible evidence all the facts which were put in issue by the plea of not guilty. The mere fact that an accused refuses to consent to the recording of an admission cannot, however, affect the nature of his statement. Such an admission does not apply as sufficient proof of the fact to which it has reference. At the end of the case the court considers the evidential value of the admission in the light of the evidence as a whole — *Sesetse* 1981 (3) SA 353 (A). See also *Shivute* 1991 (1) SACR 656 (Nm).

The judicial officer is entitled to question the accused only where it is not clear from such statement to what extent the accused denies or admits the allegations which comprise the charge against him. Where it is clear from the accused's statement which elements of the charge he admits and which he denies, the judicial officer is not entitled to question the accused regarding the facts upon which he relies to substantiate his denial of the charge or elements thereof — *Muzikayifani* 1979 (3) SA 661 (D); *Herbst* 1980 (3) SA 1026 (E).

Admission of facts made during an explanation of plea and formally recorded as admissions in terms of s 220, constitute sufficient proof of such facts. 'Sufficient proof' does not mean 'conclusive proof' but proof in the sense that no further or better proof is required. Any fact admitted by the accused, but not formally recorded with the consent of the accused, will have to be proved by the State — not as conclusively, perhaps, as an allegation which is expected to be disputed has to be proved, but, regard being had to the *onus* resting upon the State, to such a degree, nevertheless, as to amount to the discharge of that burden. It amounts to probative material and there is no impediment preventing a trial court from making use of the material afforded by such a statement against the accused. Such informal admissions do not, however, require additional proof before they may be used against the accused, because they are made in court. What is stated above does not mean that other statements made by an accused at the enquiry in terms of s 115 have no evidential value at all. On the contrary, the court must consider whatever the accused has said and such statements form part of the probative material — *Mjoli* 1981 (3) SA 1233 (A). The statement in terms of s 115 may, however, not be used in favour of an accused. It is, therefore, not evidential material in his favour — *Mothlaping* 1988 (3) SA 757 (NC). An accused may also be cross-examined regarding the contents of his statement where, for example, he later deviates from it in his evidence and it can have an effect on his credibility — *Sesetse* 1981 (3) SA 353 (A); *Selane* 1979 (1) SA 318 (T). *Contra*, however, *Mogoregi* 1978 (3) SA 13 (O).

When the court asks the accused under s 115(2)*(b)* whether an admission may be recorded, the accused must be properly informed regarding the effect of such a step, and that he is under no obligation to make any admission or to assist the State in proving the case against him. See *Evans* 1981 (4) SA 52 (C) and *Daniëls* 1983 (3) SA 275 (A); cf 1977 *SACC* 3.

According to *Klaasen* 1978 (1) SA 355 (C), s 209 (conviction may follow on confession by accused) is applicable if an accused should make a 'confession' during the 'plea explanation' procedure. Such a 'confession' will have to be confirmed in a material respect or the commission of the offence will have to be proved by other evidence. See, however, 1978 *THRHR* 207 and 1978 (1) *De Jure* 181. *Klaasen*, however, was overruled in *Talie* 1979 (2) SA 1003 (C).

3.3.3   *Accused's participation*

It is irregular for a court to put questions directly to an accused who is represented. An accused is entitled to legal representation, and the legal practitioner is in fact acting as a shield, presenting his own knowledge on behalf of his client. It appears that s 115(1) and (2) provide that a court may put questions directly to an accused, but s 115(3) makes it quite clear that the practitioner may act on behalf of his client and answer questions — *Salie* 1986 (2) SA 295 (C). *Contra K* 1982 (4) SA 422 (B). Where a legal adviser replies on behalf of the accused, either orally or in writing, to any question put by the court, the accused is required to declare whether he confirms such reply or not — s 115(3).

What an accused says in his explanation of plea may under no circumstances be used against a co-accused, except when the accused repeats his allegations in his explanation of plea in evidence under oath in which event it is in fact evidence — *Ngobeni* 1981 (1) SA 506 (B). Even an admission as envisaged by s 220, made during plea explanation, can under no circumstances be admissible against a co-accused — *Long* 1988 (1) 216 (NC).

The other question raised by s 115 is whether the court may draw an adverse inference from an accused's failure to make a statement at the stage of plea; also, whether the prosecution may cross-examine the accused on his failure to do so. Cf also *M* 1979 (4) SA 1044 (B). If an accused elects to remain silent or is advised to remain silent his choice is susceptible of being interpreted as a wish to hear what the State could prove in order to adapt his evidence thereto. His credibility is put in a bad light. But before such an inference is drawn he must have the opportunity during cross-examination to explain his silence. If he does not testify he has only himself to blame that there is no explanation for his silence before court, but it is then of minor importance as silence after the State's case has been closed is of much more importance than silence at the beginning — Hiemstra 321.

With regard to the accused's right to remain silent, note that the position where an accused has pleaded not guilty and is then questioned is quite different from that where he has actually pleaded guilty. On the plea of not guilty the questioning is primarily directed at establishing the issues in the case, and it is necessary that the accused should be protected from inadvertently jeopardising his plea of not guilty. On the plea of guilty the accused has already admitted the State's case. The questioning by the court is not primarily directed to self-incrimination by the accused, but indeed to the protection of the accused against the consequences of an unjustified plea of guilty. An explanation of the accused's right to remain silent would conflict with the whole spirit of s 112(1)*(b)* — Nkosi 1984 (3) SA 345 (A).

Section 115 has a dual purpose: First, an invitation to indicate the basis of his defence and, secondly, questioning to ascertain which allegations in the charge are in dispute. In respect of both, the accused must be informed by the court of his right to remain silent — *Salie* 1986 (2) SA 295 (C).

Merely to state in an explanation of plea that 'everything is in dispute' means in effect: 'None of the things alleged by the State happened. It is all fabricated.' If the accused subsequently says that some of the allegations are true, his credibility will be seriously affected. If he does not wish to reduce the issues in dispute, he must refuse to give an explanation of his plea. Then he exposes himself to an adverse inference although, should he enter the witness-box, he will be given an opportunity to explain his silence — *Mathope* 1982 (3) SA 33 (B); *K* 1982 (4) SA 422 (B).

3.3.4 *Committal to regional court*

Where an accused pleads not guilty in a magistrate's court, the court shall, subject to the provisions of s 115, at the request of the prosecutor made before any evidence is tendered, refer the accused for trial to a regional court having jurisdiction. The record of the proceedings in the magistrate's court shall upon proof thereof in the regional court be received by the regional court and form part of the records of that court — s 115A.

Cf s 116 regarding the committal of an accused for sentence by a regional court after conviction in a magistrate's court following on a plea of not guilty. Note that the provisions regarding the committal of an accused by a magistrate of a magistrate's court for sentence by a regional court in terms of s 116(1) are the same as those in s 114(1). See *Selebogo* 1984 (2) SA 486 (NC). Cf further *Sethuntsa* 1982 (3) SA 256 (O); *Bron* 1986 (4) SA 394 (C).

3.3.5 *Amendment of plea of not guilty*

An accused may at any stage change his plea of not guilty to one of guilty to the offence charged, with the leave of the court — *Alli* 1958 (2) SA 50 (C). Leave is seldom refused in such cases. In such a case s 112 is then also applicable — *Abrahams* 1980 (4) SA 665 (C); *Sethoga* 1990 (1) SA 270 (A). After pleading not guilty and once evidence has been led the accused may change his plea to one of guilty, make oral admissions and then be found guilty — *Adam* 1993 (1) SACR 62 (E).

Where an accused pleads not guilty and then seeks to change his plea to guilty after evidence has been led, acceptance by the prosecutor of the plea at that stage of the proceedings does not have the same effect as acceptance of a plea before commencement of the trial in that the prosecutor is no longer *dominus litis* and the court is not bound by his acceptance of the plea of guilty. Once the accused pleads not guilty it is the court's duty to determine the issues raised between the State and the accused by the latter's plea and the prosecutor cannot interfere with that duty and compel the court to enter a plea of guilty on a lesser charge thereby seeking to limit the *lis* between the State and the accused. Any acceptance by the prosecutor of a plea of guilty to a lesser offence can accordingly take place only with the court's consent — *Sethoga* 1990 (1) SA 270 (A).

3.3.6 *The procedure in essence*

The 'plea explanation' (a term also adopted by the Supreme Court of Appeal — *Imene* 1979 (2) SA 710 (A) at 717G) procedure contained in s 115 — which originated in the proposal by Mr Justice Hiemstra in 1963 that our system of criminal procedure be reformed to bring it into line with the Continental inquisitional process — is undoubtedly the most controversial provision in the 1977 Code and must be approached with great caution (*Mathogo* 1978 (1) SA 425 (O)). Its purpose is to shorten the proceedings by making it unnecessary for the prosecutor to call evidence on matters which are not in dispute. It should be noted that the questioning is discretionary only. Cf *Bepela* 1978 (2) SA 22 (B). No doubt, in most cases a judicial officer would deem it desirable to invite an accused to indicate the basis of his defence, more particularly where he feels that it may assist an undefended accused to bring out his defence before any evidence is led in order that the court may be able to assist him by ensuring that the defence is properly put to State witnesses or to safeguard him from the suggestion that he is fabricating his evidence if he were to depose to facts not put by him to State witnesses in cross-examination — *Herbst* 1980 (3) SA 1026 (E); *Kibido* 1988 (1) SA 802 (C). One thing seems clear: extensive questioning of an accused by the presiding officer will result in the setting aside of the proceedings on appeal, on the basis that the latter 'descended into the arena' — cf *Yuill v Yuill* [1945] 1 All ER 183. It is clear that s 115 does not contemplate any form of cross-examination. What is contemplated is an objective attempt at determining the facts which are really in dispute, with, if necessary, questions for clarification — *Seleke* 1980 (3) SA 745 (A).

With regard to both the pleas of guilty and of not guilty, see in general Van der Merwe, Barton & Kemp *Plea Procedures in Criminal Trials* (1983). Time and again, this work touches upon the significance of ss 112 and 115 in relation to the inquisitorial approach to criminal procedure.

3.4 Prior conviction or acquittal

3.4.1 *Basic principle*

It is a deep-seated principle of any civilised system of criminal law that no person shall be punished more than once for the same offence. This basic principle is also part of our Constitution (s 35(3)*(m)*):

> 'Every accused person has the right to a fair trial, which includes the right . . . not to be tried for an offence in respect of an act or omission for which that person has previously been either acquitted or convicted.'

The plea that a person has already been convicted of the same offence is known as *autrefois convict*. The law goes even further and provides that no person shall be in *jeopardy* of being tried for and convicted of the same offence more than once (the so-called principle of 'double jeopardy'). The Latin maxim is: *Nemo debet bis vexari pro una et eadem causa* — no person shall be harassed twice for the same cause. An accused may evade a second prosecution even though he was acquitted previously on the same charge by pleading *autrefois acquit*.

Section 108 provides that if an accused pleads any plea other than the plea of guilty he is by such plea without any further form deemed to have demanded that the issues raised by such plea shall be tried by the court. The *onus* of proving a plea of previous conviction or previous acquittal rests upon the accused. Proof of the previous trial is usually rendered by producing the record (or a copy thereof) and by oral evidence that the accused is the same person who was previously tried.

3.4.2 *Autrefois convict*

The essentials of this plea are that the accused had previously been convicted —

(1) of the same offence;

(2) by a competent court.

It is often stated as a third requirement that the accused must have been found guilty *upon the merits*. However, it is superflous to state this here as a requirement: it is apparent that a conviction can be based only 'upon the merits'. We accordingly discuss the concept of 'the same offence'.

In order to ascertain whether the offence is the same as that of which the accused has previously been found guilty, the court will pay attention to the true essence of the offence and not to technicalities; it is the *ratio decidendi* of the previous judgment which is binding — *Manaṣewitz* 1933 AD 165; 1934 AD 95. It will be sufficient if the offences are substantially the same. This test is not a formal one: the question is *not* whether the nomenclature of the respective offences coincides.

The plea is also available where the offence with which the accused is now charged is a lesser one than that of which he had been convicted, and the current offence is one of which he could have been convicted on the previous charge — *Long* 1958 (1) SA 115 (A). Illustrations: If the accused had previously been convicted of murder, he cannot now be charged with culpable homicide. If the accused had previously been charged with murder and convicted of assault, he cannot now be charged with culpable homicide. (Conviction of the latter two offences is competent upon a charge of murder.)

On the other hand, the plea is not available where it was impossible at the previous trial to prefer the more serious charge now presented. Thus, if the victim of an assault dies after the accused has already been convicted of assault, the accused may be indicted for murder or culpable homicide. See Gardiner & Lansdown 372. Likewise, conviction of negligent driving of a motor vehicle is not a defence on a charge of culpable homicide — *Dayzell* 1932 WLD 157; *Gabriel* 1971 (1) SA 646 (RA) at 652–5. But where it was possible to prefer the more serious charge the plea should prevail, for example where a person is charged with murder after he has already been convicted of culpable homicide. Cf *Tieties* 1990 (2) SA 461 (A) and see in general *Sepiri* 1979 (2) SA 1168 (NC).

According to *Motsepa* 1982 (1) SA 304 (O) the plea of *autrefois convict* can only be pleaded after the accused has already been sentenced in the first trial. Therefore, if an accused changes his plea of guilty on a lesser charge to not guilty after conviction but before sentence is imposed, and is then found guilty of the more serious crime, a plea of *autrefois convict* will fail — *Mahomed* 1994 (2) SACR 171 (N).

3.4.3   *Autrefois acquit*

The essentials of the plea of *autrefois acquit* are that the accused has previously been acquitted —

(1)   of the same offence with which he is now charged;

(2)   by a competent court; and

(3)   upon the merits.

If these three factors were present the accused is said to have stood in jeopardy, ie was in danger of having been convicted. Cf *Bizi* 1971 (1) SA 502 (RA) at 503. For a plea of *autrefois acquit* to be sustained if an accused is charged again, there must have been a trial or a prosecution followed by an acquittal. The proceedings in terms of s 119 (cf Chapter 11) are not to be regarded as the start of or part of the subsequent trial — *Singh* 1990 (1) SA 123 (A).

Regarding the concept of 'a competent court', cf *Mogatsi* 1970 (1) PH H74 (Botswana HC) where a plea of *autrefois convict* failed, the court holding that the conviction of the accused by a headman dealing summarily with him on a charge of rape had not been a conviction by a court of competent jurisdiction.

The remarks made under the heading of *autrefois convict* regarding the concept of 'the same offence' are equally applicable here. The plea can also be relied upon where the offences are substantially the same. See *Long* 1958 (1) SA 115 (A) 117:

> 'It is not enough to support the plea that the facts are the same in both trials. The *offences* charged must be the same, but substantial identity is sufficient. If the accused could have

been convicted at the former trial of the offence with which he is subsequently charged there is substantial identity, since in such a case acquittal on the former charge necessarily involves acquittal on the subsequent charge.'

Another way of putting it is that he must legally have been in jeopardy on the first trial of being convicted of the offence with which he was charged on the second trial. Cf *Watson* 1970 (1) SA 320 (R).

If at the trial there is not a substantial difference between the facts alleged in the charge and the facts proved by the evidence, the accused may be convicted (at any rate, where the charge is amended); should he be acquitted he may therefore plead *autrefois acquit* when subsequently charged on an amended charge. See *Manasewitz* 1933 AD 165, 1934 AD 95. An illustration of this principle is to be found in *Vorster* 1961 (4) SA 863 (O). The accused was initially charged with driving a lorry, OP 181, in Rabie Street, Luckhoff, while drunk. According to the evidence led at the first trial the accused attempted to drive another motor vehicle with a different registration number. The prosecutor stopped the case and the accused was acquitted. At the second trial it was alleged that the accused drove a light delivery van, OP 351, in Barnard Street, Luckhoff, on the same day. His plea of *autrefois acquit* was upheld on appeal upon the ground that the variation between the averments in the charge sheet and the evidence led (at the first trial) was not material and that he stood in jeopardy of being convicted.

If the accused has previously been acquitted on an indictment for murder and is now indicted on the same set of facts and convicted of assault, he may avoid conviction with a plea of *autrefois acquit*. The reason for this is that upon a charge of murder he might have been convicted of assault. The principle here is that there exists substantial identity of subject-matter when the crime charged in the second indictment would have been a competent verdict on the first indictment. But even though the offence alleged in the second indictment would not have been a competent verdict on the first indictment, it is still possible that the offences charged in the two indictments are similar enough to found a plea of *autrefois acquit*. The court must consider the essential ingredients of the criminal conduct respectively charged in the two indictments, and apply the test used in *Kerr* (1907) 21 ECD 324, namely whether the evidence necessary to support the second indictment would have been sufficient to procure a legal conviction upon the first indictment — *Ndou* 1971 (1) SA 668 (A); *Nyati* 1972 (4) SA 11 (T). Even if a plea of *autrefois acquit* fails on the latter ground (ie because the evidence necessary for the second indictment would not have been sufficient to procure a conviction on the first indictment), the court still has a discretion to prevent the second trial from proceeding on the basis that a trial should not be allowed to proceed in piecemeal fashion to the prejudice of the accused. The policy is that if an accused could have been charged with the two offences at the first trial, he should have been so charged — he should not be tried in two separate trials. See *Khoza* 1989 (3) SA 60 (T).

It is required that the acquittal must have been 'on the merits'. This means that the court (whether at the trial or ultimately upon appeal) must have considered the merits of the case, whether in fact or in law, and must not have acquitted the accused merely because of a technical irregularity in the procedure. See *Bekker* 1926 CPD 410; *Manasewitz* 1933 AD 165; *Moodie* 1962 (1) SA 587 (A); *Naidoo* 1962 (4) SA 348 (A); *Rudman* 1992 (1) SACR 70 (A). Where the trial proves abortive because of such an irregularity, the accused may be brought to trial *de novo* and the plea of *autrefois acquit* cannot prevail. Note that even where the merits have in fact been considered by the trial court, the irregularity may be of such a nature as to preclude a valid consideration of the merits. See *Moodie's* case at 597. An acquittal is 'on the merits' even if the State has led no evidence at all, because the real distinction is between an acquittal on the merits and an acquittal on a technicality *Mthetwa* 1970 (2) SA 310 (N) at 315E–F. Even when a court errs in law in acquitting an accused, the acquittal is 'on the merits' — *Bizi* 1971 (1) SA 502 (RA) at 504. It is not always easy to decide whether an irregularity is merely technical or not. In *Moodie's* case there was a tenth man present at the jury's deliberations. The Supreme Court of Appeal held that this constituted such a gross departure from established rules of procedure that the accused had not been properly tried. In other words the court held that the trial was a nullity and on that account it did not consider the merits at all. Compare *Rudman* 1992 (1) SACR 70 (A). For a further example, see *Mkhise* 1988 (2) SA 868 (A), where the accused's 'legal representative' falsely masqueraded as an advocate.

In *Naidoo's* case, the interpreter at the trial was not sworn in in respect of three witnesses, with the result that their evidence could not be taken into account. This in itself did not constitute so gross a departure from established rules of procedure as to render the trial *per se* a nullity. The court on appeal therefore considered the rest of the evidence which had been properly adduced, and came to the conclusion that it could not be said that the jury would inevitably have convicted on that evidence. In this case, therefore, the plea of *autrefois acquit* was upheld when the accused was re-indicted.

From these two cases it can be seen that the question of whether the acquittal can be said to have been on the merits, depends to a large extent on the nature of the irregularity. See also ss 313 and 324.

Section 322(3) now provides that where a conviction is set aside on the ground that a failure of justice has resulted from the admission of evidence otherwise admissible but not properly placed before the trial court due to some defect in the proceedings, the court of appeal may remit the matter to the trial court with instructions to deal with any matter, including the hearing of such evidence, as the court of appeal may think fit. This innovation is to overcome the objections to the result of *Naidoo's* case (see further under 'Appeal').

With regard to defective charge sheets, it is submitted that s 88 affects the plea of *autrefois acquit*. Prior to the enactment of this section the accused was in no jeopardy of being convicted where the charge was fatally (materially) defective. Since the enactment of this section, however, conviction can lawfully take place (unless the accused objects to the charge and it is not amended). It can therefore be said that the accused is in jeopardy of being convicted on a materially defective charge. Should he be acquitted on the merits in these circumstances the plea of *autrefois acquit* must be upheld. See *Makhutla* 1969 (2) SA 490 (O), for an example of the opposite situation.

The plea of *autrefois acquit* can be sustained even where it is based on the judgment of a foreign court — *Pokela* 1968 (4) SA 702 (E).

It is even possible to raise this plea after the commencement of the trial. It is easily conceivable that there could be a case where the existence of a previous acquittal could be discovered during the course of a hearing and after the accused has pleaded. The accused will then be entitled to raise a plea of previous acquittal at this stage — *Mkhuzangewe* 1987 (3) SA 248 (O).

In *Burns* 19 SC 477 it was held that a plea of *autrefois acquit* cannot be raised for the first time on appeal, but in *Mgilane* 1974 (4) SA 303 (Tk) the court considered this rule, when applied rigidly and especially in the case of an unsophisticated and uneducated person who is not represented, to be 'repugnant to one's feeling of fair play and justice'. See also *Kgatlane* 1978 (2) SA 10 (T).

3.4.4 *Section 106 and the pleas autrefois acquit/convict*

Section 106(4) provides, inter alia, that an accused who has pleaded to a charge is entitled to demand that he be acquitted or convicted. We have already pointed out that this may result in an acquittal 'on the merits' even if the State did not lead any evidence — see the reference to *Mthetwa* in the previous section. For instance, this may happen if the accused has pleaded, there have been several postponements, the State witnesses are still not available and the court (in the regular exercise of its discretion) refuses a further postponement. The accused is acquitted 'on the merits', there being simply no evidence against him.

The above scenario can occur only if the accused has pleaded before a tribunal which has the power to find him guilty or not guilty on a particular charge, ie if the tribunal is hearing the accused with this in mind. In other words, the accused must have been 'in jeopardy'. Some of the plea proceedings which we have dealt with do not conform to the aforegoing and consequently cannot be used as a springboard for the pleas of *autrefois acquit/convict*, for example a plea in a magistrate's court on a charge justiciable in a superior court (s 119) and the equivalent procedure relating to the regional court (ss 122A–122D). For example, if an accused pleads not guilty in a magistrate's court in terms of s 122A, is committed for trial in the regional court in terms of s 122D, but the case is withdrawn in the regional court before plea and the matter sent for retrial in the magistrate's court, a plea of *autrefois acquit* should not succeed in the last-mentioned court. See *Attorney General, Eastern Cape v Linda* 1989 (2) SA 578 (E); *Lubbe* 1989 (3) SA 245 (T); *Singh* 1986 (4) SA 263 (C); *Hendrix* 1979 (3) SA 816 (D); *Singh* 1990 (1) SA 123 (A).

The right given to an accused to demand an acquittal or discharge in terms of s 106(4) should not be denied him by careless or negligent actions by the state which cause infinite delays — *Lethopa* 1994 (1) SACR 553 (O).

3.5 Pardon by the President

The accused may plead that he has received a pardon from the President for the offence charged — s 106*(e)*. The President has the powers entrusted by the Constitution and legislation, including those necessary to perform the functions of Head of State and head of the national executive — s 84(1) of the Constitution. These powers include pardoning or reprieving offenders and remitting any fines, penalties or forfeitures — s 84(2)*(j)*.

3.6 Plea to the jurisdiction of the court

Such a plea may be based on an allegation that the offence was committed outside the area of jurisdiction of the court or that some condition precedent necessary to confer jurisdiction on the court has not been satisfied, for example, where the authority of the magistrate's court to try certain military offences was derived by law from the written direction of a military official, a conviction was quashed in the absence of proof that such a direction had been given — *O'Carroll* 17 ECD 79.

In the case of *Giuseppe* 1943 TPD 139 the conviction of certain prisoners of war on charges of theft was set aside on proof that the provisions of Article 60 of the Geneva Convention (requiring, *inter alia*, that at the commencement of a judicial hearing of a prisoner of war the detaining state must notify the representative of the protecting state as soon as possible and at any rate before the date fixed for the hearing) had not been complied with.

A plea of diplomatic immunity presumably also falls under this subsection — *Penrose* 1966 (1) SA 5 (N) at 6C.

If during a trial it appears that the accused is before a court by which he is not properly triable, he is not by reason thereof entitled to an acquittal, but the court may at the request of the accused direct that he be tried before the proper court and remand him to such court. If the accused fails to request removal, the trial must proceed and the verdict and judgment are valid. See s 110 and *Meyers* 1946 AD 57. In *Nqunelo* 1948 (4) SA 428 (O), the Crown (state) successfully appealed against an acquittal in such circumstances.

This section (s 106(1)(*f*)) does not affect the plea to the jurisdiction as affecting the right of the court to try a case which is by law placed beyond its jurisdiction. If the plea to the jurisdiction is dismissed, the court will not grant an interdict restraining the presiding officer from proceeding with the case. The proper course for the accused to follow is to appeal — *Lawrence v A R M Johannesburg* 1908 TS 525.

3.7 Discharge from prosecution

Section 204 of the Code deals with the immunity accorded to accomplices who give satisfactory evidence for the State in criminal proceedings. According to this section, if the prosecutor informs the court that any person called as a witness on behalf of the State will be required to answer questions which might incriminate him, the court must inform such witness that he will be obliged to answer such questions but that if he answers 'frankly and honestly' he will be discharged from liability to prosecution. If the witness does in fact answer the questions put to him frankly and honestly, the court must discharge him from prosecution. Cf *Waite* 1978 (3) SA 896 (O); *Bosman* 1978 (3) SA 903 (O). An accomplice should not be granted a discharge from prosecution directly after the completion of his evidence and before the conclusion of the case — *Mnyamana* 1990 (1) SACR 137 (A).

This section constitutes an exception to the rule that a witness in criminal proceedings may not be compelled to answer any question which might expose him to a criminal charge — s 203.

Where as accused at his trial relies on the provisions of the Indemnity Act 35 of 1990 in order to be discharged from prosecution, such reliance is neither an objection to the charge as envisaged by section 85 of the Criminal Procedure Act, nor does it fall within the ambit of s 106. However, if reliance is placed on the Indemnity Act it is a special defence which has to be dealt with by the trial court through evidence — *Gqozo* 1994 (1) SACR 253 (Ck).

3.8 Lack of authority of the prosecutor

This plea relates to the *locus standi* of the prosecutor to act. It will most probably occur with private prosecutions where a municipality must, for instance, brief a prosecutor to act. An advocate appearing on behalf of the director of public prosecutions may be asked for his delegation. The prescription of an offence may probably also be raised with this plea — Hiemstra 269.

3.9 Lis pendens

The *lis* or case pending in another court against the accused must be a criminal case. This plea is not recognised in the Code, but the general powers of postponement of the trial can be exercised on such a plea, which cannot have anything but a delatory effect. If the other trial is completed and a plea of *autrefois acquit or convict* does not then become effective, the fact that the other trial took place will be irrelevant at the trial where the plea of *lis pendens* has been raised. Cf *Lubisi* 1980 (1) SA 187 (T); *Motsepa* 1982 (1) SA 304 (O). See also *Mayisa* 1983 (4) SA 242 (T).

3.10 Pleas in the case of criminal defamation

These pleas are the same as the defences in a civil case — subject to the remarks already made.

3.11 Plea as to an order of court on an unreasonable delay in a trial

In terms of s 342A, a court before which criminal proceedings are pending, must investigate any delay in the completion of proceedings which appears to the court to be unreasonable and which could cause substantial prejudice to the prosecution, the accused or his/her legal adviser, the state or a witness. The court must consider a number of factors such as the reasons advanced for the delay, whether anybody is to blame, the duration for the delay, the effect of the delay on the administration of justice or the accused or the witnesses, and the adverse effects if the prosecution is stopped or discontinued.

If the court finds the delay to be unreasonable, the court may order, in the case where the accused has not yet pleaded, that the case be struck off the roll and the prosecution not to be resumed or instituted *de novo* without the written instruction of the attorney-general. If the accused is charged again, he/she may raise a special plea that the trial was stayed by a order of court made in terms of s 342A(3)*(c)*.

4 AFTER PLEADING, ACCUSED ENTITLED TO VERDICT

Once an accused has pleaded, he is entitled to demand that he be either acquitted or found guilty, excepting where specially provided for in the Act or in any other law — s 106(4). This sub-section will apply only where the court as it was constituted at the time that the plea was entered, remains so constituted and retains its legal authority up to the time when it passes sentence. The following instances are examples of when an accused will not be entitled to acquittal or conviction:

(1) Where the magistrate has recused himself from the trial — *Punshon v Wise NO* 1948 (1) SA 81 (N); *Magubane v Van der Merwe NO* 1969 (2) SA 417 (N); *Suliman* 1969 (2) SA 385 (A).

(2) Where separation of trials takes place — s 157.

(3) Where a trial is referred to a regional court, or is converted into a preparatory examination — ss 116 and 123.

(4) Where the magistrate dies, resigns, or is dismissed — *Mhlanga* 1959 (2) SA 220 (T). In this case it was held that also where the magistrate is transferred the accused is not entitled to a verdict. See also *De Koker* 1978 (1) SA 659 (O); *Makgetle* 1980 (4) SA 256 (B). For a contrary decision, see *Gwala* 1969 (2) SA 227 (N), where it was held that since a magistrate who has been transferred may by administrative measures be placed in a position to finalise cases which had been initiated before him, another magistrate is not competent to hear the *case de novo*. A transfer is not equivalent to death, recusal or dismissal. Therefore, s 106(4) applies. In *Tlailane* 1982 (4) SA 107 (T), *Gwala* was followed in this connection, and Mhlanga rejected. Incapacity of a magistrate persisting for a considerable period is treated in the same way as death of a magistrate. The accused may be tried de novo before another magistrate — *Makoni* 1976 (1) SA 169 (R).

(5) Where it appears that the accused is before the wrong court.

(6) Where the director of public prosecutions makes an application in terms of s 13 that a private prosecution be stopped and that the accused be prosecuted *de novo* by the State.

(7) Where a youth is referred to the Children's Court (s 254) or where an enquiry is held in terms of the Prevention and Treatment of Drug Dependency Act 20 of 1992 (s 255).

(8) If a court finds that an accused, because of a mental disorder, is not capable of understanding the proceedings so as to make a proper defence, the court must direct that the accused be detained in a mental hospital or a prison pending the signification of the decision of the Minister, and if the court so directs after the accused has pleaded to the charge, he will not be entitled to be acquitted or convicted. If the court makes such a finding after the accused has been convicted but before sentence is passed, the court must set aside the conviction — s 77(6). After recovery, the accused may again be charged and tried.

(9) Where an accused has pleaded in terms of s 119 — *Hendrix* 1979 (3) SA 816 (D); *Singh* 1986 (4) SA 263 (C).

(10) Where the prosecution has been stopped by the prosecutor without the required consent of the director of public prosecutions or any person authorised thereto by the director of public prosecutions in terms of s 6*(b)* — *Prokureur-Generaal, Venda v Magistraat Streekafdeling* 1982 (2) SA 659 (V).

The question of whether an accused who is acquitted in terms of s 106(4) may be retried must be answered on the basis of the principles relating to *autrefois acquit*.

CHAPTER 15

Miscellaneous matters relating to the trial

		Page
1	WHO MAY ATTEND THE TRIAL?	223
2	WITNESSES	224
	2.1 Securing attendance of witnesses	224
	2.2 Recalcitrant witness	225
3	TRIAL OF MENTALLY ABNORMAL PERSONS	226
4	TRIAL OF DRUG-ADDICTED PERSONS	226
5	ADJOURNMENT (POSTPONEMENT)	226
6	SPEEDY TRIAL	227

The Constitution and this chapter:

Section 35 — Arrested, detained and accused persons

(3) Every accused person has a right to a fair trial, which includes the right —

. . .

(c) to a public trial before an ordinary court; . . .

See 1, below.

---

1 WHO MAY ATTEND THE TRIAL?

The general principle is that the conduct of criminal trials should take place in open court and in the presence of the accused: an accused's right to a fair trial includes the right to a public trial — s 35(3)*(c)* of the Constitution. This means that the public is generally entitled to be present — cf *Magqabi v Mafundityala* 1979 (4) SA 106 (E). As in the case of preparatory examinations, there are exceptions to this rule.

In terms of s 153(1) all courts are given the power to exclude the public whenever it appears to be in the interests of the security of the state or good order, or public morals, or the administration of justice. The court may also order that a witness testify behind closed doors if it feels that there is a likelihood of his coming to harm as a result of his testifying — s 153(2). A court may *mero motu* or on application by the prosecutor order that a witness or an accused with his/her consent, give evidence by means of a closed circuit television or similar electronic media, but only if any of these facilities are readily available or obtainable — s 158(2)–(3). Section 153 does not authorise the court, however, to order the withholding of the identity of a witness from the defence *Leepile* (5) 1986 (4) SA 187 (W). *Contra*, however, *Pastoors* 1986 (4) SA 222 (W). In *Nzama* 1997 (1) SACR 542 (D&CLD) the court ordered that the witness should be permitted to testify behind closed doors; that the witness be excused from disclosing his real name to the court and was permitted to adopt any pseudonym for the purposes of the trial; that no person be permitted to reveal the witness' identity and that his evidence be published only to the extent that it did not or may not disclose or tend to disclose his identity. For the principles involved when trials are held in camera— see *Niesewand* (1) 1973 (3) SA 581 (RA) and cf also *Sekete* 1980 (1) SA 171 (N).

In addition, s 153(3) provides for the exclusion of the public, at the request of a complainant, where an accused is charged with committing or attempting to commit an indecent act towards any other person, or extortion (either at common law or in terms of a statute). Judgment and sentence, in such cases, however, must be given in open court unless the court is of the opinion that the complainant's identity would thereby be revealed.

Finally, s 153(4), (5) and (6), provides safeguards against young persons being adversely affected by criminal trials. No person other than the accused, his parent or guardian or legal representative, or persons whose presence is necessary for the conduct of the trial may be present at the trial of a person under 18 years of age without special authority from the presiding officer. Persons under the age of 18 are not entitled to attend any criminal trial unless they are actually giving evidence (in which case the court may be cleared of all members of the public) or unless they are specially authorised to be present. See also *Klink v Regional Court Magistrate NO* [1996] 1 All SA 191 (SECL) regarding the cross-examination of child witnesses, where the court found that a proper balance can be achieved between the protection of a child witness and the rights of an accused to a fair trial by allowing the witness to testify in congenial surroundings and out of sight of the accused— see also s 158(4) as amended by Act 86 of 1996.

Once the public has been excluded from a trial in terms of s 153, special circumstances must exist before this ruling is relaxed. The court must be satisfied that such relaxation will not cause harm to the witnesses or their relations— *Mothopeng* 1979 (4) SA 367 (T).

2 WITNESSES

2.1 Securing attendance of witnesses

Either the prosecutor or the accused may compel the attendance of witnesses by way of a subpoena. (See s 179 *et seq* dealing with witnesses generally.) In certain circumstances the court itself may also cause witnesses to be subpoenaed. (See s 186 and below.) If a witness fails to obey a subpoena, he may be arrested and brought before the court— s 188. Whenever a person is likely to give material evidence in criminal proceedings, and there is reason to believe that he is about to abscond, or has absconded, such person may be arrested (upon a warrant), and be committed to prison— s 184.

Whenever the attorney-general thinks that there is any danger that a potential State witness in respect of specified offences may be tampered with or intimidated, or that such witness may abscond, or whenever he deems it in the interest of the witness or of the administration of justice, he may apply to a judge in chambers for an order that such witness be detained pending the relevant proceedings — s 185. The witness may then be detained until the conclusion of the case or six months after his arrest (see the regulations pertaining to protective custody in *Government Gazette* No 14196 of 31 July 1992 — *Regulation Gazette* No 4916). The offences in respect of which these powers apply are murder, arson, kidnapping, child-stealing, robbery, sedition, public violence, housebreaking, whether under the common law or a statutory provision, with intent to commit an offence, offences in terms of the Intimidation Act 72 of 1982 and any conspiracy, incitement or attempt to commit any of the above-mentioned offences and treason — s 185 read with Part III of the Second Schedule to the Act. (This section is generally known as the '180-day clause'.) Note the similar drastic provisions in connection with the detention of witnesses in the Internal Security Act 74 of 1982.

2.2 Recalcitrant witness

In the case of a recalcitrant witness in a criminal trial (ie someone who refuses to take the oath or refuses to answer questions), s 189 empowers the court to institute a summary enquiry, and if such a person does not have a 'just excuse' for his refusal, he may be sentenced to a maximum imprisonment of 2 years or where the criminal proceedings relate to an offence referred to in Part III of Schedule 2, to a maximum imprisonment of five years. This may happen repeatedly. (Such a person will not, however, be sentenced to imprisonment unless the judge, regional court magistrate or magistrate is also of the opinion that the furnishing of such information is necessary for the administration of justice or the maintenance of law and order — s 205(4).) Appeal is possible. The primary criminal case may be concluded in the meantime. The following requirements have to be met before a witness may be sentenced to imprisonment for refusing to take the oath as a witness or, having taken the oath, for refusing to answer questions put to him: the witness must have refused to take the oath or to testify; a proper enquiry must have been held into the refusal; and there must have been no just excuse for his failure or refusal — *Seals* 1990 (1) SACR 38 (C). In *Attorney-General, Transvaal v Kader* 1991 (2) SACR 669 (A) it was held that it is sufficient justification if a witness were to find himself in circumstances in which it would be humanly intolerable to have to testify. A 'just excuse' in terms of s 189 is a wider concept than 'lawful excuse'. See also *Sithole* 1991 (4) SA 94 (W). In *Molobi* 1976 (2) SA 301 (W) it was held that a witness's sympathy with an accused's political ideals does not constitute a just excuse. A witness's fear for his safety and that of his family is also not a just excuse. The demands of society and the interest of the administration of justice require that a witness should nevertheless give evidence — *Moloto* 1991 (1) SACR 617 (T). However, if it is not a proven necessity for the welfare of the community that the information be required specifically from the appellant, the excuse will be considered just — *Cornelissen; Cornelissen v Zeelie NO and another* 1994 (2) SACR 41 (W). See also *Mthenjane* 1979 (2) SA 105 (A); *Haysom v Additional Magistrate* 1979 (3) SA 155 (C). A witness does not, however, have to answer any incriminating questions — s 203. Cf also *Wessels* 1966 (3) SA 737 (C).

Section 189 proceedings are not trials but they are still judicial proceedings and the rules of justice must be complied with. The witness has a right to

(1)   a fair opportunity to prepare for the proceedings; and

(2)   legal representation.

Should the witness refuse or be unable to obtain legal representation, the court must explain to him the phrase 'just excuse' and allow him the opportunity to address the court or to adduce evidence — *Bekisi* 1992 (1) SACR 39 (C). See also *Heyman* 1966 (4) SA 598 (A); *Wessels* 1966 (4) SA 89 (C); *Smit v Van Niekerk NO* 1976 (4) SA 304 (E).

3   TRIAL OF MENTALLY ABNORMAL PERSONS

If at any time *after the commencement of any trial* it appears or is alleged that the accused is not of sound mind, he must be dealt with in the manner provided by the Act in regard to mental disorder — see ss 77–79 in this regard and Chapter 14 (above). See also *Manupo* 1991 (2) SACR 447 (C); *Mokie* 1992 (1) SACR 430 (T); *Mphela* 1994 (1) SACR 488 (A). This means that the court must grant an adjournment for a medical examination. If necessary the accused should be referred to an institution for observation. See *Nell* 1969 (1) SA 143 (A) (where the accused fell forward in the dock and later collapsed and started foaming at the mouth) and the comment on psychopaths in Chapter 14.

The question of whether an accused was fit to stand trial can be raised for the first time even after conviction and sentence; and there is no onus on the accused to prove his mental defect — *Ebrahim* 1973 (1) SA 868 (A).

4   TRIAL OF DRUG-ADDICTED PERSONS

If it appears during the trial that the accused is probably a person such as is described in s 21(1) of the Prevention and Treatment of Drug Dependency Act 20 of 1992, the trial may be stopped and an inquiry in terms of s 22 may be held — s 255 of the Criminal Procedure Act. If the charge against the accused is withdrawn, conversion of the proceedings becomes impossible as it can only be converted during a trail — *In re Vorster* 1997 (1) SACR 269 (EC).

5   ADJOURNMENT (POSTPONEMENT)

If necessary a court may adjourn or postpone a case till a later date — ss 168 and 169. The court's powers to do so are regulated by s 170. When the court considers an application for postponement, whether it be by the State or the defence, the following two basic principles have to be considered:

(1)   it is in the interest of society that guilty men should be duly convicted and not discharged due to an error which could have been avoided had the case been adjourned; and

(2)   that an accused is deemed to be innocent and therefore has a right, once charged, to a speedy hearing.

When it appears that the State neglected to call a witness, the court may in its discretion hold this negligence against the State — *Geritis* 1966 (1) SA 753 (W).

A court of appeal will not interfere with a lower court's decision to adjourn a case, provided the discretion to do so was exercised judicially (ie without caprice, bias or the application of wrong principles, but on judicial grounds and for sound reasons) — *Zackey* 1945 AD 505; *Zimba* 1975 (2) PH H122 (N). Where a magistrate refused to adjourn a case to afford an accused the opportunity to find witnesses, the case was remitted for retrial (the accused had only 8 days in which to prepare for the trial) — *Levin v Whitelaw NO* 1928 TPD 357. If a refusal to adjourn amounts to the exclusion of relevant evidence, the conviction will be set aside — *Hatch* 1914 CPD 68. When the accused's legal representative is absent and it is not due to the fault of the accused, the case must be adjourned or a subsequent conviction will be set aside — *Seheri* 1964 (1) SA 29 (A). (This exposition is found in Hiemstra 428–30.)

If an accused fails to attend the trial on the date to which the case had been adjourned, he will be guilty of an offence, unless he satisfies the court that his failure to attend was not due to his fault — s 170. At such a summary enquiry, the court should explain this onus and his rights to him (including his rights to furnish evidence in terms of s 151) — *Bkenlele* 1983 (1) SA 515 (O).

An application for a postponement on the ground that an application to the executive for indemnity in terms of the Indemnity Act 35 of 1990, has not yet been decided upon, is no valid reason to curb the director of public prosecutions' duty to prosecute or to stand in his way to direct that the prosecution should continue — *Hlatswayo v Attorney-General, Witwatersrand* 1994 (1) SACR 232 (W).

6 SPEEDY TRIAL

Included in the concept of a fair trial, is the right of every accused person to have his/her trial commenced and concluded without unreasonable delay — s 35(3)*(d)* of the Constitution. The critical question is whether a lapse of time is reasonable taking into consideration the nature of the prejudice suffered by the accused, the nature of the case and systematic delay. Pre-trial incarceration of five months for a crime which has a maximum sentence of six months clearly points in the direction of unreasonableness. But it will be difficult to establish prejudice if an accused has constantly consented to postponements — *Sanderson v Attorney-General, Eastern Cape* 1998 (1) SACR 227(CC) (also reported at 1998(2) SA 38 (CC)). See also, *Wild v Hoffert* 1998 (2) SACR 1 (CC).

The appropriate remedy for an infringement of the right to a speedy trial, eg, a stay of prosecution, is to be determined in the light of the circumstances of each particular case — *Wild v Hoffert* 1998(2) SACR 1 (CC).

CHAPTER 16

Joinder and separation of trials

Page

1 INTRODUCTION 228

2 SEPARATION OF TRIALS 228

   2.1   The common-law position 228

   2.2   The position under the Criminal Procedure Act 229

   2.3   Grounds upon which separation may be applied for 229

3 JOINDER OF PERSONS CHARGED SEPARATELY 231

1 INTRODUCTION

As indicated previously, persons charged with the same offence or separate offences alleged to have been committed at the same time and place or at the same place and about the same time, may be charged jointly in the same indictment. Joinder of more than one person may afford problems for the prosecutor since it is a principle of our law that no person can be compelled either by the prosecutor or by a co-accused to give evidence in the case in which he appears—*Sas* 1918 CPD 346; *Chamane* 1962 (2) SA 428 (A). Now, it may happen that after the trial has commenced the prosecutor realises that in order to bring sufficient evidence against accused A he requires co-accused B as witness against A. He may not call B as witness against A, however. Joinder may also afford problems for the accused. A and B are indicted jointly for murder. The evidence is very strong against A, but not so strong against B. A has made a confession, which is admissible in evidence only against him, in which he laid all the blame upon B. B may now fear that the court will unconsciously be influenced against him by the strong evidence against A. May the prosecutor and the accused demand a separation of trials?

2 SEPARATION OF TRIALS

2.1 The common-law position

It was a rule of common law that where persons were jointly charged, a separation of trials was incompetent once the State had joined issue with the accused. Where A and B were charged jointly and both pleaded not guilty, the prosecutor could accordingly not apply for a separation of trials with a view to calling A as witness against B. Where, however, one or more of the accused had pleaded guilty, the view was held that the State did not join issue with the accused. If a separation of trials took place and the verdict was pronounced in the case of the accused who pleaded guilty, he (or they) could, therefore, give evidence against the other accused. See the decisions quoted by Hiemstra 406–7; Du Toit *et al* 22.14–15.

2.2 The position under the Criminal Procedure Act

A change was brought about in the common-law position by the provisions which are at present contained in s 157. In terms of this section the court may now at any time during the trial, on the application of the prosecutor or any of the accused, or *mero motu* (cf *Ndwandwe* 1970 (4) SA 502 (N)), direct that separate trials take place. (The Supreme Court of Appeal in *Goosen* 1988 (4) SA 5 (A), without referring to any authorities, held that a court cannot *meru moto* order a separation of trials without an application of the parties concerned.) The court may in such a case abstain from giving a judgment in regard to any of the accused. (An application for such separation may be repeated in the course of the trial, eg when a confession by one accused which implicates the other accused is handed in—*Libaya* 1965 (4) SA 249 (O).)

If the court has ordered a separation of trials, the trial of an accused may be concluded and *thereafter* he may be called as a witness against the remaining accused. The first-mentioned accused need not be *sentenced* (if convicted) in order to be a competent witness. But it is *desirable* that he should first be sentenced. If the witness is sentenced, the possibility is smaller that he will fabricate testimony in the hope of receiving a lesser penalty. See *Ex parte Minister of Justice: In re R v Demingo* 1951 (1) SA 36 (A). Where a separation of trials is ordered the trial of the accused which was discontinued must be commenced *de novo*.

In passing we wish to draw your attention once again to the rule that where an accomplice is produced as a witness by and on behalf of the public prosecutor, and submits to being sworn as a witness, and answers fully to the satisfaction of the court all lawful questions, he is absolutely freed from all liability to prosecution for such offence. The testimony of such a witness was formerly referred to as 'King's evidence'. Although it is perhaps hardly justifiable on ethical grounds for a criminal to go scot-free while his associates in crime must pay for their offences, the practical administration of justice requires this. It is better that one accomplice evades liability and the others are convicted than that all of them go free due to a lack of evidence.

2.3 Grounds upon which separation may be applied for

In most cases application for separation is made by the defence, since the State is free to act against the accused individually ab initio. It is undesirable for separate trials to take place if the only purpose is to call as witness someone accused of an offence arising from the same set of facts, and if such a procedure gives rise to injustice, prejudice or the apparent prejudice of an accused, the convictions which are eventually made will be set aside—except in the case of accomplices who become 'State witnesses'.

Note the following aspects:

(1) As a general rule accused persons who are charged jointly should be tried jointly. See *Bagas* 1952 (1) SA 437 (A) 441F–G:

> 'It is expedient that persons charged with the same offence should be tried together and a Court of Appeal will not lightly interfere with an order made by a presiding judicial officer that they be so tried. To succeed an appellant will have to show that

in some manner the dice were loaded against him by reason of the joint trial; that he suffered, or probably suffered prejudice to which he should not have been made subject. Such prejudice is not presumed.'

(2) The question whether separation should be allowed lies in the discretion of the presiding judicial officer. This discretion must be exercised in a judicial manner, ie not arbitrarily, but taking into account and considering all relevant facts— *Bagas* (above). The interests of justice, which is a wide concept, has to be promoted. It encompasses the interests of the individual accused, as well as—or as against—the wider interests of society—*Shuma* 1994 (4) SA 583 (ECD).

(3) The mere possibility of prejudice is not sufficient to justify an order for separation of trials. It must be established that the joint trial will probably do the accused an injustice—*Nzuza* 1952 (4) SA 376 (A).

(4) The fact that evidence is adduced at a joint trial which is admissible against one accused but inadmissible against another and that this evidence may incriminate the latter (eg a confession by the former) is an important consideration in an application for the separation of trials, but it is not the only consideration. Our courts' attitude is that they are able to distinguish between evidence which is admissible against one accused but inadmissible against the other. See, eg, *Witbooi* 1994 (1) SACR 44 (Ck).

(5) Justice requires that the State should not be unduly prejudiced in the presentation of its case. If a real danger exists that a separation of trials will hinder the State to such an extent in the presentation of its case that a miscarriage of justice may result and a guilty person may be released, this consideration is decisive—*Kritzinger* 1952 (4) SA 651 (W).

(6) In *Groesbeek* (1) 1969 (4) SA 383 (O) two accused, husband and wife, were indicted jointly for the murder of the previous husband of the woman. In an application for a separation of trials it was contended that there was a possibility of prejudice in a joint trial by virtue of the rule that a husband and wife cannot testify against each other. This would have the effect, so it was argued, that evidence given by the wife in her own defence would not be admissible against the husband; therefore the husband could not cross-examine his wife on such evidence. Being hampered in his cross-examination he would not be ensured a fair trial. The court upheld these contentions and granted a separation of trials. This decision has been neutralised by s 196(2) of the Act which provides that the evidence which an accused may give in his own defence at joint criminal proceedings shall not be inadmissible against a co-accused 'by reason only that such accused is for any reason not a competent witness for the prosecution against such co-accused'.

(7) Where co-accused blame one another it would often be in the interest of justice to try them together in order to enable the court to hear all the evidence and better to allocate the various degrees of guilt—cf *Solomon* 1934 CPD 94.

(8) If one of two or more co-accused has pleaded guilty, the best course is to separate the trials and to dispose of the trials of those who pleaded guilty first of all—*Pietersen* 1947 (1) SA 56 (GW); *Zonele* 1959 (3) SA 319 (A). In *Somciza* 1990 (1) SA 361 (A) it was affirmed that where one accused pleads guilty and the other accused (who has pleaded not guilty) needs him as a witness, their trials

should be separated since the first accused cannot be compelled to testify as long as he remains a co-accused. However, where both State and accused prefer a joint trial, despite the fact that some accused pleaded guilty and others not guilty, the neglect to order separation of the trials will not constitute an irregularity—*Mkize* 1960 (1) SA 276 (N). Cf *Lemmert* 1969 (2) PH H210 (NC). However, in *Liscoxo* 1974 (2) SA 356 (O) and in *Ndwandwe* 1970 (4) SA 502 (N) it was held that under such circumstances the court should *mero motu* order a separation, regardless of any request by any of the parties—especially if the accused is unrepresented and ignorant of the provisions of s 157. See also *Ntuli* 1978 (2) SA 69 (A).

Refusal to order a separation when an accused wants to call a co-accused as witness for the defence but the latter refuses to testify (in terms of s 196(1)*(a)* which provides that an accused may only be called as a witness on his own application), limits the accused in his defence and may have the consequence that his conviction will be reversed by a higher instance—*Mbelu* 1974 (1) PH H38 (N). See also *Shuma* 1994 (4) SA 583 (ECD), where it was also stated that a proper refusal to order a separation of trials does not amount to an infringement of an accused's constitutional right to a fair trial in terms of s 25(3) of the Constitution of the Republic of South Africa 200 of 1993 (currently s 35(3)).

3 JOINDER OF PERSONS CHARGED SEPARATELY

At common law, where persons were charged separately, the rule was that they had to be separately tried. It was not permissible to join the trials, nor did consent of the accused confer jurisdiction—*Ngwatya* 1949 (1) SA 556 (EDL); *Riet* 1970 (1) PH H94 (NC); *Sithole* 1966 (2) SA 335 (N). In *Harper* 1909 TS 361, the court nonetheless ordered a joinder of trials in extraordinary circumstances where a man and woman were indicted separately: the man for residing in a brothel, and the woman for keeping the brothel. The man wanted to conduct his own defence as well as that of the woman. The State applied for joinder and both accused consented. In granting the application, Innes CJ pointed out that the State could have indicted the accused jointly *ab initio*. See also *Xolo v Attorney-General of the Transvaal* 1952 (3) SA 764 (W) where the same principle was laid down.

Section 157(1) of the Criminal Procedure Act now provides that an accused 'may be joined with any other accused in the same criminal proceedings at any time before any evidence has been led in respect of the charge in question'. This section permits joinder of accused after arraignment but before the prosecutor has commenced leading evidence. If evidence has been led and joinder is regarded as desirable, the whole proceedings have to be commenced *de novo*—*Kabele* 1974 (3) SA 223 (NC). If the prosecutor objects to joinder, it appears that his objection, as *dominus litis*, is final—cf *Xolo v Attorney-General of the Transvaal* (above).

It has been held in *Ngobeni* 1981 (1) SA 506 (B) that other accused may be joined after explanation of plea and questioning of an accused. The court must, however, fully inform the accused of all that has already taken place in court before asking him to plead. In *Hartkopf* 1981 (1) SA 992 (T) it was held, however, that as a general rule all steps in the proceedings should take place in the presence of all the accused.

CHAPTER 17

The conduct of the trial

Page

~~omit~~ 1 INTRODUCTION   233

2 THE CASE FOR THE PROSECUTION   234

   2.1 Opening of the State's case   234

   2.2 Evidence for the State   234

3 DISCHARGE OF ACCUSED AT THE CLOSE OF THE STATE CASE   237

4 THE DEFENCE CASE   240

   4.1 The accused's rights to be explained   240

   4.2 Witnesses for the defence   241

   4.3 The accused's right to silence   242

   4.4 Unsworn statement by the accused   243

   4.5 Formal admission by the accused   243

   4.6 Re-examination of witnesses   243

5 REBUTTING EVIDENCE BY THE STATE   243

6 CALLING OR RECALLING WITNESSES BY COURT, AND QUESTIONING BY COURT   244

7 RECORDING OF EVIDENCE   245

8 ADDRESS BY PROSECUTOR AND DEFENCE   246

The Constitution and this chapter:

Section 35—Arrested, detained and accused persons

(3) Every accused person has a right to a fair trial, which includes the right—

. . .

   (h) to be presumed innocent, to remain silent, and not to testify during the proceedings;

         See 4.1 and 4.3, below.

   (i) to adduce and challenge evidence;

   (j) not to be compelled to give self-incriminating evidence; . . .

         See 2.2 and 4.3, below.

   (k) to be tried in a language that the accused person understands or, if that is not practicable, to have the proceedings interpreted in that language;

         See 2.2 below.

---

1 INTRODUCTION

The accused has pleaded and all the preliminaries to which reference has been made have been observed, the trial proceeds. The Criminal Procedure Act lays down certain rules of procedure which should be observed, but the trial is otherwise subject to the management of the judicial officer presiding over it. All orders given in the judicial discretion of the presiding judge or other judicial officer for the proper conduct of the trial must be obeyed by the parties, the court staff and the public, who are all, in case of wilful disobedience, liable to be committed or fined summarily for contempt of court.

A famous formulation regarding the course of a criminal trial is that of Lord Hewart in *Sussex Justices* [1924] 1 KB 256 at 259:

> '. . . [I]t is not merely of some importance, but of fundamental importance, that justice should both be done and be manifestly seen to be done. . . . The rule is that nothing is to be done which creates even a suspicion that there has been an improper interference with the course of justice.'

This eloquent passage has been repeated frequently, sometimes in a modified form, by our courts: *Sallem* 1987 (4) SA 772 (A); *Marx* 1989 (1) SA 222 (A) 225. One facet of the maxim that justice must be seen to be done is the requirement that witnesses and accused persons must be treated courteously by the court, the defence, and the prosecution—Cf *Abrahams* 1989 (2) SA 668 (E) and see Chapter 13.

The concept of 'justice' in its procedural sense is closely related to the idea of legality (see Chapter 1); it is not a concept which presupposes that the accused is not guilty, but rather one which refers to a quality of the proceedings. Cf *Mushimba* 1977 (2) SA 829 (A) at 844. It is illustrated clearly in *Dozereli* 1983 (3) SA 259 (C), where an accused was asked, contrary to s 197, why he had been in prison before (this section prohibits information regarding previous convictions, with certain exceptions, in the trial stages prior to sentencing). The reviewing court stated that this is not excusable, even though the magistrate affirmed that he had not based the conviction on this information; it also does not matter whether the accused is really guilty or not. The only question is whether the basic right of the accused to a fair trial has been affected by the irregularity to such a degree that it cannot in principle be said that justice was done. (*In casu* the reviewing court set the conviction aside.)

Apart from what is stated in the following paragraph the standards which a judicial officer should maintain in the questioning of witnesses and the accused have been summarised in *Mabuza* 1991 (1) SACR 636 (O) as follows:

(1) The court should not conduct its questioning in such a manner that its impartiality can be questioned or doubted.

(2) The court should not take part in the case to such an extent that its vision is clouded by the 'dust of the arena' and it is then unable to adjudicate properly on the issues.

(3) The court should not intimidate or upset a witness or the accused so that his answers are weakened or his credibility shaken.

(4) The court should control the trial in such a way that its impartiality, its open-mindedness, its fairness and reasonableness is manifest to all who have an interest in the trial, in particular the accused.

A judicial officer can only properly fulfil his demanding and socially important duties if he guards against his own actions, is attentive to his own weaknesses (such as impatience), personal opinions and whims, and continually restrains them.

In terms of s 35(3) of the Constitution of the Republic of South Africa 108 of 1996 every accused is entitled to a fair trial. This embraces fairness, not only to the accused, but also to society as a whole, which usually has a real interest in the outcome of a case—*Sonday* 1995 (1) SA 497 (C) 507.

2   THE CASE FOR THE PROSECUTION

2.1   Opening of the State's case

Before any evidence is led the prosecutor is entitled to address the court for the purpose of explaining the charge and opening the evidence intended to be adduced for the prosecution *but without comment thereon*—s 150(1). Although this subsection does not expressly say so, the prosecutor's address (except in cases where argument is necessary on an objection) is heard after the process of arraignment is completed. The subsection clearly comes into operation only where an accused has pleaded not guilty and the prosecutor intends to lead evidence—*Sethole* 1984 (3) SA 620 (O).

In practice it is considered unnecessary for the prosecutor to deliver such address in simple cases. In complicated cases an address by the prosecution at the opening of the case can be of great assistance to the court. The prosecution is expected to give a summary of the essential features of the case for the State so that the court will be in a position to appreciate the significance of each item as it is presented in the light of the evidence which is still to be presented by the State.

The prosecutor should avoid any reference to evidence which may not be admissible or to any contentious matter which may prejudice the case of the accused. Such matters should be dealt with, as a rule, when they arise in the course of the trial and, if necessary, in the absence of the assessors.

2.2   Evidence for the State

The manner in which the examination in chief of witnesses should be conducted and the nature of the questions which may be put in the course of such examination are part of the law of evidence.

The presiding officer must make sure that the accused understands the language used by witnesses. But where the accused through his conduct leads the court to assume that he understands the language used, he will not easily, after his conviction, be able to claim a review on the ground of an irregularity because he did not understand the proceedings—*Geidel v Bosman* 1963 (4) SA 253 (T). Where the language used by the witnesses is not one of the official languages, an interpreter must translate the evidence. The interpreter must be sworn in, either upon taking office or at the commencement of the case in which he acts as interpreter. If he is not sworn in, it amounts to an irregularity which may render the trial abortive—*Naidoo* 1962 (2) SA 625 (A). For a general discussion of the role of an interpreter see *Mabona* 1973 (2) SA 614 (A).

There are now eleven official languages at national level—s 6(1) of the Constitution. Every accused has the right to be tried in a language which he or she understands or, failing this, to have the proceedings interpreted to him or her— s 35(3)*(k)* of the Constitution.

Every criminal trial must take place, and the witnesses must give their evidence *viva voce* (ie orally), in open court in the presence of the accused, except in so far as specific provision to the contrary is made by law—s 152. In terms of s 212 evidence of certain formal matters may be given by way of affidavit (eg pathology reports and fingerprint reports) subject to the right of the opposing party, which may be either the accused or the State, to object against such evidence.

The prosecutor may then examine the witnesses for the prosecution and where any document may be received in evidence before any court upon its mere production, the prosecutor shall read out such document in court unless the accused is in possession of a copy of such document or dispenses with the reading thereof—s 150(2).

Statements made by witnesses at a preparatory examination may *not* be proved in this manner, even where the accused admits the facts in the record. See *Nzuza* 1963 (3) SA 631 (A), where the accused was convicted of murder, having admitted all the facts contained in the record of the preparatory examination, which was read out by the prosecuting counsel. The Supreme Court of Appeal quashed the conviction, holding that the accused could not by his consent validate the invalid procedure adopted.

Section 213 of the Criminal Procedure Act (based on s 9 of the English Criminal Justice Act of 1967) introduced a far-reaching change to the general rule that evidence at a criminal trial must be given *viva voce*. It provides that a written statement made by a witness will, in certain circumstances, be admissible as evidence to the same extent as oral evidence given by such person. Such statements must be served upon the opposing party, who may, at least two days before the commencement of the proceedings object to the statement being tendered in evidence. Where the opposing party is the accused (who might well be undefended) the statement must be accompanied by a written notice setting out that he has the right to object. Should no objection be raised, the statement may 'upon the mere production thereof' be admitted as evidence at the proceedings. The court may, however, *mero motu* or at the request of either the State or the accused, order the witness concerned to attend court to give evidence *viva voce*. An *accused* may not make use of the provisions of s 213—he must himself testify under oath or not at all.

Another exception to the rule that evidence must be given *viva voce* is to be found in the Civil Aviation Offences Act 10 of 1972, relating to 'hi-jacking' and other offences in connection with aviation. This Act provides that a statement in writing made on oath outside the Republic by a person whose evidence is required and who cannot be found in the Republic, may be submitted as evidence. It is required, however, that such statement must have been made in the presence of the accused and to a competent judicial or consular officer (s 7 of the Act).

The right to read out the accused's evidence or statement made at a preparatory examination is reserved for the prosecution only. If the accused wants to give evidence at the trial he has to do so from the witness-box, where he is subject to cross-examination. But the statements of the accused made at the preparatory examination form part of the evidence at the trial (where the prosecutor has read out the record) and must be considered by the court, even where the accused gave no rebutting evidence at the trial—*Ngutshane* 1952 (4) SA 608 (N).

As regards the calling of witnesses by the prosecutor and the nature of the evidence (eg admissions and confessions by the accused), the following aspects are important:

It is accepted practice that the prosecutor at a superior court trial is not obliged to call all the witnesses who made depositions at the preparatory examination. Where the cross-examination of a witness at the preparatory examination has shown that any such witness may be of importance to the defence, the prosecutor should, in any event, secure his presence at the trial so that he may be called by the defence or by the court.

In particular, the prosecutor is not bound to call witnesses whom he believes to be untruthful, hostile to the prosecution or in league with the accused.

The function of a prosecutor is to present the matter to the court fully and fairly and to conduct the case with judicial discretion and a sense of responsibility—not in a vindictive spirit or with any excessive zeal in trying to get a conviction, but as an officer of the court charged with the serious duty of assisting the court in arriving at the truth—cf _Jija_ 1991 (2) SA 52 (E). When a State witness gives evidence at variance with a statement in the possession of the prosecutor, the prosecutor must, if the discrepancy is a material one, immediately make the statement available to the defence or, where the accused is unrepresented, disclose the discrepancy to the court —_Xaba_ 1983 (3) SA 717 (A).

The prosecutor is free to call at the trial a witness or witnesses although such witnesses have not given evidence at the preparatory examination and even though their names do not appear on the list which an attorney-general has to supply to an accused who is arraigned in a superior court—s 144(3). Wherever practicable he should give notice that such witness or witnesses will be called and a copy of their statements should be served on the defence—_Keller and Parker_ 1914 CPD 791. If due notice has not been given a postponement will, where necessary, be granted to the accused to prepare his defence on such new evidence.

Once a State witness is in the witness-box, the prosecutor may not interview the witness privately, at least not without informing the court before doing so and explaining why it is necessary to do so—_Wise_ 1975 (1) SA 597 (RA).

In undefended cases it is the duty of the prosecutor to present before the court any information favourable to the accused which may come to his notice. In defended cases, the prosecutor should place such information at the disposal of the legal representative of the accused—_Van Rensburg_ 1963 (2) SA 343 (N).

The defence is entitled to cross-examine each and every State witness—see s 35(3)_(i)_ of the Constitution. The right of cross-examination also exists in respect of a co-accused who has elected to testify. It is the duty of a court to assist an unrepresented and unsophisticated accused who shows an insufficient understanding of his right to cross-examination and the consequences of a failure to exercise it— _Khambule_ 1991 (2) SACR 277 (W); _Namib Wood Industries v Mutiltha_ 1992 (1) SACR 381 (Nm). It is accepted practice that co-accused persons exercise their right to cross-examine their co-accused or his witness in numerical order before the State is given the opportunity to cross-examine. Cf _Langa_ 1963 (4) SA 941 (N); _Lesias_ 1974 (1) SA 135 (SWA). It is the duty of the presiding officer to grant an accused, especially an undefended accused, sufficient opportunity fully to cross-examine a State witness in a manner acknowledged as reasonable cross-examination. There must be no suspicion at all that the defence was hampered in its cross-examination (eg that excessive interference with the defence's cross-examination took place)— _T_ 1990 (1) SACR 57 (T).

The nature and extent of cross-examination is not always clear to an accused and it is unfair to expect that he/she performs as competently as an experienced legal practitioner. In circumstances where the magistrate is aware of the accused's defence it is desirable for him to assist the accused by means of pertinent questions directed to State witnesses—*Maseko* 1993 (2) SACR 579 (A).

The power to refuse a request to recall a witness for cross-examination or even for further cross-examination is a power that should be exercised sparingly by presiding officers, and then only when it is clear that the request is made frivolously or as part of delaying tactics—*Kondile* 1974 (3) SA 774 (Tk). See also *G* 1992 (1) SACR 568 (B). Where an accused has already cross-examined the State witnesses and put his defence to them, he suffers no prejudice if the court refuses the request to recall a witness for further cross-examination made by his legal representative who was appointed subsequently—*M* 1976 (4) SA 8 (T).

Where the defence proposes to submit another version of any fact or event testified to by a witness for the prosecution, there normally rests a duty upon the defence to put its version to the State witness whose evidence the defence will contradict in the course of its own case. It is only as a result of proper cross-examination on these lines that the court will be placed in a position to estimate the relative acceptability of the two versions. If this rule is not followed, it may necessitate the recalling of State witnesses and unnecessary waste of time—*M* 1970 (3) SA 20 (RA). This difficulty is experienced almost daily in the criminal courts of South Africa where undefended accused are unaware of the proper way in which to conduct their defence. A court should treat such an accused with careful patience. A court should assist a struggling undefended accused with his cross-examination; to draw an adverse inference from his failure to cross-examine would be unfair—*Sebatana* 1983 (1) SA 809 (O); *Mngomezulu* 1983 (1) SA 1152 (N).

Assertions made on behalf of the accused during his cross-examination of State witnesses and which are intended to reflect the defence case, may, in exceptional circumstances, have the effect of curing the deficiency in the case made out by the State where the evidence adduced by the State is insufficient to establish a *prima facie* case—*Offerman* 1976 (2) PH H215 (E).

There exists no absolute rule that failure to cross-examine a witness precludes the party in question from disputing the truth of that evidence—*Chigwana* 1976 (4) SA 26 (RA). A decision not to cross-examine, however, may often be a perilous one and should be taken only after careful consideration—*Gobozi* 1975 (3) SA 88 (E).

After every witness for the prosecution has been cross-examined, the State may re-examine these witnesses on any matter arising from cross-examination—s 166(1).

After all the evidence for the prosecution has been disposed of, the prosecutor must close his case. A presiding officer does not have the authority to close the State's case if the prosecutor is not willing to do so. If the prosecutor, however, after an appliction by him for the postponement of the trial has been refused, refuses to lead evidence or to close the State's case, it is presumed that the State's case is closed, and the judicial officer should continue with the proceedings as if the prosecutor has indeed closed the State's case—*Magoda* 1984 (4) SA 462 (C).

3 DISCHARGE OF ACCUSED AT THE CLOSE OF THE STATE'S CASE

It is provided in s 174 that if, at the close of the case for the prosecution, the court considers that there is *no evidence* that the accused committed the offence charged or any other offences of which he may competently be convicted, it may return a verdict of not guilty.

The concept 'no evidence' is to be interpreted in this instance as 'no evidence on which a reasonable man could properly convict'—*Shein* 1925 AD 6 at 9. The evidence referred to here, includes only evidence which is led by the State and does not include admissions by the accused under s 115(2)*(a)*—*Beckett* 1987 (4) SA 8 (C).

The background to s 174 is outlined in *Cooper* 1976 (2) SA 875 (T) at 888 et *seq.* The origin of this procedure is to be found in the historical difference between the functions of a judge and a jury. The jury was the only adjudicator of the facts. In the past, no appeal against the finding of a jury on the facts existed. The judge had to exercise control over the jury and see to it that they carried out their duties properly. If the judge was of the opinion that there was insufficient evidence on which a reasonable man could convict the accused, he would withdraw the case from the jury after the State had closed its case. The accused would then be discharged. This was to ensure that the jury did not convict without sufficient evidence. The judge's role was to decide which material qualified as evidence that might be considered by the jury. The function of the jury was to decide what weight it would attach to certain evidence in arriving at a decision. The judge did not, therefore, weigh the evidence, but simply presumed that State witnesses were telling the truth. The situation remains the same: the credibility of witnesses is not relevant at this stage in the proceedings—*Dladla* (2) 1961 (3) SA 921 (D); *Cooper* (above) at 889. When there are conflicting inferences to be drawn from the evidence, the judge does not at this stage make use of the rules of logic laid down in *Blom's* case (1939 AD 188): these rules are applied at the end of the trial to ascertain whether the accused is guilty beyond a reasonable doubt—*Cooper* (above) at 890.

The *modus* of the test applied at the end of the State's case is subjunctive; reference is made to the evidence on which 'a reasonable man—might convict'—*Gascoyne v Paul & Hunter* 1917 TPD 170. The *modus* is subjunctive (evidence on which a reasonable man 'might'—not 'will'—convict), because the question of a conviction is at this stage purely hypothetical or speculative, since one is not dealing with facts which, at the end of the trial, are regarded as having been proved—*Cooper* (above) at 890.

There are two levels on which the discretion may be exercised: first, the presiding officer must decide if there is sufficient evidence (in the above sense) to place the accused on his defence; secondly, if the answer to the first question is negative, he must decide whether he nevertheless intends putting the accused on his defence or not—see *Kritzinger* 1952 (2) SA 401 (W). In this case the accused on whose behalf the application had been made in terms of s 174 (then s 221(3), Act 31 of 1917) was discharged, since it appeared unlikely that the Crown would be able to strengthen its case against him in the course of the trial. See also *Sikumba* 1955 (3) SA 125 (E); *Campbell* 1991 (1) SACR 435 (Nm).

The existence of the second level of the exercise of discretion has, however, been questioned. According to the Natal Court in *Mall* 1960 (2) SA 340 (N), it is doubtful whether the discretion of the court (at the conclusion of the State's case) amounts to more than this, namely, that it is for the court to decide whether the evidence before it is such that a reasonable man might convict upon it. If there is a discretion in the sense in which it was understood in *Kritzinger's* case, this discretion should be exercised judicially. It would not be a judicial exercise of this discretion to refuse to discharge an accused person if the case against him depended solely upon the evidence of an accomplice in circumstances in which corroboration was required, but was lacking. 'It would be wrong to put him on his defence in the expectation that he would or might provide the corroboration', according to Caney J in *Mall's* case. If, however, in the light of the facts of the case, there are reasonable grounds to believe that the State case might be supplemented during the defence case, this would be a ground for refusing discharge. See *Campbell* 1991 (1) SACR 435 (Nm) and—for a different approach—*Phuravhatha* 1992 (2) SACR 544 (V). For this reason it would seldom happen that only some of the accused would be so discharged, for it would often be possible that they would incriminate one another. A confession of one accused in which he implicates a co-accused is inadmissible as evidence against him, but can be taken into account in the application for discharge—*Mondlane* 1987 (4) SA 70 (T). (It would, however, be unfair to subject accused persons, against whom nothing has been proved, to a long and costly trial; in such a case a court would, in its *discretion*, probably discharge them at the conclusion of the State's case.) See *Shuping* 1983 (2) SA 119 (B).

In *Mathebula* 1997(1) SACR 10 (W) the question was raised whether after the Constitution had come into operation it could be said that an accused was given a fair trial if, at the close of the State's case wherein no evidence was tendered to implicate him in the alleged crime, the trial was then continued owing to the exercise of a discretion in the hope that some evidence implicating him might be forthcoming from the accused himself or his co-accused (who made a statement to the police implicating the accused). It was decided that such a discretionary power to continue the trial would fly in the face of the accused's constitutional rights to freedom, to be presumed innocent and to remain silent, not to testify and not to be a compellable witness (cf s 35(3)*(h)* and *(j)* of the Constitution). It would constitute a gross unfairness to take into consideration possible future evidence which may or may not be tendered against the accused either by himself or by other co-accused and for that reason decide not to set him free after the State had failed to prove anything against him. See, also, *Jama* 1998 (2) SACR 237 (N). However, *Mathebula's* case was not followed in *Makofane,* 1998 (1) SACR 603 (T), where it was decided that no provision of the interim Constitution (and also the 1996 Constitution) detracts from the basic principles. What the Constitution demands is that the accused be given a fair trial, and fairness is ultimately an issue which has to be decided by the presiding officer upon the facts of each case. See, also, *Hudson* 1998(2) SACR 359 (W) where it was emphasised that the discretion to discharge the accused should be exercised judicially and not arbitralily or capriciously.

Refusal of the court to discharge the accused upon the conclusion of the State's case is not in itself a ground for appeal or review if the accused is eventually found guilty, except where such refusal amounts to an irregularity (on the ground that the court exercised its discretion improperly), whereby the accused was prejudiced. See *Mkize* 1960 (1) SA 276 (N). In the last-mentioned case the court intimated that where there is one accused only, there is practically no possibility of prejudice. 'The reason is that the remedy is in the accused's own hands. If his application for discharge is refused, all he has to do is to close his case. If he chooses to effect self-immolation, or to commit forensic hara-kiri giving evidence incriminating himself, that is his own fault.' (281G–H) Where there is more than one accused, the possibility of prejudice is stronger, in that the other accused may give evidence whereby the accused who applies for discharge will be incriminated.

If an accused's application for discharge at the end of the State's case is successful, the director of public prosecutions (or public prosecutor) may appeal in terms of s 310. (This section is dealt with fully in Chapter 21.) The magistrate's finding as to the facts may not be questioned, the State may appeal only on a question of law. If the appeal is upheld the case is remitted to the court *a quo* and the trial is proceeded with. For an example, see *Rossouw* 1971 (3) SA 222 (T).

No rule of practice, that an accused must be informed that he may apply for his dismissal when the State has closed its case, has yet developed—*Ngcube* 1976 (1) SA 341 (N) at 344; the court may dismiss the accused *mero motu*—*Mkize* (above). If, in the case of an undefended accused, there is no evidence on record upon which a reasonable man could convict the accused, the court *should* indeed act *suo motu*— failure to do so would be irregular—*Zimmerie* 1989 (3) SA 484 (C); *Mashele* 1990 (1) SACR 678 (T). Cf Peta 1982 (4) SA 863 (E); *Amerika* 1990 (2) SACR 480 (C).

A court has a duty to inform an unrepresented accused in a trial where there are multiple charges of his right to apply for his discharge in respect of a charge for which there is no evidence upon which the accused can be convicted—*Manekwane* 1996(2) SACR 264 (EC). Where a judge or magistrate acts with assessors, only he may decide whether to grant a discharge; it being a question of law—*Magxwalisa* 1984 (2) SA 314 (N).

4   THE DEFENCE CASE

4.1   Accused's rights to be explained

If the accused is not discharged at the close of the State's case, the procedure laid down in s 151(1) should be followed. In terms of this subsection the judge or magistrate must ask the accused (or his representative) if he intends leading evidence for the defence. In *Vezi* 1963 (1) SA 9 (N) at 11, this rule was extended: not only must an undefended accused be informed that he is entitled to call witnesses or to give evidence himself, but also that he may remain silent. See also *Mdodana* 1978 (4) SA 46 (E) at 48. Because an accused is a procedural subject in South African law and not an object of inquiry, it is essential for him to be informed of his rights so that he may make an informed and meaningful choice at this most important stage of the proceedings—Cf Van Rooyen May 1976 *De Rebus* 207. The mere setting out of the various procedural alternatives (mentioned in s 151) without placing it in the context of that particular case, is no explanation of the accused's rights: the purpose of the explanation, especially in the case of an unsophisticated and undefended accused, is in fact to counteract the accused's relative lack of skills in litigation—*Zulu* 1990 (1) SA 655 (T). (In this case the accused was invited to the witness-stand although there was not a shred of evidence against her at the closing of the State's case.) If the accused was not adequately informed of his rights (eg through an interpreter if necessary) and this is not properly recorded, the conviction may be set aside at higher instance. See *Sibia* 1947 (2) SA 50 (A). The fact that the accused's rights have been explained should be properly recorded—*Motaung* 1980 (4) SA 131 (T). It is the task of the presiding judicial officer to explain the rights to an unrepresented accused and such duty cannot in the ordinary course be delegated to an interpreter—*Malatji 1998(2) SACR 622 (W)*.

Section 35(3)*(h)* of the Constitution provides that every accused person has a right to a fair trial, which includes the right to remain silent and not to testify during the proceedings. In terms of s 35(3)*(i)* and *(j)* every accused has the right to adduce and challenge evidence and not to be compelled to give self-incriminating evidence. 'Fairness' is an issue which has to be decided upon the facts of each case, and the trial judge or magistrate are the persons best placed to take that decision—*Key v Attorney-General, Cape Provincial Division* 1996(4) SA 187 (CC). The concept of a 'fair trial' embraces fairness, not only to the accused but also to society as a whole, which usually has a real interest in the outcome of a case—*Sonday* 1995(1) SA 497 (C). It involves many things. To mention but a few, it involves the right to be tried within a reasonable time, the right to legal representation, the right to be fully informed of the charge laid, the right to cross-examine witnesses, the right to call witnesses, and the right to have evidence excluded in certain circumstances—*Strowitzki* 1995(2) SA 525 (NmHC). Apart from the right to legal representation at State expence, the common-law principles have not been broadened or accentuated by the codification of the right to a fair trial in the Constitution. It is really a restatement of the principles applied by the Courts in the past—*Klein* 1995(3) SA 848 (W). An unrepresented accused must, therefore, be assisted by the Court. When he experiences difficulty during cross-examination, the court must help the accused in clarifying the issues, formulating the questions, and putting his or her defence properly to the witnesses. Similarly, where an undefended accused through incompetence or ignorance fails to cross-examine a witness on a material issue, the presiding officer should question the witness in order to reduce the risk of a failure of justice—*Simxadi* 1997(1) SACR 169 (C). A serious disregard of the bounds of fair cross-examination of an unrepresented accused conflicts with the ideas underlining the concepts of justice which are the basis of all civilised systems of criminal justice—*Hendricks* 1997(1) SACR 174 (C). The Court must also assist an undefended accused to question a witness called by the accused who is able to shed light on an important point in dispute—*Moilwa* 1997(1) SACR 188 (NC).

If the accused answers in the affirmative (ie that he intends to testify in his own defence) he shall, except where the court on good cause shown allows otherwise, be called as a witness before any other witness for the defence—*Nene* (1) 1979 (2) SA 520 (D). If the accused decides, after other evidence on behalf of the defence has been led, to testify himself, the court may draw such inference from the accused's conduct as may be reasonable in the circumstances—s 151(1)*(b)*.

The court must also inform the accused that he does not necessarily have to give evidence from the witness-box, but may do so from the dock—*Mhalati* 1976 (2) SA 426 (Tk); see *Mpofu* 1970 (2) SA 162 (RA) and *Tsane* 1978 (4) SA 161 (O). Section 151(1)*(a)* provides that if the accused should wish to lead evidence, he (or his representative) may address the court on the evidence to be led, but may not comment on the evidence.

In practice, the defence very rarely avails itself of the right to open by addressing the court. This is because, in most cases, the full defence version will have been put to the State witnesses in cross-examination and will be known to the court.

4.2 Witnesses for the defence

The accused or his legal representative must then call and examine the witnesses for the defence. It is undesirable that a witness be present in court before he gives evidence, as this might affect the weight of his evidence—*Manaka* 1978 (1) SA 287 (T).

In terms of s 35(3)*(h)*, *(i)* and*(j)* of the Constitution every accused person has a right to a fair trial which includes the rights to remain silent, not to testify during the proceedings, to adduce and challenge evidence and not to be compelled to give self-incriminating evidence.

Once a client has placed his case in the hands of counsel, the latter has complete control. If counsel persuades the accused not to give evidence, the accused may not subsequently on appeal challenge the correctness of the verdict on this ground—*Matonsi* 1958 (2) SA 450 (A). If the accused insists on going into the witness-box in spite of his advocate's advice to the contrary, the advocate should withdraw from the case. It will constitute an irregularity, however, if the accused has not been consulted as to whether he wants to give evidence or not—*Majola* 1982 (1) SA 125 (A).

Where an accused is not intellectually developed and is unrepresented, the court must be exceptionally careful in refusing a request to call a witness, and before it decides on such a refusal it should make certain that such a witness cannot possibly adduce relevant evidence. If the court is not careful in fulfilling this obligation, a miscarriage of justice can occur—*Tembani* 1970 (4) SA 395 (E). A court should not refuse an undefended accused's request to call witnesses even if the court believes the accused is adopting delaying tactics or if there is uncertainty about the whereabouts of the witnesses—*M* 1990 (2) SACR 131 (B) and cf Selemana 1975 (4) SA 908 (T).

Where there is no proof that certain witnesses are available, the court may not draw an adverse inference from the failure of the accused to call them—*Phiri* 1958 (3) SA 161 (A).

The prosecution will be entitled to cross-examine each witness called by the accused and also the accused if he elects to give evidence. Cross-examination of the accused by the State should be conducted with courtesy and without prejudice to the accused. It should not be conducted in an intimidating, offensive or mocking manner. Questions should be asked in such a way as to afford the accused full opportunity to answer them. Improper cross-examination by the prosecutor may lead to the accused's conviction being set aside on appeal or review. See *Nkibane* 1989 (2) SA 421 (NC). See *Gidi* 1984 (4) SA 537 (C) for guidelines to proper cross-examination. Although there may be occasions when a prosecutor may safely decide not to cross-examine an accused person or a defence witness, such a decision is normally a perilous one, since courts will be loath to reject a defence version which went untested and unchallenged by cross-examination—*Gobozi* 1975 (2) PH H99 (E). A judicial officer is entitled to question witnesses for the defence in order to clarify unclear aspects of the case, but he may not cross-examine them—*Van Niekerk* 1981 (3) SA 787 (T). Lengthy questioning of an accused by a judicial officer is *per se* a relatively neutral factor. A more important factor is the manner of questioning. It would constitute an irregularity when questions put to an accused are so belligerent or intimidating, or are so repetitive or confusing, as to amount to judicial harassment—*Gerbers* 1997 (2) SACR 601 (SCA). See also *Matthys* 1999 (1) SACR 117 (C) where it was stressed that a presiding judicial officer should not descend into the arena and thus committing a serious irregularity clearly prejudicing the accused.

4.3 The accused's right to silence

The accused cannot be compelled to give evidence on his own behalf. In England he was until recently not even entitled to give such evidence. The position now is that an adverse inference may in appropriate circumstances be drawn against the accused if he fails to give evidence on his own behalf—*Dube* 1915 AD 557. This inference should not, however, be pressed too far—*K* 1956 (3) SA 353 (A) at 358. Any finding that an accused's silence constitutes evidence of guilt will be directly in conflict with s 35(3)*(h)* of the Constitution. No adverse inference can be made against an accused merely by virtue of his exercise of his right to remain silent. The exercise of this right has, however, certain consequences, for instance that it leaves the *prima facie* evidence of the State uncontested. If it can be said, taking everything into consideration, including the lack of gainsaying evidence against a *prima facie* case, that the State has proved its case beyond a reasonable doubt, the accused has to be found guilty—*Scholtz* 1996(2) SACR 40 (NC); *Brown* 1996(2) SACR 49 (NC). The accused must be informed about this—*Khomunala* 1998 (1) SACR 362 (VHC). The right to silence has been partly affected by the introduction in 1977 of the 'plea-explanation' procedure at arraignment, in terms of s 115. The rights to be presumed innocent, to remain silent during plea proceedings or trial and not to testify during trial are enshrined in the right to a fair trial—see s 35(3)*(h)* of the Constitution. An accused, furthermore, has the right not to be a compellable witness against himself or herself (s 35(3)*(j)* of the Constitution) and has to be informed of his or right to remain silent when arrested (s 35(1)*(a)*).

4.4 Unsworn statement by the accused

Until 1977 an accused was entitled to make an unsworn statement from the dock, inlieu of giving evidence under oath. This had the advantage of not being subject to cross-examination but also had the disadvantage that it did not carry the same weight as sworn testimony. This right has now been abolished—an accused must either testify under oath or not at all. Cf, however, the position to the contrary at a preparatory examination in Chapter 11 (above).

4.5 Formal admission by the accused

An accused or his counsel may admit any fact placed in issue. This absolves the State of the duty of proving such fact—s 220. Cf *Maweke* 1971 (2) SA 327 (A).

4.6 Re-examination of witnesses

After every witness has been cross-examined by the other party, the party who called the witness may re-examine the witness, ie on any matter raised during the cross-examination of that witness—s 166(1).

5 REBUTTING EVIDENCE BY THE STATE

If the defence, during the course of its case, introduces new matter which the prosecution could not reasonably have been expected to foresee, the State may be permitted, after the close of the defence case, to present rebutting evidence in respect of such matter—*Lipschitz* 1921 AD 282; *Christie* 1982 (1) SA 464 (A) at 476. In *Sinkankanka* 1963 (2) SA 531 (A) the trial judge, with the consent of the defence, allowed the State to lead evidence during presentation of the defence case. The Supreme Court of Appeal held that there was no prejudice to the defence in the circumstances of the case.

Where, however, the defence has by the nature of its cross-examination or otherwise given an indication of the matter which it proposed to raise in the course of its defence, the court will, as a rule, not grant permission to the State to lead rebutting evidence after the close of the defence case—*Lukas* 1923 CPD 508. If the prosecution reasonably requires a postponement in order to obtain evidence dealing with such matter (which has come to its knowledge in the course of the State's case) or to cause necessary investigations to be made, the prosecutor should not close his case, but should apply for such postponement before closing his case. If the application is considered by the court to be reasonable, it will be granted and the necessity for leading rebutting evidence after the defence case has been closed can in this way be obviated.

Unless the most exceptional circumstances arise, the State will not be allowed to introduce still further fresh matter in the course of its rebuttal, since the introduction thereof would unduly interfere with the finality of criminal proceedings—*Bersin* 1912 CPD 969.

6 CALLING OR RECALLING WITNESSES BY COURT, AND QUESTIONING BY COURT

As already pointed out, a duty is cast on the court by s 167 of the Act to subpoena and examine or recall and re-examine any person if his evidence appears to the court to be essential to the just decision of the case. The above-mentioned duty arises only when the court is of the opinion that the evidence in question is essential. The effect of this is that the court is in reality given a discretion as to whether it will call such a witness. Initially the court held the view that this section was intended solely to supplement some formal defect in the State's (or in the defence's) case. This was soon held not to be the position—*Hepworth* 1928 AD 265, and *Omar* 1935 AD 230. It has been said that a criminal trial is not a game. In other words, an accused who is in reality guilty should not be discharged because of some defect in the State's case, nor should an innocent man be convicted because of some omission, mistake or technicality. See also *Mbata* 1956 (4) SA 735 (N) and *Mgotywa* 1958 (1) SA 99 (E). However, this power should be sparingly used, since it is generally not the function of the court to build up a case which a lax prosecutor has neglected to establish. Even such a prosecutor may now (with the consent of the director of public prosecutions) save a situation which he may almost have bungled by his initial negligence, ie by converting the trial in a magistrate's court into a preparatory examination in order to give himself the opportunity to supplement an omission or to remedy a mistake made in the course of a summary trial (see *Bham v Lutge* 1949 (3) SA 392 (T) and the discussion on preparatory examinations and Chapter 11 above).

In *D* 1951 (4) SA 450 (A) a member of the jury suggested the desirability of calling a witness who had been called at the preparatory examination but not by either party at the trial. The judge refused to act upon this suggestion, and after the accused had been convicted, it was argued on appeal that the presiding judge had been obliged in terms of s 247 (now 167) to call the witness in question. The court held that it was for the presiding judge (alone) to decide whether he would act upon the suggestion of the jury and that the judge was under no obligation in the circumstances to call the witness, and finally that no good ground existed for holding that the judge had not exercised his discretion properly. From this judgment one may infer that if the judge exercises his discretion improperly, this would constitute an irregularity which, in a particular instance, may result in the conviction being set aside. For example, a magistrate who, during the course of the trial, orders that the case should be investigated afresh to obtain evidence, exceeds his powers under s 167—*Klumalo* 1972 (4) SA 500 (O).

If the court does call a witness in terms of s 167, the party adversely affected by his evidence should be given an opportunity of rebuttal and any party desiring to cross-examine such a witness should normally be allowed to do so—*Chili* 1917 TPD 61; *Soni* 1973 (1) PH HS20 (N).

The interpretation of s 167 by our courts leaves no doubt that the accusatorial system is firmly embedded in South African criminal procedure. The accusatorial system, which was taken over from English law, implies that the presiding officer plays a relatively passive role during the trial. In the inquisitorial system practised in Europe, the judge is far more active in questioning witnesses, including the accused. In our system of criminal procedure, a presiding officer is entitled to put questions during the trial to clarify an issue, but in general it is undesirable that he should participate extensively in the questioning of a witness and, so to speak, descend into the arena—*Roopsingh* 1956 (4) SA 509 (A); *Adriantos* 1965 (3) SA 436 (A). Where an accused is unrepresented, however, a judicial officer may quite properly take some part in the examination of witnesses—*Sigwahla* 1967 (4) SA 566 (A) 568. Lengthy questioning of defence witnesses *per se* does not amount to an irregularity. It is not improper to ask numerous questions clarifying aspects of evidence or eliminating uncertainty, which do not create the impression of bias—*Mohase* 1998 (1) SACR 185 (O). Questioning of the accused by the court, leading to self-incrimination or aggravation of punishment, is irregular unless the accused chose to testify—*Grotes*; *Jawuka* 1970 (1) SA 368 (C); *Mngadi* 1973 (4) SA 540 (N); *Eshumael* 1973 (2) PH H83 (RA). However, for the purposes of sentence the presiding officer may endeavour to elicit information favourable to the accused—*Sithole* 1974 (2) SA 572 (N).

The court may, however, only recall and re-examine an accused that has testified at the proceedings—s 167. Where neither the State nor the defence has adduced any evidence and the accused, in the absence of any evidence, should be acquitted and discharged, it is irregular for the presiding officer to call a witness in terms of either s 167 or s 186—*Kwinika* 1989 (1) SA 896 (W).

7 RECORDING OF EVIDENCE

The presiding officer has the duty to ensure that the evidence and all proceedings are faithfully recorded, because the record is the only source from which can be determined whether the proceedings were in accordance with justice—*K* 1974 (3) SA 857 (C). Cf *Komani* 1974 (2) PH H85 (C). It frequently happens that a witness demonstrates an incident in court, eg how the accused had stabbed at the deceased. It is the duty of the presiding officer and of counsel to see that the demonstration is described in detail in the record—*Nkombani* 1963 (4) SA 877 (A). In all cases where the age of the accused is of material importance to the proper adjudication of a case, presiding officers should properly record the same so that the method of age determination appears adequately from the record—*Kumalo* 1991 (2) SACR 694 (W). Where a magistrate has made a mistake in the recording of the evidence he cannot correct the mistake after sentence as he is then *functus officio*. The High Court alone can correct the mistake in a substantive application on notice of motion by either the prosecutor or the accused, and this applies also to obvious mistakes— *Booi* 1972 (4) SA 68 (NC); *Brandt* 1972 (4) SA 70 (NC).

As to the possible procedures when the record of the proceedings is lost, see *Mankaji* 1974 (4) SA 113 (T); *Catsoulis* 1974 (4) SA 371 (T); *Whitney* 1975 (3) SA 453 (N); *Seleke* 1978 (1) SA 993 (T); *Stevens* 1981 (1) SA 864 (C); *Malope* 1991 (1) SACR 458 (B); *Fredericks* 1992 (1) SACR 561 (C).

8 ADDRESS BY PROSECUTOR AND DEFENCE

After all the evidence has been adduced, the prosecutor may address the court, after which the accused or their/his counsel may address the court—s 175.

This section does not make it obligatory for the court to enquire of the accused or his legal representative whether he wishes to address the court, but this notwithstanding, such an enquiry should be made and the response thereto recorded—*Parmanand* 1954 (3) SA 833 (A); *Brand* 1975 (2) PH H138 (T).

If the accused is aware of his rights in this respect, but owing to his own fault fails to exercise them, failure on the part of the judicial officer to invite him to address the court will not be an irregularity—*Cooper* 1926 AD 54; *Kamffer* 1965 (3) SA 96 (T).

However, if the accused is deprived of the opportunity to address the court by the conduct of the judicial officer, it will be a fatal irregularity, unless it is clear that he has not been prejudiced—*Parmanand* (above) and *Breakfast* 1970 (2) SA 611 (E)— and the consequences will be the same if he or his representative is not allowed to address the court on a material issue—*Cooke* 1959 (3) SA 449 (T).

As far as a legal representative is concerned, the general rule is that if he wishes to address the court, he must intimate it without delay if he is not invited to do so by the court—*Blokland* 1946 AD 940; *Bresler* 1967 (2) SA 451 (A). On the other hand, if a judicial officer is deprived of the advantage of hearing the defence attorney's argument because he did not invite him to address the court, with the result that the judicial officer paid insufficient attention to material matters in the case, it may lead to a reversal upon appeal—*Sitlu* 1971 (2) SA 238 (N); *Mutambanengwe* 1976 (2) SA 434 (RA).

There seems to be a tendency to regard the failure of a court to afford an accused an opportunity to address the court as a gross and fatal irregularity—*Mabote* 1983 (1) SA 745 (O). Where, however, an accused refuses to address the court, he/she loses or abandons such right—*Vermaas* 1997 (2) SACR 454 (T).

If the accused or his legal representative raises a matter of law, the prosecutor may reply, and he may also, with the leave of the court, reply on any matter of fact raised by the accused in his address—s 175(2).

CHAPTER 18

The verdict

		Page
1	INTRODUCTION	247
2	THE VERDICT	247
	2.1 Introduction	247
	2.2 Competent verdicts (general rules)	247
	2.3 Competent verdicts (specific provisions)	248
	2.3.1 Verdict of guilty of attempt or being an accessory after the fact	248
	2.3.2 Competent verdicts on a charge of murder and attempted murder	249
	2.3.3 Competent verdicts on a charge of rape or attempted rape	249
	2.3.4 Competent verdicts on a charge of robbery	249
	2.3.5 Miscellaneous remarks	250
3	AMENDMENT OF VERDICT	250

1 INTRODUCTION

Although a criminal trial may, in a sense, be considered to have ended only after the accused has been finally sentenced, it is convenient to divide the proceedings in the trial court into two distinct compartments and to treat as the trial only that portion of the proceedings during which the issues between the prosecution and the accused are presented to the court for its consideration. After the completion of that portion of the proceedings the issues have been finally formulated and supported by the evidence at the disposal of both parties and the court now has to deliver its verdict.

2 THE VERDICT

2.1 Introduction

The formal and procedural aspects of the verdict have already been discussed, ie that it should be given in open court.

2.2 Competent verdicts (general rules)

A very sensible provision is included in the Criminal Procedure Act in connection with the verdict in order to prevent prosecutions from ending in futility. Section 270 provides as follows:

'If the evidence on a charge for any offence not referred to in the preceding sections of this Chapter does not prove the commission of the offence so charged but proves the commission of an offence which by reason of the essential elements of that offence is included in the offence so charged, the accused may be found guilty of the offence so proved.' (Our emphasis.)

All the essential elements of the lesser offence of which it is sought to convict the accused, must, however, be included in the offence actually charged. In addition, all the elements of the lesser offence must be proved—an accused may not be convicted of a lesser offence, as a sort of consolation prize to the State, where he has not been shown to have committed it. Cf also *Mei* 1982 (1) SA 299 (O); *Mbatha* 1982 (2) SA 145 (N).

The phrase 'any offence not referred to in the preceding sections of this chapter' has the effect that where the offence charged is specifically dealt with in the Act and the competent verdicts listed in the Act, the provisions of s 270 are excluded—*M* 1979 (2) SA 167 (T). To take an example, if an accused is charged with culpable homicide arising from the negligent driving of a motor vehicle and the evidence led proves only negligent driving, the accused may not be convicted, because the competent verdicts on a charge of culpable homicide are specially listed in s 259 and negligent driving is not one of them. (In such a case, prosecutors would be well advised to charge reckless/negligent driving in the alternative.) Before the introduction of the Criminal Procedure Act 51 of 1977 such a verdict would have been competent, due to the different wording of the phrase—*Ndwandwe* 1976 (1) SA 323 (N); *Hiemstra* 644–5.

On the other hand, it is clear that an accused charged with treason may be convicted of sedition in terms of s 270 (if this is proved) as the competent verdicts on a charge of treason are not specifically dealt with in the Act. See also *Viljoen* 1923 AD 90.

Although it is not necessary that a competent verdict should formally be mentioned in the indictment, it is desirable, in order to avoid prejudice to an accused, that he should be informed of the competent verdicts which can be brought in against him—*Velela* 1979 (4) SA 581 (C). An undefended accused should in some manner be forewarned of the pitfalls of a competent verdict—*Jasat* 1997(1) SACR 489 (SCA). The right to be informed with sufficient detail of the charge in terms of s 35(3)*(a)* of the Constitution includes the right to be informed of competent verdicts on a charge. A failure to inform an accused person of a competent verdict amounts to a violation of s 35(3)*(a)* and is therefore a fatal irregularity which vitiates the proceedings where the accused was convicted of an offence which constitutes the competent verdict—*Chauke* 1998 (1) SACR 354 (VHC).

2.3 Competent verdicts (specific provisions)

The Criminal Procedure Act contains a whole series of provisions in which competent verdicts on a particular charge are set out expressly. We shall discuss some of these provisions by way of illustration only.

2.3.1 *Verdict of guilty of attempt or being an accessory after the fact*

Any person charged with an offence may be found guilty of an attempt to commit that offence, or of an attempt to commit any other offence of which he may be convicted on the charge, if such be the facts proved—s 256. Thus where A is charged with rape, he may be convicted of attempted indecent assault.

A person may not, after having been tried on a charge of having committed any offence, thereafter be tried on a charge of having attempted to commit such offence, since he was at the first trial already in jeopardy of being convicted of such attempt.

In order to meet the position which arose as a result of *Mlooi* 1925 AD 131 (in which case it was held that an accessory after the fact is not a *particeps criminis* in the true sense), it was specially enacted that a verdict of being an accessory after the fact is a competent verdict on a charge of having committed such offence, provided that the facts proved are such as to justify such a conviction. In the absence of any punishment specifically provided for by law, the court is authorised to impose any punishment which is, however, in no case to be more severe than that to which the principal offender would under any law be subject—s 257. See also *Gani* 1957 (2) SA 212 (A).

The legislature did not specially stipulate in this context that having been an accomplice *before* the commission of the offence is a competent verdict on a charge of having committed such offence. This was not necessary, since it is a clear principle of our law that an accessory before the fact can be charged and punished as a principal—*Peerkhan and Lalloo* 1906 TS 798, and Parry 1924 AD 401.

2.3.2 *Competent verdicts on a charge of murder and attempted murder*

Culpable homicide;
assault with intent to do grievous bodily harm;
common assault;
robbery;
public violence;
pointing a fire-arm, air-gun or air-pistol;
exposing an infant; and
disposing of the body of a child with intent to conceal the fact of its birth—s 258.

2.3.3 *Competent verdicts on a charge of rape or attempted rape*

Assault with intent to do grievous bodily harm;
indecent assault;
common assault;
incest;
the statutory offence of unlawful carnal intercourse, or of committing any immoral or indecent act, or the soliciting or enticing of an immoral or indecent act with a girl under a specified age; and
the statutory offence of unlawful carnal intercourse, or of committing any immoral or indecent act, or the soliciting or enticing of an immoral or indecent act with a female idiot or imbecile—s 261(1).

2.3.4 *Competent verdicts on a charge of robbery*

Assault with intent to do grievous bodily harm;
common assault;
pointing a fire-arm, air-gun or air-pistol in contravention of any law;
theft;

receiving stolen property knowing it to have been stolen;

possession of goods without being able to give a satisfactory account of such possession (in terms of s 36, Act 62 of 1955); and

acquiring or receiving stolen property without having reasonable cause to believe that the person disposing of the property is the owner or duly authorised by the owner (in terms of s 37, Act 62 of 1955)—s 260.

In *Montsoa* 1952 (3) SA 511 (T) an example is given of circumstances in which a person charged with a major offence cannot be found guilty of a lesser offence comprised in the major offence. The court held that the predecessor of this section did not empower the court, when a man is charged with robbery, to find him guilty of a theft committed at a different time and at a different place, even though the two offences are not far separated in either time or place. In this case the theft of which the magistrate had convicted the accused occurred some short time *before* the alleged robbery and was therefore unconnected with the robbery. Cf also *Mabaso* 1980 (2) SA 790 (O). On a charge of robbery an accused can be convicted of assault with intent to do grievous bodily harm *and* theft, or common assault and theft—s 260.

2.3.5 *Miscellaneous remarks*

In each of the above-mentioned cases the evidence necessary to constitute the lesser offence must be before the court, since the provisions in question are not intended to empower the courts to convict the accused without the necessary proof of his guilt on the lesser offence.

In cases where a possibility exists of the accused being found guilty of a similar offence to the one charged, the prosecutor should, if a verdict of guilty of the second offence is not a competent verdict on a charge of having committed the first offence, specifically include the second offence as an alternative count in the indictment or charge. An accused should, therefore, be charged with driving a vehicle while under the influence of intoxicating liquor ('drunken driving') and alternatively driving a vehicle while the concentration of alcohol in his blood is not less than 0,08 g per 100 ml of blood—s 122 of the Road Traffic Act 29 of 1989.

It should be pointed out, finally, that where an accused person is found guilty of any one of the above-mentioned offences on which a verdict on a charge of a major offence is competent, it is unnecessary for the prosecutor to apply for a corresponding amendment of the charge, since the charge is regarded as comprising all the subsidiary charges to support the relevant competent verdicts.

3 AMENDMENT OF VERDICT

When by mistake a wrong judgment or sentence is delivered or passed, the court may, before or immediately after it is recorded, amend the judgment or sentence— ss 176 and 298. The interpretation of this section by the courts is that it is applicable only when the mistake made by the court is one which is inherent in the judgment or sentence, eg where the court has no jurisdiction or if the judgment is unrelated to the merits of the case. Where incorrect facts have been placed before a court upon which the court has imposed a proper sentence, the court may not correct such sentence as being a wrong sentence in terms of s 289 when the truth is later discovered—*Swartz* 1991 (2) SACR 502 (NC); *Malesa* 1990 (1) SACR 260 (T).

The words 'immediately after' are not synonymous with 'instantaneously', but indicate a reasonable period. What a reasonable time is will depend on the circumstances. The amendment of a judgment on the day after it was delivered is, however, not an amendment within the ambit of this subsection—*Mitondo* 1939 EDL 110. See also *Moabi* 1979 (2) SA 648 (B).

After a reasonable time has elapsed the judge or magistrate is *functus officio*, and no longer has the power to amend the mistake. Once the magistrate has passed a sentence that he was empowered to pass, he is *functus officio* and s 298 is in no way applicable—*Sikeliwe* 1962 (1) SA 408 (E). He ought to try to prevent the failure of justice by reporting the position to the High Court and by requesting review by virtue of s 304(4). Where the case is subject to automatic review he ought to draw the attention of the High Court to his error. The magistrate is not authorised *mero motu* to set aside a wrong conviction—*Malesa* 1990 (1) SACR 260 (T). However, a judicial officer is permitted to effect linguistic or other minor corrections to his pronounced judgment without changing the substance thereof. This common law approach should be read in conjunction with s 176—*Wells* 1990 (1) SA 816 (A).

PHASE THREE: THE SENTENCE

CHAPTER 19

The sentence

		Page
1	INTRODUCTION	258
2	CONCEPTS	259
	2.1 Sentence	259
	2.2 Punishment	259
	2.3 Sentencing	259
	2.4 Offender/criminal/accused	259
	2.5 Offence/crime	259
3	THE SENTENCE DISCRETION	259
4	GENERAL PRINCIPLES WITH REGARD TO SENTENCING	260
5	PENAL PROVISIONS	260
	5.1 General	260
	5.2 The Adjustment of Fines Act 101 of 1991	260
	5.3 Minimum sentences	261
6	THE PRE-SENTENCE INVESTIGATION	261
	6.1 General	261
	6.2 Previous convictions	262
	6.3 The accused on sentence	262
	6.4 The duty to supply information	262
7	ABSENCE OF JUDICIAL OFFICER	263
8	MITIGATING AND AGGRAVATING FACTORS	263
	8.1 Youth as a mitigating factor	263
	8.2 Previous convictions as an aggravating factor	264
9	CONSTITUTIONAL MATTERS	264
	9.1 The death penalty	264
	9.1.1 General remarks	264
	9.1.2 The relevant constitutional provisions	264
	9.1.3 The crucial question	264
	9.1.4 The main arguments for and against the death penalty	265

9.1.5   Arbitrariness in the imposition of the death penalty . . .   265
9.1.6   The death penalty in foreign law   265
9.1.7   Public opinion   266
9.1.8   Cruel, inhuman and degrading punishment   266
9.1.9   The limitation clause   266
9.1.10 Deterrence   266
9.1.11 Prevention   267
9.1.12 Retribution   267
9.1.13 Balancing the objects of punishment with the rights of the
        accused   267
9.1.14 Conclusion   267
9.2   Corporal punishment   268

10 THE FORMS OF PUNISHMENT WHICH MAY BE IMPOSED . .   268
10.1   Introduction   268
10.2   Imprisonment   268
10.2.1 General   268
10.2.2 The role of mitigating factors   269
       10.2.2.1 Youthfulness   269
       10.2.2.2 No criminal record   269
10.2.3 The value of imprisonment   269
10.2.4 The various forms of imprisonment   269
       10.2.4.1 Ordinary imprisonment for a term determined
                 by the court   270
       10.2.4.2 Imprisonment for life   271
       10.2.4.3 Declaration as a dangerous criminal   271
       10.2.4.4 Declaration as an habitual criminal   272
       10.2.4.5 Periodical imprisonment   272
       10.2.4.6 Section 276(1)*(i)*-imprisonment   273
10.2.5 Sentences for more than one crime   273
10.2.6 Further provisions on imprisonment   274
10.2.7 Reduction of sentence   274
10.3   Fine   275
10.3.1 General   275
10.3.2 When are fines imposed   275
10.3.3 The amount of the fine   275
10.3.4 Determining the means of the offender   276
10.3.5 Recovering the fine   276
       10.3.5.1 Imprisonment in default of payment   276
       10.3.5.2 Deferment of payment of the fine   277

		10.3.5.3	Further relief after the start of the prison term	277
		10.3.5.4	Other methods of recovery	277
	10.3.6	To whom does the fine go?	278
10.4	Correctional supervision	278
	10.4.1	General	278
	10.4.2	The nature of correctional supervision	278
	10.4.3	The various forms of correctional supervision	279
	10.4.4	The penal value of correctional supervision	279
	10.4.5	Factors influencing the imposition of correctional supervision	280
	10.4.6	The execution of correctional supervision	280
10.5	Committal to a treatment centre	281
10.6	Juvenile offenders	281
10.7	Caution and discharge	281
11	SUSPENDED AND POSTPONED SENTENCES	282
11.1	General	282
11.2	Exclusionary provisions	282
11.3	Postponement of passing of sentence	282
11.4	Suspension of sentence	282
11.5	The conditions	283
11.6	Breaching the conditions	284
12	COMPENSATION AND RESTITUTION	284
12.1	Compensation	284
12.2	Restitution	285

The Constitution and this chapter:

Section 9—Equality

(1) Everyone is equal before the law and has the right to equal protection and benefit of the law.

(2) Equality includes the full and equal enjoyment of all rights and freedoms . . .

(3) The state may not unfairly discriminate directly or indirectly against anyone on one or more grounds, including race, gender, sex, pregnancy, marital status, ethnic or social origin, colour, sexual orientation, age, disability, religion, conscience, belief, culture, language and birth.

. . .

(5) Discrimination on one or more of the grounds listed in subsection (3) is unfair unless it is established that the discrimination is fair.

See 3, below.

Section 10—Human dignity

Everyone has inherent dignity and the right to have their dignity respected and protected.

See 9.1, below.

Section 11—Life

Everyone has the right to life.

See 9.1, below.

Section 12—Freedom and security of the person

(1) Everyone has the right to freedom and security of the person, which includes the right—

   (a) not be deprived of freedom arbitrarily or without just cause;

   . . .

   (d) not to be tortured in any way;

   (e) not to be treated or punished in a cruel, inhuman or degrading way.

See 5.3 and 9.1, below.

Section 35—Detained, arrested and accused persons

(2) Everyone who is detained, including every sentenced prisoner, has the right—

   (e) to conditions of detention that are consistent with human dignity, including at least exercise and the provision, at state expense, of adequate accommodation, nutrition, reading material and medical treatment; . . .

(3) Every accused person has a right to a fair trial, which includes the right—

   . . .

   (n) to the least severe of the prescribed punishments if the prescribed punishment for the offence has been changed between the time that the offence was committed and the time of sentencing; . . .

Compare 5, below.

Section 36—Limitation

(1) The rights in the Bill of Rights may be limited only in terms of law of general application to the extent that the limitation is reasonable and justifiable in an open and democratic society based on human dignity, equality and freedom, taking into account all relevant factors, including—

   (a) the nature of the right;

   (b) the importance of the purpose of the limitation;

   (c) the nature and extent of the limitation;

   (d) the relation between the limitation and its purpose; and

   (e) least restrictive means to achieve the purpose.

(2) Except as provided in subsection (1) or in any other provision of the Constitution, no law may limit any right entrenched in the Bill of Rights.

See 9.1 and 9.2, below.

1 INTRODUCTION

Determining a suitable sentence is one of the most difficult tasks a judicial officer has to face. What makes it particularly difficult is the fact that it involves so many (often contradictory) factors. The judicial officer imposing sentence has to make a value judgment and determine how much weight every fact and factor should be afforded, and these considerations must then be converted into a sentence of some kind and some extent. In this process the personality of the sentencing official plays an important role.

2 CONCEPTS

A few preliminary remarks on some of the concepts that will be used in this chapter are apposite.

2.1 Sentence

The sentence is any measure applied by a court to the person convicted of a crime and which finalises the case, except where specific provision is made for reconsideration of that measure. Conditions of suspended sentences are not included here. A caution, however, does amount to a sentence.

2.2 Punishment

Punishment is used here in the usual sense of the word, namely as something which is unpleasant to experience, except that it is limited to measures imposed by a court after conviction. Some sentences do not constitute punishment, such as most suspended sentences and a caution. Some forms of punishment are not sentences, for example where community service is imposed as condition for the suspension of sentence. Most forms of punishment will nevertheless be sentences.

2.3 Sentencing

Sentencing is the imposition of a sentence by the court, on a particular offender.

2.4 Offender/criminal/accused

These terms are used to describe the person who is accused or convicted of having committed the crime. Although a theoretical distinction may be drawn between these concepts, no such a distinction will be drawn for the purposes of this chapter and the terms will therefore be used interchangeably.

2.5 Offence/crime

These terms are used to describe the action which caused the offender to be tried and sentenced in court. For present purposes the concepts are used as synonymous.

3 THE SENTENCE DISCRETION

A court has wide ranging powers to impose sentences. In deciding how to exercise this power in a specific case, the court exercises a *discretion*, which involves making a choice from various possibilities. In the case of sentencing these 'possibilities' consist of the various types of sentences, and normally also the measure (or quantity) of the type of sentence decided upon.

This discretion may not be exercised arbitrarily; a court is expected to act within the limits prescribed by the legislature and in accordance with the guidelines laid down by higher courts. The basic requirement set by the Supreme Court of Appeal is that the discretion must be exercised reasonably and judicially—cf *Pieters* 1987 (3) SA 717 (A).

According to Du Toit *Straf in Suid-Afrika* (1981) 127, the existence of the sentencing discretion is a pillar of our law of sentencing which should be guarded jealously by everybody involved. The main advantage of a wide discretion is that the courts can adapt their sentences to provide for the slightest differences between cases. The disadvantage is that, should the same case be heard by two different judicial officers, there may be a vast difference in the sentences that are imposed. Therefore, the wider the discretion, the less consistent the sentences will be, while inconsistency was described in *Marx* 1989 (1) SA 222 (A) as something which is generally viewed as unjust. In the United States of America this injustice has led to a radical new way of thinking and *sentencing guidelines* are widely used. These guidelines determine the form and the duration of the sentences for a long list of crimes and the discretion of courts to deviate from them is strictly limited. The courts in South Africa do not, however, take kindly to a restriction of their sentencing powers by the legislature—cf *Toms; Bruce* 1990 (2) SA 802 (A) at 822C–D. However, since s 9 of the Constitution emphatically stresses the equality of all people before the law, our courts could in future set great store upon equal treatment for equal offenders, also during the sentencing phase.

4 GENERAL PRINCIPLES WITH REGARD TO SENTENCING

The general principles of sentencing was set out in a nutshell in *Rabie* 1975 (4) SA 855 (A) at 862G, namely that:

> 'Punishment should fit the criminal as well as the crime, be fair to society, and be blended with a measure of mercy according to the circumstances.'

Furthermore, all sentences should take into account the (so-called) main purposes of punishment, namely retribution, deterrence, prevention and rehabilitation. Of these purposes deterrence has for a long time been considered the most important (see e g *B* 1985 (2) SA 120 (A) at 124), but in *Nkambule* 1993 (1) SACR 136 (A) at 146C it was pointed out that this was an oversimplification, as the position is not static.

As stated above, every sentence should fit the criminal as well as the crime and be fair to society. The process through which this is achieved is known as personalisation (or individualisation) of punishment. This process is considered to be the main reason for leaving sentencers with such a wide discretion.

In this chapter we investigate only certain procedural aspects of sentencing and leave the substantive aspects aside. We place specific emphasis on the statutory framework supplied by the Criminal Procedure Act 51 of 1977.

5 PENAL PROVISIONS

5.1 General

Most statutory offences are enacted with an attendant penal provision. Imprisonment may normally be imposed for these crimes only if it is specifically provided for. The same goes for a fine. If a penal provision provides for a fine *or* imprisonment (e g R1 000 or 1 year's imprisonment), the court has a discretion to impose either a fine or imprisonment, but not both. It may not, for instance, impose imprisonment directly *and* as an alternative to a fine. For that possibility to exist, the penal provision should prescribe a fine or imprisonment, *or both*—cf *Arends* 1988 (4) SA 792 (E) at 794I–795B.

5.2 The Adjustment of Fines Act 101 of 1991

All penal provisions must, however, be read together with the provisions of the Adjustment of Fines Act 101 of 1991. This Act replaces, with some exceptions, all existing penal provisions by using the maximum term of imprisonment prescribed for a particular offence as basis for calculating the maximum amount of the fine that may be imposed. The ratio between fine and imprisonment is determined by the standard jurisdiction of the magistrate's court, which is R20 000 for each 12 months' imprisonment at present. A penal provision allowing a penalty of 'not more than R1 000 or 6 months' imprisonment' should thus be construed as providing for 'not more than *R10 000* or 6 months' imprisonment'. This ratio also applies to penal provisions which merely provide for the imposition of a fine without reference to a maximum amount—see Terblanche *The guide to sentencing in South Africa* (1999) 49–54.

5.3 Minimum sentences

Statutes which prescribe minimum sentences have been few and far between in South African law for some decades, but the position has changed with the passing of s 51 of the Criminal Law Amendment Act 105 of 1997. This provision, in essence, provides for the imposition of minimum sentences for a wide range of the more serious crimes. For premeditated murder, and rape and robbery where aggravating factors are involved (all these factors are circumscribed), life imprisonment is prescribed. Specific minimum terms (down to 5 years' imprisonment) are also prescribed for a wide range of other crimes, especially when committed by gangs or crime syndicates, or by law enforcement officers. Only High Courts and regional courts may impose these sentences. The sentencing courts are also not allowed to suspend any part of these minimum sentences—s 51(5).

If the sentencing court is satisfied that there are 'substantial and compelling circumstances' why a lesser sentence than that prescribed is justified in a particular case, it is permitted to impose such lesser sentence, after recording these circumstances on the record—s 51(3)*(a)*. This provision is similar to provisions which applied to minimum sentences which were in operation during the 1960's and 1970's. Furthermore, these minimum sentences are not applicable to an offender of under the age of 16 years and, if the court decides to impose these sentences on an offender of younger than 18 years old, it will have to record its reasons for doing so. In this fashion the courts are discouraged from imposing the minimum sentences on children.

A novel feature of this provision is that it is intended to apply for a limited period of two years (s 53) only, although the President is allowed to extend this period with the concurrence of Parliament.

The constitutionality of some of these provisions are certainly questionable. With regard to minimum sentences, the Namibian High Court found in *Vries* 1996 (2) SACR 638 (Nm) that a prescribed sentence which is grossly disproportionate to the severity of the crime, in the view of contemporary society, will be unconstitutional. This may indeed happen, for example, to the provision that a law enforcement officer (which is widely defined in this Act) has to be sentenced to 15 years' imprisonment for dealing in a small quantity of drugs.

6 THE PRE-SENTENCE INVESTIGATION

6.1 General

As has been mentioned, the discretion of imposing a suitable sentence lies with the sentencing officer. However, the sentencing officer can not do so without sufficient factual information on which this decision can be based. Tradition seems to require the State and the accused to supply this information. However, s 274(1) places the court in the centre of this process and empowers the court, before passing sentence, to allow evidence which will assist the court in determining a proper sentence. The term 'evidence' used here is usually not interpreted in the strict sense of the word, neither is the law of evidence strictly observed—cf *Zonele* 1959 (3) SA 319 (A) at 330F.

6.2 Previous convictions

What normally happens in practice is that, after conviction, the State will indicate whether the accused has any previous convictions. The Criminal Procedure Act deals with this procedure in ss 271 to 273. If there are previous convictions, they are usually proved simply by handing in the accused's fingerprint record (the so-called SAP69), which, according to s 272 is *prima facie* proof of previous convictions. The court must enquire from the accused whether he admits the previous convictions. Should he deny them (which rarely happens) the prosecutor may tender evidence to prove that the previous convictions are his. The court will then decide the matter on the evidence—cf *Mchunu* 1974 (1) SA 708 (N).

Section 271A provides that certain previous convictions 'fall away' after a period of 10 years if the offender has not committed a fairly serious crime within that period. According to *Zondi* 1995 (1) SACR 18 (A) such a previous conviction loses its validity and cannot be considered for purposes of sentencing at all. The convictions that fall away are those for

(1) less serious crimes (where more than six months' imprisonment without the option of a fine may not be imposed) and

(2) any offence for which the passing of sentence was postponed in terms of s 297(1)*(a)*, or for which the accused was merely cautioned and discharged.

In any case, the importance of previous convictions declines with time.

6.3 The accused on sentence

After the previous convictions have been dealt with, the accused is given the opportunity to supply evidence in mitigation of sentence. In less serious cases, mitigating features are frequently described by the accused or his legal representative simply by addressing the court from the bar. It has on occasion been stated that the address on sentence should not include facts; the latter should first be proven by evidence under oath—cf *Gough* 1980 (3) SA 785 (NC) at 786H. This approach is not consistently followed, however. What is clear is that s 274(2) obliges the court to afford the accused an opportunity to address the court on sentence. After all the evidence on behalf of the accused has been led, the State will normally be allowed the opportunity to lead evidence and to address the court on sentence.

6.4 The duty to supply information

It has been mentioned above that tradition seems to require that the State and the accused have to supply the information necessary for the court to decide on a suitable sentence. This tradition was taken to the extreme in *Khambule* 1991 (2) SACR 277 (W) where it was decided that it is a serious irregularity for the court to ask the accused whether he has any previous convictions, if the State does not produce a list of previous convictions. It may be accepted that an accused person, who is aware of his rights, will normally take the opportunity to provide the court with information in mitigation of sentence. However, the State should not stand by passively as the accused gives a one-sided picture to the court—cf *Smith* 1971 (4) SA 419 (T). A criminal trial does not have a conviction as its ultimate aim, but rather a suitable sanction. The prosecutor does not fulfil his role as representative of 'the people' when the accused is convicted, but only once he has done everything in his power to ensure that the accused receives an appropriate sentence.

However, in the final analysis it is the court that has to impose the sentence. It has the discretion; a discretion which cannot be exercised properly unless all the information necessary to make such an important decision is at the disposal of the court. In comparison with the attention given to determining the guilt of the accused, the sentencing process is often neglected, which is why decisions requiring the court not to adopt a passive role in this regard (cf *Shirindi* 1974 (1) SA 481 (T)), must be welcomed. It is also for this reason that the courts themselves are expected to decide whether a pre-sentence report by a probation officer should be called for in a particular case—cf *Jansen* 1975 (1) SA 425 (A).

7 ABSENCE OF JUDICIAL OFFICER

Criminal proceedings are frequently postponed after conviction and before sentence is passed. This often happens because the State needs more time to obtain a list of an accused's previous convictions or because a pre-sentence report has been requested, to name but two reasons for such postponements. Sentence also sometimes has to be imposed anew, after the case has been on review or appeal. Section 275 provides that any judicial officer of the same court may, if the judge or magistrate who has convicted the accused is 'not available', pass sentence after consideration of the evidence. However, the judicial officer must be 'materially absent', whether due to recusal, transfer, leave, death or serious illness—cf *Lukele* 1978 (4) SA 450 (T).

8 MITIGATING AND AGGRAVATING FACTORS

When considering sentence the court must take mitigating and aggravating factors into consideration. A large number of such factors have already been accepted by our courts (see e g Hiemstra *Suid-Afrikaanse Strafproses* (1987) 590–604). Only two of these are discussed here.

8.1 Youth as a mitigating factor

As a general principle, juveniles are sentenced more leniently than adults. The reason for this approach is that juveniles cannot be expected to act with the same measure of responsibility as adults, that they lack the necessary experience and insight and are therefore more prone to commit thoughtless acts—*Solani* 1987 (4) SA 203 (NC) at 220E. In *Jansen* 1975 (1) SA 425 (A) at 428A the importance of determining the most appropriate sentence in the case of a juvenile was stressed, because the

'. . . interests of society cannot be served by disregarding the interests of the juvenile, for a mistaken form of punishment might easily result in a person with a distorted or more distorted personality being eventually returned to society'.

8.2 Previous convictions as an aggravating factor

A person who is convicted time and again of similar offences will progressively be punished more severely. This is because the offender, by continuing to commit offences, displays a disregard for the law and because it is believed that the heavier a penalty is, the more likely it is to deter the offender from committing more crime. In the past very heavy penalties were sometimes imposed for minor offences, based solely on the number of previous convictions for similar offences. However, this approach has been criticised in a number of decisions in which it was stressed that the *seriousness of the particular crime* should be afforded more weight, and that the previous convictions should not be over-emphasised—cf *Barnabas* 1991 (1) SACR 467 (A).

9 CONSTITUTIONAL MATTERS

Two of the earlier decisions of the Constitutional Court struck down as unconstitutional two well-known forms of punishment. These were the death penalty and corporal punishment.

9.1 The death penalty

9.1.1 *General remarks*

The decision of *Makwanyane* 1995 (2) SACR 1 (CC) was not necessarily a popular decision. It goes beyond only discussing the death penalty and contains a good deal of material on the interpretation of the Constitution, on the understanding of rights such as the right to dignity, and the right not to be subjected to cruel or inhumanly treatment, etc.

The discussion which follows gives a brief overview of the main considerations which brought the court to its decision. Even though each of the eleven judges wrote a separate judgment, these considerations have been adequately dealt with in the main judgment by Chaskalson P.

9.1.2 *The relevant constitutional provisions*

In essence, the decision revolves around the interpretation of sections 9 ('every person shall have the right to life'), 10 ('every person shall have the right to respect for and protection of his or her dignity') and 8(1) ('every person shall have the right to equality before the law and to equal protection of the law') of the interim Constitution (the corresponding provisions in the 1996 Constitution are ss 11, 10 and 9(1)). The court found that any punishment should meet the requirements of these provisions (para [11]). These requirements should, in turn, be used to give meaning to section 11(2) (s 12(1)*(d)* and *(e)* of the Constitution), which prohibits 'cruel, inhuman and degrading treatment or punishment'.

9.1.3 *The crucial question*

Although, given the ordinary meaning of the words, the death penalty was considered a cruel and inhuman and degrading punishment, the crucial question which faced the Court was whether it was such *within the meaning of section 11(2) of the interim Constitution* (para [26])—s 12(1)*(e)* of the 1996 Constitution).

9.1.4 *The main arguments for and against the death penalty*

Para [27] of the judgment deals with the main arguments related to the death penalty:

'The principal arguments advanced by counsel for the accused in support of their contention that the imposition of the death penalty for murder is a "cruel, inhuman or degrading punishment," were that the death sentence is an affront to human dignity, is inconsistent with the unqualified right to life entrenched in the Constitution, cannot be corrected in case of error or enforced in a manner that is not arbitrary, and that it negates the essential content of the right to life and the other rights that flow from it. The Attorney General argued that the death penalty is recognised as a legitimate form of punishment in many parts of the world, it is a deterrent to violent crime, it meets society's need for adequate retribution for heinous offences, and it is regarded by South African society as an acceptable form of punishment. He asserted that it is, therefore, not cruel, inhuman or degrading within the meaning of s 11(2) of the Constitution.'

Some of these arguments will now be discussed, as they were dealt with by the court.

9.1.5 *Arbitrariness in the imposition of the death penalty*

Section 277 of the Criminal Procedure Act provided for the imposition of the death penalty for extremely serious crimes. Before it could be imposed, however, the sentencing court had to find death to be the only proper sentence for the particular crime, with due regard to the presence or absence of mitigating and/or aggravating factors—cf *Masina* 1990 (4) SA 709 (A). After assessing the factors which used to influence the imposition of the death penalty under section 277, Chaskalson P found that this process allowed for more consistency of sentencing, than, eg the jury system in the United States of America. However, thousands of people were charged with murder every year, but less than 1 per cent of these had been sentenced to death. The inference was unavoidable:

'It cannot be gainsaid that poverty, race and chance play roles in the outcome of capital cases and in the final decision as to who should live and who should die' (para [51]).

Chaskalson P continued that all the inconsistencies inherent in any judicial system, such as good and bad prosecutors, severe and lenient judges, judges who favour the death penalty and those who favour its abolition, and other imperfections, mean that error cannot be excluded (para [54]). In ordinary criminal cases such a system has to be accepted as a matter of necessity, but with the death penalty the error is not reversible, which reduces this acceptability.

9.1.6 *The death penalty in foreign law*

The death penalty has been abolished (for murder) in almost half the countries of the world, including countries such as Namibia, Mozambique and Angola. In most of the countries where the death penalty is retained, it is hardly ever used. Nevertheless, there is no doubt that the death penalty is not prohibited by public international law (par [36]).

In the United States, the death penalty itself has not been held to be unconstitutional—*Gregg v Georgia* 428 US 153 (1976). It is specifically mentioned in the Fifth Amendment to the American Constitution, even though the Eighth Amendment prohibits cruel and unusual punishment. Every state of the United States has its own criminal justice system, which has to conform to the Constitution. If the specific statute which authorised a state's courts to impose the death penalty did not allow for sufficient discretion to be exercised in this process, or where too wide a discretion was allowed, the death penalty had been struck down by the Supreme Court (para [42]).

9.1.7   Public opinion

As the director of public prosecutions had argued that the meaning of the phrase 'cruel, inhuman and degrading' should be interpreted in accordance with the attitudes of the South African society, the court had to consider the importance of public opinion in reaching its decision:

> 'Public opinion may have some relevance to the enquiry, but in itself, it is no substitute for the duty vested in the Courts to interpret the Constitution and to uphold its provisions without fear or favour. If public opinion were to be decisive there would be no need for constitutional adjudication. The protection of rights could then be left to Parliament, which has a mandate from the public, and is answerable to the public for the way its mandate is exercised, but this would be a return to parliamentary sovereignty, and a retreat from the new legal order established by the 1993 Constitution' (para [88]).

As far as Chaskalson P is concerned, the constitutional court has been established also to protect the rights of minorities whose rights cannot be protected by the ordinary democratic process. These minorities include 'social outcasts and marginalised people of society' (*ibid*).

9.1.8   Cruel, inhuman and degrading punishment

In terms of the Constitution, the death penalty would be unconstitutional if it is found either to be cruel, inhuman *or* degrading. Ultimately, the court concluded:

> 'The carrying out of the death sentence destroys life, which is protected without reservation under s 9 of our Constitution, it annihilates human dignity which is protected under s 10, elements of arbitrariness are present in its enforcement and it is irremediable' (para [95]).

As a result the court found the death penalty to be cruel, inhuman and degrading punishment in terms of our Constitution.

9.1.9   The limitation clause

The next question the court had to answer was whether imposing death as punishment could, despite being cruel, inhuman and degrading punishment, be justified for murder. This would have been the case had it been shown to be both reasonable and necessary, as required by section 33 of the interim Constitution. The court decided the following to be required in applying section 33 to this case:

> 'Respect for life and dignity which are at the heart of s 11(2) are values of the highest order under our Constitution. The carrying out of the death penalty would destroy these and all other rights that the convicted person has, and a clear and convincing case must be made out to justify such action' (para [111]).

The main arguments in favour of justification were that the death penalty deters better than other forms of punishment, that it ensures the protection of prison warders and inmates, and that it meets the needs for retribution (para [112]).

9.1.10   Deterrence

It was argued in court that the rise in crime since the announcement of the moratorium on the execution of the death penalty could be attributed to this moratorium. This argument did not impress the court, however, as many other factors could also have attributed to the rise in crime. The court observed that

'[t]he greatest deterrent to crime is the likelihood that offenders will be apprehended, convicted and punished. It is that which is presently lacking in our criminal justice system; and it is at this level and through addressing the causes of crime that the State must seek to combat lawlessness' (para [122]).

Eventually the director of public prosecutions had to concede that there was no proof that the death penalty was a greater deterrent to violent crime than life imprisonment (para [127]), and the court could not find that the deterrent effect of the death penalty was sufficient to justify the infringement of basic rights in the fashion that it infringed those rights.

The court was at pains to emphasise its empathy with victims of crime:

'The need for a strong deterrent to violent crime is an end the validity of which is not open to question. The state is clearly entitled, indeed obliged, to take action to protect human life against violation by others . . . The level of violent crime in our country has reached alarming proportions. It poses a threat to the transition to democracy, and the creation of development opportunities for all, which are primary goals of the Constitution . . . It is of fundamental importance to the future of our country that respect for the law should be restored, and that dangerous criminals should be apprehended and dealt with firmly. Nothing in this judgment should be understood as detracting in any way from that proposition' (para [117]).

9.1.11 *Prevention*

The court maintained that prevention may be achieved through means other than the death sentence. Although gaol murders occur, they are insufficient in number to justify the existence of the death penalty for all cases (para [128]).

9.1.12 *Retribution*

Retribution was considered to be of secondary importance. The 'natural indignation' of the community can also be expressed by means other than the death penalty, such as a long term of imprisonment (para [129]).

9.1.13 *Balancing the objects of punishment with the rights of the accused*

The objects of punishment mentioned in the previous paragraphs have to be balanced with the individual's rights:

'In the balancing process, deterrence, prevention and retribution must be weighed against the alternative punishments available to the state, and the factors which taken together make capital punishment cruel, inhuman and degrading: the destruction of life, the annihilation of dignity, the elements of arbitrariness, inequality and the possibility of error in the enforcement of the penalty' (para [135]).

Criminals do not forfeit most of their rights in terms of the Constitution. Whether they loose any of these rights depends on whether it is justifiable as penalty in terms of section 33 of the interim Constitution (para [143]—currently s 36).

9.1.14 *Conclusion*

The court's main findings are summed up in the following terms:

'The rights to life and dignity are the most important of all human rights, and the source of all other personal rights in Chapter Three. By committing ourselves to a society founded on the recognition of human rights we are required to value these two rights above all others. And this must be demonstrated by the State in everything that it does, including the way it punishes criminals. This is not achieved by objectifying murderers and putting them to death to serve as an example to others in the expectation that they might possibly be deterred thereby' (para [144]).

In the end the court found most of the provisions of section 277 to be unconstitutional. The same goes for all corresponding provisions which may have been in force in any part of South Africa. All death penalty provisions have subsequently been repealed by the Criminal Law Amendment Act 105 of 1997.

9.2 Corporal punishment

Section 294 of the Criminal Procedure Act 51 of 1977 made provision for the imposition of corporal punishment on juvenile male offenders (up to 21 years of age). The Constitutional Court declared the whole of section 294 to be invalid and of no force and effect in *Williams* 1995 (2) SACR 251 (CC); 1995 (7) BCLR 861 (CC). Thereafter, the Abolition of Corporal Punishment Act 33 of 1997 abolished corporal punishment completely, by scrapping all references thereto in all statutes.

10 THE FORMS OF PUNISHMENT WHICH MAY BE IMPOSED

10.1 Introduction

Section 276 lists the sentences which may generally be passed. These basically consist of the following:

(1) imprisonment (in various forms and for various terms);

(2) committal to a treatment centre;

(3) a fine; and

(4) correctional supervision.

To this list should be added the various ways in which a juvenile may be treated in terms of s 290, and the provisions of s 297, which provide for

(1) the suspension of a sentence on various conditions;

(2) the conditional or unconditional postponement of the imposition of a sentence; and

(3) a caution and discharge.

10.2 Imprisonment

10.2.1 *General*

One of the first decisions a court has to make when sentencing the offender, is whether to remove him from society or whether to punish him within the community. The latter kinds of sentences are often described as 'alternatives to imprisonment', even though they are clearly punishment in their own right. The decision to remove the offender from the community is one of the most difficult decisions to be made during sentencing and one for which there is disappointingly little guidance provided to the sentencing court. A careful search through the law reports will reveal only that the seriousness of the particular crime is a very important, but also very inexact factor. Any aggravating factor, such as previous convictions or the brutality of the crime, may be used as reason for imposing imprisonment. Conversely, the presence of mitigating factors may dictate a decision not to imprison.

10.2.2   *The role of mitigating factors*

The decision not to imprison is often based on the presence of one or more mitigating factors. These include the following:

10.2.2.1   Youthfulness

Juveniles are not readily imprisoned (see the discussion in para 8.1 above and cf *Willemse* 1988 (3) SA 836 (A)).

10.2.2.2   No criminal record

First offenders are also not readily imprisoned. It is generally felt that they should be given another opportunity to show that they can live a life without crime—cf *Kelly* 1993 2 SACR 492 (A) 493*j*. That does not mean that a first offender who has committed a serious crime cannot be imprisoned and it does in fact often happen— cf *Victor* 1970 (1) SA 427 (A).

10.2.3   *The value of imprisonment*

Imprisonment is *indispensable* in the sense that it enables a court to remove a person who constitutes a danger to society from the community. Apart from this advantage, imprisonment is characterised by its disadvantages:

(1)   It is very expensive. Prisons cost millions of rand to erect and maintain. The inmates have to be provided with an internationally acceptable standard of living. A whole state department with a huge budget has to be financed, while the next of kin of the prisoners often have to be supported financially by the state or other welfare organisations.

(2)   Many of the people with whom the offender is incarcerated are hardened criminals. It should be evident that the prospects of rehabilitation in such an environment can only be slim. Although psychological and welfare services are available to prisoners, these are limited and their rehabilitative value has not been sufficiently proven.

(3)   The entire prison environment with its discipline and subculture is not conducive to preparing the prisoner to live in a free society. You do not teach someone to fly by locking him up in a cage.

10.2.4   *The various forms of imprisonment*

The Criminal Procedure Act 51 of 1977 makes provision for several 'forms' of imprisonment. The various forms are, however, really descriptions of different *terms* of imprisonment, rather than completely separate kinds of punishment. Whether any of these forms may be imposed in a particular instance, will depend on the statutory provisions which regulate the imposition thereof, and on the statutory provisions applicable to the particular crime. The various forms will be discussed briefly in the following paragraphs.

10.2.4.1   Ordinary imprisonment for a term determined by the court

This is the most common form of imprisonment. All criminal courts have the power to impose a term of imprisonment for most crimes, limited only by their general jurisdiction, and/or by the prescribed punishment for the particular crime. In the case of *common law crimes*, only the general jurisdiction applies—regional courts are limited to 15 years' imprisonment and district magistrates' courts to 3 years—s 92 of the Magistrates' Courts Act 32 of 1944. Subject to the minimum term of imprisonment (see below), superior courts may impose any term of imprisonment. In the case of *statutory crimes* the general jurisdiction also applies, but always subject to the penal provisions contained in the statute. Quite a number of these provisions specifically empower lower courts to impose terms exceeding the general jurisdiction, for example s 64(1) of the Drugs and Drug Trafficking Act 140 of 1992.

Sometimes, but normally only in the case of serious statutory crimes, the prescribed punishment refers to imprisonment only, or otherwise requires the imposition of imprisonment (eg s 17*(e)* of the Drugs and Drug Trafficking Act 140 of 1992 for dealing in most illegal drugs). In these instances imprisonment has to be imposed, and only the term of imprisonment is in the discretion of the court. However, due to exceptions created by sections 276(3)*(a)*, 290, 296 and 297 of the Criminal Procedure Act, it is actually only a fine that may not be imposed in such cases.

In terms of s 284 no court may impose a sentence of less than four days' imprisonment, unless the sentence is that the offender be detained until the rising of the court. It was decided in *Msimango* 1972 (3) SA 145 (N) that a court 'rises' as soon as it has disposed of a case and the offender is therefore entitled to his release before the next case is called. To call this 'imprisonment' is clearly a fiction.

Within this statutory framework a court which has decided to impose imprisonment, is expected to determine the most appropriate term of imprisonment, based on the general principles of sentencing. This implies that the more serious the offence, or the more dangerous the criminal, the longer the period of imprisonment will be, and *vice versa*—cf *Holder* 1979 2 SA 70 (A). The term of imprisonment must always be stipulated by the court.

In the past longer terms that 25 years' imprisonment were rarely imposed—cf *M* 1993 (1) SACR 126 (A) 134. However, after the abolition of the death penalty this position has dramatically changed, and sentences of 40 years are quite readily imposed for serious crime. In *Smith* 1996 (1) SACR 250 (E) the court referred to a sentence of 75 years which had been imposed already, but warned that the courts should not impose ridiculously long sentences.

Most prisoners are eventually released, but courts are not supposed to take the normal prison release policy into account when determining an appropriate prison term (cf *S* 1987 (2) SA 307 (A)). This approach by the courts has at times been severely criticised (see eg Mihálik 'Executive Manipulation of Prison Sentences' (1988) 105 *SALJ* 494). The release regime is described in Chapter VI of the Correctional Services Act 8 of 1959. Prisoners with sentences of more than 1 year imprisonment may only be considered for release on parole after having served half their sentences. 'Parole' is described in s 1 of the Correctional Services Act as the 'conditions under which a prisoner may be placed'.

Sentences of imprisonment may normally be imposed in conjunction with other forms of punishment such as fines and correctional supervision. A term of imprisonment may also normally be partly or fully suspended in terms of s 297 of the Criminal Procedure Act (see par 11 below).

10.2.4.2 Imprisonment for life

Life imprisonment was expressly inserted into s 276 of the Criminal Procedure Act by the Criminal Law Amendment Act 107 of 1990. It can only be imposed by the high courts. When the death penalty was still in place, life imprisonment was considered to be a valuable alternative to the death sentence and was imposed in cases of extreme seriousness (where the protection of society was imperative), but where the death penalty was not considered to be the only proper sentence—cf *Mdau* 1991 (1) SACR 169 (A). This should basically still be the guiding principle.

With the abolition of the death penalty, life imprisonment is the most severe sentence which our courts can impose—cf *Smith* 1996 (1) SACR 250 (E) 256*i*.

Life imprisonment is an indeterminate sentence, because when it is imposed, it is unknown for how long the offender will be imprisoned. In terms of the Correctional Services Act 8 of 1959 (after the coming into operation of Act 87 of 1997) the prisoner has to serve at least 25 years in prison, after which he may be considered for release on parole. This consideration will be performed by the court in which the sentence was imposed, with the assistance of a report by the parole board. This is a substantial change to the previous situation, when the release of all prisoners were left exclusively in the hands of the Department of Correctional Services.

10.2.4.3 Declaration as dangerous criminal

Section 286A provides for the declaration of a person as a dangerous criminal. This provision has been included mainly to provide for sentences for psychopaths. Such sentences are indeterminate, except that the court has to determine a date when the offender has to appear before the court again. Only regional and superior courts may impose such a sentence. The duration of the initial imprisonment of the offender may not exceed the court's general jurisdiction—s 287B(1)*(b)*.

The sentence may only be imposed if the court 'is satisfied that the said person represents a danger to the physical or mental well-being of other persons and that the community should be protected against him . . .'—s 286A(1).

In *T* 1997 (1) SACR 496 (SCA) the court referred to a number of considerations for the imposition of this sentence:

> 'This . . . punishment [is] ideally suited to a case . . . where the crime itself is not so serious as to warrant a sentence of life imprisonment, where the convicted person represents a danger to the physical and mental well-being of other persons sufficiently serious to warrant his detention for an indefinite period and where there is a possibility that his condition may improve to such an extent that that would no longer be the case.'

The parole board dealing with the prisoner's case must submit a report to the court on the date determined by the court for the reappearance of the dangerous criminal—s 63 of the Correctional Services Act 8 of 1959. This report should deal with, *inter alia*, the conduct of the prisoner, his adaptation, training, mental state and the possibility of a relapse into crime.

When the prisoner reappears in court, the court has to reconsider the original sentence, taking into account the parole board's report, but also any other evidence which may be adduced at the hearing. The court then has to decide whether to order the continued incarceration, or the release of the offender. The release of the prisoner may be conditional, and the sentence may also be converted into correctional supervision at this stage.

10.2.4.4   Declaration as an habitual criminal

Within the rather specific statutory framework of s 286 of the Criminal Procedure Act, a superior or regional court may declare an offender to be an habitual criminal only if the court is *satisfied* that—

(1)   the person *habitually* commits offences, and that

(2)   the community should be *protected* against him.

Both requirements must be met. The second requirement prevents a person who repeatedly commits petty offences from being declared an habitual criminal—cf *Makoula* 1978 (4) SA 763 (SWA). The statutory framework furthermore removes this form of imprisonment from a court's discretion if

(1)   the offender is under the age of 18 years, and if

(2)   the court is of the opinion that the offender deserves imprisonment for a period exceeding 15 years.

Although not a statutory requirement, it is a rule of practice not to declare an accused to be an habitual criminal unless he has previously been warned that such a sentence might be imposed on a further conviction—*Mache* 1980 (3) SA 224 (T). Despite this rule, the courts may impose such a sentence even where no warning has been given. However, a court will be particularly careful before imposing it in such a case—cf *Shabalala* 1984 (2) SA 234 (N).

A person who has been declared an habitual criminal is kept in a prison for at least seven years—s 65(4) of Act 8 of 1959. He may thereafter be considered for parole if the parole board finds that, for some reason (such as that there is a reasonable probability that the prisoner will abstain from committing crime in future), it is desirable that the prisoner be placed on parole. Owing to the provision that the court may not impose this form of imprisonment when it considers more than 15 years' imprisonment to be appropriate, 15 years should be the maximum duration of such imprisonment. Longer incarceration will probably be unconstitutional.

10.2.4.5   Periodical imprisonment

Periodical imprisonment is a form of imprisonment by which prisoners are imprisoned for short periods only (between 24 and 48 hours at a time). After every period of incarceration they are released to continue their normal existence. Because they are usually imprisoned over week-ends it has also become known as 'week-end imprisonment', but they can be imprisoned at any time, also during the week. The important aspect of periodical imprisonment is its intermittent character—the prisoner may not be held for long periods at a time in order to complete the total sentence rapidly. Unlike ordinary imprisonment, periodical imprisonment is imposed for a period expressed in hours.

Regarding the statutory framework, s 285(1) of the Criminal Procedure Act provides that periodical imprisonment may be imposed on conviction of an offence other than an offence for which a minimum punishment is prescribed. It is also imposed 'in lieu of any other punishment'. Initially this was held to mean that no other form of punishment may be imposed in combination with periodical imprisonment, but in *Visser; Nkwandla* 1990 (1) SACR 183 (E) it was held that it may be used as alternative for a fine since its imposition would then be 'in lieu of' the fine. The duration of periodical imprisonment may not exceed 2 000 hours, but may also not be less than 100 hours.

When periodical imprisonment was introduced in our law in 1959 (by Act 16 of 1959), it was highly praised as a severe form of punishment which nevertheless does not disrupt the family life of the prisoner. Courts were prompted to impose it as often as possible—cf *Botha* 1970 (4) SA 407 (T). For a number of reasons, however, it is today only occasionally imposed.

Periodical imprisonment involves more administration than ordinary imprisonment, but the authorities deal with the periodical prisoner in basically the same fashion as ordinary prisoners.

10.2.4.6   Section 276(1)*(i)*-imprisonment

If an offender has been imprisoned in terms of s 276(1)*(i)* of the Criminal Procedure Act, the Commissioner of Correctional Services is empowered to release that prisoner, during the course of his sentence, on correctional supervision. The sentencing court basically provides the Commissioner with this discretion by making clear in some way that the imprisonment is imposed in terms of this provision. The court must be satisfied that imprisonment for a maximum term of five years is appropriate for the offender's crime, before it can exercise this option (s 276A(2)*(a)*). This limit provides an indication of the seriousness of the crimes for which the legislature considered this sentence to be suitable—*Blank* 1995 (1) SACR 62 (A). As a result, if more than five years' imprisonment is required to suitably punish the offender, this option is not available—*Randell* 1995 (1) SACR 404 (O). The maximum term of this form of imprisonment is also restricted to five years—(s 276A(2)*(b)*). This does not mean, however, that more than five years may not be imposed if the accused is convicted of more than one crime—*Gouws* 1995 (1) SACR 342 (T).

In *Flanagan* 1995 (1) SACR 13 (A) the court found imprisonment of four years to be a suitable sentence but, because the appellant was found to be someone who could eventually gain by a sentence of correctional supervision, the sentence was imposed in terms of section 276(1)*(i)*. Correctional supervision is discussed in par 10.4 below.

What happens in practice is that the prisoner is evaluated immediately as he starts his prison term. The parole board has to advise the Commissioner on the advisability of releasing the prisoner on correctional supervision. The prisoner has to serve at least one-sixth of the total sentence, before he can be released. From the moment of release the offender is treated as a 'probationer' (a person under correctional supervision). If the probationer does not comply with the condition of his correctional supervision, he may be arrested and imprisoned to complete the rest of his prison sentence—s 84B of Act 8 of 1959.

10.2.5   *Sentences for more than one crime*

Offenders are often, during the same trial, convicted of more than one crime and the question is whether this fact should influence sentencing at all. The trial court retains its full sentencing jurisdiction for every separate crime the accused has been convicted of. For example, an offender who has been convicted of theft, assault and arson may be sentenced to three years' imprisonment on every count by a magistrate's court. In such cases, however, it may happen that, despite the individual sentences being suitable, the total punishment becomes unduly severe. The court then has to reduce what is called the *cumulative effect* of the various sentences in some way.

The preferred method is to order the whole or part of the sentences to run concurrently. In terms of s 280(2) of the Criminal Procedure Act all sentences of imprisonment are executed in the order in which they were imposed and the next sentence commences after the completion of the previous one, unless the court orders that they are to run concurrently. In the past only sentences of *imprisonment* may have been ordered to run concurrently (*Mngadi* 1991 (1) SACR 313 (T)), but with the insertion of s 280(3) in the Criminal Procedure Act this is now also possible with regard to correctional supervision.

There are two further methods of restricting the cumulative effect of multiple sentences. *First*, every sentence may be reduced so that the total sentence is not excessive. An objection against this approach is that the sentences for each individual crime may seem inadequate when viewed in isolation. *Secondly*, some or all of the counts can be taken together for purposes of sentencing. The Criminal Procedure Act does not specifically provide for this method, but it is part of our practice and is often used—see Hiemstra 692. The main problem with this method is that difficulties may develop on review or appeal if some of the convictions are set aside, or some misdirection took place during sentencing—cf *Young* 1977 (1) SA 602 (A) and *Keulder* 1994 (1) SACR 91 (A). It is also not desirable to take convictions in respect of divergent counts together for the purpose of sentence (cf *S* 1981 (3) SA 377 (A)). A court which takes different counts together, must also ensure that the eventual sentence is a competent one for every crime the offender has been convicted of—cf *Hayman* 1988 (1) SA 831 (NC).

The suspension of a portion of the sentence was employed as a further method of countering the cumulative effect of sentences in *S v Coales* 1995 (1) SACR 33 (A).

10.2.6 *Further provisions on imprisonment*

Some statutes may still provide for brief maximum periods of imprisonment, e g one month's imprisonment. In order to bring about uniformity with regard to maximum penalties for minor statutory offences, s 281*(b)* of the Criminal Procedure Act provides that any reference in a statute to a maximum period of imprisonment of less than three months must be construed as a reference to a period of three months.

Whenever any sentence of imprisonment is set aside on appeal or review and any other sentence of imprisonment is thereafter imposed, the latter sentence may, if the court is satisfied that the person concerned has served any part of the first sentence, be ante-dated to a specified date which shall not be earlier than the date on which the first sentence was imposed—s 282.

10.2.7 *Reduction of sentence*

Once an offender has been sentenced by a court and the questions of review or appeal have been finalised, the matter is out of the hands of the courts and the sentence can be modified only by administrative action by the Department of

Correctional Services. Its powers in this respect are prescribed by the Correctional Services Act 8 of 1959 and various office bearers may authorise the release of prisoners who have served various portions of their sentences. Executive interference with prison sentences has been severely criticised for a long time (cf *Madizela* 1992 (1) SACR 125 (N)), but one has to accept that, within reasonable limits, it is part of the reality within which the sentencing official has to exercise his or her discretion.

10.3 Fine

10.3.1 *General*

The fine is the sentence most commonly imposed in South African courts. It is a simple form of punishment and very commonly used for less serious offences. It consists of ordering the offender to pay an amount of money to the State as punishment for his crime.

10.3.2 *When are fines imposed*

As is the case with imprisonment, courts generally enjoy a wide discretion to impose fines as punishment. If a particular statute does not mention a fine in its penal provisions, it may not be imposed at all. Most penal provisions, however, provide for the imposition of fines.

If a court may impose a fine, three factors are generally decisive for the decision to impose a fine or not. *First*, the crime should not be so serious that imprisonment is called for, and *secondly*, the offender must have some financial means (or have access thereto) with which a fine can be paid—cf *Frans* 1924 TPD 419. With no means at his disposal, a fine will usually simply result in the offender's imprisonment. A *third factor* comes into play when crimes are committed for financial gain. In such cases a fine may be imposed which would indicate to the offender that crime does not pay— cf *Van Rooyen* 1994 (2) SACR 823 (A).

10.3.3 *The amount of the fine*

The amount of the fine imposed is, depending on any relevant statutory provisions, normally left to the discretion of the court. The magistrates' and regional courts are limited in this respect by the scope of their ordinary or specifically increased jurisdiction. The ordinary jurisdiction currently stands at R60 000 for magistrates' courts and R300 000 for regional courts—s 92(1)*(d)* of Act 32 of 1944 read with GN R1411 of 30 Oct 1998.

In assessing the *quantum* of the fine, the court should normally be guided by the accused's means. It goes without saying that where a court has decided to impose a fine with the intention of keeping the accused out of prison, it would serve no purpose to impose a fine completely beyond his means—cf *Ncobo* 1988 (3) SA 954 (N). On the other hand, it has frequently been held that the indigence of the accused does not warrant so moderate a fine that it does not reflect the gravity of the offence in question—cf *Bhembe* 1993 (1) SACR 164 (T). This approach, although widely applied, may in future have to be reconsidered. The fine punishes every man differently according to his financial ability. The same fine will punish the poor much more heavily than the middle class, who in turn will be more severely affected than the rich. The question is, therefore: From the point of view of which of these classes of people must the fine seem to reflect the gravity of the offence? The answer should be simply that the court must determine how heavily the fine should punish the offender, and then determine the amount that will punish that particular offender as heavily as he deserves. This principle has long been accepted by countries employing the day-fine system (such as Germany) and has also been accepted, for a brief period, as *unit fines* by Britain in its Criminal Justice Act 1991 (see Wasik & Taylor *Blackstone's Guide to the Criminal Justice Act* 2 ed (1994) 82ff). The one exception is crimes committed for illegal gain, in which case the real financial ability of the accused is usually unknown and the seriousness of the crime substantial, which should then be reflected by the amount of the fine—*Ntakatsane* 1990 (2) SACR 382 (NC).

In *Bersin* 1970 (1) SA 729 (R) it was held that the amount of the fine may be slightly increased to make provision for a wealthy offender. No direct recent and local authority is available on this point, but it may be accepted that the level of the fine may be set appreciably higher for such an offender, who would otherwise go almost scot-free.

The appropriate course of action if the offender simply does not have the means to pay a fine, is another vexed question. Various decisions have made various suggestions, which range from that it is an anomaly that has to be accepted (cf *Lekgoale* 1983 (2) SA 175 (B)), to that another form of punishment should then be imposed—cf *Ncobo* 1988 (3) SA 954 (N). The latter method has not found general acceptance. In *Van Rooyen* 1994 (2) SACR 823 (A) 827F it was at any rate decided that it cannot be stated categorically that a fine which is above the financial resources of the offender may never be imposed. However, with the recent addition of correctional supervision to the list of available sentences, this problem should be partly relieved, because more forms of punishment are available.

10.3.4 *Determining the means of the offender*

The court has to make purposeful inquiries to determine the means of the accused—cf *Sithole* 1979 (2) SA 67 (A). If necessary, it will require the accused to sell or pledge his assets in order to obtain the necessary funds for the fine—*De Beer* 1977 (2) SA 161 (O). The means of the offender consists of cash, savings, monthly income and other possessions, but income and available cash are often regarded as the main criteria.

In the past it was frequently held that, because it is the accused who is to be punished, only his ability to pay a fine must be considered and not that of his family and friends. Recently, however, there is a tendency to allow for assistance to be taken into consideration—cf *Nxumalo* 1992 (2) SACR 268 (O) at 271G and *Bhembe* 1993 (1) SACR 164 (T) at 168A.

10.3.5 *Recovering the fine*

If the accused can pay the fine immediately, the recovery of the fine does not, of course, present any problem. Various measures are, however, employed to recover the fine once it has been imposed:

10.3.5.1 Imprisonment in default of payment

Although it is not required, almost all fines are imposed with an alternative period of imprisonment already added to the sentence. This has become generally known as *alternative* imprisonment and the imposition thereof is authorised by s 287(1), which applies even if the penal provision does not specifically mention imprisonment. The total period of imprisonment imposed by any court, however, may never exceed the limits of that court's jurisdiction. If the court, for example, imposes a period of direct imprisonment (whether suspended or not) in addition to a fine, as well as alternative imprisonment, the total period of imprisonment may not exceed the maximum period that may be imposed by the court—cf *Moyage* 1958 (3) SA 400 (A).

The ratio between the fine and alternative imprisonment should always be 'reasonable' (cf *Tsatsinyana* 1986 (2) SA 504 (T)), although the exact meaning of this reasonableness is far from clear.

As explained above, a court may order that two or more terms of imprisonment should run concurrently. All sentences of fines must, however, be cumulative. In *Sitebe* 1934 AD 56, it was held that since fines cannot be ordered to run concurrently, two sentences of imprisonment in default of payment of such fines can also not be ordered to run concurrently, but it has since been held that it is competent to order two or more terms of alternative imprisonment to run together—*Lalsing* 1990 (1) SACR 443 (N) and *Mngadi* 1991 (1) SACR 313 (T).

What normally happens in practice is that, if the offender cannot pay his fine immediately, he is detained to undergo the alternative imprisonment, unless payment of the fine is deferred.

10.3.5.2 Deferment of payment of the fine

The court may, in terms of s 297(5), defer payment of the fine, or order its payment in instalments, but not for longer than five years after the imposition of the sentence. In *Molala* 1988 (2) SA 97 (T) and *Mosia* 1988 (2) SA 730 (T) courts were urged to use this discretion to accommodate people without the funds to pay the fine immediately. In this way such people are afforded the opportunity to stay out of prison.

10.3.5.3 Further relief after the start of the prison term

When an offender has started serving the alternative imprisonment, the court may at any stage before the termination of the imprisonment order the release of the person convicted on condition that he pay the rest of the fine as determined by the court—s 297(6)*(a)*.

In terms of s 287(4) the Commissioner may release a prisoner undergoing alternative imprisonment on correctional supervision at any time, unless the court specifically withdraws this power, and unless the alternative imprisonment exceeds five years. Alternatively, the Commissioner may refer the prisoner back to the court for reconsideration of the sentence.

10.3.5.4 Other methods of recovery

Sections 287(2), 288 and 289 provide further methods through which fines may be recovered, including attachment and sale of movable (and even immovable) property, deductions from salary, etc. These measures are hardly ever utilised (see Du Toit *et al* 28–28).

10.3.6 *To whom does the fine go?*

Except in cases where statutory authority exists for such an order, a court is not entitled to direct that any portion of the fine should go to the complainant in the case or to an informer or anybody else. The fine must go to the State. Compensation to the victim is discussed below in paragraph 11.1.

10.4 Correctional supervision

10.4.1 *General*

In 1991, by way of Act 122 of 1991, the legislature introduced a new form of sentence into our law of sentencing. This new sentence is called correctional supervision. The name is rather descriptive of what it entails, namely the supervision of the offender (called the 'probationer') with the view of correcting the wrongdoer and the wrongdoing. The enthusiasm with which it has been received by some judges is clear from the following dictum in *Omar* 1993 (2) SACR 5 (C):

> '[Correctional supervision is] . . . an excellent acceptable alternative, having regard to the present day emphasis on the rehabilitation and reformation of offenders, to direct imprisonment'.

10.4.2 *The nature of correctional supervision*

Correctional supervision is described rather blandly in s 1 of the Criminal Procedure Act as a 'community-based' form of punishment. This means that it is punishment which is executed within the community—where the offender would normally work and live. The term 'correctional supervision' is a collective term for describing the various measures which may be included in such punishment. This was pointed out in the very important decision *R* 1993 (1) SACR 209 (A) 220H (also reported in 1993 (1) SA 476 (A)). These various measures are called 'programmes' by the Department of Correctional Services (s 84E Act 8 of 1959) and 'conditions' by the courts.

The standard measures of correctional supervision would normally include house arrest, monitoring and community service. These three measures form the main penal components of the punishment and will, according to *Omar* 1993 (1) SACR 5 (C), seemingly only be disregarded in exceptional circumstances. Various other measures aimed at the education and rehabilitation of the offender and at correcting the wrongdoing, such as compensation of the victim, supervision by a probation officer and the presentation of various life skill courses, may also form part of the sentence—s 84 of Act 8 of 1959. The content of the main penal measures requires some illumination:

(1) **House arrest** can be equated to confinement at home—it requires of the probationer to stay at home. Exceptions would normally be made to allow the probationer at least to go to work, to do some shopping and to attend religious gatherings.

(2) **Community service** is service rendered in the interest of the community without receiving any remuneration. It may consist of the cleaning of parks or pavements, or working in a hospital or any public institution. For the purposes of correctional supervision, 16 hours' community service would typically be required every month.

(3) **Monitoring** simply entails that some state official will check whether the probationer actually complies with the condition of the sentence. Any step which is mainly aimed at this end, would amount to monitoring.

10.4.3 *The various forms of correctional supervision*

A sentencing court has various options in imposing correctional supervision:

(1) It can be imposed as a sentence in itself, just as a fine or imprisonment can be imposed—s 276(1)*(h)* of the Criminal Procedure Act. This may not be done without a report by a probation or correctional officer and it may not exceed three years—s 276A(1). This would be the standard form of correctional supervision.

(2) It can be imposed as a condition to a suspended sentence or to postponement of sentencing (see below par 11.5). This option would normally only be used if the court finds that a particular need for the individual deterrence of the accused exists—Terblanche (1992) 5 *SACJ* 254. All the other requirements of postponed or suspended sentences also apply here, including the fact that the period of postponement or suspension is limited to a duration of five years.

(3) Imprisonment may be linked to correctional supervision in the sense discussed in para 10.2.4.6 above.

(4) When the Commissioner of Correctional Services is of the opinion that a *prisoner* is a suitable candidate for correctional supervision (cf *Leeb* 1993 (1) SACR 315 (T)), he may apply to the court which initially imposed the imprisonment, to consider imposing correctional supervision in lieu of the remaining term of imprisonment—s 276A(3).

10.4.4 *The penal value of correctional supervision*

One of the many important points raised in *R supra* by Kriegler AJA is that correctional supervision is not a 'soft option'. Because of its various components, which include restraints on the freedom of the offender, it has a high penal content. This has the effect that punishment for serious crimes need not be confined to imprisonment any more—cf also *Kotze* 1994 (2) SACR 214 (O). Its penal effect can be lessened by reducing the strictness of the conditions, and the opposite may be achieved by the increasing this strictness, for instance by increasing the duration of community service which should be performed and by reducing the time which the probationer is allowed outside his house every week.

Because of its high penal content, correctional supervision will normally not be imposed if a fine or suspended sentence or other lighter form of sentence is sufficient punishment for the crime. For the same reason it is not surprising that it has already been imposed for crimes which are normally regarded as very serious, such as murder (*Potgieter* 1994 (1) SACR 61 (A); *Larsen* 1994 (2) SACR 149 (A)); rape (*A* 1994 (1) SACR 602 (A)); sexual molesting of children (*R supra*); major theft (*Sibuyi* 1993 (1) SACR 235 (A)) and drunken driving (*Croukamp* 1993 (1) SACR 439 (T)). A word of warning was, however, sounded in *Ingram* 1995 (1) SACR 1 (A) at 9F:

'As correctional supervision under s 276(1)*(h)* can . . . only be imposed for a period not exceeding three years, it is not a sentence that readily lends itself to the very serious category of crimes (which would normally call for higher sentences) and should therefore not be too lightly imposed in such cases.'

For the same reason correctional supervision was considered not to be a sufficient punishment for fraud involving R8,5 million in *Flanagan* 1995 (1) SACR 13 (A), and a sentence of four years' section 276(1)*(i)*-imprisonment was imposed.

The latest trend seems to indicate a move away from correctional supervision, and the Supreme Court of Appeal has often refused to impose it even from crimes which would in the past not have been considered to be too serious. It has regularly been emphasised lately that correctional supervision should be imposed with care, so that its 'coinage is not debased'—cf *Maritz* 1996 (1) SACR 405 (A) 418C.

10.4.5 *Factors influencing the imposition of correctional supervision*

The first important factor influencing the imposition of correctional supervision, is that it may be imposed for *any* offence (s 276(3)*(b)*). However, in *Strydom* 1994 (2) SACR 456 (W) it was decided that it could not be imposed if the penal provision provides for imprisonment only. Correctional supervision may also be imposed in conjunction with any other form of punishment.

Once it has been established that the particular crime is not too serious to be punished by correctional supervision (see above para 10.4.4), it is not so much the nature of the crime as the kind of person who has committed it, which will determine whether correctional supervision should be imposed (see Krugel and Terblanche *Praktiese Vonnisoplegging* (1997) 1104). In *Omar* 1993 (2) SACR 5 (C) it was found that the kind of offender for whom correctional supervision may be suitable may

'. . . vary from the first offender with no inborn criminal tendencies who has strayed into criminal activities, to the offender with criminal leanings who may have offended more than on one occasion but by reason of his employment, domestic and other circumstances is likely to . . . be a suitable candidate for correctional supervision.'

Kriegler AJA decided in *R* 1993 (1) SACR 209 (A) 221*h* that the legislature distinguishes between two kinds of offenders, namely those who should be removed from the community through imprisonment, and those who deserve punishment but need not be removed from the community. This is an important consideration when correctional supervision is considered.

Another factor which has been stressed by our courts is the rehabilitative value of correctional supervision. Whereas it undoubtedly has a greater potential of achieving the rehabilitation of the offender than, for example, imprisonment has, one should be careful not to have too high expectations in this regard (cf Terblanche (1993) 6 *Consultus* 67). Otherwise one might well find that when former probationers begin to reappear in the courts with sentences of correctional supervision on their list of previous convictions, sentencing courts will stop imposing this sentence, convinced that correctional supervision 'does not work'.

When a court has decided to impose correctional supervision, it must determine the composition of the sentence. The conditions of the sentence may not be left to the discretion of the Department of Correctional Services. The court should consequently prescribe which of the programmes which may be included in a sentence of correctional supervision (see par 10.4.2 above), should apply in a specific case—*Ndaba* 1993 (1) SACR 637 (A).

10.4.6 *The execution of correctional supervision*

Correctional supervision is executed by the personnel of the Department of Correctional Services in accordance with the provisions of Chapter VIIIA of the Correctional Services Act 8 of 1959.

Section 276A(4) of the Criminal Procedure Act makes provision for the situation where the probationer proves not to be a suitable candidate for correctional supervision. In such a case the Commissioner (or someone delegated by the Commissioner—*Sebiya* 1994 (1) SACR 129 (O)) or a probation officer should provide the court with a motivated recommendation why the probationer is not suitable to be subject to correctional supervision. If the court finds the probationer to be unfit, it may impose any other proper sentence, limited only to its jurisdictional limits.

10.5 Committal to a treatment centre

In terms of s 296 of the Criminal Procedure Act an offender may be committed to a treatment centre in addition to or instead of any other sentence. The treatment centres are presently established in terms of the Prevention and Treatment of Drug Dependency Act 20 of 1992. The court must be satisfied that the accused is someone who manifests any of the deviations mentioned in s 21(1) of Act 20 of 1992 (for instance, dependence on alcohol in consequence whereof his own or his family's welfare is harmed) and in order to do so should investigate the matter fully. This investigation must at least include a probation officer's report. Detention in a treatment centre is for an indefinite period, but if the offender is not released within 12 months certain reports have to be supplied to the Director-General of Welfare.

10.6 Juvenile offenders

Section 290 of the Criminal Procedure Act makes provision for different methods of dealing with juvenile offenders. This section provides that, in the case of an offender under the age of 21 years old, the court may, instead of imposing any punishment upon him for that offence, order:

(1) that he be placed under the supervision of a probation or correctional officer; or

(2) that he be sent to a reformatory—s 290(1).

If the young offender is younger than 18 years old, he may also be placed in the custody of another suitable person. The Act also allows the court to issue an order in terms of s 290 if it sentences the juvenile offender to a fine—s 290(2). No other combination of sentences is possible. Because a section 290-sentence is imposed 'instead of imposing any punishment', it has been held that it may be imposed instead of a prescribed minimum sentence as well—*Hattingh* 1978 (2) SA 826 (A).

Being sent to a reformatory (or reform school) is a severe punishment which resembles imprisonment. It should not be imposed without first obtaining a probation report on the offender and, generally, also not if the offender is a first offender, or have not committed a serious crime—*M* 1998 (1) SACR 384 (C).

A court which makes an order in terms of this section may order that the person who is to be sent to a reform school be detained in a place of safety until such time as the order of the court can be put into effect—s 290(4).

10.7 Caution and discharge

Subject to the same exceptions as are discussed below in para 11.2, a court may discharge any offender with a mere caution—s 297(1)*(c)*. This is the lightest sentence which the law permits—cf *Magidson* 1984 (3) SA 825 (T). Although the discharge has the effect of an acquittal, the conviction is still recorded and counts as a previous conviction.

11   SUSPENDED AND POSTPONED SENTENCES

11.1   General

Sentences are frequently *suspended*, which means they are imposed in full but, subject to certain conditions, not executed. A sentence that is wholly suspended is not executed unless the conditions for its suspension have been broken by the offender. Sentences can also be partly suspended. In such cases the unsuspended part is executed, but the suspended part not, unless the conditions are not complied with.

Courts are generally also empowered to *postpone* the imposition of sentence. This may be done conditionally or without any conditions. In such a case the offender is released, but may be ordered to appear before the court at some later date.

The whole statutory framework for these forms of punishment is contained in s 297, which is criticised by Hiemstra 732 for the mass of words the reader has to wade through before getting to the main purpose of the particular provision.

11.2   Exclusionary provisions

Any court may, according to s 297, postpone sentencing or suspend any sentence, for any offence *except* an offence for which a *minimum penalty* is prescribed—see par 5.3 above. In these cases the sentences may *only* be *partly* suspended—s 297(4).

11.3   Postponement of passing of sentence

The court may postpone the passing of sentence for a period not exceeding five years and release the offender unconditionally, or on one or more conditions (which are discussed in para 11.5 below). The offender may then be ordered to appear before the court if called upon before the expiry of the relevant period. If the offender is not called to appear before the court, or if the court finds that the conditions have been met, no sentence is imposed and for record purposes the result of the trial is a caution.

11.4   Suspension of sentence

All imposed sentences may be suspended, although it is mostly done with imprisonment and sometimes also with fines. The suspension of most other forms of sentence (except perhaps correctional supervision) will hardly ever make any sense.

Suspended sentences have two main functions:

(1)   to serve as alternative to imprisonment in situations where the offender cannot afford a fine and where other forms of punishment are improper, mainly because the offence was not particularly serious; and

(2)   to serve as individual deterrent to the offender as it hangs like a sword over his head—cf *Allart* 1984 (2) SA 731 (T).

The maximum term for which a sentence may be suspended is five years. In the Free State exceptional circumstances are required before the maximum of five years is employed (cf *Nabote* 1978 (1) SA 648 (O)), but this is not required in the other divisions—cf *Cobothi* 1978 (2) SA 749 (N); *Van Rensburg* 1978 (4) SA 481 (T).

The Free State point of view gives the impression that it is unreasonable to expect of people not to commit crime, which is why this view cannot be supported.

Where part of a sentence of imprisonment has been suspended, the period of suspension runs from the date on which the person is released from prison after serving the unsuspended portion, and not from the date of imposition of the sentence—*Ex parte Minister of Justice: In re Duze* 1945 AD 112. The result is that the prisoner is not under threat of the suspended portion of the sentence, a situation which has on occasion been criticised—*Mbombo* 1984 (1) SA 390 (D).

A suspended sentence is inextricably linked to its conditions of suspension. Without conditions it would not be a legally enforceable form of sentencing.

11.5 The conditions

When considering the conditions of suspension it is useful to distinguish between *negative* and *positive* conditions (even though our courts do not use this distinction, but see Hiemstra 732). *Negative* conditions are the most common conditions and require of the offender not to repeat the crimes specified. *Positive* conditions require positive action by the offender in order to fulfil the conditions of suspension. When positive conditions are imposed, they are usually combined with a negative condition as well.

Any condition of suspension has to conform to three basic requirements:

(1) It must be *related to the committed offence*. This relationship must be clear—cf *Tshaki* 1985 (3) SA 373 (O). This requirement is aimed mainly at negative conditions, so that a sentence for assault is, for example, not suspended on condition that the accused does not commit theft. It may not always be possible to link a positive condition to the kind of offence, as would be the case if community service were imposed for a theft (see Hiemstra 739).

(2) It must be stated *clearly and unambiguously*, so that the offender will know exactly what is expected of him—cf *Xhaba* 1971 (1) SA 232 (T). It is undoubtedly more clear to specify the crimes which an accused should not repeat rather than to use phrases such as 'crimes of which force is an element' or 'crimes of which dishonesty is an element'—cf *Mjware* 1990 (1) SACR 388 (N) and *Goeieman* 1992 (1) SACR 296 (NC).

(3) The conditions must be *reasonable*—cf *Gaika* 1971 (1) SA 231 (C). It should not be worded in such a way that a petty offence may trigger a severe suspended sentence. In several reported cases the accused was convicted of dealing in dagga and sentenced to a (partly) suspended term of imprisonment on condition that (*inter alia*) the accused was not found guilty of the possession of dagga. One can hardly argue that these two offences are not sufficiently related, but possession of a minute amount of dagga would normally breach the conditions upon which the (usually) severe sentence for dealing in dagga was suspended. For this reason it has become customary to include an extra condition for the latter offence, such as 'for which imprisonment, without the option of a fine, of more than four months is imposed'—cf *Adams* 1986 (3) SA 733 (C); *Herold* 1992 (2) SACR 195 (W).

Examples of positive conditions include compensation, community service, correctional supervision, submission to instruction or treatment, the attendance of courses or treatment at specified centres, etc.

Community service consists of any service rendered without remuneration, which is to the benefit of the community—s 297(1)*(a)*(i)*(cc)*. It is in actual fact a different form of punishment which is imposed under the guise of a condition of suspension. It is a form of punishment with many advantages (cf *Mogora* 1990 (2) SACR 9 (T) at 17C–F): it is not restricted to less serious offences, but can be imposed for serious offences where appropriate—cf *Van Vuuren* 1992 (1) SACR 127 (A). However, community service is not normally appropriate for recidivists or offenders who are suffering from some form of personality disturbance—*Abrahams* 1990 (1) SACR 172 (C).

Compensation may also be brought about by suspending an imposed sentence on condition that the victim is compensated. This approach was promoted in *Charlie* 1976 (2) SA 596 (A) and *Edward* 1978 (1) SA 317 (NC).

11.6 Breaching the conditions

Elaborate provision has been made for the procedure to be followed if any condition is breached. When a court has to consider whether a suspended sentence should be put into operation, the *audi alteram partem* rule is applied and the offender must be given the opportunity to lead evidence and to make representations—cf *Zondi* 1974 (3) SA 391 (N). If it is found that the offender did not comply with his conditions, the court may put the suspended sentence into operation, or may suspend it further on appropriate conditions. This decision is not subject to appeal, but as it amounts to an exercise of a discretion, it has to be done in a judicial manner, and is subject to review—*Callaghan v Klackers NO* 1975 (2) SA 258 (E).

12 COMPENSATION AND RESTITUTION

12.1 Compensation

The Criminal Procedure Act makes provision for compensation to the victims of crime in various ways. One of these procedures is contained in s 300. It provides that any convicted person who has caused damage to or loss of property of another person through his crime may, in certain circumstances, be ordered to compensate the victim. Such an order then has the effect of a civil judgment. For this purpose the court should shed its criminal approach and function completely as a civil court. The amount of compensation which may be ordered in the High Court is unlimited, but in the case of the regional and magistrates' courts it is presently limited to amounts of R300 000 and R60 000 respectively. These amounts are determined by the Minister of Justice by way of notices in the *Government Gazette*.

A court may act in terms of s 300 only when requested to do so by the injured party (cf *Dhlamini* 1967 (4) SA 679 (N) at 679G) or the prosecutor acting on the intructions of the injured person (there must be proof of this authorisation—cf *Vanmali* 1975 (1) SA 17 (N)). What follows thereafter is a separate enquiry into the amount of damages, which is civil in nature. The court should explain to the parties (including the victim—cf *Makhae* 1974 (1) SA 578 (O)) what is taking place and must afford them the opportunity to lead evidence and to present argument. The usual calculation of the amount of damages applies as in civil claims. Evidence already led at the criminal trial is also taken into consideration—cf *Maelane* 1978 (3) SA 528 (T).

The compensation order may be given only in respect of direct loss or damage—cf *Mokwaka* 1969 (2) SA 484 (O). In *Du Plessis* 1969 (1) SA 72 (N), the court intimated that motor collision cases would be inappropriate for an award in terms of s 300 where this would necessitate a lengthy enquiry into contributory negligence. An order to pay compensation is also clearly inappropriate where the accused is sent to prison for a substantial period of time and he has no assets—*Baloyi* 1981 (2) SA 227 (T).

A person in whose favour an award has been made may, within 60 days, renounce the award and, where applicable, make a repayment. If such renunciation is not done, the accused may not later be held liable in civil proceedings in respect of the injury for which the award was made—s 300(5).

Since an order for compensation in terms of s 300 has the effect of a civil judgment, a sentence of imprisonment in default of payment cannot be imposed in the alternative—cf *Msiza* 1979 (4) SA 473 (T).

12.2 Restitution

Section 301 provides that the court may order, at the request of a *bona fide* buyer, that he (the buyer) be compensated out of money taken from the convicted thief when the latter was arrested, provided of course that the buyer returns the goods to the owner thereof.

PHASE FOUR: POST-VERDICT AND POST-SENTENCE REMEDIES

CHAPTER 20

Review

		Page
1	INTRODUCTION	292
1.1	Right to review and review in general	292
	1.1.1 Review: a constitutional right	292
	1.1.2 When will review proceedings be more appropriate than appeal proceedings?	293
	1.1.3 Categories of review procedures	293
1.2	Judicial review in terms of the Constitution	295
	1.2.1 The origin, nature and extent of judicial review	295
	1.2.2 Limitation of constitutional rights and the approach thereto	296
	1.2.3 *Locus standi* and remedies in constitutional matters	297
	1.2.4 Access to competent courts relating to constitutional matters	298
2	THE DIFFERENCE BETWEEN APPEAL AND REVIEW PROCEDURES	299
3	REVIEW IN TERMS OF THE CRIMINAL PROCEDURE ACT	300
3.1	Automatic review	300
	3.1.1 General	300
	3.1.2 Magistrate's court sentences subject to automatic review	301
	3.1.3 Procedure on review	303
	3.1.4 Automatic review and the right to appeal	304
3.2	Extraordinary review	304
3.3	Review of proceedings before sentence	305
3.4	Set down of case for argument	305
3.5	Review in person and the constitutional invalidity of review by virtue of a judge's certificate	306
	3.5.1 The position before *Ntuli*	306
	3.5.2 The position after *Ntuli*	306
4	REVIEW IN TERMS OF THE SUPREME COURT ACT	307
4.1	Review at the instance of the accused	307
	4.1.1 General	307
	4.1.2 Grounds for review	308

    4.1.3 Procedure   308

  4.2   Review at the instance of the prosecution   309

5 FUNCTIONS AND POWERS OF A COURT OF REVIEW   309

  5.1   General   309

  5.2   Powers of court in terms of s 304   310

  5.3   Powers of court in terms of s 312   311

  5.4   The High Court's inherent review jurisdiction   312

  5.5   Judicial review powers and the Constitution   312

        5.5.1 Powers concerning the constitutional validity of the law . . .   312

        5.5.2 Exclusion of unconstitutionally obtained evidence   312

6 EXECUTION OF THE SENTENCE PENDING REVIEW   313

7 RETRIAL WHERE CONVICTION IS SET ASIDE   313

8 DECLARATORY ORDER   314

The Constitution and this chapter:

Section 8—Application of rights

(1) The Bill of Rights applies to all law, and binds the legislature, the executive, the judiciary and all organs of state.

(2) A provision of the Bill of Rights binds a natural or a juristic person if, and to the extent that, it is applicable, taking into account the nature of the right and the nature of any duty imposed by the right.

(3) When applying a provision of the Bill of Rights to a natural or juristic person in terms of subsection (2), a court—

  (a) in order to give effect to a right in the Bill, must apply, or if necessary develop, the common law to the extent that legislation does not give effect to that right; and

  (b) may develop rules of the common law to limit the right, provided that the limitation is in accordance with section 36(1).

(4) A juristic person is entitled to the rights in the Bill of Rights to the extent required by the nature of the rights and the nature of that juristic person.

See 1.2, below.

Section 9—Equality

(1) Everyone is equal before the law and has the right to equal protection and benefit of the law.

See 1.2 and 3.5, below.

Section 35—Arrested, detained and accused persons

(3) Every accused person has a right to a fair trial, which includes the right—

  . . .

  (o) of appeal to, or review by, a higher court.

  . . .

(5) Evidence obtained in a manner that violates any right in the Bill of Rights must be excluded if the admission of that evidence would render the trial unfair or otherwise be detrimental to the administration of justice.

See 1.1 and 5.5, below.

Section 36—Limitation of rights

(1) The rights in the Bill of Rights may be limited only in terms of law of general application to the extent that the limitation is reasonable and justifiable in an open and democratic society based on human dignity, equality and freedom, taking into account all relevant factors, including—

   (a) the nature of the right;

   (b) the importance of the purpose of the limitation;

   (c) the nature and extent of the limitation;

   (d) the relation between the limitation and its purpose; and

   (e) less restrictive means to achieve the purpose.

(2) Except as provided in subsection (1) or in any other provision of the Constitution, no law may limit any right entrenched in the Bill of Rights.

See 1.2, below.

Section 38—Enforcement of rights

Anyone listed in this section has the right to approach a competent court, alleging that a right in the Bill of Rights has been infringed or threatened, and the court may grant appropriate relief, including a declaration of rights. The persons who may approach a court are—

(a) anyone acting in their own interest;

(b) anyone acting on behalf of another person who cannot act in their own name;

(c) anyone acting as a member of, or in the interest of, a group or class of persons;

(d) anyone acting in the public interest; and

(e) an association acting in the interest of its members.

See 1.2, below.

Section 172—Powers of courts in constitutional matters

(1) When deciding a constitutional matter within its power, a court—

   (a) must declare that any law or conduct that is inconsistent with the Constitution is invalid to the extent of its inconsistency; and

   (b) may make any order that is just and equitable, including—

      (i) an order limiting the retrospective effect of the declaration of invalidity; and

      (ii) an order suspending the declaration of invalidity for any period and on any conditions, to allow the competent authority to correct the defect.

(2) *(a)* The Supreme Court of Appeal, a High Court or a court of similar status may make an order concerning the constitutional validity of an Act of Parliament, a provincial Act or any conduct of the President, but an order of constitutional invalidity has no force unless it is confirmed by the Constitutional Court.

   (b) A court which makes an order of constitutional invalidity may grant a temporary interdict or other temporary relief to a party, or may adjourn the proceedings, pending a decision of the Constitutional Court on the validity of that Act or conduct.

   (c) National legislation must provide for the referral of an order of constitutional invalidity to the Constitutional Court.

> *(d)* Any person or organ of state with a sufficient interest may appeal, or apply, directly to the Constitutional Court to confirm or vary an order of constitutional invalidity by a court in terms of this subsection.
>
> See 1.2 and 5.5, below.
>
> Section 173—Inherent power
>
> The Constitutional Court, Supreme Court of Appeal and High Courts have the inherent power to protect and regulate their own process, and to develop the common law, taking into account the interests of justice.
>
> See 1.1 and 5.4, below.

1   INTRODUCTION

1.1   The right to review and review in general

1.1.1   *Review: a constitutional right*

Section 25(3)*(h)* of the interim Constitution of the Republic of South Africa, Act 200 of 1993, entrenched every accused person's right to a fair trial, which included the right to have recourse, by way of appeal or review, to a higher court than the court of first instance. Section 35(3)*(o)* of the final Constitution of the Republic of South Africa, Act 108 of 1996, confirms this right. It guarantees, as a component of every accused person's right to a fair trial, the right of review or appeal by a court of higher instance. The omission of the words 'to have recourse' from s 35(3)*(o)* of the Constitution which appeared in s 25(3)*(h)* of the interim Constitution, brings no dramatic changes. It does, however, clarify that it is not the right of *recourse* that must be guaranteed and protected, so much as the right to a reappraisal of the proceedings by means of review or an appeal.

At first blush it does not seem as though the provisions of the interim and the final Constitutions have added to, or extended the ambit of the rights which an accused enjoyed under the previous constitutional and legal dispensation when those rights were not entrenched in a Bill of Rights as is the position now. It is, however, submitted that the entrenchment of the right to review or appeal to a court of higher instance, has strengthened the capacity of the courts to enforce standards of fairness and due process of law (see 'Procedural Rights' in Van Wyk *et al* (eds) *Rights and Constitutionalism: The new South African Legal Order* 1994 (Juta) 413). The courts are now empowered to intervene and set aside legal proceedings which do not conform to these standards. In *Ntuli* 1996 (1) BCLR 141 (CC) the Constitutional Court per Didcott J held that the concept of fairness is no longer restricted by the rules set by legal standards which were applicable before the Constitution came into force. At that time, fairness to the accused meant that the accused was '. . . not entitled to a trial which is fair when tested against abstract notions of fairness and justice' (per Nicholas AJA in *Rudman; Mthwana* 1992 (1) SA 343 (A) at 387 A–B). The main enquiry was whether a failure of justice had resulted. This was resolved by applying two alternative tests, namely, if the court would have convicted inevitably had there been no irregularity, then there was no failure of justice to vitiate the trial. On the other hand, if the irregularity was such a gross departure from established rules of procedure, that it could not be said that the accused had been properly tried, then a failure of justice resulted *per se* (see *Mtyuda* 1995 (5) BCLR 646 (E) and chp. 21, section 3.11). Sections 25(3) of the interim Constitution and 35(3) of the final Constitution removed the restriction on the meaning of the concept of fairness and enlarged the enquiry: fairness does not entail enquiring whether there was a failure of justice in that sense, but whether the trial was fair. The result is that criminal trials in the pre-trial and trial phase must now be conducted not only in compliance with previous standards or requirements, but also in conformity with these expanded notions of basic fairness and justice. The emphasis is now on whether there was a fair trial. Trials must be conducted according to acceptable standards. In *Zuma* 1995 (2) SA 652 (CC) at 651J–652A the Constitutional Court held that the right to a fair trial conferred by the Constitution '. . . embraces a concept of substantive fairness which is not to be equated with what might have passed muster in our criminal courts before the Constitution came into force'.

1.1.2 *When will review proceedings be more appropriate than appeal proceedings?*

An accused person who is dissatisfied with the outcome of his or her criminal trial in a lower court (ie a district or regional court), may bring the matter before a provincial division of the High Courts, or a local division of the High Courts having jurisdiction, either by way of an appeal or a review. In general, an accused seeking redress from a decision or order made by a court of first instance, in that she/he challenges the correctness of his or her conviction and/or sentence, should appeal against such conviction and/or sentence. However, where an irregularity in the criminal proceedings against the accused person is involved, such person should seek relief by way of review. In *Mwambazi* 1991 (2) SACR 149 (Nm,) the court explained when a specific procedure—appeal or review—would be apposite.

1.1.3 *Categories of review procedures*

There are various types of review procedure, but three distinct categories were pointed out in *Johannesburg Consolidated Investment Company v Johannesburg Town Council* 1903 TS 111. The first category deals with the type of review proceedings that are statutorily enacted by means of which the proceedings of inferior courts are brought before the High Court as a court of higher instance for a re-examination of irregularities or illegalities of the proceedings in the court *a quo*. These are the types contemplated by s 24 of the Supreme Court Act 59 of 1959, and various provisions (see below) of the Criminal Procedure Act 51 of 1977. In terms of s 19(1)*(a)*(ii) of the Supreme Court Act 59 of 1959 a provincial or local division having review jurisdiction may exercise powers of review with regard to lower court proceedings in respect of specified irregularities committed before or during lower court proceedings. Section 24(1) of the Supreme Court Act regulates the grounds on which review procedure may be instituted. These are:

(1) absence of jurisdiction by the court;

(2) interest in the cause, bias, malice or corruption by the presiding judicial officer;

(3) gross irregularity in the proceedings; and/or

(4) the admission of inadmissible or incompetent evidence, or the rejection of admissible or competent evidence.

The court hearing a review under this section is confined to the relevant provisions of the Act and beyond this it may not go. The procedure under the Supreme Court Act, contrary to that provided for by the Criminal Procedure Act, is strictly formal and also expensive (Hiemstra 764). An irregularity in the proceedings of a lower court that does not appear from the record of the proceedings may be brought under review supported by an affidavit setting out the grounds, facts and circumstances on which the applicant relies.

The Criminal Procedure Act provides for various ways in which the High Courts may review criminal proceedings in lower courts, and by whom such review procedure may be instituted. The following review procedures are provided for under this Act:

(1) automatic review in terms of s 302;

(2) extraordinary review in terms of s 304(4);

(3) review of proceedings before sentencing in terms of s 304A;

(4) set down of case for argument in terms of s 306.

The second category of review procedure is of common law origin and includes the High Courts' common law inherent jurisdiction to review, which power is acknowledged in s 173 of the Constitution. These courts are endowed with an inherent jurisdiction to review the proceedings of lower courts, administrative authorities or tribunals and to set aside or to correct errors in the proceedings if it appears to be in the interest of justice, or to test the validity of proceedings of such institutions in order to prevent injustices or miscarriages of justice. However, the courts's inherent power must be exercised sparingly and may not be used to correct mistakes made by any one of the parties, and certainly not in order to rectify a failure of the prosecution to lead important evidence (*Ntswayi* 1991 (2) SACR 397 (C)). (See *Siwela* 1981 (2) SA 56 (T) and *Mokoena* 1983 (2) SA 312 (O) for examples on the application of this power, and see also the discussion in the chapter on appeals paragraph 1.3 below. According to *Zungu* 1984 (1) SA 376 (N), the inherent review jurisdiction is included in the statutory provisions of ss 19(1)*(a)* and 19(3) of the Supreme Court Act 59 of 1959.) The Supreme Court of Appeal has no common law jurisdiction to review the proceedings of any superior court. This means that, unless an aggrieved party brings a matter before the Supreme Court of Appeal by way of appeal, that court has no jurisdiction. In criminal cases the Supreme Court of Appeal has no power to review any proceedings of superior courts which may not be brought before it by way of an appeal, an appeal by virtue of a special entry of an irregularity or illegality in the procedure, or an appeal by means of the reservation of a question of law.

The third category of judicial review has been referred to as that category which comprises reviews provided for by other legislation. The jurisdiction to review conferred upon a court or a judge thereof through such legislation, is a power of review which, according to the view expressed by Innes CJ in *Johannesburg Consolidated Investment Company v Johannesburg Town Council* 1903 TS 111 at 116, is 'far wider than the powers which it possesses under either of the review procedures [ie the categories above] to which I have alluded.' Consequently, although this was not held in the above case, with regard to the third category, the grounds of review must differ and cannot be the same in respect of both this category and the others. With the implementation of the interim Constitution on 27 April 1994, a power of judicial review had been conferred upon the High Courts or its judges (excluding the Appellate Division of the Supreme as it was called then) which could be brought under the umbrella of this third category mentioned by Innes CJ (as he then was), although that Court presumably did not have constitutional legislation in mind. In *Magano v District Magistrate, Johannesburg (2)* 1994 (2) SACR 307 (W) Van Blerk AJ held that a review by a superior court of a decision of a lower court which is alleged to be an infringement of a fundamental human right, is of a wide-ranging nature and of the type where the court could enter upon and decide the matter *de novo*.

1.2 Judicial review in terms of the Constitution

1.2.1 *The origin, nature and extent of judicial review*

The concept of judicial review within a constitutional legal system was first introduced by Judge John Marshall in the well-known American case of *Marbury v Madison* 5 U.S. (1 Cranch) 137 (1803), where the learned judge established the judicial power to set aside a statute or provision thereof, as unconstitutional.

With the introduction of the interim Constitution, South Africa was set on a democratic-constitutional course which is confirmed by the final 1996 Constitution (the 'Constitution'). In the same manner as the interim Constitution, the final Constitution ranks the Constitution and the rule of law as supreme authority and law of the country, and all other laws or conduct are subject to the Constitution. Any law (whether a statute of Parliament or a rule of the common or customary law), or conduct, inconsistent with the provisions of the Constitution shall be invalid to the extent of the inconsistency (ss 2, 8(1) and 172(1) of the Constitution). The Constitution binds all persons, legislative, executive and judicial organs of the state on all levels of government (ss 8(1) and (2) read with s 239 of the Constitution). (The interim Constitution did not apply horizontally *inter partes*. It appears from reading s 2 and s 8(2) that vertical application is now provided for. On the vertical and or horizontal application of the Constitution, see *Du Plessis v De Klerk* 1996 (3) SA 850 (CC), 1996 (5) BCLR 658 (CC) and Woolman and Davis 'The Last Laugh: *Du Plessis v De Klerk* Classical Liberation, Creole Liberalism and the Application of Fundamental Rights under the Interim and the Final Constitutions' 1996 *SAJHR* 361.) Declaring the Constitution the supreme law of the country, departed decisively from Westminster tradition based on the sovereignty of Parliament. The Constitution is now 'sovereign'. The supremacy of the Constitution implies, in broad terms, that when any norm or rule of statute or common law is in conflict with the Constitution, that law or rule ceases to be valid law and lacks binding force. However, such law does not lapse automatically, but will continue to exist until such time as it is declared unconstitutional (see item 2 of the transitional arrangements in Schedule 6 to the Constitution). As the cornerstone of democracy in South Africa, the Constitution guarantees the fundamental human rights entrenched in the Bill of Rights in chapter 2 thereof and demands that the state shall respect, protect, promote and fulfil the rights in the Bill of Rights, although these rights may be limited (s 7 of the Constitution).

The Constitutional Court, the High Courts of South Africa and the Supreme Court of Appeal are now entrusted with the responsibility of ensuring that the democratic ideals and the values of the new constitutional order in South Africa are enforced, and that the fundamental human rights set out in chapter 2 of the Constitution are protected, by virtue of their judicial review powers. The power of judicial review has been said to be a necessary part of a democratic system in order to protect individual rights against powers that may ignore, undermine, harm or infringe basic guarantees (see Davis D, Chaskalson M, De Waal J 'Democracy and Constitutionalism: The role of constitutional interpretation' in Van Wyk *et al* (eds) *Rights and Constitutionalism: The new South African Legal Order* 1994 (Juta) 1 ff for a discussion). These courts have the power to review actions by government and the conduct of persons, and to review the constitutional validity of legislation by Parliament—a power that had been denied all courts during the former system based on the sovereignty of parliament.

Contrary to the provisions of the interim Constitution which denied constitutional jurisdiction to the Supreme Court of Appeal, the final Constitution acknowledges the Supreme Court of Appeal as a separate constitutional entity, empowered with jurisdiction to decide the constitutional validity of any conduct or any law to the extent of the inconsistency of the law or conduct. However, if the invalidation concerns an Act of Parliament or a provincial Act, the order of constitutional invalidity made by any competent court must be confirmed by the Constitutional Court (s 172(2)*(a)* of the Constitution).

1.2.2 *Limitation of constitutional rights and the approach thereto*

No right, whether entrenched or not, can be absolute and unqualified. The rights of others and the needs of society may restrict these rights. Section 7(3) of the Constitution explicitly recognises this fact by providing that the rights in the Bill of Rights are subject to the limitations contained or referred to in s 36 or elsewhere in the Constitution. It is the task of the courts to lay down the meaning, content and extent to the said rights within the ambit of the limitation clause.

Section 36(1) prescribes the criteria determining any limitation of fundamental rights. When an infringement, denial or breach or threat of an entrenched right or freedom is alleged, a two-stage approach in determining its constitutional validity has to be followed. The first stage of the inquiry is to determine whether the right or freedom has been infringed or violated. This will lead to an investigation into the nature and scope of the particular right, bearing in mind that the court will have 'to promote the values which underlie an open and democratic society based on freedom and equality', as is required by section 39(1) of the Constitution. If the answer to the first question is in the affirmative, then the second stage is to decide to what extent such infringement or violation is reasonable and justified in terms of the limitation provisions (s 36 of the Constitution). The onus to prove the limitation, on a balance of probabilities, rests on the party alleging that the applicant's right is limited. This is the approach adopted in *Qozeleni v Minister of Law and Order* 1994 (2) SACR 340 (E) which was approved by the Constitutional Court in *Makwayane* 1995 (3) SA 391 (CC); *Zuma* 1995 (1) SACR 568 (CC); *Mbatha; Prinsloo* 1996 (2) SA 464 (CC). The party alleging a limitation of the right in question will argue that the contested conduct or law is nevertheless acceptable, because it can be justified as law of general application and that the basis of the limitation is reasonable and justifiable. The final determination will then hinge on the limitation clause and not on the provision which entrenched the right. Section 36(1) provides the mechanisms and guidelines for the courts having jurisdiction, to decide the constitutionality of a specific issue. Section 36 has to be applied in all instances concerning the infringement of a fundamental right or freedom. Note that s 35 of the Constitution sets out important additional limitation grounds, such as 'substantial injustice' (ss 35(2)*(c)* and 35(3)*(g)*), and if the 'interests of justice require otherwise' (s 35(1)*(f)* and 35(5))). If a right entrenched in the Bill of Rights is to be limited, it may only be limited by law of general application, if such limitation:

(1) is reasonable, and

(2) justifiable in an open and democratic society based on human dignity, equality and freedom, and

(3) all relevant factors are taken into consideration, including—

   (a) the nature of the right;

   (b) the importance of the purpose of the limitation;

   (c) the nature and extent of the limitation;

   (d) the relation between the limitation and its purpose; and*(e)*less restrictive means to achieve the purpose.

1.2.3 *Locus standi and remedies in constitutional matters*

(i) *The meaning of a 'constitutional matter' and related issues*

A constitutional matter includes any issue involving the interpretation, protection or enforcement of the Constitution.

   In *Friedman (2)* 1996 (1) SACR 196 (W) the court stated that a court retains the discretion to refuse to entertain a constitutional challenge before the accused pleads. Such discretion is only to be exercised in exceptional cases, after taking certain factors into consideration. The factors to be taken into account are (1) the prospects of success of the constitutional challenge; (2) the possible length of delay of the trial and (3) the possible prejudice to the accused, if the constitutional challenge is not decided immediately.

(ii) *Who has locus standi, what relief is sought and when?*

Section 38 of the Constitution provides that when an infringement of or a threat to any right entrenched in the Bill of Rights is alleged, any person mentioned below shall be entitled to apply to a competent court for appropriate relief, which may include a declaration of rights. (See 8 below for a discussion on a declaration of rights.) The relief available to an applicant includes an order of constitutional invalidity of a law; the suspension of such order for a period to allow for the rectification of the constitutional defect in a law; to adjourn the constitutional proceedings pending a decision of the Constitutional Court; the exclusion of unconstitutionally obtained evidence; a temporary interdict or other temporary relief. (In *Ferreira v Levin NO* 1995 (2) SA 813 (W), the court held that an application for temporary relief will only be granted if the applicant can show that the issue of the validity of the Act is urgent and serious.) When there is an infringement of, or threat to, a constitutionally entrenched right, the appropriate relief must be found in our common law and the statutes on a case by case basis. The court may develop the common law to the extent that legislation does not give effect to a fundamental right and, if necessary, develop rules of the common law to limit the right, provided that the limitation is in accordance with section 36—see s 8(3) of the Constitution.

In terms of s 38 of the Constitution competent courts (on constitutional matters in terms of s 172) are—

- the Constitutional Court as a court of final instance (and in certain circumstances, a court of first instance),
- the Supreme Court of Appeal,
- the provincial or local division of the High Courts, and
- lower courts, where the validity of legislation is not in issue

may in terms be approached for relief by any of the persons mentioned hereunder when an infringement of, or threat to, any right entrenched in Chapter 2 is alleged, namely

    (1)   a person acting in his/her own interest

    (2)   an association acting in the interests of its members

    (3)   a person acting on behalf of another person who is not in a position to seek such relief in his/her own name

    (4)   a person acting as a member of, or in the interest of, a group or class of persons

    (5)   a person acting in the public interest.

Any person or organ of state with a sufficient interest may apply by motion procedure or appeal directly to the Constitutional Court to confirm or vary an order of constitutional invalidity of an Act of Parliament or provincial Act by a competent court (s 172(2)*(d)* of the Constitution).

Juristic persons are entitled to the rights contained in the Bill of Rights where, and to the extent that, the nature of the rights permits. Therefore, as a 'person', a juristic person is entitled to seek relief in terms of the Constitution (cf s 8(4) of the Constitution).

In *Magano v District Magistrate, Johannesburg (2)* 1994 (2) SACR 307 (W) the court considered the question whether application of s 7(4)*(a)* of the interim Constitution (now s 38) should be restricted to recognised grounds of review enumerated in s 24(1) of the Supreme Court Act (see above) and whether such grounds are of a wide-ranging nature. The court held that s 7(4)*(a)* does not determine the nature of or the grounds for relief, but the circumstances when such relief may be sought, ie when a person's constitutional rights are disregarded or infringed. If s 7(4) were to be limited to those situations that arise as a result of the grounds enumerated in s 24, it would seriously hamper the courts' powers (in terms of the Constitution) to review proceedings in lower courts. Section 38, therefore, should not be restricted to the grounds mentioned in s 24(1), but should be interpreted to allow a person to obtain relief whenever there is an infringement of a fundamental right.

1.2.4 *Access to competent courts relating to constitutional matters*

Access to courts competent to hear constitutional matters, may be gained in the following ways:

(a) With regard to the Constitutional Court:

    (1) by means of an appeal from a court of a status higher than a lower court (s 172(2)*(d)*);

(2) by means of a referral by a provincial or local division of a High Court or any high court of appeal or by the Supreme Court of Appeal (s 172(2)*(b)* and *(c)*); or

(3) by means of direct access on application or on appeal from any court if the interest of justice requires it (s 167(6)*(a)* and *(b)*).

(b) With regard to the High Courts, access to provincial or local divisions for the purposes of deciding a constitutional issue is by means of review or appeal or on application for relief (s 169).

(c) The Supreme Court of Appeal may only be approached by means of an appeal, unless an issue was specifically referred to this court by legislation.

(d) Lower courts may only decide constitutional issues where the validity of any statutory legislation is not in issue (see chapter 21 par 1.2.2—applicable here, *mutatis mutandis*).

2 THE DIFFERENCE BETWEEN APPEAL AND REVIEW PROCEDURES

Although there is a difference between appeal and review procedure, both are inherently aimed at setting aside a conviction or sentence. Correct procedure should, however, be used. As mentioned above, an appeal is the correct way to challenge a conviction or sentence or both. An appeal is concerned with the substantive correctness of the decision based on the facts or merits of the case on the record and the law relevant to such facts. Should a party feel aggrieved about an irregularity involved in arriving at the conviction, the best procedure is to seek redress by way of review. A review is concerned with the validity of the proceedings. According to *Ellis v Morgan; Ellis v Dessai* 1909 TS 576 at 581, an irregularity in the proceedings

'does not mean an incorrect judgment; it refers not to the result, but to the methods of a trial, such as, for example, some high-handed or mistaken action which has prevented the aggrieved party from having his case fully and fairly determined'.

Not only irregularities that arise from high-handedness but also a bona fide mistake, denying the accused a fair trial, will amount to an irregularity in the proceedings. If a party wishes to attack the proceedings on one or more grounds of review and also the correctness of the magistrate's findings on the facts or the law—or both—he may appeal *and* apply for review—*Ellis* (above).

The difference between appeal and review procedure when constitutional issues are involved, is basically the following:

(1) An appeal may be brought against the findings of a lower court on any point of law and or fact. A review in terms of the Supreme Court Act, on the other hand, can be brought only on the ground of specific procedural irregularities (see below, under 'Grounds for review').

(2) In an appeal the parties are confined to what appears on the record, but in a review it is permissible to prove any of the grounds for review (including alleged irregularities that do not appear on the face of the record) by affidavit.

'Indeed, if the right to file affidavits did not exist, it would often be impossible to show that any irregularity had been committed; the legal and competent evidence, which had been rejected, would not appear on the record, nor is it likely that the proceedings would show that the judge had an interest in the cause or that he acted maliciously or corruptly'—Gardiner & Lansdown 748.

(3) Furthermore—

> 'While any question of law or fact, or any gross irregularity appearing on the face or the record, may be raised by means of an appeal, the accused who brings the matter before the court by way of review, is confined to the specific grounds for review. On review he will not be allowed to argue that the presiding officer went wrong on a point of law, unless the error affected one of the grounds for review (eg where the magistrate incorrectly decides that the law conferred jurisdiction upon him which he actually does not have). The applicant may not argue on review that the magistrate's decision is wrong on the facts—although a total absence of any evidence to justify the magistrate's finding, is such a gross irregularity as to afford a ground for review'— Gardiner & Lansdown 749; *Hlatswayo* 1947 (4) SA 755 (O) on a similar note.

(4) While an appeal must be brought within a certain time, there is no such limit in the case of a review. However, a court of review will not condone the bringing of the matter under review after an unreasonable period has elapsed since conviction—Gardiner & Lansdown 749. In the case of a long delay, the court will exercise its discretion to hear the review only if a satisfactory explanation for the delay is given—*Zwane v Magistrate, Maphumulo* 1980 (3) SA 976 (N).

(5) Appeal is tantamount to a retrial on the record, while in the case of a review, facts could be brought to the notice of the court by means of an affidavit in order to prove the irregularity and the enquiry is then whether the proceedings have been in accordance with justice and/or whether the accused has been prejudiced by the irregularities in the proceedings (however, see the constitutional implications of such an enquiry as discussed in chapter 21 par 3.11).

(6) A court has no inherent appellate jurisdiction and its powers on appeal are statutorily limited. It is therefore not possible to invoke the court's appellate powers by any other means other than as set out in the relevant statutory provisions. Only a superior court of first instance enjoys inherent review jurisdiction. The court's inherent review jurisdiction is an overriding jurisdiction and may be invoked irrespective of the procedure instituted. When considering an appeal or a statutory review, the court may resort to its inherent review jurisdiction.

(7) An appeal is lodged by way of a notice of appeal whereas a review is sought by way of a notice of motion whereby the respondents are called upon to show cause why the decision or proceedings should not be reviewed and corrected or set aside.

3 REVIEW IN TERMS OF THE CRIMINAL PROCEDURE ACT

3.1 Automatic review

3.1.1 *General*

The law of criminal procedure provides that certain sentences of magistrates' courts must be reviewed by the provincial or local division of the High Courts in the ordinary course of events, without the accused requesting it. Review of sentences as a matter of course is known in practice as 'automatic review'—the term that is favoured here. Automatic review is of South African origin and is a praiseworthy development, because it ensures that the High Court constantly controls the administration of justice in magistrates' courts (see (1962) 79 *SALJ* 267 *et seq*).

The process of automatic review is based on two fundamental principles namely judicial experience and the extent of the sentence. The premise is that the less judicial experience the presiding officer has, the more restricted his proficiency and skill will be, and the greater the danger of incorrect conduct and sentences. In district courts, experience in sentencing above a certain limit is restricted by the limited extent of cases adjudicated in such courts—*Mokubung; Lesibo* 1983 (2) SA 710 (O). Consequently, no provision is made in the Act for the automatic review of sentences imposed by superior courts, as is the case with sentences of regional courts. (A sentence of a fine or imprisonment imposed by a regional court in terms of s 108(1) of Act 32 of 1944 for contempt of court is an exception to the above rule—see s 108(2) of the Magistrates' Courts Act 32 of 1944 and cf—*Nxane* 1975 (4) SA 433 (O).)

Although automatic review procedure is termed 'review', the reviewing judge is not limited to the investigation of irregularities but may pay attention to all aspects that are subject to appeal. However, in an automatic review, the judge is confined to the record of the proceedings (Hiemstra 770).

3.1.2 *Magistrate's court sentences subject to automatic review*

The following sentences are subject to automatic review:

(1) Sentences of imprisonment (including detention in a reformatory and a rehabilitation centre—*Dalton* 1978 (3) SA 436 (O); *MacDonald* 1978 (4) SA 200 (T)) for a period exceeding three months if imposed by a judicial officer who has not held the substantive rank of magistrate or higher for seven years, or which exceeds a period of six months, if imposed by a judicial officer who has held the substantive rank of magistrate or higher for seven years or longer, are subject to automatic review—s 302(1)*(a)*(i). Section 302 does not apply in respect of any sentence of imprisonment (detention) imposed by a military court, which sentence is automatically reviewable by a Court of Military Appeals in terms of s 34 of the Military Discipline Supplementary Measures Act 16 of 1999. Note that the words 'has held the substantive rank' in the section, are wide enough to include a magistrate's previous term of office—*Botha* 1978 (4) SA 543 (T). (In *Heskwa* 1992 (2) SACR 95 (C) the desirability of the practice propounded in *Botha* (above) was questioned and the court suggested an amendment of s 302, providing that the seven-year period should have been served during the immediately preceding ten years.) However, the judicial officer should actually have served as *magistrate* for the required period and the fact that he has been regarded as a magistrate for the required period is irrelevant for the purposes of s 302(1)*(a)*(i), *Heskwa* (above).

Direct imprisonment and any suspended imprisonment, if imposed, must be added to determine the reviewability of the sentence. In the same manner a suspended period of imprisonment is subject to automatic review if it exceeds the prescribed period. Likewise, if a suspended sentence of imprisonment does not exceed the prescribed limit, the sentence is not subject to automatic review—*M* 1990 (2) SACR 217 (T).

(2) A sentence of a fine that exceeds the amount determined by the Minister from time to time by notice in the *Government Gazette* for the respective judicial officers referred to in subsection 302(1)*(a)*(i) above is subject to automatic

review—s 302(1)*(a)*(ii). From 1 May 1992 sentences that in the case of a fine exceed the amount of R2 500,00 if imposed by a judicial officer who has not held the substantive rank of magistrate or higher for seven years, or which exceed the amount of R5 000,00 if imposed by a judicial officer who has held the substantive rank of magistrate or higher for seven years or longer, are subject to automatic review—s 302(1)*(a)*(iii).

For the purpose of automatic review, it is irrelevant whether a fine is coupled with an alternative imprisonment whether suspended or not and whether the fine is paid or not—*Melani* 1991 (2) SACR 611 (NC); *Afrikaner* 1992 (2) SACR 408 (C). All sentences of fines above the prescribed limit and imposed by magistrates of district courts render the proceedings automatically reviewable and it is irrelevant whether the fine is paid or not.

In order to compute sentences that are appropriate for automatic review, each sentence on each separate count must be considered a separate sentence. The fact that the aggregate of the sentences imposed in respect of more than one count in the same proceedings or criminal trial exceeds the prescribed periods or amounts, does not render those sentences below the statutory prescribed limits, subject to automatic review—s 302(2).

A sentence is not subject to automatic review if the accused was assisted by a legal adviser—302(3). If the accused was assisted during the trial, but not at the time of sentence, either because the legal adviser had withdrawn or the accused had withdrawn the legal adviser's mandate, the proceedings are nevertheless subject to automatic review—*Mboyany* 1978 (2) SA 927 (T). It is submitted that where there is doubt or where the legal adviser is absent at *any stage during the trial* for such a period that his absence could have made a difference to the outcome of the trial, automatic review would be the proper course (but see Hiemstra 770 for a different viewpoint).

An automatic review is performed either by a court of review of the appropriate provincial or local division having jurisdiction, or in chambers by one of the judges thereof. An automatic review does not affect an accused's right of appeal against such a sentence, whether before or after confirmation thereof by the judge or court reviewing it. If an accused has appealed against a conviction or sentence and has not abandoned the appeal, the automatic review of a sentence is suspended and shall cease to apply concerning such an accused when judgment is given—s 302(1)*(b)*.

Not all orders of a lower court are automatically reviewable. When a person is convicted and it appears that the convicted person has not complied with a condition of suspension imposed as part of a sentence of a previous conviction, the putting into effect of such suspended sentence is an administrative decision and is not a 'sentence'. The High Courts may review it only by virtue of its common law power of review upon notice of motion—*Van Staden* 1975 (2) PH H103 (T). Similarly, an order made under s 77(6) (detention of an accused in a psychiatric hospital or a prison pending the signification of the decision of a judge in chambers) is not subject to automatic review—*Blaauw* 1980 (1) SA 536 (C). The proceedings in an inquest conducted before a magistrate in terms of the Inquests Act 58 of 1959 as amended, in order to investigate the cause of death of a deceased person, are not criminal proceedings and accordingly not reviewable in terms of the Criminal Procedure Act—*In re Mjoli* 1994 (1) SACR 336 (T).

3.1.3 *Procedure on review*

After a reviewable sentence has been passed, the clerk of the court must transmit the record to the registrar of the provincial or local division having jurisdiction, not later than one week after the determination of the case. There should be no delay in transmitting the record as any delay can seriously prejudice an accused—*Raphatle* 1995 (2) SACR 452 (T). The magistrate may append to the record such remarks as she considers desirable. The accused is entitled, within three days after conviction, to supply any written statement or argument in support of his/her case to the clerk of the court to be transmitted to the registrar with the record—s 303 and see also *Brunette* 1979 (2) SA 430 (T). As soon as possible, the registrar must submit all these papers to a judge in chambers for his consideration—s 303.

A judge who receives the documents in chambers must certify on the record that the proceedings are in order if in his opinion, the proceedings were in accordance with justice. ('Proceedings' comprise both the conviction and sentence and a court of review is accordingly empowered to review both conviction and sentence even though the case is referred for rectification of the sentence only—*Rothman* 1990 (1) SACR 170 (O).)

If the judge is uncertain whether the legal rules were complied with during the magistrate's court proceedings, he requests a statement from the magistrate who presided at the trial setting forth his reasons for convicting the accused and for the sentence imposed. Usually the director of public prosecutions will also be approached for his comments—cf s 304(1); Hiemstra 775. If the judge has no further doubts, he signs the certificate.

Magistrates ought not to regard a query directed by a judge as an unnecessary irritation, to be disposed of as quickly as possible. When a judge directs a query, it means that he/she is *prima facie* not satisfied that justice was done. The magistrate can, by furnishing proper reasons, contribute to the removal of the judge's initial doubt, and to the confirmation of the conviction and/or sentence—*Joale* 1998 (1) SACR 293 (O).

However, if the judge is still in doubt or is uncertain or it appears from the outset to the judge that the proceedings were not according to justice, two judges (sitting as a court of review) must consider the proceedings and deliver judgment—cf s 304(2)*(a)*; Hiemstra 775. Where the review of the proceedings is a matter of urgency, the court of review considers the proceedings without obtaining a statement from the magistrate. This would be the case where the judge is of the opinion that the proceedings were clearly not in accordance with justice and that delaying the review procedure may be to the accused's prejudice.

The test that a court of review applies in automatic review procedure is whether justice has been done. If it has, the sentence will be confirmed even though there were technical irregularities—*Addabba; Ngeme; Van Wyk* 1992 (2) SACR 325 (T). The confirmation of proceedings on review requires a finding only that the proceedings were in accordance with justice although not necessarily in accordance with law, for example the proceedings might be confirmed on review although a rule of criminal procedure was disregarded—*Ndlovu* 1998 (1) SACR 599 (W).

If the court of review desires to have any question of law or fact in the case argued, it may direct it to be argued by the director of public prosecutions and by such counsel as the court may appoint for the accused. The queries by the reviewing judge, the magistrate's reply and all other communication must be included in the case record—*Ntshingila* 1980 (3) SA 883 (N).

Lost record

It may sometimes happen that the record of a case is mislaid. In such an event, the court of review may order that the clerk of the court submits the best secondary evidence obtainable as to the nature of the original evidence and proceedings *(Van Sitters* 1962 (4) SA 296 (C)), or, that the case be sent back to the court to hear evidence in order to reconstruct the record—*Dlomo* 1969 (1) SA 104 (N). This also applies to an appeal. In *Biyana* 1997 (1) SACR 332 (T), the court held that in order to reconstruct a lost record, the recall of witnesses who had given evidence during the trial would be irregular. However, the clerk of the court may obtain affidavits from such witnesses, as well as from other persons concerned with the trial. However, if no record exists and the record cannot be reconstructed, the conviction and sentence must be set aside. The matter may not be referred back to the trial court for a *de novo* trial—*Fredericks* 1992 (1) SACR 561 (C).

3.1.4   *Automatic review and the right to appeal*

The provisions relating to automatic review are suspended in respect of an accused who has appealed against a conviction or sentence. If the accused person abandons his or her appeal, the sentence will nevertheless be reviewed. Once judgment has been given on appeal, no automatic review can take place—s 302(1)*(b)*.

If the proceedings have already been certified by a judge in terms of s 304(1), when the notice of appeal by the accused reaches the registrar, the certificate will be withdrawn to allow an accused to prosecute his or her appeal—cf *Disler* 1933 CPD 405. There is no inconsistency in criminal proceedings being set aside on appeal after they have been confirmed on review, since the test applied on review is different from the criteria applied on appeal. A judge is at liberty to withdraw his certificate if he discovers afterwards that he made a mistake or if admissible fresh evidence is discovered after the proceedings have been confirmed—*Madlelana* 1936 EDL 140. In *Makebe* 1967 (1) SA 464 (N), it was held that if, after a judge has confirmed a conviction and sentence on automatic review, it appears that justice demands that the sentence be altered, it is competent for the review court to deal with the matter, although the reviewing judge is no longer able to withdraw the certificate because he is no longer a judge. (Here the magistrate failed to impose a compensatory fine besides a term of imprisonment.)

3.2   Extraordinary review

Where it has been brought to the notice of a provincial or local division of the High Courts having jurisdiction or any judge thereof that the criminal proceedings in which the sentence was imposed, were not in accordance with justice, such court or judge shall have the same powers in respect of such proceedings as if the record of it has been laid before such court or judge according to the procedure on automatic review—s 304(4). These provisions will apply where the criminal proceedings are not subject to automatic review, either because they do not qualify in terms of the provisions of s 302 or the sentences have been imposed in a regional court—cf *Eli* 1978 (1) SA 451 (E). The provisions of this subsection enable the director of public prosecutions, a magistrate, or the accused to bring irregularities in the proceedings under review, by bringing it to the notice of a judge in chambers for him to act according to s 303 or s 304—cf *Hlope* 1962 (2) SA 607 (T). However, a matter that has been finally disposed of on appeal, may not be brought on review in terms of s 304(4)—*Mtombeni* 1946 TPD 401.

The question that the High Court must consider when a matter comes before it on review in terms of s 304(4), is whether there are considerations of equity and fair dealing that compel the court to intervene to prevent a probable failure of justice. Evidence to this effect should be placed before the court—*Cedras* 1992 (2) SACR 530 (C). See also *Addabba; Ngeme and Van Wyk* (above). Care must be taken to prevent s 304(4) being used as a cheap form of appeal—*Matsane* 1978 (3) SA 821 (T); *Ferreira* 1978 (4) SA 30 (T).

No time limit is set by s 304(4) and cases have been reviewed even after a lapse of four years since conviction—cf *Fouché* 1953 (3) SA 201 (C). In *Callaghan v Klackers* 1975 (2) SA 258 (E) the provincial division requested *mero motu* the record of a magistrate's decision that was delivered 18 months earlier, for the purposes of review.

3.3 Review of proceedings before sentence

If a magistrate or regional magistrate after conviction but before sentence is of opinion that the proceeding in which a conviction has been brought are not in accordance with justice or that doubt exists whether the proceedings are in accordance with justice, such magistrate or regional magistrate shall, without sentencing the accused, submit the record and the reasons for his opinion for review by a judge in chambers—s 304A. This applies irrespective of whether the conviction has been entered by himself or someone else—cf *Abrahams* 1991 (1) SACR 633 (O); *Hlongwane* 1990 (1) SACR 310 (NC). The judge shall have the same powers as if the matter has been placed before him in terms of s 303. Meanwhile the case is postponed, pending the outcome of the review proceedings.

Section 304A should not be applied so sparingly as to be a dead letter. It must, however, be applied only rarely where the continuation of the case would constitute a failure of justice, and real and substantial prejudice would be caused against the accused—*Makhubele* 1987 (2) SA 541 (T). If *a conviction* has not been entered, the provisions of s 304A are not available—*Burns* 1988 (3) SA 366 (C). In proper and rare cases the High Courts could by virtue of its inherent powers to restrain irregularities in lower courts, grant relief by way of review, interdict or *mandamus* against the decision of the magistrate in unterminated proceedings in a lower court. The possibility that grave injustice or failure of justice would result must be likely before the High Court would exercise its inherent power—*Van Niekerk v Van Rensburg* 1976 (2) SA 471 (T); Hiemstra 764. The court will not exercise its inherent review jurisdiction where its decision will be of academic interest only.

The introduction of s 304A brought an end to a series of conflicting decisions dealing with the problem whether a magistrate who doubts the correctness of a conviction, should first impose a sentence although he knows that it would be set aside on review.

3.4 Set down of case for argument

After an accused has been convicted, he/she may in terms of s 306 bring the magistrate's court proceedings under review by way of setting down for argument his/her case before a provincial or local division with jurisdiction. This type of review is restricted to those cases that are in any event automatically reviewable. However, it creates an alternative review procedure for those accused who are not content with the procedure provided for in s 303 namely the submission of a written statement or argument. However, the accused may not have his case set down after he has submitted a written statement or argument for consideration—*Simelane* 1958 (2) SA 302 (N); Hiemstra 781. In *Simelane* it was decided that the procedure set down in s 306 may only be used in the case of an alleged irregularity. The accused is naturally free to bring the matter under review on any of the grounds mentioned in s 24 of the Supreme Court Act 59 of 1959. The procedure created in s 306 is, however, much simpler than those in terms of Act 59 of 1959.

In terms of s 306(1) the accused enrols the case before the record of the proceedings has been transmitted to the provincial or local division for automatic review. Whenever a case is set down for consideration, the accused must notify the director of public prosecutions in writing of the date on and court before which the matter is set down for argument. Such notification must be given more than seven days before the argument and the accused must also state the grounds upon which the setting aside or the alteration of the sentence is to be sought.

3.5 Review in person and the constitutional invalidity of a review by virtue of a judge's certificate

3.5.1 *The position before Ntuli*

Before December 1996 no person convicted by a lower court of an offence and undergoing imprisonment for that, or any other offence, was entitled to prosecute in person any proceedings for review. A prisoner could not argue in person his or her case on review (or on appeal), unless a judge of the provincial or local division with jurisdiction had certified that reasonable grounds existed for such a review—s 305. This was done in order to avoid a flood of abortive reviews. A judge's certificate was a necessary prerequisite for a prisoner to conduct his case on review without the assistance of a legal representative. Through this requirement, the legislature devised a method to prevent prisoners from abusing the legal process in order to escape the walls of prison—cf *Muniohambo* 1983 (4) SA 791 (SWA). Prisoners assisted by legal counsel and other sentenced persons were not subject to these restrictions, and had an automatic right of appeal or review which led to an unequal treatment between this and other classes of sentenced persons.

The judge could have granted his certificate though the proceedings have been confirmed on review—*Muniohambo* (above). Since the nature of an appeal differs from that of review, the prisoner was expected to indicate clearly whether she/he required the certificate in order to bring the matter under review or on appeal. (Du Toit *et al* 30–14.)

3.5.2 *The position after Ntuli*

The constitutional validity of s 309(4)*(a)* was referred to the Constitutional Court in *Ntuli* 1996 (1) SACR 94 (CC). The Constitutional Court was required to decide whether this section violated s 25(3)*(h)*(which provided for a right of review or appeal to a court of higher instance) and s 8 (the equality clause) of the interim Constitution (currently sections 35(3)*(o)* and 9, respectively, of the 1996

Constitution). Although the court dealt primarily with the provisions of s 309(4)*(a)*, it is submitted that the judgment must inevitably apply to a review by virtue of s 305. The Constitutional Court held that the provision which required prisoners to obtain a judge's certificate, is inconsistent with the constitutional rights guaranteed by the said sections and held s 309(4)*(a)* to be unconstitutional and invalid. Parliament was required to correct the said invalid provision before 30 April 1997, during which time the provision would remain in force pending the correction or the expiry of the period so specified.

The rationale for the court's decision may be restated as follows: Firstly, the requirement to obtain a judge's certificate prevents an applicant from the excercise of his constitutional right of having the opportunity to have recourse by way of an appeal or review, which right envisages, as a minimum, 'the opportunity for an adequate reappraisal of every case and an informed decision on it' (at 101*d–e*). Secondly, the requirement that a judge's certificate has to be obtained, differentiates between two groups of sentenced persons who want to prosecute a review or appeal. The first group consists of those in prison who have no legal counsel to act on their behalf. The second group consists of sentenced persons who are not incarcerated and those that are fortunate enough to have lawyers to represent them in their appeals or reviews. The opportunity to have recourse to relief by way of an appeal or review is denied only those in the first group and this group labours under the greatest disadvantage in the prosecution and management of their appeals and reviews. In addition, the inherent danger that worthy appeals and reviews are stifled by this process and never attract the judicial attention that they deserve, exposes the process of having to obtain a certificate as offending against the right to equal protection and benefit of the law.

The provisions of s 309(4)*(a)* (which includes s 305), remained in force until the specified date without being amended. Through government's failure to cure the defect in time, or to apply timeously for an extension of the order suspending the declaration of invalidity, the Constitutional Court refused to grant any further extension. (See *Minister of Justice v Ntuli* 1997 (2) SACR 19 (CC).)

Sections 309(4)*(a)* and 305 were repealed on 28 May 1999 in terms of the Criminal Procedure Amendment Act 76 of 1997. Although s 309 was amended to provide for leave to appeal, the same does not apply to reviews. Any sentenced prisoner may, therefore, without legal assistance, have his or her conviction by and or sentence of a lower court reviewed by a High Court.

4 REVIEW IN TERMS OF THE SUPREME COURT ACT

4.1 Review at the instance of the accused

4.1.1 *General*

Apart for the indirect manner by which a review may be brought to the High Courts in terms of ss 304(4), 305 and 306, the Criminal Procedure Act does not provide for a review of lower court proceedings at the instance of the accused. The power of the High Courts to review lower courts' proceedings is regulated by s 19(1)*(a)*(ii) of the Supreme Court Act 59 of 1959. The authority to review is vested in the provincial divisions and the Witwatersrand local division of the High Courts—s 19(2). The power to review lower courts' proceedings is, however, limited by statute to the grounds set out in s 24 of the said Act (see below). These grounds deal exclusively with irregularities of the proceedings and the procedure to be followed is formally embodied in rule 53 of the Uniform Rules of Court. (These rules regulate the conduct of the proceedings of the provincial and local divisions of the High Courts of South Africa and are here called the Supreme Court Rules.)

4.1.2 *Grounds for review*

The grounds in terms of s 24(1) of the Supreme Court Act upon which the proceedings in any lower court may be brought under review before a provincial or local division having jurisdiction are:

(1) absence of jurisdiction on the part of the court, for example where the offence is one that cannot be tried by the court, or where the court imposed a punishment beyond its jurisdiction, or where the offence was committed outside the court's territorial area of jurisdiction;

(2) interest in the cause, bias, malice or corruption by the presiding judicial officer. This ground deals with irregularities which are founded on a lack of good faith or ulterior motive on the part of the magistrate;

(3) gross irregularity in the proceedings; and

(4) the admission of inadmissible or incompetent evidence, or the rejection of admissible or competent evidence.

4.1.3 *Procedure*

A matter should be brought under review within a reasonable time which will depend in each case on the relevant circumstances. The onus of establishing an unreasonable delay is on the party alleging it. The court has a discretion to either condone the delay or refuse to entertain the application for review.

As a rule, review will not be granted in unterminated proceedings. It may, however, be granted where the interests of justice demand it and the High Court avails itself of its inherent power to correct the proceedings in a lower court at any stage thereof to prevent an injustice— *Lubisi* 1980 (1) SA 187 (T); *Malakwana* 1975 (3) SA 94 (O); *Shezi* 1984 (2) SA 577 (N). An accused may seek either a review or interdict or *mandamus* against the magistrate's decision in order to compel the magistrate to adopt the legal procedure.

The procedure to be followed for bringing criminal matters under review is by way of notice of motion directed and delivered to the presiding officer, magistrate and to all parties affected. The procedure is embodied in Rule 53 of the Supreme Court Rules. Rule 53 must also be followed in cases where the High Court's inherent power of review is sought. The applicant (accused or other party requesting a review) calls upon such persons—

(1) to show cause why the inferior court's decision or proceedings should not be reviewed, corrected or set aside, and

(2) to despatch, within 15 days after receipt of the notice of motion, to the registrar of the High Court, the record of such proceedings sought to be corrected or set aside, with such reasons as he is by law required or wants to give, and to notify the applicant that he has done so.

The notice of motion set out the decision or proceedings sought to be reviewed and must be supported by an affidavit setting out the facts on which the applicant relies. Within ten days the applicant may amend or vary the terms of the notice of motion by means of a fresh notice of motion with supporting affidavits. The respondent may oppose the granting of the order prayed in the notice of motion.

4.2 Review at the instance of the prosecution

Although there is no express provision in the Supreme Court Act or the Criminal Procedure Act regarding review at the instance of the prosecution, there is nothing in the Supreme Court Act or the Supreme Court Rules that confines a prayer for review to the accused to the exclusion of the prosecution. The provincial or local division of the High Courts with jurisdiction may review an alleged procedural irregularity at the instance of the prosecution. See for example *Attorney-General v Magistrate, Regional Division, Natal* 1967 (4) SA 680 (N) where the director of public prosecutions successfully brought an application for review of proceedings of a regional court which improperly converted a case into yet another preparatory examination although a preparatory examination had already been held and the matter had been forwarded by the director of public prosecutions for trial to the said court. See also *Monchanyana* 1968 (1) SA 56 (O). Although these cases are not clear on the specific manner of review procedure, these reviews probably fall within the type contemplated by s 19(1)*(a)*(ii) on any of the grounds referred to in s 24(1) of Act 59 of 1959. However, s 304(4) provides an easier mechanism for the prosecution to notify the High Court of irregular proceedings and to seek relief from such Court.

5 FUNCTIONS AND POWERS OF A COURT OF REVIEW

5.1 General

Upon automatic review, the function of the court is solely to decide whether the proceedings were in accord with the demands of justice. The evidence is not considered as carefully as upon appeal and the same weight is not attached to technical points—cf *Butler* 1947 (2) SA 935 (C). This is equally applicable to all kinds of review, since a review is concerned only with the question whether the proceedings are in accordance with the demands of justice—*Hlatswayo* 1947 (4) SA 755 (O). The interests of the convicted person and those of the State are considered—*Zulu* 1967 (4) SA 499 (T). Here, however, the court refused to exercise its discretion in favour of the State to correct an error that the magistrate had made when imposing the sentence, so that a more severe punishment would have to be imposed. In the circumstances, the court held that justice towards the convicted person outweighed justice to the State. See further 1975 *Annual Survey* 484–5; Hiemstra 775.

The question whether the proceedings were according to justice must, in general, be decided according to circumstances which prevailed when the proceedings took place. It is only in exceptional circumstances that the court will take cognisance of circumstances that occurred after the completion of the proceedings and alter the sentence on this account—*Sithole* 1988 (4) SA 177 (T); *Marx* 1989 (1) SA 222 (A). A decision is right or wrong according to the facts in existence at the time it is given, not according to new circumstances subsequently coming into existence—*Verster* 1952 (2) SA 231 (A).

The functions and powers of a court on review as set out hereunder are applicable irrespective of the type or manner of review which is brought before the review court. The absence of specific provisions in the Supreme Court Act regarding that court's powers and functions, suggests that the provisions of s 304(2)*(b)* and *(c)* apply equally to reviews brought under the Supreme Court Act.

5.2 Powers of court in terms of s 304

The powers of the court of review in terms of ss 304(2)*(b)* and *(c)* and 304(3) are as follows:

(1) The court may confirm, alter or quash the conviction. In *Isaacs* 1970 (4) SA 397 (NC) at 399 the court observed (*obiter*) that where the sentence of a magistrate's court is confirmed upon review, this fact signifies only that there were no grounds for the High Court to interfere with that sentence. It is not to be regarded as a sentence that the High Court would necessarily have imposed in the first place, nor that such confirmed sentence establishes any criterion or norm.

(2) The court may confirm, reduce, alter or set aside the sentence or any order of the magistrate's court. Accordingly, the court of review has the power to correct a penalty imposed or the conditions of suspension of the sentence. In doing so the court cannot render either the penalty or the conditions of suspension more onerous where that sentence or order was a competent one—*Morris* 1992 (2) SACR 365 (C). A court of review has no jurisdiction to increase a sentence—*Haasbroek* 1969 (1) SA 356 (O). Only on appeal may sentences be increased. If the sentence imposed by the magistrate's court is unjustified, it must be substituted for the appropriate and legal one, although it would result in a heavier sentence than the sentence previously imposed by the magistrate—Hiemstra 716. Evidently the sentence so imposed may not be beyond the lower court's punitive jurisdiction—cf *Freedman* 1921 AD 603. The court of review may impose the proper sentence but would normally refer the matter back to the lower court for the imposition of a suitable sentence in the presence of the accused—*Zulu* 1967 (4) SA 499 (T). Where there is a possibility of the review court substituting another conviction for a more serious one with the effect that a heavier sentence than that imposed in the lower court might have to be imposed, the accused ought, in all fairness, to be given prior notice of the court's intention and counsel ought to be appointed to represent the accused—*Zulu* (*supra*) at 500; *Viljoen* 1989 (3) SA 965 (T). See also *Annual Survey* 484–5.

(3) If the accused was convicted on one of two or more alternative counts, the court may, when quashing the conviction, convict on an alternative count;.

(4) The court may set aside or correct the proceedings, or generally give such judgment or impose such sentence or make such order as the magistrate could or should have given, imposed or made. This provision provides the court of review with the jurisdiction to substitute a conviction for a more serious offence and to impose a suitable sentence—cf *E* 1953 (3) SA 314 (A); *Mokoena* 1984 (1) SA 267 (O); *E* 1979 (3) SA 973 (A) 977D; *Morgan* 1993 (2) SACR 134 (A); Hiemstra 777. Also in terms of this power the court may amend on review or appeal, the charge sheet to a conviction on another charge according to

the provisions of s 86 only if the proposed amended charge corresponds to the original charge and if the accused is not prejudiced by the amendment. The practical aspects in deciding whether prejudice will result, such as legal cost and the trauma involved in a retrial, must also be kept in mind—*Mahlangu* 1997 (1) SACR 338 (T).

(5) The court may remit the case to the magistrate's court with instructions to deal with any matter in such manner as the court may think fit.

(6) The court may make such order affecting the suspension of the execution of any sentence or admitting the person convicted to bail or, generally, affecting any matter or thing connected with such person or the proceedings about him as to the court seems calculated to promote the ends of justice.

(7) *Further evidence:* A court of review may at the sitting thereof hear any evidence and for that purposes summon any person to appear and to give evidence or to produce any document or other article—s 304(2)*(b)*. When further evidence is allowed, a trial cannot be completed and it is in the interests of justice that finality is reached in criminal cases. Therefore, further evidence would not readily be allowed except on good cause. The fresh evidence must be such as to shed new light on facts that existed at the trial in the court *a quo*—*Verster* 1952 (2) SA 231 (A). When an application for further evidence, by either the accused or the prosecution, is entertained, there are two requisites that the court has to consider: first, that the applicant produces reasonably sufficient reasons why such evidence was not led at the trial and, secondly, that the evidence sought to be adduced be of material interest in the case—*De Beer* 1949 (3) SA 740 (A); *Zackey* 1945 AD 505. The court will receive further evidence where such evidence is clearly relevant and the genuineness and reliability of the further evidence are not disputed by the other party—*Noemdoe* 1993 (1) SACR 264 (C). Generally the magistrate would be directed to take such further evidence, such a course is more convenient for the parties—cf *Brunette* 1979 (2) SA 430 (T). The circumstances of the case would dictate the decision of the court of review and the conviction and sentence may be set aside and referred for further evidence (*Schutte* 1926 TPD 172) or the conviction may be left standing and the magistrate directed to report to the court upon the fresh evidence, which is then considered with the evidence already on record—*Barlow* 1924 CPD 202. An example of a case in which the leading of further evidence was allowed is *Bernhardt* 1967 (3) SA 174 (T), where an undefended juvenile alleged that he was forced to plead guilty and the court accepted as a possibility, that the allegation was *prima facie* true.

(8) If the court desires to have a question of law or fact, arising in any case, argued, it may direct such question to be argued by the director of public prosecutions and by such counsel as the court may appoint—s 304(3).

5.3 Powers of court in terms of s 312

Apart from the powers of the court in terms of s 304(2), a conviction and sentence may be set aside on review (or on an appeal) on the ground that any provision of ss 112(1)*(b)* or 112(2) or 113 was not complied with—s 312. The case must be remitted to the court where the sentence was imposed and such court directed to either question the accused as is required by s 112(1)*(b)* or (2) or to correct the plea when it is clear that the trial court should have had doubts as envisaged by s 113— cf *Addabba; Ngeme; Van Wyk* 1992 (2) SACR 325 (T).

5.4 The High Court's inherent review jurisdiction

Although the courts are slow to interfere in unterminated criminal proceedings, the High Court's inherent power to restrain illegalities in lower courts could be exercised in exceptional cases—cf *Pitso v Additional Magistrate, Krugersdorp* 1976 (4) SA 553 (T) and *Lubisi* 1980 (1) SA 187 (T).

5.5 Powers of judicial review and the Constitution

5.5.1 *Powers concerning the constitutional validity of the law*

In terms of s 172 of the Constitution, a high court when deciding a constitutional matter within its power must declare that any law (whether statutory law, common law or customary law) or conduct (of a person or state organ) that is inconsistent with the Constitution is invalid to the extent of its inconsistency. It may make any order that is appropriate, just and equitable, including an order limiting the retrospective effect of the declaration of invalidity and an order suspending the declaration of invalidity for any period and on any conditions, to allow the competent authority to correct the defect. High Courts or courts of similar status may make orders concerning the constitutional validity of an Act of Parliament, a provincial Act or any conduct of the President, but any such orders of constitutional invalidity must be confirmed by the Constitutional Court. It is clear that the only issues that may be referred to the Constitutional Court without prior decision, are issues concerning the constitutional validity of Acts by Parliament or provincial Acts or the conduct of the President. See also the discussion in chapter 21 par 1.2.2.

5.5.2 *Exclusion of unconstitutionally obtained evidence*

The Constitution demands a fair trial for any accused person and the presiding officials are tasked with ensuring that trials are conducted fairly. Fairness is an issue which has to be decided upon the facts of each case, and the presiding official is the person best placed to take that decision—*Ferreira v Levin; Vryenhoek v Powell NO* 1996 (1) SA 984 (CC). Ultimately, if evidence is obtained in a manner that violates any right in the Bill of Rights, it must be excluded if the admission of that evidence would render the trial unfair or otherwise be detrimental to the administration of justice—s 35(5) of the Constitution. The court of review may, by virtue of its judicial powers of review, exclude such evidence if the presiding official has exercised his discretion in an irregular manner which affected the fairness of the trial. In *Key v Attorney-General, Cape of Good Hope Provincial Division* 1996 (6) BCLR 788 (CC), Kriegler J summarised the powers of exclusion in the following manner: 'At times, fairness might require that evidence unconstitutionally obtained be excluded. But there will also be times when fairness requires that evidence, albeit obtained unconstitutionally, nevertheless be admitted.' Compare also section 1.2, above on judicial review.

6 EXECUTION OF THE SENTENCE PENDING REVIEW

The execution of any sentence brought under review is not suspended pending the review, unless the magistrate (in his discretion) grants bail—s 307. The manner of review does not effect this provision at all.

7 RETRIAL WHERE CONVICTION IS SET ASIDE

Whenever conviction and sentence of a lower court are set aside on review on the ground—

(1) that the court that convicted the accused was not competent to do so; or

(2) that the charge sheet on which the accused was convicted was invalid or defective in any respect; or

(3) that there has been any technical irregularity or defect in the procedure,

proceedings in respect of the same offence to which the conviction and sentence referred may be instituted *de novo*. The new trial could be either on the original charge, suitably amended where necessary, or upon any other charge as if the accused had not been previously arraigned, tried and convicted. Such proceedings must then be instituted before some judicial officer other than the one who recorded the conviction and passed the sentence set aside on appeal or review—s 313, read also with s 324 (see also chapter 21 par 3.13)

Although proceedings are not lightly set aside because of irregularities of a formal nature, some irregularities are of such a serious nature that the courts will consider that the proceedings have not been in accordance with justice and fairness, will set aside the conviction. Where the irregularity is clearly a matter of substance and not a matter of form only and constitutes such a gross departure from established rules of procedure that the accused has not been properly tried, it is *per se* a failure of justice— *Raphatle* 1995 (2) SACR 452 (T). In this case, the failure of the court to explain to the accused his rights or to record the full detail of such explanation once given, was held to be a failure of justice. In *Mabuza* 1991 (1) SACR 636 (O) 638*e* it was held that public policy is an important consideration on the question of whether a presiding officer in his conduct as judicial officer has committed an irregularity and that the accused was thereby prejudiced to such an extent that a failure of justice has occurred. If there was such a failure of justice, the demands of justice and also of public policy will require that the proceedings are to be set aside. *In casu* the regional court magistrate questioned the accused in a fashion that was described by the High Court as severe cross-examination and *inquisitorial* in nature. Other instances of irregular proceedings that were considered not to be in accordance of justice are: those where the magistrate was clearly biased and indicated that he was satisfied of the guilt of the accused before the State had even closed its case (*Berkowitz v Pretoria Municipality* 1925 TPD 113); where A was charged with stock-theft, and B, awaiting trial on the same charge, was called as a witness for the state (*Thompson* 1911 EDL 98); where the then director of public prosecutions had remitted two accused separately, but the magistrate tried them together and the court was satisfied that one accused had been prejudiced— *Engelbrecht* 1923 CPD 586. Where a prosecutor in a trial later assumed the role of magistrate and sentenced the accused, a gross irregularity would clearly result (*Louw* 1981 (4) SA 939 (E)).

The provisions of s 313 must be read in conjunction with the principles involved in *autrefois acquit* and *autrefois convict*.

8 DECLARATORY ORDER

As mentioned above, criminal proceedings should not, unless in the case of grave injustice, be interrupted to take an illegal or irregular ruling of the magistrate on review. Legal rights or obligations can, however, be decided in the interim by means of a declaratory order. Section 19(1)*(a)*(iii) of the Supreme Court Act 59 of 1959 provides that, besides any powers or jurisdiction that may be vested in the provincial or local division of the Supreme court, it shall have power in its discretion and at the instance of any interested party to inquire into and decide any existing, future or contingent right or obligation despite the fact that such person cannot claim relief consequential upon the determination. Such interested parties could also be the accused or the prosecuting authority. A declaratory order can also be granted although there is no *existing* dispute between the parties concerned but the dispute must be still alive—*JT Publishing (Pty) Ltd v Minister of Safety and Security* 1996 (12) BCLR 1599 (CC). The courts however, will not deal with or pronounce upon abstract, hypothetical or academic points of law in proceedings for a declaratory order. The applicant must show that he has a tangible, real and justifiable interest in the determination of his or her rights and obligations.

Where an appeal or a review *might* not cover the rights or obligation in question on which clarity is required, a declaratory order may be requested—*Ex parte Attorney-General, Bophuthatswana* 1980 (3) SA 292 (B).

In *Attorney-General of Natal v Johnstone* 1946 AD 256, the court discussed the propriety of relief by means of a declaratory order. It is highly questionable whether relief by way of a declaratory order is appropriate in relation to a matter in which criminal proceedings have been instituted—*Sita v Olivier* 1967 (2) SA 442 (A). Where involved statutory provisions that could be interpreted in different ways are in question, and there is a resultant risk of repeated criminal proceedings against the applicant, the court may grant a declaratory order although the applicant's rights or obligations were in issue at a concluded criminal trial—*Johnstone* (above). In *Ex parte Prokureur-Generaal, Transvaal* 1978 (4) SA 15 (T) the then director of public prosecutions requested a declaratory order concerning his authority under s 75 to decide upon the court in which to prosecute an accused.

CHAPTER 21

Appeal

		Page
1	GENERAL	318
	1.1 Historical background	318
	1.2 Right of appeal	319
	1.2.1 General	319
	1.2.2 Access to the High Courts in respect of appeals against decisions and orders of lower courts and of constitutional issues	320
	1.2.3 Access to the Supreme Court of Appeal and the Full Courts in respect of appeals against decisions and orders of High Courts	323
	1.2.4 Access to the Constitutional Court	325
	1.2.4.1 General	325
	1.2.4.2 Ways of access to the Constitutional Court	326
	1.3 No appeal before conviction	329
	1.4 Appeal against sentence	330
	1.5 Appeal on the facts	332
	1.6 Difference between an appeal on facts and an appeal on a question of law	333
	1.7 Appearance of the appellant	333
	1.8 Withdrawal of appeal	334
	1.9 Publication of proceedings	335
	1.10 Inspection *in loco*	335
	1.11 Aspect first raised on appeal	335
	1.12 Record of the proceedings	336
2	APPEALS TO PROVINCIAL AND LOCAL DIVISIONS OF THE HIGH COURTS	337
	2.1 To which division?	337
	2.2 When may an accused appeal?	337
	2.3 Notice and prosecution of appeals	338
	2.4 Amendment of grounds of appeal	339
	2.5 Condonation of late noting or late prosecution of appeals	340

Omit — 1.1

Omit (1.7, 1.8, 1.9, 1.10, 1.11, 1.12)

Omit (2.3, 2.4)

Omit   →2.6   Prosecuting an appeal in person   341

        2.7   When may the prosecution appeal?   341

               2.7.1   Appeal against a bail decision   341

               2.7.2   Appeal restricted to a question of law   342

               2.7.3   Appeal against sentence   343

        2.8   Powers of court of appeal   344

Omit   2.9   Execution of sentence pending appeal   347

        2.10   Remission for new sentence   347

        2.11   Fresh trial   347

3   APPEALS TO THE FULL COURT AND THE SUPREME COURT
     OF APPEAL   348

        3.1   Jurisdiction and constitution of: 348

               3.1.1   The Supreme Court of Appeal   348

               3.1.2   The Full Court   348

        3.2   Right of appeal to the Supreme Court of Appeal   350

        3.3   Appeals to the Supreme Court of Appeal in cases that originated in
               a lower court   351

        3.4   Application for leave to appeal   353

               3.4.1   By whom, when and against what may an application for
                       leave to appeal be made?   353

               3.4.2   To whom must the application be made?   354

               3.4.3   Grounds of appeal   354

               3.4.4   When leave to appeal should be granted   355

               3.4.5   If leave to appeal is refused   355

        3.5   Application for condonation   356

        3.6   Application for leave to lead further evidence   357

        3.7   Appeal on special entry of irregularity or illegality   358

        3.8   Reservation of questions of law   360

        3.9   Appeal by the prosecution to the Supreme Court of Appeal   361

               3.9.1   Appeal against decisions by a High Court on bail   361

               3.9.2   Appeal limited to a question of law   362

               3.9.3   Appeal against sentence by a High Court   363

Omit   →3.10   Powers of the Supreme Court of Appeal   363
partly
        3.11   Statutory limitations on the powers of the Supreme Court of Appeal   367

               3.11.1 Setting aside or alteration of conviction on ground of
                       irregularity   367

               3.11.2 Inherent jurisdiction of the Supreme Court of Appeal   369

        3.12   Execution of sentence pending appeal   369

        3.13   Proceedings *de novo* when conviction is set aside on appeal   370

The Constitution and this chapter:

Section 34—Access to Courts

Everyone has the right to have any dispute that can be resolved by the application of law decided in a fair public hearing before a court or, where appropriate, another independent and impartial tribunal or forum.

See 1.2.2, below.

Section 35—Arrested, detained and accused persons

(3) Every accused person has a right to a fair trial, which includes the right—

. . .

(o) of appeal to, or review by, a higher court.

. . .

(5) Evidence obtained in a manner that violates any right in the Bill of Rights must be excluded if the admission of that evidence would render the trial unfair or otherwise be detrimental to the administration of justice.

See 1.2, below.

Section 36—Limitation of rights

(1) The rights in the Bill of Rights may be limited only in terms of law of general application to the extent that the limitation is reasonable and justifiable in an open and democratic society based on human dignity, equality and freedom, taking into account all relevant factors, including—

(a) the nature of the right;

(b) the importance of the purpose of the limitation;

(c) the nature and extent of the limitation;

(d) the relation between the limitation and its purpose; and

(e) less restrictive means to achieve the purpose.

(2) Except as provided in subsection (1) or in any other provision of the Constitution, no law may limit any right entrenched in the Bill of Rights.

See 1.2, below.

Section 38—Enforcement of rights

Anyone listed in this section has the right to approach a competent court, alleging that a right in the Bill of Rights has been infringed or threatened, and the court may grant appropriate relief, including a declaration of rights. The persons who may approach a court are—

(a) anyone acting in their own interest;

(b) anyone acting on behalf of another person who cannot act in their own name;

(c) anyone acting as a member of, or in the interest of, a group or class of persons;

(d) anyone acting in the public interest; and

(e). an association acting in the interest of its members.

See 1.2.4, below.

Section 170—Magistrates' courts and other courts

Magistrates' Courts and all other courts may decide any matter determined by an Act of Parliament, but a court of a status lower than a High Court may not enquire into or rule on the constitutionality of any legislation or any conduct of the President.

See 1.2.2, below.

Section 171—Court procedures

All courts function in terms of national legislation, and their rules and procedures must be provided for in terms of national legislation.

Section 172—Powers of courts in constitutional matters

(1) When deciding a constitutional matter within its power, a court—

    (a) must declare that any law or conduct that is inconsistent with the Constitution is invalid to the extent of its inconsistency; and

    (b) may make any order that is just and equitable, including—

        (i) an order limiting the retrospective effect of the declaration of invalidity; and

        (ii) an order suspending the declaration of invalidity for any period and on any conditions, to allow the competent authority to correct the defect.

(2) *(a)* The Supreme Court of Appeal, a High Court or a court of similar status may make an order concerning the constitutional validity of an Act of Parliament, a provincial Act or any conduct of the President, but an order of constitutional invalidity has no force unless it is confirmed by the Constitutional Court.

    (b) A court which makes an order of constitutional invalidity may grant a temporary interdict or other temporary relief to a party, or may adjourn the proceedings, pending a decision of the Constitutional Court on the validity of that Act or conduct.

    (c) National legislation must provide for the referral of an order of constitutional invalidity to the Constitutional Court.

    (d) Any person or organ of state with a sufficient interest may appeal, or apply, directly to the Constitutional Court to confirm or vary an order of constitutional invalidity by a court in terms of this subsection.

See 1.2.2–4, below.

1 GENERAL

1.1 Historical background

According to Roman-Dutch law, the general rule was that neither the prosecution nor a convicted person could appeal in criminal cases. This rule was regarded as so self-evident that when William of Orange referred an application for leave to appeal to the Supreme Court of Holland, the reply was that practically throughout the Christian world, the rule was that convicted persons could not appeal. If appeals were allowed, the reply naively continued, convicted criminals would only be enabled to commit further crimes while their appeals were pending! See *Grundlingh* 1955 (2) SA 269 (A). The harshness of this rule was somewhat alleviated by statute both in the Netherlands and at the Cape. In both countries, until after the second British occupation, the right to appeal in criminal cases was far more restricted than the right to appeal in civil cases. During the period 1652 to 1806, the *Raad van Justitie* was the court of appeal for lower courts. At the payment of an amount of 25 rixdollars (£1 7s 6d), the accused was allowed a right of rehearing (*re-auditie*), which rehearing was based on the record of the trial. Fresh evidence could not be adduced at the rehearing. No *re-auditie* was allowed where the accused had confessed or where the sentence did not exceed a prescribed minimum. In addition to rehearing, appeals lay from the College of Landdrost and Heemraden, to the Circuit Court (or the Court of Justice) to the High Court of Appeals as the highest court. The decision of the latter was final, but the governor retained the right to pardon an unsuccessful appellant. During the period 1910 to 1955, a further appeal was available to the Privy Council, with the leave of the Privy Council only. (Cf Dugard J *South African Criminal Law and Procedure Volume 1V Introduction to Criminal Procedure* Juta & Co (1970) 18ff.)

Until 1879 no appeal was allowed in criminal cases tried in superior courts, but afterwards appeals were allowed with leave and only to the extent provided for. A special entry was allowed to be made if the proceedings were irregular, as well as the reservation of any question of law for decision by the appeal court. Leave to appeal against the facts was not allowed.

Although no right of appeal initially existed, it was generally accepted later that any person who felt aggrieved by his or her conviction or sentence in an inferior court, had a right of appeal to a superior court, provided that the appeal was noted and prosecuted in accordance with the rules of the court. (Van Zyl *The Theory of Judicial Practice* (1923) 539ff.) Today the right of appeal against decisions of lower and High Courts is governed by statute and the Constitution (cf *Grundlingh* (above); *Sefatsa v Attorney-General, Transvaal* 1989 (1) SA 821 (A)).

1.2 Right of appeal

1.2.1 *General*

After the decision in *Minister of Justice v Ntuli* 1997 (2) SACR 19 (CC), all convicted persons (whether legally represented or in prison) had an unlimited or absolute right of appeal to a court of higher instance against a decision or order of a lower court. (Section 309(4)*(a)* and by implication also s 305 of the Act that prohibited a person who had been convicted by a lower court and was undergoing imprisonment, from prosecuting in person any appeal relating to such conviction unless a judge has certified that there were reasonable grounds for the appeal (the so-called 'judge's certificate'—see chap. 20 par 3.5), was declared invalid by the Constitutional Court on the score of its inconsistency with the 1993-Constitution—*Ntuli* 1996 (1) SA 1207 (CC); *Minister of Justice v Ntuli* 1997 (3) SA 772 (CC).) However, the position was drastically changed by ss 1 to 3 of the Criminal Procedure Amendment Act 76 of 1997 which came into operation on 28 May 1999, whereby the former unlimited right of appeal is amended in favour of a limited right of appeal. The amendment brings the procedure regarding appeals from lower courts' decisions in line with those noted against decisions made by High Courts, sitting either as courts of first instance or as courts of appeal. Such appeals are not as of right and leave to appeal has to be obtained (see s 315(4)). The reasons for the amendment to the Act are, according to the Department of Justice, that unlimited appeals will give rise to a backlog in hearing appeals by the already overburdened High Courts and place a too heavy burden on state funds which will eventually cause infringements of constitutional rights and weaken the judicial system. Whether these amendments will improve the criminal justice system is questionable in the light of the following: the skills, abilities and experience of magistrates especially in district courts are not comparable to that of judges (a fact which is substantiated by the necessity for the present system of automatic reviews) and the mandatory provisions of s 309D allowing the granting of legal aid or legal representation for the unrepresented convicted accused who wants to appeal against his or her conviction or sentence, will place a tremendous burden on state funds.

It is trite law that no right is absolute and restrictions are set by the rights of others and by the legitimate needs of society. In order to facilitate these claims, the Constitution provides for the limitation of rights through a general limitations clause in s 36, whereby constitutional rights may be limited by law of general application and on certain constitutionally recognised grounds. The justification for a limitation of a fundamental right must be established by the party relying therein and it is not for the party challenging it to show that it was unjustifiable (see *Zuma* 1995 (1) SACR 568 (CC)).

The criteria for an acceptable limitation of the rights entrenched in the Bill of Rights are measured against those enumerated in s 36 of the Constitution, namely, that they must be reasonable and justifiable in an open and democratic society based on human dignity, freedom and equality. In addition, certain factors mentioned in s 36(1)*(a)–(e)* must also be considered in any appraisal of the reasonableness and justifiability of the limitation. A competent court must apply these criteria when deciding any alleged infringement of an alleged constitutional right. In the same manner, the constitutional validity of a limited right of appeal must be assessed according to the said criteria. The right to an unlimited right of appeal was the subject of dispute in a number of cases adjudicated under the new constitutional dispensation.

The right to have recourse to a court of higher instance does not allow of the application of the principle of peremption to be extended to criminal cases. The principle of peremption means that the right of an unsuccessful litigant to appeal against an adverse judgment or order, is said to be perempted if he, by unequivocal conduct inconsistent with an intention to appeal, shows that he acquiesces in the judgment or order. It is fundamental to criminal procedure that a hearing will not be denied a person who can show a reasonable probability that he might have been wrongly convicted—*Marwane* 1981 (3) SA 588 (B).

Note that although every accused person, in terms of s 35(3)*(d)* of the Constitution, has a right to a fair trial, which includes the right to have his/her trial begin and conclude without unreasonable delay, such a delay does not necessarily call for a remedy. While undue delay in the hearing of criminal appeals, is obviously undesirable, particularly when an appellant is in custody, it does not follow that an undue delay constitutes an infringement of the constitutional right to a fair trial—*Pennington* 1997 (4) SA 1076 (CC).

1.2.2 *Access to the High Court in respect of appeals against decisions and orders of lower courts and of constitutional issues*

An accused who now wishes to appeal against a conviction or sentence or order made by a lower court must apply within 14 days or a longer period as extended on good cause shown, to the trial court for leave to appeal against the decision or order made by such lower court. The court must inform every accused who is unrepresented at the time of his or her convictions and sentence of the accused's right in respect of appeal, legal representation and the correct procedures to give effect to these rights—s 309D(1).

The application for leave to appeal must be heard by the trial magistrate whose decision or order is the subject of the prospective appeal or another magistrate if the former is unavailable—s 309B. Every application for leave to appeal must set forth clearly and specifically the grounds upon which the accused desires to appeal— s 309B(3). If the appeal is not noted and prosecuted within the period and manner prescribed by the Act and rule 67 of the Rules for Magistrates' Courts, condonation must be sought on application and on good cause shown, with the magistrate against whose decision or order the appeal is lodged—s 309(2)*(b)*. This provision amends the former position whereby condonation for the late filing and prosecution of an appeal had to be sought from the High Courts. The court in deciding on condonation, should assess the prospect of success on appeal. The accused should explain in an affidavit clearly and under oath why the appeal was not timeously noted—*Thobakgale* 1998 (1) SACR 703 (W).

Notice of the date set for the hearing of the application of leave to appeal must be given to the relevant director of public prosecutions and to the accused— s 309B(2)*(b)*. However, an accused may apply verbally for leave to appeal immediately after the passing of the decision or order, in which case he or she must state the grounds upon which the accused desires to appeal—s 309B(3). Such application must be taken down in writing to form part of the record.

Further evidence may be received by the court hearing the application for leave to appeal if the application for leave to appeal is accompanied by an affidavit stating that

(1) further evidence which would presumably be accepted as true, is available

(2) that if accepted the evidence could reasonably lead to a different decision or order, and

(3) save in exceptional cases, that there is a reasonable acceptable explanation for the failure to produce the evidence sought before the close of the trial— s 309B(4).

It is not in the interests of the administration of justice to allow further evidence on appeal when the only evidence sought to be adduced, is that contained in affidavits made by persons recanting their evidence at trial—*H* 1998 (1) SACR 260 (SCA).

If an application for leave to appeal, an application for an extension of the period referred to in s 309B(1) within which an appeal must be noted and prosecuted, an application to call further evidence on appeal or an application for condonation is refused, the accused person has 21 days within which to petition the judge president of the High Court having jurisdiction, against such refusal and submit any one or all of the applications mentioned, as the case may be—s 309C. The unrepresented accused whose application for leave to appeal is refused, must be informed by the presiding officer of his or her right concerning petition, legal representation and the correct procedures involved to give effect to these rights—s 309D(2). A petition is to be considered in chambers by two judges designated by the judge president or if the two judges differ in opinion, the petition must be considered by the judge president or by any other judge designated by the judge president. In considering the petition, the application may be refused or granted. If the application for condonation is granted, the judges may direct that an application for leave to appeal be made within the period set by them to the trial court.

If it is alleged in a lower court that a law is invalid because it is inconsistent with the provisions of the Constitution, the jurisdiction of the lower court to decide the issue should be determined with due regard to the provisions of s 170 of the Constitution. In terms of s 170, lower courts are not competent to decide the constitutional validity of *any statutory legislation*. In terms of ss 98(3) and 103(2) of the interim Constitution, lower courts were not competent to rule on the validity of 'any law or provision of such law', and had to decide the matter on the assumption that the law or provision was valid. The jurisdiction of lower courts to decide constitutional issues was not clear and conflicting judgments were given. In *Qozeleni v Minister of Law and Order* 1994 (3) SA 625 (E), it was held that these courts had jurisdiction to decide all constitutional issues, while in *Bate v Regional Magistrate, Randburg* 1996 (7) BCLR 974 (W) it was held that lower courts had no jurisdiction to decide any constitutional issues where an infringement of constitutional rights was alleged. (See also *Scholtz* 1996 (2) SACR 623 (C) where it was held that a magistrate's court was able to venture on constitutional territory otherwise reserved for the Constitutional or High Courts, when acting in terms of the Magistrates' Courts Act or the Criminal Procedure Act only.) Unfortunately, the final Constitution does not bring absolute clarity either.

A constitutional matter (which includes any issue involving the interpretation, protection or enforcement of the Constitution) that could arise in a lower court can be divided into five groups of issues. They are:

(1) where the constitutionality of legislation promulgated by parliament or by a province or the conduct of the President is disputed;

(2) where the constitutionality of municipal legislation is disputed;

(3) where the constitutionality of regulations other than those mentioned in (1) or (2) is disputed;

(4) where the constitutionality of legal rules is disputed;

(5) where the constitutionality of the conduct or activities of a person or organ of the state is challenged.

When the constitutionality of national, provincial or municipal legislation (mentioned in groups (1) and (2) above) is challenged, the lower court, in terms of s 170, does not have jurisdiction to decide the issue. If constitutional issues raised in the lower court fall within the jurisdiction of a High Court, the latter court must, in terms of s 172(1) of the Constitution, deal with it and give judgment, unless it involves the validity of an Act of parliament, a provincial Act or the conduct of the President. The High Court is now obliged to make a ruling, unlike previously under the interim Constitution, whereby it had the power to refer the validity of an issue falling within its jurisdiction to the Constitutional Court. The present position solves the numerous problems experienced during the period when the interim Constitution was in force, when a large number of Constitutional judgments arose on account of referrals of constitutional issues referred to the Constitutional Court by the High Courts without them first reaching a decision (see paragraph 1.2.4.1, below).

If the constitutional validity of an Act of Parliament, a provincial Act or conduct of the President is challenged, the High Court is not obliged to give a ruling and the issue may be referred to the Constitutional Court. If the High Court does make a ruling, any order of constitutional invalidity lacks force until it is confirmed by the

Constitutional Court. If the constitutional validity of a common law rule or the conduct of a person or organ of the state (ie the third, fourth and fifth groups mentioned above), is challenged in a lower court, it seems as though a lower court is competent, in terms of s 170, to decide its constitutionality. However, such interpretation in so far as common law rules are concerned, is somewhat ironic. Firstly, in that it grants the lower courts the jurisdiction to declare a common law offense unconstitutional and invalid should the court find that it unjustifiably infringes a constitutional right, yet the constitution denies the lower courts the jurisdiction to enquire into the constitutionality of municipal legislation. (In terms of s 117 of the Criminal Procedure Act 51 of 1977 and 110 of the Magistrates' Courts Act 32 of 1944 as amended, lower courts have jurisdiction to rule on the validity of municipal legislation, but these provisions are now clearly inconsistent with the Constitution and invalid in this respect.)

Secondly, as it is trite law that other courts are not bound by a lower court's judgment, an untenable situation of fragmentation and legal uncertainty will arise if an accused is charged with common law offence A in one magisterial district, but cannot be charged in another district with that same common law offence A, because the latter lower court declared it unconstitutional and invalid. It is inconceivable that the framers of the Constitution intended to confer this authority on lower courts.

1.2.3 *Access to the Supreme Court of Appeal and to the Full Courts in respect of appeals against decisions and orders of High Courts*

The law does not allow an absolute right of appeal against a decision or order of a provincial or local division of a High Court as a court of first instance. The Criminal Procedure Act provides that in the case of a matter heard by a High Court as a court of first instance, no appeal shall lie against the conviction, sentence or order thereto as a matter of course. Leave to appeal must be applied for in all instances—s 315(4) and cf s 316. In determining whether or not to allow an application for leave to appeal, the main consideration is whether or not the applicant has a reasonable prospect of success on appeal (see below, para 3.4.4).

When an appellant wants to appeal against the judgment or order of the provincial or local division having jurisdiction, given on appeal, leave to appeal has first to be obtained from the division against whose judgment or order it is appealed. Where such leave is refused, leave may be requested from the Supreme Court of Appeal— s 20(4) of the Supreme Court Act 59 of 1959. In terms of s 166*(c)* of the Constitution, a Full Court is also a provincial division of the High Courts, created specifically by an Act of parliament to hear appeals from High Courts. Leave to appeal against the judgment of this court, has to be requested directly from the Supreme Court of Appeal (see section 3.12 below, for a discussion).

Section 35(3) of the Constitution entrenches a general right to a fair trial and section 35(3)*(o)* guarantees a specific right to appeal to, or review by, a higher court. The provision reads that every accused person has a right to a fair trial, which includes the right 'of appeal to, or a review by, a higher Court'. There is no substantial difference between s 35(3)*(o)* of the Constitution and s 25(3)*(h)* of the interim Constitution even if the wording is not identical. Section 25(3)*(h)* provided that included in the right to a fair trial, was the right 'to have recourse by way of appeal or review to a higher court than the court of first instance'. The first question which arose after the interim Constitution Act 200 of 1993 came into effect, was whether in view of the provisions of s 25(3)*(h)*, an accused acquired an absolute right of appeal. Secondly, the question was investigated whether the accused's right to appeal or review, could be limited by the condition contained in the provisions of ss 315(2)*(a)* and 316(1) of the Criminal Procedure Act, namely:

(1)   that the accused has to be granted leave to appeal to the Supreme Court of Appeal or to the Full Court of the provincial division of a High Court before she/he may appeal (s 316), and

(2)   that in order to succeed with such an application for leave to appeal, the accused has to convince the court hearing the application that she/he has a reasonable prospect of success on appeal (see also par 3.4.4, below).

In *Nocuse* 1995 (1) SACR 510 (Tk) the court considered the second condition above and held that such a test meets all the requirements of a valid limitation enunciated in s 33 of the interim Constitution. The court decided that the right of appeal afforded an accused in terms of s 25(3)*(h)* of the interim Constitution must be construed as being a right of appeal only in those cases where there is a reasonable prospect of success on appeal. In *Van Schoor* 1995 (2) SACR 515 (E) it was submitted on behalf of the appellant (the accused) that s 25(3)*(h)* of the Constitution allows the accused an automatic right of appeal to a Full Court of a provincial or local division and that ss 315(2) and 316(1) have been repealed by necessary implication or, alternatively, that the said sections are unconstitutional to the extent that they infringe upon the accused's automatic right of appeal. The court did not decide the matter because it was of the opinion that the issue had to be argued before the appropriate Full Court and that whatever decision it might give would, in any event, have had no binding force on such Full Court. The court decided that the matter need not to be referred to the Constitutional Court. The court held that the High Court has a discretion in terms of s 102(1) of the Constitution whether or not to refer an issue to the Constitutional Court and that it would be pointless and contrary to the interest of justice to refer to the Constitutional Court the question of whether ss 315(2) and 316(1) are unconstitutional to the extent that they preclude an appeal, because the appellant has no reasonable prospect of success in an appeal.

In *Strowitzki* 1995 (1) SACR 414 (NmH) the argument by counsel for the defence that where an application deals with the fundamental rights of an individual, the courts should lean towards granting the individual an automatic right of appeal if, and when, his or her application for leave has failed, was rejected. The court held that, as a matter of practicality, there has to be a screening process for such appeals, otherwise the Appellate Courts will be inundated with futile appeals. However, in *Rens* 1996 (1) SACR 105 (CC) par 18–25 the constitutional questions came to a head, and the Constitutional Court held that ss 25(3)*(h)* and 102(11) should be construed in such a way as to harmonise with one another and that leave to appeal procedures must be consistent with the broad criterion of fairness demanded by s 25(3) of the Constitution. The court held that procedure prescribed by s 316(1) does not offend against the provisions of s 25(3)*(h)* although it requires the trial judge to pronounce on the prospects of success on appeal against his/her own judgment. The court found that the trial court is not required to say that his/her own judgment is wrong, but simply to decide whether another court may reasonably come to a different conclusion. The underlying purpose of these limiting requirements, is to protect the appeal courts—either the Supreme Court of Appeal or the Full Court of the provincial or local division—against the burden of dealing with appeals in which there are no prospects of success (see par 7 and par 20 of the judgment). The court also found that the procedure prescribed by s 316(1) is fair because it allows the accused a doubled opportunity of recourse to a higher court, namely either with the leave of the trial court, or with leave to appeal by the Chief Justice by way of petition. On the issue of whether a denial to persons tried in a higher court of an absolute right of appeal is discriminatory and in breach of the provisions of s 8 of the interim Constitution, the court found that the fact that appeals from the High Courts are treated differently from appeals from magistrates' courts, is due to the difference in the standing and functioning of the courts and that the purpose of the leave to appeal procedure, being the protection of the higher courts from having to deal with unmeritorious appeals, is legitimate and rational and not inconsistent with the provisions of s 8 of the Constitution.

1.2.4 *Access to the Constitutional Court*

1.2.4.1 General

The Constitutional Court is the highest court in all constitutional issues, and has the inherent power, in the interests of justice, to protect and provide for its own process and to develop the common law. This court also gives final judgment on whether an Act of parliament, a provincial Act or the conduct of the President is constitutionally valid, and as such, no order of unconstitutionality given by the Supreme Court of Appeal, the High Court or a court with similar status has any force unless it is confirmed by the Constitutional Court (s 167(5) of the Constitution). The jurisdiction of the Constitutional Court is dealt with in Chapter 2. See also *Pennington* 1997 (4) SA 1076 (CC).

The Constitutional Court may, in terms of ss 38 and 172 of the Constitution, be approached for relief by any person (which may include juristic persons—see s 8(4)), with sufficient interest in the matter to be admitted as a party, if any right entrenched in Chapter 2 of the Constitution is infringed or threatened. Those with *locus standi in iudico* are—

(1) anyone acting in their own interests;

(2) anyone acting on behalf of another person who cannot act in his own name;

(3) anyone acting as a member of, or in the interest of, a group or class of persons;

(4) anyone acting in the public interest;

(5) an association acting in the interests of its members;

(6) any party having an interest in an appeal or a matter where the right of direct access has been invoked or any other matter before the Constitutional Court may either with the written consent of all the parties in the matter or on an application to be admitted, with the leave of the President of the Court, obtain access to the court as *amicus curiae* with the competence of making a written submission to the court (rule 9 of the Rules of the Constitutional Court published in *Government Gazette* 18944 of 29 May 1998—to which reference is made as the 'Rules');

(7) any person or organ of state with sufficient interest may appeal directly or apply directly to the Constitutional Court to confirm or vary an order of

constitutional invalidity given by a court in respect of parliamentary or provincial legislation or the conduct of the President (s 172(2)*(d)* of the Constitution). ('Organ of the state' is defined in s 239 of the Constitution and, broadly speaking, includes any functionary of the state or any person performing public functions or any state department, but not a judicial officer or a court.)

1.2.4.2 Ways of access to the Constitutional Court

(a) *Direct access to the Constitutional Court*

Direct access according to s 167(6)*(a)* of the Constitution to the Constitutional Court by a member of the public shall be allowed in exceptional circumstances only, and must be in the interest of justice (see *Zuma* 1995 (1) SACR 568 (CC)). It will be in the interest of justice for a constitutional issue to be decided first by the Constitutional Court without being considered by other courts, where there are compelling reasons that it should be done—*Ferreira v Levin No; Vryenhoek v Powell NO* 1996 (1) SA 984 (CC). This will ordinarily be the case where the matter is of such urgency or of such importance that the delay necessitated by the application of the ordinary procedures, would prejudice the public interest or prejudice the ends of justice and good government. In terms of rule 17 of the Rules of the Constitutional Court an application for direct access as contemplated in s 167(6)*(a)* of the Constitution must be brought by way of a notice of motion supported by an affidavit setting forth the facts upon which the applicant relies for relief. The application must set out the grounds on which it is contended that it is in the interests of justice that an order for direct access be granted, the relief sought, the grounds upon which such relief is based and whether oral evidence must be heard or not.

In terms of sections 79, 80, 121 and 122 of the Constitution, direct access to the Constitutional Court is permitted in the case of specific members or bodies of the national executive authority concerning applications on the constitutional validity of the whole or part of an Act of Parliament or of a province or the referral of a Bill.

An application for direct access to the Constitutional Court has to be made according to the Rules.

The Constitutional Court may, on sufficient cause shown, condone any failure to comply with the rules (rule 31).

(b) *Direct access to the Constitutional Court by means of an appeal or confirmation without the leave of the Constitutional Court*

A state organ or a person may according to s 172(2)*(d)* of the Constitution, directly approach the Constitutional Court where, any competent court has declared in terms of s 172(2)*(a)* legislation promulgated by Parliament (or by a province) or the conduct of the President unconstitutional and invalid.

The registrar of a court which has made an order of constitutional invalidity, shall within 15 days of such order, lodge with the registrar of the Constitutional Court, a copy of such order. A person or state organ who wishes to appeal against such order or to have it confirmed by the Constitutional Court, must within 21 days after the order has been made, lodge a notice of appeal (in the case of an appeal) or lodge an application for confirmation (in the case where confirmation is sought) with the registrar of the Constitutional Court and lodge a copy thereof with the court which has made the order—rule 15 of the Rules.

(c) *Access to the Constitutional Court by means of an appeal with the leave of the Constitutional Court*

The Constitutional Court may be approached on appeal with the leave of the Court in the following instances:

(1) In an application according to s 167(6)*(b)* for leave to appeal *directly* to the Constitutional Court against a decision on a constitutional matter (other than a order of constitutional invalidity in terms of s 172 of the Constitution) given *by any court other than the Supreme Court of Appeal*, the appellant or litigant who is aggrieved by the decision of the court and who wishes to appeal directly to the Constitutional Court, must apply within 15 days after the decision or order to the court who gave the decision to certify that

   (a) it is in the interest of justice for the matter to be brought directly to the Constitutional Court, and

   (b) there is reason to believe that the Constitutional Court may give leave to the appellant to note an appeal against the decision on such matter—rule 18(2) of the Rules.

The application must be in writing, signed by the appellant, and it must state the grounds on which the decision is disputed, the decision against which the appeal is made and what constitutional matter is raised—rule 18(3) of the Rules.
   If it appears to the judge or judges hearing the application that—

   (i) the constitutional issue is one of substance on which a ruling by the Constitutional Court is desirable;

   (ii) the evidence in the proceedings is sufficient to enable the court to dispose of the matter without referral back for further evidence; and

   (iii) there is a reasonable prospect that the court will reverse the decision given by any court other than the Supreme Court of Appeal or materially alter such decision, if permission for leave to appeal is granted

the court must certify whether in the opinion of the court it is in the interest of justice for the appeal to be brought directly to the Constitutional Court and whether the requirements mentioned above have been met or failing which, which of such requirements have been satisfied and which have not been so satisfied (rule 18(6) of the Rules).

(2) An appeal to the Constitutional Court on a constitutional matter against a judgment or order of the Supreme Court of Appeal shall be granted only *with the special leave* of the Constitutional Court made to it by way of an application. The appellant or litigant, who is aggrieved by the decision of the Supreme Court of Appeal and who wishes to appeal to the Constitutional Court, must apply within 15 days after the judgment against which the appeal is sought and after giving notice to the other parties concerned, lodge with the registrar of the Constitutional Court an application for leave to appeal—rule 20 of the Rules. The application must be in writing, signed by the appellant and it must state the

grounds on which the decision is disputed, the decision against which the appeal is made and what constitutional matter is being raised—rule 20(3) of the Rules.

The Constitutional Court may decide summarily on the application for leave to appeal whether or not to grant the appellant leave to appeal. If the Constitutional Court is not in term, the President of the Constitutional Court may in cases of urgency grant leave to appeal only but may not refuse such leave—rule 18(10) of the Rules.

(d)   *Access to the Constitutional Court by way of referral*

(i)   The position according to the 1993-Constitution

Referrals of constitutional issues were made by the provincial or local divisions of the High Courts (ss 102(1), 102(8), 102(14) and 103(4) of the 1993 interim Constitution) or by the Supreme Court of Appeal (s 102(6)). Only constitutional issues could have been referred.

A competent constitutional referral required the following (reference made here to the rules of the Constitutional Court refer to the now repealed rules of 5 January 1995):

(1)   The provincial or local division could, on request of a party before the court or *mero motu*, refer a constitutional matter or dispute to the Constitutional Court. The judge (or judges at the hearing of appeal or review proceedings) had to formulate the issue or issues on which a ruling was sought from the Constitutional Court, provided it was within the exclusive jurisdiction of the Constitutional Court.

(2)   The referring court had to give reasons:

   (a) why the judge or judges considered the issue, even in the case of a substantial issue:

   (i) to be decisive for the case; and

   (ii) in the interest of justice that the matter be referred—s 102(1) of the interim Constitution; and

   (b) why the referring provincial or local division opined that there was a reasonable prospect that the relevant law or provision was invalid—this was not an express requirement of s 102(1) but was held in *Mhlungu* above, par 59, to be implicitly contained therein. See also rule 22 of the Rules read with ss 102(1) and 103(4) of the interim Constitution.

(3)   Before a referral could have been made, the provincial or local division first had to make a finding on any evidence which was relevant to the issue (s 103(4)*(a)*; *Vermaas; Du Plessis* (above) par 15 thereof). A constitutional matter raised in the provincial or local division or in the Supreme Court of Appeal that was regarded as of public importance, could have been referred in terms of s 102(8), provided the case had been disposed of by such court and if that court had been of the opinion that the constitutional issue was of sufficient public importance that a ruling should be given therein by the Constitutional Court—see s 102(8) and, on a referral in terms of this sub-section, see *Zantsi v The Council of State* 1995 (4) SA 615 (CC). If it was in the interest of justice that

a constitutional issue raised in an appeal be determined before the appeal was decided by the Supreme Court of Appeal, the constitutional issue was then first determined and thereafter the appeal continued before the Supreme Court of Appeal if it was still necessary to do so. (Cf rule 23 of the Rules read with s 102(6) and (7) of the interim Constitution.)

(ii) The position according to the 1996-Constitution

The 1996 Constitution limits referrals to a minimum. The Supreme Court of Appeal, a High Court or a Full Court must in terms of the 1996 Constitution, refer for confirmation an order concerning the constitutional inconsistency and invalidity of an Act of Parliament, a provincial Act or any conduct of the President to the Constitutional Court or may refer for decision such legislative enactments. Any other constitutional issue must be decided by any competent court and the decision by the court cannot be referred. Consequently, when a common law offence is declared to be constitutionally invalid by any other court, the Constitution does not provide for an obligatory referral. The undesirable consequences of this are pointed out in *National Coalition for Gay & Lesbian Equality v Minister of Justice* 1998 (2) SACR 556 (CC) at paras. 3, 79–82.

1.3 No appeal before conviction

The general rule is that an appeal should not be decided piecemeal and usually the court of appeal will exercise its powers only after termination of the criminal trial. In the normal course of events it is preferable to reach finality in the disposal of cases: that all issues should be decided during a single session so that a final judgment can be given at the end of the proceedings which disposes of the case as a whole. The approach that a case should not be heard piecemeal, also applies to the final disposal of the appeal—cf *Adams* 1959 (3) SA 753 (A). Furthermore, there is no statutory provision to note and to prosecute an unterminated criminal trial—*Wahlhaus v Additional Magistrate, Johannesburg* 1959 (3) SA 113 (A) at 119F. In exceptional cases, however, the court of appeal will, even before the termination of the trial, exercise its inherent power to prevent irregularities in lower courts: for example, where a magistrate unreasonably denies the accused the opportunity to obtain legal representation or where other irregularities occur. This power should be sparingly used—*Wahlhaus* (above). Where grave injustice might otherwise result or where justice might not by other means be attained, the High Court will not hesitate to interfere—Gardiner & Lansdown 750; *Goncalves v Addisionele Landdros, Pretoria* 1973 (4) SA 587 (T). In *Malinde* 1990 (1) SA 57 (A) at 67B it was held that although the High Court does not possess inherent power to enhance the substantive jurisdiction which it has by virtue of statutory provisions, there is no doubt that this court possesses an inherent power to regulate its procedure in the interest of the proper administration of justice. (In that matter, after conclusion of the trial, the Supreme Court of Appeal granted an order to separate the hearing of the special entry from the whole of the appeal.) The High Courts' inherent power to regulate and protect their own process is confirmed by the Constitution—s 173.

Whenever the High Court is approached to exercise its inherent powers to prevent irregularities in lower courts, the court may grant a *mandamus* (ie an order directing the magistrate to act as ordered) or an interdict (ie an order directing the magistrate not to act in a certain manner). Cf *Bailey* 1962 (4) SA 514 (E) where the magistrate improperly refused to recuse himself. See also *Ncukutwana v Acting Additional Magistrate, Lady Frere* 1968 (1) SA 140 (E) where a magistrate unreasonably refused to allow the defence attorney to record the court proceedings by means of a tape recorder.

If, however, the magistrate performs his functions in a proper and regular way procedurally, but comes to a wrong conclusion on the merits, no application may be made to the court of appeal before conviction—*Ginsberg v Additional Magistrate, Cape Town* 1933 CPD 357; *Marais* 1959 (1) SA 98 (T). It follows that, if the grounds for complaint are such that they can afford an effective basis for relief in appeal or review proceedings after the trial, such an interlocutory application will not be entertained—*Van Heerden* 1972 (2) PH H74 (E).

In matters heard before a High Court, an appeal based on a question of law reserved (see below) cannot take place unless the trial has been concluded—*Adams* 1959 (3) SA 753 (A).

The general rule that no appeal should lie to the Supreme Court of Appeal, whether by means of a special entry, reserved question of law or in the ordinary way unless the accused is first sentenced, may, however, also be departed from in exceptional circumstances. See *Majola* 1982 (1) SA 125 (A), where it appeared before sentence that the appellant had never been consulted by his legal adviser as to whether he wanted to give evidence or not.

1.4 Appeal against sentence

Although an appeal court is vested with jurisdiction to reduce a sentence, it is to be noted that a court of appeal, whether the Supreme Court of Appeal or the provincial or local division with appeal jurisdiction, does not have a general discretion to ameliorate the sentences of trial courts. Principles derived from judicial precedent regulate the powers of the appeal court on appeal against sentence. It is the trial court that has the discretion to impose a proper sentence—*Whitehead* 1970 (4) SA 424 (A) 435. The mere fact that the court of appeal would have imposed a lighter sentence if the punishment were within its discretion is not in itself sufficient reason for the court to intervene.

A court of appeal cannot interfere with a sentence unless the trial court has not exercised its discretion judicially, that is in a proper and reasonable manner—*Kock* 1988 (1) SA 37 (A); *S* 1988 (1) SA 120 (A); *Tshoko* 1988 (1) SA 139 (A). This will be the case:

(1) where the sentence is vitiated by an irregularity (eg where a magistrate imposes a sentence beyond his penal jurisdiction)—cf *Pillay* 1977 (4) SA 531 (A);

(2) where the trial court misdirects itself (eg by taking into consideration irrelevant factors). See, for example, *Runds* 1978 (4) SA 304 (A). A mere misdirection does not suffice to warrant interference by a court of appeal. The misdirection must be of such a nature, degree or seriousness that it vitiates the trial court's decision on sentence—*G* 1989 (3) SA 695 (A); *Mtungwa* 1990 (2) SACR 1 (A);

(3) where the sentence is so severe that no reasonable court would have imposed it—*Anderson* 1964 (3) SA 494 (A). Over the years different tests have been applied for determining whether an imposed sentence is such that the court of appeal is competent to interfere. Thus, the Supreme Court of Appeal has asked

itself whether the sentence appealed against induces 'a sense of shock'; in some cases again the question was whether the sentence was 'startlingly inappropriate', and then again in other cases whether there was 'a striking disparity' between the sentence imposed and the sentence which the Supreme Court of Appeal would have imposed, had it acted as a court of first instance. Other criteria applied by the Supreme Court of Appeal are whether 'no reasonable court would have imposed the sentence which was imposed by the trial court' or 'whether the trial court has reasonably exercised the discretion conferred upon him'—cf *M* 1976 (3) SA 644 (A). The different formulations may be combined into the one crucial question that needs to be answered, that is, whether the trial court could reasonably have imposed the sentence which it did—*Pieters* 1987 (3) SA 717 (A) at 734C–H; *Gross* 1982 (1) SA 593 (A); *S* 1988 (1) SA 120 (A). Therefore, the fundamental approach to an appeal on sentence is that a court of appeal will interfere with an imposed sentence only, if it is satisfied that the trial court exercised its discretion improperly or unreasonably—*Pieters* (above). Obviously this applies only if no misdirection occurred.

In an appeal against sentence on the ground that the sentence imposed on the appellant is disturbingly inappropriate when compared with the sentence imposed in a different trial on another accused for the same crime, the question, whether the sentence appealed against is disturbingly inappropriate, must obviously be answered on the basis of a comparison between that sentence and the lesser sentence which was imposed on a convicted person who played an equal part in the commission of the same crime and who shared comparable personal circumstances. Even if there is a striking difference between the two sentences when they are compared, it does not necessarily mean that interference is justified. Interference is justified only if the lighter sentence is a reasonably or commonly imposed sentence. Where the lighter sentence is unreasonable or clearly inappropriate and the heavier sentence is in all circumstances an appropriate one, interference with the latter sentence would be improper—cf *Marx* 1989 (1) SA 222 (A).

A court of appeal has no jurisdiction to impose on appeal a sentence which, at the time of sentencing the accused, was not a competent one for the trial court to impose. If, at the time of sentence, the jurisdiction of a trial court in respect of punishment which is regulated by legislation is altered by statute (eg where an ameliorating amendment replaces a compulsory minimum sentence with a discretionary one), the appeal court is bound by the legal position as it existed at the time of the trial— *Smith (2)* 1987 (4) SA 768 (A); *Loate* 1983 (3) SA 400 (T). On the other hand, once the sentence is set aside on appeal on the ground of an irregularity, misdirection or inappropriateness, the court of appeal is competent to impose a sentence which was not available to the trial court at the time of sentencing the accused—*E* 1992 (2) SACR 625 (A). In this case, the Supreme Court of Appeal imposed a sentence of correctional supervision although this punishment was not in operation when the accused was sentenced. Cf also *Prokureur-Generaal, Noord-Kaap v Hart* 1990 (1) SA 49 (A).

The law confers upon the Supreme Court of Appeal and provincial or Witwatersrand local division jurisdiction to increase a sentence on appeal— ss 309(3) of the Criminal Procedure Act and 22 of the Supreme Court Act 59 of 1959. A court may increase the sentence on appeal even though the appeal is against conviction only *F* 1983 (1) SA 747 (O). This power is conferred upon the court to see that justice is done because 'it is just as much in the interest of justice that a guilty person should be adequately punished as that he should be convicted'—*Grundlingh* 1955 (2) SA 269 (A) at 277H. Rules of practice dictate that notice should be given to the accused, should an application requesting an increase of sentence be brought by the prosecution or where the court *mero motu* considers a possible increase of sentence where the court of appeal is *prima facie* of the view that there is a prospect that such an increase may eventuate. (Hiemstra 805). In *Sonday* 1994 (2) SACR 810 (C) the practice of the courts to give notice of a possible increase in the sentence even though such increase was not requested by the prosecution, was alleged to be invalid and to constitute a violation or threatened violation of an appellant's constitutional right of access to a court that is entrenched in s 22 (now, s 34) of the Constitution and the right to a fair trial—more specific—the right to have recourse by way of appeal to a court of higher instance than the court of first instance (s 25(3)*(h)*— now, s 35(3)*(o)*—of the interim Constitution). The court held, holding the allegations to be devoid of merit, that the power to increase a sentence on appeal is a well established rule in our law and that the practice to give notice is no indication that the Court has already made up its mind to dismiss the appeal even before hearing the appellant's argument or that the court has taken over the role of the prosecution in respect of sentence.

In the exercise of this power to increase a sentence on appeal, the general principles with regard to appeals against sentence are applied. Therefore, a sentence will be increased only if the trial court has exercised its discretion unreasonably or improperly, or misdirected itself—cf *Molorane* 1954 (2) PH H150 (O); *Fischer* 1955 (2) PH H186 (C); *De Vos* 1970 (2) SA 590 (C) at 591C; *Du Toit* 1979 (3) SA 846 (A) at 856B. Careful consideration of the offence, the offender and the interests of society forms an integral part in deciding on a possible increase in sentence. Naturally, a court of appeal will not lightly increase a sentence even though that court would have imposed a heavier sentence—*Du Toit* (above) at 855H. (See 'Powers of court of appeal', below.)

1.5   Appeal on the facts

A court of appeal is usually loath to interfere with the findings of the trial court on questions of fact (*Francis* 1991 (1) SACR 198 (A)). The reason behind this approach is that the trial court is in a better position than the court of appeal to make reliable findings on credibility. It enjoys an advantage over the court of appeal in that it sees and hears the witnesses in the atmosphere of the court and is therefore better equipped to assess the demeanour, appearance and personality of the witnesses. Where the findings of fact by the trial court are based to any great extent on the impressions made by witnesses, a court of appeal will be particularly unwilling to upset the findings on the facts and will do so only if the court is convinced that they are wrong—cf *Dube* 1929 AD 46; *Macaba* 1939 AD 66; *Kristusamy* 1945 AD 549 and *Robinson* 1968 (1) SA 666 (A). It is well-established law that if there is no misdirection on the facts, there is a presumption that the trial court's evaluation of the evidence as to the facts is correct, and that a court of appeal will interfere only if it is convinced that the evaluation is wrong— *Mkohle* 1990 (1) SACR 95 (A); *Mlumbi* 1991 (1) SACR 235 (A). In determining whether the trial court's findings of fact were clearly wrong, the evidence ultimately had to be assessed as a whole—*Hadebe* 1998

(1) SACR 422 (SCA). In special cases where there are circumstances which convince the court of appeal that, having made every allowance for observations as to the demeanour of witnesses, the court *a quo* should have entered a different finding, an appeal on the facts will be allowed—*Mpeta* 1912 AD 568 and cf *Dhlumayo* 1948 (2) SA 677 (A) on the general principles that should guide a court of appeal in an appeal purely on the facts.

The demeanour of witnesses in court is, however, only one of various factors which play a part:

> '[I]t must now be regarded as settled law that the demeanour of a witness whilst testifying is in many cases the decisive and determining factor in the search for the truth. It is however difficult to conceive of a case where it is the only factor; for even where great stress is laid on the demeanour of a certain witness one knows by experience that the setting, the surrounding circumstances, the probabilities, the inferences, all go towards creating that subtle, pervasive and undefinable atmosphere at a trial from which the witness emerges as the symbol of truth'—*Abels* 1948 (1) SA 706 (O) at 708.

It is desirable that the court should place on record in what respect or respects the demeanour of a witness is unsatisfactory. The reasons given by the court must be those of the majority (ie assessors and presiding officer) and not of the presiding officer alone—*Kalogoropoulos* 1993 (1) SACR 12 (A) and see also *Belinsky* 1925 AD 363 and *Khaile* 1975 (3) SA 97 (O). If the question is whether a correct inference has been drawn from the facts, which facts are not themselves in dispute, the court of appeal is in as favourable a position as the trial court. Similarly, the court of appeal can determine just as well as the trial court whether corroborative evidence (where this is required) is present.

1.6 Difference between an appeal on facts and an appeal on a question of law

It is not always easy to distinguish between an appeal on a question of fact and one on a question of law. In an appeal on a question of fact, it is the duty of the court of appeal to retry or rehear the case on the record before the court with such other evidential material as it may have decided to admit and then decide for itself whether there is a reasonable doubt about the appellant's guilt.

In an appeal on a question of law the question is not whether the *court of appeal would have made the same finding* but whether the trial court *could* have made such a finding. The question of law, therefore, cannot be whether the *evidence* supports the finding of the court, because that would be a question of fact.

Where the prosecution appeals in terms of s 310(1) or applies in terms of s 319(1) for the reservation of a question of law for the consideration of the Supreme Court of Appeal, the question of law may not be formulated in such a fashion that a question of fact is masquerading as a question of law. This is illustrated by the case of *Magmoed v Janse van Rensburg* 1993 (1) SACR 67 (A), where a purely factual question was formulated as a legal one, by asking whether a particular inference is the only possible inference to be drawn from a given set of facts. See also *Colgate-Palmolive* 1971 (2) SA 149 (T) at 154 and *Coetzee* 1977 (4) SA 539 (A).

1.7 Appearance of the appellant

If an appellant who has noted and prosecuted his appeal, fails to appear, the following courses of action are open to the court of appeal:

(1) It may summarily dismiss the appeal.

(2) It may strike the appeal off the roll—*Hlongwa* 1993 (2) SACR 225 (A). Where an appeal has been struck off the roll, it will be reinstated only if a substantive application is brought, indicating a reasonable prospect of success—*Tshapo* 1967 (3) SA 100 (N).

(3) It may postpone the appeal if there is reason to believe that the appellant has been prevented from appearing through no fault of his own—cf *Mohapi* 1990 (1) SACR 573 (O); *Letweli* 1982 (2) SA 666 (NC), where guidelines were laid down on the procedure to be followed where attorneys withdraw after noting an appeal, or are unable to obtain instructions or are requested not to proceed with same, or have to request a postponement. If the appeal has no prospect of being successful, the court will not grant a postponement for the appointment of counsel—*Joseph* 1967 (2) SA 539 (N).

(4) It may hear the appeal. In various cases where the appellant has failed to appear and where the circumstances mentioned in (3) above are not present, the Supreme Court of Appeal has, of its own accord, heard the appeal. Provincial or local divisions having jurisdiction, would be competent to hear the appeal by virtue of s 304(4) as if it had been brought before it on review—*Hlope* 1962 (2) SA 607 (T). See in general *Govender* 1955 (2) SA 130 (N); *Grundlingh* 1955 (2) SA 269 (A), especially at 276; *Beck* 1958 (4) SA 250 (C); *Solomon* 1966 (3) SA 145 (A).

1.8 Withdrawal of appeal

Generally it may be said that an accused must have a right to withdraw his appeal. However, it is necessary that this right should be curtailed by the courts, especially where an increase in sentence is considered. Although the prosecution of an appeal commences with the notice of appeal (*Du Toit* 1979 (3) SA 846 (A) at 855C), it is reasonable that certain time limits should be set, within which the appellant may reconsider his decision to appeal. Where the prosecution of an appeal has progressed to the point where the court of appeal has taken cognisance of the matter or where the appeal is called for argument in open court, the appellant may not withdraw the appeal without the leave of the court. The court may in its discretion decide to dispose of the case—cf *Grundlingh* 1955 (2) SA 269 (A); *Wilken* 1971 (3) SA 488 (A); *Williams* 1963 (1) SA 761 (T) at 786–9; *Rost* 1980 (2) SA 528 (SWA).

In the normal course of events, judges of the provincial and local divisions (having appeal jurisdiction), seldom have the opportunity due to their specific circumstances, to study well in advance the relevant documents pertaining to the appeal, especially with a view to decide whether or not notice of increase should be given. The South African Law Commission has therefore recommended in 1994 in Working Paper 42: *Simplification of the Criminal Procedure*, that the withdrawal of criminal appeals in the local and provincial divisions should be placed on firm foundations. It recommended that it ought not be possible to withdraw an appeal without leave of the court of appeal once it has been set down for hearing. (These recommendations have however, not yet been implemented.)

It was held in *Du Toit* 1979 (3) SA 846 (A) with regard to the question whether an appellant is entitled unilaterally to withdraw his appeal subsequent to the date of setdown, that, as far as appeals to the Supreme Court of Appeal are concerned, practical and equitable reasons would require an appellant to obtain *leave to withdraw* his appeal only in those instances where either the Supreme Court of Appeal or the state had already given notice that an increase of sentence would be considered by the Supreme Court of Appeal or sought by the state. These practical and equitable reasons are equally relevant to appeals noted to a provincial or local division—*Kirsten* 1988 (1) SA 415 (A). In *Kirsten* it was further held that a withdrawal of an appeal (in cases where leave of the court of appeal is not required) need not be embodied in a formal notice. All that is required is that an appellant must decide to withdraw his appeal and that such decision must be conveyed to the court of appeal and the state. Consequently, should an appellant give notice in his heads of argument—which have been filed with the court of appeal—that the appeal is withdrawn in its entirety, then that court would not be entitled to increase the appellant's sentence.

1.9 Publication of proceedings

Since an appeal is a continuation of the trial, the provisions of ss 153 and 154 concerning exclusion of the public and prohibition of publication also apply to appeals—*Ex parte X* 1938 AD 244.

1.10 Inspection in loco

A court of appeal may hold an inspection *in loco*—*Carelse* 1943 CPD 242.

1.11 Aspect first raised on appeal

In *Herschel* 1920 AD 575 at 581, the Supreme Court of Appeal made the following pronouncement about an aspect of the case which was raised, not during the trial, but on appeal for the first time:

> 'In criminal appeals from magistrates' courts formal defects apparent on the face of the charge sheet cannot be relied upon for the first time on appeal; objection to them must be made by way of exception before plea. *Material defects of such a nature that the charge sheet discloses no crime may be relied upon on appeal, even though the point was not taken at the trial.* But where the charge sheet, thought materially defective, does disclose a crime . . ., then the defect cannot be relied upon if, in the opinion of the Court of Appeal, it could, if timeously taken, have been remedied by amendment without prejudice to the accused in the conduct of his defence.' (Emphasis was added and the example was omitted.)

Subsequently this view was followed in numerous decisions. In *Myburgh* 1922 AD 249 it was held that objections to formal defects, 'apparent on the face of the charge', must be made by way of exception to the charge sheet before plea. (The *dictum* in *Herschel's* case pertains to both charge sheets in lower courts and indictments in superior courts—*Preller* 1952 (4) SA 452 (A)). In *Tucker* 1953 (3) SA 150 (A) it was held that the court of appeal will set aside the conviction where the charge sheet discloses a material defect, even if the accused has pleaded guilty.

The effect of *Herschel's* case and later decisions on defective charge sheets was considerably influenced by the enactment in 1959 of s 88 of the Criminal Procedure Act. This section provides as follows:

> 'Where a charge is defective for want of an averment which is an essential ingredient of the relevant offence, the defect shall, unless brought to the notice of the court before judgment, be cured by evidence at the trial proving the matter which should have been averred.'

The *dictum* (the italicised portion of the quoted passage) in *Herschel's* case therefore applies only if the defect has not been cured by evidence.

The trial court also has the power to amend a charge even if it discloses no crime. See s 86 and *Crause* 1959 (1) SA 272 (A). The trial court's power to amend the charge sheet is limited by the possibility of prejudice to the accused—*Crause (supra)* at 281; *Alberts* 1959 (3) SA 404 (A). Thus, if the accused objects to a materially defective charge during the trial, and the trial court alters the charge without prejudice resulting to the accused, he cannot on appeal rely on the fact that the charge was defective. However, the fact that an accused person is entitled under the Constitution to a fair trial which includes the right to be informed with sufficient particularity of the charge (s 35(3)*(a)*) may well cause a court of appeal to take a different stance.

On appeal the charge sheet or the indictment may also be amended if the court is satisfied, first that the proposed amendment is an amendment as envisaged by s 86 and secondly that the accused would not be prejudiced—cf *Barkett's Transport (Edms) Bpk* 1988 (1) SA 157 (A). Although the test regarding prejudice is the same during the trial as on appeal, a court of appeal will be less inclined to grant an amendment on appeal for the obvious reason that evidence would already have been given and the trial conducted on a different basis to that which it would have perhaps been conducted, had the amendment been granted at the trial—*Ndhlovu* 1991 (2) SACR 322 (W).

1.12 Record of the proceedings

It is important, for purposes of appeal, to have a reliable record of the proceedings of the trial court. Where there is an error in the record of the proceedings or the certified transcript thereof, the accused or the prosecutor may within a certain time period, apply to the court to correct such error (rule 66(6) of the Magistrates' Courts Rules of Court). Such application must be brought in open court—*De Wet v Greeff NO* 1991 (2) SACR 17 (T). If the time limit specified in rule 66(6) has expired, an application may be brought in the High Court—*Slabbert* 1958 (1) SA 275 (O). If essential evidence has been omitted from the record and cannot be supplemented satisfactorily, the accused's appeal must succeed—*Collier* 1976 (2) SA 378 (C); *Marais* 1966 (2) SA 514 (T). However, a court of appeal will not be inclined to set proceedings aside on the basis of a mere speculation that the missing parts of the record of the proceedings that could not be reconstructed, were material evidence. There must be some indications in the record itself or by way of affidavits made by the appellant of the materiality of the missing evidence—*S* 1995 (2) SACR 421 (T).

Where it is impossible to reconstruct a lost record and the lost portion contains evidence which is of material importance to the adjudication of the appeal, the appeal ought to succeed and the conviction and sentence set aside. In such circumstances it is not permissible to refer the matter back to the trial court for a trial *de novo*—*Fredericks* 1992 (1) SACR 561 (C).

The final responsibility to ensure that all copies of the record of proceedings are in all respects properly before the court and suitable for such purposes, rests with the appellant or his attorney—*Ngxitho* 1979 (1) SA 1037 (O); rules 49A(7) and 51(3) of the Supreme Court Rules.

After conviction a court may not amend certain portions of the record. At the conclusion of the trial the presiding officer is *functus officio* and unable to amend the record *mero motu*—*Mpopo* 1978 (2) SA 424 (A).

2 APPEALS TO PROVINCIAL AND LOCAL DIVISIONS OF THE HIGH COURTS

2.1 To which division?

In a criminal matter an appeal from a lower court must be brought to the provincial or local division having jurisdiction. Since 1982, the Witwatersrand Local Division has had jurisdiction to hear appeals (see Act 105 of 1982). The provincial or local division in whose area of jurisdiction the lower court trial was held, has jurisdiction, irrespective of where the offence was committed—*Ex parte die Minister van Justisie: In re S v De Bruin* 1972 (2) SA 623 (A). In terms of s 13(2)*(a)*(i) of the Supreme Court Act 59 of 1959 an appeal against a judgment or order of a lower court to the provincial or local division of the High Courts must be heard by not less than two judges. In the case of an appeal against a decision of a lower court on a bail application, irrespective of whether it is an appeal lodged by the accused against the refusal to grant bail or an appeal by the prosecution against the court's decision to grant the accused bail, such appeal shall be heard by a single judge—ss 65(1)*(b)* and 65A(1)*(b)* of the Criminal Procedure Act.

When the appellant wishes to appeal against a judgment or order of the provincial or local division given on appeal, leave of the court against whose judgment or order the appeal is to be made, must be applied for or where such leave has been refused, leave of the Supreme Court of Appeal must be requested—s 20(4) of the Supreme Court Act 59 of 1959.

2.2 When may an accused appeal?

The general principle is that an accused may appeal with leave from the trial court, against any conviction (even if he/she is discharged with a mere warning after having been found guilty) and any resultant sentence or order of the lower court— s 309(1)*(a)*. The following are exceptions to this general principle:

(1) A fugitive convicted person may not appeal—*Isaacs* 1968 (2) SA 184 (A). The reason for this is that, by his/her flight the convicted person puts himself, as it were, beyond the jurisdiction of the court. While he/she thus disregards the legal process, he/she cannot invoke it for any legal relief—*Molotsi* 1976 (2) SA 404 (O); *Nkosi* 1963 (4) SA 87 (T); *Kennedy* 1967 (1) SA 297 (C).

(2) A third party who has an interest in a verdict of guilty or in a subsequent order has no *locus standi* to appeal. An example is *Raftopulos* 1952 (4) SA 85 (T), in which case the accused was found guilty of gambling in that he unlawfully had a pin-table in his shop. The magistrate ordered that the table be forfeited to the state, but it appeared later that the table was the property of a certain R. R appealed against the order of forfeiture, but the court held that he had no power to do so. R in this case had not been found guilty by the court and could therefore not rely on s 309.

(3) A finding of not guilty because the accused lacked criminal capacity is not an appealable verdict where the finding was made in consequence of an allegation made *by the accused*—s 78(8).

(4) An accused may not appeal against the putting into operation of a suspended sentence—*Khalpy* 1958 (1) SA 291 (C); *Khan* 1961 (1) SA 282 (N); *Gasa v Regional Magistrate for the Regional Division of Natal* 1979 (4) SA 729 (N).

(5) An appeal may not be continued after the death of the accused because all appeal proceedings then lapse—Vos 1914 CPD 139; *Tremearne* 1917 NPD 117. The same applies where the proceedings were brought by the State, save possibly where the State should derive some pecuniary benefit in the event of the appeal being upheld—*January; Prokureur-Generaal, Natal v Khumalo* 1994 (2) SACR 801 (A). If an appellant dies before judgment is given on appeal, and the judgment of the court *a quo* affects his estate (eg where the sentence is a fine), the court of appeal has jurisdiction to pronounce judgment—*P* 1972 (2) SA 513 (NC); *Molotsi* 1976 (2) SA 404 (O). When a fine is imposed, it provides the executor of the deceased with the necessary *locus standi* to prosecute the appeal—*Von Molendorff* 1987 (1) SA 135 (T) (not approving *Vos* 1914 CPD 139) and see also s 288.

(6) No appeal may be lodged against an exception which has been rejected (where no verdict followed)—*Mackeson* 1939 PH L21 (C).

(7) No appeal lies against an administrative order (eg an order in terms of s 12 of Act 75 of 1969, declaring a person unfit to possess a firearm—*Lombard* 1951 (3) SA 842 (E); *Vaz* 1975 (1) SA 52 (T)).

2.3 Notice and prosecution of appeals

Magistrates' Courts Rule 67 prescribes the steps that accused persons should take to note an appeal in terms of s 309B. An application for leave to appeal must be noted in writing within 14 days after the date of the conviction, sentence or order in question. It must be accompanied by a statement of the grounds of appeal set out clearly and specifically the grounds whether of fact or law or both fact and law, on which the application and appeal is based (s 309B(3)). Notice must be given to all the parties concerned.

The steps for the noting of the appeal are taken in the magistrate's court but those for the prosecution of the appeal are taken in the court of appeal. The prosecution of an appeal relates to the enrolment for hearing of the appeal, heads of argument and the filing of copies of the record of the proceedings (cf rule 51 of Supreme Court Rules).

As mentioned above, the statement of the grounds of appeal must set out clearly and specifically the grounds on which the appeal is based. The question then is: when does the statement comply with this requirement? At the time of writing no judgment had been given on this point. One could, however, glean some guidance from case law applicable at the time when an appeal against a lower court's decision was considered a matter of right, without requesting leave to appeal.

In *Meyer* 1950 (1) PH H88 (O), a full bench refused to allow an appellant to put forward a special substantive legal argument which had not been specifically mentioned in the notice of appeal and on which the State had not prepared any argument—cf *Phillips* 1949 (2) SA 671 (O). The court may, with the consent of the State and if the State's case will not thereby be prejudiced, allow the grounds of appeal to be supplemented so that a particular point of law may be argued. If the State is not prepared to give its consent, a substantial application must be made to the court—cf *Breytenbach* 1954 (2) SA 10 (O).

In *Breytenbach's* case appeal was noted against the conviction in its entirety on the grounds that '*(a)* it was bad in law, and *(b)* it was against the preponderance of evidence'. These general grounds were held to be sufficient, but it was pointed out that the case was a relatively simple one, as the magistrate gave a ruling on only one prominent point of law and made only two findings on fact. Each case has to be decided in the light of its own circumstances.

A similar notice was held to be bad in *Horne* 1971 (1) SA 630 (C), a case containing several issues and conflicts of fact. The governing principle is that the magistrate must know what the issues are which are to be challenged so that he can deal with them in his reasons for judgment; counsel for the State must be duly informed so that he can prepare and present arguments which will assist the court of appeal in its deliberations; finally, that the court itself should be apprised of the grounds so that it can know what portions of the record to concentrate on and what preparation, if any, it should make in order to guide and stimulate argument in court—*Horne (supra)* at 631–2.

A notice of appeal which embarrasses the court and the State will therefore not be entertained. Accordingly, the safest course would be to set out fully every separate ground of objection in the notice of appeal—cf *Breytenbach* (above) at 13; *Hoosen* 1953 (3) SA 823 (N); *Sibiya* 1957 (1) SA 247 (T); *Zive* 1960 (3) SA 24 (T); *Kruger* 1970 (2) SA 233 (N); *Cohen* 1970 (2) SA 231 (N); *Mhlongo* 1970 (2) SA 235 (N); *Horne* (above).

A notice of appeal which does not comply with the requirements of the rules is in fact not a notice of appeal at all, and the matter should be considered on the basis that no appeal was noted—*Hoosen* (above), *Kruger* (above); and *Zive* (above). Consequently the appeal will be struck off the roll—*Zive* (above).

The onus of satisfying the court that the notice of appeal is in order rests on the appellant. If it is not in order, the only expedient is to apply for condonation of the late noting of an appeal. In such a case the appellant must, *inter alia*, convince the court that he has a reasonable prospect of success. A magistrate is fully entitled to disregard an inadequate notice of appeal—*Hoosen* (above). The magistrate may not, however, express his disapproval of the way grounds of appeal are drawn, by refusing to comply with his duty to state the facts he found proved and his reasons for judgment, unless the grounds of appeal are so defective that he cannot fully or properly comply with this duty—*Noah* 1959 (3) SA 530 (E).

2.4 Amendment of grounds of appeal

An accused person may amend his statement of grounds of appeal within the prescribed time (see rule 67(7) of the Magistrates' Courts Rules). The accused is entitled to do this and need not obtain leave. After the prescribed period has expired, however, the accused must apply for leave before the magistrate against whose decision or order the appeal is to be noted (s 309(2)). Good cause must be shown why the period should be extended for the amendment of the statement. It is within the court's discretion to grant or refuse such application. It will grant it more readily if the appellant does not put off making his application until the last minute. When an amendment is made, notice must be given to the prosecutor (rule 67(8)). The High Court may expand the statement on petition (s 309C).

Where the accused has noted an appeal against the *sentence*, the court does not have the power to order an amendment of the statement of the grounds of appeal to include an appeal against the *conviction*. Technically there is no application for leave to appeal against the conviction that could be amended. The only remedy in such a case is to apply for condonation for late noting of appeal. (Cf *Diedericks* 1960 (4) SA 730 (O) and see also *Langa* 1981 (3) SA 186 (A).)

2.5 Condonation of late noting or late prosecution of appeals

The Magistrates' Courts Rules prescribe certain time limits within which an appeal should be noted. If an appeal is not noted within these time limits, condonation for late noting should be applied for.

In terms of s 309(2) the magistrate has the power to extend the period within which the appeal must be noted or prosecuted. The grounds on which the courts will condone the late application, noting and grant an extension, are in the discretion of the court. In *Rheeders v Jacobsz* 1942 AD 395, the court expressed its approval of the view 'that the Court will take a liberal view of the matter but must be careful to see in each instance that there is some reasonable ground for the exercise of its discretion in favour of the applicant'.

In criminal cases the courts are more accommodating about granting condonation than in civil cases because it is desirable that an accused should be given every reasonable opportunity to present his case as fully as he wishes to the court of appeal—*De Vos* 1975 (1) SA 449 (O).

In *Cairn's Executors v Gaarn* 1912 AD 181 at 186 it was stated:

> 'It would be quite impossible to frame an exhaustive definition of what would constitute sufficient cause to justify the grant of indulgence. Any attempt to do so would merely hamper the exercise of a discretion which the rules have purposely made very extensive, and which is highly desirable not to abridge. All that can be said is that the applicant must show . . . "something which entitles him to ask for the indulgence of the Court". What that something is must be decided upon the circumstances of each particular application.'

In *Abdool Latieb & Co v Jones* 1918 TPD 215 at 216, it was said:

> 'I think when we find that there has been gross negligence or absolute indifference as to whether the appeal is or is not set down, we ought to say that good cause has not been shown. But when we come to the conclusion that there has been a bona fide mistake due to misunderstanding, or that for some excusable reason the appeal has not been set down at the proper date, we ought to come to the assistance of the litigant.'

The mere fact that the accused is impecunious is not by itself sufficient ground for extension of the period—*Jacobs v The Attorney-General* 1918 CPD 526; *Fisher* 1973 (4) SA 121 (R).

In *Matsatebe* 1949 (2) SA 105 (O), the accused was an ignorant person who could neither read nor write. He was not acquainted with the statutory provisions concerning appeals and he apparently received a false impression from prison officials. The court found that he had not been negligent. (His application for leave to appeal was refused, however, because there was no reasonable prospect of a successful appeal.) In *Anderson* 1949 (4) SA 629 (C) the court granted condonation on the ground of negligence on the part of the accused's attorney. See also *Mall* 1953 (1) SA 118 (SWA) and cf *Heyns* 1958 (2) SA 253 (E).

In *De Vos* 1975 (1) SA 449 (O) condonation to alter the grounds of appeal was granted where the applicant *bona fide* alleged that he did not appreciate a substantial point of law when he timeously noted an appeal on another point.

In *Van Niekerk* 1967 (4) SA 269 (SWA) it was held that the mere fact that another person in identical circumstances successfully appealed against a conviction, was not sufficient reason for condonation. In this case A and B were jointly charged. A noted an appeal, but B did not. A's appeal succeeded. B then (five months after his conviction) applied for condonation. His application was refused because of absence of an acceptable explanation for his failure to appeal timeously. Cf also *Franco; Lasovsky* 1974 (4) SA 496 (RA).

2.6 Prosecuting an appeal in person

As is pointed out in chapter 20, at present a person is entitled to prosecute his appeal in person. The position was previously regulated by s 309(4)*(a)* read with s 305 which provided that 'no person who has been convicted by a lower court of an offence and is undergoing imprisonment for that or any other offence shall be entitled to prosecute in person any proceedings for the appeal relating to such conviction, sentence or order, unless a judge of the provincial or local division having jurisdiction has certified that there are reasonable grounds for appeal'.

The noting of an appeal was a prerequisite for the issuing of a judge's certificate— *Absalom* (above) at 159E. In *Thos* 1976 (2) SA 408 (O) the background to and procedure involved in obtaining the judge's certificate was set out.

The purpose of the provisions of s 309(4)*(a)* was to prevent convicted prisoners from abusing the process of court by being released from prison under guard at state expense to argue in person frivolous and unnecessary appeals in a court of appeal, thus also impeding prison authorities in the execution of their duties—*Nel* 1960 (4) SA 228 (O); *Hassen* 1956 (3) SA 106 (N); *Gibbs* 1959 (2) SA 84 (C); *Pillay* 1958 (4) SA 27 (N); *Muniohambo* 1983 (4) SA 791 (SWA). The constitutionality of the provisions of s 309(4)*(a)* was referred to the Constitutional Court in *Ntuli* 1996 (1) SACR 94 (CC). The Constitutional Court held that the requirement that a judge's certificate has to be obtained by a prisoner, is inconsistent with the constitutional rights embodied in s 25(3)*(h)*(relating to recourse by way of appeal or review, (now, s 35(3)*(o)*) and s 8(1) (that is the clause dealing with equal treatment and protection by the law, (now, s 9) of the interim Constitution. The court held that the requirement that a judge's certificate has to be obtained, operates as a restriction on the full access to the High Court and inhibits an adequate reappraisal of such cases, which are enjoyed by those who are free to prosecute their similar appeals to finality (see para 23). The court remarked that the idea of prisoners lodging appeals for no better reason than to take an excursion to the court to argue a bad appeal, is fanciful and probably exaggerated (see para 23 ff of the judgment). The Constitutional Court held that the provisions of s 309(4)*(a)* are unconstitutional and invalid and required Parliament to correct the said invalid provisions before 30 April 1997 during which time the provisions remained in force pending the correction or the expiry of the period so specified. The rationale of the judgment is discussed in chapter 20 paragraph 3.5. In *Minister of Justice v Ntuli* 1997 (2) SACR 19 (CC) the court refused the application for an extension of the period of suspension in order to correct the Act, and the constitutional invalidity of s 309(4)*(a)* became effective.

2.7 When may the prosecution appeal?

2.7.1 *Appeal against a bail decision*

Following English law, our law is slow in allowing the prosecution a right of appeal. The prosecution may therefore not appeal against an acquittal on the facts (merits) of the case—*Brash* 1911 AD 525; *Gasa* 1916 AD 241. However, there is an exception to the rule: Section 65A allows the director of public prosecutions to appeal against the decision of a lower court to release an accused on bail or against the imposition of a condition of bail as contemplated by s 62. The right to appeal is subject to leave to appeal granted by a judge in chambers in terms of s 310A. A decision to grant an accused bail is a factual one and consequently an appeal against such decision turns on the facts. The appeal may be heard by a single judge of a local division— s 65(1)*(b)–(c)*.

The prosecution may, except for an appeal against a bail decision which right of appeal is in any event only available to the director of public prosecutions, appeal against questions of law decided by a lower court and against a sentence imposed by a lower court only. As far as the right to appeal against a decision on sentence, such right is of limited application—see below.

2.7.2   *Appeal restricted to a question of law*

When a lower court in criminal proceedings has given a decision in favour of the accused on any question of law, the director of public prosecutions or any other prosecutor may appeal against such decision. This includes an order by the court in favour of the accused to either amend or quash the charge or to deliver particulars to the charge (see s 85(2) read with s 310(1)). For examples of such appeals see *Van Heerden* 1949 (4) SA 949 (N); *Kungeka* 1954 (4) SA 76 (E); *C* 1955 (1) SA 464 (T); *Zoko* 1983 (1) SA 871 (W).

The legal competency of a court in terms of s 174 to grant an application for a discharge at the close of the case for the prosecution is a legal question. Differently stated, the decision of the trial court, namely that there is no evidence upon which a reasonable man could convict at the close of the case for the prosecution, is one of law. This is so because the forming of an opinion as envisaged by s 174 does not involve the exercise of a discretion properly so called, but merely an evaluation of the evidence and its relevance to the essentials of the crime which the prosecution must prove—*Attorney-General, Venda v Molepo* 1992 (2) SACR 534 (V), following *Thielke* 1918 AD 373 at 376. (Cf also *Attorney-General, Zimbabwe v Mzizi* 1992 (2) SACR 582 (Z) at 583*c–d*.)

Section 310 provides that when a lower court has in any proceedings given a decision in favour of the accused on any question of law, the director of public prosecutions or other prosecutor may require the judicial officer to state a case for the consideration of the court of appeal, setting forth the question of law and his decision thereon. If evidence has been heard, his findings of fact in so far as they are material to the question of law must also be stated. It is not sufficient merely to set forth the reasons for his finding. But if the reasons which he has given make it quite clear what the question of law is, this will be sufficient—*Foley* 1953 (3) SA 496 (E). The director or national director of public prosecutions or other prosecutor may then appeal against the lower court's decision. It is not for the director himself to state the question of law: this must be set forth in the case stated by the magistrate or regional magistrate—*Saib* 1975 (3) SA 994 (N); *Petro Louise Enterprises* 1978 (1) SA 271 (T).

In an appeal in terms of s 310 (and s 311—see below) the court of appeal will, as a general rule in deciding the appeal, confine itself to the findings of fact as reflected in the case stated by the judicial officer but that is not a hard and fast rule. In some cases the court of appeal (or Supreme Court of Appeal) may have recourse to the facts of the case as disclosed at the trial—cf *Attorney-General, Transvaal v Flats Milling Co (Pty) Ltd* 1958 (3) SA 360 (A).

Where the prosecution appeals, the accused must be notified of the appeal— *Van Wyk* 1960 (2) SA 106 (C). The procedure regarding the noting of an appeal by the prosecution and related procedure, is set out in Rule 67(9)–(15) of the Magistrates' Courts Rules. Non-compliance with the Rules could be condoned—cf *Heyns* 1958 (2) SA 253 (E).

The prosecution may not appeal in order to obtain a decision on a purely academic question which will not affect the outcome of the case— *Attorney-General, Transvaal v Raphaely* 1958 (1) SA 309 (A); *Attorney-General, Transvaal v Flats Milling Co (Pty) Ltd* (above); *Attorney-General, Transvaal v Lutchman* 1959 (2) SA 583 (A); *Suid-Afrikaanse Uitsaaikorporasie* 1991 (2) SA 698 (W). The purpose of an appeal by the prosecution in terms of s 310 is not only to clarify a legal question but also to ensure that justice is done—*Lusu* 1953 (2) SA 484 (A) at 494F–H. To distinguish between a question of law and a question of fact can at times be difficult as is borne out by the case of *Attorney-General, Transvaal v Kader* 1991 (4) SA 727 (A).

Unlike the position regarding the reservation of a question of law in terms of s 319, the requisite of a total acquittal is not present where the director of public prosecutions (or other prosecutor) appeals against the decision of a lower court on a question of law—cf *Seekoei* 1982 (3) SA 97 (A). The prosecution may appeal on a legal question where the lower court has convicted the accused of a lesser offence which is a competent verdict on the offence actually charged—*Zoko* 1983 (1) SA 871 (N) at 875E–H. The decision to acquit the accused on the offence actually charged, is a decision *in favour of the accused* as envisaged by s 310. (In *Zoko's* case the accused was charged with culpable homicide but convicted of assault with intent to do grievous bodily harm. The evidence showed that the killing was committed with the intention to kill. The regional magistrate erroneously found that the accused could only be found guilty of an offence that requires *mens rea* in the form of intention and not of culpable homicide that requires negligence only.)

If the appeal is allowed, whether wholly or in part, the court of appeal may itself impose such sentence or make such order as the lower court should have imposed or made. The court of appeal may also remit the case and give certain directions. If the case is remitted, the presiding officer who gave the decision must reopen the case (after giving notice to both parties) and deal with it in the same manner as he should have dealt with it if he had given a decision in accordance with the law laid down by the court of appeal—s 310(4) and (5).

If the prosecutor's appeal is not upheld and refused by a provincial or local division of the High Courts, the prosecution may *with the leave of such court* appeal to the Supreme Court of Appeal. See s 311; s 20(4) of Act 59 of 1959; *Attorney-General, Transvaal v Nokwe* 1962 (3) SA 803 (T).

2.7.3 *Appeal against sentence*

The director of public prosecutions may appeal also against a *sentence* imposed upon an accused in a criminal case in a lower court—s 310A. (In view of the fact that the Act does not mention any other prosecutor and it has to be inferred that the right to appeal a sentence is not available to a private prosecutor or any other prosecutor under statutory right. Compare the wording of s 311 with that of s 310A.) Section 310A(1) permits an appeal against the sentence by the prosecutor, provided that an application for leave to appeal has been granted by a judge in chambers. A written notice of such an application together with the grounds for the application must be lodged with the registrar of the High Court within 30 days of the passing of sentence. Condonation may be granted on just cause if the time limits have not been complied with—*Attorney-General, Venda v Maraga* 1992 (2) SACR 594 (V) at 600*f–i*. The accused may lodge a written submission to the judge hearing the application.

It has been pointed out that s 310A does not restrict the prosecution's right to appeal to instances where the sentence imposed is unfair to the State but it is also appropriate where an incorrect sentence or a sentence against binding authority has been imposed and the director of public prosecutions wishes to bring the matter to the attention of the High Court—*Maseti* 1992 (2) SACR 459 (C). In *Maraga* (above) the court warned that an appeal by the director of public prosecutions against a sentence should not be too readily instituted. Where the appeal against sentence is dismissed, provision has been made to order the accused's costs to be borne by the State—s 310A(6).

Section 310A is designed to widen the powers of the director of public prosecutions in connection with the increase of a sentence on appeal and not to restrict them. However, s 310A did not repeal the established practice whereby the prosecution may request an increase of sentence when the accused brought an appeal—*Kellerman* 1997 (1) SACR 1 (A).

In the absence of a provision similar to that of s 311, it has to be concluded that the legislature did not intend the give the director of public prosecutions the right to a further appeal or a further application for leave to appeal against sentence to be brought before the Supreme Court of Appeal once the appeal against sentence has been dismissed by a provincial or local division or leave to appeal has been refused by the judge. The decision of the court or judge would then be final. If an incompetent sentence were to be upheld by the appeal court, the director of public prosecutions would, it seems, have no redress in terms of this section.

On the question of whether the State should be allowed to appeal on the facts, see Van Rooyen 'Appeals by the State in Criminal Cases—some Policy Considerations' 1970 *CILSA* 360; *Report of the Commission of Inquiry into Criminal Procedure and Evidence* by Botha J (RP 78/1971).

2.8   Powers of court of appeal

The powers of the provincial or local divisions of the High Courts sitting as courts of appeal are regulated by s 304(2) read with s 309(3) and s 22 of the Supreme Court Act 59 of 1959. These powers are the following:

(1)   The court *may hear further evidence*. The power to hear further evidence is derived from s 304(2)*(b)* and s 22*(a)* of the Supreme Court Act 59 of 1959. Section 22*(a)* provides that a provincial or local division shall have the power on the hearing of an appeal to receive further evidence, either orally or by deposition before a person appointed by such division, or to remit the case to the court of first instance for further hearing, with such instructions as regards the taking of further evidence or otherwise as to the division concerned seems necessary. A court of appeal may exercise this power on its own initiative

(*mero motu*) or at the request of the appellant. A request for leave to lead further evidence must be made simultaneously with the appeal. The court will not consider a request for leave to lead further evidence after the appeal has been dismissed—*D* 1953 (4) SA 384 (A) at 391. Section 304(2)*(b)* read with s 309(3) provides that the court of appeal may summon any person to appear and to give evidence or to produce any document or other article. The court does not have to hear the evidence itself but may remit the matter to the court of first instance with instructions as to the hearing of new evidence (cf s 22 of the Supreme Court Act 59 of 1959). Normally the remittal for the hearing of further evidence will only be ordered where the desired evidence is of a mere formal or technical character; or is such as would prove the case without delay and without real dispute; or where it has been omitted at the trial not deliberately but by oversight and where, in addition, a satisfactory explanation is furnished as to why the desired evidence had not been adduced in the first instance—*Mokgeledi* 1968 (4) SA 335 (A) at 339; *Gumede* 1992 (2) SACR 237 (N). The fundamental enquiry involved in whether to allow the hearing of further evidence, is whether the true interests of justice require a case which has been completed to be reopened for the hearing of further evidence because it is in the interest of justice that finality should be reached in criminal cases (see *Roux* 1974 (2) SA 452 (N) at 454H).

(The powers of the Supreme Court of Appeal to hear further evidence is similarly regulated by s 22 of the Supreme Court Act 59 of 1959 and the discussion on the Supreme Court of Appeal's powers with regard to the hearing of further evidence in terms of this section applies *mutatis mutandis* to such powers of the provincial or local division having appeal jurisdiction and sitting as a court of appeal. See below, 'Application for leave to lead further evidence' and 'Powers of the Supreme Court of Appeal'.)

(2) The court may *confirm, alter or quash the conviction*. If the accused was convicted on one of two or more alternative counts, the court may, on quashing that conviction, convict the accused on the other alternative count or on one or other of the alternative counts. However, where the prosecutor has *withdrawn* alternative charges after conviction on the main charge, the court, on quashing that conviction, may not consider the alternative charges—*Conradie* 1972 (2) PH H109 (T).

(3) The court may *confirm, reduce, alter or set aside the sentence or order*. If the appeal is noted against sentence only, the court of appeal has no jurisdiction to extend the ambit of the notice of appeal to include an appeal against conviction—*Matshoba* 1977 (2) SA 671 (A) at 677D; *Abrahams* 1990 (2) SACR 420 (A).

(4) The court may correct the proceedings of the lower court.

(5) The court may generally give such judgment or impose such sentence or make such order as the lower court should have given, imposed or made on any matter which was before it at the trial of the case in question. If punishment-tempering provisions are enacted by an amendment Act, after the imposition of sentence and before the hearing of the accused's appeal against his sentence, the court of appeal would be entitled to impose a sentence according to the new punishment measures. The *ratio* behind this is that when setting aside an original sentence by a court of appeal, the status of the accused at that stage is

juridically the same as that of an unsentenced accused—*Prokureur-Generaal, Noord-Kaap v Hart* 1990 (1) SA 49 (A).

(6)   The court may remit the case to the magistrate's court with instructions to deal with any such matter in such manner as the court of appeal may think fit. When a conviction and sentence has been set aside due to non-compliance with the provisions of subsec (1)*(b)* or subsec (2) of s 112, or on the ground that s 113 should have been applied, the court of appeal is in terms of s 312 obliged to remit the case to the court by which the sentence was imposed and direct that court to comply with the provisions in question or to act in terms of s 113, as the case may be—s 312(1). Section 312(1) obliges a court of appeal to set aside the conviction and sentence and remit the matter to the court *a quo* in circumstances where the trial court did not questioned the accused or did not question the accused properly in order to satisfy itself that the accused had admitted the allegations in the charge or where the trial court erroneously did not apply the provisions of s 113 where it was clear that the court should have had doubts as to the accused's plea of guilty.

(7)   The court may make an order affecting the suspension of the execution of a sentence against the person convicted or his admission to jail or, generally, affecting any relevant matter or proceeding which the court of appeal deems calculated to promote the ends of justice.

(8)   Sentence may be *increased* on appeal. In addition to the powers of the court of appeal to set aside the conviction and sentence, or to reduce the sentence, the court also has the power to increase the imposed sentence or to impose another form of sentence in lieu of or in addition to such sentence—s 309(3). But the court of appeal may not exercise its power to increase the sentence of a lower court (or to impose another form of sentence in lieu of or in addition to such sentence) where the appeal is based *solely upon a question of law*—s 309(3). The practice is for the court to notify the appellant that it will consider increasing the sentence if the appeal fails—*Abrahams* 1983 (1) SA 137 (A) at 148C and see para 1.4 above. It is also a rule of practice that the director of public prosecutions must give notice of his intention to apply for an increase in sentence. See *Swanepoel* 1945 AD 444 at 451; *Naidoo* 1987 (3) SA 834 (N); *Du Toit* 1979 (3) SA 846 (A). In *Kellerman* 1997 (1) SACR 1 (A) the court confirmed *obiter* the rules of practice that an accused is not empowered to withdraw, without leave, his appeal once it has been set down for hearing and when notice of a request for a proposed increase of sentence has been lodged by the director of public prosecutions.

The approach of a court of appeal when considering whether a sentence should be increased is to compare the sentence it would have imposed with that actually imposed by the court *a quo*. If in such comparison it appears that the difference is substantial, the court has a duty to interfere with the sentence—*De Vos* 1970 (2) SA 590 (C); *Human* 1979 (3) SA 331 (E); *Du Toit* above. A court of appeal does not have the jurisdiction to increase, on appeal, a sentence beyond the penal jurisdiction of the trial court—*Louw* 1990 (3) SA 116 (A) at 126B; *Peter* 1989 (3) SA 649 (CkA).

The power of the court of appeal to increase the sentence may be exercised also where the appeal is against the *conviction* only (and not against the sentence as well, or against the sentence only)—cf *Deetlefs* 1953 (1) SA 418 (A); *F* 1983 (1) SA 747 (O). On an appeal against *sentence* only, a court of appeal has no power to substitute a conviction of a more serious crime—*Tladi* 1989 (3) SA 444 (B). (See also the discussion in para 1.4 above.)

(9) The court of appeal has the power to give any judgment or make any order which the circumstances may require—s 22*(b)* of the Supreme Court Act 59 of 1959. Consequently, the court may give such judgment or impose such sentence as the trial court should have given or imposed (s 304(2)(iv) read with s 309(3)). The court of appeal may, therefore, substitute a more serious offence for the offence of which the accused was convicted in the court *a quo*. This power is, however, limited—*Morgan* 1993 (2) SACR 134 (A) at 160*(c)*—162*(g)*. On conviction on appeal of the more serious offence, the sentence may be increased or the matter may be remitted to the trial court for the imposition of a proper sentence—cf *E* 1979 (3) SA 973 (A) at 977D–E. In *V* 1953 (3) SA 314 (A) the accused was charged in the alternative and found not guilty on the main charge but guilty on the alternative charge. On appeal the court held that the conviction should be set aside, that the accused was guilty on the main charge and that the court of appeal was entitled to convict the accused (appellant) on the main charge. The court of appeal remitted the case to the magistrate for sentence. See also *Du Toit* 1966 (4) SA 627 (A). However, where an accused is convicted on one charge and acquitted on another substantive charge and he appeals against his conviction, the court of appeal has no power to alter the verdict of not guilty to one of guilty—*Phewa* 1962 (3) SA 370 (N); *Motha* 1987 (1) SA 374 (T). This is not a case of a main and alternative charge as in *V's* case, but of two substantive independent charges.

2.9 Execution of sentence pending appeal

The execution of any sentence is not suspended pending appeal unless the court which imposed the sentence sees fit to order that the convicted person be released on bail—see s 307(1), read with s 309(4). Prior to 1963, a convicted person was entitled to bail as of right—*Sisulu* 1963 (2) SA 596 (W). The court now has a discretion whether to grant bail or not. Steps may be taken to cancel bail where the convicted person is about to abscond—*Allie v De Vries NO* 1982 (1) SA 774 (T).

Although the execution of a *sentence* is not suspended, an appeal suspends the operation of an order as, for example, an order which authorises the suspension of a driver's licence—*Abraham* 1964 (2) SA 336 (T).

2.10 Remission for new sentence

When a case is remitted on appeal to that lower court which originally tried the matter, for an altered sentence or an addition to a sentence, such sentence need not be passed by the judicial officer who originally passed sentence—s 275.

2.11 Fresh trial

In terms of s 324, read with s 313, proceedings may be instituted again when a conviction of a lower court is set aside on any of the following grounds:

(1) the court was not competent to convict; or

(2) the charge sheet was invalid or defective; or

(3) there was a technical irregularity in the proceedings.

The proviso in s 309(3) restricts the instituting of fresh proceedings on the grounds of irregularities. It provides that, notwithstanding that the court is of opinion that a point may be decided in favour of the appellant, no conviction or sentence may be reversed or altered by reason of any irregularity or defect in the record or proceedings, unless it appears to the court of appeal that a failure of justice has in fact resulted. However, where proceedings are void *ab initio*, a court of appeal will not hesitate to intervene *mero motu* and set the proceedings aside— *Prinsloo* 1970 (3) SA 550 (O). The proviso contained in s 309(3), must be read in the context of the constitutional demand for a fair trial. See also the discussion relating to the proviso contained in s 322 in para 3.11.1 below.

When a trial is instituted afresh on any of the above grounds, a plea of *autrefois acquit* will be of no avail to an accused if he is prosecuted again on the same charge. However, s 313 must be interpreted in consonance with the principles regarding double jeopardy or *autrefois acquit*. (The discussion in par 3.11.1 'Setting aside or alteration of conviction on ground of irregularity' below applies *mutatis mutandis*.)

3 APPEALS TO THE FULL COURT AND THE SUPREME COURT OF APPEAL

3.1 Jurisdiction and constitution of:

3.1.1 *The Supreme Court of Appeal*

The composition and jurisdiction of the Supreme Court of Appeal are arranged in general terms by the Constitution in s 168 thereof. Accordingly, the court consist of a Chief Justice, Deputy Chief Justice and a number of judges determined by legislation. The Supreme Court of Appeal may, contrary to the 1993 Constitution, decide any appeal of whatever matter even constitutional matters. It is the highest court of appeal except in constitutional matters and may decide only—

(a) appeals;

(b) issues connected with appeals; and

(c) any other matter that may be referred to it in circumstances defined by an Act of Parliament.

The quorum of the Supreme Court of Appeal shall be five judges in all criminal matters. The Chief Justice or, in his absence, the senior available judge of the Supreme Court of Appeal, may direct that a criminal appeal, save a criminal matter arising out of proceedings instituted before a special criminal court constituted under s 148 of the Criminal Procedure Act, be heard before a court consisting of three judges—s 12 of the Supreme Court Act 59 of 1959.

In respect of appeals and questions of law reserved in connection with criminal cases heard by a provincial or local division or a special High Court, the court of appeal shall be the Supreme Court of Appeal, except in so far as the provisions regarding appeals before a Full Court provide otherwise—s 315(1).

3.1.2 *The Full Court*

'Full court' means a court of a provincial division, or the Witwatersrand local division of the High Court, sitting as a court of appeal and constituted before three judges—s 315(5)*(b)* read with s 13(2)*(a)*(ii) of the Supreme Court Act 59 of 1959 and s 166*(c)* of the Constitution. A Full Court is a court of appeal and not a court of first instance and consequently a criminal trial cannot be conducted before such a court. In relation to appeals from provincial or local divisions as courts of first instances, the words 'court of appeal' means either a Full Court or the Supreme Court of Appeal. Only provincial divisions has each a Full Court, except in the case of the Witwatersrand local division where the judge president may direct a Full Court for that local division as well. The powers of a Full Court are the same, unless otherwise stated, as that of a provincial division sitting as a court of appeal. An appeal which is to be heard by a Full Court shall, in terms of s 315(3), be heard—

(1) in the case of an appeal in a criminal case heard by a single judge of a provincial division, by the Full Court of the provincial division concerned;

(2) in the case of an appeal in a criminal case heard by a single judge of a local division other than the Witwatersrand Local Division, by the Full Court of the provincial division which exercises concurrent jurisdiction in the area of jurisdiction of the local division concerned;

(3) in the case of an appeal in a criminal case heard by a single judge of the Witwatersrand Local Division

   (a) by the Full Court of the Transvaal Provincial Division, unless a direction by the judge president of that division under *(b)* applies to it; or

   (b) by the Full Court of the said *local* division if the said judge president has so directed in the particular instance.

A Full Court must be distinguished from a 'full bench'. The latter means that whenever it appears to the judge president or, in his absence, the senior available judge of any division, that any matter, which is being heard before a court of that division, ought, in view of its importance be heard before a court consisting of a larger number of judges, he may direct that the hearing be discontinued and commenced anew before a court consisting of so many judges as he may determine—s 13(3) of the Supreme Court Act 59 of 1959. This is commonly called a full bench trial. However, the term 'being heard' in this section, includes the hearing of an appeal and therefore an appeal in terms of s 309 may also be heard by a full bench (ie before more than the required number of (two) judges) of a provincial or local division as a court of appeal, if so ordered by the judge president of the provincial division. The enlargement of a Full Court would hardly be allowed for the obvious reason that if the matter is of such importance, leave to appeal should have been granted to the Supreme Court of Appeal and not to a Full Court—see the criterion for an appeal to a Full Court, below.

If an application for leave to appeal in a criminal case, heard by a single judge of a provincial or local division (irrespective of whether he sat with or without assessors) is granted under s 316 (see below), the court or judge or judges granting the application shall, if he/they or the majority of them is/are satisfied that the questions of law and of fact and the other considerations involved in the appeal (such as public importance) are of such a nature that the appeal does not require the attention of the Supreme Court of Appeal, direct that the appeal be heard by a Full Court—s 315(2)*(a)*. The criterion for allowing an appeal to the Full Court depends largely on whether the appeal is without obvious difficulties—see *Sinama* 1998 (1) SACR 255 (SCA).

Any such direction by the court or a judge of the provincial or local division may be set aside by the Supreme Court of Appeal, on application (by way of a petition addressed to the Chief Justice) by the accused or the director of public prosecutions or other prosecutor within 21 days after the direction was given (or such longer period as may on application to the Supreme Court of Appeal on good cause be allowed)— s 315(2)*(b)–(c)*. An appeal against the judgment or order of a Full Court given on appeal in terms of s 315(3), shall be allowed only with the special leave of the Supreme Court of Appeal on application either by the accused or by the prosecution.

It is suggested that s 315(2)*(a)* does not give a Full Court jurisdiction to hear unsuccessful appeals from lower courts heard by a provincial or local division of a High Court. The wording of this section refers specifically to 'a criminal case heard by a single judge'. Consequently, in view of the fact that all appeal cases before High Courts (except for appeals against decisions on bail which are specifically provided for in ss 65 and 65A and as such *sui generis*), are heard by at least two judges, the submission must be correct. Only matters heard by a High Court (excluding a special High Court because such court sits with more than a single judge (see s 148(3)*(a)*), as a court of first instance may be adjudicated by a Full Court as a court of appeal. Section 316(1A)*(a)* may give rise to a different interpretation of s 315(2)*(a)*, although this is highly unlikely. The section provides as follows:

> '316(1A)*(a)* No appeal shall lie against the judgment or order of a Full Court given on appeal to it in terms of section 315(3), except with the special leave of the Supreme Court of Appeal on application made to it by the accused or, where a Full Court has for the purposes of such judgment or order given a decision in favour of the accused on a question of law, on application on the grounds of such decision made to that division by the director of public prosecutions or other prosecutor against whom the decision was given'.

The reference to the decision on a question of law being decided in favour of the accused, may suggest that the appeal by the state to the High Court was decided in favour of the accused and the prosecution now wishes to appeal further and accordingly support an argument that the legislature intended an appeal from a lower court. This argument is, however, unfounded in view of the fact that s 311 allows the prosecution, when unsuccessful with its appeal to the High Court, access to the Supreme Court of Appeal only.

A Full Court has *no jurisdiction* to hear an appeal in the following instances:

(1) where it has been directed by the court hearing the application for leave to appeal that the questions of law or of fact or other considerations require the attention of the Supreme Court of Appeal;

(2) where leave to appeal on a special entry of irregularity or illegality against the proceedings of a High Court has been granted;

(3) where a question of law has been reserved by a High Court;

(4) where an appeal is brought against the judgment or order of a provincial or local division of the High Court given on appeal;

(5) where an appeal is lodged against a decision or order given by a special High Court.

3.2 Right of appeal to the Supreme Court of Appeal

Section 315(4) provides that appeals with regard to proceedings in High Courts as courts of first instance, shall lie only as provided in ss 316–319 and shall not be as *of right*, that is, leave to appeal must first be obtained. Sections 20(4)*(b)*, 20(5)*(a)* and 21 of the Supreme Court Act 59 of 1959 provide *inter alia* that there is no appeal to the Supreme Court of Appeal on a decision given by any provincial or local division on an appeal to such division, except with the leave of the court against whose decision the appeal is to be made. The automatic right of appeal to the Supreme Court of Appeal which existed in the case where a sentence of death was imposed, had lapsed when the death penalty was declared to be invalid and unconstitutional by the Constitutional Court (cf s 316A). A criminal matter may be taken on appeal to the Supreme Court of Appeal in the following manner:

(1) In cases *tried in lower courts* and taken on appeal by the prosecution or the accused to a provincial or local division with appeal jurisdiction, a further appeal to the Supreme Court of Appeal is possible only with the leave of the provincial or local division concerned or, where such division refuses leave, then with the leave of the Supreme Court of Appeal itself.

(2) In cases *tried in High Courts*, appeals to the Supreme Court of Appeal are possible in the following circumstances only:

   (a) where leave to appeal against a conviction and/or sentence or order following thereon, is granted by the trial court—s 316(1). Where leave to appeal is refused, the Supreme Court of Appeal may be approached by way of petition addressed to the Chief Justice;

   (b) where an application for appeal on grounds of a special entry is *granted* by the trial court based on an alleged irregularity or illegality—ss 317 and 318. Where an application for a special entry is refused, the Supreme Court of Appeal may be approached by way of petition addressed to the Chief Justice;

   (c) where a question of law is reserved by the trial court either *mero motu* or at the request of the prosecution or the accused—s 319. Here too, a further remedy is available in that the Supreme Court of Appeal may be approached by petition if the trial court refuses to reserve a question of law;

   (d) where the state has been given leave to appeal against sentence—s 316B; and

   (e) where a matter is brought to the Supreme Court of Appeal by the Minister for decision of the Supreme Court of Appeal concerning a question of law, where the Minister is doubtful as to the correctness of any decision given by any High Court in any criminal case, or where conflicting decisions on a question of law in criminal matters were given by different divisions—s 333. There are no legal consequences for an accused as a result of this procedure. See Chapter 2 for a discussion.

(3) Matters decided on appeal by a Full Court may only be brought to the Supreme Court of Appeal with leave by the Supreme Court of Appeal.

3.3   Appeals to the Supreme Court of Appeal in cases that originated in a lower court

An appeal against a judgment or order of the court of a provincial or local division having appeal jurisdiction in a matter which originated in a lower court, and which was brought before that division on appeal, is regulated by ss 20(4)*(b)*, 20(5)*(a)* and 21 of the Supreme Court Act 59 of 1959. These sections provide *inter alia*, as has been mentioned, that there is no appeal to the Supreme Court of Appeal on a decision given by any provincial or local division on an appeal to such division, except with the leave of the court against whose decision the appeal is to be made. The provincial or local division against whose decision an appeal is made, may grant or refuse the appellant bail—s 309(5) of the Criminal Procedure Act.

Every application for leave to appeal must set out, clearly and specifically, the grounds upon which the accused desires to appeal. The grounds of appeal to the Supreme Court of Appeal need not coincide with the grounds of appeal from the court to the provincial or local division—*Attorney-General, Transvaal v Flats Milling Co (Pty) Ltd* 1958 (3) SA 360 (A).

Where leave to appeal is not applied for within the prescribed time, application for condonation of delay in applying for leave must accompany the accused's application for leave to appeal. (See the discussion below, under 'Application for leave to appeal'.)

If a provincial division refuses leave to appeal, the accused may, by petition addressed to the Chief Justice, submit his application for leave to appeal to the Supreme Court of Appeal. The petition is considered by two judges of the Supreme Court of Appeal designated by the Chief Justice. The judges considering the petition may in terms of s 21 of the Supreme Court Act—

(1) grant or refuse the application; or

(2) refer the application to the Supreme Court of Appeal for consideration, whether upon argument or otherwise, and the Supreme Court of Appeal may then grant or refuse the application.

The decision of the majority of the judges or of the Supreme Court of Appeal as the case may be, is final. With regard to the procedure to be followed when a petition is lodged with the Supreme Court of Appeal under s 21, see *Summers* 1956 (2) SA 786 (A) and rule 52 of the Supreme Court Rules.

Notice of the date fixed and of the place appointed for such hearing, if a hearing is ordered, is given to the applicant and the respondent by the registrar of the Supreme Court of Appeal.

Where a provincial division refuses to grant an order condoning the late noting of an appeal to the Supreme Court of Appeal, the only remedy is a petition to the Supreme Court of Appeal against such refusal. The High Court's leave for such petition and appeal is not required—*Tsedi* 1984 (1) SA 565 (A); *Absalom* 1989 (3) SA 154 (A). Where the Supreme Court of Appeal has reversed on appeal a local or provincial division's refusal to grant condonation, it does not have the power to hear the appeal on the merits. *No provision has been made for an appeal directly to the Supreme Court of Appeal against a conviction by a lower court.* After the reversal of the local or provincial division's refusal of condonation, the matter must be remitted to the local or provincial division for the hearing of the application for leave to appeal unless leave to appeal has been requested simultaneously with the petition for condonation (see also *N* 1991 (2) SACR 10 (A). However, the Supreme Court of Appeal may direct, if it is deemed expedient, that an application for leave to appeal shall be submitted by petition to the Chief Justice as if it had been refused by the trial judge (or other judge)—s 316(8)*(c)*(i).

Where leave to call further evidence is applied for after a provincial division has dismissed an appeal, the Supreme Court of Appeal may be approached directly for leave to lead such evidence—cf s 22 of the Supreme Court Act 59 of 1959 and *Schawol* 1956 (1) SA 310 (T).

The national or director of public prosecutions or other prosecutor may appeal against a decision given on appeal by a provincial or local division in a matter arising in the lower court, if such division has given a decision in favour of a *convicted* accused on a *matter of law*, after having obtained the necessary leave to appeal. Such leave must be obtained from the provincial or local division concerned. If such leave is refused, the director of public prosecutions may petition the Supreme Court of Appeal for leave. See s 311(1), read with s 20(4)*(b)* of the Supreme Court Act 59 of 1959; *Attorney-General, Transvaal v Nokwe* 1962 (3) SA 803 (T) (*contra Dave* 1954 (4) SA 736 (A)). (See also 'Appeal by prosecution to the Supreme Court of Appeal' below.) If the prosecution succeeds in an appeal to the provincial or local division brought in terms of s 310(2) against the decision of the lower court, such division may grant the accused leave to appeal to the Supreme Court of Appeal in terms of s 21(1) of the Supreme Court Act—cf *Webb* 1956 (2) SA 208 (A).

3.4 Application for leave to appeal

3.4.1 *By whom, when and against what must an application for leave to appeal be made?*

(1) An accused convicted before a High Court may, within a period of 14 days of the passing of any sentence or order as a result of such conviction, apply for leave to appeal to the trial court—s 316(1). However, a refusal of an application for bail, following a conviction and sentence by a High Court, is not an appealable order—*Heller* 1970 (4) SA 679 (A).

(2) Leave to appeal against a judgment or order given on appeal by a court of a provincial or local division, must be applied for by the appellant within 15 days after the date the judgment or order was given—see rule 49(1)*(a)* and *(b)* of the Supreme Court Rules read with s 21(2) of the Supreme Court Act 59 of 1959.

(3) An accused who is found not guilty by reason of mental disorder at the time when he committed the act may appeal against such finding if the finding was not made in consequence of an allegation by the accused that he was mentally disordered—s 78(8) read with s 78(2) and (6).

(4) An accused convicted of any offence before *a High Court* on a plea of guilty may, within 14 days of the passing of any sentence, apply for leave to appeal against any *sentence or any order* following thereon only—s 316(1)*(b)*. Notwithstanding this provision, an accused who pleaded guilty in a High Court to a charge of murder was previously not denied an appeal against a *conviction* which was based on such a plea. This was allowed in terms of s 316A read with s 112(1)*(b)*. Section 112(1)*(b)* provides that despite a plea of guilty, the sentence of death shall not be imposed unless the guilt of the accused has been proved 'as if he had pleaded not guilty'. (See *Mavhungu* 1981 (1) SA 56 (A); and cf also *Mamba* 1957 (2) SA 420 (A) at 422A.) After the demise of the death penalty, the legal position with regard to such appeal against a conviction following a plea of guilty appears to be somewhat uncertain.

(5) Leave to appeal before termination of the trial is, in principle, not allowed—see par 1.3 above.

(6) The director of public prosecutions may within a period of 14 days of the passing of the decision, apply for leave to appeal against the decision of a High Court to release an accused—s 65A(2). The director of public prosecutions may not appeal the imposition of any condition of bail as contemplated in s 65(1)*(a)*—s 65A(2)*(a)* read and compared to s 65A(1)*(a)*.

3.4.2   *To whom must the application be made?*

(1) If the conviction was by a special High Court, application for leave to appeal is made to that court or any judge who was a member of that court. If no such judge is available, application is made to any judge of the provincial or local division within whose jurisdiction the special High Court sat—s 316*(a)*.

(2) If the conviction was by any other court, application is made to the judge who presided at the trial. If he is not available, application is made to another judge of the division concerned. In the case of conviction before a circuit court, application is made to that court, but if it is not in session, it may be made to a judge of the provincial or local division of which the judge of the circuit court was a member—s 316(1)*(b)*.

(3) If leave to appeal is sought against any judgment or order of the court of a provincial or local division given on appeal, application for leave to appeal is to be made to the court against whose judgment or order the appeal is to be made—s 20(4)*(b)* of Supreme Court Act 59 of 1959.

(4) If the accused fails timeously to approach the court that passed sentence for leave to appeal, he may approach another court, provided that his application is *bona fide*. See *Makhali v Minister of Justice* 1957 (4) SA 322 (T).

(5) If leave to appeal is sought against a decision to release an accused on bail, the director of public prosecutions may apply for leave to appeal to the court who gave the decision in the same manner as an accused convicted by a High Court—s 65A(2)*(b)* read with s 316.

3.4.3   *Grounds of appeal*

An application for leave to appeal must set forth, clearly and specifically, the grounds upon which the accused desires to appeal. This also applies to an application brought by the director of public prosecutions. If the party applies verbally for leave immediately after the passing of sentence by a High Court, he must state the grounds and they must be taken down in writing and form part of the record—s 316(2) and see rule 49(1)*(a)* and *(b)* of the Supreme Court Rules and *Hlatswayo* 1982 (4) SA 744 (A).

When leave to appeal is granted, the leave may be limited to particular grounds of appeal. But if leave to appeal is granted generally, without restricting the grounds, all issues may be canvassed on appeal—*Jantjies* 1958 (2) SA 273 (A). Where leave to appeal has been granted on limited grounds, the Supreme Court of Appeal may be approached for an extension of such grounds. The Supreme Court of Appeal has the power to grant leave to appeal on wider grounds than those allowed by the trial judge—*Mpompotshe* 1958 (4) SA 471 (A) at 473. A local or provincial division does not, however, have the power to grant leave for the extension of grounds of appeal after leave to appeal has been granted on particular grounds by that division—*Van H* 1959 (3) SA 648 (T).

The question whether the Supreme Court of Appeal may allow an appellant who appealed against the *sentence* imposed by a lower court to appeal against the *conviction*, was raised in *L* 1960 (3) SA 503 (A), but left undecided. In *Abrahams* 1990 (2) SACR 420 (A), it was held that the Supreme Court of Appeal cannot assume jurisdiction under s 22 of the Supreme Court Act 59 of 1959, to set aside a conviction where there is an appeal against the sentence only. Where the trial court has granted leave to appeal to the Supreme Court of Appeal against the conviction, the Supreme Court of Appeal may interfere with the sentence—*Mazibuko* 1978 (4) SA 563 (A) at 565.

3.4.4 *When leave to appeal should be granted*

In determining whether or not to grant an application for leave to appeal, the dominant criterion is whether or not the applicant has a reasonable prospect of success on appeal. The mere circumstance that a case is 'arguable' is insufficient, unless the term 'arguable' is used in the sense that there is substance in the argument advanced on behalf of the applicant. In the nature of things, it is always somewhat invidious for a judge to have to determine whether a judgment which he has himself given may be considered by a higher court to be wrong. That, however, is a duty imposed by the legislature upon judges. The primary consideration in an application for leave to appeal is therefore whether or not (both in relation to questions of fact and of law) there is a reasonable prospect of success—cf *Baloi* 1949 (1) SA 523 (A); *Kuzwayo* 1949 (3) SA 761 (A) at 765; *Shaffee* 1952 (2) SA 484 (A); *Ackerman* 1973 (1) SA 765 (A). The judge is thus faced with no easy task, but he must exercise his power judicially and objectively, and ask himself whether there is a reasonable prospect that another court might come to a different conclusion—*Sikosana* 1980 (4) SA 559 (A).

The *mere possibility* that another court might come to a different conclusion is not sufficient to justify the granting of leave to appeal—*Ceaser* 1977 (2) SA 348 (A) at 350. Nevertheless, in *Milne and Erleigh* (3) 1950 (4) SA 599 (A), the court took into consideration that a number of difficult and novel questions of law were involved. See also *Muller* 1957 (4) SA 642 (A).

Leave to appeal may, however, be granted even if there is no prospect of success on the existing record, if there is a reasonable prospect that leave to adduce further evidence will be granted and that, if it is, the result may be different—*Jantjies* 1958 (2) SA 273 (A).

If the application is refused, the judge must furnish his reasons for refusal—s 320, *Sikosana* (above) and see *White* 1952 (2) SA 538 (A). The fact that an accused pleaded guilty before the court of first instance does not mean that leave to appeal will never be granted. See *In re Clark* 1958 (3) SA 394 (A); *Mavhungu* 1981 (1) SA 56 (A). The mere fact that the State does not oppose an application is not a proper ground for granting leave to appeal—*Mosia* 1971 (2) PH H135 (A).

3.4.5 *If leave to appeal is refused*

Where an application for leave to appeal against a judgment, sentence or order given by a High Court as a court of first instance is refused, the accused has another legal remedy namely to apply to the Supreme Court of Appeal for leave to appeal. Such application must be made within 21 days after refusal by the High Court, and is made by petition addressed to the Chief Justice. If the accused has not applied within 21 days, he may on good cause be allowed to apply later—s 316(6).

The petition may be considered in chambers by two judges of the Supreme Court of Appeal designated by the Chief Justice or in case of a difference of opinion by the Chief Justice or by any other judge of the Supreme Court of Appeal to whom it has been referred by the Chief Justice—s 316(7). The judges considering the petition may—

(1) call for further information from the judge who heard the application for leave to appeal or who presided at the trial;

(2) order that the application be argued before them;

(3) whether they have taken the above-mentioned steps or not, grant or refuse the application; or

(4) refer the matter to the Supreme Court of Appeal for consideration, whether upon argument or otherwise. The Supreme Court of Appeal may then grant or refuse the application.

The decision of the Supreme Court of Appeal, or of the judges thereof considering the petition, to grant or refuse any application for leave to appeal is final.

If the accused applies to the *trial court* for leave to appeal only against his *sentence* and that is refused, he cannot later apply to the Supreme Court of Appeal for leave to appeal against his *conviction*—*Cassidy* 1978 (1) SA 687 (A).

Notice must be given to the director of public prosecutions and the accused of the date fixed for the hearing of the application—s 316(10).

3.5 Application for condonation

Leave to appeal must be applied for within the prescribed time limits, unless condonation is obtained for the late filing of notice of appeal. Section 316(1) specifically makes provision for an application for leave to appeal within such extended period as may on good cause be allowed.

In an application to condone a defective procedure, the court will not grant condonation where the appellant has no reasonable prospect of success on appeal, and accordingly, the court is entitled to consider the merits of the appeal— *Mofokeng v Prokureur-Generaal, OVS* 1958 (4) SA 519 (O). In *Tsedi* 1984 (1) SA 565 (A) the Supreme Court of Appeal indeed took into consideration the absence of any prospect of success in rejecting the appellant's application for condonation. The test of whether there are reasonable prospects of success on appeal is a lesser one than that which has to be applied in deciding whether the appeal ought to succeed or not—*N* 1991 (2) SACR 10 (A) at 13*(b)*–*(c)*. (On the subject of condonation see the discussion under the heading 'Condonation of late noting or late prosecution of appeals' in the previous section.) See also *Matsatebe* 1949 (2) SA 105 (O); *Boya* 1952 (3) SA 574 (C); *Kgolane* 1959 (4) SA 483 (A); *Kashire* 1978 (4) SA 166 (SWA).

If an application for condonation is refused, the accused may, within a period of 21 days of such refusal, or within such extended period as may on good cause be allowed, by petition addressed to the Chief Justice submit his application for condonation—s 316(6). See also s 21(2) and (3) of the Supreme Court Act 59 of 1959 with regard to a petition to the Supreme Court of Appeal for leave to appeal or for condonation against the refusal of the provincial or local division of the High Court. The rules relating to a petition for leave to appeal apply *mutatis mutandis* to a petition for condonation.

Where condonation is granted by the Supreme Court of Appeal it may direct, if they deem it expedient, that an application for leave to appeal shall be submitted by petition to the Chief Justice as if it had been refused by the trial judge (or other judge)—s 316(8)*(c)*(i).

3.6 Application for leave to lead further evidence

When applying to the trial court or another judge of a provincial or local division for leave to appeal, a convicted person may also apply for leave to lead further evidence—s 316(3). This section by implication requires that the context of the evidence be placed before the court—*Loubscher* 1979 (3) SA 47 (A).

However, it is in the interest of justice that finality be reached in criminal cases. Once the facts have been decided upon, the case will not lightly be reopened—cf *De Jager* 1965 (2) SA 612 (A); *Yusuf* 1968 (2) SA 59 (A). Because of the finality principle it is a general principle regarding further evidence is that such evidence should be allowed in exceptional circumstances only, although a certain measure of leniency towards applications for the hearing of further evidence is apparent in certain cases (Hiemstra 800–1). In exceptional cases the court might come to the relief of the accused if it is satisfied that there is a reasonable probability that he would not be convicted if given the opportunity of a further hearing—*Ford* 1974 (2) PH H39 (N); *Myende* 1985 (1) SA 805 (A). (On this aspect, see the discussion below under 'Powers of the Supreme Court of Appeal'.)

Prior to 1968, a provincial or local division of the High Courts had no power of its own without the authority of the Supreme Court of Appeal, to hear any fresh evidence after conviction and sentence. Such power was first granted by s 24 of Act 9 of 1968—the then s 363(3) of Act 56 of 1955. (Section 316(3) is consonant to the provisions of the repealed s 363(3) of Act 56 of 1955.) However, even though the provincial or local division prior to 1968 had no statutory power for the hearing of further evidence, it was the practice of the Supreme Court of Appeal to remit a case to the trial court for the hearing of further evidence where a conviction and sentence were set aside on appeal because fresh evidence had become available—cf *De Jager* (above). Today this situation is remedied by s 316(3).

When an application under s 316(1) for leave to appeal is brought, it must be shown by affidavit—

(1) that further evidence which would presumably be accepted as true, is available;

(2) that if accepted, the evidence could reasonably lead to a different verdict or sentence; and

(3) save in exceptional cases, that there is a reasonably acceptable explanation for the failure to produce the evidence before the close of the trial—s 316(3). The failure of a legal representative to call available witnesses is not an acceptable explanation—*N* 1988 (3) SA 450 (A); *Venter* 1990 (2) SACR 291 (NC).

The *onus* of satisfying these requirements rests upon the appellant. It is not in the interests of the proper administration of justice that further evidence should be allowed on appeal, or that there should be a re-trial for the purpose of hearing that further evidence, when the only further evidence was that contained in affidavits made after trial and conviction, by persons who recanted the evidence they gave at the trial. Some good reason has to be shown why a lie was told in the first instance, and a good reason has to be given for thinking that the witness would tell the truth on the second occasion—*H* 1998 (1) SACR 260 (SCA).

Normally the courts demand that all three requirements are to be fulfilled. Although an application for leave to lead further evidence may be brought in terms of s 316(3), it can be made only in conjunction with a competent application for leave to appeal. If leave to appeal has been refused with final effect, an application for leave to lead further evidence is incompetent—*Ebrahim* 1972 (2) SA 61 (C); *Gavanozis* 1979 (1) SA 1020 (W). Furthermore the trial judge is empowered only to hear such evidence and not to set aside the conviction and sentence even if it is clear that the conviction cannot stand—*Masinda* 1981 (3) SA 1157 (A) at 1165B. Nevertheless, the court is entitled to express an opinion on issues affected by the new evidence and to furnish the court of appeal with the reasons for such an opinion— *Tsawane* 1989 (1) SA 268 (A).

If an application for leave to call further evidence is refused, the accused may (just as in the case of condonation or leave to appeal) petition the Chief Justice—s 316(6). Where the judges considering the petition are of the opinion that the application for leave to call further evidence should have been granted, they may set aside the refusal of the court *a quo* and remit the matter in order that further evidence may be received—s 316(8)*(c)*(ii).

If an accused discovers further evidence after the trial court has already *refused* an application for leave to appeal, the remedy of further evidence in terms of s 316(3) is exhausted. If *leave to appeal* was *granted* but leave to lead further evidence refused, an accused may approach the Supreme Court of Appeal in terms of s 22 of the Supreme Court Act 59 of 1959, and the Supreme Court of Appeal may grant leave to lead further evidence. If, however, the Supreme Court of Appeal has already refused a petition for leave to lead further evidence in terms of s 316(6) (see above), the Supreme Court of Appeal has no jurisdiction to act in terms of s 22 of the Supreme Court Act and the only remedy available to the accused is as contemplated by s 327.

For criticism of the provisions of s 316(3) see *Masinda* 1981 (3) SA 1157 (A) and the South African Law Commission's Working Paper 42 (1994) *Simplification of the Criminal Procedure.*

The Constitutional Court has the power under rule 19 of the Constitutional Court Rules to admit new evidence on appeal. This Court should not, however, save in exceptional circumstances, permit disputes of fact or expert opinion to be raised for the first time on appeal—*Lawrence* 1997 (4) SA 1176 (CC).

3.7 Appeal on special entry of irregularity or illegality

Irregular proceedings or proceedings not according to law in a lower court may be taken on review before the High Court. However, there is no review procedure for irregular proceedings in trials in a High Court but it does not leave the accused without a remedy: the Criminal Procedure Act makes provision for a so-called special entry on the ground of which the accused may, if convicted, take his/her case to the Supreme Court of Appeal. This procedure is necessary because an irregularity will often not appear from the record, and the accused will therefore not be able to rely on it if he takes the case on appeal. With a special entry the accused may request during or after the trial, that the irregularity be entered on the record. Naturally, the trial judge himself will have to consider the application based on the alleged irregularity and this may influence him in his decision.

Two types of irregularity are possible; those *relating* to the trial, and those that arise *during* the trial. In the latter type of irregularity, for example, a refusal of the judge to allow proper cross-examination—to use an extreme example—the judge himself will be aware of what has happened. The first type of irregularity, for example where an assessor gained extra-curial information detrimental to the accused, will have to be proved by evidence—*Matsego* 1956 (3) SA 411 (A). Cf also *Suliman* 1969 (2) SA 385 (A). Where the prosecution fails to disclose a material divergence from the witnesses' statements, it is an irregularity in the proceedings for the purposes of s 317(1)—*Xaba* 1983 (3) SA 717 (A).

Where the irregularity in question clearly appears *ex facie* the record and a general and unqualified leave to appeal has been granted, it is unnecessary for a special entry to be made in that respect—*Ncaphayi* 1990 (1) SACR 472 (A); *Xaba (supra)*.

Section 317(1) provides that if an accused thinks that any of the proceedings in connection with or during his/her trial before a High Court are irregular or not according to law he/she may, during the trial or within a period of 14 days after the conviction, apply for a special entry to be made on the record stating in what respect the proceedings are alleged to be irregular or not according to law. The court is bound to make such a special entry upon such application, unless the court or judge to whom the application is made is of the opinion that the application is not made *bona fide* or that it is frivolous or absurd (*Sefatsa v Attorney-General, Transvaal* 1988 (4) SA 297 (T)), or that the granting of the application would be an abuse of the process of the court.

Section 317 is concerned with irregularities or illegalities *in respect of procedure*. Questions of law cannot, therefore, form the subject of a special entry.

If a special entry is made on the record, the accused may, if convicted, appeal to the Supreme Court of Appeal against conviction on the ground of the irregularity or illegality. The accused must, within 21 days after the entry is made (or within such extended period as may on good cause shown be allowed) give notice of appeal to the registrar of the Supreme Court of Appeal and to the registrar of the provincial or local division—s 318(1).

If the accused fails to make the application within the prescribed period of 14 days, he/she may on good cause shown be allowed to make the application later— s 317(1). Usually an application for a special entry is made to the judge who presided at the trial, but it may also be made to another judge—s 317(2) and (3). The terms of a special entry are settled by the court which, or the judge who grants the application—s 317(4). (For the formal requirements with reference to the wording of a special entry, see *Kroon* 1997 (1) SACR 525 (A).)

If an application for a special entry is refused, the accused may, within a period of 21 days of such refusal (or within such extended period as may on good cause shown be allowed), by petition addressed to the Chief Justice, apply to the Supreme Court of Appeal for a special entry to be made on the record. The same applies to refusal of an application for condonation—s 317(4).

Where an application for leave to appeal has been refused by the Chief Justice, the accused may not, *on the same grounds*, apply for a special entry to be made— *Serumula* 1962 (3) SA 962 (A). See also *Swanepoel* 1979 (1) SA 478 (A).

In considering the appeal on a special entry the court must heed the proviso to s 322(1) in terms of which the accused's conviction and sentence are not to be set aside by reason of the irregularity unless it appears to the Supreme Court of Appeal that a failure of justice has in fact resulted from the irregularity. The question would then be whether the irregularity in question is of the kind that *per se* vitiates the proceedings as in *Moodie* 1961 (4) SA 752 (A), or whether it is of the kind, as in *Naidoo* 1962 (4) SA 348 (A), which requires consideration of whether on the evidence and credibility findings, unaffected by the irregularity, there was proof of the accused's guilt beyond reasonable doubt—*Xaba* (above) at 735–6; *Ncaphayi* (above). The constitutionality of the proviso contained in s 322(1), is discussed below in par 3.11.1 and is *mutatis mutandis* applicable here.

3.8   Reservation of questions of law

It is possible that in the course of a trial in a High Court a question of law relative to that particular case may arise. The court itself may be uncertain about the law regarding a particular point, for example whether certain evidence is admissible, or whether certain actions constitute a crime—cf *Coetzee* 1977 (4) SA 539 (A). See also *Goliath* 1972 (3) SA 1 (A) where the question of law, as to whether the defence of compulsion could ever in law constitute so a complete defence to a charge of murder as to entitle an accused to an acquittal, was reserved.

If such question of law arises during a trial in a High Court, the court may, of its own motion or at the request of either the prosecutor or the accused, reserve that question for the consideration of the Supreme Court of Appeal. The court then states the question reserved, and directs that it be specially entered in the record and that a copy of it be transmitted to the registrar of the Supreme Court of Appeal— s 319(1). The grounds upon which any exception or objection to an indictment is taken are deemed to be questions of law which may be reserved—s 319(2).

The request for reservation of a question of law must be made after conclusion of the trial (ie after conviction or acquittal)—*Adams* 1959 (3) SA 753 (A); *Groesbeek* (2) 1969 (4) SA 445 (O); *Mene* 1978 (1) SA 832 (A). Since a question of law can be brought by the accused only if convicted, and a verdict in terms of s 78(6) (that the accused committed the offence charged, but was mentally disordered) does amount to an acquittal, a question of law cannot be reserved by the accused where such verdict is brought—*Ngema; Cele* 1960 (1) SA 137 (A).

The question of law must appear from the record—*Mulayo* 1962 (2) SA 522 (A). Section 319 limits the ambit of questions of law to be reserved to questions which arose 'on the trial' by a High Court of any person for any offence. That entails: the prosecution of the accused for an offence allegedly committed by that accused; the defence set up by that accused to avoid conviction; and any sentence imposed following upon a successful prosecution. Accordingly, the State would not be able to reserve a question of law, in terms of s 319, to administrative orders like where a forfeiture order is made and the State is dissatisfied with the order—*Pineiro* 1992 (1) SACR 287 (Nm).

There must have been an actual trial. In *Tucker* 1953 (3) SA 150 (A) it was decided that even with a plea of guilty a trial takes place within the meaning of the section. (The contrary viewpoint was taken in *Ex parte Laher: In re Laher* 1960 (2) SA 32 (W), but it cannot be regarded as binding authority.)

Section 319 does not make provision for any period of time within which the application must be brought. In *Haarmeyer* 1970 (4) SA 113 (O) it was held that the application must be made as soon as possible after the judgment, or at any rate within a reasonable time. The further procedure to be followed when a question of law is reserved for the matter to be set down for hearing in the Supreme Court of Appeal, is the same as in the case of a special entry. When the trial court refuses to reserve a question of law at the request of the accused, the accused may, by petition to the Chief Justice, submit an application to the Supreme Court of Appeal— s 319(3) read with s 317(5).

Where the accused was convicted, a question of law may not be reserved that could have an adverse effect upon the accused in respect of such conviction. A question of law can thus be reserved on the application of the prosecutor only in the following instances:

(1) where there has been a *conviction* and the question of law may be to the advantage of the accused—*Solomons* 1959 (2) SA 352 (A); *Adams* 1959 (3) SA 753 (A) at 764G–H). The question of law may not be academic but must have a practical effect on the accused's conviction—*Magmoed v Janse Van Rensburg* 1990 (2) SACR 476 (C); or

(2) where the question of law may have a bearing upon the validity of the sentence imposed. In *Ntuli* 1975 (1) SA 429 (A) the Supreme Court of Appeal sanctioned the right of the State to ask for a reservation of a question of law *adverse to the accused*, in relation to a sentence which was incompetent; and

(3) where there has been an *acquittal*. By 'acquittal' is meant a complete acquittal, that is a finding whereby the accused is set completely free. A question of law can, therefore, not be reserved where an accused is found guilty in terms of a competent verdict—*Seekoei* 1982 (3) SA 97 (A). The quashing of an indictment does not qualify as an acquittal for the purposes of s 322(4)—*Mene* 1978 (1) SA 832 (A). Where the prosecution succeeds on appeal on an acquittal, the provisions of s 322(4) will apply in that the Supreme Court of Appeal may allow the accused to be reindicted in terms of s 324.

The primary benefit today of this procedure, whereby a question of law is reserved, is that it provides the State with the same opportunity to appeal on a point of law as it has when it appeals a decision of a lower court on a point of law in terms of s 310. The section is of little use to the accused, as he may raise the same points in an ordinary appeal in terms of s 316.

3.9 Appeal by the prosecution to the Supreme Court of Appeal

3.9.1 *Appeal against decisions by a High Court on bail*

Generally, the Criminal Procedure Act does not allow the prosecution, in respect of a criminal trial held in a High Court or in a lower court, to appeal against a decision on the merits or facts of a case and consequently no provision is made for an application by the prosecution for leave to appeal *on the facts*. Only an accused may appeal on the merits of a case, and similarly, only an accused may apply for a special entry. However, the position has been changed with the introduction of the Criminal Procedure Second Amendment Act 75 of 1995 in the sense that it inserted s 65A into the Criminal Procedure Act, whereby an appeal by the director of public prosecutions against the decision of a High Court to release an accused on bail (but not against the decision of the court to impose any condition of bail) may be taken on appeal to the Supreme Court of Appeal. A decision of a court to grant bail is based on certain facts and an appeal against such a decision is accordingly, inherently an appeal on the facts. The director of public prosecutions has to apply for leave to appeal in terms of s 316 and all the provisions of s 316 apply *mutatis mutandis*. It is suggested that this right of the prosecution to appeal against a factual decision is *sui generis* and is not to be seen as the beginning of a process of erosion of due process of law in our adversarial system. The court may order the prosecution to pay the accused's cost to defend such an appeal or the application for leave to appeal—s 65A(2)*(c)*.

3.9.2 *Appeal limited to questions of law*

In respect of legal issues the prosecution may, like an accused, apply for the reservation of a question of law for decision by the Supreme Court of Appeal. Previously a question of law could be reserved only when it might result in a decision in favour of the accused (see *Herbst* 1942 AD 434), but since 1948 it has also been possible to reserve a question of law where the final decision of the Supreme Court of Appeal may be in the prosecution's favour. See *Gani* 1957 (2) SA 212 (A). Should the provincial or local division give a decision in favour of an accused on the facts and not on the law, the Supreme Court of Appeal will strike the appeal off the roll on the ground that it was incompetent for the prosecution to appeal. However, should it appear from the record that the court gave a decision in favour of the accused on a matter of law, then it is the duty of the director or the national director of public prosecutions to consider whether or not the court erred in law, see *Attorney-General, Transvaal v Moores (SA) (Pty) Ltd* 1957 (1) SA 190 (A).

The director (or other prosecutor) may in terms of s 311 appeal to the Supreme Court of Appeal on a point of law against a decision decided in favour of a *convicted* accused. To decide whether a question of law was decided in the accused's favour, the judgment of the provincial or local division concerned, is relied upon. Leave to appeal will first have to be obtained from the appropriate court. In order for the court to grant leave to appeal to the Supreme Court of Appeal, a case must be made out, based on legal arguments, what the legal questions are that are to be argued—cf *Mosterd* 1991 (2) SACR 636 (T).

Where the Supreme Court of Appeal decides in favour of the prosecution, it may order that a prosecution be instituted *de novo* against the accused. The Supreme Court of Appeal cannot substitute a conviction for an acquittal. See s 322(4) read with s 324. Where the appeal was brought before the Supreme Court of Appeal in terms of s 311, the powers which the Supreme Court of Appeal enjoys when it has decided the matter in favour of the appellant depend upon whether it was the director (or other prosecutor) or the accused who originally appealed against the decision of the lower court. If the accused had successfully appealed against the lower court's decision, and the director of public prosecutions in turn had succeeded with an appeal to the Supreme Court of Appeal in terms of s 311, it may restore the conviction, sentence or order of the lower court whether in its original form or amended form—s 311(1)*(a)*; Du Toit *et al* 30–43. However, if the director originally appealed to the provincial division, which appeal was rejected, but succeeded on a subsequent appeal to the Supreme Court of Appeal, the Supreme Court of Appeal must give such decision or take such steps as the provincial or local division ought to have taken—s 311(1)*(b)*; Du Toit *et al* 30–43.

The prosecution authority may approach the Minister of Justice to invoke the decision of the Supreme Court of Appeal in terms of s 333. Although s 333 does not allow the prosecution a remedy but allows the Minister to invoke the Supreme Court of Appeal's decision (see discussion of s 333 in Chapter 2), the Minister would not be unwilling to exercise his rights in terms of the said section, especially where the prosecution has exhausted its remedies and legal uncertainty exists regarding the correctness of a certain decision. In *Ex parte Minister van Justisie: In re S v Suid-Afrikaanse Uitsaaikorporasie* 1992 (2) SACR 618 (A) the State had to approach the Minister regarding an uncertainty in the law concerning a decision of the local division in respect of the liability of a company for a crime that requires proof of negligence only. The accused was found not guilty in the lower court and the prosecution's appeal was dismissed. Due to the requirement in s 311(1) that a decision must have been given in favour of a *convicted* accused, the State's remedies were exhausted and approaching the Minister was the only alternative left.

3.9.3 *Appeal against a sentence of a High Court*

The prosecution may also apply for leave to appeal against sentence. Regarding an appeal by the director of public prosecutions against a sentence imposed by a High Court, s 316B provides that the director of public prosecutions may appeal to the Supreme Court of Appeal against a sentence imposed upon an accused in a criminal case in a High Court. Leave to appeal must be obtained and the provisions of s 316 are *mutatis mutandis* applicable. The State may be ordered to pay the costs of the accused—s 316B(3).

3.10 Powers of the Supreme Court of Appeal

(1) In respect of appeals in matters originating in an inferior court, the Supreme Court of Appeal has the same powers as the provincial division—see above.

(2) In addition, the Supreme Court of Appeal has the powers in case of an appeal against a conviction or any question of law reserved to—

 (a) allow the appeal if it thinks that the judgment of the trial court should be set aside on the ground of a wrong decision of any question of law or that on any ground there was a failure of justice; or

 (b) give such judgment as ought to have been given at the trial or impose such punishment as ought to have been imposed at the trial; or

 (c) make such other order as justice may require: These powers are subject to the proviso that, even if the Supreme Court of Appeal is of the opinion that any point raised might be decided in favour of the accused, no conviction or sentence shall be set aside or altered by reason of *any irregularity or defect in the record or proceedings*, unless it appears to the court of appeal that a failure of justice has in fact resulted from such irregularity or defect—s 322(1). The proviso relates to an irregularity in the record or the proceedings. Such an irregularity is of the kind set out in s 317(1). Irregularities or defects based on infringements of constitutional rights should not be subject to the proviso as they are to be regarded as *per se* a failure of justice violating a fair trial or alternatively, if the consequences of the proviso is to be regarded as a limitation of a constitutional right to any component of a fair trial, it must muster the criteria set by s 36 of the Constitution in that it must be reasonable and justifiable. Compare *Pretorius* 1991 (2) SACR 601 (A) where the trial court misdirected itself in

disallowing certain cross-examination. The Supreme Court of Appeal held that such a misdirection with regard to evidence is not an 'irregularity or defect in the record or proceedings' as intended in the proviso to s 322(1). The proviso relates only to irregular or illegal departures from those formalities, rules or procedure, in accordance with which the law requires a criminal trial to be initiated or conducted—*Mofokeng* 1962 (3) SA 551 (A) at 557G; *Alexander (1)* 1965 (2) SA 796 (A) at 809. (See also below, par 3.11.1: 'Setting aside or alteration of conviction on ground of irregularity'.)

(3) The Supreme Court of Appeal has the power to impose a punishment more severe than that imposed by the court *a quo*—s 322(6). Prior to 1963, the Supreme Court of Appeal could not increase a sentence imposed by a High Court, although it had the power to increase a sentence in a case which originated in a lower court—see *Deetlefs* 1953 (1) SA 418 (A); *Theunissen* 1952 (1) SA 201 (A); *Mofokeng* 1962 (2) SA 385 (A). The Supreme Court of Appeal is still vested with this power. The Supreme Court of Appeal is furthermore empowered to increase a sentence although there is no appeal against sentence—*Citizen Newspapers (Pty) Ltd* 1981 (4) SA 18 (A). The principles relevant to an increase of sentence are the same as those mentioned under the powers of provincial divisions. The Supreme Court of Appeal has no jurisdiction to consider a sentence imposed by a lower court if an appeal against sentence was not lodged previously with a provincial division, that is if there was no decision on appeal by a provincial division in respect of the sentence—*Maepa* 1974 (1) SA 659 (A).

(4) The Supreme Court of Appeal also has the power to remit the case for *the hearing of further evidence* or to hear further evidence itself. The powers of the court arise 'on the hearing of an appeal' and not before there is an appeal. These powers are conferred on it by s 22 of the Supreme Court Act 59 of 1959, which provides as follows:

> 'The appellate division or a provincial division or a local division having appeal jurisdiction, shall have power—
>
> *(a)* on the hearing of an appeal to receive further evidence, either orally or by deposition before a person appointed by such division, or to remit the case to the court of first instance, or the court whose judgment is the subject of the appeal, for further hearing, with such instructions as regards the taking of further evidence or otherwise as to the division concerned seems necessary; and
>
> *(b)* to confirm, amend or set aside the judgment or order which is the subject of the appeal and to give any judgment or make any order which the circumstances may require.'

When s 22 of the Supreme Court Act is invoked, the Supreme Court of Appeal has the power to receive further evidence itself, either orally or by appointing a person to hear such evidence, or to remit the case to the court of first instance. In the latter case the conviction and sentence are set aside and the trial court instructed to adjudicate the case; to give judgment and impose sentence afresh after hearing the further evidence. It is only in very rare circumstances that the Supreme Court of Appeal will itself hear evidence on appeal; the usual course is to set aside the conviction and remit the case to the trial court—*Njaba* 1966 (3) SA 140 (A).

The hearing of further evidence will be sanctioned in exceptional cases only. The mere fact that a miscarriage of justice may have taken place is not sufficient to justify the admission of fresh evidence in cases where the evidence was available at the trial. There must be some possible explanation based on allegations that may be true why the evidence was not put before the court—*Van Heerden* 1956 (1) SA 366 (A) at 371; *Foley* 1926 TPD 168 at 171 and *Carr* 1949 (2) SA 693 (A). Generally speaking, there must be a possibility, amounting almost to a probability, that a miscarriage of justice will take place unless the additional evidence is led—*Sittig* 1929 TPD 669 at 678. In *De Jager* 1965 (2) SA 612 (A), the requirements were summarised as follows, as now embodied in s 316(3):

(1) There should be some reasonably sufficient explanation, based on allegations which may be true, why the evidence which it is sought to lead was not led at the trial.

(2) There should be a *prima facie* likelihood of the truth of the evidence.

(3) The evidence should be materially relevant to the outcome of the trial.

In appropriate cases the Supreme Court of Appeal nevertheless has the power to relax strict compliance with the requisite mentioned in (1) above, but will only in rare instances exercise that power—*Njaba* above and see *Lehnberg* 1976 (1) SA 214 (C).

The question whether the Supreme Court of Appeal may direct the leading of still further evidence after the trial court had already heard further evidence, was answered *obiter* in the negative in *Mdlalose* 1972 (1) PH H10 (A).

An application for the hearing of further evidence in terms of s 22 of the Supreme Court Act 59 of 1959 and an application for leave to lead further evidence in terms of s 316(3) of the Criminal Procedure Act, differ in the following aspects: In terms of s 316(3) leave to lead further evidence may be applied for only in combination with an application for leave to appeal. In terms of this section leave to hear further evidence may not be brought on its own. If leave to appeal and to lead further evidence has been refused, the Supreme Court of Appeal may be approached in terms of s 316(6). Section 22 does not demand a simultaneous application and the Supreme Court of Appeal may be approached in terms of s 22 in circumstances where leave to appeal has already been granted before the further evidence came to light. Section 22 does however, demand that the appeal must be before the Supreme Court of Appeal in order for them to hear further evidence. Leave to appeal must therefore have been granted or at least have been petitioned in order for the appeal to be before them. The Supreme Court of Appeal has no power to order further evidence to be heard if leave to appeal has already been refused with final effect by the Supreme Court of Appeal—*Sibande* 1958 (3) SA 1 (A); *Maharaj* 1958 (4) SA 246 (A).

In the past the court was prepared to permit new evidence or to remit the case in the following instances:

(1) *On the ground of previous false evidence*

The court will not allow new evidence to be heard in such cases, unless it is satisfied that

(a) the evidence was false; and

(b) it was upon such false evidence that judgment had been obtained—*Solomon* 1905 TS 711 at 713.

(2) *On the ground of previous erroneous evidence*

It is possible that after trial a witness may make further investigations and come to the conclusion that he made a mistake during the trial. Typical examples are to be found in *Mhlongo* 1935 AD 133 and *Carr* 1949 (2) SA 693 (A). In the latter case the accused was convicted of the murder of a child and sentenced to death. On appeal to the Supreme Court of Appeal leave was granted to admit new evidence about the conclusion which might be drawn from certain marks on the throat of the deceased. In this case a doctor who had given evidence for the (then) Crown had later begun to have doubts about the conclusion which he had drawn when giving evidence. After hearing the evidence, Greenberg JA stated (at 699):

> '[I]t must be emphasised that the inadequate presentation of the defence case at the trial will only in the rarest instances be remediable by the adduction of further evidence at the appeal stage. However serious the consequences may be to the party concerned of a refusal to permit such evidence to be led the due administration of justice would be greatly prejudiced if such permission were lightly granted.'

(3) *On the ground of new facts coming to light in a subsequent trial*

In *Kgolane* 1959 (4) SA 483 (A), a number of accused were convicted of murdering, *inter alia*, one J. Two months afterwards a great number of other accused from the same area were charged in a regional court with public violence resulting from the same acts which led to J's murder. The regional magistrate held an inspection *in loco* and made plans of the place where the offence was committed. One of these plans was of the spot where J had been killed. This plan gave rise to doubt whether the eye-witnesses who gave evidence at the murder trial could, in view of the peculiar nature of the premises, in fact have seen what had happened. These facts were by way of petition brought to the attention of the Supreme Court of Appeal, which remitted the case for further evidence.

(4) *On the ground of a serious and pardonable misapprehension on the part of the accused as to the calling of witnesses in his defence*

See *Nkala* 1964 (1) SA 493 (A), where the accused, an ignorant tribesman, being somewhat distrustful of his *pro Deo* counsel, failed to have witnesses called to support his *alibi*. In *Dhadhla* 1964 (2) SA 623 (T) the court ordered a case to be reopened where the accused was a juvenile female and, through her ignorance, failed to present her defence properly. A court will not, however, grant an application where the evidence was available at the time of the trial but was not led and the risk of a conviction was run deliberately—*Steyn* 1981 (4) SA 385 (C).

(5) *On the ground of 'very exceptional circumstances'*

In *Njaba* 1966 (3) SA 140 (A) the accused was convicted of murder and sentenced to death, largely on the strength of a confession made by himself. He did not testify during his trial, but thereafter it appeared that at the time of the murder he had been in prison. The false confession was apparently made at the instigation of a warder and the matter was remitted although there was no reasonably sufficient explanation why the rebutting evidence was not led at the trial.

In *Turner* 1976 (1) PH H107 (A), on appeal against sentence, an affidavit of a neurosurgeon was included with regard to a serious brain operation which the accused had undergone and which indicated that he had not been criminally responsible. The Supreme Court of Appeal set aside the sentence and remitted the case for further evidence. In general, the allegation of the accused that his legal representative conducted his case in an unsatisfactory manner would not be an acceptable excuse for the failure of the defence to call certain witnesses—*N* 1988 (3) SA 450 (A) at 460. See further *Jatham* 1968 (3) SA 311 (N); *Cebekulu* 1976 (2) PH H132 (A).

Injudiciousness or inexperience on the part of a legal representative is not an adequate reason for the failure to lead the evidence. In exceptional circumstances the court might grant an application to lead further evidence but it is in the public interest, and in the interest of the administration of justice, that accused persons be bound by the actions of their legal representatives—*Venter* 1990 (2) SACR 291 (NC); cf *Louw* 1990 (3) SA 116 (A).

(6) *On the ground of a misunderstanding or oversight by the state*

In *Pretoria Timbers Co (Pty) Ltd* 1950 (3) SA 163 (A) at 178, Schreiner JA said: 'I see no reason for restricting that [the court's] discretion so as to prevent the Court from hearing evidence that may supply a fatal deficiency in the Crown's case.' But the courts are loath to grant an application on the part of *the State* to have a case remitted in order to be able to adduce evidence that will remedy a fatal deficiency in its case. See *Letuli* 1953 (4) SA 241 (T); *Mosala* 1968 (3) SA 523 (T). In *O'Brien* 1970 (3) SA 405 (C), however, it was held that justice required the case to be remitted for further evidence to be led by the State where the evidence was formal in its nature, readily available, and hardly likely to be disputed. On the other hand, if the prosecutor consciously elects not to apply for the reopening of the State's case in order to lead further evidence, it is not a proper case for remittal—*Stevens* 1983 (3) SA 649 (A).

3.11 Statutory limitations on the powers of the Supreme Court of Appeal

3.11.1 *Setting aside or alteration of conviction on ground of irregularity*

The Supreme Court of Appeal is not bound or competent to simply set aside or alter a conviction or sentence by reason of any irregularity or defect in the record or proceedings. This may be done only where it appears to the court of appeal that a failure of justice has, in fact, resulted from such irregularity or defect—s 322(1). In *Moodie* 1961 (4) SA 752 (A) the following rules were formulated in respect of irregularities and the proviso in s 322(1) (compare the proviso in s 309(3) which is identical):

(1) The general rule with regard to irregularities is that the court will be satisfied that there has in fact been a failure of justice if it cannot hold that a reasonable trial court would inevitably have convicted had there been no irregularity.

(2) In an exceptional case, where the irregularity consists of such a gross departure from established rules of procedure that the accused has not been properly tried, this is *per se* a failure of justice, and it is unnecessary to apply the test of enquiring whether a reasonable trial court would inevitably have convicted had there been no irregularity.

(3)   Whether a case falls within (1) or (2) depends upon the nature and degree of the irregularity.

Accordingly, it amounts to this, that a distinction should be drawn between irregularities that are *per se* a failure of justice that vitiate a trial without reference to the merits of that case and other less serious and less fundamental irregularities. In the case of the latter, the remaining evidence is considered and weighed by the appeal court, while in the case of the irregularities which are fatal *per se*, the conviction is set aside, irrespective of the strength of the evidence for the prosecution (cf *Ponyana* 1981 (1) SA 139 (TSC)). In the collectively decided cases of *Mkhise; Mosia; Jones; Le Roux* 1988 (2) SA 868 (A) 872G Kumleben AJA held, with regard to what the learned judge of appeal termed as 'fatal irregularities', that judicial decisions on the nature of irregularities indicate that the enquiry in each case is whether the irregularity is of so fundamental and serious nature that the proper administration of justice and the dictates of public policy require it to be regarded as fatal to the proceedings in which it occured. The presence or absence of prejudice in a particular case is not a relevant consideration in deciding in the first place on the fundamental significance of the irregularity.

Where the irregularity is not fatal *per se*, the appeal court thus considers, apart from the evidence which is affected by the irregularity or defect, whether there is still sufficient evidence to prove guilt beyond a reasonable doubt. Cf *Naidoo* 1962 (4) SA 348 (A); *Bernardus* 1965 (3) SA 287 (A); *Tuge* 1966 (4) SA 565 (A); *Yusuf* 1968 (2) SA 52 (A); *Rall* 1982 (1) SA 828 (A). Compare also the discussion in Chapter 14 under the heading *autrefois acquit* and the discussion of s 324 below.

Where a conviction and sentence are set aside by the court of appeal on the ground that a failure of justice has in fact resulted from the admission against the accused of evidence otherwise admissible but not properly placed before the trial court by reason of some defect in the proceedings, the court of appeal may remit the case to the trial court with instructions to deal with any matter, including the hearing of such evidence, in such manner as the court of appeal may think fit—s 322(3).

The effect of the provisions of s 322(1) could have constitutional implications in that it could be perceived as a limitation of an accused's constitutional right to a fair trial. On the strength of such an interpretation, s 322(1) will have to bear the scrutiny of the requirements of the limitation clause embodied in s 36(1) of the Constitution. In *Klein v Attorney-General* 1995 (2) SACR 210 (W) at 222*c* and 224*a* the court assumed, without deciding thereon, that s 322(1) is a justifiable limitation of the constitutional right to a fair trial. *In casu* an application for an order staying a criminal prosecution in a regional court was brought after the accused was arraigned on several charges. The order was sought on the basis that the accused's right to a fair trial was made impossible due to the fact that the prosecution obtained information of a confidential and privileged nature and therefore had knowledge of the defence the accused intended to raise during the trial. The court held that there has never been a principle that a violation of any of the specific rights encompassed by the right to a fair trial would automatically preclude the trial. Such a rigid principle would operate to the disadvantage of law enforcement and to the prejudice of the society which the law and the Constitution is intended to serve. Before any remedy can be enforced the nature and extent of the violation of the right must be properly considered in accordance with the rules enunciated per Holmes JA in the *Moodie's* case above.

A less compromising approach was adopted in *Solo* 1995 (1) SACR 499 (E) at 509*a–c* where Erasmus J was of the opinion that irregularities occurring during criminal proceedings (*in casu* the refusal of the presiding officer in the court *a quo* to grant the accused a postponement in order to obtain legal counsel) are, since the coming into operation of the interim Constitution, no longer adjudicated according to the demands of s 322(1)—or s 309(3) with a similar effect—but according to the provisions of the Constitution and more particularly ss 25(3) and 33 of the Constitution. The court held that an appeal must succeed if the accused's right to a fair trial has been infringed, unless the court finds that such right has been limited by law of general application as intended by s 33(1) of the Constitution. Support for the approach adopted in *Solo* (above) could be found in the remarks made by Kentridge AJ in *Zuma* 1995 (1) SACR 568 (CC) at 579*h* that s 25(3) of the interim Constitution (now, s 35(3)) requires criminal trials to be conducted in accordance with notions of basic fairness and justice. It is the task of all courts hearing criminal trials or criminal appeals to give content to that notions and not simply to enquire whether there has been an irregularity or illegality, that is a departure from the formalities, rules and principles of procedure according to which the law requires a criminal trial to be initiated or conducted, as the law was before 27 April 1994.

However, it is suggested that whichever way alleged irregularities in proceedings are approached, the effect thereof would be the same. A gross irregularity will invariably cause an injustice which in any event suggests a constitutional infringement and reflects negatively on the fairness of the trial. In *Mvelase* 1996 (8) BCLR 1055 (N) the court held that an infringement during trial of any of the fundamental rights embodied in s 25(3) (now, s 35(3)) of the interim Constitution, has the same effect as a fatal irregularity vitiating the trial as a whole. However, in *Smile* 1998 (1) SACR 688 (SCA) the court held that it is not every constitutional irregularity committed by the trial court that justifies the court in setting aside the conviction on appeal. Whether or not there has been a fair trial must ultimately be answered having regard to the particular circumstances of each case.

3.11.2 Inherent jurisdiction of the Supreme Court of Appeal

The Supreme Court of Appeal is a creature of statute and it used to have no inherent or common-law jurisdiction in criminal matters beyond the provisions of the Criminal Procedure Act and the Supreme Court Act—cf *Sefatsa v Attorney-General, Transvaal* 1989 (1) SA 821 (A); *Abrahams* 1990 (2) SACR 420 (A); *Mamkeli* 1992 (2) SACR 5 (A). However, in terms of the Constitution this court's jurisdiction is no longer strictly limited to statutory law, but it does have an inherent jurisdiction to protect and regulate its own process, and to develop the common law, when and if the common law is pertinent to an issue.

3.12 Execution of sentence pending appeal

The execution of a sentence imposed by a High Court is not suspended by reason of an appeal against a conviction or by reason of a question having been reserved for consideration of the Supreme Court of Appeal, except where the High Court from which the appeal is made thinks fit to order that the accused be released on bail, or that he be treated as an unconvicted prisoner until the appeal has been heard and decided—s 321.

With regard to the effect of the suspension of the execution of the sentence on the ultimate calculation of the term of sentence to be served, see the proviso in s 321(1).

3.13   Proceedings *de novo* when conviction is set aside on appeal

Section 324 provides that proceedings may be instituted *de novo* when a conviction is set aside by the court of appeal on one of the following grounds:

(1)   The court which convicted the accused was not competent to do so;

(2)   The indictment on which the accused was convicted was invalid or defective; or

(3)   There was some other technical irregularity or defect in the procedure.

If a new trial is instituted, the judge or assessor before whom the original trial took place may not take part in the new trial.

This section is interpreted in consonance with the common-law rules regarding *autrefois acquit*—*Naidoo* 1962 (4) SA 348 (A); and see par 3.11.1, above.

CHAPTER 22

Mercy, indemnity and free pardon

		Page
1	GENERAL	371
2	REOPENING OF CASE AND POWERS OF THE PRESIDENT ...	372

The Constitution and this chapter:

Section 84—Powers and functions of President

(1) The President has the powers entrusted by the Constitution and legislation, including those necessary to perform the functions of Head of State and head of the national executive.

(2) The President is responsible for—

. . .

    (j) pardoning or reprieving offenders and remitting any fines, penalties or forfeitures; . . .

See 1, below.

---

1 GENERAL

The Constitution of the Republic of South Africa, Act 108 of 1996, empowers the President of the Republic, subject to, and in accordance with the Constitution, to pardon or reprieve offenders and to remit any fines, penalties or forfeitures— s 84(2)*(j)* read with s 83 of the Constitution. Although these powers are statutory regulated, they are derived historically from the royal prerogatives of the President's erstwhile predecessor, the British monarch, and are presently, still generally regarded as having the character of prerogatives. The power to reprieve and to extend mercy are an integral part of our criminal justice system and a constitutional mechanism to protect the system and the people against injustices and mistakes.

Section 325 of the Criminal Procedure Act affirms *ex abundanti cautela* the President's prerogative by providing that nothing contained in the said Act shall affect the powers of the President to extend mercy to any person. In accordance with international tradition neither the Constitution nor the Criminal Procedure Act lays down specific criteria according to which the prerogatives are to be exercised and it is clear that the President has a wide discretion when exercising these powers. The only clear limitation is that the President cannot act contrary to the Constitution (see *President of the RSA v Hugo* 1997 (1) SACR 567 (CC). Nothing prevents the President from granting mercy *mero motu*, but generally the President is petitioned for mercy by the convicted person or by someone on his or her behalf. Prior to the

Constitutional Court declaring the death penalty unconstitutional in 1995 (and thereby invalidating all corresponding legislative provisions), the Criminal Procedure Act even provided, with regard to convicted persons under the sentence of death, that the Minister of Justice could have submitted a petition for mercy in cases where such persons had not requested or desired a petition for clemency—cf s 325A (now repealed).

Convicted persons have no right to be pardoned or reprieved and also have no right to be heard in respect thereof, but may only *hope* for the indulgence of the President—*Rapholo v State President* 1993 (1) SACR 421 (T). The prerogative of commuting any punishment is therefore that of the President. In practice, however, the President will not exercise his prerogative of mercy without considering a report from the Minister of Justice containing the recommendations of the attorney-general, the presiding officer of the trial court and that of the State Law Advisers. This does not detract from the fact that it remains an executive act which ought not to be influenced by the judiciary. However, the conduct of the President in exercising his powers in terms of s 84, remains subject to the Constitution and as such subject to judicial review (see ss 8(1) and 2). However, the Constitutional Court must confirm any decision of a court declaring the conduct of the President in terms of the Constitution invalid (s 172(2)*(a)* of the Constitution). Where the sentences of a group of prisoners are reprieved by the President, the courts will not likely interfere with such conduct unless satisfied that the decision was motivated by bad faith or was so irrational that no reasonable executive authority could have reached such conclusion (*Kruger and Another v Minister of Correctional Services* 1995 (1) SACR 375 (T)); or that the discretionary exercise of the President's powers was done in an irregular manner because it violated the constitutional rights of others in a unreasonable and unjustified manner (see *President of the RSA and another v Hugo* 1997 (1) SACR 567 (CC) concerning the unique release of female prisoners who had had children under the age of 12 years, in terms of Presidential Act no 17).

In addition to the President's prerogatives, the Indemnity Act 35 of 1990 and the Further Indemnity Act 151 of 1992 empowered the President (the 'State President', as he then was) to grant to any person or category of persons either temporary amnesty or immunity, or conditionally or unconditionally permanent indemnity. Such immunity or indemnity was granted against arrest, prosecution, detention and legal proceedings. (The distinction between the various kinds of indemnities or immunities was discussed in *Rapholo* (above).) Furthermore, in terms of Act 151 of 1992 the President could, after consultation with the National Council on Indemnity, release certain prisoners serving imprisonment for life or other sentences of long-term imprisonment. The power to grant immunity or indemnity in terms of these Acts was subject to certain time limits and was generally associated with political objectives and aimed at the promotion of political reconciliation in South Africa. See also the Promotion of the National Unity and Reconciliation Act 34 of 1995. Since 17 May 1996 the Indemnity Act is no longer in force.

2   REOPENING OF CASE AND POWERS OF THE PRESIDENT

Before 1948 it was generally assumed that the Supreme Court of Appeal had extraordinary jurisdiction to come to the assistance of a convicted person in order to prevent material and serious injustice, even though no remedy existed. In *Milne and Erleigh (6)* 1951 (1) SA 1 (A), the Supreme Court of Appeal held *obiter* that the assumption of such jurisdiction could be justified only when the legislature had not provided a remedy. See *Sibande* 1958 (3) SA 1 (A) where the existence of the Supreme Court of Appeal's extraordinary jurisdiction in criminal matters was questioned and also *Maharaj* 1958 (4) SA 246 (A); *Ngema; Cele* 1960 (1) SA 137 (A); *Mofokeng* 1962 (3) SA 551 (A); *Heller* 1970 (4) SA 679 (A).

In *Mokoena v Minister of Justice* 1968 (4) SA 708 (A), the accused was convicted of murder and sentenced to death. He appealed unsuccessfully to the Supreme Court of Appeal. Thereafter a witness who had given material evidence at the trial declared under oath that he had lied. On the strength of this information Mokoena's execution was postponed but the President decided against commuting the sentence of death. By this time Mokoena had exhausted his remedies under the Criminal Procedure Act, and therefore instituted civil proceedings for the setting aside of his conviction and sentence in the provincial division, which were dismissed. On a petition to the Supreme Court of Appeal it was held that our common law does not allow a convicted person to have his case reopened by way of a claim for *restitutio in integrum* in order to prove that he had been convicted on false evidence. However, the Chief Justice pointed out that there was a deficiency in our criminal procedure in that no provision had been made for a procedure whereby the condemned person could petition the then State President for the hearing of further evidence after the recognised judicial procedures had been exhausted or were no longer available.

This deficiency has been remedied by s 327, which was first introduced into our criminal justice system by Act 51 of 1977.

Since the courts are created by statute, the powers and functions of the High Courts and the Supreme Court of Appeal with regard to the reopening of a criminal matter and the hearing of further evidence are governed by the Criminal Procedure Act and the Supreme Court Act. Not even the Supreme Court of Appeal itself has an extraordinary jurisdiction to reopen a case after it has been finalised by the Supreme Court of Appeal—*Sefatsa v Attorney-General, Transvaal* 1989 (1) SA 821 (A), nor can it usurp powers that are not bestowed upon it by the Legislature—*Mamkeli* 1992 (2) SACR 5 (A). The reopening of such a matter is only possible by virtue of the provisions of s 327.

Section 327 provides that if a person convicted of any offence in any court has exhausted all the recognised legal procedures regarding appeal and review, or if they are no longer available to him, such person may submit a petition, supported by affidavits, to the Minister of Justice, stating that further evidence has become available which materially affects his conviction or sentence. The Minister may, if he considers that such evidence, if true, might reasonably affect the conviction, refer the petition and affidavits to the court which convicted the accused.

The court thereupon receives the affidavits and may permit the examination of witnesses in connection with the further evidence as if it were a normal criminal trial (the presence of the accused is not essential, however) and assesses the value of such evidence. The findings of the court regarding the further evidence do not form part of the proceedings. The court finally advises the President whether and to what extent the further evidence affects the conviction. The President thereupon considers the finding or advice, and may then—

(1) direct that the conviction be expunged, effectively giving the accused a free pardon; or

(2) commute the conviction to a lesser one and adjust the sentence accordingly.

No further appeal, review or proceedings are permitted in respect of proceedings, findings or advice of the court in terms of s 327. Similarly no appeal, review or proceedings shall lie against the refusal by the Minister to issue a direction to the trial court or by the President to act upon the finding or advice of the court—s 327(7).

See, with regard to the application of s 327, *Hoosain v Attorney-General, Cape (1)* 1988 (4) SA 137 (C); *Hoosain v Attorney-General, Cape (2)* 1988 (4) SA 142 (C); *Sefatsa v Attorney-General, Transvaal* 1988 (4) SA 297 (T); *Sefatsa v Attorney-General, Transvaal* 1989 (1) SA 821 (A).

Schedules to the Criminal Procedure Act

(Only those schedules relevant to the contents of the text are recorded.)

SCHEDULE 1

A list of offences appearing in the first schedule to the Criminal Procedure Act is given below. These offences relate to ss 40, 42 and 49.

(See the discussion thereof in the text.)

Treason
Sedition
Public violence
Murder
Culpable homicide
Rape
Indecent assault
Sodomy
Bestiality
Robbery
Kidnapping
Childstealing
Assault, when a dangerous wound is inflicted
Arson
Malicious injury to property
Breaking or entering any premises, whether under the common law or a statutory provision, with intent to commit an offence
Theft, whether under the common law or a statutory provision
Receiving stolen property knowing it to have been stolen
Fraud
Forgery or uttering a forged document knowing it to have been forged
Offences relating to the coinage
Any offence, except the offence of escaping from lawful custody in circumstances other than the circumstances referred to immediately hereunder, the punishment wherefor may be a period of imprisonment exceeding six months without the option of a fine
Escaping from lawful custody, whether the person concerned is in such custody in respect of any offence referred to in this Schedule or is in such custody in respect of the offence of escaping from lawful custody
Any conspiracy, incitement or attempt to commit any offence referred to in this Schedule

SCHEDULE 2

PART II

(The offences mentioned in this part of Schedule 2, relate to ss 59 and 72.)

Treason
Sedition
Murder
Rape
Robbery
Assault, when a dangerous wound is inflicted
Arson
Breaking or entering any premises, whether under the common law or a statutory provision, with intent to commit an offence
Theft, whether under the common law or a statutory provision, receiving stolen property knowing it to have been stolen, fraud, forgery or uttering a forged document knowing it to have been forged, in each case if the amount or value involved in the offence exceeds two hundred rand
Any offence under any law relating to the illicit dealing in or possession of precious metals or precious stones
Any offence under any law relating to the illicit possession, conveyance or supply of dependence-producing drugs
Any offence relating to the coinage
Any conspiracy, incitement or attempt to commit any offence referred to in this Part

SCHEDULE 2

PART III

(The offences mentioned in this part of Schedule 2 relate to ss 59, 61, 72, 184, 184 and 189.)

Sedition
Public violence
Arson
Murder
Kidnapping
Childstealing
Robbery
Housebreaking, whether under the common law or a statutory provision, with intent to commit an offence
Contravention of the provisions of Section 1 and 1A of the Intimidation Act, 1982 (Act 72 of 1982)
Any conspiracy, incitement or attempt to commit any of the above-mentioned offences
Treason

Selected sections, Constitution of the Republic of South Africa, Act 108 of 1996

Section 1—Republic of South africa

The Republic of South Africa is one, sovereign, democratic state founded on the following values:

. . .

(c) Supremacy of the constitution and the rule of law.

Section 2—Supremacy of Constitution

This Constitution is the supreme law of the Republic; law or conduct inconsistent with it is invalid, and the obligations imposed by it must be fulfilled.

Section 8—Application of rights

(1) The Bill of Rights applies to all law, and binds the legislature, the executive, the judiciary and all organs of state.

(2) A provision of the Bill of Rights binds a natural or a juristic person if, and to the extent that, it is applicable, taking into account the nature of the right and the nature of any duty imposed by the right.

(3) When applying a provision of the Bill of Rights to a natural or juristic person in terms of subsection (2), a court—

(a) in order to give effect to a right in the Bill, must apply, or if necessary develop, the common law to the extent that legislation does not give effect to that right; and

(b) may develop rules of the common law to limit the right, provided that the limitation is in accordance with section 36(1).

(4) A juristic person is entitled to the rights in the Bill of Rights to the extent required by the nature of the rights and the nature of that juristic person.

Section 9—Equality

(1) Everyone is equal before the law and has the right to equal protection and benefit of the law.

(2) Equality includes the full and equal enjoyment of all rights and freedoms. . . .

(3) The state may not unfairly discriminate directly or indirectly against anyone on one or more grounds, including race, gender, sex, pregnancy, marital status, ethnic or social origin, colour, sexual orientation, age, disability, religion, conscience, belief, culture, language and birth.

. . .

(5) Discrimination on one or more of the grounds listed in subsection (3) is unfair unless it is established that the discrimination is fair.

Section 10—Human dignity

Everyone has inherent dignity and the right to have their dignity respected and protected.

Section 11—Life

Everyone has the right to life.

Section 12—Freedom and security of the person

(1) Everyone has the right to freedom and security of the person, which includes the right

(a) not to be deprived of freedom arbitrarily or without just cause;

(b) not to be detained without trial;

(c) to be free from all forms of violence from either public or private sources;

(d) not to be tortured in any way; and

(e) not to be treated or punished in a cruel, inhuman or degrading way.

(2) Everyone has the right to bodily and psychological integrity, which includes the right

   . . .

(b) to security in and control over their body; . . .

Section 13—Slavery, servitude and forced labour

No one may be subjected to slavery, servitude or forced labour.

Section 14—Privacy

Everyone has the right to privacy, which includes the right not to have

(a) their person or home searched;

(b) their property searched;

(c) their possessions seized; or

(d) the privacy of their communications infringed.

Section 21—Freedom of movement and residence

(1) No one may be deprived of property except in terms of law of general application, and no law may permit arbitrary deprivation of property. . . .

Section 28—Children

(1) Every child has the right

   . . .

(g) not to be detained except as a measure of last resort, in which case, in addition to the rights a child enjoys under sections 12 and 35, the child may be detained only for the shortest appropriate period of time, and has the right to be

   (i) kept separately from detained persons over the age of 18 years; and

   (ii) treated in a manner, and kept in conditions, that take account of the child's age.

Section 32—Access to information

(1) Everyone has the right of access to

   (a) any information held by the state; and

   (b) any information that is held by another person and that is required for the exercise or protection of any rights.

Section 34—Access to courts

Everyone has the right to have any dispute that can be resolved by the application of law decided in a fair public hearing before a court or, where appropriate, another independent and impartial tribunal or forum.

Section 35—Arrested, detained and accused persons

(1) Everyone who is arrested for allegedly committing an offence has the right—

   (a) to remain silent;

   (b) to be informed promptly—
      (i) of the right to remain silent; and
      (ii) of the consequences of not remaining silent;

   (c) not to be compelled to make any confession or admission that could be used in evidence against that person;

   (d) to be brought before a court as soon as reasonably possible, but not later than—
      (i) 48 hours after the arrest; or
      (ii) the end of the first court day after the expiry of the 48 hours, if the 48 hours expire outside ordinary court hours or on a day which is not an ordinary court day;

   (e) at the first court appearance after being arrested, to be charged or to be informed of the reason for the detention to continue, or to be released; and

   (f) to be released from detention if the interests of justice permit, subject to reasonable conditions.

(2) Everyone who is detained, including every sentenced prisoner, has the right—

   (a) to be informed promptly of the reason for being detained;

   (b) to choose, and to consult with, a legal practitioner, and to be informed of this right promptly;

   (c) to have a legal practitioner assigned to the detained person by the state and at state expense, if substantial injustice would otherwise result, and to be informed of this right promptly;

   (d) to challenge the lawfulness of the detention in person before a court and, if the detention is unlawful, to be released;

   (e) to conditions of detention that are consistent with human dignity, including at least exercise and the provision, at state expense, of adequate accommodation, nutrition, reading material and medical treatment; and

   (f) to communicate with, and be visited by, that person's—
      (i) spouse or partner;
      (ii) next of kin;

      (iii) chosen religious counsellor; and

      (iv) chosen medical practitioner.

(3) Every accused person has a right to a fair trial, which includes the right—

    (a) to be informed of the charge with sufficient detail to answer it;

    (b) to have adequate time and facilities to prepare a defence;

    (c) to a public trial before an ordinary court;

    (d) to have their trial begin and conclude without unreasonable delay;

    (e) to be present when being tried;

    (f) to choose, and be represented by, a legal practitioner, and to be informed of this right promptly;

    (g) to have a legal practitioner assigned to the accused person by the state and at state expense, if substantial injustice would otherwise result, and to be informed of this right promptly;

    (h) to be presumed innocent, to remain silent, and not to testify during the proceedings;

    (i) to adduce and challenge evidence;

    (j) not to be compelled to give self-incriminating evidence;

    (k) to be tried in a language that the accused person understands or, if that is not practicable, to have the proceedings interpreted in that language;

    (l) not to be convicted for an act or omission that was not an offence under either national or international law at the time it was committed or omitted;

    (m) not to be tried for an offence in respect of an act or omission for which that person has previously been either acquitted or convicted;

    (n) to the benefit of the least severe of the prescribed punishments if the prescribed punishment for the offence has been changed between the time that the offence was committed and the time of sentencing; and

    (o) of appeal to, or review by, a higher court.

(4) Whenever this section requires information to be given to a person, that information must be given in a language that the person understands.

(5) Evidence obtained in a manner that violates any right in the Bill of Rights must be excluded if the admission of that evidence would render the trial unfair or otherwise be detrimental to the administration of justice.

Section 36—Limitation of rights

(1) The rights in the Bill of Rights may be limited only in terms of law of general application to the extent that the limitation is reasonable and justifiable in an open and democratic society based on human dignity, equality and freedom, taking into account all relevant factors, including—

    (a) the nature of the right;

    (b) the importance of the purpose of the limitation;

    (c) the nature and extent of the limitation;

    (d) the relation between the limitation and its purpose; and

    (e) less restrictive means to achieve the purpose.

(2) Except as provided in subsection (1) or in any other provision of the Constitution, no law may limit any right entrenched in the Bill of Rights.

Section 37—States of emergency

(1) A state of emergency may be declared only in terms of an Act of Parliament, and only when—

  (a) the life of the nation is threatened by war, invasion, general insurrection, disorder, natural disaster or other public emergency; and

  (b) the declaration is necessary to restore peace and order.

(2) A declaration of a state of emergency, and any legislation enacted or other action taken in consequence of that declaration, may be effective only—

  (a) prospectively; and

  (b) for no more than 21 days from the date of the declaration, unless the National Assembly resolves to extend the declaration. The Assembly may extend a declaration of a state of emergency for no more than three months at a time. The first extension of the state of emergency must be by a resolution adopted with a supporting vote of a majority of the members of the Assembly. Any subsequent extension must be by a resolution adopted with a supporting vote of at least 60 per cent of the members of the Assembly. A resolution in terms of this paragraph may be adopted only following a public debate in the Assembly.

(3) Any competent court may decide on the validity of—

  (a) a declaration of a state of emergency;

  (b) any extension of a declaration of a state of emergency; or

  (c) any legislation enacted, or other action taken, in consequence of a declaration of a state of emergency.

(4) Any legislation enacted in consequence of a declaration of a state of emergency may derogate from the Bill of Rights only to the extent that—

  (a) the derogation is strictly required by the emergency; and

  (b) the legislation—

    (i) is consistent with the Republic's obligations under international law applicable to states of emergency;

    (ii) conforms to subsection (5); and

    (iii) is published in the national Government Gazette as soon as reasonably possible after being enacted.

(5) No Act of Parliament that authorises a declaration of a state of emergency, and no legislation enacted or other action taken in consequence of a declaration, may permit or authorise—

  (a) indemnifying the state, or any person, in respect of any unlawful act;

  (b) any derogation from this section; or

  (c) any derogation from a section mentioned in column 1 of the Table of Non-Derogable Rights, to the extent indicated opposite that section in column 3 of the Table.

Table of Non-Derogable Rights

1 Section number	2 Section title	3 Extent to which the right is protected
9	Equality	With respect to unfair discrimination solely on the grounds of race, colour, ethnic or social origin, sex, religion or language
10	Human dignity	Entirely
11	Life	Entirely
12	Freedom and security of the person	With respect to subsections (1)*(d)* and *(e)* and (2)*(c)*
13	Slavery, servitude and forced labour	With respect to slavery and servitude
28	Children	With respect to: — subsection (1)*(d)* and *(e)*; — the rights in subparagraphs (i) and (ii) of subsection (1)*(g)*; and — subsection 1*(i)* in respect of children of 15 years and younger
35	Arrested, detained and accused persons	With respect to: — subsections (1)*(a)*, *(b)* and *(c)* and (2)*(d)*; — the rights in paragraphs *(a)* to *(o)* of subsection (3), excluding paragraph *(d)*; — subsection (4); and — subsection (5) with respect to the exclusion of evidence if the admission of that evidence would render the trial unfair

(6) Whenever anyone is detained without trial in consequence of a derogation of rights resulting from a declaration of a state of emergency, the following conditions must be observed:

(a) An adult family member or friend of the detainee must be contacted as soon as reasonably possible, and informed that the person has been detained.

(b) A notice must be published in the national Government Gazette within five days of the person being detained, stating the detainee's name and place of detention and referring to the emergency measure in terms of which that person has been detained.

(c) The detainee must be allowed to choose, and be visited at any reasonable time by, a medical practitioner.

(d) The detainee must be allowed to choose, and be visited at any reasonable time by, a legal representative.

(e) A court must review the detention as soon as reasonably possible, but no later than 10 days after the date the person was detained, and the court must release the detainee unless it is necessary to continue the detention to restore peace and order,.

(f) A detainee who is not released in terms of a review under paragraph (e), or who is not released in terms of a review under this paragraph, may apply to a court for a further review of the detention at any time after 10 days have passed since the previous review, and the court must release the detainee unless it is still necessary to continue the detention to restore peace and order.

(g) The detainee must be allowed to appear in person before any court considering the detention, to be represented by a legal practitioner at those hearings, and to make representations against continued detention.

(h) The state must present written reasons to the court to justify the continued detention of the detainee, and must give a copy of those reasons to the detainee at least two days before the court reviews the detention.

(7) If a court released a detainee, that person may not be detained again on the same grounds unless the state first shows a court good cause for re-detaining that person.

(8) Subsections (6) and (7) do not apply to persons who are not South African citizens and who are detained in consequence of an international armed conflict. Instead, the state must comply with the standards binding on the Republic under international humanitarian law in respect of the detention of such persons.

Section 38 — Enforcement of rights

Anyone listed in this section has the right to approach a competent court, alleging that a right in the Bill of Rights has been infringed or threatened, and the court may grant appropriate relief, including a declaration of rights. The persons who may approach a court are—

(a) anyone acting in their own interest;

(b) anyone acting on behalf of another person who cannot act in their own name;

(c) anyone acting as a member of, or in the interest of, a group or class of persons;

(d) anyone acting in the public interest; and

(e) an association acting in the interest of its members.

Section 39 — Interpretation of Bill of Rights

(1) When interpreting the Bill of Rights, a court, tribunal or forum—

(a) must promote the values that underlie an open and democratic society based on human dignity, equality and freedom;

(b) must consider international law; and

(c) may consider foreign law.

(2) When interpreting any legislation, and when developing the common law or customary law, every court, tribunal or forum must promote the spirit, purport and objects of the Bill of Rights.

(3) The Bill of Rights does not deny the existence of any other rights or freedoms that are recognised or conferred by common law, customary law or legislation, to the extent that they are consistent with the Bill.

Section 84—Powers and functions of President

(1) The President has the powers entrusted by the Constitution and legislation, including those necessary to perform the functions of Head of State and head of the national executive.

(2) The President is responsible for

. . .

(j) pardoning or reprieving offenders and remitting any fines, penalties or forfeitures; . . .

Section 165—Judicial authority

(1) The judicial authority of the Republic is vested in the courts.

(2) The courts are independent and subject only to the Constitution and the law, which they must apply impartially and without fear, favour or prejudice.

Section 170—Magistrates' Courts and other courts

Magistrates' Courts and all other courts may decide any matter determined by an Act of Parliament, but a court of a status lower than a High Court may not enquire into or rule on the constitutionality of any legislation or any conduct of the President.

Section 171—Court procedures

All courts function in terms of national legislation, and their rules and procedures must be provided for in terms of national legislation.

Section 172—Powers of courts in constitutional matters

(1) When deciding a constitutional matter within its power, a court—

(a) must declare that any law or conduct that is inconsistent with the Constitution is invalid to the extent of its inconsistency; and

(b) may make any order that is just and equitable, including—

(i) an order limiting the retrospective effect of the declaration of invalidity; and

(ii) an order suspending the declaration of invalidity for any period and on any conditions, to allow the competent authority to correct the defect.

(2) *(a)* The Supreme Court of Appeal, a High Court or a court of similar status may make an order concerning the constitutional validity of an Act of Parliament, a provincial Act or any conduct of the President, but an order

of constitutional invalidity has no force unless it is confirmed by the Constitutional Court.

(b) A court which makes an order of constitutional invalidity may grant a temporary interdict or other temporary relief to a party, or may adjourn the proceedings, pending a decision of the Constitutional Court on the validity of that Act or conduct.

(c) National legislation must provide for the referral of an order of constitutional invalidity to the Constitutional Court.

(d) Any person or organ of state with a sufficient interest may appeal, or apply, directly to the Constitutional Court to confirm or vary an order of constitutional invalidity by a court in terms of this subsection.

Section 173—Inherent power

The Constitutional Court, Supreme Court of Appeal and High Courts have the inherent power to protect and regulate their own process, and to develop the common law, taking into account the interests of justice.

Section 179—Prosecuting authority

(1) There is a single national prosecuting authority in the Republic, structured in terms of an Act of Parliament, and consisting of

    (a) a National Director of Public Prosecutions, who is the head of the prosecuting authority, and is appointed by the President, as head of the national executive; and

    (b) Directors of Public Prosecutions and prosecutors as determined by an Act of Parliament.

(2) The prosecuting authority has the power to institute criminal proceedings on behalf of the state, and to carry out any necessary functions incidental to instituting criminal proceedings.

(3) National legislation must ensure that the Directors of Public Prosecutions

    (a) are appropriately qualified; and

    (b) are responsible for prosecutions in specific jurisdictions, subject to subsection (5).

(4) National legislation must ensure that the prosecuting authority exercises its functions without fear, favour or prejudice.

(5) The National Director of Public Prosecutions

    (a) must determine, with the concurrence of the Cabinet member responsible for the administration of justice, and after consulting the Directors of Public Prosecutions, prosecution policy, which must be observed in the prosecution process;

    (b) must issue policy directives which must be observed in the prosecution process;

    (c) may intervene in the prosecution process when policy directives are not complied with; and

    (d) may review a decision to prosecute or not to prosecute, after consulting the relevant Director of Public Prosecutions and after taking representations

within a period specified by the National Director of Public Prosecutions, from the following:
   (i) The accused person.
   (ii) The complainant.
   (iii) Any other person or party whom the National Director considers to be relevant.
(6) The Cabinet member responsible for the administration of justice must exercise final responsibility over the prosecuting authority.
(7) All other matters concerning the prosecuting authority must be determined by national legislation.

References to the
Criminal Procedure Act

Section	Page
1	32, 99, 119, 162
2(1)	45
2(2)	45
5(1)	54
5(2)	54
6(a)	66
6(b)	62, 66, 200, 206, 222
7	67
7(1)(a)	69, 71
7(1)(b)	69, 71
7(1)(c)	69, 71
7(1)(d)	69, 71
7(2)(a)	71
7(2)(b)	71
7(2)(c)	71
8	67
8(1)	67
8(2)	68
8(3)	68
9(1)	71
9(1)(a)	71
9(1)(b)	71
9(2)	71
9(2)(a)	71
9(2)(b)	71
9(3)	71
10(1)	69
10(2)	69
10(3)	70
11	71
11(1)	72
11(2)	72
12(1)	69
12(2)	72
13	72, 222
14	69
15(1)	72
15(2)	72
16(1)	72
16(2)	72
17	72

Section	Page
18	66
18(1)	58
19	12, 124
20	12, 90, 125, 130, 133
21	12, 126, 128, 133
21(1)	125, 126
21(1)(a)	90, 129
21(2)	126
21(3)(a)	126
21(3)(b)	127
21(4)	128
22	120, 126
22(a)	129
22(b)	28
22(1)(b)	90
23	12, 131
23(2)	131
24	90, 126, 130
25	126, 127, 128
25(1)	126, 127, 128, 129, 133
25(2)	128
25(3)	129
26	90, 118
27	90, 118, 119, 131
27(1)	118, 131
27(2)	132
28	133
28(1)	133
29	132
30	133
31	133
31(1)(a)	133
31(1)(b)	134
31(2)	134
32	133
33	133
34	133
34(1)	133
35	133
35(1)	134
36	133, 134

Section	Page
37	121
38	93
39	99
39(1)	97, 113
39(2)	97, 99
39(3)	113
40	12, 100
41	90, 119
41(1)	103, 119
41(2)	103, 119
42	12, 90, 104
42(1)	97, 104
42(2)	97, 104
42(3)	97, 104, 110
43	12, 90
43(2)	98
43(3)	98
44	99
45	98
46	99
47	108
47(1)	108
47(2)	108
48	131
49	12, 90
49(1)	108, 112, 113
49(2)	109
50	98, 105, 107, 139
50(1)	98, 106, 110
50(1)(a)	99, 141
50(1)(d)	106
50(2)	106
50(3)	106
50(6)	141, 152
50(6)(b)	141
50(6)(c)	142
50(6)(d)	142
50(6)(i)(bb)	141
51	113
51(1)	110
52	104
54	63, 81
54(1)	94
54(2)(a)	94
54(2)(b)	94
54(3)	171
55	149

Section	Page
55(1)	94, 96
55(2)	95, 96
55(2A)	94
55(3)	95
55(3)(b)	95
56(1)	96
56(1)(c)	82
56(2)	96
56(3)	96
56(4)	96
56(5)	96
57	95, 96
57(1)	81, 82
57(4)	82
57(7)	82
57A(1)	82
57A(4)	96
58	137, 148
59	114, 139, 149
59(1)(a)	139, 140
59(1)(b)	139
59(1)(c)	140
59(2)	140
59A	139
59A(1)	140, 141
59A(3)	140, 141
59A(4)	141
59A(5)	141
59A(6)	141
59A(7)	141
60	114, 141, 149, 152
60(1)(a)	141
60(1)(c)	139, 152
60(2)(a)	152
60(2)(b)	152
60(2)(c)	152
60(2)(d)	152
60(3)	152
60(4)	144
60(4)(a)	144, 154
60(4)(b)	144, 145
60(4)(c)	144, 146
60(4)(d)	144, 146
60(4)(e)	144, 147
60(5)	144
60(5)(a)	145
60(5)(b)	145, 154

Section	Page	Section	Page
60(5)(c)	145, 154	65(4)	143
60(5)(d)	145	65A	350, 361
60(5)(e)	145	65A(1)(a)	143, 354
60(5)(f)	138, 145	65A(1)(b)	337
60(5)(g)	145	65A(2)	354
50(5)(h)	145	65A(2)(a)	143, 354
60(6)	144, 145	65A(2)(b)	354
60(6)(a)	145	65A(2)(c)	362
60(6)(b)	145	65A(3)	143
60(6)(c)	145	66(1)	150
60(6)(d)	145	66(2)	150
60(6)(e)	145	66(3)	150
60(6)(f)	145	67(1)	150
60(6)(g)	145	67(2)	150
60(6)(h)	145	67A	137, 152
60(6)(i)	145	68	158
60(6)(j)	145	68(1)	151
60(7)	144, 146	68(2)	151
60(8)	144, 146	68A	151
60(8A)	147	69(1)	149
60(9)	144, 147	69(2)	150
60(10)	152	69(3)	149
60(11)	152, 156	70	151
60(11)(a)	137, 152, 156, 157, 158	71	158
60(11)(b)	137, 152, 156, 157	72	95, 114, 158
60(11A)	157	72(1)	114
60(11B)(a)(i)	154	72A	158
60(11B)(a)(ii)	154	73	77
60(11B)(b)	154	73(1)	74
60(11B)(c)	154, 155	73(2)	74
60(11B)(d)(i)	154	73(3)	74
60(11B)(d)(ii)	154	74	74
60(12)	148	75	160, 314
60(13)(a)	149	75(1)(b)	159
60(13)(b)	149	75(1)(c)	159
60(14)	155	75(2)	159
62	140, 148, 149, 1	76(1)	171
62(f)	149	76(2)	161
63	152	76(3)	161
63(1)	149	77	9, 15, 67, 164, 200, 226
64	141	77(6)	222, 302
65	350	77(6)(a)	200
65(1)(a)	142, 354	77(6)(b)	201
65(1)(b)	142, 337	78	15, 67, 226
65(1)(c)	142	78(2)	201, 353
65(2)	142	78(6)	201, 353
65(3)	142	78(6)(b)	200

Section	Page
78(8) 337, 353	
79 . . . . 15, 67, 200, 226	
79(2)(b) 200	
80 171	
81(1) 183	
81(2) 183	
83 . . . . 178, 179	
84(1) 172	
84(3) 172	
85 . . . . 199, 202, 220	
85(1) 202	
85(2) 202	
86 . . . . 199, 311, 336	
86(1) 173, 176, 177	
86(4) 177	
87 174	
88 . . . . 175, 202, 218, 335	
92(1)(c) 172	
92(2) 172	
105 199	
106 . . . . 160, 162, 202, 220	
106(1)(e) 219	
106(1)(f) 220	
106(4) 219, 221, 222	
107 203	
108 215	
109 199	
110 . . . . 186, 220	
110(1) 38	
111 . . . . 36, 39, 54, 186	
112 . . . . 10, 16, 160, 162, 203, 206, 214, 215	
112(1) 203	
112(1) 206	
112(1)(a) 204	
112(1)(b) . . . 161, 183, 184, 204, 205, 207, 210, 213, 311, 312, 353	
112(2) 204, 207, 311	
112(3) 207	
113 . . . . 205, 208, 210, 311, 312, 346	
113(1) 208	
113(2) 208	
114(1) 209, 214	
114(2) 209	
114(3)(b) 209	
115 . . . . 10, 16, 160, 161, 162, 193, 200, 206, 213, 215, 243	

Section	Page
115(1) 210, 213	
115(2) 213	
115(2)(a) 210, 238	
115(2)(b) 211	
115(3) 199, 213	
115A 214	
116 . . . . 214, 221	
116(1) 214	
117 323	
118 208	
119 . . . . 160, 161, 162, 163, 216, 219, 222	
120 161	
121 162	
121(1) 161	
121(1)(b) 150	
121(2)(a) 161	
121(2)(b) 161	
121(3) 161	
121(3)(c) 164	
121(4) 161	
121(5) 161	
121(5)(aA) 162	
121(6) 161	
121(7) 161	
122 162	
122(1) 161	
122(2)(ii) 164	
122(3) 162	
122(4) 162	
122A 160, 162, 163, 219	
122B 219	
122C 219	
122C(1) 160	
122C(2) 160	
122D 160, 219	
123 . . . . 160, 163, 221	
123(a) 164	
123(b) 164	
124(a) 164	
124(b) 164	
127 164	
128 164	
130 . . . . 163, 164	
131 . . . . 163, 164	
137 . . . . 162, 165	
139 . . . . 164, 165	

Section	Page
140	165
141	165
142	163
144(1)	96, 171
144(2)	96, 171
144(3)	96, 171, 236
144(3)(a)	174
144(4)	171
144(4)(a)	96
144(4)(b)	96
145(1)(b)	187
145(4)	188
145(4)(a)	188
146	188
147(1)	187, 188
147(1)(a)	187
148	32, 33
148(3)(a)	350
149	186
150(1)	234
150(2)	235
151	240
151(1)	240
151(1)(a)	241
151(1)(b)	241
152	235
153	223, 335
153(1)	223
153(2)	223
153(3)	224
153(4)	224
153(5)	224
153(6)	224
154	335
155	183
156	183, 184
157	221, 229, 231
157(1)	184
158	80
158(2)	223
158(3)	223
158(4)	223
159(1)	80, 81, 200
159(2)	81
159(2)(a)	81
159(3)	81
160(2)	81

Section	Page
160(3)	81
162	120, 192
162(1)	192
163	120, 192
164	120, 192
165	120
166(1)	237, 243
167	244, 245
168	226
169	186, 226
170	226
174	188, 237, 238
175	246
175(2)	246
176	250, 251
179	120, 224
180	120
181	120
184	224
185	125
185(1)(b)	61
185(2)	61
185(3)	61
185(4)	61
185A	63
186	224, 245
187	120
188	120, 224
189	120, 121, 225
191	120
196(1)(a)	231
196(2)	230
197	190, 194, 233
203	121, 220
204	120, 203, 220
205	120, 121
205(1)	120
205(3)	120
205(4)	120, 225
209	212
211	193
212	235
213	235
217(1)(b)(ii)	8
217(3)(b)	188
220	211, 212, 243
235	155

Section	Page
254	67, 222
255	67, 222, 226
256	249
257	249
258	249
259	248
260	250
261(1)	249
270	247, 248
271	262
271A	262
272	262
273	262
274(1)	262
274(2)	262
275	207, 263, 347
276	41, 42, 268, 271
276(1)(h)	279
276(1)(i)	273, 280
276(3)(a)	270
276(3)(b)	280
276A(1)	279
276A(2)(a)	273
276A(2)(b)	273
276A(3)	279
276A(4)	281
277	265
280(2)	274
280(3)	274
281(b)	274
282	274
284	270
285(1)	272
286	272
286A	271
286A(1)	208, 271
287(1)	277
287(2)	277
287(4)	277
287B(1)(b)	271
288	277
289	277
290	281
290(1)	281
290(2)	281
290(4)	281
294	268

Section	Page
296	270, 281
297	282
297(1)(a)	262
297(1)(a)(i)(cc)	284
297(1)(c)	281
297(4)	282
297(5)	277
297(6)(a)	277
298	250, 251
300	47, 284
300(5)	285
301	47, 285
302	294, 304
302(1)(a)(i)	301
302(1)(a)(ii)	302
302(1)(a)(iii)	302
302(1)(b)	302, 304
302(2)	302
302(3)	302
303	305, 306
304	305
304(1)	303
304(2)	311, 344
304(2)(a)	303
304(2)(b)	310, 311, 344, 345
304(2)(c)	310
304(3)	310
304(4)	251, 304, 305, 307, 309
304A	305
305	319, 341
306	294, 305, 306, 307
306(1)	306
307	313
307(1)	347
309	337, 349
309(1)(a)	337
309(2)	339, 340
309(2)(b)	321
309(3)	331, 344, 345, 346, 347, 348, 367
309(4)	347
309(4)(a)	319, 341
309(5)	352
309B	321, 338
309B(1)	321
309B(2)(b)	321
309B(3)	321, 338, 369

Section	Page
309B(4)	321
309C	321, 339
309D	319
309D(1)	320
309D(2)	321
310	240, 342, 343, 361
310(1)	333, 342
310(2)	353
310(4)	343
310(5)	343
310A	342, 343, 344
310A(1)	344
310A(6)	344
311	342, 343, 344, 350, 362, 363
311(1)	353
311(1)(a)	362
311(1)(b)	362
312	311, 346
312(1)	346
313	218, 313, 314, 347
315	34, 35
315(1)	348
315(2)	324
315(2)(a)	324, 349, 350
315(2)(b)	350
315(2)(c)	350
315(3)	349
315(4)	319, 323, 350
315(5)(b)	349
316	323, 324, 349, 354, 361, 362, 363
316(1)	324, 325, 351, 353, 356, 357
316(1)(a)	354
316(1)(b)	353, 354
316(1A)(a)	350
316(2)	354
316(3)	357, 358, 365
316(6)	355, 356, 358, 365
316(7)	356
316(8)(c)(i)	352, 357
316(8)(c)(ii)	358
316(10)	356
316A	337, 340, 351
316B	338, 350, 351, 363
316B(3)	363
317	351, 359
317(1)	359, 363
317(2)	359
317(3)	359
317(4)	359
317(5)	361
318	351
318(1)	359
319	343, 351, 360
319(1)	333, 360
319(2)	360
319(3)	361
320	355
321	369
321(1)	370
322	194, 348
322(1)	359, 363, 364, 367, 368, 369
322(3)	218, 368
322(4)	361, 362
322(6)	364
324	218, 313, 347, 361, 362, 370
325	371
325A	372
327	358, 373
327(7)	374
328	94, 98
329	94, 96
330	94
331	99
332(5)	184
333	34, 351, 362, 363
334	99
336	179
341	82
342	47
342A	221
342A(3)(c)	203, 221

Subject index

access to court 24
accusatorial model 15
accused
  arraignment 198
  attendance at trial 94
  bodily features 121
  discharge at close of state's case 237
  fairness to 192
  formal admission 243
  misbehaviour 80
  presence of 79
  review at instance of 307
  rights of 9, 10
    explained 240
  trial in absence of 80
  trial in presence of 79
  unsworn statement 243
address by prosecutor and defence 246
adjournment of trial 226
admission of guilt 81
appeal
  accused, by 337
  aspect first raised on 335
  bail 142
  condonation 340, 356
  Constitutional Court, to 326
  conviction, not before 329
  evidence
    further 357
    new 364
  facts, on 332
  fresh trial 347
  full court, to 348
  grounds of 339, 354
  historical background 318
  in person, prosecuting 341
  judge's certificate 341
  leave to 353
  powers of court 344, 363
    limitations 367
  proceedings *de novo* 370
  prosecution, by 341, 361
  provincial and local divisions, to 337

appeal — *(continued)*
    question of law, on 333
    record of proceedings 336
    reservation of question of law 360
    review — difference 299
    right of 319, 350
    sentence
        against 330, 343
        execution of — pending appeal 347
    special entry 358
    Supreme Court of Appeal, to 323, 348
    withdrawal 334
arraignment of accused 198
arrest 96
    duty to 108
    effect of 107
    force to overcome resistance 108
    interrogation, for 114
    justifiable homicide 109
    motive for 97
    peace officer, by 100
    private person, by 104
    procedure after 105
    requirements for 97
    resisting 108
    search for effecting 130
    warrant
        with 98
        without 99
arrestee
    rights of 24
    search of 131
assessors 173
autrefois acquit 216
autrefois convict 215
bail
    amount 149
    appeal 142
    application 141
        evidentiary rules 152
    cancellation and forfeiture 150
    conditions 148
        amendment 149
        discretionary special 149
    effect 137
    factors considered 144
    money 149
    nature of 138
    police, granted by 139
    prosecution, granted by 140

bail — *(continued)*
  right to 137
  risk 144
Bill of Rights 18
bodily features of accused 121
caution and discharge 281
charge
  splitting 178
  withdrawal 62
charge sheet 170
  amendment 176
  correction 176
  defect cured by evidence 175
  form and substance 171
  lodgment and service 170
  negativing exceptions etc 173
  particulars 174
children, rights of 24
civil action for damages 27
committal to treatment centre 281
compensation and restitution 284
compounding of minor offences 82
Constitutional Court 31, 325
constitutional principles 28
corporal punishment 268
correctional supervision 278
court
  access to 24
  appeal — see appeal
  constitution of 186
  courtesy in 191
  impartiality and fairness 190
  open 223
  questioning by 244
  recusal 194
  review — see review
  special 33
  venue of 186
  witnesses called or recalled by 244
courtesy in court 191
crime
  reporting of 63
crime control model 16
criminal defamation, plea in the case of 221
criminal procedure
  function of 5
  history of 15
  models 16
  system, as 14
cross-examination of witness 236, 237, 242, 244

dangerous criminal, declaration as 271
death penalty 264
declaratory order 302
defence
  address by 246
  case 240
detention
  interrogation, for 114
director of public prosecutions
  accountability 56
  appointment 51
  control of representatives 61
  discretion of 65
  independence 48
  office of 47
  policy 55
  powers of 57, 61
  suspension and removal from office 52
discharge
  caution and 281
  close of state's case, at 237
  prosecution, from (plea) 220
discretion
  director of public prosecutions 65
  police bail 139
  prosecute, to 65
  sentencing 259
district court, meaning of 33
diversion of criminal trial 67
double-functional rules 13
'drastic procedure' 24
drug-addicted person, trial of 226
due process model 16
duplication of convictions 178
emergency, state of 24
equality before the law 21
escape from lawful custody 113
evidence
  further — on appeal 357
  law of 5
  recording of 245
exclusionary rule 6, 27
extradition 114
fairness (in court) 190
force
  arrest 108, 109
  search 131
fine 275
freedom and security of the person 23
guilty plea 203

habeas corpus 26
habitual criminal, declaration as 272
High Court 32
  divisions 32
history of criminal procedure 15
human rights — see Bill of Rights
immunity 372
impartiality of court 190
imprisonment 268
indemnity 371
indictment 96, 170
  see also: charge sheet
information, access to 23
innocence, presumption of 6
inquisitorial model 16
interception and monitoring 121
interdict 27
interdictum de libero homine exhibendo 26
internal security
  search warrant 127
interrogation 117
  detention for 114
joinder
  accused, several 183
  offences 183
  persons charged separately 231
judge's certificate
  appeal 341
  review 306
Judges' Rules 5
jurisdiction 31
  appellate 32, 34
  extraterritorial 39
  offences, in respect of 35
  sentencing 41
  territorial 36
  validity of statutorial provisions 42
jurisdiction of the court, plea to 219
jury trial 189
justice 190
juvenile
  assistance by parent or guardian 74
  imposing punishment on 281
  release 158
law
  adjectival 5
  substantive 5
legal assistance, right to 74
legal guilt 6
legal representation 74

legality, principle of 6, 7, 26, 28, 45, 190
life, right to 22
life imprisonment 271
lis pendens 221
lower court
  meaning of 33
magistrate's court
  meaning of 33
mandamus 27
mentally abnormal person, trial of 200, 226
monitoring, interception and 121
name and address, obtaining 119
national prosecuting authority 47
nolle prosequi 68
not guilty plea 210
pardon by President 371
  plea 219
particulars, further 174
periodical court 33
periodical imprisonment 272
plea
  accused entitled to verdict after 221
  amendment of 207, 209, 214
  autrefois acquit 216
  autrefois convict 215
  criminal defamation 221
  discharge from prosecution 220
  dispensed with 199
  explanation of 210
  guilty 203
  jurisdiction of the court, plea to 219
  lack of authority of prosecutor 220
  lis pendens 221
  not guilty 210
  pardon by President 219
  prior acquittal 216
  prior conviction 215
plea in magistrate's court
  charge justiciable in regional court 160
  charge justiciable in High Court 160
police
  bail granted by 139
  powers 12
  prosecutor, co-operation with 62
postponement of trial 226
powers
  reasonableness when exercising 90
preparatory examination 162
pre-trial examinations 159
previous convictions 262, 264

prima facie case 7
proof, quantum of 7
prosecution (of crime) 45
  civil actions and 46
  discharge from (plea) 220
  institution of criminal proceedings 51
  legal ethics 66
  national prosecuting authority 47
  prescription 66
  private 67
  public 47
  stopping 66
prosecutor
  address by 234, 246
  appointment 59
  control by director of public prosecutions 61
  discretion to prosecute 64
  dominus litis, as 64
  lack of authority (plea) 220
  opening address 234
  police, co-operation with 62
punishment 259
  forms of 268
reasonable grounds 12, 90
reasonableness
  exercise of powers, in 90
rebutting evidence 243
Rechtsstaat 26
recording of evidence 245
recusal 194
re-examination of witness 243
regional court
  committal of accused
    sentence, for 208
    trial, for 213
  meaning of 33
release
  juvenile accused 158
  warning, on 114, 158
remedies 25
reopening of case 372
reprieve 371
reservation of question of law 360
restitution, compensation and 284
review
  accused, at instance of 307
  appeal — difference 299
  automatic 300
  conviction set aside — retrial 313
  extraordinary 304

review — *(continued)*
   functions and powers of court 309
   judge's certificate, by virtue of 306
   judicial 295
   prosecution, at instance of 309
   right to 292
   sentence
     before 304
     execution pending 313
right(s)
   access to information 23
   accused, of 24
   appeal, right of 319
   arrestee, of 24
   bail, to 137
   children, of 24
   counsel, to 74
   freedom and security of the person 23
   human dignity, to 21
   individual, of 19
   life, to 22
   privacy, to 23
   questioned, not to be 121
   relative/absolute 11
   remain silent, to 8, 121
   review, to 292
   vindication of 88
rule of law 6, 26
schedules to Criminal Procedure Act 375
search 124
   arrest, to effect 130
   arrested person 124, 131
   border control 129
   cordoned off area 129
   force 131
   occupiers of premises 130
   roadblock or checkpoint 130
   unlawful 132
   warrant
     with 125
     without 128
seizure
   articles susceptible to 124
   disposal and forfeiture of articles 133
self-incrimination, privilege against 8
sentencing
   discretion 259
   information required 262
   jurisdiction 41
   mitigating and aggravating factors 263

sentencing — *(continued)*
  pre-sentence investigation 261
  sentence 258
    postponed 282
    suspended 282
separation of trials 228
silence, right to 8, 121, 242
special entry, appeal on 358
special superior courts 33
splitting of charges 178
state's case 234
  discharge at close 237
  evidence for state 234
  opening address 234
summons 94
superior court
  meaning of 32
  special 32
treatment centre, committal to 281
trial
  adjournment 226
  attendance 223
  conduct of 233
  drug-addicted person 226
  mentally abnormal person 226
  postponement 226
  separation 228
venue of the court 186
verdict
  accused entitled to — after plea 221
  amendment of 250
  competent 247
warning
  appear in court, to 114
  release on 114, 158
whipping 268
witness
  attendance, securing 224
  called or recalled by court 244
  cross-examination of 236, 237, 242, 244
  defence, for 241
  questioning by court 244
  recalcitrant 225
  re-examination of 243
  refusal to testify 120
  state, for 234
written notice to appear 95